More praise for LEVIATHAN

Eric Jay Dolin was awarded the 2007 J. Byrne Waterman Award, by the New Bedford Whaling Museum, in recognition of outstanding contributions to research and pedagogy in the arts, humanities, and sciences.

"I thought I learned everything I needed to know about whaling from Melville, but I was wrong. Eric Jay Dolin's *Leviathan* exposes the rise and fall of the industry inspired by the great beasts of the deep. . . . The excitement of the stories in this magnificently researched saga build and build. . . . I read every word."
—Dava Sobel, author of *Longitude* and *Galileo's Daughter*

"The whaling business left behind a singularly rich history—one abrim with adventure, danger and profit—of men who went down to the sea in ships to hunt the mightiest creatures who ever lived. That story is told, and told very well indeed, by Eric Jay Dolin. . . . Mr. Dolin handles this long, complex tale with great skill, both as a historian and as a writer (the bibliography and illustrations are splendid too). Thanks to his firm command of the tale's narrative drive, *Leviathan* is thoroughly engaging." —John Steele Gordon, *Wall Street Journal*

"Engrossing account . . . at once grand and quirky, entertaining and informative." —*Publishers Weekly*, starred review

"Anyone whose knowledge of whaling begins and ends with *Moby-Dick* will get a solid education from Mr. Dolin."
—William Grimes, *New York Times*

"Eric Jay Dolin's lively and thorough history spans the rise, golden age, and decline of what was once one of New England's distinctive industries. . . . Dolin chose to take on the subject in its broadest form, and if he leaves us wanting more, that is what good history does."
—David Waldstreicher, *Boston Globe*

"This volume reads like a history of America through whaling . . . with a historian's diligence and a trivia nut's eye for oddities. He reels in the big one."   —Troy Patterson, *Entertainment Weekly*

"Eric Jay Dolin has written a remarkable book, broad in its scope but sharp in focus. . . . Numerous attempts have been made in the past one hundred years to cover the subject all at once, however, only Dolin has managed to synthesize the enormous array of historical sources into one cohesive narrative."   —Michael P. Dyer, librarian and maritime historian, New Bedford Whaling Museum

"Captivating . . . what ultimately distinguishes *Leviathan* is Dolin's ability to show that, for generations, whaling was far less the romantic adventure of popular imagining (both past and present) than a purely, unapologetically economic engine helping to drive a young country from ambitious, increasingly aggrieved colony to world power. . . . Dolin's book, filled with killing and death, bravery and ingenuity, greed and hubris, brings a murky, myth-shrouded past to vivid, messy life."   —Ben Cosgrove, *Salon*

"This book's achievement is a comforting completeness on a subject that remains uncomfortably resistant to closure."
                                —Neal Mathews, *San Diego Union-Tribune*

"Fascinating. . . . Terrific. . . . Wonderful study."
                        —Tony Lewis, *Standard Times* (New Bedford, MA)

"Unputdownable encyclopedic account. . . . It's a ripping yarn."
                        —Mark Austin, *Daily Yomiuri* (Japan)

"A riveting story and one that invites discussion of the history of human predation in the world's oceans."
                                —Timothy J. Runyan, *Sea History*

The History of
Whaling in America

ERIC JAY DOLIN

LEVIATHAN

W. W. NORTON & COMPANY

New York London

To Lily and Harry

Copyright © 2007 by Eric Jay Dolin

All rights reserved
Printed in the United States of America
First published as a Norton paperback 2008

For information about permission to reproduce
selections from this book, write to Permissions,
W. W. Norton & Company, Inc.,
500 Fifth Avenue, New York, NY 10110

Manufacturing by RR Donnelley, Harrisonburg
Book design by Barbara M. Bachman
Production manager: Julia Druskin

LIBRARY OF CONGRESS
CATALOGING-IN-PUBLICATION DATA

Dolin, Eric Jay.
    Leviathan : the history of whaling in America /
Eric Jay Dolin. —1st ed.
        p.   cm.
    Includes bibliographical references and index.
    ISBN 978-0-393-06057-7 (hardcover)
1. Whaling—United States—History. I. Title.
    SH383.2.D65   2007
    639.2′80973—dc22   2007006113

ISBN 978-0-393-33157-8 pbk.

W. W. Norton & Company, Inc.
500 Fifth Avenue, New York, N.Y. 10110
www.wwnorton.com

W. W. Norton & Company Ltd.
Castle House, 75/76 Wells Street London W1T 3QT

1 2 3 4 5 6 7 8 9 0

Few of us realize how much we owe the whalers, the prominant part they played in our history, the prosperity and wealth they brought to the infant Republic, or the influence their rough and ready lives had upon the civilization, exploration, and commerce of the globe.

—A. Hyatt Verrill, *The Real Story of the Whaler*, 1916

And God created great whales.   —Gen. 1:21

CONTENTS

PART THREE: DISASTER AND
DECAY, 1861–1924

Introduction

PAINTING BY WILLIAM EDWARD NORTON SHOWING THE
WHALESHIP *CONCORDIA*, OUTWARD BOUND IN CHOPPY SEAS
ON BUZZARDS BAY, MASSACHUSETTS.

FOR MORE THAN A THOUSAND YEARS MEN HAVE PURSUED THE leviathans of the deep, yet of all the nations that have done so, none has a more fascinating whaling history than does the United States. From the moment the Pilgrims landed until the early twentieth century, whaling was a powerful force in the evolution of the country. Much of America's culture, economy, and in fact its spirit were literally and figuratively rendered from the bodies of whales. Thousands of American ships manned by tens of thousands of men killed hundreds of thousands of whales, which were processed into products and profits that in turn created great fortunes and spurred the formation and growth of the nation.

American whale oil lit the world. It was used in the production of soap, textiles, leather, paints, and varnishes, and it lubricated the tools and machines that drove the Industrial Revolution. The baleen cut from the mouths of whales shaped the course of feminine fashion by putting the hoop in hooped skirts and giving form to stomach-tightening and chest-crushing corsets. Spermaceti, the waxy substance from the heads of sperm whales, produced the brightest- and cleanest-burning candles the world has ever known, while ambergris, a by-product of irritation in a sperm whale's bowel, gave perfumes great staying power and was worth its weight in gold.

The heroic and often tragic stories of American whalemen were renowned. They sailed the world's oceans and brought back tales filled with bravery, perseverance, endurance, and survival. They mutinied, murdered, rioted, deserted, drank, sang, spun yarns, scrimshawed, and recorded their musings and observations in journals and letters. They survived boredom, backbreaking work, tempestuous seas, floggings, pirates, putrid food, and unimaginable cold. Enemies preyed on them in times of war, and competitors envied them in times of peace. Many whalemen died from violent encounters with whales and from terrible miscalculations about the unforgiving nature of nature itself. And through it all, whalemen, those "iron men in wooden boats" created a legacy of dramatic, poignant, and at times horrific stories that can still stir our emotions and animate the most primal part of our imaginations. "To produce a mighty book, you must choose a mighty theme," proclaimed Herman Melville, and the epic story of whaling is one of the mightiest themes in American history.[1]

This book was sparked by an image. A large oval box in my house is painted with a primitive, powerful whaling scene. The image shows a whaleship with its sails unfurled, three whaleboats filled with men, and two whales that appear to be unnaturally buoyant, seemingly floating on top of the waves. Many times I gazed at that painting and wondered what it was like actually to go whaling. Having gone through the academic ritual of reading *Moby-Dick* in school, I already knew about whaling, especially its golden age during the mid-1800s. But the painting continued to stir my curiosity, and soon I discovered that there were libraries devoted to whaling, providing almost unlimited material for a historical narrative. This book, then, is my attempt to weave that material into a maritime tapestry that attempts to do justice to America's rich whaling heritage.

Whaling today is a highly controversial and emotionally explosive issue. The debate between those who favor commercial whaling and those who think it is barbaric and must be eliminated is played out, often daily, in the news. And even though America has an important and vocal role in that debate, it is not a subject that is covered here. Instead *Leviathan* seeks to re-create what whaling was, not to address what it is or should be now. Similarly this book does not pass judgment on American whalemen by applying the moral, ethical, and cultural sensitivities of modern times to the actions of those who operated and existed in a bygone era—one that ended during the early days of the American conservation movement and well before anyone had heard of environmentalism. While it is true that a few whalemen worried about driving whales to extinction, their concern revolved more around the viability of their industry than the need to protect another species. To the whalemen whales were swimming profit centers to be taken advantage of, not preserved. So if you are looking for commentary on whether whaling should continue, you will be disappointed. But if you want to appreciate and marvel at the way in which whaling influenced the course of American history, read on.

Part One

ARRIVAL *and*
ASCENT

1614–1774

Chapter One

JOHN SMITH GOES
WHALING

JOHN SMITH'S MAP OF NEW ENGLAND, 1616.

ONLY THIRTY-FOUR YEARS OLD IN 1614, CAPT. JOHN SMITH ALREADY had enough adventures to fill many lifetimes. He had survived a shipwreck, pirated in the Mediterranean, crisscrossed Europe, and fought with the Dutch against the Spanish and with the Hungarians against the Turks. Twice wounded in battle, he had beheaded three men in duels. Once made a slave by a Turkish pasha, he had also helped to found Jamestown, Virginia, where his encounter with the Indian princess Pocahontas became legend. Even if, as many have argued, some of Smith's exploits were apocryphal, his was still a fantastically interesting and dramatic life.

Now Smith yearned for another adventure. What he wanted more than anything was to travel back to America. Virginia, his first choice for a destination, was off-limits. He had left Virginia in 1609, and the overseers of that colony had made it clear that he would not be welcomed back. Still open to Smith, however, was that vast expanse of the North American continent that fell between the thirty-eighth and the forty-fifth lines of latitude, commonly referred to as the northern part of Virginia, an area that England's King James I had chartered for colonization eight years earlier.[1] "As I liked Virginia well," Smith later wrote, "though not their proceedings; so I desired also to see this country, and spend some time in trying what I could finde."[2]* Finally, on March 3, 1614, Smith stood at the bow of a ship heading back to the New World.

Four English merchants—Marmaduke Roydon, George Langam, John Buley, and William Skelton—underwrote Smith's voyage to that portion of the northern part of Virginia that lay between the forty-first and forty-fifth lines of latitude, which he would later christen New England.[3] Their enthusiasm for this venture was fueled by the dream of finding gold, the precious yet elusive metal that had been the driving force behind so many explorations of the world. The talk of there being gold in New England was in large part due to a story that had been making the rounds in England ever since 1611, when Capt. Edward Harlow captured four American Indians and hauled them back to London. One of the Indians, named Epenow, was, said Smith, "of so great a stature, he was shewed . . . for money as a wonder."[4] It was not Epenow's size, however, that impressed his captors most, but his tale of gold on Martha's Vineyard, the island from which he had been forcibly taken. Given that gold has never been found on Martha's Vineyard, many have wondered what Epenow was thinking. He might have assumed that the brilliant yellow streaks in the sands of Gay Head, the cliffs at the west end of the island, were evidence of the precious metal, not knowing that they were by-products of weathering and erosion.

*The original, often archaic, and sometimes mystifying spellings have been retained throughout this book.

Another take is that Epenow created the story, telling the Englishmen that only he knew where to find the gold, as a means of gaining passage back home. If this second story is true, it was an excellent gambit, for when another group of English adventurers enlisted Epenow as a guide, he jumped ship off Martha's Vineyard and swam to shore. Epenow's motives notwithstanding, his story had an electrifying effect. When Roydon heard the story and shared it with his associates, Smith's return engagement to America was launched. If there was gold on Martha's Vineyard, there might be gold in other parts of New England as well, and if the merchants were lucky, Smith and his men would find it.[5]

No matter how alluring, gold was a slender reed on which to hang the success of an entire voyage. The goals of the endeavor were thus broadened to include more conventional ways of making money, with Smith's ultimate charge being to turn a profit by taking "Whales and . . . [making] tryalls of a Myne of Gold and Copper," and if neither of these schemes succeeded, then "Fish and Furres" were to be their "refuge." Smith doubted that they would find gold—or copper, for that matter—believing that dangling such prospects before the merchants' eyes was simply "a device" to get them to fund the voyage.[6] But the prospect of taking whales, unlike gold, was no convenient fiction. From the discoveries of earlier voyagers, Smith knew that whales swam in New England's waters.

One such voyager was Bartholomew Gosnold, who had departed from Falmouth, England, in the spring of 1602, with hopes of establishing a foothold for a colony in America.[7] On the other side of Cape Cod, which Gosnold so named because of the incredible abundance of cod in local waters, he and his men landed on Cuttyhunk Island, where they found "many huge bones and ribbes of whales" along the beach.[8] Three years later, George Waymouth, another Englishman bent on colonization, sailed to America, first sighting land near Cape Cod, then sailing north along the coast of Maine. While Gosnold had merely seen whalebones, Waymouth brought back a story of an Indian whale hunt, which one of his men described as follows.

One especiall thing is their manner of killing the Whale, which they call Powdawe; and will describe his forme; how he bloweth up the water; and that he is 12 fathoms long; and that they go in company of their King with a multitude of their boats, and strike him with a bone made in fashion of a harping iron fastened to a rope, which they make great and strong of the barke of trees, which they veare out after him: then all their boats come about him, and as he riseth above the water, with their arrowes they shoot him to death: when they have killed him and dragged him to shore, they call all their chief lords together, and sing a song of joy.[9]

Written accounts of Gosnold's and Waymouth's voyages included lists of the valuable commodities that intrepid American colonists could reap from nature, with whales prominently featured.[10] Smith was familiar with these voyages, but they weren't his only sources of intelligence about whales in America.[11] For many years European fishermen had plied the coastal waters off northern New England in search of cod, the piscine equivalent of gold, as well as other fish. Although few if any of these trips were recorded in writing, it is implausible that some of the fishermen didn't report whale sightings once they returned home.[12] Smith not only knew there were whales off New England, but was also confident that they could bring him and his backers great wealth.

JUST WHEN HUMANS BEGAN viewing whales as objects worthy of pursuit will never be known. As historian Gordon Jackson quipped, "The origins of whaling are hidden in the mists of mythology and are, perhaps, best left there."[13] The first close-up encounter between people and whales was likely not at sea but on an unknown beach where a whale, either dead or dying, had washed ashore, no doubt astonishing and scaring the locals. People learned to take advantage of these occurrences by cutting up whales for food and using their body parts and bones for building materials or other purposes. At some point men took to the water to hunt whales. Ancient cave carvings and drawings offer possible evidence of such encounters; and the Greeks, Romans, and Phoenicians ate whale meat, which may have been obtained through hunting instead of random strandings. This fragmentary history, however, offers only glimpses and whispers rather than a clear image of how whaling began. To get onto firmer ground one needs to look to the Basques, the ancient people inhabiting the mountainous region between Spain and France, who are widely credited as being the first to make a business of whaling. Perhaps as early as the seventh or eighth centuries, the Basques built stone towers along the coast, which they used to scan the Bay of Biscay for whales. When one was sighted, the men, alerted by the smoke of a fire or the beating of drums, ran to the water's edge and set off in their small boats, harpoons at the ready. And the whale they pursued was the right whale.[14]

At first glance the right whale, which grows to a length of sixty feet and can weigh as much as eighty to one hundred tons, appears to be an ungainly animal. In fact, though massively built, the right whale is quite graceful, moving fluidly albeit somewhat lazily through the water. Its enormous mouth takes up roughly a quarter of its body's length and contains a truly remarkable mechanism for gathering food. Hanging down from the upper jaw are hundreds of strips of baleen, a keratinous material that when viewed from the side resembles a comb with hairlike fringes on the inner edge. These strips, which were referred to as "whalebone" or "whale finnes" by whalemen, can reach lengths of ten feet. When feeding, right whales swim at the surface or at depth with their mouths wide open, taking in huge drafts of water filled with small copepods, krill, and other zooplankton. Having corralled its meal, the whale closes its mouth and thrusts up its massive tongue, while the tightly packed baleen, sievelike in action, strains the food as the water escapes in a torrent. With a swallow the feeding loop begins again, and for a mature adult this daily cycle continues until the whale's mighty hunger is satisfied and between two and three tons of food have been consumed.[15]

Herman Melville noted that right whales in the southern oceans feasted on swarms of yellowish copepods, calling the whales "morning mowers, who side by side slowly and seethingly advance their scythes through the long wet grass of marshy meads . . . making a strange, grassy, cutting sound; and leaving behind them endless swaths of blue upon the yellow sea."[16] This somewhat mellow, almost bucolic image contrasts sharply with the sheer panic that the sight of a right whale feeding at the surface could provoke in an unseasoned whaleman. On first witnessing the whale's huge mouth, half jutting out of the water, he might reasonably be scared senseless, not realizing that right whales have neither the interest nor the ability to eat men, for their throats are so small that they cannot admit anything bulkier than a slurry of pint-size creatures.[17]

The right whale's name is a bit of a puzzle. The most-oft-repeated story is that it is so named because it was the "right," as in the "correct," whale to hunt. Generally docile and relatively slow moving, right whales could be easily approached by men in boats. Right whales rarely dive for long periods of time and tend to surface close to where they last submerged, making them eminently trackable. On being killed, rather than sink, as did many other whales, the right whale usually floated, thereby giving its attackers the opportunity to attach ropes to the carcass and tow it to shore for processing. Best of all, the right whale produced copious amounts of oil, baleen, and meat, items for which there was ready demand.[18] Despite this highly plausible rationale, nobody actually knows how the right whale got its name. The earliest references to the right whale offer no indication why it was called that, and some who have studied the issue point out that the word "right" in this context might just as likely be intended "to connote 'true' or 'proper,' meaning typical of the group."[19]

Their reputation for docility notwithstanding, right whales were not always easy marks; once harpooned they could quickly become a dangerous adversary. With surprising speed and tremendous force and agility, a right whale can swing its powerful tail in a great arc, and if a boat was in the way it could be dashed to bits.[20] Despite the potential dangers of hunting right whales, once the Basques discovered these creatures, they did not look back. It is not clear exactly how the forces of supply and demand transformed the Basques, who had long been accomplished fishermen, into whalemen, but the role of the Catholic Church figures prominently. As historian Mark Kurlansky points out, among the church's edicts was one forbidding its followers from eating "'red-blooded' meat on holy days . . . arguing that it was 'hot,' associated with sex, which was also forbidden on holy days." The church, however, had no problem with its followers eating meat that came from animals that lived under water, for such meat was viewed as "cold" and, apparently, unlikely to excite libidinous passions. This dispensation even extended itself to the tails of beavers because, the reasoning went, they were often immersed in water and therefore were "cold." Of course the church was wrong about whales—and beavers for that matter. But the church's distinction, though biologically faulty, proved to be a bonanza for the Basques who did a brisk business supplying whale meat, along with other "cold" products such as cod, to Catholics on their holy days, which at the time included 166 days out of the year.[21]

In the ensuing centuries the Basques actively sold an impressive array of whale products throughout Europe. Whale meat, salted or fresh, called *craspois* or *lard de Carême*, was widely consumed in England and France, and used in Spain as an ingredient in soup. Flexible yet sturdy, baleen gave form to skirts and provided ornamentation for knight's helmets and bristles for brushes. The massive vertebrae and ribs of the whales were used for seats and fences. The precious tongue was served to clergymen and royalty. Whale oil served as a lubricant, it was combined with tar and oakum to caulk ships, and it aided in the making of soap and paint and the cleaning of coarse wool used for clothes. When it was burned, whale oil, called *Lumera* in the marketplace, became an important source of light. And even the excrement of whales was used to make red fabric dyes.[22]

The Flemings, the Icelanders, the Norwegians, and the French all went whaling in medieval times, but it was the Basques who dominated this burgeoning industry.[23] What we can ascertain is that around 1540 they extended their operations across the North Atlantic to the coasts of Labrador and Newfoundland, where, during the 1560s and 1570s, it is estimated that more than one thousand Basque whalemen produced as much as five hundred thousand gallons of whale oil each year.[24] The English watched the Basques' success with covetous eyes, and by the end of the 1500s they too entered the whaling industry, as a means of meeting domestic demands for whale products while at the same time building their economic might.[25] The earliest English whaling voyages ventured to Newfoundland and Iceland, but it was not until 1611, when the English turned their sights farther north to the edge of the Arctic Circle, that their own whaling industry was truly born.

The explorer Henry Hudson was largely responsible for alerting the English to the possibilities of whaling. In 1607 the London-based trading giant the Muscovy Company had given Hudson the task of finding the fabled northern route to the Far East. He had no luck on that count, his progress arrested by the formidable and impenetrable Arctic ice pack, but he did see huge concentrations of whales around the island of Spitsbergen.[26] Those whales looked similar to the right whales, but were in fact bowheads, a different species—larger and more rotund than right whales, reaching sixty-five feet in length and some-times weighing more than one hundred tons.[27] With a layer of blubber that can extend to twenty inches thick, the bowhead produces more oil per foot than the right, and possesses the longest baleen of all whales, with strips reaching fourteen feet. As the bowhead became more important to the economies of Europe, its standing rose to the point where it was referred to simply as "the Whale."[28]

The leaders of the Muscovy Company were disappointed that Hud-son didn't find the northern passage, but his discovery of whales intrigued them. When another expedition went north in 1610, one that confirmed and expanded on Hudson's observations, the Muscovy Com-pany committed to going whaling. Over the next couple of years the company's whaleships expanded their operations off Spitsbergen, but they did not have the hunting grounds to themselves. News about the Muscovy Company's success spread fast, and Dutch and Basque whale-ships headed north to share in the bounty. The presence of these "inter-lopers" incensed the Muscovy Company, and to better secure its claims to this new branch of whaling, the company asked for, and in fact received in 1613, a royal charter from King James I, which gave it the exclusive right to Spitsbergen's whales. With this charter in hand and the determination to defend its turf, the Muscovy Company sent seven heavily armed whaleships to Spitsbergen during the 1613 season, one of which, the *Tigris*, had twenty-one guns and was designated the lead enforcer.[29]

Although the word spread that the Muscovy Company was pre-pared to fight, the interlopers were not so easily cowed, and the sum-mer of 1613 proved to be unusually crowded up north. The Muscovy Company's seven ships were rudely joined by nearly twenty others from various countries. The ensuing season was rife with altercations, threats, and boardings, all of which were orchestrated by the English. Many of the interlopers were run off the grounds, and others had their cargoes seized; in one instance an entire Dutch ship, with Englishmen making up part of the crew, was taken to London and later released. Arguing that the English had no right to claim sole possession of the whaling grounds off Spitsbergen, the Dutch whalemen were particu-larly angry about the way their ships had been treated by the English. After all, Hudson didn't discover Spitsbergen; a Dutchman by the name of Willem Barents had done so in 1596. He, like Hudson, was sent on an ill-fated voyage to find a northern route to the Far East. When Barents crossed the eightieth parallel he came upon a mountainous and craggy land, and using this topography as a guidepost, he named it Spitsbergen, which in Dutch means "pointed hills" (or mountains). So, from the Dutch perspective, it was the English who were the interlopers. To reassert their claim to the area, the Dutch did what the English had done. They formed a whaling company and obtained a monopoly from their government to the Spitsbergen grounds. During the summer of 1614 the Dutch decided to enforce their monopoly by sending fourteen whaleships north, escorted by four men-of-war, each boasting thirty guns. There the Dutch were met by the equally determined and defended fleet from the Muscovy Company. But rather than fight and risk war, the English and the Dutch divided the whaling grounds between them and sought to keep all other interlopers out.[30]

JOHN SMITH AND THE BACKERS of his voyage to New England knew the broad history of whaling, and about England's efforts to establish itself as a whaling power. Therefore having whaling as one of the voyage's main goals was very attractive indeed, providing as it did another potential avenue for England to expand its stake in this growing industry. It was with great expectations, then, that John Smith, along with forty-five men and boys on two ships sailed down the river Thames, through the English Channel, and embarked on a journey across the Atlantic Ocean. They arrived at Monhegan Island, off the coast of Maine, in late April 1614, where their hopes of whaling were soon dashed. Despite having brought along Samuel Cramton, who had been chosen specifically for his skill as a whaleman, as well as other crewmembers who were also "expert in that faculty," Smith wrote that he and his men "found this Whale-fishing a costly conclusion. We saw many and spent much time in chasing them, but could not kill any. They being a kinde of Jubartes, and not the Whale that yeelds Finness [baleen] and Oyle as wee expected."[31] The type of whale that Smith wanted was either a right or, possibly, a bowhead. These "Jubartes," on the other hand, were likely fin or humpback whales.[32] Neither of these species would have excited a whaleman of the day because, as compared with right or bowhead whales, they have very short strips of baleen and produce much less oil. And fin whales in particular would have been a very hard target to kill. Second in size to only the blue whale, the fin, called the "greyhound of the sea," could attain speeds of twenty knots for up to fifteen minutes, giving it the ability to elude Smith's men in their small whaleboats.[33]

Failures at whaling and finding no precious metals, Smith and his men opted for other targets—fish and furs; But their timing was off. "By our late arrival and long lingring about the Whale," Smith commented, "the prime of both those seasons [fish and furs] were past ere wee perceived it." Still, Smith's men managed to catch nearly fifty thousand pounds of fish and were able to trade for many furs, making the trip partially successful, though not profitable enough to defray its cost.[34] The mediocre material fortunes of the voyage didn't concern Smith much, nor did it dampen his excitement about New England. While his men fished, and in between his stabs at trading "trifles" to the Indians in exchange for animal skins, Smith eagerly surveyed New England's coast in a small boat with eight of his crew.[35] Exploring and mapping were what Smith loved most, and while doing so he dreamed of the role this region might have in expanding what later became the British Empire, and of the part he might play in that development. The section of the coast that most stirred Smith's imagination was Massachusetts, and specifically the area surrounding Boston, which he called "the Paradise of all those parts." Of Plymouth he said that it had "an excellent good harbor, good land; and no want of anything but industrious people."[36]

Smith sailed back to England on July 18, 1614. Had his fortunes been different, however, Smith might not have set sail at all. Years later he wrote that if the whaling had proved successful, he would have stayed in New England "with ten men to keep possessions of those large territories."[37] The mind reels to think how America's history might have changed had Smith's men caught some whales. But the whales did not provide a reason for Smith to remain, and by the end of August he was back in London.

Smith's experience fueled his desire to return. So great was his need for grand adventure that he wrote that he "would rather live . . . [in New England] than any where," and if the colony "did not maintaine it selfe . . . let us starve."[38] Smith's first chance to return came in March 1615, but not long after his ship departed Plymouth, England, it was caught in a lashing gale that shattered the masts and caused the ship to leak at a tremendous rate. Continuing the voyage was out of the question. The new goal was survival—getting the ship back to port—which Smith and his men were able to do after rigging a new mast and patching the hull. Despite this failure Smith convinced his backers to underwrite him again, and in June of that year he stood on the deck of another ship seeking the shores of New England. But this voyage ended no better. Within a couple of weeks Smith's ship was captured by French pirates, and Smith thus began his imprisonment aboard the *Sauvage*.[39]

Rather than bemoan his situation, Smith started writing "to keepe my perplexed thoughts from too much meditation of my miserable estate."[40] He wrote about the subject that was dearest to his heart—New England—and the prospects it held for colonization. After three months Smith made a daring escape. He tucked his manuscript under his shirt, stole one of the ship's small boats, and rowed it ashore off the coast of France. French officials questioned Smith about his strange odyssey and then released him, and not long thereafter, Smith, with his manuscript, left for London, arriving there in January 1616.[41] Smith tried to generate interest for another voyage to New England, but finding no backers who were willing bet on a man whose last two efforts had ended in disaster, Smith decided on a different approach. He added to his manuscript, which was published in June 1616, titled *A Description of New England*. Smith hoped that this book would generate excitement about colonization, especially with investors who could offer him the command of yet another ship.

A Description of New England was in equal parts travelogue and sales pitch. It included a handsome and detailed map of New England, stretching from what is now Cape Cod to the northern reaches of Maine. Looking at the map some four hundred years later, one is struck by its accuracy. Although many of the details are off, some considerably so, it is a brilliant rendition given the tools and time at Smith's disposal, and it far outshone contemporary maps of the region. In one corner is a striking picture of Smith dressed in the finest military garb, his left hand resting lightly on his sword. With a full beard and mustache, and a dark mane of hair swept back from his forehead, Smith looks out with the firm and steely gaze of a man who is confident in himself and his place in the world.[42] Just to the left of center of the map, out in the ocean, a sea serpent, or perhaps a stylized whale, appears, its head in view, spouting water in an arc from a hole in its nose.

One of the map's most distinct features is its place-names. In an effort to tie New England more tightly to old England in the public's mind and at the same time enhance the prospects for colonization, Smith gave Prince Charles (sixteen at the time and later to become King Charles I) the honor of renaming many of the "the most remarkable places" in New England, changing "their barbarous names for such English, as posteritie might say Prince Charles was their Godfather."[43] Thus, Cape Cod became Cape James, Accomack became Plimoth, and the Massachusetts river became the river Charles. Although *A Description of New England* found a curious and receptive audience in England and throughout Europe, it did not facilitate Smith's return. Indeed, it could be argued that by writing it, Smith might have helped to ruin one of the best chances he had to venture back across the Atlantic—namely, the opportunity to lead a group of religious dissenters called Pilgrims to the New World.

THE PILGRIMS HAD ESTABLISHED themselves in northern England in the early 1600s by separating from the Church of England. This was a bold, illegal, treasonous, and heretical act that made them the target of scorn and reprisals. Rather than stay in a country where they were clearly not wanted, the Pilgrims emigrated to Holland in 1608. Although the Dutch were more tolerant, the Pilgrims decided, after a decade of living in Holland, that to reach their full potential as a community they needed to leave. They had, as historian Samuel Eliot Morison has written, "a vision of a colony overseas where they could make a decent living, worship as they thought right, and lead the New Testament life."[44] That vision led the Pilgrims' leaders back to England, where they obtained a land patent from the Virginia Company, which would allow them to settle near the mouth of the Hudson River.[45]

The Pilgrims met with Smith to discuss their trip, and even though he would rather have led a band of seasoned and skilled pioneers to New England, Smith was so desperate for an American voyage of any kind that he leaped at the chance to become a part of this admittedly questionable and risky expedition.[46] That Smith had no other commission at the time certainly added to his desire to join this endeavor. But Smith's offer to join the Pilgrims as a guide and military commander was rebuffed, with the job going to Myles Standish instead. Smith later claimed that his own work, including *A Description of New England*, played at least a partial role in denying him the position. "My books and maps were much better cheape to teach them," wrote Smith, "than my selfe."[47]

The Pilgrims departed from Plymouth, England, on September 6, 1620, on board the *Mayflower*.[48] Smith's failure to secure participation in the voyage was particularly ironic given that when the Pilgrims arrived in America, they saw whales aplenty. But unlike the whales Smith had so frustratingly encountered off the coast of Maine in 1614, the whales the Pilgrims saw were whales worth catching.

Chapter Two

"THE KING OF WATERS,
THE SEA-SHOULDERING WHALE"

A 1704 ENGRAVING ILLUSTRATING JOHN MONCK'S 1620 VOYAGE
TO SPITSBERGEN, SHOWING A "WHALE FEMALE AND THE
WINDLAIS WHEREBY THE WHALES ARE BROUGHT ON SHORE."

AT DAYBREAK ON NOVEMBER 9, 1620, AFTER MORE THAN TWO
months of stormy seas, the passengers of the *Mayflower* sighted shore,
which they deemed a "goodly" land that was "woodded to the brinke of
the sea." Unfortunately they also realized that they were in the wrong
place. Their patent had permitted them to settle in the vicinity of the
Hudson River, but here they were near the tip of Cape Cod, far north of
where they were supposed to be. Joyful though they were on reaching
land, the Pilgrims decided to coast farther south to finish the journey

to which they had originally agreed. But less than a day later, after a harrowing attempt to sail beyond the elbow of the Cape through treacherous shoals, the master turned the *Mayflower* around and headed back. If they were going to settle in the New World, New England was going to have to be the place, patent or no. To give some semblance of order to their new endeavor, the Pilgrims quickly drafted and signed the Mayflower Compact, in which they announced their intention to "plant the first Colony in the Northerne parts of Virginia," and bind themselves "together into a civill body politike, for our better ordering and preservation." No sooner had they completed this historic document, than on the morning of November 11, the weary wanderers dropped anchor in modern-day Provincetown Harbor. Almost immediately, whales surrounded the ship.[1]

The abundance of whales caused great frustration. "Every day," wrote one of the passengers, "we saw Whales playing hard by us, of which in that place, if we had instruments and meanes to take them, we might have made a very rich returne, which to our great griefe we wanted. Our master and his mate, and others experienced in fishing, professed we might have made three or foure thousand pounds worth of Oyle." One whale surfaced near the ship and floated there listlessly, with the sun glinting off its back. Thinking that it might be dead, and apparently wanting proof of this surmise, two men went for their guns and prepared to shoot it. When one of the men fired, his "musket flew in peeces, both stocke and barrell." Amazingly nobody was hurt, though quite a few people were nearby. The whale, oblivious to the commotion, finally "gave a snuffe and away."[2]

It is not surprising that the men of the *Mayflower* lacked the "instruments and meanes" to pursue whales. While the Pilgrims had always intended to go fishing in the New World, the fish they wanted to catch were not whales, the vaunted "Royal fish," as they were called in England, but the equally prized though much more diminutive cod.[3] It is impossible to know from the Pilgrims' written accounts what type of whales greeted the *Mayflower*, but in all likelihood they were right whales. The men seemed to be familiar with the species, and certainly right whales, which had been the mainstay of European whaling for centuries, would have been a familiar sight to men "experienced in fishing." The men noted, furthermore, that they preferred fishing for these whales than to go "Greenland Whale-fishing."[4] That was a logical comparison to make. Right whales and Greenland, or bowhead, whales, were really the only two species of consequence hunted at the time. And the bowhead had recently taken center stage as the preferred whale for the English, the Dutch, and other nations, all of whom were struggling to gain the upper hand in the whaling grounds off Spitsbergen.[5] Assuming, then, that the whales milling about the *Mayflower* were right whales, the men's preference to hunt for them made perfect sense. Although right and bowhead whales share many favorable characteristics from the whalemen's perspective—foremost among them being that they are relatively slow moving, easy to kill, usually float when dead, and provide large amounts of oil and baleen—there is still the issue of location. Even to see, much less hunt, bowheads one had to go to where they lived, and that meant braving the freezing and treacherous waters of the Far North.

The men of the *Mayflower* not only professed a preference for whaling off Cape Cod but boldly proclaimed that they would "fish for Whale here" the next winter. Before the Pilgrims could make it to the next winter, however, they had to survive the one that lay in store. The weather was getting colder, the food supply on board the *Mayflower* was dwindling, and many of the passengers were sick, with most suffering "vehement coughs." Some argued for going no farther and settling on the Cape, not far from where they had first anchored. There was a good harbor there, and the area appeared to be easily defended. Indeed, the search for a better location seemed a foolhardy undertaking now that "the heart of Winter and unseasonable weather" were imminent. There were also the whales to consider. Some of the passengers pointed out that "Cape Cod was like to be a place of good fishing, for we saw daily great Whales of the best kind for oyle and bone, come close aboord our ship, and in fayre weather swim and play about us." But the majority agreed with Robert Coppin, one of the *Mayflower*'s mates, that before making such a fateful decision they should explore one more location, "a great Navigable river and good harbour in the other head-land of this bay." Coppin remembered the place well. Years earlier he and his shipmates came ashore there, and while they were trading with the Indians, one of the "wild men" stole a harpoon, causing the Englishmen to label the place Thievish Harbor. So on December 6, a band of explorers began sailing the *Mayflower*'s shallop, or small boat, west along the coast of the Cape's inner arm, toward what they hoped would be Thievish Harbor. At dusk, having made good progress and with their clothes frozen "like coats of Iron," they headed toward the shore and saw movement on the beach.[6]

A dozen or so Indians were "busie about a blacke thing," which the explorers could not quite discern. Seeing the white men approach, the Indians ran back and forth as if gathering their things, and then disappeared into the woods. The explorers pulled ashore farther up the beach, where they spent the night behind a hastily constructed barricade, while sentries kept watch for unwelcome visitors. The next morning the explorers set out to "discover this place" and came upon a "great fish, they called a '*Grampus*,' dead on the sands." Two more were found dead at the bottom of the bay under a few feet of water. "They were some five or sixe paces long, and about two inches thicke of fat, and fleshed like a Swine." Later that day the explorers solved the mystery of the "black thing" that had so interested the Indians. It was another grampus, which the Indians had been cutting into "rands or pieces, about an ell long, and two handfull broad." In their haste to depart, they had left some pieces behind. Having found so many of these "great fish" that day, the explorers decided to call this place Grampus Bay.[7]

The grampus would later go by various names, including "blackfish," "cowfish," "pothead," and "puffin pig," though we know it today as the pilot whale.[8] In contrast to right and bowhead whales, the pilot whale has teeth, not baleen, in its mouth; feeds on squid and schooling fish; and is a relatively small whale, reaching twenty feet in length and nearly four tons in weight. Henry David Thoreau described pilot whales, somewhat ungenerously, as being "remarkably simple and lumpish forms for animated creatures, with a blunt round snout or head, whale-like, and simple stiff-looking flippers," and skin that was "smooth shining black, like India-rubber."[9] The pilot whale's jawline angles upward toward the back of its mouth, giving it, as another writer called it, "an innocent, smiling expression," a feature it shares with many of the smaller whales, including dolphins.[10]

That the Pilgrims were familiar with pilot whales, having a ready name for them, makes sense, since this widely distributed species is found on both sides of the Atlantic. In speculating on how these "great fish" had died, the explorers thought that they had been "cast up at high water, and could not get off for the frost and ice."[11] While this might have kept the pilot whales from returning to open water, and thereby surviving, it is just as likely that these animals had, in effect, killed themselves. This is not to say that the pilot whales sought death in the way that a human being might choose suicide; it's just that the pilot whales' behavior sometimes ends in a self-imposed death sentence, and nobody knows why. For centuries humans have been baffled by pilot whales periodically stranding themselves on beaches.[12]

Scientists have offered many theories to explain this behavior. Perhaps whales strand because they are ill and disoriented, or their navigation systems are disrupted by perturbations in the Earth's magnetic field or sonar, or they are too aggressive in chasing prey into the shallows, or they simply get lost in the mazelike inlets and bays along the coast and can't find their way out before the tide recedes. It is even possible that the gregariousness of pilot whales and the strong social cohesion of their pods are partly to blame for some of the larger strandings, especially if after one or more whales become stranded, others in the same pod refuse to leave the beached individuals behind and therefore get stranded themselves. Whatever causes pilot whales to follow this deadly course, this behavior is most prevalent in the waters surrounding Cape Cod, for that long, curvaceous arm of land leads the world in strandings.[13]

The Pilgrims' discovery of the pilot whales on the beach elicited a response similar to the one they had had on seeing their first whales from the deck of the *Mayflower*. This time, though, instead of lacking the instruments to take the whales, they lacked only the "time and meanes" to boil down the whales' blubber, a process they reckoned would "have yeelded a great deale of oyle."[14] For a second time these newcomers had seen valuable whales yet could not exploit the situation. Thwarted, they returned to the task at hand, finding a good location to settle. The next morning the Pilgrims skirmished with the local Indians and then departed in their shallop, leaving behind a stretch of sand that would thenceforth be known as First Encounter Beach. That night, after losing its rudder and its mast to a savage sea, the crippled shallop, with the explorers hanging on tight and thankful to God, limped into Plymouth Harbor. Although this was not the Thievish Harbor that Coppin had hoped to gain, it was a safe and good harbor, and it became the place where the Pilgrims finally and permanently stepped ashore.[15]

There is no evidence that any of the men on board the *Mayflower* went whaling the year following their arrival. Nor is there any indication that any of the colonists who came ashore in New England during the 1620s or early 1630s took up harpoons and got into boats to hunt for whales. During those early years the colonists were consumed by other tasks, such as harvesting fish from coastal waters and crops from the land. While the colonists appear to have had neither the inclination nor the infrastructure to pursue whales at sea, they undoubtedly looked for them on the beach, taking advantage of what the currents and the tides ushered in.[16] And they had good reasons for doing so. Whale oil had for centuries proved itself as an excellent illuminant, and the possibility of using such oil in that way must have looked attractive, especially given the lighting alternatives. Burning slivers of wood or pine knots from the pitch pine trees, which grew in great numbers, was a ready option, and one that the colonists and the Indians commonly used. This "candlewood" or "lightwood" was, as one contemporary noted, "so full of the moysture of Turpentine and Pitch, that they burne as cleere as a Torch."[17] But the turpentine and pitch that weren't consumed during combustion dripped from the wood, leaving behind a sticky, black mass, and candlewood also created thick plumes of sooty smoke; neither of these features commended this fuel for indoor use. And some observers were none too pleased with the light that candlewood threw off, claiming that "it makes the people pale."[18] Another illuminant was oil from the livers of fish, primarily cod. This too was plentiful, but it also smelled rancid and gave off only a middling amount of light.

One lighting alternative that was not readily available to the early colonists was tallow, or animal fat, which could be used to make candles. Tallow was scarce because there were precious few domesticated animals, the main source from which this substance was usually rendered.[19] There was, of course, the option of importing tallow candles from England, but that was cost prohibitive for all but the wealthiest individuals. Assessing all their lighting options, the colonists would have viewed whale oil quite favorably. Poured into a crude lamp of the time, or simply pooled in a dish, with a wick sticking out, whale oil provided a dependable and superior light.

The date on which the first colonist cut into a beached whale and boiled its blubber into oil is not known, but by 1635, John Winthrop, the founding governor of the Massachusetts Bay Colony, wrote in his journal that "Some of our people went to Cape Codd & made some oyle of a whale which was cast on shore: there were 3: or 4: cast, as it seemes there is allmost everye yeare."[20] This enterprising use of whales fit in well with the plans of English promoters of colonization. In 1622 the Council for New England, which had received a royal charter to the region in 1620, sent a report to the king's son, in which they did their best to showcase the benefits of colonizing New England and thereby transforming it into an economic engine that would admirably serve old England. Turning its attention to the bounty from the sea, the council highlighted the "great numbers of whales, and other merchantable means to raise profit to the industrious inhabitants or diligent traders."[21] The importance of whales to the future prosperity of New England was reconfirmed seven years later, in 1629, when the Massachusetts Bay Company received its charter from the Crown, granting it the rights to a great chunk of land along the coast, as well as to "all Fishes, royall fishes, whales, balan, sturgions, and other fishes of what kind or nature soever that shall . . . be taken in . . . the saide seas or waters" in and around Massachusetts Bay.[22]

However enterprising the colonists were in capitalizing on drift whales, they were not the first Americans to do so. The butchered pilot whale the Pilgrims inspected on First Encounter Beach proved that. The Indians had for many years, and undoubtedly many centuries before that, viewed stranded whales as a commodity, cutting them up and putting parts of the animals to good use, including the meat, blubber, bones, tendons, teeth, flukes, and skin.[23] The Indians' use of drift whales raises a controversial question: Did the Indians hunt for whales at sea? If saying something over and over again makes it true, then the answer is a resounding yes. Numerous authors have stated plainly and without reservation that the Indians were America's first whalemen.[24] One wrote that "the first white men to explore the coast of New England found red whalers at work. In every clan and tribe along the coast were men accustomed to killing whales."[25] Another author was more specific and bold in his conclusions, stating that the American Indians were skilled at killing not just any whales, but sperm whales, the most formidable whale in the ocean.[26] The problem with such claims is that there is very little evidence to support them. The only written documentation that Indians in New England pursued whales before the

Europeans arrived is the description of the Indian whaling hunt in the book documenting the Waymouth expedition. Although this account is fascinating, and it appears to be a reasonable description of how a whale hunt could be prosecuted, it is not entirely convincing on its own. And, as one historian notes, it "does not appear to be first-hand," casting further doubt on its reliability.[27] As for archaeological support that New England Indians hunted whales, while examples of bone- or stone-tipped spears and harpoons have been unearthed in the region, even some that are thousands of years old, they could have been employed in hunting seals rather than whales.[28]

The only other early written account of Indians along the east coast of America hunting whales is by Joseph de Acosta in his *History of the Indies*, published in 1590, which tells an extraordinary story of whaling off Florida. According to Acosta the Indians paddled their canoes alongside a whale, and one of them leaped onto the whale's neck and thrust "a sharpe and strong stake . . . into the whales nosthrill [blow-hole]," causing the whale to "furiously beate the sea . . . [and run] into the deepe with great violence, and presently [rise] againe." The Indian, relying on seemingly supernatural powers, remained firmly attached to the whale's back, and when it resurfaced, he resumed the attack, driving a second stake into the other blowhole to "take away" the whale's "breathing." The Indians then tied a cord around the whale's tail and towed it into shallow water, where they surrounded the "conquered beast" to collect their "spoils," cutting its "flesh in peeces . . . [and] using it for meate." Although Acosta's story was repeated many times, few believed it. Not only were the details too fantastic, but the story was not based on an eyewitness account and instead was relayed to Acosta by "expert men."[29]

The idea that New England's Indians went whaling before the colonists arrived is by no means far-fetched. Other native peoples, with tools and skills not dissimilar to the ones available to the eastern tribes, hunted whales well before Europeans were even aware that New England existed. A thousand years ago the Thule Inuits, using bone-tipped harpoons, were whaling in the Canadian Arctic for bowhead and beluga whales from skin-lined boats.[30] And the Indians Waymouth encountered had arrows that possibly could have been used to hunt whales, which were described by an eyewitness as being made of ash or witch hazel, "big and long, with three feathers tied on . . . headed with the long shank bone of a Deere, made very sharpe with two fangs in [the] manner of a harping iron. They have likewise Darts, headed with bone. . . . These they use very cunningly, to kill fish, fowle and beasts."[31] As for being able to approach a whale in its element and react to and defend against its fury, the coastal Indians of New England possessed the canoe-handling talents to have done so. Still, if the New England Indians had an independent whaling tradition, it most certainly would have continued after the colonists arrived. Yet none of the accounts of the region written by Europeans during the early years of colonization mention Indian whaling. The lack of evidence, of course, does not prove that Indians didn't have a tradition of whaling, rather it simply means that we cannot say with any confidence that they did.[32]

While the New England colonists and, most likely, the local Indians focused their attention on drift whales, the Dutch took whaling in America to the next level.[33] On December 12, 1630, two Dutch ships, the *Walvis* (whale) and the *Salm* (salmon), departed from the Dutch port of Texel and began their voyage to a small parcel of land located at the mouth of the Delaware River, in the vicinity of Cape Henlopen. The Dutch West India Company, the ship's owners, set two goals for the expedition. The first and primary one was to hunt for whales in and around Delaware Bay, and boil their blubber to produce oil that could be sent back to Holland for use in manufacturing soap. The second goal was to establish a permanent Dutch settlement in the area.

Efforts to establish a settlement on the Delaware coast, in an area that was called Swanendael, or Valley of the Swans, proceeded reasonably well, with the construction of a few buildings and fortifications. But the whaling was a complete bust. Capt. Pieter Heyes, whose job it was to oversee the whaling, abandoned his responsibility, claiming that the whaling season had passed despite the fact that plenty of them were seen swimming just offshore. The only whale that Heyes encountered up close was dead on the beach, from which he and his men extracted a pitifully small amount of oil. Thus, when the *Walvis* returned to Texel in September 1631, Heyes had almost nothing to show for his trip.

The Dutch West India Company, upset about the outcome of its first whaling expedition, decided to launch another, and placed David de Vries, an accomplished sea captain, in charge. The *Walvis* was joined by the *Eikhoorn* (squirrel), and the two ships, after a series of mishaps

and delays, finally reached Swanendael in December 1632. After landing and helping to set up the shore-based whaling station, de Vries left
on the *Eikhoorn* to explore the area, while another captain stayed
behind on the *Walvis* to oversee the whaling. From December through
March the men of the *Walvis* harpooned seventeen whales but killed
and brought in only seven, and those were the smallest of the bunch,
leading de Vries to remark that "the whale fishery is very expensive
when such meager fish are caught."[34] De Vries's disappointment notwithstanding, the men of this expedition made history, becoming the
first Europeans to hunt whales successfully in America.

Despite the poor performance of the Dutch, and the limited nature
of whaling activities in New England, there was no doubt that whaling
was going to play an increasingly important role in America's development. There were simply too many whales to ignore. Immigrants saw
them on their way to America, and settlers saw them from the shore.
When a ship traveling to New England in 1629 passed near Cape
Sable, off the southern tip of Nova Scotia, the Reverend Francis Higginson wrote in his journal, "In the afternoon we had a cleare sight of
many islands and hills by the sea shoare. Now we saw . . . a great store
of great whales puffing up water as they goe, some of them came neere
our shipp; this creature did astonish us that saw them not before; their
back appeared like a little island."[35] Soon after Higginson arrived in
Massachusetts in 1630 he wrote that "the aboundance of Sea-Fish are
almost beyond beleeving, and sure I should scarce have belleved it
except I had seene it with mine owne Eyes. I saw great store of
Whales, and Crampusse."[36] Five years later, on a clear July afternoon,
the minister Richard Mather reported seeing off the coast of New England "mighty whales spewing up water in ye ayre, like ye smoake of a
chimney, and making ye sea about them white and hoary, as is said [in]
Job . . . of such incredible bigness y^t I will never wonder y^t ye body of
Jonas could bee in ye belly of a whale."[37]

And each whale represented a potential path to earning a livelihood. One of the first visitors to note this relationship was William
Morrell, an Episcopal clergyman who arrived in Plymouth in 1623.
Finding that the locals didn't lack for religious leadership, Morrell
abandoned his first calling and busied himself during the following
year by studying the local animals, plants, and people. So smitten was
he with his surroundings that he wrote a long and flowery poem about

New England, which was published in 1625.[38] In a couplet devoted to whales, Morrell captured the primary animating force that would drive future whaling activities in America.

> *The mighty whale doth in these harbours lye,*
> *Whose oyle the careful mearchant deare will buy.*[39]

About five years after Morrell published his poem, another young Englishman, by the name of William Wood, arrived in Massachusetts. He too wrote down what he saw, and in 1634, after returning to England, he published *New England's Prospect*, a relatively short, wide-ranging book about the unfolding colonial experience. In the chapter devoted to fish, Wood included a poem to illustrate the range of commodities that were plentiful off the New England coast. The poem led with the line, "The king of waters, the sea-shouldering whale."[40] And in subsequent years "the king of waters" did not disappoint.

Chapter Three

ALL ALONG THE COAST

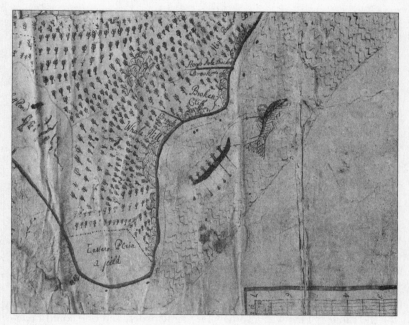

DETAIL FROM 1722 MAP SHOWING MEN IN A WHALEBOAT, HARPOONING A
WHALE OFF GARDINER'S ISLAND, NEAR THE TIP OF LONG ISLAND.

THE COLONISTS WHO LOOKED FOR DRIFT WHALES WERE PATIENT
people. They had no choice. Drift whaling was an uncertain pursuit.
Whales floated to shore neither reliably nor predictably. Yet these random events occurred often enough in America to engage the intense
interest of the people who lived near the sea. The clearest sign that
drift whaling had become an important occupation in the colonies was
the rise of government oversight. As the colonies grew and new com-

munities sprouted along the coast, local authorities began to view drift whaling as an enterprise that needed to be regulated so that disputes could be settled, profitability ensured, and order maintained. Nowhere were such authorities more active than in Massachusetts and on Long Island. By virtue of their locations these two areas took most seriously the very imprecise and fickle art of taking advantage of washed-up whales.

It is possible that the first local ordinance pertaining to drift whales was written in Massachusetts sometime during the 1630s. Governor Winthrop's casual reference in his journal that, in 1635, "Some of our people went to Cape Codd & made some oyle of a whale which was cast on shore," and his additional comment that as many as four whales were cast up there each year, provides at least a hint of potential trouble that might have necessitated government intervention. After all, Winthrop's "our people" belonged to the Massachusetts Bay Colony, while the people and lands of Cape Cod came under the aegis of the Plymouth Colony. Although these two colonies would eventually merge into the greater state of Massachusetts, at this time they remained separate entities. And while there is no record of the Plymouth Colony objecting to their Massachusetts Bay Colony brethren sailing over and taking their valuable whales, it is certainly plausible to think that there might have been some formal agreement between the colonies sanctioning and/or regulating such cross-border acquisitions.[1] We do know that by 1641 the Great and General Court of Massachusetts Bay ordered that "any Whale, or such like great fish cast upon any shore, shall be safely kept, or improved where it cannot be kept, by the town or other proprietor of the land, till the Generall Court shall set Order for the same."[2] This was a somewhat vague order, and one could imagine the lucky finder not wishing to keep watch over the animal or "improve" upon it (boil it for oil) until the colonial authorities were alerted and then arrived to sort things out. When the people of Southampton, Long Island, took up the issue of drift whales, they proved to be much more specific in their instructions than their peers to the north.

SOUTHAMPTON WAS FOUNDED in 1640 by a small group of settlers from Lynn, Massachusetts. Drawn to the area primarily to farm the land, these newcomers soon realized that there was also a ready bounty offered by the sea—drift whales. Over the next four years fights over who owned such whales were frequent enough that the Southampton General Court stepped in to keep the peace. On March 7, 1644, the court ordered that the town be divided into four wards of eleven persons each, and when a whale was found, each ward was required to offer two people, chosen by lot, to do the honors of cutting it up. Once the cutters took their double shares of the blubber, to compensate for "their payne," the remaining spoils were divided equally among the other able-bodied inhabitants. To ensure that no whale went unclaimed, the court established an early-warning system. After every storm Mr. Howell, Mr. Gosmer, and Mr. Bond were to select two people "to view & espie if there be any whales cast up."[3] If those viewers failed to carry out this responsibility, they would be fined ten shillings or whipped— Southamptonites were not ones to be trifled with. A year later a finder's fee was established as an incentive to encourage people to report drift whales. The first person who told the magistrate that there was a whale on the beach received a five-shilling reward, but if the whale was so puny that it was not worth five shillings, the finder got to keep the carcass. Was such a find to be reported on Sunday, however, the reward would be forfeited, courtesy of a clause in the law that was designed to keep people from spending the Lord's day on the beach looking for whales. With this detailed set of regulations, Southampton became the first colonial town in America to organize, albeit loosely, the process of drift whaling. It is fitting that this event took place on Long Island, for this elongated spit of land looks very much like a whale, its head lying near New York City and its mighty flukes splayed at the other end.[4]

Detailing every evolutionary twist and turn of drift-whale regulations in the colonies would be a tedious endeavor. When one steps back from the minutiae of the laws passed, however, a single theme appears. Generally speaking all the regulations focused on determining who would profit from the whales. First in line was the finder of the whale, who would get either a financial payoff or a part of the whale for his services. Thus enticed, many coastal residents became beachcombers on a mission. Then there were the cutters, sometimes Indians, who butchered and processed the whale so that the oil and baleen could be distributed. They were either chosen on a rotating basis or were appointed to their jobs, receiving payment as well.[5] Cutting up a whale was not pleasant, and some men figured out ways to avoid the task. In East Hampton, Long Island, for example, Thomas James and Lion Gardiner, the town's minister and a large landowner, respectively, were willing to keep on the lookout for whales, but avoided the next stage in the process by agreeing to "give a quart of licker apiece to the cutters of every whale, and be free from cuttinge"—then as now, wealth has its privileges.[6] The next stop in the drift-whale distribution system was the town where the whale washed ashore, and since whales were viewed as communal property, the oil was usually distributed more or less equally among its inhabitants, the latter group often being defined as householders or landowners.[7]

A town's claim to the whale, however, was not always all encompassing. In many instances the Indians sold their lands to the colonists with the proviso that they would retain the rights to various parts of the whales that were cast up. Sometimes this meant that the Indians were given the fins and flukes of the whales, items they held in reverence and used in religious ceremonies.[8] Other times the Indians' demands were more substantive, such as when a local chief on Martha's Vineyard sold a parcel of land to an Englishman and transferred with the property "four spans round in the middle of every whale that come upon the shore of this quarter part and no more."[9] And of course not all whales drifted ashore within a town's official limits. The vast majority of the coast during this era was not settled. In those wide-open spaces the policy on drift whales was essentially first come, first served.[10] Whoever processed the whale got the benefits, thereby creating an incentive for whale prospectors.

Once the finders, the cutters, the townspeople, the Indians, and the prospectors got what they were due, there could still be others waiting in line. In the Plymouth Colony of Massachusetts it was the colonial government that stepped forward in 1652 with its hand out. Noting that the cost of maintaining the colony was on the rise, and that "by God's providence many whales" were cast ashore on beaches within its jurisdiction, the colony saw no reason why it should not share in the profits. In other words the government would continue to run the colony, but the towns would have to chip in to defray the costs. To that end the court ordered that for every whale cast on shore, bought from an Indian, "or taken on drift att Sea and brought to shore," one barrel of "marchantable oyle," which was an amount equivalent to 31.5 gallons, had to be paid to the colonial treasury and delivered to Boston, whence the oil would be sold and shipped to England.[11]

At one point, however, the colony got greedy. In June 1661 the common understanding that the drift whales washing up within the town limits belonged to the town, with only a small part of the profits going to the colony, was turned on its head. Instead the colony proposed that it would take the lion's share of the whale's oil, and pay the town merely two hogsheads, or four barrels of oil, for processing each whale. Needless to say this idea didn't sit well with the towns, and they argued strenuously against it. The colony took heed of the complaints, rethought its position, and ultimately capitulated. On October 1, 1661, Constant Southworth, the treasurer of the colony, wrote to the towns of Barnstable, Sandwich, Eastham, and Yarmouth to make amends. His letter began with a most conciliatory salutation, "Loving Friends." Southworth went on to say that in light of the towns' failure to accept the colony's proposal, it was his duty to propose another solution. All controversy would be set aside for the present season, he promised, if the towns would "duely and trewly pay to the" colony one hogshead of oil for every whale that was cast ashore. While this was certainly better than the original proposal, it doubled the amount of oil due to the colony from one barrel to two.[12] Still, it was for the most part an acceptable solution to the towns, and it became the standard for many years.

In 1662 the Plymouth Colony proposed that men of God, too, should benefit from drift whales and receive a portion of the oil the towns produced to encourage the local ministry. The court's persuasive powers, however, were quite limited. In the near term at least, the only town that answered the call was Eastham.[13] Reflecting on Eastham's decision nearly two hundred years later, Henry David Thoreau wrote:

No doubt, there seemed to be some propriety in thus leaving the support of the ministers to Providence, whose servants they are, and who alone rules the storms; for, when few whales were cast up, they might suspect that their worship was not acceptable. The ministers must have sat upon the cliffs in every storm, and watched the shore with anxiety. And, for my part, if I were a minister I would rather trust to the bowels of the billows, on the back-side of Cape Cod, to cast up a whale for me, than to the generosity of many a country parish that I know. You cannot say of a country minister's salary, commonly, that it is 'very like a whale.' Nevertheless, the minister who depended on whales cast up must have had a trying time of it. . . . Think of a whale having the breath of life beaten out of him by a storm, and dragging in over the bars and guzzles, for the support of the ministry![14]

Locally obtained whale oil and whalebone quickly got swept into the stream of domestic and international commerce. By the 1640s, perhaps earlier, whale oil had become a staple commodity, and baleen could be found in many local shops. The rise of whale oil as a component of international trade was recognized by entrepreneurs interested in obtaining English goods. Undoubtedly one of the first of these individuals was Samuel Maverick, an Englishman who had settled on Noddles Island (modern day East Boston) in the late 1620s. By 1641 he had already begun sending colonial whale oil to the port of Bristol, England, where his agent would use the oil to purchase goods that would then be shipped back across the Atlantic.[15]

EVENTUALLY THE COLONISTS became impatient waiting for whales. Why rely on Providence, stormy weather, or the inexplicable and doomed meanderings of pilot whales as the only means to obtain whale oil and whalebone? Thus the colonists, slowly at first, then with increasing regularity, took to the sea in their boats and went whaling, or to be more precise, went shore whaling within a few miles of the beach. Although shore whalemen would occasionally kill a humpback whale, and certainly take advantage of the opportunity to drive a school of pilot whales ashore, it was the right whale that they viewed as the ultimate grail.[16]

The exact date and location of the first colonial shore-whaling trip is unknown.[17] It is possible that it took place off Connecticut as early as 1647, for that is when the General Court in Hartford passed a resolve giving a Mr. Whiting the right to "prosecute a design for the taking of whale," and to have the sole right to such business for the period of seven years.[18] But there is no record of Mr. Whiting taking advantage of this monopoly. The first shore-whaling trip may just as well have departed from Southampton in 1650, when the General Court there gave John Ogden the "free liberty without interruption from the Inhabitants of Southampton to kill whales" upon the Atlantic Ocean within the town's limits, also for a period of seven years.[19] Proof of Ogden's success, however, is similarly lacking. Nevertheless, there is little doubt that shore whaling began at least as early as the 1650s. The evidence for this comes from a petition sent to King Charles II of England in 1672, in which the three towns at the eastern end of Long Island informed the king that although "they had endeavored above these twenty years" to be successful in whaling, they "could not bring it to any perfection till within these 2 or 3 yeares last past."[20] From this admittedly inauspicious beginning, shore whaling spread along the coast. Up through the end of the seventeenth century and into the beginning of the next, the number of boats engaged in shore whaling increased as did the number of whales towed to shore.

The rise of shore whaling did not mean the end of drift whaling. Instead the colonists simply added shore whaling to their repertoire, and continued to scan the beaches for surprises. If anything, shore whaling contributed to the growth of drift whaling, because when whales struck at sea escaped their pursuers, they often drifted ashore after succumbing to their wounds. According to one account from 1700, a woman walking along the beach between East Hampton and Bridgehampton came across thirteen stranded whales, a few of which, no doubt, had been harpooned by men in boats. The rise of shore whaling also spawned organizational changes. Whereas drift whaling was a communal activity organized to dispose of common property, shore whaling was the active pursuit of profit by a select group of people who, understandably, had little interest sharing the fruits of their investment and labor with those who had no role in the hunt. Thus small groups of men partnered with one another, pooled their resources, and launched whaling companies.[21]

Such companies motivated their workers by promising them a portion of the proceeds from the whales they caught, called a "lay," which was usually paid in money, whale oil, or whalebone, although sometimes other forms of payment were used. Shore whaling relied heavily on Indian labor, and many of the authors who claim that the Indians were America's first whalemen also indicate that the Indians taught the colonists how to whale, but there is no evidence for this. What is far more likely is that the colonists employed Indians not as teachers but because they were cheap labor, and certainly skilled and strong enough to perform the more menial tasks they were almost always assigned, such as rowing and processing the whales on shore.[22] Indians were also sought because the alternative sources of labor were somewhat limited. African Americans would one day become a mainstay of the whaling industry, but that time was still far in the future. And the only other laborers, white Europeans, were not always interested in being shore whalemen. "The problem with the economy of colonial America," historian T. H. Breen has observed, "was that no one was willing to serve as a common laborer."[23]

Indian labor proved so essential to the whaling industry that special laws were passed to ensure that Indians were available for the hunt. In 1708, for example, New York passed an act for the "Encouragement of Whaling," which said that any Indian who was signed on to go whaling should not "at any time or times between the First Day of November and the Fifteenth Day of April following, yearly, be sued, arrested, molested, detained, or kept out of that Imployment by any person or persons whatsoever."[24] As Indian labor grew scarcer, the competition for the most skilled Indians increased, leading the employers to offer them additional inducements to sign on. In 1672, for example, John Cooper of Southampton hired two Indian crews to go whaling on his behalf from November 16 to April 16. His contract with the Indians stipulated that in addition to half of the oil from the trip, they would also receive "broadcloth; trucking-cloth britches; poringers; spoones; shott, powder, and, when they need it, each Boats crew, 3 gills of liquor at sixpence ye gill."[25] A year later the Southampton General Court stepped in to halt the escalation of these bidding wars by placing a cap on Indians' wages. Anyone who hired an Indian to go whaling, the court ordered, "Shall not give him . . . above one Trucking Cloath coat for each Whale, hee and his company Shall Kill or half of the Blubber, without the Whale bone."[26] Although many Indians willingly engaged in shore whaling, and some even bargained for better wages, the relationship between the Indians and their employers was hardly simple. Liquor was often used as an inducement to work, with the colonists exploiting the Indians strong desire for and addiction to firewater. Indians also frequently became indebted to the whaling company owners and had little choice but to continue in their employ until they could buy back their freedom.[27]

No matter where shore whaling took root, similar techniques were used. Lookouts scanned the horizon for cresting whales and telltale spouts, often while sitting atop a tall timber pounded into a dune and fitted with a platform. When a whale came into view, the lookout cried, "Whale off!" or "Whale in the bay!" or placed a piece of cloth called a "weft" on a pole, and the whalemen came running. One, two, or sometimes more whaleboats, each with the usual complement of six men, would then shove off, and the men would begin rowing toward deeper water. As the boat approached the whale, the men became silent so as not to startle it and cause it to swim away. If oars were in the water they were used gently, or sometimes replaced with paddles. Once the boat closed in on the whale, the harpooner grabbed the tool of his trade and stood poised at the bow ready to strike when the time was right. His harpoon was a double-barbed iron dart, with a two-foot shank, mounted on a pole made from a hardwood sapling. Thick enough for a man to wrap his hand around and up to six feet long, the pole was rough-hewn, often with the bark still on, to provide a solid grip. The harpoon, which whalemen called an iron, was attached to a hemp or manila line or warp a hundred or more fathoms long, which lay coiled in a tub at the bottom of the boat. Although the best harpooners might have been accurate from a distance of tens of feet, the goal was to get as close as possible to the whale so that the harpoon could be thrown or thrust with enough force to penetrate the whale's fibrous skin and blubber. If the harpooner had the time and the talent, he would launch a second harpoon into the wounded whale. Despite their considerable size and sharp tips, harpoons were not designed to kill the whale; instead they were meant to hold fast to the whale to keep it from escaping. To perform this function the harpoon had to be strong enough to withstand the tremendous forces that the whale could bring to bear as it tried to wrench free, and it was not uncommon for the whale's contortions to cause a harpoon to loose its grip.[28]

The moments after the harpoon found its mark were the most dangerous part of the hunt. With one flick of its mighty tail flukes, the enraged whale could destroy the boat, flinging the men into the water, possibly injuring or killing a few, and leaving the rest, few of whom could swim, struggling to stay afloat. More commonly the struck whale would take off, and what happened next depended on what the whalemen chose to do with the harpoon line. Some fastened it to a large, buoyant block of wood, called a drogue, which tired the whale by creating drag and making it difficult for the whale to dive. Other whalemen kept the line attached to the boat, thereby, in effect, turning the boat into a large drogue. If the harpoon was tethered to the boat, the men had to be especially alert. Were the whale to dive, and the men failed to pay out the rope fast enough, the boat could easily be dragged under. To help avoid this possibility a crewmember stood by with a hatchet at the ready to cut the line if need be.

A whale barreling along at the surface would take the men on the proverbial Nantucket sleigh ride, a bone-jarring, terrifying, and at times, no doubt, exhilarating trip over the waves.[29] As soon as the whale tired, the men pulled alongside it—"wood to blackskin"—whereupon one of them grabbed the lance, a long, teardrop-shaped and extremely sharp steel knife mounted on a pole, which was used to finish off the whale. The goal was to strike hard and deep to pierce the lungs, or the "life" of the whale, and then churn the lance to do the most damage. Success would show itself as a geyser of crimson blood gushing from the whale's blowhole, which caused whalemen to cry out, "Chimney's afire!"[30] Now came the whale's final flurry, in which it began swimming frantically in ever tighter circles, thrashing its tail, and posing its final danger to the whalemen, who backed off their boat to keep it from being damaged by the dying animal's final exertions. When the whale exhaled its last breath, it turned on its side, fin out, as the whalemen called it. One of the men cut a hole in the whale's flukes, into which was inserted a T-shaped wooden toggle attached to a rope, and the crew began the long, wearying tow back to shore. Writing in 1725 Paul Dudley, an eminent jurist and naturalist from Massachusetts, observed, "The Whale is sometimes killed with a single stroke, and yet at other Times she will hold the Whale-men in Play, near half a Day together, with their Lances, and sometimes will get away after they have been lanced and spouted Blood, with Irons in them, and Drugs fastened to them, which are thick boards about fourteen inches square."[31]

The processing of the whales followed a familiar routine. Once the whale came to rest on the sand, the cutters began their work. Sharp knives sliced through the blubber as it was peeled off the animal in great heavy strips. The blubber was then hauled higher up the beach using ropes and, in many instances, a winchlike device called a crab, which the men strained to turn. The men also cut off the whale's lips to get at the strips of baleen, which were sheared from the roof of the mouth. This was brutal, dirty, and tiring work, which could take a couple of days or more. Spattered with blood and oil, and soaked in salt water, the men often had to contend with the weather, fighting the winds of winter or the heat of summer. And if the cutting didn't begin immediately, the process of decay would create a noisome stench, forcing the men to fight nausea as well as fatigue. Undoubtedly one of the worst experiences was when the men had to cut into a drift whale that had been dead for days. The carcass, bloated with the gases of decomposition, was like a very taut balloon full of the foulest-smelling vapors imaginable. One unlucky man would be given the task of puncturing the "balloon," and, with a mighty *whoosh*! the gases would escape, enveloping the area in a malodorous cloud.

The baleen and blubber were loaded onto carts and taken from the beach for processing, while the rest of the carcass, including all the meat, was left to rot in the water. The colonists' failure to take advantage of such a large and ready source of protein is a bit puzzling. If a single pilot whale has the same caloric content as thirty-six deer, as has been calculated, then just imagine how many calories a large right whale could provide.[32] Why did the colonists, with ever more mouths to feed, look askance at this enormous bounty from the sea? After all, for centuries their European ancestors had consumed whale meat, and well before that, other cultures, such as those of the Greeks and the Romans, had done the same. And by many accounts whale meat, or at least the meat of certain whales, is edible if not quite tasty.[33] Yet, while some colonists did eat whale meat, they were an extreme minority. Perhaps the reason for this can be gleaned from the words of the famed English whaleman, William Scoresby, who noted that, "to the refined palate of a modern European, the flesh of a whale, as an article of food, would be received with abhorrence."[34] Although Scoresby was writing in 1820, he certainly could have been describing a shift in taste that had already been under way for quite some time.

Not everyone ignored the whale carcasses floating in the shallows. Even if whale meat did not suit the palates of the colonists, perhaps it could serve another purpose. Where others saw waste, Thomas Houghton, a Boston merchant, saw profit. In the early 1700s he came up with some novel ideas for utilizing whale meat, or as he said, "improving the lean of the whales."[35] The most interesting was that of taking whale meat and mixing it with "other things" to produce saltpeter, the main ingredient in gunpowder. Houghton did not offer any details as to how such improvements would be achieved, but that did not stop the provincial government from granting him a four-year monopoly to prove his case. If Houghton ever did anything with this grant, he clearly failed to execute his business plan, for the lean of the whales remained what it had always been in the colonies—something to be left behind after the valuable blubber and baleen had been stripped from the carcasses and taken to the tryworks for processing.[36]

At the tryworks the baleen was dried and prepared for shipping, while the blubber was cut into small pieces and placed in large iron pots suspended over a wood fire to be "saved," or rendered into oil.[37] As the oil melted out of the blubber, the skin and any meat left behind, called "cracklins," would rise to the surface of the pot, where they would be scooped off and fed to the fire below or sometimes be eaten by the men. "Trying out" a whale was a slow process. It could take many days for a tryworks, burning around the clock, to process all the blubber of a large whale.[38] After the oil in the pots cooled, it was poured into casks for storage or shipping. A whale's yield depended on its size. The governor of New York, writing about right whales in 1708, said, "A Yearling will make about forty Barrils of Oyl, a Stunt or Whale two years old will make sometimes fifty, sometimes Sixty Barrils of Oyl, and the largest whale that I have heard of in these Parts, Yielded one hundred and ten Barrils of Oyl, and Twelve hundred Weight of Bone."[39]

While the processing of a whale was a time of great joy because of the profits it represented, it was also a time of great discomfort and concern. Fully stoked tryworks filled neighboring areas with a stench of boiling blubber and posed a fire threat. In Southampton the situation became so bad that on March 4, 1669, the town issued a public order to limit olfactory distress and the potential for blazes.[40] Even when the tryworks were not operating, they could be a nuisance on account of the whaling waste that accumulated around them. To address that problem, the town of East Hampton passed an ordinance in April 1674 that sought to reduce those "unsavourie and noisome smells" by requiring that "all whale scrapps that are at the several mens tryringe places shall bee all buried in the ground by the 15th of this instant upon the penaltie of 5 shillings."[41]

The hunting season for shore whaling usually ran from late fall or early winter through early spring, which allowed men to engage in farming, fishing, and other pursuits during the rest of the year. This diversification was important, for although a good season could generate considerable profits, shore whaling was usually a supplementary, rather than a sole, source of income. Some towns, such as East Hampton, took steps to ensure the availability of young men to man the boats and tend the tryworks. When the town hired a schoolmaster in 1675, his instructions were to start classes on August 16, keep them going until the end of December, and then let the pupils go whaling until April 1, at which time school would go back into session until August.[42] Shore whaling required so much local labor that it could be hard to find men to perform other tasks. That was the situation that faced Capt. John Thacher, in 1694, when he was looking for recruits on Cape Cod to fight in the French and Indian War. He wrote to Governor Stoughton, "All our young and strong men are imployed in whaling and mostly have their rendivous remote from the towns." But even when Thacher did track down these men, he had a tough time getting their attention, not because they were so devoted to whaling, but because they were motivated to avoid military service. "If they see any man coming towards them," Thacher continued, they "presently mistrust, make a shoute and run into the thickets."[43]

Shore whaling proved to be a highly variable business. Some years inevitably were good, others bad. According to a recent survey of historical records, the largest single-year catch of right whales on Long Island was 111 in 1707. This yielded an impressive four thousand barrels of oil. Yet, the very next year, Long Islanders caught far fewer whales and produced only six hundred barrels of oil.[44] This variability notwithstanding, shore whaling was a very attractive business opportunity. In 1683, for example, William Penn wrote to a group of land developers with encouraging news. "Mighty whales roll upon the coast, near the mouth of the Bay of Delaware; eleven caught and worked onto oyle one season. We justly hope a considerable profit by a whalery, they being so numerous and the shore so suitable."[45]

Despite the economic vagaries of shore whaling, it became a growing source of overseas trading revenue near the end of the seventeenth century. A glimpse into the transatlantic trade is offered by the notes of John Hull, a Boston shipowner. In 1675 Hull dispatched Capt. John

Harris, on board the *Sea Flower*, to Long Island. Once there Harris was to trade or sell the commodities he had on board and obtain whale oil and whalebone from the Long Islanders. The *Sea Flower*'s next stop was England, where Harris was to get the best price for his cargo and then either go to France if the sale had been profitable enough to justify more lavish expenditures, or just load up on English cargo and return to Boston.[46]

THE FORTUNES OF THE COLONIAL WHALING trade were not lost on England. In 1688 Edward Randolph, one of the king's commissioners, visited the colonies to report on their economic progress. Focusing on the situation in Massachusetts, Randolph wrote, "New Plimouth Colony have great profit by whale killing. I believe it will be one of our best returnes, now beaver and peltry fayle us."[47] Randolph had good reason to be pleased with the rise of whaling in the colonies because colonial whale oil filled a void in England's economy. When the London-based Muscovy Company first sent its ships north to Spitsbergen in the early 1600s, it had high hopes of creating a whaling empire. But its hopes were soon crushed by the Dutch, who became the preeminent whalemen of the day.[48] The British whale fishery, in contrast, limped along and produced very little. With its own ships performing so miserably, England had to look elsewhere to meet local demands for whale oil and baleen. Not only did England have strong trading ties with the colonies, but it also created a tax policy that favored colonial oil over that supplied by the Dutch. Beginning in 1673 England placed a duty of nine pounds per ton on Dutch oil in an effort to stem its flow into the country. In contrast the duty on oil imported from the colonies was set at only three shillings per ton.[49] The political and economic logic was inescapable: Given the choice between paying more for the oil of an erstwhile enemy and competitor and buying cheaper oil from fellow countrymen, English merchants increasingly opted for the latter.

The success of shore whaling also commanded the attention of Cotton Mather, the famed Congregational minister of the North Church in Boston. In his magnum opus, the *Magnalia Christi Americana; or, the Ecclesiastical History of New-England*, published in 1702, Mather marveled at "the catching of *Whales*, whose *Oil* is become a *Staple-Commodity* of the Country . . . [and] the desperate hazards run by the

Whale-Catchers in their thin *Whale-Boats.*"[50] Fourteen years later
Mather decided that whalemen needed to honor the God who created
the whales by becoming better Christians and sharing their success
with the church. "May it not be a service unto the Kingdome of God,"
Mather noted in his diary on October 18, 1716, "if I address our
numerous Tribe of *Whale-Catchers*, with some suitable Meditations,
that may have a Tendency to make them sensible to their Obligations
to live unto God?"[51] His essay, titled "The Thankful Christian," is
addressed "unto *All* that have received the Favours of Heaven; But more
especially unto them, who after the good successes of a WHALING-
Season, would Express their Gratitude unto God their SAVIOUR." In
the course of forty-three pages Mather not only offers up a great
amount of information on the biology, behavior, and religious history
of the "*Fish* of the Cetaceous Kind," but he also makes clear why whalemen in particular might have cause to dig deep into their pockets when
deciding how much of their income to share with the church:

> The *Whales* are a *Fish*, that sometimes are found of a very Stu-
> pendous Magnitude, My Brethren, You that Encounter those
> mighty *sea-monsters* and Extend the *Empire of Mankind*, unto a
> Victory and a Dominion over those formidable Animals; most
> certainly, *You* ought upon some Accounts to be *Christians of the
> First Magnitude. . . . Give unto the Lord*, O ye Subduers of the
> *Mighty*, . . . He is the Creator and the Governour of those
> Mighty *Fishes*, which He has delivered into your Hands. . . . Hav-
> ing Survived your *Whaling-Season*, your Thankful Souls may
> say, *This is the Lords-doing, and Marvellous in our Eyes!*

Having made every effort to rouse his readers to action, Mather ends
his treatise by urging them to give no less than a "Tenth Part" of their
earnings to the church.[52]

Shore whaling quickly became a controversial business, particularly
as it related to ownership of whales killed at sea. Disagreements rarely
arose when the whales were successfully towed back to land. However,
when a whale was harpooned but lost by its pursuers, only to wash
ashore later, then things could prove nettlesome, especially when the
whale no longer had a harpoon in it.[53] Who then did the deed? Even
when a harpoon was still embedded in the whale, ownership could be

contested, for in the early years of shore whaling few whalemen marked their harpoons. The Plymouth Colony attempted to remedy this by requiring, in 1688, that "each company's harping iron and lance be distinctly marked on ye heads and sockets with a poblick mark: to ye prevention of strife."[54] That certainly helped, but it didn't solve the problem. So in 1690 the colony decided to get some eyes on the ground to gather the relevant facts. The court appointed individuals to "inspect and view the whales, and for the "prevention of contests and suits by whale killers," the court laid down a series of regulations that were designed to clarify who owned the whales in the event that a controversy arose. Moreover, anyone who defaced a whale by "cutting, stabbing, or lancing" it before the inspector could investigate would lose the right to the whale and be fined ten pounds, payable to the colony.[55] Poaching was another source of controversy in shore whaling. In some instances one colony would invite whalemen from another to come whaling, with the proviso that those whalemen give part of their profits to the host government. Conflicts arose, however, when whalemen from one colony whaled in another without paying for that privilege.[56]

The most interesting shore-whaling controversy pitted the whalemen of Long Island against a string of governors of New York. These two groups regarded whales very differently. Simply put, the whalemen believed it was their right to dispose of the whales as they saw fit, while the governors did not. This fundamental disagreement began in the early 1670s with the passage of two laws. One, making the most of the claim that whales were "Royal Fish," required Long Islanders to pay the governor of New York, who, after all, was the duly appointed representative of the king, one-sixteenth of the oil and whalebone they procured from drift whales. The second law required Long Islanders wishing to export such oil and whalebone to do so through the port of New York.[57] The Long Islanders viewed these laws with contempt and, for the most part, did not comply. The whaling towns on eastern Long Island, by virtue of their lineage and their original patents of ownership, bore a more natural affinity to their brothers and sisters to the west and north, in Connecticut and Massachusetts, than they did to New York, and it was to those other colonies that they sent virtually all their oil and whalebone. This illegal trade quickly became an open secret, greatly angering New York's governors, but for many years, try as they might, they failed to halt it.

When Edward Hyde, or, as he was better known, Lord Cornbury, became the governor of New York in 1702, he renewed the government's claim to the "Royal Fish," and threw in a few twists of his own. Long Island whalemen now had to purchase a license to go shore whaling, give the governor a share of the profits from drift *and* live-caught whales, and export *all* oil and whalebone through New York.[58] Cornbury's decision to reinvigorate and expand on his predecessors' claims on whales was largely self-interested. During his term as governor, which lasted until 1708, Cornbury amassed a record that, according to one historian, "rendered himself not only odious but despicable.... As he came here in the most indigent circumstances, hunted out of England by a host of hungry creditors, some of whom had been ruined by his profligacy, he was bent on getting as much money as he could squeeze out of the purses of an insulted people."[59] Unfortunately for Cornbury, his plan to squeeze the Long Island whalemen wasn't working. In 1703 he wrote to the Lords of Trade complaining that

there has for some time been no Trade between the City of New Yorke and the East-end of Long Island, from whence the greatest quantity of Whale oyl comes. And indeed, the people of the East End of Long Island are not very willing to be persuaded to believe that they belong to this province. They are full of New England principles. They choose rather to trade with the people of Boston, Connecticut, and Rhode Island, than with the people of New Yorke.[60]

Ineffectual or not, Cornbury's laws infuriated many Long Island whalemen, including Samuel Mulford. Born in 1644, Mulford spent his first few years in Southampton and the balance of his life in East Hampton. Growing up in these towns, Mulford was surrounded by men involved in whaling, including his father, who owned whaleboats and in whose employ he had learned some of his whaling skills. As early as 1681 Mulford was fitting out shore-whaling boats of his own, and by the turn of the century he was running a whaling company that employed twenty-four men. By every estimation Mulford had a striking personality. To his critics he was dangerous, rash, and pigheaded. But to those who knew him best, he was an honest man, who was strong willed, fought for what he believed in, said what was on his mind, rarely took no for an answer, and, most of all, stood up for his himself and his fellow Long Islanders. Mulford viewed Cornbury, as well as many of the governors who had preceded him, as riding roughshod over the people. Cornbury's demands of whalemen were, as Mulford saw them, just another in a long line of such insults that Long Islanders had been forced to endure.[61]

Rather than fight Cornbury directly, Mulford sailed to England in 1704 to plead his case with Cornbury's superiors, and to get the new laws on whaling repealed. This was, as historian Robert Ritchie noted, "a rather audacious thing to do."[62] Mulford was a relatively obscure representative of an equally obscure colonial town, and there he was doing an end run around a royal governor, who, it should be pointed out, was closely related to Queen Anne as well as various highly placed personages in the British government. Unfortunately, there is no record of Mulford's activities during this trip, or the reception he got, but he did not achieve his primary goal. The law remained in place, and the whalemen continued flouting it, while Cornbury continued to try to compel compliance, with little success. In 1708, on the eve of his departure as governor, Cornbury repeated, in a letter to his superiors in London, what had by then become a plaintive cry, that the "illegal trade—carried on between New England, Connecticut, and the East End of Long Island" continued unabated.[63] As it turned out, Mulford's skirmish with Cornbury and his 1704 visit to London were only a dress rehearsal for a later and much more momentous engagement. Only this time his adversary was Governor Robert Hunter, who came to power in 1710.

Following in Cornbury's footsteps, Hunter ordered that Long Island whalemen take out licenses, export their oil and whalebone from New York, and share their profits. This, along with other measures aimed at restricting the Long Islanders' rights and opportunities to trade freely with whomever they pleased, ignited fresh protests from the eastern towns. It did not help matters when Hunter then sent sheriffs to seize whales to ensure that the Crown received its due. Mulford, who now represented East Hampton in the New York Assembly, took up the cause once again, and set his sights on Hunter. In a dramatic speech before the assembly, on April 2, 1714, Mulford laid out his many grievances about Hunter's laws. He railed against the restrictions on whaling and the levying of taxes that he thought were being foisted on the citizenry without their consent. He was angry that while the government of New York was claiming poverty, the governor was earning a salary that was far greater than the combined salaries of the governors of Massachusetts, Connecticut, and Rhode Island. He implied that rather than being used to defray the costs of government, the taxes were being embezzled by government officials.[64] He was incensed by the requirement that the Port of New York alone serve as the conduit through which Long Island goods must move, believing that it stymied, rather than encouraged business. Not only did this force Long Island merchants to travel upward of one hundred miles before they could sell their goods, but it also meant that they had to run the bureaucratic gauntlet at the port.

If Mulford had stopped at that point, the resulting battle with Hunter would have been heated enough. But Mulford took the brazen step of having his speech printed and distributed, thereby rendering moot any immunity from retaliation he might have had as an elected official simply stating his opinions within the confines of the assembly. Hunter pounced on the opening, having Mulford arrested and charged before the Supreme Court of New York with printing and "dispersing a false scandalous and malicious libel . . . with an intent to raise Sedition amongst the people."[65] While many of Mulford's peers in the assembly no doubt agreed with him, they, too, were quite upset about his decision to publish the speech, and, as a result, they expelled him from the legislature. And those weren't Mulford's only problems. While all this was going on, he was also defending himself in court against another charge brought by Hunter, that he had violated New York law by taking whales without a license and, in effect, appropriating the Crown's goods for his own purposes.[66]

Far from vanquished, Mulford returned to East Hampton, whereupon his loyal and like-minded supporters promptly re-elected him. Back in the assembly in 1716, Mulford convinced his colleagues to intervene on his behalf to have the legal cases against him dropped. The assembly's petition to Hunter told of the "great Hurt, Damage, and Inconveniency" that the proceedings were causing Mulford, and, further, requested that the governor take into account Mulford's "great Age," the distance he lived from New York City, and "other considerations" in deciding to free him from prosecution.[67] Hunter responded that, if Mulford openly apologized for his transgressions, the suit would be dismissed.[68] Rather than admit something he didn't believe, Mulford upped the ante, and secretly departed for England to plead his case yet again.

To conceal his departure, the seventy-one-year-old Mulford first sailed to Newport, and then walked to Boston, where he boarded a ship to London. At this point in the story, legend and fact become intertwined. It was during this visit that Mulford supposedly earned his nickname, "Fishhook." He was, it is said, dressed rather plainly, and on getting off the boat in London, Mulford, with his "unsophisticated appearance," proved to be an appealing target to the local pickpockets, who promptly divested Mulford of some of his property. Greatly annoyed by this thievery, Mulford repaired to a local tailor and had him sew fishhooks into his pockets, so that the next person who went exploring would find a nasty surprise. According to the legend, the local papers became aware of Mulford's so-called "Yankee Trick," and soon his fame spread throughout London, with even the king being counted as one of Mulford's admirers.[69] While there is no evidence that such events took place, they certainly are nevertheless in character with the man. And fishhooks or no, Mulford made the most of his time in London, submitting a petition to the king and urging all the officials he met with to overturn Hunter's laws.

In the petition Mulford noted that New York law had long required whalemen to pay a duty on drift whales. Ignoring history, Mulford added that he and his fellow Long Islanders had no problem with this system and had been more than happy to give the "Crown the benefit of all drift whales." Mulford's real objection, he said, was with the governors' extending their reach and demanding profits from and control over the disposition of whales caught at sea. He pointed out that ever since the inception of the colony of New York, and through their patent from the king, the people of East Hampton and the surrounding areas had been given "the priviledge and benefit of fishing for whale & applying ye same to their own use as their undoubted right and property." Mulford argued that the new licensing, exporting, and duty requirements took away that right and property, and they had done so without the consent of the governed. He ended his petition claiming that unless these laws were overturned, the whale fishery would suffer, because "the person concerned will not be brought to the hardship of waiting out at sea many months, & the difficulty of bringing into New York the fish, and at last paying so great a share of their profit."[70]

When Hunter learned of Mulford's trip, he wrote to the Lords of Trade, telling them his side of the case and urging them to not to listen to Mulford, whom he variously called, "that poor troublesome old man," an "enemy to the Publick [and] . . . a Crazed man."[71] Hunter said that Mulford was the only one to "dispute" the Crown's "right" to part of the profits from whale fishing, and that many of his peers had "voluntarily" purchased licenses.[72] To learn the truth from Mulford, Hunter invited the Lords to "bluff him."[73] But Hunter underestimated his adversary. The lords found Mulford's arguments compelling because, as Breen points out, they "transformed" Mulford and his peers into "true Englishmen" fighting for "ancient rights and liberties" against "a gang of corrupt hirelings"—all of which were ideas that resonated with men who ruled England.[74] Then, in a turn that must have caused Hunter to seethe, the lords shifted the burden of proof back to the governor. "You intimate in your letter," they wrote to Hunter, "that the Whale fishery is reserved to the Crown by your Patents: as we can find no such thing in your Commission, we desire you will explain what you mean by it." The Lords further requested Hunter to provide an account of any duties that he had received and to what purposes they had been applied. And lest there be any doubt about the support of the Lords of Trade for whaling in the colonies, they added, "Upon this occasion we must observe to you, that we hope you will give all due incouragement to that Trade."[75]

In subsequent years heated letters sailed back and forth between London and New York, which alternately ascribed blame, elicited and offered legal opinions, requested reconsideration, and encouraged resolution. Hunter continued to attack Mulford, and at one point, after noting that Mulford had managed to secure only a few signatures to support his cause, wrote, "If the voice of a whole Province is not judged of force sufficient to disprove the simple allegations of one crazed old man, it will be in vain for me to endeavor any more at being pronounced innocent."[76] Meanwhile Mulford stayed resolute in his unwillingness to pay a single shilling to the Crown from the profits he gained through whaling. Unfortunately we don't know how this controversy was resolved. Once Hunter returned to England in 1719, the flow of correspondence and the rhetoric on this issue diminished rapidly. It appears, though, that there was at least a partial resolution in 1720, when Governor William Burnet wrote to the Lords of Trade stating that he had decided to remit the percentage due to the Crown from the whale fishery, but he still intended to enforce the requirement that all whalemen be licensed, thereby maintaining the integrity of the king's rights while having a "good effect on the country."[77]

Crusty till the end, Samuel Mulford died in 1725, at the age of eighty-one. In him, and the lives of the other Long Islanders who supported him, we can see glimpses of the spirit that animated the American Revolution, and hear faint echoes of the future rallying cry, "No taxation without representation." We can also detect signs of the beginning of the end of an era in whaling. Although men would continue shore whaling for centuries more, a fundamental shift in American whaling had begun by the 1720s. The industry was moving in a new direction. And leading the way was Nantucket island.

Chapter Four

NANTUCKET,
THE "FARAWAY LAND"

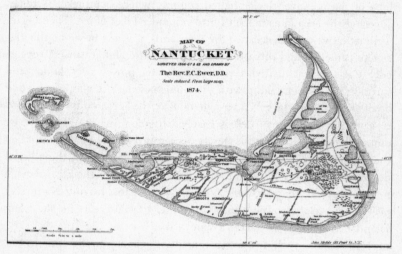

MAP OF NANTUCKET, DRAWN BY THE REVEREND F. C. EWER, 1874.

NANTUCKET, OR NATOCKETE AS THE LOCAL WAMPANOAG INDIANS called it, translates from the Indian language as "faraway land" or "the far-off place," and it lives up to its name.[1] "Take out your map and look at it," Herman Melville exclaimed. "See what a real corner of the world it occupies; how it stands there, away off shore, more lonely than the Eddystone lighthouse."[2] A crescent-shaped island just thirteen miles long and seven miles wide at its farthest reaches, Nantucket is roughly thirty miles from Woods Hole on Cape Cod, and fifteen miles from the larger island of Martha's Vineyard.

According to one Wampanoag legend, Nantucket was born of a

great giant's irritation. When this giant, called Mashop, lay down to sleep one night on the ample bed provided by Cape Cod, all was fine. But during the night his moccasins filled with sand. This irritating discovery upon waking led Mahsop to fling his moccasins out to sea. The one that landed nearest to Cape Cod became Martha's Vineyard and the one further out, Nantucket.[3]

Albeit less fanciful, Nantucket's geological origins are just as interesting as the legend. Toward the end of the last Ice Age, about fifteen to twenty thousand years ago, as the world began warming, the southern edge of the Laurentide glacier stopped advancing. The edge of one lobe of the massive glacier halted roughly where Nantucket is today, covering the area in as much as fifteen hundred feet of ice. Then began a climatic two-step that lasted for thousands of years, in which the glacier first melted and retreated, and then refroze and advanced, repeatedly. Each time it melted, rivers of icy water flowed over, under, and through the glacier, taking with them much of the silt, clay, gravel, and boulders that the glacier had gouged out of the earth on its southward trek. As these rivers of debris reached the edge of the glacier, they dumped their load onto the slowly accreting alluvial plain, and when the glacier refroze and advanced, it pushed and mounded the alluvial deposits into ridges, hills, and other landforms. When the glacier made its final retreat, its meltwater filled up the oceans, leaving Nantucket peeking above the waves, along with other glacial creations like Long Island, Cape Cod, and Martha's Vineyard.[4]

Nantucket's path toward colonization began in the late 1640s, when Thomas Mayhew of Martha's Vineyard, imbued with and wanting to share the Holy Spirit, began visiting Nantucket to convert the Wampanoags to Christianity. At the same time Vineyarders were in the habit of using Nantucket as a pasture for their sheep and cattle. But it was not until the late 1650s that colonists started eyeing Nantucket as a candidate for permanent English settlement, when a small group of men from the Merrimack Valley, which sits astride today's Massachusetts–New Hampshire border, approached Mayhew with a proposal to buy land on the island. Mayhew was the man to talk to because he had recently purchased a large part of Nantucket himself. Although many of the prospective purchasers were prosperous members of their communities, and therefore had much to lose in moving off shore, they had, as historian Edward Byers points out, a variety of compelling reasons for wanting to relocate.[5] Some felt hemmed in by the commercial opportunities available on the increasingly crowded and competitive mainland. Some were enticed by the idea of launching a community on their own terms, where success and failure would rest squarely on their shoulders. And still others saw relocation as a way to escape the strict Puritanism and, at times, the reproach of their peers. So on July 2, 1659, this group of men, nine in all, purchased a great swath of Nantucket from Mayhew for thirty pounds and two beaver hats—one for Mayhew and one for his wife.[6]

The first contingent of settlers sailed for Nantucket in October 1659, on a small and heavily provisioned boat. On board were Thomas Macy, his wife, Sarah, and their five children, along with Edward Starbuck, James and Tristram Coffin, and twelve-year old Isaac Coleman. Macy gave out the greatest sigh of relief as the boat departed, for he was leaving some trouble behind. It began earlier that year, when Macy, a Baptist, extended the hand of kindness to four Quakers who were passing by his home on a summer's day, on their way to a nearby town. When it started raining Macy invited the Quakers inside to stay dry. Although the Quakers' stay was brief, it was long enough to be noticed by the local Puritan officials, who were quite upset and pointed out to Macy that he had broken a law that fined anyone five pounds for every hour that they entertained Quakers. Macy was ordered to appear before the court and pay up, but instead he wrote the court a letter in which he said that he wanted to come in person and answer the charges, but he couldn't just yet, being "very ill" and not having the money to "hire a horse" for transportation. Although Macy paid the fine, he never did appear before the court, choosing instead to make haste to Nantucket and start a new life beyond the Puritans' watchful eyes.[7]

Macy and his fellow travelers hugged the coast down to Cape Cod, and then sailed through Boatmeadow Creek, a waterway that, until a storm cut it off in 1770, sliced through the Cape near Eastham.[8] They stopped briefly at Martha's Vineyard, enlisting the aid of a pilot to guide them on the final leg of the journey. Soon after leaving the safety of the Vineyard's Great Harbor, the small boat and its passengers were enveloped in a storm, whose ferocity started Sarah wailing about witches and demons that must have brought the terrible weather down on them. According to legend, Macy turned to Sarah and yelled, so as to be heard above the tempest, "Woman, go below and seek thy God. I fear not the witches on earth or the devils in hell!"[9] A short while later the boat reached Nantucket's shores, and in the ensuing years other settlers followed and the English population began to grow.

Surrounded by water and closer than the mainland to the migration routes of whales, Nantucket was a natural repository for an uncertain but fairly steady stream of drift whales. The Wampanoag Indians became involved in drift whaling very early on, stripping the blubber and meat from the carcasses and using the bones as tools. Thus, when the English settled Nantucket, drift whaling was already a going concern on the island, and for many years thereafter, the Indians jealously guarded their rights to drift whales, often selling land to the English but retaining ownership of all the whales cast ashore.[10] Although the exact date is unknown, it was probably sometime during the late 1660s that a "scrag" whale—perhaps an immature or sickly right whale or an Atlantic gray whale—swam into one of Nantucket's harbors.[11] This unexpected arrival sent a wave of excitement throughout the small community of settlers, few of whom, if any, had ever thought of attacking a whale, much less doing so. According to Nantucket historian Obed Macy, the would-be hunters "caused [a harpoon] to be wrought"[12] This took some time, and fortunately there was plenty of that. The whale remained in the harbor for three days, which was a fateful decision on its part. On the third day a few men boarded a boat with the harpoon and nervously set off to meet the whale, which they dispatched and brought to shore. This encouraged the Nantucketers to think about launching shore-whaling operations, but they knew they couldn't do it on their own. Their success with the scrag—call it beginner's luck—did not suddenly transform the Nantucketers, most of whom were merchants and farmers, into expert whalemen. If they were going to go whaling, they needed professional help, and the person they turned to was James Loper, of East Hampton, Long Island.[13]

It was understandable that Nantucketers looked to Long Island in this matter. Nantucket was, at the time, part of New York, and towns on the eastern end of Long Island were already famous for whaling. The choice of Loper also made sense. His family had emigrated from Holland in the 1640s, and they brought with them knowledge of the whaling industry that had made their homeland the world's preeminent whaling power. Soon after settling in East Hampton, Loper made good use of that knowledge and established himself as one of the area's most successful whalemen.[14] The Nantucketers tried mightily to woo Loper to their island "to carry on a design of Whale Citching."[15] They offered him land, livestock rights, as well as a one-third ownership in the whaling company that he was supposed to establish, which would enjoy short-term monopoly rights to whaling on the island. In return Loper would have to remain on the island for two years. Obtaining workers in this manner was an integral part of Nantucket's master development plan. The island's founders knew that they didn't have the skills necessary to take full advantage of all the opportunities for generating profit that the island could provide. So, early on they set out to acquire those skills by offering enticements to mainlanders who would agree to stay on the island for a period of years, during which time they would establish their operations and, it was hoped disseminate their skills to the broader population. The original agreement, or compact, among the founders called for recruiting ten "necessary tradesmen, and seamen," and Loper was an excellent prospect.[16]

Loper accepted the attractive offer but then, for reasons unknown, backed out. Nantucketers didn't reach out again right away but waited eighteen years until 1690, when they invited Ichabod Paddock, of the Cape Cod town of Yarmouth, "to instruct them in the best manner of killing whales and extracting their oil."[17] This invitation came at a critical time for the Nantucketers, who were finding it increasingly difficult to thrive on their small island. The glacial lottery had left Nantucket with a particularly sandy and gravelly soil that was short on organic material and therefore not very fertile. Making matters worse, when the rains fell, the water quickly percolated through the soil and out of reach of thirsty roots. Decades of farming, grazing, and tree cutting had further diminished the productivity of the lands, while, at the same time, the expanding population was placing greater demands on those lands to produce more. Nantucketers supplemented the produce from the land with the bounty from the sea, but that was not sufficient. By 1690, when Nantucketers contracted Paddock, they had clearly set their sights on whaling as their lifeline to future prosperity. According to local lore, it was then that a few Nantucketers stood on a hill at the southern edge of the Island and spied whales "spouting and sporting with each other, when one observed, *'there,'* pointing to the sea, *'is a green pasture where our children's grand-children will go for bread.'*"[18]

We know more about the myth of Paddock than the man himself.

The facts are sketchy. He left Yarmouth and arrived on Nantucket in 1690, and he returned to Yarmouth by 1710, at the latest, and possibly earlier than that.[19] We can infer that he must have had quite a reputation as a whaleman, for the shrewd Nantucketers surely would not have employed an amateur. The legend of Ichabod Paddock, on the other hand, is far richer.[20] It begins with a "giant battle-scarred" bull sperm whale named Crook-Jaw, "a monster who would make two hundred barrels of oil if he'd make a thimble." Like a boxer who is totally outmatched, Paddock repeatedly went at old Crook-Jaw but never could land a blow. His harpoons were but great big toothpicks to this old bull, whose skin they bounced off without leaving so much as a scratch. Paddock was not one to shy away from a challenge, and he especially didn't like his reputation as a whaleman being sullied by a seemingly invincible whale, so the next time Crook-Jaw came into view, Paddock grabbed a knife and dove into the sea. When Paddock reached Crook-Jaw, instead of stabbing him he waited until the whale's mouth opened wide, and swam in. Rather than find himself in the whale's stomach, Paddock was shocked to see a door, which he entered. There, sitting at a dimly lit table, were two figures playing cards; One, a beautiful, green-eyed, blond-haired mermaid, and the other the devil. The devil "slammed his cards on the table, and sparks singed their edges and sent little wisps of blue smoke curling upward." He stared angrily at Paddock for a moment, cursed him, and then disappeared. Paddock apologized for barging in like that, and asked the mermaid what they were playing for. "You," she responded with a laugh. What the mermaid did with (or to) her winnings is not recorded for posterity, but Paddock did not leave until the next morning, and one can only assume they weren't up all night playing cards. Paddock's crew feared the worst, but being very well trained they had stayed by the strangely listless Crook-Jaw through the night, and when Paddock reappeared after dawn they were very happy to see him, and a bit surprised that he was sporting such a wide grin.

The rumors about Paddock's underwater trysts eventually made their way to Paddock's wife, a beautiful woman with a well-developed sense of jealousy. She gave Paddock a new harpoon to take on his next voyage, and also asked that Paddock take her father with him. Paddock agreed, and soon after they left port, Crook-Jaw appeared. Paddock's father-in-law grabbed the new harpoon and launched it with a mighty throw. Paddock wasn't alarmed. He had hurled plenty of harpoons at Crook-Jaw, and all had bounced off, and he was sure that this one would too. This harpoon, however, hit its mark and drove deep into Crook-Jaw's side. It was a mortal blow, and soon Crook-Jaw lay dead in the water. Watching his men cut into the whale, Paddock braced for what he thought they would find. But there was nothing there save for "a strand of seaweed which had been bleached to the color of Eastham corn, a shell of plum-blossom pink, and two round sunsqualls [a kind of jellyfish] of pure emerald green." Years later Paddock's wife came clean about her role in vanquishing Crook-Jaw and, more to the point, the mermaid who had stolen her husband's heart: The harpoon she had given him, which her father had thrown at Crook-Jaw, was made of silver, "the only metal that could pierce the heart of a witch."[21]

Whatever Paddock taught the Nantucketers about whaling, they learned their lessons well. Over the next four decades shore whaling on Nantucket expanded dramatically and quickly became the major employer of men on the island. Historian Nathaniel Philbrick writes, "By 1700, anyone who could hold an oar—English and Indian alike—was involved in the whale fishery."[22] So important did shore whaling become that Nantucketers, who were already quite concerned that uncontrolled cutting of their trees was going to deforest the entire island, decided in 1694, despite their fears, to allow cedars to continue to be cut down as long as they were to be used only "for whale boats or the like."[23]

Indians played a crucial role in the expansion of shore whaling in two ways. First they agreed to sell prime coastal land to the Nantucketers, on which the latter established many of their whaling stations. Second, and more important, the Indians provided the Nantucketers with much-needed labor. As the eighteenth century dawned, there were about three hundred Englishmen on Nantucket, and roughly eight hundred Indians, a ratio that not only allowed but encouraged colonists to use Indians as labor multipliers in the whaling business.[24] While eight hundred might seem to be a large number, it pales in comparison with the population of Indians that were on Nantucket when the first settlers arrived some forty years earlier; a number estimated to be between fifteen hundred and three thousand, which led John Winthrop to refer to Nantucket at the time as "an island full of Indians."[25] During the seventeenth century Nantucket's Indians were decimated by the potent force that had ravaged other tribes who came into contact with the Europeans—the spread of new diseases for which the Indians had neither a built-in immunity nor any ready cures. The diminution of Nantucket's Indian population would continue for many years, but around 1700, during the rise of Nantucket's shore-whaling fortunes, there were still more than enough to man the boats. And, by all accounts, they were excellent workers. According to Obed Macy, "The Indians, ever manifesting a disposition for fishing of every kind, readily joined with the whites in this new pursuit, and willingly submitted to any station assigned them. . . . Nearly every boat was manned in part, many almost entirely by natives."[26]

The relationship between the whites and Indians in Nantucket's shore-whale fishery was far from equal. According to historian Daniel Vickers, "The English were masters; the Indians were servants; and between the two groups there was no mobility at all."[27] The Indians did not own the boats that they rowed, nor did they have equal rights to the spoils of their labor. Like their peers in the other colonies, they took the lays or other inducements that the white owners gave them. And even though this system provided Indians with a cut of the profits, it was far less than the whites received.[28] An old Nantucket Indian story about shore whaling highlights the basic inequality between the two groups. Zaccheus Macy tells of a small fleet of whaling boats that were just offshore, when

the wind came round to the northward, and blew with great violence, attended with snow. The men all rowed hard, but made little head way. In one of the boats there were four Indians and two white men. An old Indian in the head of the boat, perceiving that the crew began to be disheartened, spake loud in his own tongue and said, *Momadichhator auqua sarshkee sarnkee pinchee eyoo sememoochkee chaquanks wihchee pinchee eyoo*: which in English is, "Pull ahead with courage: do not be disheartened: we shall not be lost now: there are too many Englishmen to be lost now."[29]

Thus bolstered the men rowed even harder, and they finally made it safely back to shore. On its face, this story evokes a relationship between the Indians and the white men that is almost paternalistic, but, according to Philbrick the story is really "a kind of insider's alongshore whaling joke," which makes a wholly different point. "By saying that there are 'too many Englishmen to be lost now,' the old man is implying that two different standards existed for English and Indian Nantucketers. Indian whalemen died; English whalemen didn't." The Indians, in other words, "were expendable" in the Nantucketers' quest for whales.[30]

Shore whaling flourished on Nantucket throughout the late seventeenth and early eighteenth centuries. The names of those engaged in whaling read like a who's who of the island's most prominent families, including the Swains, the Coffins, the Gardners, and the Folgers.[31] Profits from shore whaling were a boon to the local economy, with a single good-size whale providing each member of a whaleboat's crew with a payday equal to that which a shore-based worker might earn in a half a year.[32] The extent to which whaling pervaded the character and inclinations of Nantucketers can be glimpsed in a news item from the period. On October 4, 1744, the *Boston News-Letter* reported that a forty-foot whale had washed ashore on Nantucket.[33] When three local men happened upon the animal, they did not simply look at it, nor did they run to tell others. Instead their first impulse was to secure the prize as quickly as possible. Not having any "proper instruments" on hand, the men took out their "Jack-Knives" and went in for the kill. The high point for shore whaling was 1726, when eighty-six whales were taken, eleven of which were brought in on one extraordinary day. After that banner year, however, Nantucket's shore-whaling fortunes declined. Like the Long Islanders before them, the Nantucketers' success proved to be their undoing, as the whales near shore became scarcer with each passing year. By 1760, said Obed Macy, the era of shore whaling on Nantucket had come to an end.[34]

The exact date of Nantucket's most important shore-whaling trip is not known, but it was likely sometime around 1712. That is when Macy claims that Capt. Christopher Hussey and his men sailed out of Nantucket's main harbor in search of right whales. The men and their small boats were no match for a strong northerly wind that quickly rose, and they were blown a considerable distance out to sea, far from the sight of land, where they soon "fell in with" a school of sperm whales.[35] Rather than rue their predicament, the men attacked and killed one of the whales, and with the aid of a fair turn in the weather they were able to tow it ashore.

One serious problem with this account is that in 1712 Christopher Hussey was only six years old. Although Nantucketers are properly revered for their whaling acumen, one has to admit that a six-year old, even a Nantucketer, is not quite ready for the responsibility of being a whaleman. According to Nantucket historian Elizabeth Little, in another version, the first Nantucketer to harpoon a sperm whale was not Christopher but, most likely, Bachellor Hussey, who would have been about twenty-seven at the time. Bachellor, along with a few other Nantucketers had among their 1712–14 whaling accounts with a local merchant entries labeled "permaseta," which appears to signal that they were trading in spermaceti oil.[36] Despite such evidence there are still lingering doubts about the veracity of Macy's story, and whether any Hussey in fact "fell in with" sperm whales in the manner described. The questions of depth and behavior pose problems. Sperm whales are an open-ocean species, preferring to stay in waters that are at least many hundreds and, more commonly, thousands of feet deep. Although we don't know how far Hussey was blown offshore before encountering the school of sperm whales, he and his men would have had to have been nearly thirty miles from Nantucket before even reaching areas as deep as three hundred feet, which would still be considered not much more than an uncomfortably shallow puddle for sperm whales. From that distance it is almost inconceivable that Hussey's men would have been able to row a dead whale to shore. Of course there have been instances of sperm whales being sighted closer to the coast, and perhaps a school of them did skirt Nantucket just as Hussey and his men were being pushed out to sea. In the end, however, the veracity of the story is irrelevant, for as marine historian and artist Richard Ellis points out, the story of Christopher Hussey "has been told so many times that it probably no longer matters whether it really happened."[37] Even if it wasn't Hussey who discovered the sperm whale's haunts beyond the horizon, some event around this time, and possibly an accidental offshore encounter, clearly caused Nantucketers to begin pursuing sperm whales intentionally, rather than leaving it up to chance.[38]

The Hussey incident was not the first time Nantucketers had seen a sperm whale. Some years earlier one had washed ashore on the southwestern part of the island, setting off the whaling equivalent of a gold rush, with various parties claiming ownership of the valuable prize.[39] The Indians, being the first on the scene, thought that the whale should belong to them; for it was their discovery and "finders-keepers" seemed to be the fairest law to apply. The English, however, objected, arguing that when they purchased the original rights to the island they also obtained the rights to all occurrences such as this. Next came the local inspector of whales, who attempted to seize the "Royal Fish" for the king.[40] The final claimant was Richard Macy, the grandfather of Obed Macy. He had heard his Indian servant talking about the whale. Before anyone else arrived Macy, a hulk of a man, said to be "the strongest . . . in the county," took his sledgehammer and knocked all of the beautiful teeth out of the whale's head and hid them, "believing that they were of great value." A sharp debate ensued, with each claimant presenting his case for receiving part of the spoils. Particular attention was focused on the teeth, and many of those present threatened to "whip" Macy unless he gave them up. Macy responded that if he was forced to give up the teeth, he would "take the whole company one by one and handle them as a woman would her child."[41] Not surprisingly, all claims to the teeth were immediately dropped. As for the rest of the whale, "it was finally settled that the white inhabitants should share the prize equally amongst themselves," yet another indication that Indian rights were easily trammeled. That done, the whale was cut up and hauled to the tryworks. They took special care with the spermaceti oil "procured from the head" of the whale, deeming it a valuable curative and "worth its weight in silver."[42]

ALTHOUGH THE HUSSEY STORY serves as the marker for the birth of the sperm whale fishery in America, it is hardly the first instance of humans hunting this species. One historian claims that the Phoenicians pursued sperm whales in the eastern Mediterranean as far back as 1000 B.C. and in doing so provided background material for the biblical tale of Jonah.[43] Marco Polo, writing in the thirteenth century, claimed that the people of Madagascar caught great numbers of sperm whales.[44] And when the Muscovy Company told one of its whaling captains, in 1611, to be on the lookout for sperm whales during his voyage to Spitsbergen, because they were "good" whales to hunt, it was advice based on experience.[45] Clearly men had been hunting sperm whales long before Hussey's time. Indeed, Hussey can't even claim to have been the first colonist to have thought, albeit not in a premeditated manner, about hunting sperm whales. In 1688, Timotheus Vanderuen, commander of the brigantine *Happy Return*, out of New York, petitioned Edmund Andros, the royal governor of the Dominion of New England, for "License and Permission" to take twelve whalemen "upon a fishing design about the Bohames Islands, And Cap florida, for sperma Coeti whales." But there is no record of this trip having been taken. Thus, Hussey, Christopher, or Bachellor, apocryphal or not, holds the distinction of being the first colonial whaleman to kill a sperm whale, the most storied whale in the ocean.

Chapter Five

THE WHALE'S WHALE

WATER CASCADING OFF THE CRESCENT-SHAPED FLUKES OF A SPERM WHALE.

MOBY-DICK HAD TO BE A SPERM WHALE. NOT JUST BECAUSE THE sperm whale is the only type of whale known to have sunk ships deliberately—a critical element to be sure—but because it is the only whale whose biography was fantastic enough to sustain the grand and sweeping novel that bears his name. From virtually every perspective the sperm whale is an astounding animal. Its size, its shape, its behavior, its physiology, its mighty tooth-studded jaw, its powerful tail, its grace and beauty are all wonders to behold. And in death this hulking leviathan provided the whaling industry both with its most unusual products and some of its greatest profits. The sperm whale, more than any other whale, has captured the public's imagination, to the point that when the average person envisions a whale, it is the sperm whale that they most often see. Whether this is a relic of Moby-Dick's great fame or the result of the inherent power that sperm whales certainly possess is open to debate. But whatever the reason, the sperm whale clearly is the whale's whale.

The sperm whale specializes in extremes, earning it a string of superlatives. It is the biggest of the odontocytes, or toothed whales, a group that includes pilot whales, killer whales, and a wide range of dolphins. The largest male or bull sperm whales reach lengths of just over sixty feet, and weigh as much as fifty tons. No whales exhibit greater disparities between the sexes than do sperm whales, with the females, or cows, being much smaller than their male counterparts, growing to forty feet in length and eighteen tons in weight. Sperm whales have the largest skull of any whale, the largest head of any animal, and the largest brain of any species, which can tip the scales at twenty pounds. They dive deeper than any other whale, regularly descending many thousands of feet—at times well over a mile; and they can stay under the water for upward of an hour. The sperm whale's skin, which can reach a depth of fourteen inches, is the thickest of any animal, and its tail is, in proportion to its body, the largest of all the whales, and arguably the most stunning. "In no living thing," opined Melville, "are the lines of beauty more exquisitely defined than in the crescentic borders of these flukes."[1]

The sperm whale goes by different names in other languages. The English "sperm whale" therefore becomes *cachalot* in French, *Pottfisch* in German, *spermhval* in Norwegian, and *makko-kuzira* in Japanese. But from the perspective of science, through the unifying power of taxonomy and systematics, one expects a particular animal to have a single scientific name, expressed as a unique genus and species that holds steady across the globe. And by and large that is the case for the sperm whale. After a tortuous history, in which the sperm whale has been given a dizzying array of taxonomic classifications, most scientists now call it *Physeter macrocephalus*. The genus *Physeter* means "blower" in Greek, and refers to the sperm whales' single, powerful spout, while the species tag, *macrocephalus*, is Greek for "big head." There are, however, still a few who identify the sperm whale as *Physeter catodon*. This is not a bad name, and in fact it is fairly descriptive, given that *catodon* is Greek for "lower tooth" or "teeth in lower jaw." But *macrocephalus* seems much more appropriate because the sperm whale's most impressive feature is its gargantuan, bulbous head, which takes up roughly a third of its body length, and which led the British at one time to refer to sperms as anvil-headed whales.[2]

On closer inspection, however, calling a sperm whale's head a head seems a bit odd, because the usual physical structures one associates with that part of the body are more than a little off kilter. The brain, the eyes, the bulk of the skull, and the ears are not where one would expect them to be. Instead of these features being clustered toward the top, or at least the middle, of the head, they are quite a distance from the forward end of the whale. And then, to confuse matters further, the blowhole, or nose of the whale, is near the tip of the head, on the top and slightly off center. The two structures that give the sperm whale's head much of its great mass and its torpedo shape are the spermaceti organ, or case, and the junk. The spermaceti organ is a cavernous, liquid-filled compartment encased in a "beautiful glistening membrane" and a thick layer of muscle.[3] It can contain as much as three tons, or twenty-three barrels, of spermaceti, which means the "sperm or seed of the whale" in Latin.[4] The junk lies beneath the spermaceti organ, and also contains spermaceti, although in lesser amounts and more solidified form.[5] Spermaceti isn't whale sperm, but the men who first named this substance can be excused for thinking that this might be the case. In situ and at body temperature, spermaceti is a semitransparent rose-tinted or slightly yellowish liquid, but once exposed to cool air or water it crystallizes into a milky-white waxy mass that, indeed, looks very much like sperm. John Smith noticed this liquid-to-wax transformation when he wrote about a sperm whale driven ashore in Bermuda in the 1620s, remarking that "the water in the Bay where she lay, was all oily, and the rocks about it all bedashed with Parmacity [spermaceti], all congealed like ice."[6]

There are many theories about the function of the spermaceti organ, among them that it regulates buoyancy, generates sound, or is involved in echolocation. Some believe that it helps the whales absorb nitrogen and thereby avoid the debilitating impacts of the bends during their deep dives and ascents. The most intriguing theory is that the head of the sperm whale is designed to be a battering ram, and that the oil-filled spermaceti organ and the junk act as giant shock absorbers to cushion the blow of a collision. The evolutionary purpose of this design would most likely be to allow males to butt heads with one another in the hope of winning the affection or, at least, the sexual attention of females. This theory also explains why some bull sperm whales were able to plow, headfirst, into relatively massive whaleships, sending the ships to the bottom, while still being able to swim away to fight another day.[7]

The spermaceti organ is just one example of how little we know about sperm whales. Indeed, the entire field of cetology is rife with unanswered questions. Roger Payne, a man who has devoted his life to the passionate study of the great whales, once concluded that "conducting scientific research on this most difficult of groups can be compared to viewing a whale through a keyhole. The bulk of the animal glides past from time to time while we try desperately to figure out what on earth it is." And, of all the whales that humans have studied, the sperm whale is arguably the one that hides it secrets most jealously. This was true more than 150 years ago, when Melville wrote that "the sperm whale, scientific or poetic, lives not complete in any literature. Far above all other hunted whales, his is an unwritten life;" and it is just as true today.[8]

The spermaceti organ and the junk rest within the scooplike embrace of the skull, which whalemen referred to as the "sleigh," the "chariot," the "coach," and the "trough."[9] Beneath the skull is the sperm whale's most famous feature—its long, narrow jaw, which is studded on the bottom with anywhere from thirty-nine to fifty large, slightly curved, conical teeth, distributed in two rows. In large bulls these teeth can be huge, reaching a length of ten inches and weighing two pounds or more. The teeth in the top of the jaw, in contrast, are vestigial and protrude only slightly, if at all, beyond the gum line. One might reasonably think that the sperm whale's massive teeth are used in eating or chewing food, but that doesn't appear to be the case. The sperm whale's jaw can only grasp but not chew, and most of the whale's prey is relatively small and swallowed whole without being bitten first. Further confounding the dining hypothesis is that younger animals, whose teeth have yet to come in, as well as adults with grossly misshapen jaws seem to have no problem feeding despite not being able to rely on their teeth for help. It seems that the evolutionary force that led to such large teeth had more to do with fighting than feeding, with the great white gashes and scars that crisscross the head of many bull sperm whales offering evidence that the teeth are used in combat or, if not that, some extremely serious play.[10]

The eyes of the sperm whale, which some have likened to those of an ox, are behind and above the corner of the jaw, on either side of the body. Traveling farther down the animal, there is a change in the texture of the skin. While the head is smooth, much of the trunk of the sperm whale's body is covered with undulating, relatively shallow ridges. The purpose of these corrugations is unclear, but some think they might reduce drag or help the whale's body withstand pressure during deep dives.[11] At the far end of the animal is the graceful and powerful tail. "It has a hardness almost of iron," wrote whaleman William M. Davis, "with elasticity greater than steel; and urged by a thousand horse-power, it becomes the terror of the puny bipeds in their fragile boats."[12]

Another part of the sperm whale's anatomy or, more accurately, the bull sperm whale's anatomy which has often been an object of fascination is its penis. Although this might have something to do with the seminal nature of the whale's name, it is more the result of a very popular and much-copied drawing done in 1598 by Hendrik Goltzius.[13] That year a fairly sizable bull sperm whale washed ashore at Katwijk, Holland, and came to rest on its side. As evidenced by a contemporary engraving of Goltzius's drawing, this stranding generated great excitement among the local population. Men and women surrounded the animal, with some pointing to this or that feature, while others simply stared. The most interesting scene in the engraving is near the midsection of the whale, where two men and a woman stand admiring the animal's enormous penis, which extends five to seven feet, its tip resting on the sand. One of the men leans toward the whale and uses his staff, apparently to measure the organ's size. The other man's left arm is draped around the women's back, drawing her near, while his other arm is outstretched, palm upward, toward the penis, as if to say "behold." Yet another man, finding the protruding penis less interesting than useful, has leaped on its base and is using it as a ladder to get on top of the whale.

More than four hundred years later another sperm whale's penis would excite similar interest among observers. On January 17, 2004, a fifty-six-foot bull sperm whale washed up on a beach in Taiwan. Seeing an opportunity to use the carcass for educational purposes, a group of local marine biologists, employing the services of fifty workmen and powerful cranes, managed to get the fifty- to sixty-ton whale onto a flat-bed truck for transport to a nearby nature preserve, where a necropsy was to be performed. By the time the truck started its trip, nine days later, the decomposition process was well advanced, causing gases to build up to dangerous levels within the carcass. While traveling through the downtown streets of a nearby city the whale exploded, splattering blood and guts on cars, motorcycles, the street, and the windows of nearby businesses, creating a horrific scene that was caught on film and shown by media outlets worldwide. When the whale, still chained to the flatbed, finally reached the nature preserve, an entirely different scene played out. The *Taipei Times* reported that more than one hundred local residents, "mostly men, have reportedly gone to see the corpse to 'experience' the size of its penis," which, like the whale in Katwijk, was protruding quite a distance from its body.[14]

Melville devoted an entire chapter in *Moby-Dick* to the sperm whale's penis, which, he noted, was called the "grandissimus" by whale-men. "Had you stepped on board the *Pequod* at a certain juncture of this post-mortemizing of the whale," wrote Melville, "and had you strolled forward nigh the windlass, pretty sure am I that you would have scanned with no small curiosity a very strange, enigmatical object, which you would have seen there, lying along lengthwise in the lee scuppers. Not the wondrous cistern in the whale's huge head; not the prodigy of his unhinged lower jaw; not the miracle of his symmetrical tail; none of these would so surprise you, as half a glimpse of that unaccountable cone,—longer than a Kentuckian is tall, nigh a foot in diameter at the base, and jet-black as Yojo, the ebony idol of Quee-queg." Melville then has the "mincer," or the crewman on board who is charged with chopping the blubber into small pieces, slice off the penis's skin, stretch it, dry it, and cut two holes in it, thereby trans-forming the now leathery skin into a cassock or coat. "The mincer now stands before you," continued Melville, "invested in the full canonicals of his calling. Immemorial to all his order, this investiture alone will adequately protect him, while employed in the peculiar functions of his office."[15]

Sperm whales range in color from black to gray to bluish-gray to brown, depending on the specimen and the person offering the descrip-tion. A few were pure white. Of course, this immediately brings Moby-

Dick to mind, but Moby-Dick was not a true albino. Melville describes the star leviathan of his novel as having "a peculiar snow-white wrinkled forehead, and a high, pyramidical white hump," but "the rest of his body was so streaked, and spotted, and marbled with the same shrouded hue, that, in the end, he had gained his distinctive appellation of the White Whale."[16] Thus, while Moby-Dick was white enough to be called such, he was not white all around. Besides Moby-Dick, the most famous white whale is, in fact, Mocha Dick, who was purportedly a role model for Melville when he created his toothy protagonist. Mocha Dick lived off the coast of Chile, near the island of Mocha, and was, according to a contemporary chronicler, as "white as wool." He was a massive bull sperm whale—"more than seventy feet from his noodle to the tip of his flukes"—and "renowned monster" that had destroyed numerous boats and outwitted the many men who had tried to catch him during the early to mid-nineteenth century.

With each purported encounter Mocha Dick's reputation grew. His reign of terror extended the length and width of the Pacific Ocean. On rounding Cape Horn, whalemen would ask one another, "Any news from Mocha Dick?" and they would dream of slaying the legend.[17] His fame extended well beyond the whalemen's fraternity, to the popular press and then into the casual conversations of friends and strangers. Ralph Waldo Emerson wrote in his journal of a stagecoach ride in which a mariner told him and his fellow passengers "of an old bull sperm whale which he called a white whale . . . who rushed upon the boats which attacked him & crushed the boats to small chips with his jaws."[18] The sheer volume of material on Mocha Dick and the number of people who claimed to be on intimate terms with him and his ferocious disposition lends support to the notion that he did indeed exist. But determining where the reality ends and the myth begins is not a task for the fainthearted. Even the rumors of his death are separated by many years, and in some instances decades, and the honor of vanquishing this "stout gentleman" is variously accorded to a range of would-be conquerors. In the end Mocha Dick, like his literary relative Moby-Dick, will remain for the ages a whale that was larger than life.

Sperm whales exhibit a great range of interesting behaviors. Being highly social animals, they often congregate in large groups that include a mix of immature males and females along with older cows. The mature male bulls, by contrast, are solitary animals, rejoining the groups only for mating. As many as five or six hundred sperm whales have been seen in a single gathering.[19] "A large party of Cachalots, gamboling on the surface of the ocean," noted one seasoned nineteenth-century observer, "is one of the most curious and imposing spectacles a whaling voyage affords: the huge size and uncouth agility of the monsters, exhibiting a strange combination of the grand and the ridiculous."[20]

Sperm whales are also noisy animals. They use clicks for echolocation, and their patterns of clicks, called codas, are believed to play a role in communication. Some of these clicks are quite powerful and can travel through the water with sufficient intensity to jar nearby divers. Whalemen often heard the clicks through the hulls of their ships and, thinking that they sounded like someone hammering, referred to sperm whales as "carpenter fish."[21] One of the most dramatic behaviors of sperm whales is breaching, in which they catapult themselves into the air. Charles Darwin witnessed this off the coast of Tierra del Fuego during his voyage on the *Beagle*. "There was a curious spectacle," wrote Darwin, "of very many Spermaceti whales, some of which were jumping straight up out of the water; every part of the body was visible excepting the fin and the tail. As they fell sideways into the water, the noise was as loud as a distant great gun."[22] Sperm whales also engage in spy hopping—lifting their heads into the air; lobtailing—raising their flukes out of the water and bringing them down in a thunderous splash; and settling—which is sinking rapidly without the use of the tail or pectoral fins.[23] This last behavior frustrated many whalemen. "I have seen the sperm-whale at rest suddenly seem a mass of lead," wrote Davis, "and sink from the head of the boat so rapidly that the harpoon was darted, but not delivered."[24]

The most fascinating of the sperm whales' behaviors is feeding, which is also probably the least understood. The mystery lies not in where they eat or what they eat. We know that sperm whales descend to great depths, where they dine primarily on squid and, to a much lesser extent, various fish, including sharks, rays, and tuna.[25] Of all the delicacies that sperm whales pursue, none generates as much awe and fascination as the giant squid, an elusive and imposing animal that can measure up to sixty feet long and weigh as much as a ton. Epic battles between sperm whales and giant squid are a staple of many dramatic tales of the deep. Nineteenth-century adventure writer and whaleman

Frank T. Bullen, who claims to have witnessed such an event, offered a somewhat melodramatic description, in which "a very large sperm whale was locked in deadly conflict with a cuttle-fish, or squid, almost as large as himself, whose interminable tentacles seemed to enlace the whole of his great body. The head of the whale especially seemed a perfect net-work of writhing arms.... All around the combatants were numerous sharks, like jackals round a lion, ready to share the feast, and apparently assisting in the destruction of the large cephalopod. So the titanic struggle went on, in perfect silence as far as we were concerned, because, even had there been any noise, our distance from the scene of conflict would not have permitted us to hear it."[26]

While this account is probably fiction, there are real battles between sperm whales and giant squid, although they usually take place at great depths, not at the ocean's surface. The traces of these clashes are often found on a whale's head in form of large saucer-shaped scars inflicted by the squid's barbed and powerful suckers. The squid that make up the bulk of the sperm whale's diet, however, are a much smaller species that are just a few feet long and usually weigh no more than three pounds.[27]

What we still don't fully understand is how sperm whales catch their prey. There are no pictures or film of sperm whales eating. We cannot follow them on their great descents. The relatively small squid they consume are bioluminescent, thus the whales can see them in the virtual darkness of the deep; but seeing is one thing, catching is another. The squid, with their jet-propelled locomotion and great ability to shift direction instantly, are too fast and agile for the sperm whales to chase down. How, then, do the whales capture the squid? As one comes to expect with sperm whales, there are many theories but few answers. The sounds that sperm whales make might be focused into a powerful pulse of sound, or sonic boom, which stuns the squid, allowing the whales to gather them up at a leisurely pace. Perhaps the whale's white teeth or the bright white flesh on the inside and the edges of its mouth act as beacons, luring the squid into the whale's maw, although how this could be accomplished in the absence of light is unclear. A variation on the whiteness theme has the squid's bioluminescence somehow being rubbed onto the whale's mouth, thereby creating or amplifying the beacon affect. Yet another theory is that the whale opens its bottom jaw to nearly a ninety-degree angle, and the squid grab on to the jaw as the whale swims by, only to be scooped up when the jaw closes. However they do it, sperm whales are very successful predators. Dissections of sperm whale stomachs have revealed as many as thirty thousand squid beaks, the hard mouthparts that squid use to capture food. And with each squid providing two beaks, that translates into fifteen thousand individuals.[28]

Among the more unusual items that have been found in a sperm whale's stomach are shoes, rubber boots, toy cars and toy guns, bundles of insulated wire, dolls, coconuts, cosmetic jars, flesh from baleen whales, and fishing nets.[29] But surely the most unusual item is a man. Some have claimed that the "great fish" that swallowed Jonah was none other than a sperm whale, and, of course, this is possible since its gullet is large enough to allow a full-grown man to pass through it.[30]

Leaving Jonah and the whale aside, there are more recent stories of man-eating sperm whales, and the most fantastic is that of James Bartley. According to a letter submitted to *Natural History* magazine in April 1947, Mr. Bartley was a young seaman aboard the *Star of the East*, a whaleship cruising near the Falkland Islands in 1891, when the call rang out that a large bull sperm whale was surfacing nearby. Bartley, along with his mates, jumped into a whaleboat and began the pursuit. The whale introduced itself to its attackers by smashing their boat to pieces, and in the process Bartley disappeared. The next morning the whale was killed and towed to the ship. During the cutting in, the men noticed that the whale's stomach was moving. They quickly sliced open the undulating organ and were astonished to find Bartley, still very much alive, but unconscious and curled up in a ball. After a lengthy recovery of four weeks, Bartley told the others what happened. Apparently the whale had scooped him up and swallowed him whole. The last things Bartley remembered before coming to on the ship were sliding down the whale's slippery throat—"the walls of which quivered at his touch"—and then finding himself in the stomach, the great heat from which "drained all his strength." And not only that, the powerfully acidic digestive juices in the whale's stomach had "permanently bleached Bartley's face, hands, neck, and arms as white as snow." As to how Bartley survived such a seemingly hopeless situation, a range of possibilities had been proposed, which were thought to have worked in concert. The first was that the whale's teeth had "missed" Bartley; second, that he had remained "quiet" on account of being unconscious; and third, that because the whale was killed quickly, its body temperature had rapidly diminished, thereby apparently keeping Bartley from being sapped of the last of his life force. The letter ended with the writer asking for an expert opinion as to the plausibility of this tale.[31]

Robert Cushman Murphy, a scientist at the American Museum of Natural History, in New York City, took up the reply. Although world famous as an ornithologist, Murphy was also extremely knowledgeable about whales and whaling, having shipped out himself aboard a New Bedford whaleship, the *Daisy*, in 1912, on its voyage to the Antarctic in search of sperm whales (Murphy was along not as a whaler, but as a scientist, in the museum's employ, collecting birds and other animals from the region).[32] Murphy admitted that a man could be swallowed by a sperm whale, and that whalemen likely had been in the past. But he added that the story was "unadulterated 'bunk,'" and that no man could survive in a whale any longer "than he would if he were held under water." Murphy also had other doubts about the veracity of the letter, including the very existence of the *Star of the East*, concluding that the story may well have been "wholly apocryphal."[33]

THERE IS NO DOUBT that some whalemen marveled at sperm whales when they saw them, and thought about their form and beauty even as they were preparing to kill them. But such musings, whether common or rare, were not foremost in the whalemen's minds. When whalemen looked at sperm whales they mainly saw three things that could make them money—blubber, spermaceti, and ambergris. The sperm whale's blubber, while not nearly as thick as that of a right or a bowhead whale, could be rendered into oil that was cleaner burning and more valuable than that which came from other whales. Spermaceti was not only a highly valuable source of oil for illumination, but it was also used for medicinal purposes, to which William Shakespeare alluded in his play *Henry IV, Part I*, when he said, "the sovereign'st thing on earth was parmaceti for an inward bruise."[34] Spermaceti was judged to be "a noble remedy in many cases," including dealing with asthma and the discomfort felt after childbirth. The preparation of spermaceti for sale as a drug began with the raw spermaceti being cooked over a flame, and poured into conical molds. Once the material in the molds cooled and the excess oil was drained away, the molds would be repeatedly heated and cooled and drained of oil until the spermaceti was white and hard. Pharmacists would then use a knife to shave off flakes of spermaceti, which would be sold to customers in search of better health. Spermaceti was also applied as a cream or lotion, and by the early 1700s it was all the rage for its purported ability to soften the skin and cure "Tumours of the Breast."[35] Spermaceti's greatest fame, however, came when manufacturers learned to make spermaceti candles, a skill that became the foundation for one of the most lucrative and fascinating branches of colonial commerce. Finally there was ambergris, sometimes called "Neptune's Treasure," the most mysterious of all the products derived from sperm whales.[36]

Ambergris is a gray or black waxy substance that is formed in the stomach or large intestine of sperm whales, and is often expelled during defecation, sometimes as small lumps the size of baseballs, and other times as large concretions weighing hundreds of pounds. It appears that ambergris is a by-product of irritation caused by squid beaks as they scratch their way through the whale's digestive system or, possibly, the result of some other malady. This simple and somewhat unappealing description offers not the slightest inkling of ambergris's illustrious history. For more than a thousand years ambergris has been a rare and exceedingly sought-after item of commerce, making it, at times, literally worth its weight in gold.[37] Egyptians burned it as incense in their temples, and the Chinese thought it to be a powerful aphrodisiac.[38] King Charles II of England favored ambergris and eggs over any other dish. Arabs placed a lump of ambergris in cups of coffee to enhance the coffee's aroma. Italians added ambergris to chocolate, and an English cookbook, published in 1747, recommended it as an ingredient in icing for "a great cake," while others used it as a flavoring for wine and cordials.[39] But it was as a fixative for perfume that ambergris achieved its most important and widespread use, serving to prolong the staying power of the scents with which it was mixed.

Even more varied than the uses of ambergris were the theories proposed for its origin. Establishing the causal connection between ambergris and sperm whales took a long time, and for many years trying to figure out where ambergris came from was a question that scores of natural philosophers tried to answer. All this conjecture was, in part, because ambergris was almost always found floating at sea or washed up on the shore, and therefore didn't appear to have an identifiable source. In 1666 a writer who had examined the literature found that there were at least eighteen different opinions as to ambergris's origin.[40] Among the candidates were sea foam; fish livers, the dung of an East Indian bird, fruit from underwater trees, a type of naphtha, a bituminous emanation from the sea floor, a type of sulfur, a sea fungus, the feces of a whale, or some sort of artificial material. In 1672, the Honorable Robert Boyle claimed that a document found on board a recently captured Dutch ship provided the answer. "Ambergreese is not the scum or excrement of the whale, but issues out of the root of a tree, which tree, howsoever it stands on the land, alwaies shoots forth its roots towards the sea, seeking the warmth of it, thereby to deliver the fattest gum that comes out of it."[41] In 1685, it was proposed that ambergris was "nothing but the wax, mixt with the Honey, which falls into the Sea, and is beat about in the Waves, between the tropics."[42] And last, but not least, there was a very old theory of Chinese origin that supposed that ambergris was "spittle" coughed up by sea dragons.[43]

All these theories notwithstanding, it was getting harder and harder to escape the conclusion that ambergris did in fact come from whales, and sperm whales to be exact. Marco Polo in the late thirteenth century was certainly one of the first persons—if not *the* first—to make the connection, stating that ambergris was "produced in the belly of the whale and the cachalot."[44] In the early 1600s the Muscovy Company informed its whaling captains that ambergris was found in the sperm whale, "lying in the entrals and guts of the same, being the shape and colour like unto Kowes dung," and because of its "good worth" it was "not slightly to be regarded." To ensure that no ambergris was overlooked, the captains were ordered "to be present at the opening of this sort of whale, and cause the residue of the said entrals be put into small caske, and bring them with you to England."[45] Over a century later, in 1724, Dr. Boylston, of Boston, published a letter in the Royal Society's *Philosophical Transactions*, which further cemented the case. "The most learned part of mankind are still at a loss about many things even in medical use; and, particularly, were so in what is called *ambergris*, until our *whale* fishermen of *Nantucket*, in *New England*, some three or four years past," discovered a twenty-pound lump of ambergris while cutting into a bull sperm whale.[46]

The debate over the origin of ambergris cooled considerably after Boylston's contribution, and toward the latter part of the 1700s, further investigations erased any claims that ambergris might come from a source other than sperm whales.[47] The most persuasive evidence, of course, came from the whalemen themselves. During the nineteenth century, when the best records were kept, nearly every year witnessed at least one American whaleship returning to port with ambergris on board. One of the most impressive hauls came in 1858, when the *Watchman* of Nantucket returned with eight hundred pounds of ambergris, stored in four casks, and sold this treasure for ten thousand dollars, which was more than half the profits from the ship's yearlong cruise.[48]

Before whalemen could examine a sperm whale to see if it contained ambergris, they had to kill one, and that was not any easy task. Finding the whales was the first obstacle to overcome. Only the keenest of lookouts were successful at this game. In contrast to right or humpback whales, whose two blowholes are located atop their head and send out a high stream of vapor that is relatively easy to spot, the sperm whale's single blowhole is located on the left side of the head, and the spout it sends forth is low to the surface, making it more difficult to discern. During the chase the plodding nature of right whales bore a striking contrast to the speed and unpredictability of sperm whales and the dangers they posed. As Thomas Jefferson noted, the spermaceti whale "is an active, fierce animal and requires vast address and boldness in the fisherman."[49] Sperm whale hunters had to move more quickly, strike more decisively, and prepare more fully for the potential that a wounded and enraged animal might attack. Whereas with right whales, whalemen were mostly concerned about being hit by the animal's tail, with sperm whales the attack could come from the tail or the head; thus the common phrase among whalemen that the sperm was "dangerous at both ends."

An enraged sperm could thrust up or bring down its tail with such awesome force that should a whaleboat be in the way it would be smashed to pieces. Such was the whalemen's healthy fear of and respect for the sperm whale's flukes that they called them the "hand of God."[50] Far more dangerous than the tail, however, was the sperm whale's jaw. To use this mighty weapon, the sperm whale would usually turn over on its back and hold the tooth-studded bottom jaw aloft as it zeroed in for the attack. Just the sight of a sperm whale "jawing-back" in this manner could cause men to leap from their boat and remain bobbing in the water until the whale had departed or, at least, closed its menacing mouth.[51] In rare instances the whale would end its attack by chomping the whaleboat in two, then chomping the remains of the boat and perhaps the unlucky crewmen as well, until satisfied that its work was done. There were also times when, instead of delivering a final blow, the whale would simply keep its lower jaw suspended over the boat for a moment or two, which must have seemed like an eternity to the terrified crew, and then roll to one side, close its mouth, and be off. And, as if the jaws were not worry enough, there was the bulbous battering ram of a head that could easily cripple a whaleboat or even the mother ship.

The colonial whalemen of the early eighteenth century, whose desires to pursue sperm whales in the open ocean were fueled by Hussey's chance discovery, knew very little about their quarry or how best to hunt them and market their products. But time and experience would prove to be exceptionally good teachers.

Chapter Six

INTO "YE DEEP"

A Perilous Ride, by J. S. Ryder, showing boatheader
about to cut the line with a hatchet to keep the whaleboat
from being dragged too far from the mother ship.

Soon after hussey's legendary voyage around 1712, nantucketers began new trips into "ye deep," as the wider ocean was called.
This required new ships, which were built by an expanding human
fleet of shipwrights, carpenters, and caulkers. New wharves were
erected in the main harbor to unload the catch. More casks were made
to store blubber and transport oil to market, and the number of coopers expanded to meet the rising demand. Great supplies of iron were
needed for harpoons and ship fittings, and blacksmiths worked their
forges longer as a result. Sails and ropes had to be made, keeping the
sail lofts and rope manufacturers busy. The whaleships needed food and
supplies, and a cadre of merchants kept them provisioned. Larger

crews, willing to spend days, weeks, or even months at sea were necessary, and many men were lured into this burgeoning profession with
promises that they would share in the profits of the whaling trips. For
nearly forty years, from roughly 1712 until 1750, Nantucket dominated
the offshore whale fishery, primarily targeting sperm whales, but also
rights and humpbacks. The number of whaleships on the island rose
from six in 1715 to sixty in 1748, and the amount of oil processed
annually grew from 600 barrels to 11,250, a nearly twentyfold increase
in production.[1] Nantucket was not alone in setting its sights on "ye
deep." Other whaling ports in Massachusetts and Rhode Island went in
search of whales in the open ocean and expanded their infrastructure
accordingly. None of them, however, came close to approaching the
breadth and depth of Nantucket's whaling fleet.

There are many reasons for Nantucket's success. The island's prime
location was an excellent launching point for deep-sea voyages, and
many of the skills that the islanders learned through shore whaling
proved equally useful in this new endeavor. The community on Nantucket, by virtue of its isolation and the high degree of interrelatedness
among its inhabitants, was tightly knit, and as the whalemen spent
more time at sea, the people they left behind, especially the women,
proved adept at keeping the community together.[2] This supportive net-
work was further enhanced by the spread of Quakerism which, by midcentury, was the predominant religion on Nantucket, and the one to
which many of the island's leading whaling merchants subscribed.
These "fighting Quakers" or "Quakers with a vengeance," as Melville
called them, had a strong work ethic and a business sense that proved
most efficacious in this emerging industry.[3] Their frugality, too, added
to their business success by enabling them to weather the bad years
with a prevailing ethos to make the most of the good. This frugality
was on display in 1737, when Thomas Chalkley, a Quaker minister, visited Nantucket and observed that "the priests who have money for
preaching; the lawyers, who have it for pleading, and the physicians,
who have money for giving receipts for health; are poor trades here on
this island."[4]

All these positive attributes of Quakerism notwithstanding, it is a
bit strange that this religion, rooted so firmly in pacifism, should have
been so instrumental in catapulting Nantucket to the front rank of
colonial whaling communities. After all, whaling, at its most elemental,

is a brutal, violent, and deadly activity, and one that a pacifist might just as soon avoid.[5] But, as is so often the case, the lure of profits trumped any moral or religious qualms. Melville speaks to this in *Moby-Dick* when Ishmael muses "how now in the contemplative evening of his days, the pious [Captain] Bildad . . . reconciled" his Quaker beliefs with his actions as a whaleman. Ishmael concludes, "I do not know; but it did not seem to concern him much, and very probably he had long since come to the sage and sensible conclusion that a man's religion is one thing, and this practical world quite another. This world pays dividends."[6]

Nantucket's success also grew out of the island's labor system and the hierarchy it imposed. The upper echelons of the whaling business remained the exclusive preserve of white Nantucketers, who were bred to be whalemen. The influences of this industry were everywhere, and few were the Nantucket boys who didn't dream of becoming a master of a whaleship. "As soon as they can talk," noted Nantucketer Walter Folger, the local boys "will make use of the common phrases, as *townor*, which is an Indian word, and signifies that they have seen the whale twice; and as soon as they are some years older, they are seen rowing in boats for diversion, which makes them expert oarsmen, a thing that is requisite in taking the whale."[7] According to a contemporary observer, the process of molding a Nantucket whaleman began when the boys were twelve, and had finished their formal schooling. First they learned the cooper's trade, then, at fourteen, they went to sea to acquire ship handling and navigation skills. "They go gradually through every station of rowers, steersman, and harpooners; thus they learn to attack, to pursue, to overtake, to cut, to dress their huge game: and after having performed several such voyages, and perfected themselves in this business, they are fit either for the counting house or the chase."[8] Of the ones who opted for the chase, the best of them would form the pool from which the masters of whaleships were chosen—the very capable leaders on whom so much of the profits of whaling depended.

Beneath the white Nantucketers were the Indians. The continued availability of Indian labor was an integral part of Nantucket's success, as well as that of other whaling communities. While Indian populations throughout the colonies continued to decline, there remained enough natives to man many whaleboats. As before, the positions they held tended to be the lowliest. The practice of extending credit played a key role in the loss of many Indians' freedom and their subsequent forced employment in the whale fishery, until such time as they could pay off their debts.[9]

While most Indians were treated unfairly, that certainly wasn't always the case. Account books from Nantucket show that between 1721 and 1756 there were Indian whalemen who annually earned four times the salary of the average seaman in Boston.[10] And there was at least one instance where a commitment to whaling allowed Indians to escape a more perilous employment. During the mid-1720s the Massachusetts colony went to war against the Abenaki Indians in yet another phase in the long-standing hostilities between colonists and Indians over land—this time in the vicinity of southern Maine. The Massachusetts contingent included Indians from Barnstable, on Cape Cod, who had signed on to fight under the condition that they be allowed to return home in the fall to go whaling. Accordingly Massachusetts governor William Dummer wrote the following note in 1724 to Col. Thomas Westbrook, who was at the time helping to orchestrate the military campaign. "Upon Sight hereof you must forthwith dismiss Cpt. Bournes Comp[y] of Indians & send them hither in one of the Sloops, That so they may lose no Time for Following the Whale Fishery, w[ch] is agreeable to my Promise made to them at Enlisting." The following year, still intent on living up to his word, Dummer penned a similar dispensation, urging that "none" of the Indians "be detained on any Pretense whatsoever."[11]

Although Indians were the predominant minority involved in whaling, they were not alone. Blacks, too, were employed in the whale fishery, with or without their consent, and almost always under inferior working conditions.[12] Such circumstances are hardly surprising, given that blacks, at the time, were viewed primarily as property and a cheap source of labor. It was hardly uncommon to see ads for whaling supplies to be placed alongside ads for slaves, as the "Advertisement" section of the *Boston News-Letter* revealed in November 1723. The first ad told of a merchant in Boston who had "lately imported from London, Extraordinary good Whale warps . . . made of the finest hemp," which were available in "Quoile" or "Quantity" for a reasonable sixteen pennies per pound. The next ad read, "A Likely Negro Woman, fit for Town or Country; to be Sold, Inquire of the Printer thereof and know further." Thus coils of rope and a black human being were tantamount: simply merchandise to be bought and sold at will. The same advertisement section included the announcement of a hefty reward for the return of "a Negro boy about 20 Years of Age, named Scipio," who had run away from his "Master" just a few days earlier.[13]

AS DEEP-SEA WHALING expanded in the early 1700s, shore whaling declined significantly. Whether hunting had decimated the near-shore populations, or the whales had shifted their traditional haunts to escape this relentless pursuit, there was no denying that up and down the coast whales were becoming scarcer. An entry from a diary written in 1762 tells the story of a sixty-year-old Truro resident who recalled when, as a much younger man, "he had seen as many whales in Cape Cod [Provincetown] harbor at one time as would have made a bridge from the end of the Cape to Truro shore, which is seven miles across and could require two thousand whales."[14] By the time those words were written, however, such days were already long gone.

With fewer whales close at hand, the trend from the teens through the 1740s was for whaleships to go farther offshore and stay out longer in search of prey. Trips progressed from days to weeks, and then to months, and the men ventured east to the margins of the Gulf Stream, south to North Carolina, and north as far as the Davis Strait, which lies between Greenland and Baffin Island. Whaleships, too, evolved from relatively small sloops of thirty-eight tons to sloops and schooners of upward of one hundred tons, and each ship usually carried a crew of thirteen men and two whaleboats. The whaleboats were twenty to twenty-five feet long, made of cedar clapboards, and so light that two men could easily maneuver them on land.[15] But this lack of bulk was much more important at sea, where the boats could be lowered away and pulled aloft quickly. And their lightness, combined with a shallow draft, allowed them to move swiftly over the water. During shore-whaling days and through the early stages of the deep-sea fishery, some whaleboats were square ended and therefore maneuverable primarily in one direction—forward. Although that design persisted until the mid-eighteenth century, it was increasingly supplanted by a much more agile type of boat, one with a V-shaped bow and stern, which was equally nimble at moving fore and aft—particularly useful attributes for a boat that not only had to maintain its stability while being towed full ahead by an angry whale, but also had to be able to back away quickly from snapping jaws or flailing flukes of the same should the need arise.[16] The double-V shape was adopted from earlier European designs, but the colonists perfected it, and it remained the whaling industry standard from then on—the perfect match of form and function.[17]

The rhythms and flow of offshore whaling differed markedly from shore whaling. For varying lengths of time, the men on board became a floating community, and relied on each other for companionship, support, and, ultimately, their lives. The boundary of this community was often extended through the process of mateship, whereby two or more whaleships would pool their efforts and share in the spoils of the hunt. As for the towns and villages that the whalemen left behind, they too had to confront a new reality. In whaling ports it was often the case that so many men from their teens through their thirties went "a-whaling" that they left behind communities comprising mainly women.[18] Still, the life of a whaleman was not yet all-consuming, as it would become in later years. Once the whaling season ended, the men returned and reentered the fabric of local life with relative ease.

Hunting whales at sea was a bit different than hunting them along the coast. After the whale was sighted, either by a man on the mast or one on deck, the call went out and the crews jumped into the whaleboats, which were then lowered, and the chase commenced to the rallying cry of "A dead whale or a stove boat!" The boatsteerer would be at the bow of the boat, pulling an oar, while the officer, or boatheader, would be at the rear, shouting directions to the crew. When the boat closed in on its prey, the boatsteerer would put down his oar, grab a harpoon, and brace his left thigh against a semicircular cut (called the clumsy cleat) in the thwart ship planking for support. His muscles taut and his heart racing, he would raise the harpoon, draw back his body like a bow, and, waiting for the best time to strike, hurl the harpoon into the whale's back or flank. Once the whale was fast to the boat, the boatsteerer and the boatheader engaged in a most curious maneuver, with the former going to the back of the boat to steer it during the chase, while the boatheader went to the front of the boat so that he would be in position to lance the whale. To stand up and change places in a whaleboat in calm conditions, with no whale about, was tricky enough, but to do so after a whale had just been harpooned was quite dangerous. Not only did the boat have a full complement of men and a great array of equipment strewn about, but also ocean conditions were often quite choppy, and the whale usually made matters worse by either thrashing about or taking off, dragging the boat behind. Nevertheless tradition was maintained, and despite the awkwardness and the dangers of switching places, the men did so just the same, and the chase was on.[19]

The harpoon line was paid out, whizzing around the wooden post at the stern of the boat, called the loggerhead, at such a tremendous speed that the men would have to douse it with seawater to keep it from scorching and igniting. The chase could last for hours and take one or more whaleboats many miles from, and sometimes well out of sight of, the mother ship. When the boat finally pulled up alongside the whale, the boatheader finished it off with deep thrusts of the lance. Then the whale was rowed back to the ship, where officers, wielding sharp cutting spades, peeled the blubber from the carcass as it rolled in the water, and the block and tackle, roused to action by the men pumping the handles of the windlass up and down, hauled the blubber onto the deck. The fate of the blubber depended on the captain's inclination and the availability of tryworks. The blubber could be cut into small pieces and stored in casks on board, ultimately to be brought back to port and tried out on shore. The longer the blubber sat in the casks, however, the more rancid it became, especially when the whaling grounds were in warmer climates, and the more rancid the blubber, the lower the grade of oil that could be produced. On trips far to the north, however, the bitterly cold air helped minimize spoilage, thus enabling the whaleship transporting raw blubber to reach port with a reasonably fresh product. For longer trips, both north and south, whalemen often brought portable tryworks along and set them up on the shore. Once the blubber was boiled down, the oil was placed in casks. This ensured a better product and enabled the ships to stay out longer, because casks of oil take up far less space than casks of blubber. Spermaceti proved much easier to handle than blubber. Already in liquid form, it could simply be ladled into casks, or if the spermaceti congealed, the whalemen would scald it before storing it.

Offshore whaling was a dangerous profession. When shore whaling was dominant, injuries were few and far between.[20] Now with longer trips, and the opportunity to row ashore for help or to escape bad weather foreclosed, injuries became more common, and fatalities increased. Between 1722 and 1742, for example, three whaleships from Nantucket, and their entire crews, were lost at sea. One of these was mastered by Elisha Coffin. He had planned to be away for a month or, at most, six weeks, but ran into bad weather, which, according to his wife, Dinah, "in all probability Swallowed him and those with him up: for they were never heard of" again.[21]

Other dangers loomed as well. Whaling vessels far from their home-ports sometimes fell victim to privateers. Capt. Solomon Sturgis and his crew, for example, sailed out of Barnstable in 1741, but encountered a Spanish privateer that promptly commandeered their ship, while setting Sturgis and most of his men free. Three years later a Nantucket whaleship heading for Boston, laden with 330 barrels of oil, lost sight of its fellow whaleships. When another ship came into view, it appeared, at first blush, to be a lightly crewed English sloop, and was in fact in the process of raising the English flag as it approached. But the Nantucket captain suspected a ruse, and he and his men loaded the whaleboats with essential items and rowed two miles to shore. It was a wise decision. Soon after the Nantucketers abandoned their ship, the visitor, a French privateer, showed its true colors and sent a boat of armed men to claim its prize.[22]

THE ONLY KNOWN firsthand account of offshore whaling before 1750 is provided by Benjamin Bangs of Brewster, Massachusetts.[23] Beginning in 1742, and for twenty years thereafter, he kept a diary of his activities, including his whaling pursuits along with a great range of mundane and momentous events in his own life and the life of the colony. Only four of the diary books have survived, out of a likely total of eight. They measure four by six inches, and are about one-quarter to one-half inch thick. Given how expensive paper was at the time, Bangs tried his best to make the most of the space by filling each page from top to bottom and side to side. His penmanship is flowing and handsome, and although more than two hundred years have elapsed since the last entry was made, the paper is in very good shape and the sepia-colored ink is bold and clear. The condition of this eighteenth-century time capsule is all the more remarkable since it was at sea for long periods, following Bangs as he traveled on the often boisterous Atlantic Ocean.

Born in 1721 on Cape Cod, Bangs began his diaries when he was twenty-two, and on the first page of the first book he proclaimed that this is "a memorandum or short Acct. of ye Life of Benj. Bangs, containing some Transactions and most Remarkables for my own Satisfaction." Of all the books that survive, it is this first one—which starts on January 1, 1742, and ends on May 31, 1749—that contains the richest source of whaling material. Bangs, whose family originally settled in the colony in 1623, provides insight into the earliest days of offshore whaling. The beginning of book 1 finds Bangs still attending school, but by March 18, 1743, he decided that he had had enough formal education and "broke up keeping school" for good.[24] Setting his sights on offshore whaling, Bangs took navigation and "plain sailing" lessons, and having gained confidence in his ability to handle himself at sea, he signed on to "go with [Captain] Sam'l Paddock whaling in a bumpkin sloop, fitted out by Esq. Paine"; so began his first offshore whaling cruise, on May 9, 1743.

Fifteen days later, after sheltering at Provincetown harbor to wait out a storm, Bangs and his mates reached the waters off North Carolina and found themselves "among ye spermacetis." This being a popular spot for whaling, there were already three other sloops in the vicinity "cutting up fish." Eager to catch up to the competition, Captain Paddock ordered the whaleboats into the water. The men killed the first sperm whale they harpooned, pulled it alongside, and started cutting in. This was an auspicious beginning. Whalemen often failed to harpoon the whales they chased or kill the whales they harpooned, and many times, days and weeks of arduous pursuit netted nothing but frustration. The "bumpkin sloop" could not avoid the vicissitudes of whaling, and it too encountered its fair share of missed opportunities. On May 30 Bangs wrote, "we are among ye fish as thick as bees and as wild, for we could strike none." And even when they struck the whales, they couldn't always finish them off. Between May 24, when they arrived at the whaling grounds, and June 2, when they departed for home, Bangs and his mates harpooned at least nine sperm whales but killed only four. After returning to Harwich and unloading its casks of oil and blubber, the sloop was reprovisioned, and on June 14 it set out on another whaling cruise, with Bangs again on board. This trip was cut short on account of having to take a sick crew member home, yet the men still managed to kill two sperms. Reflecting on the 1743 whaling season, Bangs wrote, "there are great voyages made this year in general," and his experience bears this out. Between the two cruises he was on, six sperms were caught, making seventy-three barrels of oil, and earning for the men between fifteen and twenty-five pounds, depending on their lay.

Rather than go on another cruise with Captain Paddock, Bangs decided to stay home to tend to the family farm. Although Bangs had his fill of offshore whaling for the year, when an opportunity for shore whaling arose, he took it. The whale he was after was not the right, which was already scarce in coastal waters, but rather the pilot whale or blackfish, which was still quite plentiful. In September 1743 Bangs participated in a hunt which killed about eighty blackfish, clearing "£12 a share." The next month he recorded that "our Harwich people killed 4 or 5 hundred black-fish at Mulford's clefts, and cleared £79, single share. Our old boat had one share." Such great numbers were a function of the hunting method employed. "It would," noted a late-eighteenth-century observer, "be curious indeed to a countryman, who lives at a distance from the sea, to be acquainted with the method of killing blackfish. Their size is from four to five tons weight, when full grown. When they come within our harbors, boats surround them. They are as easily driven to shore as cattle or sheep are driven on land. The tide leaves them, and they are easily killed. They are a fish of the whale kind, and will average a barrel of oil each."[25] In many instances a good pilot whale hunt could greatly improve upon an otherwise paltry whaling year. Such was the case in 1741, when more than one thousand pilot whales were taken along a stretch of Cape Cod. "This unexpected Success so late in the Year," reported the *Boston News-Letter*, "put new Life into Some who had spent all the former Season of the Year in Toil and Labour to little or no Purpose."[26] The all-time record for an American pilot whale hunt was set in 1874, when 1,405 of them were herded onto the beach in Truro.[27]

Bangs returned to offshore whaling in 1744, as captain aboard his family's sloop.[28] As he was preparing to depart on a cruise, troubling news reached Cape Cod, and Bangs's first entry for April reports of hearing about "a fight between ye English and French." That fight turned out to be King George's War, and as soon as war was declared,

colonial ships became potential targets for French cruisers and privateers. Fearful though he was of being captured, Bangs left port on
April 19, and kept one eye warily trained on the horizon for trouble.

For Bangs 1744 turned out to be a dismal year. As soon as his sloop
left Harwich, it started leaking, forcing him to turn back. A few days
after leaving port again, the leak reappeared and finally got so bad that
the sloop had to pull into Nantucket for repairs. Even if they hadn't
lost those days, it is doubtful that Bangs and his men would have had a
much better season. For whatever reason, the necessary combination of
skill and luck eluded them. Between the middle of April and the end of
June, they saw many sperm whales off the coast between North Carolina and Massachusetts but killed only two. Fortunately they were
able to add to their balance sheets when they found and cut up a sperm
whale floating dead at the surface, filling twelve hogsheads with "good
blubber." The final tally for the season was forty-eight and one-half
barrels of oil. Other colonial whaleships fared better than Bangs's
sloop. Indeed, when Bangs had arrived in Nantucket to repair his sloop,
he noted in his diary that "45 spermacetes are brought in here this day."

The holes in his ship, his men's skills, and the apparent lack of luck
were not the only things that put a crimp in Bangs's whaling season;
the war intruded as well. On April 28, 1744, his sloop was south-
southwest of Martha's Vineyard when two sperm whales appeared.
While pursuing the whales, Bangs and his men were themselves being
pursued. "There came a sloop down upon us," wrote Bangs, "and
chased us 4 hours close upon the wind, our boats towed, [and] we a
bitterly scared. They are within a mile of us and by their looks we
judge them Enemy. They could not come up to us and so left us at
night." Nearly two months later, after Bangs had brought his oil into
Boston, rather than head home immediately he decided to stay in port a
while longer "on account of ye enemy who are very plenty on our
coast, so that we dare not stir." And a week later Bangs summed up the
season, stating, "Whaling voyages are not so good this year as last
year. Ye noise of ye war spoils us all."

In the remaining years covered by the first book, which extends to
1749, Bangs went whaling a few more times. He primarily chased
sperm whales and on one occasion, off the coast of Virginia, claimed to
have seen "thousands of them," which proved virtually impossible to
catch because they acted "like porpuses" and were "exceedingly wild."

Bangs repeatedly mentions sailing with other whaleships at sea, yet none of the ships he was on, as far as can be told, engaged in the common practice of mateship. The enemy continued to be a problem and not only hampered many of Bangs's voyages but also took away some unfortunate whalemen as prisoners. Although much of Bang's diary concerns whaling, its many other entries are just as interesting. He records weddings and many deaths, including a commentary on the widow Hopkins's boy, who "tore out his guts with a plough and died." In October 1747 he "saw a negro man hanged on Roxbury Neck for shooting another," and on April 20, 1749, he noted that "Deacon Taylor at Chatham hanged himself but was cut down and is not quite dead yet." Bangs liked rum and spoke fondly of getting "boozed," and not so fondly of having to "keep sober." He feared being forced to join the militia and take up arms on behalf of England, and he was awed by an "earthquake [that] was heard all over New England." Whether Bangs went whaling between 1749 and 1759 is not known, since the books covering those years are missing. By the 1760s, however, and perhaps earlier, Bangs had already become a successful merchant in Harwich, and was outfitting whaling voyages and employing men on his own vessels.[29] He died in 1769 at the age of forty-eight, leaving a large fortune to his heirs, who had whaling to thank for much of their inheritance.

UP THROUGH THE MIDDLE of the eighteenth century, the colonial whaling industry pursued an uneven path. There were good years and bad. Sometimes the whales were plenty and the men's aim true, resulting in "greasy" trips with holds full of oil, while at other times, "clean" trips were the order of the day, with the men either not finding the whales or, if finding them, not being able to do much more than engage in fruitless pursuits and curse their failure.

Demand affected profits as well. Periodic market gluts, when the price for oil and whalebone sank, were counterbalanced by stretches where increased demand kept prices high. Despite these fluctuations, however, the overall trend was positive. More boats were bringing in more product, and prices remained strong, rising from seven pounds per ton of oil in 1730 to fourteen pounds by 1748, with many gyrations in between. Thomas Hutchinson noted this success in his contemporary *History of the Colony and Province of Massachusetts-Bay*, saying that the whale fishery is "in a more flourishing state than formerly. . . . The increase of the consumption of oyl by lamps as well as divers manufactures in Europe has been no small encouragement to our whale fishery. The flourishing state of the island of Nantucket must be attributed to it. The cod and whale fishery, being the principal source of our returns to Great Britain, are therefore worthy not only of provincial but national attention." Those "returns to Great Britain" were particularly important, for with each passing year the colonies sank deeper into debt to the mother country, in large part because, as historian Arthur M. Schlesinger pointed out, "Colonial commerce was conditioned by the fact that the Acts of Trade conceived of America as a market for British manufactures and a source of raw materials rather than as a country free to develop its own potentialities." By 1721 America's negative trade balance with Britain stood at two hundred thousand pounds and was still growing.[30] The income from whaling was an important source of currency that helped the colonists slow the debt's rise.

Although the colonies consumed a significant amount of oil and whalebone, it was primarily British demand that enabled the colonial whaling industry to grow. This is not what Britain had wanted. Ever since the late 1600s, when Britain's hopes of becoming a whaling powerhouse were destroyed by the Dutch whaling juggernaut, the British had dreamed of getting back into the business, and doing so by building their own whaling fleet that sailed from British ports. In 1724 the South Sea Company decided to revive the moribund whale fishery by outfitting ships to go to the Greenland whaling grounds.[31] Parliament encouraged this venture by eliminating, for a period of seven years, customs duties on whalebone, oil, and blubber that was caught off Greenland and imported on British ships—ones commanded by British captains and manned by crews that were at least one-third British subjects. Thus encouraged, the South Sea Company commissioned the building of twelve ships, of 306 tons each, to be ready for the 1725 whaling season. While the South Sea Company viewed this endeavor as a potentially lucrative business opportunity for itself and its shareholders, Parliament viewed it in much broader terms. Should the British whale fishery be revived, it would result in many benefits to the nation that Parliament dearly wanted to achieve. It would stanch the flow of money out of Britain to pay for oil and whalebone. Britain's shipyards would be kept busy, and so too would all the craftsmen and laborers necessary to outfit voyages. And a key "nursery" of British seamen would be created that could be tapped for service in His Majesty's Navy as needed. As a result the officers of the South Sea Company and their parliamentary backers looked to the 1725 whaling season with great anticipation and excitement.

Their enthusiasm, however, did not last long. Problems arose even before the first of the company's ships left port. It had been more than fifty years since the British last had any whaling industry to speak of, and therefore, when it came to manning the ships, few if any Britons could be found who knew anything about the business. This labor shortage forced the company to hire foreigners as crew, with the largest contingent coming from Germany. Yet despite the whaling talents of the Germans, the 1725 whaling season was a bust. The company's ships killed only twenty and a half whales, with the half coming from a whale that had been struck by two ships and, therefore, was divided between them, as was the custom. This was far short of the three-whales-per-ship ratio that the company calculated would be necessary to make a profit. The company's owners could chalk up this bad year to experience, and hold out hope that the next year would be better. After all, whaling was a game of averages, and there was that old whaling adage that one good year in seven will make up for the other six. But with each passing year, the owners' hopes dimmed. The disappointing season of 1725 was followed by seven more that were even worse. The 1730 season was particularly disastrous, with twenty-two ships catching only twelve whales. Throughout this eight-year stretch the South Sea Company failed to post a profit. Instead it continued hemorrhaging money, accruing increasing debt with each passing year. By 1732 the day of judgment beckoned. The company had invested more than £262,000 in this doomed enterprise, while earning only about £84,000, which came from the sale of oil and whalebone, as well as the sale of all of the company's ships and stores—leaving, as it were, a gaping loss of nearly £178,000.

Nobody was more shocked by Britain's failure to jump-start its whaling industry than the British. According to Scoresby, the general reaction of the day was one of "astonishment."[32] This turn of events was all the more disturbing to the British in light of the great success that the Dutch were having in the same line of work. Ever since the

British succumbed to Dutch competition at the end of the seventeenth century, Dutch whaling had been riding high. Between 1675 and 1721, the Dutch had killed 32,907 whales, making huge profits. The dominance of the Dutch continued while the South Sea Company faltered and ultimately fell under its own weight. Many reasons have been offered to explain this great disparity in whaling fortunes. The Dutch, it was said, benefited from low interest rates on money, and they were more frugal than the British and built their ships at a lower cost. In contrast to the British, the Dutch didn't have to suffer the great expense of hiring foreigners to man the boats, because with more than a century of whaling behind them, the Dutch had a large and skilled cadre of native whaling talent to draw on. And by exporting much of their whale products to other countries, the Dutch kept prices high and generated a steady stream of money flowing into their coffers. Some observers discounted all these reasons and instead focused on ability. To their way of thinking the British, and the foreign talent they hired, failed because they were simply not very good at whaling.[33]

Not ready to abandon the whaling industry, and eager to compete with their own colonies, the British tried to subsidize their way to success. Beginning in 1733 Parliament offered a bounty of twenty shillings per ton on all whaleships greater than two hundred tons that were fitted out in Britain. This didn't incite much enthusiasm for new ventures, however, and seven years later Parliament upped the bounty to thirty shillings, hoping that would turn the tide. But still the British failed to respond, and the country's whaling industry remained in a feeble state. Unable to satisfy its own needs for oil and whalebone, and not wanting to purchase the heavily taxed Dutch supplies of these products, the British continued what they had been doing for many years—namely, buying from the colonies. The colonial whalemen shared none of the disadvantages that seemed to conspire to keep the British whalemen down. Through a combination of frugality, skill, and perseverance, colonial whalemen succeeded in much the same manner as the Dutch, and were quickly chipping away at that country's dominance in the industry.[34] Although British demand for colonial whale products through the early 1730s was not particularly strong, it was steady. Then, in the mid-1730s, the British demand for—and price of— colonial whale oil started to climb.

By the early eighteenth century, London had already emerged as one of the greatest cities of the world, but also one of the darkest. It was, in fact, two cities—one by day and another by night. During the day natural light illuminated the city's streets, which were bustling with activity. But at night, when the sun went down, the streets became dark and dangerous places. The only nighttime lighting occurred between Michaelmas (September 29) and Lady Day (March 25), when contractors hired by the city were required to place lamps before every tenth house. But these lamps were lit only on "dark nights"—about twenty days per month—and then they were extinguished at midnight.[35] Thus for much of the time, when Londoners ventured out of their houses at night, if they did at all, they often rushed through the shadows, constantly looking over their shoulders, all the while fearing that they might be robbed or attacked by thieves or thugs who used darkness as an accomplice. A British historian painted a disturbing picture of one of the most notorious of London's night gangs operating at this time:

> In 1712 a club of young men of the higher classes, who assumed the names Mohocks, were accustomed nightly to sally out drunk into the streets to hunt the passers-by and to subject them in mere wantonness to the most atrocious outrages. One of their favourite amusements, called "tipping the lion," was to squeeze the nose of their victim flat upon his face and to bore out his eyes with their fingers. Among them were the "sweaters," who formed a circle round their prisoner and pricked him with their swords till he sank exhausted to the ground.[36]

London turned a corner in its fight against nocturnal lawlessness in 1736. That year the city government began levying a tax to pay for the placement and maintenance of oil lamps, called parish lamps, throughout the city, which were to be lit from sundown to sunrise. Within a couple of years the number of lamps in the city rose to fifteen thousand. Whereas under the old system the city's lamps were lit just 750 hours per year, under this new system that number increased to 5,000. Nighttime crime in London didn't stop as a result, but it was greatly reduced. The citizens of London were not the only group to benefit from this new measure. The parish lamps were greedy consumers of whale oil, and with the installation of each new lamp, the demand for colonial whale oil grew in step with colonial profits.[37]

As the whaling industry expanded, mercantile connections between colonial whaling ports and Boston strengthened, with the latter serving as the major conduit for the whale oil trade within the colonies as well as between the colonies and Britain. Not everyone, however, was happy with this arrangement. Some Nantucket whaling merchants, who watched the Bostonians profit greatly by purchasing oil on the island, transporting it to Boston, and shipping it overseas, thought that there might be a better way to conduct the transatlantic trade. If they shipped their oil and whalebone directly to London, the Nantucketers realized they could cut out the Boston middlemen and in all likelihood earn a higher price for their product. To test the waters and not risk too much on this experiment, the Nantucketers sent a single vessel to London, in 1745. The success of this voyage encouraged more in the ensuing years. This new arrangement allowed the Nantucketers to act as their own oil and whalebone salesmen in London, to good effect, and also enabled them to purchase goods, such as sailcloth and iron, directly from the suppliers at prices that were far lower than what they had traditionally paid for the same items in Boston. Nevertheless Nantucketers didn't abandon the Boston trade. While Boston's middlemen cut into the Nantucketers' profits, they also provided services of considerable value, the most important of which was using their own ships to transport the oil and whalebone, thereby assuming some of the major risks of this international trade, including shipwreck and capture.[38]

Thomas Hancock was, for a brief time, one of those Boston middlemen, and a look at his activities provides insights into the nature of the business.[39] In 1731 the twenty-eight-year-old Hancock eagerly sought to get involved in the overseas trade with London, but first he had to decide which products he could sell that would, in turn, generate the income necessary to purchase British goods for trade back in the colonies. He quickly settled on whalebone and whale oil. Before Hancock and his partners could launch their business, however, they had to pick a London representative to barter on their behalf. Choosing a good man was critical because he was the one who would have to sell the products for the best price, all without the benefit of conferring with his bosses, three thousand miles away in Boston. The great trust

placed in the hands of this man comes through in a letter that Hancock
wrote to his London representative in November 1737. "Inclosed you
have bill of lading for forty-two bundles of whalefins [baleen] to you
consigned which I wish may come safe to hand & to a good market,
youl be best Judge at what Season to Dispose of it."[40] Hancock also
looked to his London man as his eyes and ears to report on the market
trends for oil and whalebone in Europe.

Just as important to the middlemen were the ship captains who
were entrusted with the cargoes. These men, of course, had to be con-
summate sailors. The race to London was an important component of
the whaling trade, and there was a premium placed on getting there
first. The arrival of one fully loaded ship in that port could, by virtue of
flooding the market, cause the prices for oil and whalebone to fall,
meaning that the next ship that offloaded could be faced with the
prospect of having to sell its cargo for a lower price than what had been
expected. If too many ships arrived simultaneously, the resulting glut
could force the captains either to bide their time in port, hoping for the
market to shift, or to sail off to another port in search of buyers. In July
1734, for example, one of Hancock's ships failed to win the race and
had to pay the price. The ship that beat his was able to sell its oil for fifteen pounds per ton, but by the time Hancock's ship pulled in, accompanied by two other colonial whale ships laden with oil, the price per
ton had dropped to fourteen pounds. Despite this and other relatively
minor setbacks, Hancock profited handsomely from the oil and whalebone trade, but then, around 1739, he somewhat abruptly and mysteriously abandoned this line of work to pursue other business activities.

By the middle of the eighteenth century, colonial whalemen were
more adept at finding and killing whales than they were at processing
them. Both of the alternatives for obtaining oil—rendering blubber at
home port or using portable tryworks during voyages—worked, but
neither was particularly efficient. So, to squeeze more profits out of
their labors, colonial whalemen began to ask how the efficiency of their
operations might be improved. The answer they came up with was so
simple and clean that it is surprising they had not thought of it earlier.
Why not install the tryworks on the whaling vessels, with the iron
pots and brick-lined furnace built into the center of the main deck,
thereby transforming the vessels into floating factories capable of cutting in, rendering, and storing whale oil all in one place?[41]

Predictably there was opposition. Even though the fires of the try-works would be surrounded by thick layers of brick, and underlain by an enclosed water barrier, wasn't the proximity of the flames and the wood still a little too close for comfort? Such trepidation notwithstanding, this was, as Victor Hugo might later observe, an idea whose time had come. When and where the first tryworks was installed on board a colonial whaling vessel is not known. Nevertheless it was around 1750 that the colonial whaling fleet first latched onto this idea, which over time spread throughout the industry. Now colonial whalemen were not only engaged in a business of international importance, but they were also among the first, and perhaps *the* first, colonial laborers to be a part of what could reasonably be called an industrial assembly line. This one began with the man who sighted the whale and progressed through stages that included lowering the boats, killing the whale, towing it back, cutting into the carcass, hauling the blubber and baleen aboard, rendering the oil, stowing the casks below, and ultimately swabbing the deck and waiting for the next cry of "Thar she blows!"

The middle of the century witnessed yet another technical advance that had an equally profound impact on the colonial whaling industry—that is, when the colonists first made candles from spermaceti. And these weren't just any candles, but ones that burned with a brilliance, clarity, and purity that shed a most beautiful and unique light on the world.

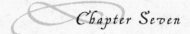
CANDLE WARS

LABEL FOR SPERMACETI CANDLES SOLD BY NICHOLAS BROWN & COMPANY,
BEAUTIFULLY ENGRAVED BY NATHANIEL HURD.

THE HISTORY OF THE SPERMACETI CANDLE INDUSTRY IS CLOAKED
in mystery, with some historians suggesting that Abraham Rodriguez
Rivera, a Portuguese Jew who had settled in Newport, was the first
person to make such candles, and that he did so around 1751. Other
evidence, however, points to Benjamin Crabb, of Rehoboth, Massachusetts, as the man who launched the industry, for in 1751, it was Crabb
who petitioned the General Court of Massachusetts for the "sole priv-

iledge" of producing spermaceti candles.[1] He averred "that he and no other person in the province, has the art of pressing, fluxing and chrystalizing of spermaceti and coarse spermaceti oyl, and of making candles of the same."[2] He also claimed to have already obtained the tools and devices necessary to make "Candles of such Transparency and Lustre in burning that they exceed all others."[3] The court assented to Crabb's request, but for reasons unknown, Crabb soon moved to Providence, where he built his candleworks and began supplying local merchants with candles. His good fortune, however, proved short lived, for not long after opening his candleworks, it burned to the ground.

If Rivera and Crabb were the only ones vying for the title of the first spermaceti candle entrepreneur, then the mystery, while interesting, would not run deep. But a tantalizing advertisement in the March 30, 1748, issue of the *Boston News-Letter* casts doubt on the primacy of either man's position.

> Sperma-Ceti Candles. To be sold by Minot's T. by James Clemens, Sperma-Ceti Candles, exceeding all others for Beauty, Sweetness of Scent when extinguished; Duration, being more than double Tallow Candles of equal size; Dimensions of Flame, nearly four Times more, emitting a soft easy expanding Light, bring the object close to the Sight, rather than causing the Eye to trace after them, as all Tallow Candles do, from a constant Dimness which they produce.[4]

The literature remains mute on who this manufacturer was, but a 1743 edition of *Chambers' Cyclopædia* indicates that spermaceti candles were introduced even earlier. There, in the second volume, about half-way through the letter *S*, is a most illuminating entry—"*Sperma-ceti candles*, are of modern manufacture: they are made smooth, with a fine gloss, free from rings and scars, superior to the finest wax-candles in colour and luster; and, when genuine, leave no spot or stain on the finest silk, cloth, or linen."[5] Having no evidence that spermaceti candles were being produced in the colonies at this time, one can nonetheless reasonably conclude that this "superior" product was of European origin. As to which European country was manufacturing spermaceti candles, the answer to this question will have to wait for the sleuthing of researchers able to comb through the libraries of Europe with great patience and an eye for faint traces of this nascent industry.

The *Chambers' Cyclopædia* comment that "Sperma-ceti candles" are of "modern manufacture" implied that it was not long before 1743 that this item first appeared on the scene. What is most surprising about this early date is that it is not even earlier. The congealing, wax-like qualities of spermaceti was already known for quite some time, as was the value of spermaceti oil as an illuminant. For decades, if not centuries, before *Chambers' Cyclopædia* first mentioned spermaceti candles, pharmacists and others in the curative arts knew how to transform spermaceti into a hardened waxy mass, from which shavings could be taken and distributed to the sick. It is not, then, too difficult to imagine some creative inventor seeing spermaceti as a prime ingredient for candles, for this curious substance was easily fashioned into various shapes and would burn brilliantly if supplied with a wick. However far back the lineage of the spermaceti candle goes, it is the American colonists who deserve credit for making such candles a valuable international commodity.

The first colonial candleworks, established by Crabb and Rivera, attracted attention, and not surprisingly, other men with money to invest sought to get into the business. One of the first was Obadiah Brown, a Quaker merchant and scion of the family that would one day found Brown University, who built a candleworks in Providence in 1753. To get a leg up on the competition, Brown hired Crabb to teach him about this new venture, but this turned out to be a poor business decision. Although Brown kept Crabb on the payroll for three years, he learned precious little of value from his erstwhile tutor. Writing about this, Brown said that he "was disappointed of the information which he expected to receive from Crabb and was obliged to learn the secret of refining [spermaceti into candles] by his own expertise."[6]

THE REFINING PROCESS began each fall when the spermaceti and oil taken from the whale's head, commonly referred to as head matter, was delivered to the candleworks, where it was placed in large copper kettles and heated, liquefying the spermaceti and removing water or other contaminants that might have been mixed in on board ship. The hot, thick liquid was drained from the kettles into casks, which were then placed in storehouses for the winter, where the cold temperatures transformed the mixture into a semisolid granular mass. When the temperature rose enough during the winter to soften this mass, the casks were opened and the contents transferred into woolen sacks that were tied off and squeezed in a large wooden screw press capable of exerting hundreds of tons of pressure. The oil that drained out of the sacks was collected and sold as winter strained sperm oil, the most valuable whale oil.

The material that remained in the sacks was reheated in the kettles and drained into casks to be stored until the warm weather returned in early spring, when the contents of the casks were shoveled into cotton bags and again set on the press. The oil that issued this time, called spring-strained sperm oil, was of lesser quality, but it still fetched a good price. The wax remaining in the sacks was brittle and dry and of a gray, brown, or yellowish cast. In such a state it could not be used to make the pure white candles that consumers demanded. To get to that point, the candlemaker boiled the wax once again and added an alkali, such as potash, which stripped away the unwanted color. Then the kettles' temperature was increased to the point where the alkali itself boiled out of solution. The now-white wax could be molded into candles or large blocks for later use.[7]

The earliest spermaceti candle manufacturers were extremely secretive. They viewed the candlemaking process as proprietary and sought to dissuade potential competitors. Nevertheless others learned the "secret of refining," built their own presses, and by the end of the 1750s there were at least ten spermaceti candleworks in the colonies. In the face of such competition the manufacturers had to distinguish themselves in the marketplace, so they wrapped and boxed their candles in ways intended to catch the eye and make it clear that theirs was a product of rare quality. The Browns of Providence, for example, swaddled their spermaceti candles in blue tissue paper and placed them in boxes adorned with a beautifully engraved label, sporting images of a sperm whale and men in a whaleboat, along with an ornately drawn frame at the edge, and text proclaiming the candles' purity in English and French.[8]

Fancy labels and colorful packaging, however, were not enough for a manufacturer to retain market share. The quality of the candles, too, had to be beyond reproach, for they were a luxury that cost more than a shilling per pound. People who pay dearly for an item do not want an inferior product. This was certainly true of the purchasers of spermaceti candles, a very discriminating group that included the affluent in the American colonies, Europe, the Caribbean islands, and African slaving ports. Benjamin Franklin, one of many satisfied customers, wrote a friend in November 1751 that he was impressed by these "new kind" of candles "to read by . . . [that] afford a clear white Light; may be held in the Hand, even in hot Weather, without softing; that their Drops do not make Grease Spots like those from common Candles; that they last much longer, and need little or no Snuffing."[9] Manufacturers went to considerable pains to assure their customers that the product was well worth the price. The Browns, in shipping an especially fine lot of candles to Philadelphia in 1759, included a note to the receiving merchant, claiming that the candles had been "made in the best manner for a gentleman of London," and they recommended them "to be equal to any made in Europe or America, the difference between these and the common sort is in their being harder & consequently freer from oil, whiter, clear and neater cast."[10]

By 1760 the candle manufacturers realized that they had a serious problem. Despite the expansion of the colonial whaling fleet and the rise in the number of sperm whales captured, the demand for spermaceti candles was so strong that it far outstripped the supply of head matter. Just a handful of the largest candle manufacturers, working at full tilt, had the capacity quickly to process all the head matter the colonial whale fishery could provide. As historian James Hedges pointed out, the manufacturers' ability to respond to this situation was constrained. They couldn't afford to get into a bidding war with one another over the limited amount of head matter, for that would only cause its price, and hence the price of the candles, to rise. And while the wealthy were willing to pay more for spermaceti candles, they were willing to pay only so much. Were the price of spermaceti candles to rise too high, all but the richest customers would replace them with other illuminants, such as right whale oil, seal oil, or tallow candles.[11]

Although the manufacturers couldn't charge more for their product, there existed an alternative to keep the price of candles in check while still remaining profitable. Namely, if they could keep the cost of the head matter from rising too fast, then their goal could be achieved.

At first, only four of the candle manufacturers joined forces, and they told the main supplier of head matter, Nantucketer Joseph Rotch, that they would only pay a certain amount, and no more, for his product. The folly of this plan, however, quickly became apparent. The four manufacturers could agree all they wanted on a ceiling price for head matter, but there was nothing to stop their competition from paying more, and therefore causing the price to rise rapidly. On November 5, 1761, the eight largest candle manufacturers in the colonies attempted to solve this problem by banding together in oligarchic fashion to form the "United Company of Spermaceti Chandlers," which came to be known as the Spermaceti Trust. Under the terms of their agreement, the manufacturers established a maximum price that they would pay per ton of head matter, which was six pounds higher than the price that "common merchantable spermaceti body brown oil" was fetching in London. They also agreed to "use all fair and honorable means" to stop potential rivals from building new candleworks. And if the trust's members were not able to keep the price of head matter from rising above the agreed-upon cap, they vowed personally to "fit out at least 12 vessels" to secure the head matter themselves. The trust was scheduled to remain in force for seventeen months, and during that time the members were to meet twice annually, "at the best tavern in Taunton" (Massachusetts), where they could share intelligence and measure the progress of their endeavor.[12]

The Spermaceti Trust, one of the the earliest industrial monopolies in the colonies and, according to one author, the "world's first energy cartel," was plagued by problems from the start.[13] Trust members accused one another of breaches of their agreement, the most egregious of which was paying more than the stipulated price for head matter. Rather than let the trust sink under an accumulating list of grievances, the members chose to regroup and clarify the terms of their association, signing revised articles of agreement on April 13, 1763. The new maximum price for head matter was now set at ten pounds above the price for "Brown oil," and members were allowed to buy only from a specific list of suppliers, thereby minimizing the likelihood of secret purchases at inflated prices. The members remained committed to stifling the competition, and instructed their agents to provide them with "the most early notice of any attempt to set up other spermaceti works," so that they could take steps to keep the interlopers from obtaining the expertise and tools, mainly the screw press, needed to launch the business. The most critical element of the new articles of agreement was the division of head matter among members. Originally the members were free to buy as much head matter as they could secure at a given price. Now members would receive a set allotment from the entire stock of head matter caught in the colonies, which was divided into one hundred parts. Thus, Nicholas Brown and Company, the largest of the manufacturers received twenty out of every one hundred barrels, while the others got smaller amounts.[14]

For the next dozen years the Spermaceti Trust endured, and so did its problems. The members' faith in one another and the trust itself was repeatedly shaken. Efforts to quash new candleworks were largely ineffectual, and by 1774 there were twenty-four different spermaceti candle manufacturers, all of whom had joined the trust. Worse still was the growing gap between the price of head matter and the price of candles.[15]

Despite these problems, the members remained committed to maintaining the trust, believing that if it were to dissolve, the situation for all of them would be much worse. Better to have an imperfect union than to open the floodgates to uncontrolled competition, which could easily push the price of spermaceti candles beyond what even the luxury market was willing to bear. As long as the trust's members could obtain head matter on reasonable terms, they could stay in business. And for many years the rise in the price for head matter notwithstanding, the trust managed to keep that price low enough so that they could still make a profit.

The trust members' worst fear was that one or more of the whaling merchants who provided the head matter would get into the candle-making business, thereby introducing a new level of competition into an already overcapitalized industry. None of the members wanted to compete against whalemen-turned-candlemakers who would, in effect, sit atop vertically integrated companies, able to provide their own raw materials, manufacture their own candles, and sell their product. When Joseph Rotch entered the candlemaking business it appeared that the trust members' worst fears were about to be realized.

Rotch was the patriarch of America's most famous whaling family. "The Rotches were to whaling," historian Joseph Lawrence McDevitt observed, "what Andrew Carnegie and John D. Rockefeller were to steel and oil." A cordwainer, or shoemaker, by trade, Rotch migrated from Salem to Nantucket around 1725. He soon put shoemaking aside and threw himself into the mainstream of the local economy by investing in various maritime enterprises, including whaling. Although Rotch might very well have risen through the ranks of Nantucket's merchant class on his own, he possessed another advantage, marrying Love Coffin Macy in 1733, a woman whose ancestors included Thomas Macy and Tristram Coffin, two of the island's founders. Not only did this marriage bring Rotch into the warm embrace of one of Nantucket's most prominent families, and thereby immediately enhance his social standing, but it also afforded him entrée to the highest echelon of the island's whaling industry. Rotch further cemented his position in local society by becoming a Quaker the same year in which he married.[16]

Rotch rose through the family firm, and in 1753 branched off on his own, bringing his sons, William, Joseph junior, and Francis into the business. By the early 1760s, the Rotches were, on their own and as agents for other whalemen, the Spermaceti Trust's main supplier of head matter. The relationship between the Rotches and the trust was tempestuous, punctuated by numerous arguments over price. But in 1768 the source of friction came from an altogether new direction, when Joseph supervised the construction of a spermaceti candleworks in Dartmouth (later New Bedford), a small Massachusetts village on the west bank of the Acushnet River. Although the candleworks was owned by Joseph Russell and Isaac Howland, Rotch was heavily involved in its operations, which particularly worried the trust, because with this turn of events the theretofore separate spheres of merchant and candlemaker merged into one. And from the trust's perspective it would be hard to imagine a more threatening competitor than the Rotch family.

Joseph Rotch's journey to New Bedford began in 1765, when he purchased a considerable amount of land there. The choice of New Bedford was well conceived. The village had been specially laid out by Russell as a future whaling center, with land set aside for shipwrights, blacksmiths, coopers, and other tradesmen. Indeed, for ten years or more Russell had been sending out a small number of whaleships from that location. New Bedford also could lay claim to many attractive features that Nantucket could not. Whereas Nantucket's main harbor was guarded by a sandbar that posed an obstacle to the navigation of large, cargo-laden vessels, New Bedford's harbor was deep and inviting. Nantucket's stands of timber were long gone, while New Bedford was surrounded by forests that could easily provide all the wood needed to build an armada of whaleships. Nantucket, surrounded by water, was isolated and vulnerable to naval attack from all sides, whereas New Bedford had the rest of the continent behind it, a very considerable asset if one was desirous of retreating from a seaborne enemy. And Nantucket's limited agricultural output and, hence, its great reliance on food imports, contrasted sharply with New Bedford, which had plenty of arable land. For all these reasons and others, New Bedford proved to be an excellent choice for expanding the Rotch empire, and in 1767 Joseph and his sons Joseph junior and Francis departed for the mainland, leaving William behind to run the family's operations on Nantucket.[17]

As soon as the New Bedford candleworks went up, it became a potential threat to the Spermaceti Trust's admittedly limited control over the candlemaking industry in the colonies. Eager to turn this threat into an asset, the trust invited the fledgling business to become part of the club. This strategy worked, and soon the New Bedford candleworks joined the trust. As it turned out, however, the trust had been worrying about the wrong Rotch.

Joseph's son William Rotch had been raised to be a whaling merchant, learning the ropes in the family firm. Although his apprenticeship didn't include the typical stint aboard a whaleship, William became immersed in nearly every other aspect of whaling, and especially the details of running an efficient and profitable business. He learned accounting, how to hire reliable captains and crews, schedule voyages, assess monetary exchange rates, and determine the most propitious time to ship oil and whalebone to market. He also learned one of the most valuable skills a whaling merchant could possess—how to grade oil.[18]

Properly grading oil was particularly important because the customers of this product were a demanding lot. One British vendor who sold whale oil on behalf of an American supplier felt slighted by a shipment he had received, and wrote the supplier begging him to "Please . . . order your People to be correct and exact, in the assorting, character and denomination of your Oil. It wou'd be of great help to us in the selling of it, and wou'd save us much cavelling here, [if you would] let the Brown Oil be call'd Brown, and the White, White; and please to let Whale Oil be distinguished from the other."[19]

Moreover William possessed a shrewdness and confidence that had, by the early 1770s, made him a key player in the industry. It is no wonder that the trust became quite concerned, then, when he built a spermaceti candleworks on Nantucket in 1771. At first William, like his father, decided to play by the rules, joining the trust and accepting the allotment of head matter doled out to his candleworks. By 1775, however, he felt that this arrangement was unfair, and he decided to exercise his power. In a letter written on January 24 he noted that despite his recommendation that his Nantucket candleworks be allotted head matter "equal in proportion to any one on the continent," the trust had given him far less than that, dividing the head matter "according to the number concerned [rather] than their interest in procuring" it. This was particularly galling to William because the amount of head matter the trust gave him was much less than what his own whaleships brought home in a below-average year. Rather than let the trust dictate terms to him, especially ones he didn't like, he issued a threat: "Now if upon consideration you still insist keeping me to the proportion you allotted me," William wrote, "I believe I shall comply with it, but I certainly know it will not be in your interest to drive me to such and unreasonable complyance."[20] At the next meeting of the trust, scheduled for March 29, 1775, there was little doubt that William's threat would be the first order of business, the rupture of the trust being what its members wanted most to avoid. When that meeting was cancelled due to poor attendance, a new date was set for April 26, but it never took place. Just a week earlier, on April 19, the first shots of the American Revolution rang out on a field in Lexington, Massachusetts. Although the spermaceti candle industry would come back strong after the war, the trust would not. Indeed, the March 29 meeting turned out to be its last.

The rise of the spermaceti candle industry and the tendentious tenure of the Spermaceti Trust coincided with and contributed to the most exciting period of the colonial whale fishery—a time when colonial whalemen led the world in whaling.

Chapter Eight

GLORY DAYS

THIS PRINT, BASED ON A PAINTING BY WILLIAM ALLEN WALL, DEPICTS *A WHALING SCENE OF 1763*, IN NEW BEDFORD (OR DARTMOUTH, AS IT WAS THEN CALLED). A WHALESHIP IS AT THE CENTER, THE TRYWORKS AT THE RIGHT, AND IN THE FORE-GROUND ARE MEN MINCING BLUBBER AND LADLING OIL INTO A CASK. SEATED AT THE LEFT, WITH HIS BACK TO THE VIEWER, IS JOSEPH RUSSELL, THE QUAKER MERCHANT WHO LAUNCHED THE WHALING INDUSTRY IN NEW BEDFORD. TO THE RIGHT AND ON TOP OF THE TRYWORKS' SHED IS THE V-SHAPED LOWER JAW OF A SPERM WHALE.

THE PERIOD BETWEEN THE 1750S AND THE EARLY 1770S WAS A dramatic time for the colonial whale fishery. Trips that once lasted days, weeks, or a couple of months now extended often to a full year, enabling whalemen to reach destinations as far away as Greenland, Guinea, and the Falkland Islands. In doing so colonial whalemen caught more whales and watched their profits rise.

The mid-eighteenth century, with an explosion of urban growth, witnessed a great social transformation in that the cities of Europe and the colonies were becoming lighted, increasingly with whale oil, at a rapid pace. The expanding chain of lighthouses dotting America's coastline relied on whale-oil lamps to guide mariners safely home. Spermaceti candles shone brightly in the houses and businesses of the well-to-do. Whale oil lubricated an ever-more-mechanical world and provided one of the main ingredients for processing the coarse cloth used to make military uniforms throughout Europe. Whalebone-supported petticoats and corsets, designed to keep the female body in line with prevailing ideas on upper-class beauty, were the rage in fashion.[1] Between 1768 and 1772, for example, the sale of whale oil and baleen provided New England with its single largest source of British sterling, accounting for just over 50 percent of all the remittances coming directly from the mother country.[2] Even in Massachusetts, where many thought cod was king, whaling had a much greater impact on the local economy.[3]

To meet the demand for whale products, the number of ships rose during this period from just over one hundred to more than three hundred. These vessels sailed from an increasing number of colonial ports, including the perennial whaling locales of Nantucket, Martha's Vineyard, Cape Cod, and Long Island, as well as newer entrants such as New Bedford, Lynn, Boston, Providence, Newport, Sag Harbor, Williamsburg, and Newbern, North Carolina.[4] Nowhere was this growth more in evidence than on Nantucket, which laid claim to roughly half of the colonial whaling fleet.

A traveler to Nantucket at this time would have witnessed a legion of whaleships arriving, unloading, or preparing for new voyages. The pungent smell of boiling blubber hung heavily in the air, perhaps offending some newcomers, but a sign to Nantucketers that these were prosperous times. The best snapshot of Nantucket comes from the pen of Crèvecoeur, a Frenchman who arrived in the colonies around 1760 and traveled widely. Using the pseudonym J. Hector St. John, and dubbed by one historian the "eighteenth-century Thoreau," Crèvecoeur wrote *Letters from an American Farmer* in 1782, providing a decidedly upbeat and somewhat idealized vision of rural America.[5] A large part of the book describes life on Nantucket, focusing mainly on the whale fishery. Calling Nantucket "a barren sandbank, fertilized with whale oil only," Crèvecoeur marveled at what such fertilization had produced:

> Would you believe that a sandy spot of about twenty-three thousand acres, affording neither stones nor timber, meadows nor arable, yet can boast of an handsome town consisting of more than 500 houses, should possess above 200 sail of vessels, constantly employ upwards of 2,000 seamen; feed more than 15,000 sheep, 500 cows, 200 horses; and has several citizens worth £20,000 sterling! Yet all these facts are uncontroverted . . . they plough the rougher ocean, they gather from its surface, at an immense distance and with Herculean labours, the riches it affords; they go to hunt and catch that huge fish which by its strength and velocity one would imagine ought to be beyond the reach of man.

So all-encompassing was the impact of whaling on Nantucket, according to Crèvecoeur, that the physical makeup of the men on the island was, in fact, transformed. "A man born here is distinguishable by his gait from among a hundred other men, so remarkable are they for a pliability of sinews, and a peculiar agility, which attends them even to old age." As to what imbued Nantucketers with these long-lasting attributes of youth, Crèvecoeur noted that some believed it was whale oil, "with which they are so copiously anointed in the various operations it must undergo ere it is fit either for the European market or the candle manufactory." Crèvecoeur found the women, too, deserving of praise and admiration, noting their essential role in keeping the economic and social fabric of the island from falling apart. "As the sea excursions [of whalemen] are often very long, their wives in their absence are necessarily obliged to transact business, to settle accounts, and, in short, to rule and provide for their families. . . . This employment ripens their judgment, and justly entitles them to a rank superior to that of other wives . . . [and upon returning, the men,] full of confidence and love, cheerfully give their consent to every transaction that has happened during their absence" and tell their wives, "Thee hast done well."[6]

Whalemen on Nantucket, despite the time they spent away from home and the responsibility they left their wives, were considered exceptionally fine marriage material. In his book, *Miriam Coffin or the Whale-Fisherman*, published in 1834, Joseph C. Hart claimed that successful whalemen were such a catch that the "daughters of some of the wealthiest men of the island ... formed a compact not to accept the addresses of sighing swains, much less to enter into the holy bands of matrimony with any but such as had been on a voyage, and could produce ample proof of successfully striking a whale."[7] Although Hart's book is fictional, and there appears to be no evidence that such a compact ever existed, the animating force behind it is plausible, and even if there was no such compact, there were certainly many Nantucket women who viewed wedding a prominent whalemen as a social coup.

Nantucket's rapidly expanding whale fishery required ever more labor. Accordingly the labor market for whalemen changed dramatically. The Indians, whom this industry relied on so much for so long, were dying out at a horrendous pace, killed in large part by the continued spread of disease. In 1700, 800 Indians inhabited the island; by August 1763, only 358; and then another epidemic struck. There is no certainty about what happened, but according to one version an Irish brig arrived at the mouth of Nantucket's main harbor carrying a cargo of death. The first sign of trouble appeared when the bodies of two women from the ship washed ashore. Suspecting that they had died of smallpox, the town decided to send a reconnaissance party to the brig, comprising men who had already had smallpox and, therefore, were inoculated against the disease. It was not smallpox they discovered, however, but yellow fever, a much more dangerous and virulent adversary. The town placed the brig in quarantine, but not before a couple of passengers came to shore for treatment, taking up residence with a local couple. From that initial foothold, the disease spread rapidly, striking down most of the town's Indians but inexplicably leaving all the whites, with one exception, unscathed.

Despite this legend's staying power, there is little evidence to support it. It could be that the disease arrived through some other avenue, perhaps on a Nantucket whaleship returning from a voyage. Even the nature of the disease itself is debatable, with other possibilities ranging from yellow fever to the plague to typhus. Whatever the cause and the exact nature of the disease, the outcome is clear. Ultimately 222 Indians died, and by 1764 the island's Indian population stood at 136. By the end of the century the island's Indians were nearly extinct.[8]

Given this decimation Nantucket's whaling merchants were forced to look farther afield for hired hands. Men were sought up and down the coast. This search for labor was aided by the improving profitability of the whaling industry, which filtered down to crewmen in the form of higher lays that were often more than the men could earn on land.[9] Whereas in earlier years white men often looked askance at joining a whaling voyage as anything other than a captain or one of the mates, now, lured by the prospect of good money, such men were entering the industry in large numbers. By the close of the colonial period, according to historian Daniel Vickers, roughly 75 percent of the oarsmen and steersman on Nantucket ships were white.[10]

Blacks also became more of a presence on whale ships and shared in the bounty. One such whaleman from Nantucket, Prince Boston, certainly lived up to his name, earning the princely sum of twenty-eight pounds as a boatsteerer on board William Rotch's sloop *Friendship* for a three-and-one-half-month voyage; a rate of pay, which Vickers points out, equaled what the captain of Britain's largest slave ship was getting at the time.[11] But it was not this particular voyage for which Boston is most remembered but for another one on board the same ship.[12] In 1769 Boston returned to port after being at sea for six months. Shortly after docking, Rotch, an ardent foe of slavery, ordered Capt. Elisha Folger to pay Prince his lay directly, instead of giving it to his purported master, John Swain. This outraged Swain, whose father had first owned Boston's family, and who claimed that he still owned Boston and was, therefore, entitled to the black man's wages. Swain sued in the Court of Common Pleas to recover the ownership of Boston and his wages, whereupon the judges awarded Boston his freedom and the money. When Swain took his case to the Supreme Court of Massachusetts, Rotch vowed to hire John Adams as his lawyer and vigorously fight the appeal. The prospect of crossing swords with Adams, not to mention growing opposition to slavery in Massachusetts, was too much for Swain, who dropped the case, remarking that he was "discouraged by the feelings of the people and the circumstances of the country."[13] In relatively short order Nantucket, and then Massachusetts, abolished slavery.

As colonial whalemen built on their success, competition arose from a quarter close at hand. Britain made another run at establishing a whaling industry based in the mother country. The arguments fueling Britain's renewed efforts were similar to those relied on in the 1720s and 1730s. Britain looked askance at relying on other nations for its whale oil and whalebone, worrying that such reliance made it more vulnerable to external shocks. Building and outfitting whaleships at British ports would benefit the local economy. And there was also the belief that the British whaling fleet would create a nursery of seamen that could be called upon to staff the navy in times of trouble, and given the number of wars and altercations that burdened the Empire, the need for seasoned seaman and a strong navy were particularly acute. The decline of the Dutch whale fishery provided another impetus to Britain. By the middle of the eighteenth century the great Dutch whaling fleet was but a shadow of its former self, the result of a combination of some particularly bad whaling seasons and the increased substitution of seed oil for whale oil in the manufacture of soaps and certain cloths, both markets in which the Dutch had loomed large. In view of all this, it seemed to be a particularly propitious time for the British to reassert themselves.

Parliament increased the bounty on whaleships fitted out in Britain to forty shillings per ton, and formerly skittish British investors rushed to collect. In the year just before the new bounty was put into place, only two British whaleships had been fitted out, but by 1756, after the bounty had been in place a mere six years, the number of ships had soared to more than eighty.[14] Yet despite the best efforts of its government, the British whaling fleet failed to succeed.

Many factors in the 1750s and early 1760s conspired to thwart British ambitions.[15] During the French and Indian War in North America, and its European counterpart, the Seven Years' War, British whaleships were frequently captured by the French and their crews forced into the enemy's service, jailed, or killed. Even when the British whaling fleet was relatively unscathed, it witnessed a few lean hunting years, which, combined with fluctuating and sometimes low prices for oil, prevented a boom. Moreover, British whalemen didn't seem to have as much aptitude for whaling as did the colonists. But maybe the problem was not skill at all but the lack of proper incentives for the crew. Unlike the colonial whalemen, British whalemen, including the captain of the ship, were usually paid a fixed salary, not a lay. Without the prospect of getting a share of the profits, British whalemen could perhaps be forgiven for not throwing their all into making each trip a success. Flat rates rarely inspire zeal.

Given these considerable drawbacks, the British whaling industry was in a steep decline by 1763, fielding only forty ships, while the colonial fishery was vibrant and growing stronger. This latter circumstance was not lost on the British, who more than ever before needed whale oil and whalebone to meet demand. Thus the British government revised its whaling regulations in 1764, lifting some of the most onerous duties on colonial whale products. Prime Minister George Grenville was well aware that an unencumbered colonial whale fishery would eclipse the British, but he supported the change in regulations for purely pragmatic reasons. "Though we resign a valuable Branch of Trade in their favour," said Grenville, ". . . the Preference is given upon truly national Considerations, when the inhabitants of *America* and of *Europe* are looked upon as one People."[16]

In the colonies the positive feelings engendered by Grenville's gesture did not last long. During the summer of 1765 Hugh Palliser, "Governor and Commander in Chief in and over the Island of Newfoundland, the Coast of Labradore and all the Territories dependent thereupon," issued a declaration in which he restricted whaling in his domain. The declaration required whaleships "to carry the useless Parts of such Whales as they may catch, to at least three leagues from shore," to avoid damaging the neighboring cod and seal fisheries. This meant that once the whale was brought to the beach and the blubber stripped, the carcass had to be towed back to sea. Whaleships were also "not to fish for any other [fish] than Whale on this Coast."[17] In Palliser's mind these were good policies because they not only protected the cod and seal fishing grounds from being contaminated by rotting carcasses, but they also retained more of the valuable cod for Britain's home-based fishing fleet.[18]

The colonists, however, had a decidedly less generous view of the declaration, and they were most upset by the command that they "fish for" whales only. Colonial whaling vessels that ventured north to the grounds of Newfoundland and Labrador were traditionally dual-use operations. When whales were scarce, the vessels fished for cod to fill their holds and cover costs. Palliser's decree eliminated the cod safety net. Soon after the decree went into force its effects could be seen in colonial whaling ports, where ships returned half empty. The anger that colonial whalemen felt was amplified by the circumstances that had reopened the northern fishing grounds. One of Great Britain's goals in the French and Indian War was to take Canada from the French. That goal was achieved in 1760, and much of the burden of fighting and defeating the French fell on the shoulders of colonial soldiers, who died alongside their British counterparts. With the French gone, colonial whaleships that had avoided Canadian waters during the war returned in force. Now, with this decree, the very waters that had been liberated with colonial blood had, for all practical purposes, been closed to the colonial whalemen. As a further insult to the whalemen, some colonial whaleships that were found to be in violation of Palliser's decree were detained and boarded by British warships, whose crews not only treated the colonials with derision, but also confiscated their cod.[19]

Hoping to correct these injustices, colonial whaleship owners petitioned Parliament to repeal Palliser's decree. London merchants who had a vested interest in the whaling trade with the colonies added their voice to the chorus calling for Parliament to act. Parliament, however, wasn't alone in hearing these complaints. Palliser was listening, too. And in August 1766 he issued a supplementary decree, in which he acknowledged colonial concerns but hardly backed down. After claiming that he and the men under his command had always assisted and encouraged colonial whaleships that fished in the region, Palliser contended that his restrictions on whaling were no different from those that had always been enforced to protect the cod fishery, and that they would, for the most part, continue to be enforced. Then, having dispensed with the conciliatory approach, Palliser gave vent to what was really bothering him and issued a threat. He argued that colonial whalemen were "guilty of . . . plundering whoever they find on the coast too weak to resist them," destroying local fishing operations, and "taking away or murdering the poor Indian Natives." As a result Palliser argued that the "Coast is in the utmost Confusion, and with Respect to the Indians is kept in a State of War." To put a halt to this Palliser proclaimed that the king's officers would be stationed along the coast, where they would apprehend all such offenders and bring them "to me to be tried." To ensure that the intended audience was sufficiently warned, Palliser ordered that his proclamation be posted in "the ports within the Province of Massachusetts, where the Whalers mostly belong."[20]

Parliament viewed the situation between Palliser and the colonists with growing alarm, and soon suspended the decrees until it could review them in full. But while the decrees had been in effect only a little more than a year, much damage was done. Faced with a hostile government to the north, and the inability to fish for cod, colonial whalemen simply ramped up their efforts to the south, where they had already been whaling with great success for years. In the lower latitudes, off the American coast, the whalemen were beyond Palliser's reach and they could pursue their trade without interference. Any satisfaction that Palliser might have gained from having scared off the colonial whalemen didn't last long. In 1767 Parliament repealed his decree, and soon whaleships from colonial ports were once again pursuing whales off the Canadian coast in increasing numbers.[21]

Dealing with Palliser was not the only obstacle confronting colonial whalemen during this period. In fact, wherever colonial whalemen fished, they faced the threat of attack. During the French and Indian War, whaling off Labrador, Nova Scotia, and in the Gulf of St. Lawrence was a treacherous occupation for any vessel with British connections. In 1756 and 1757 alone, six Nantucket whaleships were attacked and burned by the French, and the captains and crews were taken prisoner. The risk of capture was not restricted to the waters off Canada. Farther south, both French and Spanish privateers and pirates often took advantage of poorly armed and relatively slow-moving colonial whaleships. In 1771, for example, three whaleships from Dartmouth, Massachusetts, were taken by Spanish forces near Hispaniola, and their crews were sent home on another colonial whaleship.[22]

Colonial whalemen not only faced danger from enemy ships but also from whales, as attested by the infrequent but hardly rare notices of whaling related deaths in newspapers. On July 26, 1764, for example, the *Massachusetts Gazette* reported that "Jonathan Negers of Dartmouth" was thrown overboard when a whale struck his boat and then pulled him under water, breaking his arm and thigh; he "died in a few Days, after enduring the most exquisite Pain."[23] In 1766 the *Boston*

News-Letter wrote about a sperm whale near George's Bank that struck a whaleboat with such "violence" that the captain's son was thrown high into the air, landing in the whale's "devouring jaws." The boy "was heard to scream when . . . [the whale] closed her jaws, and part of his body was seen out of the mouth, when she turned, and went off."[24] Four years later John Claghorn, a whaleman from Martha's Vineyard, was killed at sea, an event immortalized in a poem inscribed on a headstone marking the grave on Martha's Vineyard, which contained the bones of John's wife, whom he had married barely a year before leaving on his final voyage.

> JOHN AND LYDIA
> THAT LOVELY PAIR
> A WHALE KILLED HIM
> HER BODY LIES HERE[25]

Not all encounters with attacking whales ended in death or even serious injury. In 1752 a nineteen-year-old oarsman on the *Seaflower* wrote in his diary how a harpooned whale went into a flurry and "made a Miserable rack of our boat in a moment." Although a few of the men "were sadly puzzled under water," none were hurt.[26] A Boston paper, in 1771, ran a story about a whaleboat that had been bitten in two by a sperm whale, which then took one Marshal Jenkins "in her mouth and went down with him; but on her rising," spit him out. Despite Jenkins's serious bruises, "he perfectly recovered." Lest anyone question the particulars of this story, the article pronounced that the account came from an "undoubted Authority."[27] Legend has it that impressions of the whale's teeth were evident on Jenkins's body for the rest of his life.

The elements themselves presented enormous danger, particularly in the Far North, where ice and the bitter cold were ever-present threats. One of the most horrific tales of this sort occurred in August 1775, when a whaleship, captained by a Mr. Warrens, made a startling discovery near northern Greenland. As Warrens's ship was dodging ice floes, a crewmember spied another ship in the distance. Warrens and a few of his men lowered a whaleboat to investigate. The mystery ship bobbed gently among the swells and presented a ghostly appearance. Its masts were bare, its hull damaged and worn, and its decks covered with snow and ice. Warrens hailed the ship but received no response.

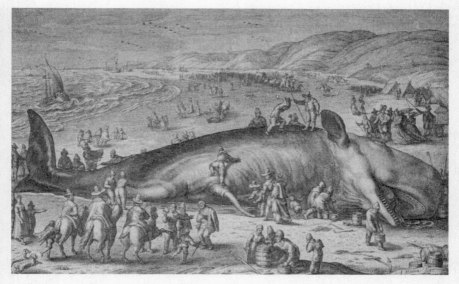

The stranding of a sperm whale on the Dutch shore near Katwijk, in 1598, was quite the event. Engraved by Jacob Matham, based on a painting by Hendrik Goltzius. COURTESY OF NEW BEDFORD WHALING MUSEUM

First European print to depict commercial whaling, possibly in Newfoundland. Engraved in 1582 by Johannes Bol, it shows European and native whalemen at work. COURTESY OF NEW BEDFORD WHALING MUSEUM

Bowhead whale drawn by British whaleman William Scoresby in 1820, and included in his classic book, *An Account of the Arctic Regions with a History of the Northern Whale-Fishery.*

Right whale and calf, depicted on a Taiji whaling scroll from Japan, circa 1850.

Humpback whale
breaching off
southeastern
Alaska.
© FRANÇOIS GOHIER

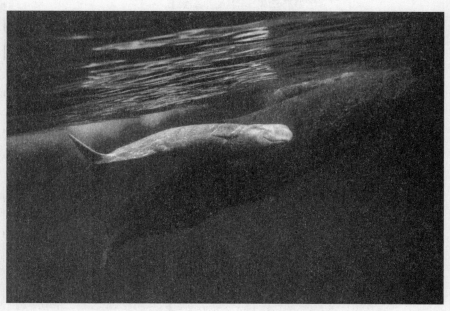

Sperm whale cow with albino calf.   © FLIP NICKLIN/MINDEN PICTURES

Capt. George A. Grant, a whaleman for thirty-three years, posing in front of a huge sperm whale jawbone at the Nantucket Whaling Museum in 1934. On display in the background are whaling tools including harpoons, cutting knives, and spades.

COURTESY OF NANTUCKET HISTORICAL ASSOCIATION

The 1786 version of the map of the Gulf Stream commissioned by Benjamin Franklin, based on information provided by Franklin's cousin, whaling captain Timothy Folger.

COURTESY OF AMERICAN PHILOSOPHICAL SOCIETY

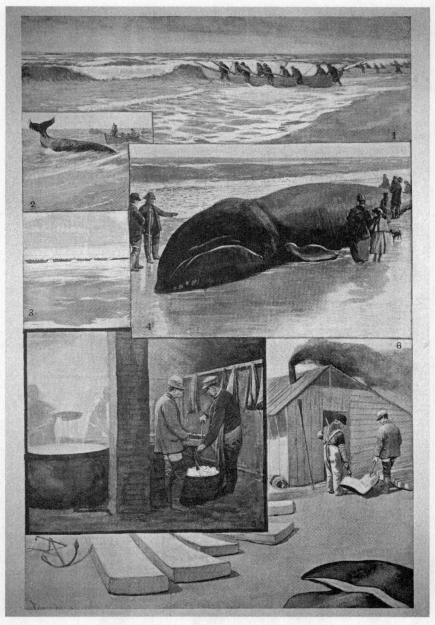

Whaling off Amagansett, Long Island. This 1897 wood engraving shows the major stages in shore whaling, including launching the boats, harpooning the whale, towing it in, hauling slabs of blubber into the tryworks, and boiling the blubber in the try-pots. COURTESY OF PEABODY ESSEX MUSEUM

Portrait of Nantucket
whaling captain
Absalom Boston.

Pair of whale-oil
lamps, circa 1833,
which have been
converted to
electricity.

This 1840 lithograph shows the ways in which whales were captured, processed, and used. Clockwise from the top is shown: "the sperm whale fishery; for light—as a guide to mariners; cutting off the blubber; commerce—spermaceti, ambergris; Manufacture—oil works; agriculture—for manure; the whalebone; for food; for light—sperm oil & candles."

COURTESY OF PEABODY ESSEX MUSEUM

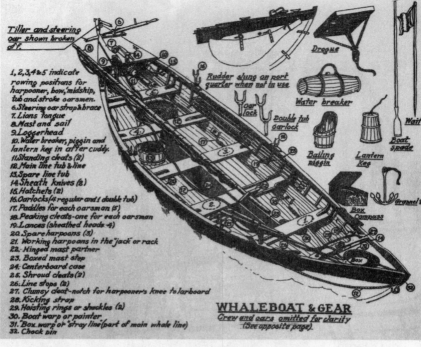

Tiller and steering
oar shown broken
off.

1, 2, 3, 4 & 5 indicate
rowing positions for
harpooner, bow, midship,
tub and stroke oarsmen.
6. Steering oar strap & brace
7. Lions tongue
8. Mast and sail
9. Loggerhead
10. Water breaker, piggin and
lantern keg in after cuddy.
11. Standing cleats (2)
12. Main line tub & line
13. Spare line tub
14. Sheath knives (2)
15. Hatchets (2)
16. Oarlocks (4 regular and 1 double tub)
17. Paddles for each oarsman (5)
18. Peaking cleats-one for each oarsman
19. Lances (sheathed heads-4)
20. Spare harpoons (3)
21. Working harpoons in the "jack" or rack
22. Hinged mast partner
23. Boxed mast step
24. Centerboard case
25. Shroud cleats (2)
26. Line stops (2)
27. Clumsy cleat-notch for harpooner's knee to larboard
28. Kicking strap
29. Hoisting rings or shackles (2)
30. Boat warp or painter
31. Box warp or "stray line (part of main whale line)
32. Chock pin

Drogue

Rudder slung on port
quarter when not in use.

Oar
lock

Double tub
oarlock

Water breaker

Bailing
piggin

Lantern
Keg

Box
Compass

Box

Waif

Boat
spade

Grapnel's

WHALEBOAT & GEAR
Crew and oars omitted for clarity
(See opposite page).

Whaleboat and gear.

From left to right: Lance,
single-flued harpoon,
double-flued harpoon,
Temple toggle harpoon,
and improved Temple
toggle harpoon. (Whalemen
called harpoons irons.)

Double-flued harpoon from
the whaleship *Norman* of
Nantucket, mangled after
tangling with a whale.

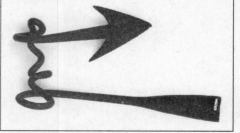

The Navigator,
by Clifford W. Ashley,
shows a whaling captain
considering his course.

Men on the
lookout for
whales.

This painting by Anton Otto Fischer shows a
whaleman poised to hurl his harpoon.

These two paintings (*left and above*) by
Charles Sidney Raleigh depict the hazards of
sperm whaling, and why sperms were said to
be dangerous at both ends.

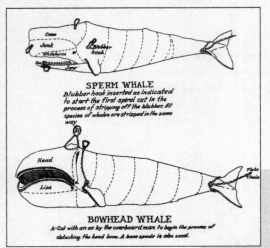

SPERM WHALE
Blubber hook inserted as indicated to start the first spiral cut in the process of stripping off the blubber. All species of whales are stripped in the same way

BOWHEAD WHALE
A-Cut with an ax by the overboard man to begin the process of detaching the head bone. A bone spade is also used.

Cutting-in patterns, drawn by John F. Leavitt. Right whales were cut in the same manner as bowheads.

© MYSTIC SEAPORT
COLLECTION, MYSTIC, CT

Boarding the case of a small sperm whale onto the main deck. Photograph by Clifford W. Ashley.

COURTESY OF NEW BEDFORD
WHALING MUSEUM

Men begin cutting into a sperm whale and raising the first blanket piece. Photograph by Clifford W. Ashley.

COURTESY OF NEW BEDFORD
WHALING MUSEUM

Hoisting the baleen, still attached to the jaw, from a bowhead whale.
Photograph by Herbert L. Aldrich.

Mincers cutting
blackfish (pilot
whale) blubber
into bible leaves,
readying it for
the try-pots.
Photograph by
Albert Cook
Church.

Eighteenth-century engraving showing the tryworks on a whaleship. The fires beneath the pots are visible through the openings near the men's feet. The man in the center is wielding a blubber fork.

The whaleship *Wanderer*, trying out, or processing, a whale at night.

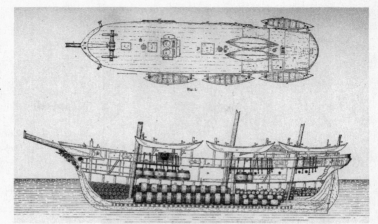

Sectional plan of the *Alice Knowles* of New Bedford.

Portside view of the steamship *Massachusetts* towing a whaleship—which is gripped in the embrace of the camels—over the bar at the mouth of Nantucket's harbor.

The Sailor's Adieu, circa 1845. A sentimental image of a scene played out thousands of times during the days of whaling in America.

Watching for Whaleships, by Margaretta Shoemaker Hinchman. Woman and child on a widow's walk waiting for their loved one to return to Nantucket from a whaling voyage.

An 1847 painting, by Joseph Fowles, of the Nantucket whaleship *Walter Scott* in a hurricane off Lord Howe Island, Australia, which the ship survived.

On boarding, Warrens went down to the cabin and found a man, holding a pen, in repose in a chair at a writing table. The man was frozen stiff, his face covered by a thin green patina of mold. On the table before him lay the ship's logbook, open to a page on which were written the following words. "November 11, 1762. We have now been enclosed in ice seventeen days. The fire went out yesterday, and our master has been trying ever since to kindle it without success. His wife died this morning. There is no relief." On further inspection Warrens found other bodies throughout the ship, none of which had moved an inch for thirteen years. Although many have, with good cause, questioned the validity of this story, labeling it apocryphal at best, its message is incontrovertible.[28] The frozen north did and would continue to send many whalemen to an early grave.

BEYOND THE DANGERS, whaling voyages were often quite tedious. It might be weeks or months until a whale was captured, followed by days of feverish activity when the whale was processed, and then another down time, usually of considerable duration. This cycle could be repeated many times. To fill the time and relieve the boredom, men would whittle, talk among themselves, and do shipboard maintenance. They would also drink, courtesy of the captains who, desirous of a contented crew, brought libation along. Rum was the drink of choice, and the amount of rum on board depended, in part, on the latitude of the trip; The farther north the trip, the more rum would be needed to assuage the chills.[29]

Another pastime was writing in journals, most of which were little more than collections of brief observations and random thoughts. Some, however, were more literary in nature, and there were a few in which the author and the medium melded to create truly surprising prose. One of the best examples of this was provided by Peleg Folger, a whaleman out of Nantucket, who began his journal in 1751, when he was eighteen years old, with the following announcement: "Many People who keep journals at Sea fill them up with some trifles or other; for my part, I [propose] in the following sheets, not to keep an over-strict history of every trifling occurrence that happens; only now and then of some particular affair; and to fill up the nest with subjects either mathematical, theological, Historical, philosophical, or poetical, or any thing else that best suits mine inclination."[30] Like all whale-men Folger often thought wistfully of home, and on August 18, 1754, while on the sloop *Phebe*, en route to the whaling grounds in the Davis Strait, he wrote of those he had left behind. "So it is fine pleasant Weather and a charming day & the Glorious Sun Shines Pretty hot and if the weather is So Pleasant at home it is a charming day for the Young Ladies to go Meeting. . . . So Remembring all at Home . . . & wishing them all well & happy & prosperous . . . while we are Drinking Flip [a heated combination of beer, molasses or sugar, and rum] & Chasing Whales . . . till we once more meet together which I hope will not be Long."[31]

Given the length of their voyages, colonial whalemen learned much about the rhythms and ways of the ocean. Indeed, Benjamin Franklin might never have gained fame for charting the Gulf Stream, that warm highway of water that slices through the Atlantic Ocean, had it not been for the knowledge gleaned from whaling expeditions. Franklin's fame came not from being the first person to reveal this natural phe-nomenon. The Gulf Stream's existence had been known for centuries before Franklin's time, with a few very crude and partial maps of it having been drawn. And many mariners and explorers had witnessed, firsthand, the power of the stream to accelerate or retard a ship's motion. But it wasn't until Franklin, a great scientist as well as a great statesman, was asked to solve the mystery that the true scope of the Gulf Stream was first mapped.[32]

The conundrum was as follows: Customs officials in London and the colonies had for years wondered why British packets traveling between Falmouth, England, and New York were often two weeks longer in transit than colonial merchant ships going from London to Rhode Island. The distances involved could not explain this major dis-crepancy. New York and Rhode Island were separated by less than a day's sail, and before leaving England, the merchant ships had to first navigate the river Thames and the English Channel, while the packets, departing from the southwestern coast of England, could simply sail into the open sea. Even more confusing was the fact that the merchant ships were usually weighted down more heavily and manned by smaller crews than were packets, and therefore should have been the slower of the two. The baffled officials' first impulse was to order that all packets go to Rhode Island instead of New York, in the hope that by merely changing the destination the transit time would be reduced. But before implementing this plan the officials turned to Benjamin Franklin, then postmaster general of the colonies, to see if he could determine what was happening.

As it turned out, this wasn't the first time Franklin had thought about the strange current in the sea. More than two decades earlier he had puzzled over why voyages from the colonies to England were "much shorter" than those going in the other direction. He had commented that he wished he had "mathematics enough to satisfy" himself that it was "not in some degree owing to the diurnal motion of the earth."[33] Taking up the issue once again in the late 1760s, Franklin was as baffled as the customs officials. Nevertheless he quickly dismissed the notion of sending the packets to Rhode Island instead of New York. At most such a move would likely shorten the trip by a day, not two weeks. Thinking that it would be best to gain insights from men who were most familiar with the Atlantic, Franklin paid a visit to his cousin Timothy Folger, a Nantucket whaling captain. Folger thought that the difference in time was because the captains of the merchant ships, who were from Rhode Island, knew about the Gulf Stream, although not by that name, while the captains of the British packets did not. This knowledge, Folger argued, came from the pursuit of whales, which liked to travel at the edges of the Gulf Stream but not within it. In pursuit of these whales, Rhode Island captains would cross from one side of the stream to the other, and in so doing they experienced the mighty power of the great "river in the ocean." Indeed, when colonial whalemen came on British packets in the midst of the Gulf Stream, they would often tell them that they were sailing against a current of up to three miles per hour and that they should exit the stream if they wished to make good time. Battling this current during a calm, Folger pointed out, meant that the ships would lose rather than gain ground; and even with strong winds on their side, as long as the ships stayed in the stream, any forward progress they made would be offset by as much as seventy miles per day. "But," Folger told Franklin, the captains of the packets "were too wise to be counseled by simple American fishermen," and they stubbornly refused to change course.[34]

Hearing this quite sensible explanation, Franklin thought it was a "pity that no notice was taken of this current upon the charts," and he asked Folger to outline it.[35] Folger did so, and he also added sailing directions on how to keep clear of the stream on voyages from Europe to North America. Armed with this valuable information, Franklin persuaded the colonial post office to create new maps and to distribute them to the captains of the British packets departing from Falmouth. To Franklin's great dismay those captains continued to disregard the maps and any advice about the Gulf Stream, apparently still thinking that they were too wise to be counseled by Americans. Nearly 250 years later, the Franklin-Folger map has stood the test of time, and despite dramatic advances in our understanding of the oceans, it still offers a surprisingly accurate outline of the Gulf Stream's path and speed.[36]

The great expansion of the colonial whale fishery in the decades preceding the Revolution brought a flood of new investment, as many American merchants flush with income from other mercantile endeavors sought to build on their fortunes by adding whale products to their inventories. One such merchant was Thomas Hancock, who, in the early 1760s, after staying out of the whale-oil market for more than two decades, decided to jump back in. He was not alone.[37] At Thomas's side, as both partner and adopted son, was his nephew, John Hancock. With the conclusion of the French and Indian War, and the subsequent rise in the demand for whale oil, both Hancocks believed that the time was right to reenter the business. Joining with other investors in 1763, the Hancocks fitted out a new ship, the *Boston Packet*, and filled it with just over two hundred tons of sperm and whale oil for the London market. Expecting to make a large profit on their first venture, the Hancocks were greatly upset when the trip provided only meager returns. There was plenty of blame to go around. The buyer hadn't brought the oil to Boston quickly enough to take advantage of the strong winter market, when the need for illumination, and therefore the price for oil, was at its highest. The *Boston Packet*'s captain had sailed too slowly, arriving in London after other ships had already offloaded and flooded the market, causing prices to drop still further. And, finally, too much of the oil on board was common, low-value whale oil.

Instead of reconsidering their decision to sell whale oil, the Hancocks redoubled their efforts. They decided that to be successful, they needed to dominate the oil market. That meant beating the competition, and the best way to do that was to purchase as much oil as possible and get it to market first. In the spring of 1764 the Hancocks went on a buying spree for oil and whalebone. Their main competitor was William Rotch, and as the season progressed the buyers for the Hancocks' and Rotch's firms engaged in a bidding war that caused the price for oil and whalebone to rise to astronomical heights. The next stage of the competition played out on the docks, where the goal for each was to get their ships filled and to London first. The Hancocks crowed loudly when their ship set sail before Rotch's ship. The stars, this time, seemed to be aligned in favor of the Hancocks, but they weren't. Although the price for oil and whalebone in London was high, John and his uncle had spent so much obtaining these products that the sale price was too close to the purchase price, leaving little room for profit. Thomas Hancock was spared this bad news, however, having died just before the Hancocks' ships arrived in London.

John Hancock, twenty-seven years old, was now the head of the house of Hancock and one of the richest men in America, on account of Thomas bequeathing him one hundred thousand pounds. Rather than reflect on his and his uncle's flawed business strategy, John forged ahead, buying all the oil and whalebone he could, regardless of price. In short order Hancock had amassed an enormous shipment for England, at a personal cost of almost seventeen thousand pounds. Once again, however, the returns were disappointing. Without a sense of his own fallibility, and plenty of money left in his coffers, Hancock was prepared in 1765 to sally forth again in search of as much oil as he could buy, whatever the price, but this time shrewder heads intervened. The London agents for Hancock and Rotch, alarmed by the recent trends in the price of oil, knew that if the two merchants continued their bidding war, the net result would be the ruin of both. Thus the agents urged Hancock and Rotch to agree to keep oil prices in check, which the men did, and 1765 proved to be less tempestuous and less competitive than the previous year.

In 1766, however, John reverted to form, and decided to strike quickly and decisively. He opened his coffers, and the money flowed freely to any merchant who had product to sell. Outspending his competitors at every turn, Hancock further depleted his fortune by roughly twenty-five thousand pounds. Characteristically confident that his strategy had worked, Hancock told his London agents that they would be in a position to dictate the terms of sale because they would be in control of nearly all the supply.

The bad news arrived before Hancock's last shipment had departed Boston. The price of oil on the London market was falling, not rising. Rather than being price setters, Hancock's London agents were forced to take what they could get. What Hancock had never considered was that colonial whalemen were not the only whalemen on the seas. At the same time as Hancock's cargoes were racing to London, so too were similar cargoes from Holland and Germany, as well as other whaling nations, including Britain. Thus, even if Hancock had managed to corner the market on colonial oil and whalebone, he still wouldn't have enjoyed a monopoly on these products. Instead of dominating the market, as he had hoped, Hancock only succeeded in saturating the market to the point where the buyers held the upper hand and suppliers watched glumly as their profits vanished.

Hancock faced this situation with a measure of equanimity; still, he was hurt by this, yet another setback. And when his agents gently suggested to him that he have his oil "inspected" before it was purchased, to make sure of its quality and avoid disappointment in London, Hancock's anger erupted. "What you mean, [Gentlemen,] I am at a loss to know. When I am in want of a *Guardian*, our laws will appoint one. . . . I will never submit to have a man sent over to inspect my business, to make me the ridicule of the merchants."[38] This bluster notwithstanding, it is clear that the debacle of 1766 had dealt Hancock's whaling-related ambitions a serious blow. The next year his shipments to London were cut by half, and in the ensuing years they continued to decline. Instead of becoming a whaling magnate, Hancock redirected his energies into politics—a focus that proved to be a boon for him as well as the nation he helped found.

The Hancocks, both Thomas and John, were not the only merchants to lose money on whaling during this pre-Revolutionary era. But for all the losers there were as many or more winners. Numerous ship's captains and whaling merchants had become wealthy men and pillars of their communities. Whale products were an increasingly important part of local and international commerce. Colonial whaleships had visited the farthest reaches of the Atlantic Ocean and were already eyeing sights even farther afield. This success was truly astonishing considering that it had been barely 150 years in the making. In that relatively brief period of time, the American whaling industry had evolved from an idea into a major force in colonial life, which contributed to the increasing independence of the colonies. And the industry appeared to be poised to grow bigger still.

Part Two

TRAGEDY *and* TRIUMPH

1 7 7 5 – 1 8 6 0

Chapter Nine

ON THE EVE OF
REVOLUTION

BOSTON MASSACRE, ENGRAVING BY PAUL REVERE.

As 1775 DAWNED, COLONIAL WHALING MERCHANTS LOOKED FOR-
ward with a combined sense of excitement and dread. They had just
experienced, from 1771 through 1774, a string of exceptionally productive and profitable years. Colonial ports had sent forth annually an
average of roughly 360 whaleships with a cumulative cargo capacity of
33,000 tons. The five thousand men who manned these ships brought

back roughly 45,000 barrels of sperm oil, 8,500 barrels of whale oil, and 75,000 pounds of whalebone each year.[1] These products had, in turn, fueled an active national and international trade that made colonial whalemen the pride of the colonies and the envy of all other whaling nations.

In the midst of this great success, however, there was great apprehension and foreboding. The building friction between the colonies and Britain had reached a critical point, and the rhetoric of accusation and retaliation was at a fever pitch on both sides of the Atlantic. All that was needed, it seemed, was a pivotal event, a spark to launch the final slide toward revolution. And regardless of how the whale merchants felt about the possibility of taking up arms, they knew that revolution, if it came to that, would result in the ruin of their business.

Problems between Britain and the colonies were hardly new, especially when the Crown took protective actions that the colonists considered unfair or punitive. The taxes levied on the whale products fell into this category, as Samuel Mulford's defiance had most eloquently shown. For the most part, however, these tensions were manageable and did not threaten the strong ties that bound Britain and the colonies. Through the middle of the eighteenth century, in fact, few, colonists viewed themselves as anything but loyal British subjects. Benjamin Franklin emphasized this point as late as 1760, claiming that it was inconceivable that the colonists, who had difficulty agreeing with one another, would ever form a united front and break from Britain.[2] Still, Franklin was not so bold as to close the door on that possibility, and as a result, he added the caveat that his assurance of continued union between Britain and the colonies was predicated on the absence of "the most grievous tyranny and oppression." As long as Britain's "government is mild and just," Franklin continued, "while important civil and religious rights are secure . . . [the colonists] will be dutiful and obedient. *The waves do not rise but when the winds blow.*"[3]

The souring of relations between Britain and the colonies accelerated shortly after the end of the French and Indian War in 1763, when the joy that the colonists felt in helping to rout the French was quickly replaced with anger over Britain's actions during the ensuing peace. In rapid succession the British implemented a series of laws that raised the colonists' ire. One barred colonists from settling west of the Appalachian Mountains in the Ohio Valley, a right they thought they had won by helping to drive the French from the continent. Another law forbade colonists from minting their own currency, while yet another forced them to provide lodging and supplies for British troops. But the worst of the lot, from the colonists' perspective, were the laws designed to force the colonies to help pay for the war and the maintenance of a colonial military force capable of staving off Indian uprisings. The first of these was the Sugar Act, passed in 1764, which not only placed stiff import duties on sugar and molasses and other materials, but also deployed the British navy to clamp down on trade between the colonies and other countries. Next came the Stamp Act of 1765, which required colonists to pay a tax on virtually all commercial and legal documents, including newspapers, bills, advertisements, and the clearance papers that whaleships, as well as all other vessels, needed before leaving port.

Parliament viewed both the Sugar Act and the Stamp Act as appropriate. After all, the cost of defending the colonies was quite high, having risen from roughly £70,000 in 1748 to more than £350,000 in 1764. Shouldn't the colonists, who benefited from such protection, share in its costs, especially when Britain's national debt was ballooning and its citizens were already paying exorbitantly high taxes to pay for repeated military entanglements? The colonies, however, viewed the situation quite differently. Having sacrificed many of their finest youth, and forced to pay off their own war debts of around £2.5 million, the colonies wondered why they needed to do more. The Stamp Act was particularly infuriating. Its fundamental premise, that Parliament—a body that included no colonial representation—could levy a direct, internal tax on the colonies without the latter's consent, ran counter to the colonists' sense of equity.[4]

All at once groups such as the Sons of Liberty, and great patriots, including Samuel Adams and James Otis, inflamed colonial passions with the rallying cry of "no taxation without representation." Unrest spread throughout the colonies. Mobs in Boston, New York, and Charleston flooded into the streets in protest. They hanged effigies of stamp collectors from trees, and many of the stamp collectors resigned rather than subject themselves to continued threats of bodily harm. Colonial merchants and their customers boycotted British goods, and the ledgers of British merchants slid into the red.

In the face of vehement anger and protest, Parliament repealed the

Stamp Act in March 1766. Before the colonists had much time to rejoice, however, Parliament made another attempt to generate revenue from the colonies. In June 1767 Parliament passed the Townshend Acts, which placed customs duties on tea, glass, paper, lead, and paint imported into the colonies. Parliament had assumed that a tax on imports, as opposed to an internal tax like the Stamp Act, would be more palatable to the colonies, but the Townshend Acts engendered another wave of protests. More boycotts of British goods ensued as merchants banded together in nonimportation agreements. Customs officials intent on collecting the tax were often attacked. And when the British sent troops to the colonies to enforce the act and keep the peace, their presence only served to inflame the colonists more. Three years later, in March 1770, Parliament repealed the notorious Townshend Acts. Rather than raise revenue, these laws had led to colonial boycotts of such force that duties collected by customs officials plummeted, worsening the financial position of British merchants, who were being cut out of one of their largest markets. But the repeal of the acts was not complete. The duty on tea remained in force, so that Parliament could show the upstart colonies that it still had the right to govern them as it saw fit. While Parliament was willing to admit the defeat of the acts, it was not willing to concede its power to tax the colonists.[5]

The virtual repeal of the Townshend Acts failed to end Britain's difficulties with the colonies. The Sugar Act, the Stamp Act, and the Townshend Acts, as well as a sprinkling of other unpopular British initiatives, had unalterably changed the way in which a growing number of colonists viewed their relationship with the mother country. For many, separation was no longer out of the question. These colonists, who had recently begun referring to themselves as Americans, had developed an identity of their own. The vast majority of them had been born in, and had never ventured beyond, the colonies. And with each passing year, colonists were becoming increasingly self-sufficient, raising their own food, making their own clothes, and building the infrastructure necessary for societal growth.

Even the need for British military protection was being questioned. With the end of the French and Indian War, the French, once a danger to the colonists, were a threat no more. The colonists had fought beside British regulars in the last war, and they had proved to themselves that they were just as capable on the battlefield. For all these reasons, the restive America that Britain faced in the early 1770s bore only a faint resemblance to the compliant colonies of previous decades.[6]

THERE WAS A CHILL in the air and a thick layer of snow on the ground in Boston on the evening of March 5, 1770. It was not the weather, however, that bothered the British sentry who was guarding the Custom House early that evening, but the small, jeering crowd gathered before him, which John Adams would claim was a "motley rabble of saucy boys, negroes and mulattoes, Irish teagues and outlandish Jack tars."[7] This was nothing new. The tensions between the British soldiers and Bostonians had been acrimonious for quite some time, and altercations were commonplace. Around nine a church bell rang, signaling a fire. People ran into the street, and lacking a conflagration to focus on, the crowd, which was soon augmented by men from the docks, turned its attention to the sentry and the eight British soldiers who had come to his aid. This small show of force only angered the crowd, which began hurling imprecations at the soldiers and hitting them with rocks and snowballs.[8] One American was reported to have shouted, "Damn you, you sons of bitches, fire. You can't kill us all."[9] Then a shot rang out, followed by others. Five colonists died that night, and six more were wounded. One of the men killed was Crispus Attucks, a former slave who had worked on a whaleship out of Boston.[10] Samuel Adams labeled the event a "bloody butchery," and the colonists came to know it as the Boston Massacre.[11] The massacre, which was captured so dramatically by Paul Revere's contemporary engraving, increased the opposition to British rule, and according to John Adams, "laid the foundation of American independence."[12]

Three years later, in 1773, Parliament passed the Tea Act, its goal being to resuscitate the insolvent British East India Company financially by allowing it to sell its surplus tea to the colonies at vastly depressed prices. To accomplish this Parliament agreed to waive British export taxes on the tea, and also allow the East India Company to sell the tea directly to the colonists, without the services of American merchants who traditionally brokered the transaction. To Parliament it seemed to be a winning policy. The East India Company would have an outlet for nearly twenty million pounds of warehoused tea, and the colonists would be able to purchase that tea for half the price of what con-

sumers in Britain would have to pay. Of course the threepenny Townshend tax on tea would still apply, but even so, the tea would be incredibly cheap. Parliament, however, made a major miscalculation: Radical
leaders argued that the Tea Act was merely a British attempt to take
over the American market for tea and thereby keep American merchants from participating in this formerly lucrative trade. And many
colonists, though interested in paying less for tea, were not interested
in doing so if it meant they still had to pay the hated Townshend tax,
small though it was.[13]

The net result of this agitation over tea was the famous Boston Tea
Party. At the end of November 1773 the ship *Dartmouth* arrived in
Boston, and it was soon followed by two others, the *Eleanor* and the
Beaver, all of them laden with tea. At first local radicals demanded that
the tea be returned to London. When that demand went unheeded,
they settled on a more dramatic course. On the evening of December
16, 1773, a group of fifty or so colonists, disguised as Indians, left the
Old South Meeting House and marched down to the waterfront where
the ships were docked. The men boarded the ships, smashed the tea
chests, and then dumped all the tea—more than ninety thousand
pounds—into the harbor. Now King George III knew exactly where
the colonists stood.

The tea party had a whaling connection. Two of the ships, the
Dartmouth and the *Beaver*, were owned, respectively, by Francis and
William Rotch, and were regularly used to transport whale oil from
Nantucket to London. In fact, before bringing the tea to Boston, the
two ships had traveled from Nantucket to London with a cargo of
whale oil. And after the *Dartmouth* and the *Beaver* were raided, they
sailed back to Nantucket, where they were again loaded with oil before
returning to London.[14]

The British reacted strongly and swiftly to the Boston Tea Party by
sending more troops to the colonies and passing the Coercive Acts in
late spring 1774, which were intended primarily to strike back at Massachusetts and punish the colony for its continued opposition to British
taxation. Among other things these acts annulled the Massachusetts
charter, giving the colonial governor even more power over the colonists, and they effectively closed off the Port of Boston from the rest
of the world until such time as the colonists paid for the losses sustained during the Boston Tea Party. Parliament and the king believed

that the Coercive Acts would break the resistance in Massachusetts and put an end to the talk of rebellion not only in that colony but in the others as well.

The situation was clearly spiraling out of control. In late 1774 American leaders at the Continental Congress in Philadelphia railed against the Coercive Acts, which were commonly referred to in the colonies as the Intolerable Acts, labeling them "unjust, cruel, and unconstitutional."[15] And while those leaders were talking protests, boycotts, and rebellion, the Crown, far from backing down, decided to maintain and even extend its stranglehold on the colonies. Given the great importance of the fisheries to the colonies it is not surprising that when Britain chose to strike again, its target was the fisheries. On February 10, 1775, the New England Trade and Fisheries Act was introduced in Parliament. This piece of legislation, commonly called the Restraining Act, was intended to "starve New England" by restricting the trade of the New England colonies to Great Britain, Ireland, and the British West Indies, and also prohibiting those colonies from fishing off Newfoundland or any other place in the North Atlantic. Reflecting on this turn of events, nineteenth-century historian George Bancroft remarked, "The best shipbuilders in the world were at Boston, and their yards had been closed; the New England fishermen were now to be restrained from a toil in which they excelled the world. Thus the joint right to the fisheries was made a part of the great American struggle."[16] If this act passed, the American whale fishery would be dealt a crippling blow.

Support for the Restraining Act ran deep in Britain, yet a determined minority, which "made amends for the smallness of their numbers by their zeal and activity," tried to keep it from passing.[17] A British statesman, on hearing the opinion voiced that England owned America's fisheries and could do with them as it wished, pointed out that, "God and nature have given that fishery to New England, and not to Old."[18] Some argued that the implementation of the bill would result in the migration of New England fishermen, including whalemen, to Britain's rivals, where they would be free to pursue their profession. Others believed that the bill violated long-held principles of retaliation. "It was said that the cruelty of the bill exceeded the examples of hostile rigour with avowed enemies; that in all the violence of our most dangerous wars it was an established rule in the marine service, to spare the coast-fishing craft of our declared enemies; always considering that we waged war with nations, and not with private men." One member of the opposition presented the colonial version of the domino theory. "Evil principles were prolific; The Boston Port Bill begot this New England Bill; this will beget a Virginia Bill; and that again will become the progenitor of others, until one by one, parliament has ruined all its colonies."[19]

Many British merchants were in line to lose valuable business should the bill pass, and they came out strongly against it. Colonial merchants hired British merchant David Barclay, a Quaker, to defend their interests in Parliament. At one point Barclay visited the Prime Minister, Lord North, to plead his clients' case. Barclay told North that the bill would be so terrible in its consequences that its passage might precipitate a revolt in the colonies. Despite arguing the point for two hours, Barclay could not convince North to back down on his support of the bill.[20] The most vocal opponents of the bill were the Nantucketers and their allies. Of all the whaling ports in America, Nantucket would be the one most injured by the passage of the bill, so dependent was it on the whaling trade, and the island's defenders fought hard to keep that from happening. Here, too, Barclay entered the fray, noting that Nantucket's residents "are peaceable and industrious, and by the principles of the majority, and the occupation of all, they are innocent subjects, [and] it appears extremely hard that they should be included in this severe punishment."[21] But Nantucket's defenders didn't pursue an all-or-nothing strategy. They argued that if the bill did pass, whalemen of Nantucket should be given a special dispensation from the law so that they could continue whaling.[22]

On March 22, 1775, Edmund Burke, the renowned British statesman and philosopher, spoke up against the Restraining Act in a 25,000-word speech to Parliament that lasted three hours. In soaring prose Burke urged his countrymen to reconcile their deep differences with the colonies and choose peace not war.[23] He did not want the colonies to become independent, but rather he hoped to maintain the colonies "in a profitable and subordinate connection with" Great Britain, and he was convinced that "prudent management," not force, was the best way to achieve that goal. Burke marveled at the spirit, activity, and sheer numbers of the colonists, but most of all he was amazed by their productivity. The "commerce of your Colonies," he told Parliament, "is out of all proportion beyond the numbers of the people." One of the divisions of commerce that he focused on in his speech was the colonial fisheries, and there he gave a place of honor to whaling.

> Look at the manner in which the people of New England have of late carried on the Whale Fishery. Whilst we follow them among the tumbling mountains of ice, and behold them pene- trating into the deepest frozen recesses of Hudson's Bay and Davis's Straits; whilst we are looking for them beneath the Arctic Circle, we hear that they have pierced into the opposite region of polar cold, that they are at the antipodes, and engaged under the frozen Serpent of the south. . . . We know that whilst some of them draw the line and strike the harpoon on the coast of Africa, others run the longitude, and pursue their gigantic game along the coast of Brazil. . . . Neither the perseverance of Holland, nor the activity of France, nor the dexterous and firm sagacity of British enterprise, ever carried this most per- ilous mode of hardy industry to the extent to which it has been pushed by this recent people; a people who are still, as it were, but in the gristle, and not yet hardened into the bone of manhood.[24]

Burke's eloquence was for naught. The Restraining Act passed with an overwhelming majority of more than three to one, and it received the king's approval on March 30. There was, however, one concession offered. Based on the pleadings both from and on behalf of Nantucket, and in light of the island's unusually strong mercantile and loyalist connections with Great Britain, Nantucketers were excluded from having to comply with the harshest terms of the act—the island's whalemen would still be able to pursue their quarry off the coast of North America.[25]

On April 5 the Marquis of Granby reacted to the general flood of punitive legislation targeting the colonies with a call to reason. "In God's name, what language are you now holding out to America? Resign your property, divest yourselves of your privileges and freedom, renounce every thing that can make life comfortable, or we will destroy your commerce, we will involve your country in all the miseries of famine; and if you express the sensations of men at such harsh treatment, we will then declare you in a state of rebellion and put yourselves and your families to fire and sword."[26] This plea, too, failed. Just eight days later the Restraining Act was extended to all of the colonies.

Before the Restraining Act could take hold, however, other events transpired to render it meaningless. On the night of April 18, 1775, a force of British regulars stationed in Boston began marching toward Concord to seize a store of colonial munitions. Soon after the British set out, two lanterns lit the belfry of the Old North Church, and, seeing the signal, William Dawes and Paul Revere set out on their fabled ride to warn the colonial minutemen that the "lobsterbacks" or "redcoats" were on their way. The next morning, on the outskirts of Lexington, the minutemen halted the British advance and would not move. Then the "shot heard 'round the world" rang out, and a skirmish ensued, leaving eight Americans dead. Before long word of the battle spread and minutemen from nearby towns converged on the British, muskets blasting. By the time the British made it back to Boston they had suffered almost 250 casualties. The American Revolution had begun.

Chapter Ten

RUIN

PORTRAIT OF WILLIAM ROTCH, SR., THE SON
OF JOSEPH ROTCH AND THE NEW NATION'S
PREEMINENT WHALING MERCHANT.

THE AMERICAN REVOLUTION DEVASTATED THE COLONIAL WHALE fishery. All along the coast, whaling operations ground to a halt as the risks of capture by the British navy escalated and many of the men needed to outfit whaleships joined the patriot cause. Historian Obed Macy recounted that when the news of the battle in Lexington arrived on the Nantucket, "sorrow was depicted on every countenance; every mind was overwhelmed with fearful anticipations, all springing from one general cause—the war."[1] The island was so wedded to whaling that to consider giving it up, even in the face of war, was unthinkable. And during the Revolution, Nantucket was the only colonial port that attempted to steer a course between the American and British forces while maintaining its whale fishery, but it largely failed in those efforts.

Nantucket's trials began almost immediately. On May 23, 1775, a ship bearing one hundred provincial soldiers landed on the island, and before departing five days later, the soldiers had commandeered a considerable amount of flour and around fifty whaleboats, the latter of which were prized for their maneuverability, stability in rough weather, and their stealth on the water, which would make them valuable when they served to ferry colonial troops and launch surprise attacks on British outposts and British ships.[2] Then, on May 29, the Continental Congress clamped down on the flow of goods to the island. Thenceforth, no "provisions or necessaries of any kind [could] be exported to the Island of Nantucket, except from the Colony of the Massachusetts Bay," and furthermore, such "provisions or necessaries" were to be only as much as was needed for the island's "internal use and no more."[3] Then, in July, the Provincial Congress placed a boycott on the export of "provisions or necessaries of any kind" to Nantucket from the continent until such time as the islanders could prove "that the provisions they have now by them, have not been, and shall not be, expended in foreign, but for domestic consumption."[4] The motivating force behind these two congressional actions was the strong suspicion that Nantucket was surreptitiously providing Britain, and more specifically, Britain's whale fishery, with valuable goods.

Of all the places in the colonies, Nantucket was perhaps the most tied to and dependent on England. Virtually all its whale products went to England, and most of the goods it needed to survive were supplied in return. Thus, although the island was physically much nearer to the colonies, financially and culturally it was much more closely aligned with England. Colonial suspicions about Nantucket's allegiance were exacerbated when the notorious Restraining Act was passed with an exemption accorded to Nantucket, a move that seemed to confirm that the islanders were on cozy terms with London. Yet another sign of the island's supposed British leanings came shortly after the battles of Lexington and Concord, when sixty loyalists from the mainland sailed to Nantucket to find a safe haven. And there is no doubt that Kezia Coffin Fanning, a young Nantucketer, spoke for many on the island when, after recounting the provincial solders' raid in May 1775, she concluded a diary entry with a rousing "God save George the King!"[5]

Despite all this Nantucket was not teeming with Tories. Most islanders were, in fact, neutral, and a significant number of them were sympathetic to the colonial cause, with some ultimately supporting the Revolution financially and fighting on its behalf. Moreover, Nantucket's dual allegiances were not at all unusual. A large number of colonists did not support the war and would rather have remained within the British fold. John Adams believed that as much as one-third of them felt this way.[6] Such distinctions, however, were not what either the Continental or the Provincial Congress took into account. Instead they saw an island full of people whose patriotism should be questioned; therefore they were a people who needed to be closely watched and regulated. Indeed, a little over a week before the Continental Congress voted to restrict trade with the island, an event took place that appeared to lend support to Congress's action. On May 19, 1775, a ship bound for Nantucket, carrying cargo for Francis and William Rotch, pulled in at Newport to purchase supplies before proceeding to Boston, which was occupied by the British at the time. According to Henry Ward, Rhode Island's secretary of state, "All the Circumstances attending this Affair concur to give the strongest Suspicions that these Provisions were purchased for Use of the Enemy."[7]

The congressional actions targeting Nantucket caused great concern on the island. The Nantucket town meeting responded in July by sending representatives to the Provincial Congress, along with a petition pleading Nantucket's side of the story. The document noted that the island's resources were not sufficient to support even one-third of "its Inhabitants with the Necessaries of life," and because of this great dependence on provisions from outside sources, Nantucket's lifeline could be summarily cut off by "any Naval power." As for taking sides in the present conflict, the petition pointed out that "The Inhabitants [of the island] are the greater part, of the people call'd Quakers, whose well known principles of Religion will not admit of their taking up arms in a Military way in any case whatever." Nantucket's goal was to avoid offending either side in the conflict, and, to that end, the island's inhabitants prayed "that a speedy & lasting reconciliation may take place to the mutual benefit of both." Finally, on the claim that Nantucket had in any way been providing support to England's whale fishery, such accusations were branded as being "without the least foundation."[8]

The petition's claim of neutrality based on religious convictions was sincere. Pacifism and the avoidance of conflict had long been hall-marks of Quakerism, and soon after the petition was written, an infamous incident proved it. The story actually began eleven years earlier, when William Rotch acquired a large amount of goods from a deceased merchant in Boston who had been indebted to him. Among the items were muskets, many with bayonets. Rotch did a brisk business selling the muskets to whalemen headed to the northern whaling grounds who wanted to hunt for waterfowl in between hunting for whales. But each time someone selected a musket with a bayonet, Rotch, a Quaker, withheld the bayonet, the purchaser's protests notwithstanding. Rotch kept the bayonets for many years and had pretty much forgotten about them until the outbreak of hostilities. But there was at least one individual on the mainland who hadn't forgotten, and with the commencement of hostilities he asked Rotch to hand over the bayonets so they could be provided to colonial troops. Rotch refused to do so because it ran counter to his religious beliefs. "As this instrument is purposely made and used for the destruction of mankind," Rotch proclaimed, "I can put no weapon into a man's hand to destroy another, that I cannot use myself in the same way."

News of Rotch's refusal spread quickly, and generated an angry response from those who viewed his stance as subversive and undermining the revolutionary cause. Despite receiving death threats, however, he would not back down. He later remarked that his preference would have been to beat the bayonets into "pruning hooks," but that not being an option, he decided instead to throw them all into the sea. That led, in August 1775, to Rotch being forced to appear before a committee of the Provincial Congress to defend his decision. Far from being apologetic, Rotch told his inquisitors that he "did it from principle," and he was "glad" to have done so. The chairman of the committee said that he believed that Rotch had provided a "candid account," and that, "everyman has a right to act consistently with his religious principles." Still, the chairman added, "I am sorry that we could not have the Bayonets, for we want them very much."[9] Although this ended the official investigation of Rotch and his bayonets, the issue continued to follow him for many years, and was often cited as proof of Rotch's and, by association, Nantucket's sympathies for the British.

Even if Nantucket had had no Quakers, and the island's opposition to the war had not been based partly on religious beliefs, the petition cited geography as a cogent reason why the island couldn't afford to take sides in the conflict. Had Nantucket declared its independence from the colonies, it would have almost certainly been only a temporary separation. With no means of protection and little hope that British forces would defend them, the renegade Nantucketers would likely have been quickly overrun by colonial forces. By the same token, had Nantucketers, many of whom considered themselves patriots, decided to cast their lot with the rebellious Americans, the danger would simply have been shifted, not eliminated. Instead of worrying about attacks from the mainland, the Nantucketers would have had to live in fear of reprisals from the omnipotent British navy. As Nantucketer Jonathan Jenkins pointed out in September 1775, "The Situation of this Island is such as will not admit of our doing anything except we pack up our all & Abandon it, we are in no way capable of defending ourselves, from even an Arm[ed] schooner with twenty soldiers on board."[10] Never had this isolated island, this "Nation of Nantucket," felt so utterly alone.[11]

Nantucket never officially took sides in the war and tried its best to remain neutral, but mainlanders nevertheless accused Nantucketers of actively supporting the British. In December 1775, for example, Governor Jonathan Trumbull of Connecticut wrote to the General Court of Massachusetts implying that Nantucket ships had been importing materials from Long Island that were ending up in British hands. "Surely," said Trumbull, "such large Supplies of provisions to the favorites of Administration looks suspicious & ought to be duly watched."[12] Although Trumbull was later persuaded by William Rotch that "nothing of that kind had taken place," other accusers never revised their opinions. Indeed, for many colonists, Nantucket's neutrality alone was reason enough to question the islanders' loyalty.[13] If Nantucket wasn't for the colonies, the argument went, surely it must be against them.

There was sufficient cause for such suspicions. Early in 1775 Francis Rotch and William Rotch, along with a few other colonial whaling merchants, had developed a plan to continue their whaling operations in the event of war. They had chosen the Falkland Islands, in the heart of the rich southern sperm-whaling grounds, as their base of operations, and planned to send fifteen to twenty whaleships there. Originally the merchants had wanted to send their fleet out of a British port, but that plan was abandoned for purely practical reasons. To be so closely aligned with the enemy would make it difficult for the merchants to crew the ships with colonial whalemen, many of whom either didn't want to take sides in the conflict or were sympathetic to the colonial cause. By establishing a new colony and port on the Falklands, the merchants hoped to create an appearance of neutrality that was persuasive enough to get crewmen to sign on. What they had more trouble gainsaying was their plans to ship their oil and whalebone primarily to British ports, a move that was hardly neutral. According to Joseph McDevitt the whalemen "rationalized" this by claming that "they were simply pursuing their occupation," and that where the merchants sold the "fishery's products was not their concern."[14] But before the merchants could launch their scheme, the General Court of Massachusetts tried to put a stop to it. On August 10, 1775, the court passed a resolution that required all whaleships, from August 15 forward, to obtain a permit from the court before going whaling.[15] A couple of weeks later the court added that to obtain such a permit, the ship's owners had to post a bond of two thousand pounds and also land its cargo at a colonial port other than those in Boston and Nantucket. Its goal was clearly to keep the Falkland fleet from supplying the British, and to ensure that no other colonial whalemen aided the enemy in any way.[16]

Despite the court's restrictions the Rotches and their partners were able to secure the necessary permits, and they launched their ships in early September 1775. Five of those ships were immediately seized by Her Majesty's ships the *Renown* and the *Experiment*, and brought to London. This forced Francis Rotch and one of his colleagues, Richard Smith, who had sailed to London to enlist Britain's support for their endeavor, not only to present the case for such support but also to plead for the return of their ships. Rotch and Smith sent petitions to the British ministry that highlighted the reasons why Britain should release the ships and provide naval protection to the Falkland fleet. They claimed that they and their colleagues had, "by a uniform conduct ever given proof of Loyalty during the disorders in America," and noted that the fleet "shall be considered British or not American."[17] Most important, they argued that their ships would provide Britain with the whale products it sorely needed, now that the whale trade between Britain and America had been curtailed. The petitions had the intended effect. The ships were released, and the Falkland fleet began operations. How successful the fleet was or how long it operated is not clearly known, but there is evidence that it may have continued until the war's end.

As the war escalated the situation on Nantucket worsened. Although earlier restrictions on trade with the island were loosened somewhat, islanders found it increasingly difficult to fill their basic needs. Ships sent to the mainland were in constant fear of being captured by British cruisers, their crews either impressed into duty or placed on dreaded prison ships, the outcome often being death. To avoid capture during such supply runs, the Nantucketers often departed during the most inclement weather, hoping that that would keep their pursuers at bay. This strategy was, not surprisingly, fraught with danger, for the ships that the Nantucketers used to shuttle back and forth were long and narrow, and built for speed not stability and durability in rough seas. Even when Nantucket's ships arrived at the mainland, they faced yet another obstacle. Many colonists despised the island's supposed Tory leanings and would not trade with the Nantucketers, causing some ships to be "sent back empty."[18]

Miserable weather only added to Nantucket's woes. During the summer of 1778, a "great storm" destroyed half the corn crop, which the people had counted on to make bread, and then in December 1778, a powerful blizzard swept over the island. Two-thirds of the sheep were either driven into the sea or buried alive in the snow, and many of the cows and horses were similarly lost, leading one of the town elders to remark that Nantucket's "stock never suffered so much in any storm in the memory of man."[19] The storm's tides and pounding waves demolished buildings and wharves, forcing Nantucketers to flee for their lives. As supplies dwindled and prices rose, many, but especially the poor, faced the constant threat of starvation. Although some Nantucketers departed the island rather than face an increasingly harsh future, most stayed, all the while praying for an end to the hostilities. Some colonial ports grudgingly, if not willingly, supplied Nantucket's ships. Merchants from the mainland often visited Nantucket to sell their products at inflated prices to the islanders who had little choice but to accept such price gouging. Quaker organizations provided relief to the Friends on the island. Nantucket merchants ramped up trade with the West Indies, sending down oil, candles, cattle, and tobacco in exchange for rum, sugar, and salt. And the cod fishery in the waters around Nantucket, which had long taken a backseat to whaling, had new life breathed into it.

The general consensus among historians is that, with the exception of the Falkland fleet, colonial whaling, both on Nantucket and other colonial ports between 1775 and early 1779, was virtually halted. Still a small number of whaling merchants carried on, obtaining permits and posting bonds. But the men on those ships kept a keen eye on the horizon, aware that British warships were eagerly patrolling the Atlantic Ocean for booty. The British were looking for bodies as well, courtesy of an onerous act of Parliament that stated that all prisoners captured on board American vessels should be required to work as seamen on British warships. To a minority of the Lords this was a foul decree. One of them called the law "a refinement in tyranny," which "in a sentence worse than death, obliges the unhappy men who shall be made captives in this predatory war, to bear arms against their families, kindred, friends, and country."[20] When whaling captain Nathan Folger was faced with such a prospect, he defiantly declared, "Hang me if you will to the yardarm of your ship, but do not ask me to be a traitor to my country!"[21]

As John Adams noted, serving on a British warship wasn't the only option offered to American prisoners of war. "Whenever an English Man of War, or Privateer, has taken an American Vessell," wrote Adams, "they have given to the Whalemen among the crew, by order of Government, their Choice, either go on board a Man of War, and fight against their Country or go into the Whale Fishery."[22] There was logic to this Hobson's choice. The war had cut off much of Britain's supply of whale products at a time when such products, especially sperm whale oil for lighting, were in great demand. Although Britain was again encouraging its whale fishery with various inducements, it realized that an even quicker way to develop its own resources was to appropriate American talent. As a result many whalemen from Nantucket and other American whaling ports, including those in New York and Rhode Island, and on Cape Cod, were impressed into the ranks of the British whaling fleet.

Adams was particularly incensed by such barbarous behavior. The Continental Congress named him a commissioner to France in November 1777, to assist Benjamin Franklin and Arthur Lee in forging an alliance with the French. But by the time Adams arrived in Paris in early April 1778, the alliance had already been struck. Not one to sit idle, Adams became heavily involved in administrative activities, including corresponding with a great range of people.[23] It was through such correspondence that Adams first learned about a large fleet of British whaleships off the coast of South America, which was being manned by hundreds of Americans, who, according to the informants, had been forced into that service against their will (although it is not clear, it is certainly possible that some of these vessels were part of the Falkland fleet). With great zeal Adams took up the cause of finding a way to free the American whalemen. In October 1778 he wrote to David McNeill, a successful American privateer, imploring him to attack the British whaling fleet. "If you have an Inclination for so glorious an Enterprize," said Adams, "I am Sure you cannot engage in one, more for the Honour and Interest of your Country."[24] In the same month, Adams and Franklin wrote to the French authorities to inquire whether they could send a frigate to overpower the fleet. Then, early in November, the commissioners wrote to the president of the Continental Congress, asking the colonies to send forth a ship to the same ends. Much to Adams's dismay, however, nobody was interested in taking up the charge.

When Adams returned to America in March 1779, he tried yet again to generate interest in his plan. On September 13, 1779, he wrote a letter to the Massachusetts Council that laid out the case in full.

> May it please your Honours: While I resided at Paris I had an opportunity of procuring from London, exact Information concerning the British Whale Fishery on the Coast of Brazil, which I beg Leave to communicate to your Honours, that if any advantage can be made of it the opportunity may not be lost.
>
> The English, the last year and the year before, carried on, this Fishery to very great advantage, off of the River Plate, in South America.... They had seventeen vessells in this Fishery, which all sailed from London, in the Months of September and October. All the officers and Men are Americans.

After listing the names of the captains and noting that, despite reports to the contrary, the fleet was not guarded by a British convoy,

Adams claimed that "a single Frigate or Privateer of Twenty-four, or even of Twenty guns, would be sufficient" to destroy or capture all of the ships, and as a result, "at least four hundred and fifty of the best kind of seamen would be taken out of the Hands of the English, and might be gained into the American service to act against the Enemy."[25] Although the council forwarded Adams's report to the Continental Congress, no further action was taken, and Adams, seeing that his plea was being ignored, dropped the issue.

As the war continued, the British became increasingly angered by the casualties inflicted upon them. The British navy responded by attacking numerous coastal communities to destroy the "rebel nests of privateers," and to gain additional supplies for British troops.[26] On September 6, 1778, the navy descended on New Bedford and ripped through the village. Stores and warehouses were looted. Guns, gunpowder, rum, rope, coffee, tea, rice, wine, tobacco, and other items were loaded onto British ships. Buildings, wharves, and a small flotilla of the ships that had made New Bedford a vital colonial port were torched. Damage estimates were in the vicinity of £105,000.[27] Having had their fill at New Bedford, the British then sailed to Martha's Vineyard for a repeat performance, arriving there on September 11, where they destroyed six ships, a salt works, and twenty-three whaleboats, while gathering up 10,574 sheep, 315 cattle, 52 tons of hay, and a variety of arms and munitions.[28] Just as the British began plundering the Vineyard, Nantucket residents received word that they were next in line. Panic swept the island as Nantucketers rushed to load whatever they could on carts and move it out of town. But the feared visit never materialized. Shortly after the British landed on Martha's Vineyard, a storm lashed the island with gale-force winds and rain. The British ships, though eager to press on, were forced to remain anchored off the Vineyard and bide their time. Then their time ran out. After three days of waiting for the weather to turn, the ships received new orders from Adm. Richard Howe; they were to return to New York immediately, and Nantucket thus was spared.[29]

Nantucket's reprieve, however, was short lived. On April 5, 1779, seven ships, led by the loyalist George Leonard, and crewed by Americans who had similarly thrown in their lot with the British, approached the island. Five of the ships anchored at the mouth of the harbor, while two of them tied up to the wharf. According to Kezia Coffin Fanning,

Leonard's orders were to determine whether the Nantucketers were "for war or peace; whether for King George or country."[30] The British authorities suspected that Nantucketers were supplying the colonists "with West India goods and military stores," and part of Leonard's task was to root out the offending parties, destroy their property, and force them to "send their submission" to the British commanders.[31] At the same time, those inhabitants whose allegiance was to the Crown were to be left alone. Leonard's force of one hundred men milled about while he met with local leaders, and then the looting began. A few Nantucketers, including William Rotch and Timothy Folger, tried to reason with Leonard, but to no avail; others just watched and worried. Then, somewhat mysteriously, and perhaps because they had heard rumors of colonial ships on their way, Leonard and his men suddenly departed, taking with them 260 barrels of sperm whale oil, fourteen hundred pounds of whalebone, and other items valued at just over ten thousand pounds.[32]

Days later Nantucketers heard rumors that Leonard was planning a return engagement, which caused them to petition the General Court of Massachusetts for permission to plead their case with the British commanders.[33] The Nantucketers received a positive reply on April 14, but by that time they had already taken action. A few days earlier Nantucketer Dr. Benjamin Tupper, had learned that Leonard was assembling his forces in Newport and that an attack on Nantucket was imminent. With this intelligence Nantucket's town meeting decided that it could not wait but immediately had to dispatch a delegation to Newport "to endeavor to avert the impending stroke threatened" by the British.[34] Thus on April 13 William Rotch, Dr. Tupper, and Samuel Starbuck sailed for Newport. On entering the harbor, the delegation could see that Leonard and his men were readying to depart. With no time to waste, the delegation requested an audience with Capt. William Dawson, who commanded the navy, and Gen. Richard Prescott, who led the army. But both men refused the meeting and ordered the delegation to depart. Dr. Tupper, however, would not be so easily dissuaded. He boarded Dawson's ship and delivered a stern rebuke. "You order us to depart. We cannot be frightened away, nor *will* we depart. We know the extent of your authority. You may make a prize of our vessel, and imprison us—much better for us to be thus treated, than to be sent away. We came here for peace, and you ought to encourage everything of this kind."[35] This gained the delegation permission to stay, but for a few days more the British would not let them leave their ship. Finally, after continually pressing the matter, the delegation was allowed to come ashore. The men asked that the raid on Nantucket be postponed until they had a chance to apply for protection from the British commanders in New York. With this permission granted, the Nantucketers sailed south.

The delegation met with considerable success in New York. Sir George Collier, the commodore of the British navy, issued orders forbidding "all privateers, . . . armed vessels, or bodies of armed men, from molesting, ravaging, or plundering, the estates, houses, or persons, of the inhabitants of the said island."[36] The delegation also obtained the release of some of the Nantucketers who had been imprisoned after being captured by British ships. Having achieved its main goals, the delegation decided to improvise. Going beyond their charge from the town, they now negotiated with Sir Henry Clinton, commander of the British army, for permission to resume business activities that had essentially been shut down by the war. If the British would halt the attacks on the island, allow islanders to resume whaling and cod fishing, and resume trade with the continent, including British-held Newport and New York, then the Nantucketers would welcome British privateers "as friends," not import "warlike or military stores," and "not be a store house for persons belonging to the continent."[37] Clinton agreed to this quid pro quo, and when the delegation returned to Nantucket, their fellow citizens pronounced the delegation's actions "entirely satisfactory to the Town and that they have fully answered the Intent and End of their Mission."[38]

Any comfort that Nantucketers felt as a result of the delegation's success was fleeting. Even before the delegation had completed its work, the General Court of Massachusetts began looking into the propriety of the delegation's meetings with the British. The impetus behind the investigation was Gen. Horatio Gates, the commander of American forces in New England. When Gates learned of Nantucket's planned negotiations with the British, from letters intercepted by his men, he exploded with rage: "As the town of Sherburne [Nantucket] is in your state," Gates wrote to the General Court on April 16, "I doubt but your Honorable Council will immediately take proper measures to prevent any Separate Treaty being made with the enemy. . . . Such Things are not only pernicious to the General Confederacy of the United States but traitorous in the Transaction."[39] Gates's letter prompted the court to summon a representative from Nantucket to defend the island's actions. The town sent Stephen Hussey, along with a petition that argued that the negotiations with the British were "unexceptionable," and were entered into "plainly & simply to endeavor to prevent further ravages and devastations." Hussey's defense was only partially persuasive. On June 23 the court found that "several of the inhabitants" of Nantucket had carried "on a correspondence & trade in an unjustifiable manner with the British Troops at Newport & New York to the injury of the cause of the United States," and that Nantucket appeared "in some measure guilty of a violation of their fidelity to said states."[40] In a move that showed that the court still had its doubts about the island's patriotism, it forbade Nantucketers from communicating with the enemy, either in writing or in person, unless the General Court granted them permission to do so.

FOR THE BALANCE OF 1779 Nantucket's situation failed to improve, as food supplies dwindled and embargoes continued to severely restrict trade with the mainland. Despite the understanding recently reached with British forces, Nantucket vessels still faced the very real prospect of attack at sea, and a number of them indeed were captured. Then Nantucket's plight worsened. Obed Macy wrote that "greater suffering was experienced by the inhabitants of Nantucket, in the year 1780, than at any other period during the revolutionary war."[41] Beginning in late December 1779, and continuing until the spring of 1780, a "hard winter" settled over the region. The ice in the harbor extended so far that for some time open water could not be seen, and the ice and snow piled so high in the swamps and on the land that it was difficult to procure any fuel. Thus the deprivations that Nantucketers had had to bear for years deepened.

With the coming of spring, however, a measure of hope returned. The word from New York was that the British forces might grant Nantucketers permits to go whaling if they were requested. Few on Nantucket believed that the General Court would willingly allow their emissaries to present such a request to the British. Faced with this dilemma the Nantucketers lied about their intentions. They promised the court that they wanted to return to New York only to regain lost property, and the court let them proceed; but once in New York the Nantucketers departed from their script and asked for and received fifteen whaling permits. When these permits were rendered useless as a result of a change in the British command, the seemingly clueless court allowed the persistent Nantucketers to use the same ruse to travel to New York yet again, whereupon more whaling permits were obtained.

The issuance of these permits buoyed the Nantucketers and gave them a reason to hope that they could hang on until the hostilities ceased. The island's fortunes did, in fact, improve. A few whaling vessels were fitted out, and the oil and whalebone brought back was enough to reinvigorate trade with the mainland and, clandestinely, with London. This turn of events, however, did not put an end to the Nantucket whalemen's problems. Permits notwithstanding, the British still targeted Nantucket whaleships, stripping them of their valuable cargo and sinking some. Nantucketers decided that the best way to address this problem would be to send yet another delegation to the British to ask for additional permits as well as protection from further attacks. Following a now-familiar routine, the General Court granted the Nantucketers permission to go to New York, where they secured twenty-four whaling permits, as well as assurances that the British would stop raiding the island.[42]

By late 1782, as the war was ending, Nantucketers decided on a new course of action. The continued harassment of their whaleships by American privateers had been particularly detrimental, and the only way they thought they could get it to stop was to obtain American whaling permits to add to those already granted by the British. On September 25, 1782, Nantucket laid its case before the General Court. The island's petition noted the war's toll on the industry, and claimed that if the islanders were not "given free liberty both from Great Britain & America to fish without interruption," this once great branch of industry would come to a complete halt. Having described the situation fully, the Nantucketers issued a barely veiled threat. If the conditions for Nantucket's whale fishery were not soon improved, they concluded, many Nantucketers would have to "quit the island . . . and the most active in the Fishery will most probably go to distant Countries, where they can have every encouragement."[43]

The General Court was sympathetic to Nantucket's situation, but it felt that the relief that Nantucketers wanted could be granted only by the Continental Congress, and therefore the petition was forwarded to that body. William Rotch and Samuel Starbuck accompanied the document to Philadelphia and acted as advocates for Nantucket's cause. In the course of lobbying for the permits, Rotch butted heads with a representative on the Massachusetts delegation from Boston, who was opposed to granting Nantucket any special privileges. Rotch later recounted the tail end of their conversation as follows:

> At last I asked him three questions, which were
> "is the whale fishery worth preserving in this Country?
> Yes.
> Can it be preserved in the present state of things by any place except Nantucket?
> No.
> Can we pursue it unless you and the British will both give us Permits.
> No
> Then pray where is the difficulty?"
> Thus we parted.[44]

The obstinate Boston representative was finally brought around by the entreaties of his fellow congressional delegates, who sided with the interests of Nantucket. Thus the petition was presented before Congress, which voted in early 1783 to approve thirty-five fishing permits for the island, which, in the end, weren't needed. The day after Congress granted the permits, Americans received the joyous news that a provisional treaty of peace had been signed in Paris. The American Revolution was over, but the American whale fishery lay in ruins.

Nantucket had taken the hardest hit. At the outset of the war, the island boasted a fleet of 150 whaleships; by the end of the hostilities fewer than 30 remained.[45] More than a thousand Nantucket seamen, the majority whalemen, were either killed or imprisoned, creating 202 widows and 342 orphaned children out of eight hundred families. Damages were estimated to be in excess of $1 million, a number that takes on greater significance when one considers that at the time an average day's pay was sixty-seven cents.[46] Although Nantucket's whaling fleet incurred the greatest losses, it did not suffer alone. Other whaling

ports, including New Bedford, Provincetown, Martha's Vineyard, Newport, and Southampton, were likewise targeted and their fleets were in
shambles. The American whale fishery had been brought to its knees,
and it remained to be seen whether it would ever regain its former
glory.

Chapter Eleven

UP FROM THE ASHES

WILLIAM ALLEN WALL PAINTED THIS SCENE OF *NEW BEDFORD IN 1807*
SOMETIME BETWEEN 1852 AND 1857. IT SHOWS THE HOUSE OF
WILLIAM ROTCH, SR., BEHIND SOME POPLARS, AND ROTCH HIMSELF
SITTING IN THE CHAISE IN THE CENTER OF THE STREET.

THE NANTUCKET WHALESHIP *BEDFORD* SAILED UP THE RIVER
Thames and docked on February 6, 1783, within sight of the Tower of
London, creating quite a commotion. At first the local customs officials
didn't know what to do. Although ended for all practical purposes, the
war was not officially over because the formal peace treaty had not
been signed, thus raising the possibility that the Americans, still technically considered rebels, should be barred from delivering their cargo.
Finding themselves in this unique and awkward situation, the customs

officials looked to the Lords of Council for guidance, and as a result of that consultation decided to let the *Bedford* unload its 487 casks of oil.

The real commotion, however, was not on account of the *Bedford's* cargo. Instead what brought many Londoners down to the docks was a symbol high on the main masthead. There, a flag with thirteen stripes fluttered in the wind, giving the *Bedford* the distinction of being the first ship ever to display America's new colors in a British port.[1] Other American whaleships soon followed the *Bedford's* lead, believing that commercial connections with Britain, so vibrant and lucrative before the war, could be revived and perhaps even strengthened now that the war was over. This optimism fueled whaling ventures from Nantucket, Sag Harbor, New London, Boston, Wellfleet, Plymouth, and other towns along the American coast. The whaling was particularly good because the whales, which had gone relatively unmolested during much of the war, were more plentiful on the grounds and less skittish, and therefore easier to kill.

For a short while, with the number of ships entering the whale fish- ery and the prices for whale oil rising, the future of whaling looked promising. But then, with crushing rapidity, the prospects of America's whalemen were dashed. The outcome of the war had irrevocably altered the political and commercial landscape, and thus the relationship between America and Britain. This wasn't altogether surprising. When Lord Cornwallis surrendered to George Washington at Yorktown on October 19, 1781, effectively ending the war and sending peace negoti- ations into high gear, the British band reportedly played a song called "The World Turned Upside Down," which had some rather arresting lyrics.

> *If ponies rode men and grass ate the cows,*
> *And cats should be chased into holes by the mouse . . .*
> *If summer were spring and the other way round,*
> *Then all the world would be upside down.*[2]

Although there is disagreement as to whether this song was actually played at Yorktown, the sentiment it expresses rang true for the time. With the end of the war the world had, indeed, been turned upside down, as American whalemen were rather painfully about to learn.[3]

The war's end sparked a spirited debate in Britain over how to deal with the Americans and their whale oil. On one side were many who thought that Britain should focus on building its own whale fishery, and on banning the Americans and their oil. Most of the arguments were well worn, and had been used to support earlier efforts to jump-start the British whaling industry. There was the strong belief that a homegrown whale fishery would serve as a nursery of seamen for the British navy; thus a thriving whaling industry was viewed as a key to maintaining Britain's supremacy on the high seas. There were also the financial benefits that would accrue from building ships in Britain and selling whale oil and baleen procured by British merchants directly to the British market, rather than sharing some of this business with the Americans. Why, after all, should the British add to American coffers and foster its whaling industry when the goal was to resuscitate Britain's whaling fleet and leave the American enterprise floundering? But the end of the war provided a new and very powerful reason for supporting the growth of a British-based whaling industry; namely, that the Americans had revolted and won, leaving Britain hoping that their erstwhile subjects and former adversaries would fail miserably in their experiment in self-government. Many a red-faced Brit, therefore, had little or no interest in establishing cordial trade relations with America, especially in the sphere of whaling, where it was believed that Britain could provide for itself.

Other Englishmen opposed shutting out the American whaling trade. Merchants in particular, who had eagerly sent their wares to the long-starved and highly receptive American markets once the war had ended, worried that the former colonists would be unable pay for what they bought if whale oil, one of their main sources for bartering and generating currency, could no longer be sold in Britain. It would be far better for all concerned if the whale oil trade between America and Britain were encouraged. The fate of the American whale fishery hung in the balance between these two contending groups. If Britain fostered trade between the two countries, America's whale fishery could thrive. But if Britain chose the other path, the American whale fishery would suffer, for Britain was far and away the single most important market for American whale oil, with London annually purchasing four thousand tons of sperm oil at a cost of three hundred thousand pounds.[4]

As it turned out, the Britain-firsters won the debate. Proof of this came in late 1783, when Britain slapped a duty of £18 3s. per ton on foreign oil. Under the heavy weight of this duty not even sperm whale oil merchants, the ones with the most valuable product to sell, could turn a profit. The duty was so high, according to William Rotch, that each ton of American sperm whale oil would have to be sold at a staggering loss of nearly £8.[5] The British tax on whale oil generated considerable concern and consternation in the American government. If the prospects for the whale fishery dimmed, so too would the prospects for America's financial future. Few political leaders were more aware of this than John Adams, who admiringly referred to the whaling industry as "our glory."[6]

In August 1785, while he was ambassador to England, Adams met with William Pitt the Younger, the prime minister, to discuss the state of trade between the two countries and to inquire about Britain's reasons for continuing a wide range of British sanctions, including the duty on oil. When the conversation turned to the subject of the whaling industry, Pitt placed Adams on the defensive. Surely, Pitt said, the Americans "could not think hard of the English for encouraging their own shipwrights, their manufactures of ships, and their own whale fishery?" Adams responded with diplomatic flair. "By no means" did the Americans begrudge the British efforts to bolster their industry, the future president replied, "but it appeared unaccountable to the people of America, that [Britain] . . . should sacrifice the general interests of the nation to the private interests of a few individuals interested in the manufacture of ships and in the whale fishery." Adams continued his appeal:

> The fat of the spermaceti whale gives the clearest and most beautiful flame of any substance that is known in nature, and we are all surprised that you prefer darkness, and consequent robberies, burglaries, and murders in your streets, to the receiving, as a remittance, our spermaceti oil. The lamps around Grosvenor Square, I know, and in Downing Street, too, I suppose, are dim by midnight, and extinguished by two o'clock; whereas our oil would burn bright till 9 o'clock in the morning, and chase away, before the watchmen, all the villains, and save you the trouble and danger of introducing a new police into the city.[7]

Adams's eloquence failed to persuade either Pitt or his government. Britain would maintain the course it had set in late 1783. Expanding the British whale fishery was a national priority, the Americans and their desire for beneficial trade relations be damned.

The Americans who were damned the most were Nantucketers. They had welcomed the end of the war and had hoped once again to ascend to the top of the international whaling aristocracy, but the tax, along with other British navigation measures that served to keep American oil out of Britain, had turned their dreams into a nightmare. The ever-resourceful Nantucketers, however, were not willing to give in. If Britain didn't want American oil, then what if Nantucket separated from America? A special committee appointed by the town in early 1785 concluded that such a move might be Nantucket's best hope for survival. The committee was unanimous in its belief "that the whale fishery cannot be preserved to this place, nor any part of that business can be carried on by the inhabitants of the island, without great loss attending it, which will of course reduce the inhabitants to a state of poverty and distress"; the only remedy was to place "the island and its inhabitants in a state of neutrality." On May 1 the town residents concurred that neutrality was "the most convenient situation that the town can be placed in," and they directed a small group of Nantucket's leading citizens to go to the Massachusetts General Court to plead the island's case. Once before the court the island's emissaries, who had been granted latitude to use their judgment in presenting the situation, chose a two-pronged approach. In addition to broaching the subject of neutrality, they also requested, more broadly, that the "government point out some method" for the island to continue its whale fishery.[8]

Not surprisingly the court took an exceedingly dim view of the secessionist murmurings, which many mainlanders considered to be treasonous, and the legislators summarily dismissed any possibility of neutrality. At the same time, however, the court was extremely sensitive to the plight of the whaling industry, and it wanted to find some means of helping the industry survive. As a result the legislators established a series of bounties on whale oil—five pounds for every ton of white spermaceti, sixty shillings for every ton of brown or yellow spermaceti, and forty shillings per ton for run-of-the-mill whale oil. Though it was hoped that such financial inducements would bolster the industry, not only on Nantucket but throughout Massachusetts, in fact just the opposite occurred. Eager to cash in, new merchants entered the industry, flooding the market with oil. This surge caused the prices of whale oil to plummet, thereby eliminating the financial benefits provided by the bounties. The main problem was that the domestic demand for oil was exceptionally weak. The war's virtual destruction of the American whaling fleet had led to a precipitous decline in the wartime supply of whale oil. Americans reacted to this shortage by switching to the use of tallow candles, which were not only plentiful but cheap.[9] With the end of the war, as supplies of whale oil increased, Americans were slow to return to their old ways. Thus, when the bounties flooded local markets with oil, there were precious few consumers waiting to buy. Although this was a most discouraging outcome, it was hardly the end of the game for Nantucket's whalemen. Even as Nantucket was considering neutrality and petitioning the court for relief, Nantucket's whaling merchants were also exploring how they might continue their business by leaving the island; the main question was where they should go. One group of Nantucketers had already faced this question some years earlier, deciding to settle roughly one hundred miles from the mouth of the Hudson River.

THE JOURNEY TO THE LITTLE HAMLET called Claverack Landing began in 1783. With the war winding down, a group of eighteen men, comprised of whalemen, artisans, and businessmen from Nantucket, Providence, and Newport, decided that the time had come for them to relocate. After witnessing the British destroy their ships and ransack their towns during the war, they wanted to settle in an area that would not be an easy target for foreign invasion but at the same time allow them to make a living. They reasoned that any location along the eastern coast of America was out of the question because it would be too exposed. Still, for them to carry on their businesses, especially whaling, and establish shipping and trade routes, a direct link to the ocean was a necessity. Claverack Landing appeared to be the perfect choice. Not only did it provide a considerable degree of built-in protection, being so far from the sea, but it was also surrounded by vast stands of large trees that were excellent for shipbuilding, as well as numerous farms, the produce from which could be the foundation for a thriving ship-borne trade.

Thus it was, in the summer of 1783, that these eighteen men, the so-called Nantucket Navigators, sent one of their own, Thomas Jenkins, to Claverack Landing to purchase land along the riverbank. Jenkins bought a couple of parcels, including a wharf, and soon the Nantucket Navigators were sailing up the Hudson River to start a new life. Not long after arriving they decided that their new community needed a new name, and they chose to call it "Hudson," after voting down the alternative of "New Nantucket."[10] Within a few years Hudson became a thriving port. One visitor in 1788 remarked that the town had come "into being through the energy and enterprise of New England emigrants . . . exhibiting a progress . . . *almost without a parallel in American history*. It had emerged from a Dutch farm into a position of a commercial city, with considerable population, warehouses, wharves and docks, ropewalks, shipping and the din of industry."[11] Much of Hudson's success was rooted in whaling, as dozens of whaleships left the port and returned with oil and whalebone. The heyday of Hudson whaling ran from the mid-1780s up through the early nineteenth century, and by the end of the War of 1812, the industry had all but petered out, only to revive again between 1830 and 1845.[12]

The Nantucket Navigators never considered moving to another country. They were ardent patriots, and although they were intent on leaving their homes, they had no interest in leaving their homeland. If they were to continue whaling it would have to be from American shores, despite the inherent difficulties.[13] The Nantucket Navigators' patriotism stood in stark contrast to the sentiments of other Nantucket whalemen, who in the postwar years decided that their primary loyalty was not to America but to their business interests. Their main goal was to find a way to sell their oil; where they did so was of secondary concern. In the summer of 1785, this motivation led a group of Nantucket whaling merchants to present Governor John Parr of Nova Scotia, where thousands of American loyalists had already relocated, with a petition requesting permission to settle there and carry on the whale fishery from the shores of Dartmouth, a small town located across the harbor from Halifax. The Nantucketers hoped that such a move would enable them to ship their oil on British-registered vessels, thereby avoiding onerous import duties, and in the process earn substantial returns. Governor Parr, who had encouraged the Nantucketer's overtures, responded with great excitement. Nova Scotia had been economically depressed since the end of the war, and Parr viewed the possibility of transplanting part of the formerly lucrative Nantucket whaling establishment as just what was needed to spur the province's financial turnaround. "The affair of the Quakers of Nantucket," wrote Parr, "is of the greatest moment in this province, their returns from the spermaceti whale fishery amounting to near £150,000 per annum." The provincial assembly not only welcomed the Nantucketers but also offered them a great range of valuable incentives. In addition to providing a total of fifteen hundred pounds and two thousand acres to assist in the relocation, the assembly vowed to treat the Nantucketers as loyalists, grant them British ship registrations, and allow them to practice their religion as they saw fit. With such favorable terms for reviving the whaling trade, Nantucketers began arriving in Dartmouth in the spring of 1786.[14]

Parr did not have long to congratulate himself on his fine show of international business acumen and diplomacy. He had urged the acceptance of the Nantucketers' petition without first having obtained London's approval for his bold policy. Unfortunately for Parr that was a major miscalculation. Many of Britain's most prominent whaling merchants, who viewed the Dartmouth fleet as potential competition in the rapidly expanding British-based southern whale fishery, strenuously opposed the new settlement. They voiced their opposition to the Board of Trade in March 1786, arguing that the Nantucketers' migration and their supposed shift in loyalty were a ruse. "We know many tricks will be played," the British merchants informed the board, ". . . for whatever fishery is carried on from any port in that part of the world will be managed by the people from Nantucket." The British whaling merchants urged the board to put a halt to the Dartmouth experiment, believing that by doing so the Nantucketers would have no recourse but to immigrate to England or else abandon their industry. And if the Nantucketers could be induced to come to England, the merchants believed that "in a very short time we shall be one people & one interest."[15]

The board was swayed, and soon thereafter Thomas Townshend, Lord Sydney, the British home secretary, gave Parr the bad news: "It is the present determination of the government," wrote Sydney, "not to encourage the southern whale fishery that may be carried on by persons who may have removed from Nantucket and other places within the American states, excepting they shall exercise that fishery directly from Great Britain." Parr was greatly dismayed by this edict, especially since he thought his actions had been in his country's best interest. "My chief motive," Parr wrote, "was to draw from the United States a branch of trade so valuable as to prevent their Emigrating to any country inimical to England."[16] Nevertheless Downing Street had spoken. As a result, by the summer of 1786 the flow of Nantucketers to Dartmouth stopped, but not before forty families had made the trek. And since Lord Sydney said nothing about what to do about the Nantucketers who had already relocated, Parr let them stay.

At the same time that Nantucket whalemen were making overtures in Nova Scotia, William Rotch and his twenty-year-old son, Benjamin, traveled to London on board the *Maria*. Rotch had embarked on this trip as a representative of Nantucket, and his primary goal was to obtain concessions from the British government that would make it possible for Nantucket's oil to gain access to the British markets. Arriving in London on July 25, 1785, Rotch was informed that the government was currently overwhelmed by having to address some thorny domestic issues, and that it would be best for Rotch to delay his meetings. Rotch took advantage of the delay by touring the coast. This was no pleasure cruise. If relocating to Britain ended up being the wisest course of action, a suitable port would have to be found. Thus Rotch used his tour to evaluate potential locations, but he did so with mixed emotions. "I heartily wish [our long journey] was over but I think shall be inexcusable to come thus far, and not be able to make some judgment of the propriety of removing to the country if necessity shall urge it."[17] Rotch was less than impressed with the ports he saw, the only exception being Falmouth, and by November he had made his way back to London.

While on tour Rotch had been kept apprised of the evolving political situation by family members, business acquaintances, and American officials. He had learned that Massachusetts had denied Nantucket's request for neutrality and was on the verge of passing a bounty for oil. He knew that Nantucketers' migration to Nova Scotia had been approved by the government there, but he was already hearing mur-

murs that powerful British merchants and trade officials were opposed to such a settlement and wanted instead to lure Nantucket whalemen with incentives to leave Nova Scotia for England. Rotch also had become aware of just how intent the British were on building their whaling industry. "The spirit of whaling," Rotch observed, "seems almost running to a degree of madness, they intend if men can be got to send out 30 ships, but at present there appears no possibility of getting men."[18] Taking these factors into account, Rotch decided on a course of action, and when he finally met with Pitt, in November 1785, he was ready to negotiate.

Pitt received Rotch warmly and listened carefully as he laid out the history that had brought him and his fellow Nantucketers to their current "ruinous situation." Rotch argued that Nantucket had wanted no part of the war, had endeavored to remain neutral, and had throughout the conflict done nothing to rebel against the mother country. "Consequently," Rotch concluded, "we remained part of your Dominions until separated by the Peace." And because of Nantucket's disposition during the war, Rotch believed that Britain should treat the island, especially its whalemen, differently, and much better than it was now treating the United States. Pitt considered Rotch's comments for a few minutes, then said, "most undoubtedly you are right Sir—Now what can be done for you?" This was just the response Rotch had been hoping for, and he jumped at the opening. After noting that current difficulties were forcing many Nantucketers to leave the island, Rotch said that many of them "wish to continue the Whale fishery, wherever it can be pursued to advantage—Therefore, my chief business is to lay our distressed situation, and the cause of it, before this Nation, and to ascertain if the Fishery is considered an Object worth giving such encouragement for a removal to England, as the subject deserves."[19]

Although Pitt did not respond to this proposal immediately, but rather referred it to the Privy Council for further study, there is no doubt that he was excited by the prospect of transplanting Nantucket whalemen to England. Ever since the beginning of the American Revolution, the British whaling industry had been endeavoring to expand its operations, and especially gain a foothold in the southern sperm whale fishery, which to that point had been nearly monopolized by American whalemen and Nantucketers in particular. To that end British whaling merchants, such as Samuel Enderby, had recruited seasoned Nantucket whalemen to work on their ships and teach the British the finer points of whaling.[20] These transfers of talent helped the British whaling industry expand to the south, but that expansion could be dramatically increased were a significant part of Nantucket's whaling industry to move to England. Rotch, of course, was well aware of British designs on Nantucket's whalemen, and despite Pitt's lack of commitment, he left the meeting confident that once the British government examined the matter more fully, it would make a generous offer to encourage the Nantucketers' removal to England. This confidence proved to be misplaced.

Rotch's downfall came at the hands of Charles Jenkinson, Lord Hawkesbury, who had been appointed by the British government to bargain with the Quaker merchant. The minute Rotch learned of Hawkesbury's appointment, he apprehended trouble. "A greater enemy to America," Rotch observed, "could not be found in that Body, nor hardly in the Nation." Rotch began the negotiations in early 1786 by spelling out just how much "encouragement" would be needed to get the Nantucketers to migrate to England. The cost for a family of five would be, Rotch said, one hundred pounds for transportation, and one hundred pounds for settlement, bringing the total for one hundred families to twenty thousand pounds. "Oh," responded Hawkesbury, seemingly taken aback, "this is a great sum, and at this time we are endeavoring to economise in our expenditures." Rotch had little sympathy for Hawkesbury's position, especially since Rotch had lost so many of his ships and their cargoes during the war. "Thou mayst think it a great sum for this Nation to pay," Rotch replied, but "*I* think two thirds of it a great sum for you to have taken from me as an individual, unjustly, and illegally." When the two met again a few days later, Rotch upped the ante, requesting that he have permission to bring thirty American whaleships to England, to which Hawkesbury responded, "Oh no, that cannot be, our carpenters must be employed . . . [the ships] must be British built." The two went back and forth on this issue without resolution, with Rotch pressing his position, and Hawkesbury emphasizing that what England really wanted was Nantucket's whalemen, not its ships.[21]

In the end, Hawkesbury made Rotch a counter offer. Instead of the twenty thousand pounds that was requested, would Rotch take thirteen thousand pounds? Hawkesbury then added that he was at the moment drafting a fishery bill and he could, if Rotch accepted the offer, insert its particulars into the bill to get the ball rolling. "Thy offer is no Object," Rotch coolly replied before leaving, "therefore go on with thy Fishery Bill, without any regard to me." Chagrined at Rotch's response, the British government quickly came back, agreeing to allow thirty American vessels to come to England as long as they were accompanied by five hundred Nantucketers. This still wasn't enough for Rotch, and he told Hawkesbury so at their final meeting, informing him that he was thinking of going to France to see what encouragement that government might give Nantucket whalemen. Rotch said he had heard a rumor that Nantucket whalemen had already signed a contract to supply France with oil. At this Hawkesbury pulled a file of papers from his bureau and began reading aloud from purported text that clearly contradicted the rumor. But Rotch was not fooled by this transparent and clumsy display. Sure that Hawkesbury had fabricated the lines he just read, Rotch replied, "it was only a vague report that I heard, and I cannot vouch for the truth of it—but we are like drowning men, catching at every straw that passes by, therefore I am now determined to go to France, and see what it is." Hawkesbury was amazed and surprised. "Ah! Quakers go to France?" Rotch answered, "Yes, but with regret," and they parted.[22]

Rotch had been less than forthcoming with Hawkesbury. His turn toward France was not based on rumors, but rather the certain knowledge that France was indeed interested in Nantucket's whale oil. Prior to the Revolutionary War, France had little domestic demand for whale oil, but after the war, the French had become significant whale oil consumers. France tried to meet this demand by expanding its own whaling fleet, with little success. Therefore the opportunity to obtain oil from Nantucket was quite appealing, and even before Rotch began his negotiations with the British, the French had begun importing oil from the island. In mid-1785 the Marquis de Lafayette, in fact, had helped broker a deal in which the French government contracted American whalemen to supply oil for streetlights in Paris. George Washington was most appreciative of the marquis' support. "Your constant attention, and unwearied endeavors to serve the interest of these United States," Washington wrote to his dear friend, "cannot fail to keep alive in them a grateful sensibility of it; and the affectionate regard of all their citizens for you. The footing on which you have established a market for whale oil must be equally pleasing and advantageous to the States which are more immediately engaged in that commerce."[23] No group of Americans was more grateful or showed its gratitude more concretely than the residents of Nantucket, who agreed to supply the milk from their cows for a period of twenty-four hours so that a five hundred-pound block of cheese could be presented to Lafayette, "as a feeble, but not less sincere, testimonial of" their feelings toward him.[24]

Yet it wasn't just American oil that the French wanted. By late 1785 the French had already begun negotiating with Nantucket whalemen to entice them to come to France, and Rotch had responded by forwarding a list of conditions necessary for Nantucketers to accept the French invitation, to which the French had responded most encouragingly. Thus, when Rotch stood before Hawkesbury at their final meeting and talked only of "vague reports" of French interest, he was lying. Rotch departed England nine months after he had arrived and sailed to France in April 1786, expecting a warm reception, and that is exactly what he got.

According to Rotch it took a mere five hours for the French to agree to his terms. In addition to building a shipyard at Dunkirk and giving the Nantucketers full control of their whaling operations, the French granted the Nantucketers freedom to practice their religion, exemption from military service, and land on which to settle. And each Nantucket ship that fitted out from Dunkirk would receive a bounty.[25] France's eagerness to reach agreement with the Nantucketers had as much to do with meeting the country's needs as it did with ensuring that France's bitter rival, Britain, didn't benefit from Nantucket's travails. Thomas Jefferson, reflecting on the negotiations between Rotch and the French, noted that "the French government had not been inattentive to the news of the British, nor insensible to the crisis. They saw the danger of permitting five or six thousand of the best seamen existing to be transferred by a single stroke to the marine strength of the enemy, and to carry over with them an art which they possessed almost exclusively. The counterplan which they set on foot, was to tempt the Nantucketois by high offer, to come and settle in France."[26]

Having achieved his goals, and looking forward to establishing whaling operations in Dunkirk, Rotch prepared to leave France, thinking that his business was settled. But the British weren't willing to give up the fight. When Rotch announced that he was going to France,

Hawkesbury was not particularly concerned. He simply didn't believe that the French could match Britain's offer, and he thought that American whalemen would much rather settle among the British than the French. After all, Americans and the British shared the same language, customs, ancestry, and history.[27] But soon after Rotch made good on his threat to parley with the French, Hawkesbury panicked, and through an intermediary sent word to Rotch in France that Parliament would soon be considering a fishery bill that would allow the Americans to bring forty whaleships to Britain, rather than the thirty that Rotch had originally requested. It wasn't enough, and when Rotch returned to London he so informed Hawkesbury. In a last-ditch effort to turn the tide, the prime minister sent an emissary to tell Rotch that he could make his own terms. But even with this blank check waved before his eyes, Rotch responded that it was too late. "I made very moderate proposals to you," Rotch said, "but you could not obtain anything worth my notice."[28] The French, on the other hand, were most accommodating. Rotch had decided: The Nantucketers were going to France.

The French offer, however, was not generous enough to induce the mass migration of Nantucketers that France had hoped for. Just nine whaling families, thirty-three people in all, relocated. Disappointed at this response, and fearful that the American whalemen might still ally themselves with the British, the French took further steps. The French realized that if American whalemen were able to carry on their trade from America, they would have no incentive to relocate to Britain. The key was to make sure that the Americans had a foreign market where they could sell their oil, and further to make sure that that market was French. To that end the French eliminated, in 1787, all duties on whale oil from the United States. But no sooner had this plan been put into effect than the British began, as Jefferson pointed out, flooding "the markets of France with their whale oils: and they were enabled by the great premiums given by their Government to undersell the French fisherman, aided by feebler premiums, and the American aided by his poverty alone."[29] Britain's main goal was to cripple the Dunkirk whale fishery, and it was on the way to doing so when the French struck back by passing an *arrêt*, or government act, that shut its ports to all foreign oil. While this move augured well for the American whalemen operating out of Dunkirk, it was a disaster for American whalemen still in the States, who were, like the British, now barred from the French market.

Jefferson, America's minister to France, watched these proceedings with alarm. His years of work to open France's ports to American oil were, with the implementation of the *arrêt*, completely undone. Jefferson demanded and was granted a meeting with government officials, at which he argued passionately for the *arrêt's* repeal, and soon thereafter the French issued another *arrêt* that allowed American oil back in, while continuing to keep oil from other countries out.[30] Notwithstanding these maneuvers, the French connection proved to be a profitable one for the Americans. The Dunkirk fleet of whaling vessels, which was dominated by the Rotches, grew from six ships in 1786 to a high of twenty-six in 1792. And American whalemen who remained stateside continued sending their products to French ports.

Meantime the British forged ahead with the expansion of their own whale fishery. Finally, after centuries of trying, the British had finally gotten the hang of whaling. Much of their success rested squarely on the strong, broad backs of the Nantucket whalemen and whaling masters who had been wooed to ship out on British whaling vessels. But credit was also due to the business acumen of the new generation of British whaling merchants, as well as the bounty system employed by the British, which made whaling ventures more financially attractive. And of course it didn't hurt that the Americans had been hobbled by the war. "Before the war," Jefferson observed, Great Britain "had not 100 vessels in the whale trade, while America employed 309. In 1786, Great Britain employed 151 vessels; in 1787, 286; in 1788, 314 . . . while . . . [America's number] is fallen to about 80. They have just changed places then, England having gained exactly what America has lost."[31]

In addition to expanding in size, the British whale fishery extended its reach across the globe. As early as 1786 British whalemen noticed that the whales off the coast of Brazil, which had been aggressively hunted for more than a decade, were becoming "wilder" and therefore more difficult to kill. At the same time, reports from merchant ships engaged in the China trade were filtering back to Britain, claiming that the Pacific Ocean was full of whales. One American whaling captain on a trading voyage to the Far East said that he "had seen more spermaceti whales about the Straights [*sic*] of Sunda and the Island of Java than he had ever seen before, so much so that he could have filled a ship of 300 tons in 3 months." Such intelligence had British whalemen dreaming of rounding Cape Horn and chasing whales in the Pacific, and on August 7, 1778, the *Emilia*, owned by the leading British whaling firm of Samuel Enderby & Sons, sailed from London. And seven months later, on March 3, 1789, the *Emilia's* first mate, Archaelus Hammond, a Nantucketer, became the first Westerner successfully to harpoon a sperm whale, or any whale for that matter, in the Pacific Ocean. By the time the *Emilia* returned to London, roughly a year later, its hold was full of oil. Reflecting on the voyage, a very satisfied Samuel Enderby wrote, "From her account the whales of the South Pacific Ocean are likely to be most profitable; the crew are all returned in good health, only one man was killed by a whale."[32] The whale fishery in the Pacific had begun.

DESPITE BRITAIN'S WHALING SUCCESS, many Britons still regretted their country's failure to lure Rotch and his fellow whalemen to England in the mid-1780s. At the head of this list was Charles Greville, a British nobleman and member of Parliament. In 1785 Greville had strongly encouraged Rotch to consider the town of Milford Haven, in Wales, as a place to establish his expatriate whale fishery. Greville's suggestion was both practical and self-serving. Milford Haven boasted an excellent port, and since Greville owned much of the land in town, he would profit handsomely if a whale fishery were established there. But before Rotch could fully consider this proposal, or any others, his negotiations with Hawkesbury ground to a halt, and Rotch left for France. Although Greville had lost this opportunity, he never lost his desire to transform Milford Haven into a whaling port, and by 1790 he devised another plan to make this happen. Why not entice the Nantucket whalemen who had settled in Dartmouth, Nova Scotia, to immigrate to Milford Haven? The British government reacted positively to Greville's suggestion, and in relatively short order it offered the Dartmouth whalemen generous incentives to relocate, which most duly accepted, and the migration to Milford Haven began in the summer of 1792. Dartmouth was devastated by this mass exodus, and not long thereafter its whaling industry withered away.[33]

At about the same time that the Dartmouth whalemen were crossing the Atlantic to their new home, William Rotch was growing increasingly alarmed at the deteriorating situation in France. The

French Revolution, which had started in 1789, was growing more violent. "I little expected," wrote Rotch, "ever to be in the midst of another Revolution after that of America was compleated," but so he was, and he had already decided that for the preservation of his business interests he would have to leave France. In the summer of 1792 Rotch met twice with Greville in London to discuss the possibility of transferring his Dunkirk fleet to Milford Haven. The prospect of such a transfer delighted Greville, and he did his best to urge the government to provide inducements to encourage Rotch to make the move. But Greville's entreaties were of little consequence. The very men of power in the government, whom he was trying to persuade, were the ones that felt most burned by Rotch's earlier decision to spurn England's relocation offers. Beyond the personal animosity directed at Rotch, there was a more basic economic reason why the government was not eager to invite him to England: The expansion of the British whaling fleet had led to a corresponding increase in the supplies of whale oil being unloaded at British ports, making it imperative for British whaling merchants to find more markets for their oil or suffer financial losses. The government feared that adding Rotch's very efficient fleet to England's would only increase the amount of oil produced without creating new markets, thereby potentially expanding the gulf between supply and demand—a gulf that was already getting wider with the recent transfer of the Dartmouth whalemen to Milford Haven.[34]

Once Rotch realized that his services were not wanted in England, he set his sights on returning to America, and on January 19, 1793, he packed up his belongings in France and sailed to London. A year later he boarded another ship to Boston, whence he made his way back to Nantucket. Rotch was home, but any plans that he had of reestablishing his whaling business on the island were soon scrapped. Although Rotch's reception in Nantucket was "more cordiale" than he had expected, many Nantucketers still harbored a deep distrust and dislike for the Rotches, primarily because of the family's decision to place their business interests ahead of all else and abandon the island for ports of opportunity in England and France.[35] Rotch did not want to remain in a place where he and his family no longer felt welcome. But much more serious to Rotch than the ill feelings of his peers was the problem of depth. Many of the whaleships of the late eighteenth century were so large that they could not float over the shallow sandbar that guarded the mouth of Nantucket's harbor. Rotch thus opted to follow in his father's footsteps, and during the summer of 1795 he relocated to New Bedford, where the harbor was deep and the people inviting.

THIS WAS A TIME of dramatic change not only for William Rotch but also for the American whale fishery. By the mid-1790s the situation in the United States was improving. Domestic demand for whale oil was on the rise. Many who had switched to the use of tallow candles during and just after the war were now returning to oil, which was increasingly being burned in better-designed lamps that gave off more light and less smoke. Spermaceti candles, too, were back in vogue, and used more widely as people decided that spending more for these candles was justified because they burned longer and brighter. The number of lighthouses along the coast expanded, as did the number of street lamps in America's cities, like Boston, Philadelphia, and New York, eager to keep up with the trends in London and Paris. Demand from overseas also rose as European countries, fearful that international conflicts might interrupt the flow of oil, stocked up by purchasing American oil.[36]

Accordingly the number of American whaleships increased, and they traveled farther afield, following Britain's lead into the Pacific Ocean.[37] Indeed, the *Rebecca* of New Bedford, one of the first American whaleships to round Cape Horn, noted that of the forty whaleships sighted during its 1791–93 voyage to the Pacific, seven were from Nantucket, and one each hailed from New Bedford, Hudson, and Boston.[38] No longer did American whalemen have the urge to migrate to other countries to pursue their trade. Rather, the trend in migration had been reversed, as many expatriate whalemen now returned for a variety of reasons, including instability overseas, homesickness, and the knowledge that the American whaling industry was picking up steam. These trends notwithstanding, American whalemen were apprehensive about the future because they knew that their continued success depended largely on forces that were out of their control. What they feared most was the United States getting embroiled in another war, and with the European balance of power rapidly crumbling, that appeared to be exactly what was going to happen.

Just two days after Rotch departed from France, Louis XVI was guillotined, on January 21, 1793, much to the delight of a cheering crowd. In short order France's revolutionary government declared war on Britain, Spain, and Holland. President George Washington, a man who would later "warn" his countrymen "against the mischiefs of foreign intrigue," wanted desperately to keep from being drawn into the growing European conflict, and he kept an eye on France, but it was Britain that worried him most.[39] Since the end of the Revolutionary War the relationship between America and Britain had been cantankerous. By 1794 tensions had increased so much, given the British navy's policy of seizing American ships and impressing American sailors, that many Americans thought another war with Britain was inevitable. The president, however, did not. Instead of declaring war, Washington sent Supreme Court Justice John Jay to London to see if he could negotiate a settlement. Although the resulting "Jay treaty," which was ratified in 1795, didn't actually solve many of the problems, it was successful in averting war with Britain. It was equally successful in angering the French. In America's hour of need during the Revolutionary War, France had allied itself with the rebellious colonies, but now the United States had chosen to negotiate a treaty with France's sworn enemy, Britain. With some justification the French viewed the Jay treaty as a repudiation of the treaty they had signed with the colonies in 1778. France responded to this diplomatic slap in the face by turning a blind eye when French privateers stepped up their attacks on American shipping in the West Indies. Then, in 1797, the French formalized this policy of harassment and officially authorized the attacks, which ultimately resulted in the French seizing more than six hundred American ships.[40]

Although an earlier American attempt to get the French to halt these attacks had failed, the newly inaugurated president, John Adams, decided to try the diplomatic route one more time. He sent Charles Cotesworth Pinckney, John Marshall, and Elbridge Gerry to Paris to negotiate a truce, but French foreign minister, Talleyrand, decided to play a most dangerous and insulting game. He granted the Americans a perfunctory fifteen-minute meeting, and then left subsequent contacts to three of his emissaries. These men, to whom the American negotiators referred as X, Y, and Z in their letters to Congress, made it clear that while Talleyrand was eager to come to some agreement, he required a bribe, or "sweetener" as it was called, of $250,000. And that was not all. The Americans would also have to loan France $10 million.[41] Pinckney, Marshall, and Gerry decried this form of extortion and cut off negotiations. When word of the "XYZ Affair" reached the United States, and the terms of the extortion became clear, the American people exploded in indignation. "The man who, after this mass of evidence, shall be an apologist for France . . . is not an American," declared Alexander Hamilton, and "the choice for him lies between being deemed a fool, a madman, or a traitor."[42] With the rallying cry "Millions for defense, but not one cent for tribute," calls for war spread throughout the country.[43] But instead of declaring war America chose to pursue an aggressive offensive policy aimed at encouraging France to decide that attacking American shipping was not in its best interest. America bulked up its navy and sent its ships forth to capture foreign armed vessels and also seize any captured American vessels. This launched the Quasi-War with France, which had a dramatic impact on American whalemen. Many whaleship owners chose to sell their ships or keep them in port rather than send them out and risk capture. Insurance rates for commercial shipping shot up, adding a further impediment to fitting out whaling voyages. And some of the owners who sent their whaleships out lost them to the enemy, with Nantucket alone losing four.[44]

The end of the Quasi-War in 1800 inaugurated another period of growth for the American whaling industry. Demand expanded, prices rose, and new vessels were launched from Nantucket, New Bedford, New London, Hudson, Sag Harbor, and other ports. This prosperity, however, proved fleeting. In 1803 a tenuous peace that had been brokered between Britain and France fell apart, and the Atlantic Ocean once again became a battleground. In 1806 France proclaimed a naval blockade against Britain, and Britain retaliated early the next year with a blockade against France. The neutrality of American vessels was increasingly ignored by the warring powers as both French and British warships and privateers seized American ships suspected of trading with the enemy. The tiny American navy was virtually helpless to stop these depredations, and without adequate protection and fearing capture, many American whaling merchants scaled back their operations; but still they went whaling, all the while pursuing profits and believing that they could ride out the storm as long as the United States didn't become further enmeshed in the European conflict. Then the situation worsened.

The USS *Chesapeake*, captained by Samuel Barron, sailed from Norfolk, Virginia, early on the morning of June 22, 1807. Later that day HMS *Leopard* bore down on the *Chesapeake* and ordered it to stop. Barron complied and a boarding party from the *Leopard*, headed by Lt. John Meade, soon arrived. Meade demanded that Barron call his crew to the main deck so that Meade could determine if any of them were deserters from the British navy and retrieve those who were discovered. Barron balked, Meade departed, and soon thereafter the *Leopard* responded by firing on the *Chesapeake* at close range. The *Chesapeake*'s decks were strewn with supplies brought on board in Norfolk, making it virtually impossible for Barron and his men to mount an effective counterattack. Realizing this, Barron surrendered, but the *Leopard*'s commander ignored this move, and instead sent another boarding party, which left with four men the British claimed were deserters. The *Chesapeake*, badly damaged and carrying four dead and eighteen wounded sailors, slowly made its way back to Norfolk.[45]

The *Chesapeake* affair outraged the American public. Since the early 1790s Americans had watched and fumed as Britain pursued its increasingly active policy of impressing Americans. The British claimed that the sailors it seized in this manner were British subjects who had deserted from the British navy and therefore deserved to be repatriated. Although that claim was true in some instances, it was equally true that many of the impressed seamen were American citizens. Such was the case with the *Chesapeake*. While one of the men forcibly removed from the ship was a British deserter, the other three were Americans.[46]

The indignation that the *Chesapeake* affair aroused led many Americans to call for war against Britain. But President Thomas Jefferson knew that the United States was woefully unprepared for war, so he pursued a different strategy. He decided to teach the British as well as the French, both of whom had violated America's neutrality and harassed its shipping, a lesson in the power of trade. On December 22, 1807, Jefferson signed the Embargo Act, which prohibited all maritime trade with other nations, and allowed shipping between American ports to continue only after shipowners posted a hefty bond to ensure that they wouldn't surreptitiously sail to a foreign port. The Embargo

Act's supporters hoped that depriving Britain and France of American goods would send their economies into a tailspin, force them to respect America's neutrality and put an end to their policies that were harming American interests.

The embargo did have a major economic impact, but unfortunately it was on America, not Britain or France. It turned out that both of those countries could get along quite well without America's goods, but America could not get along as well without Britain's and France's markets. Within a year of the act's passage, American exports dropped from $108,000,000 to $22,000,000.[47] American whalemen were hit particularly hard. With overseas markets shut and the domestic market open only to those shipowners willing to post exorbitant bonds, most whaleships remained idle, as did their crews.

By 1811 signs in the United States were increasingly pointing to an imminent war with Britain. Many Americans were outraged by Britain's continued violations of American neutrality as well as British efforts to arm Indians in the West, via Canada, and encourage them to resist American expansion along the frontier. Congress was populated with war hawks, predominantly from the West and South, who demanded "Free Trade and Sailor's Rights," but also viewed a war with Britain as a prime opportunity to wrest control of Canada from the British, and Florida from the Spanish.[48] Then, in May 1811, the USS frigate *President* fired on the British sloop-of-war *Little Belt* off the coast of Virginia. Although the captain of the *President* called this action a case of mistaken identity, and apologized, that did not pacify the British. When the British demanded reparations for the damage done to the *Little Belt*, the Americans responded indignantly that first the British would have to pay reparations for the shelling of the *Chesapeake*, and neither side offered anything. In November, President James Madison asked Congress to increase the country's military preparedness. A month later, still hoping to avoid conflict, Madison sent the warship *Hornet* to Britain with letters imploring the British to change their policies toward America or risk war. In early April 1812, after failing to receive a response from Britain, Congress, at Madison's request, placed a ninety-day embargo on all trade, which was assumed to be enough time for ships at sea to return safely to port before war was declared.[49]

Although many Americans were clamoring for war, whaling merchants most emphatically were not. They knew from grim experience that war would ruin their business. In May, Nantucket sent a letter to Congress "on the subject of our present Foreign Relations, wishing to avoid war." The document recounted the devastating impact of the Revolutionary War on the island's economy, and implored Congress to take steps to avoid the same fate again, noting that "the declaration of a Foreign War would be desolating to the Inhabitants of this Island." Of particular concern to Nantucket was that nearly 90 percent of its "mercantile capital" was at sea and 75 percent of those ships were not expected to return to port in fewer than twelve months.[50] If war were to be declared in the meantime, those ships would be subject to attack by the British navy. But the whaling merchants' concerns, which were shared by many Americans dependent on maritime trade, were drowned out by the drumbeat for war. The final turn in that direction came on May 22, when the *Hornet* returned with word that the British had refused Madison's entreaties. On June 1, feeling that he had done his best to broker a peace, Madison asked Congress to declare war on Britain. With the western and southern states leading the way, Congress obliged, and on June 18, Madison signed the declaration.[51] The War of 1812 had begun, and American whaling was heading for another crash.

Chapter Twelve

KNOCKDOWN

COMMODORE DAVID PORTER OF THE U.S. NAVY—THE PROTECTOR OF
AMERICA'S WHALING FLEET IN THE PACIFIC OCEAN DURING THE WAR OF 1812.
ENGRAVING BASED ON A PAINTING BY ALONZO CHAPPELL.

IN MANY WAYS THE WAR OF 1812 WAS A REPLAY OF THE REVOLU-
tionary War, but on a smaller scale. Dozens of American whaleships
that were at sea when hostilities broke out were captured or burned by
the British navy. Markets for whale oil and baleen were cut off or
severely compromised. All of the whaling ports in the United States

ceased operating, except Nantucket. But even this steadfast whaling community could only muster a handful of voyages, and each departure was attended by the fear that the vessels and their crews would not be seen again. Although the War of 1812 was a dark time for American whaling, it did bring to the fore two figures whose heroic actions provided the only bright spots for the crippled industry. The more noteworthy of these was Capt. David Porter, of the U.S. Navy, who led the USS *Essex* on a bold and dramatic cruise through the Pacific that damaged the British whale fishery and gave American whalemen something to cheer about.

Porter's father had been an American privateer during the Revolutionary War, and in 1796, at the age of sixteen, Porter decided to join his father on board merchant ships bound for West Indies. Two years later he enlisted in the fledgling American navy as a midshipman, eager to defend his country's shipping interests and its honor during the Quasi-War with France. Porter rose quickly through the ranks, distinguishing himself by acts of heroism and courage under fire. His rapid ascent in the navy, however, was abruptly halted in late 1803, when the ship he was on, the *Philadelphia*, ran aground in Tripoli harbor and the entire crew was captured and imprisoned for nineteen months by the Tripolitan government, which was at war with the United States. Upon his release at the war's end, Porter remained in the Mediterranean, commanding two U.S. naval ships, and then returned to America in 1807, where he took up residence for a brief time in New York City, becoming something of a man-about-town, befriending the writer Washington Irving and his circle—the "true lads of Kilkenny"—and gaining the nickname the "Second Sindbad." Porter married in 1808 and soon thereafter was named commander of the naval station in New Orleans. It was an important and at times dangerous job, enforcing the Embargo Act and protecting American shipping interests from French and Spanish privateers, but it lacked much of the drama, excitement, and challenge that Porter thrived on; and most of all it lacked a ship he could call his own. Porter wanted to get back to sea, to have men under his command, and to fight for his country. So, after two years in New Orleans, Porter headed north to secure a commission, and he was given command of the *Essex*.[1]

The *Essex* was a great ship with a proud history. Launched from Salem, Massachusetts, in 1799, it owed its existence to the good people of that town as well as their neighbors throughout Essex County. As one of the country's most important ports, Salem was heavily involved in international trade and therefore was greatly troubled by French aggression on the high seas during the Quasi War. Wanting to help the war effort and teach the French a lesson, Salem's leaders raised roughly $75,000 through public subscription to build a thirty-two-gun frigate for the U.S. Navy. In November 1798 Enos Briggs, a shipbuilder, issued a clarion call for materials in the *Salem Gazette*: "Ye Sons of Freedom!" began the advertisement. "All true lovers of the liberty of your country! step forth and give your assistance in building the frigate, to oppose French insolence and piracy. Let every man in possession of a White Oak Tree, be ambitious to be foremost in hurrying down the timber to Salem, and fill the complement wanting, where the noble structure is to be fabricated, to maintain your rights upon the Seas, and make the name of America respected among the nations of the world."[2] Step forth they did, and soon Salem's Winter Island was alive with the sounds of hammers, saws, and forges as the *Essex* took shape. The ship was launched on September 30, 1799, before an enthusiastic crowd numbering in the thousands, and the next day the *Gazette* proclaimed that the *Essex* was "well calculated to do essential service for her country."[3] In the ensuing years the *Essex* developed a solid record of achievement, and when Porter took command in August 1811, he was confident that he had a good ship. What Porter needed now was an opportunity to test himself and his crew, which the War of 1812 soon provided.

It was a daunting task. Britannia still ruled the waves and had at its disposal more than six hundred naval ships, with nearly 28,000 cannons. Of course much of Britain's nautical firepower was occupied maintaining a blockade of Europe and trying to beat back Napoleon's marauding armies, but even with Britain's attention divided between Europe and America, the American navy was outgunned to an almost comical degree. After the Quasi War, America had decided to downsize its already small navy, a policy that was only just beginning to be reversed on the eve of the War of 1812. As a result, when the *Essex* sailed, the U.S. Navy had a mere seventeen ships and 442 cannons at its command. With such a small force the navy believed that sending the ships out en masse would be foolhardy, for a single disastrous battle could destroy most if not all of them. Instead the navy settled on a strategy of dispatching its ships one at a time, hoping that through the use of stealth, speed, and skill, they could put a dent in the massive British fleet before it blockaded the American coast. Thus it was that a little more than two weeks after war was declared, the *Essex* sailed out of New York into the Atlantic. After capturing a few relatively minor prizes, the *Essex* achieved a modicum of fame on August 13, when it became the first American naval ship in the War of 1812 to take a British warship, the sixteen-gun *Alert.* Despite this victory, however, Porter was disappointed. The *Alert* had barely put up a fight. The entire action lasted a mere eight minutes before the British captain struck his colors. Porter found little honor in this. He wasn't interested in just winning, he wanted grand accomplishments. He wanted to make a name for himself by vanquishing a mighty foe. He wanted to be inscribed in the annals of naval history as a great commander who led a glorious campaign upon the seas.[4]

On October 28, 1812, the *Essex* left the capes of Delaware and headed south with new orders, to rendezvous with other American naval ships in the South Atlantic. But each time Porter appeared where he was instructed, the other ships did not. By the end of January 1813 Porter's situation was becoming tenuous. He had exhausted most of his supplies, and there were no nearby ports where he could go ashore without the risk of capture. He refused to return to the United States for fear of being seized by British warships, which he knew were now eagerly patrolling American waters. "It became absolutely necessary," Porter wrote, "to depart from the letter of my instructions; I therefore determined to pursue that course which seemed to me best calculated to injure the enemy, and would enable me to prolong my cruize."[5] That course was to round Cape Horn into the Pacific Ocean, where he could resupply the *Essex* and also harass British merchant ships. Porter kept his plans from his men for fear of causing alarm, but as the ship neared the southern tip of South America and the dangerous waters off Cape Horn, the men became increasingly agitated. To keep this unrest from growing Porter wrote a note to his crew:

SAILORS AND MARINES!

A large increase of the enemy's force compels us to abandon a coast, that will neither afford us security nor supplies; nor are there any inducements for a longer continuance there. We will, therefore, proceed to annoy them, where we are least expected. What was never performed, by a single ship, we will attempt. The Pacific Ocean affords us many friendly ports. The unprotected British commerce, on the coast of Chili, Peru, and Mexico, will give you an abundant supply of wealth; and the girls of the Sandwich Islands, shall reward you for your sufferings during the passage around Cape Horn.[6]

This bolstered the crew's spirits, but still they feared the passage around Cape Horn. Even today rounding the Horn can be a harrowing experience. The waters are unpredictable and often treacherous, and weather conditions can change rapidly.[7] As the *Essex* started its passage the waters were uncharacteristically calm, and Porter and his men began to believe that fortune was smiling down upon them and that they would make it to the Pacific unscathed. But fortune proved fickle, and soon black clouds rolled off the land and "burst upon us," Porter recounted, "with a fury we little expected." The storm "produced an irregular and dangerous sea, that threatened to jerk away our masts, at every roll of the ship." For days the leaking *Essex* battled through mountainous waves, the "piercing cold," and "almost constant rains and hails." Finally, toward the end of February, the *Essex* cleared the Cape, thus becoming the first American warship to sail in the Pacific.[8]

After a stop on the island of Mocha for provisions, the *Essex* sailed to Valparaiso, arriving in Chile in the middle of March. Porter approached the port warily, flying British colors. When he had left New York, Spain was allied with Britain, and Porter thought there might be trouble on that account, hence the ruse. But while Porter had been at sea, Chile had declared its independence from Spain, and its ports were now open to all nations. On gaining this intelligence, Porter revealed his true allegiance and was heartily welcomed by the local officials, who, he said, "looked up to the United States of America for example and protection." Days of parties and celebrations followed, and Porter and his men thoroughly enjoyed themselves. As the *Essex* was preparing to depart, Porter received valuable information from the captain of an American whaleship that had just arrived, who noted that he had recently come into contact with two armed British whaleships. The British captains had said they had no orders to attack American whaleships, but that they expected to get such orders very soon. The American whaling captain also told Porter that off the Galápagos Islands there were many American whaleships that had no idea that war had broken out between America and Britain, and therefore would "fall an easy and unsuspecting prey to the British ships."[9] On hearing this Porter immediately sailed for the Galápagos Islands.

Soon after leaving Valparaiso the *Essex* came upon the Nantucket whaleship *Charles*, and learned from its captain, Grafton Gardner, that a British and a Spanish ship had attacked and captured two other American whaleships, the *Walker* and the *Barclay*, near the Chilean port of Coquimbo. Porter, in the company of the *Charles*, set out to find the enemy ships and free the Americans. On the morning of March 26 the *Essex* sighted a ship in the distance and gave chase. It was the *Nereyda*, a Peruvian sloop-of-war disguised as a whaler, and Porter surmised that it was one of the ships that had attacked the Americans. Porter drew the *Nereyda* alongside by raising the British colors, and when a lieutenant from the Spanish ship boarded the *Essex*, he told Porter that they were cruising for American whaleships and had on board twenty-three prisoners from the *Walker* and the *Barclay*. Porter asked the lieutenant to bring the captain of the *Walker* and one of the crew of the *Barclay* to the *Essex*. This done, Porter took Captain West aside and informed him that he was actually on an American frigate. West, much relieved, told Porter that men of the *Walker* and the *Barclay* hadn't learned of the war until they were captured, and that the American vessels had been nearing the end of their voyages, with holds full of oil, when they were attacked without warning or provocation. And not only did the attackers take the ships but they also stripped the men of all their belongings. Having heard enough, Porter sprung the trap, raising the American colors and firing two cannon shots over the Spanish ship, which surrendered without a fight. Porter viewed the *Nereyda's* actions as "piratical," and he decided to send the government of Peru a very pointed message. First he ordered that all the *Nereyda's* arms and ammunition be thrown overboard, along with its light sails, so that the ship could do no more harm to American interests. Then Porter sent the ship and its crew back to Lima, along with a letter for the Spanish viceroy, which chastised the Peruvians for attacking American ships and threatening the relationship between the United States and Spanish America.[10]

A few of the liberated American prisoners decided to remain with the *Essex*, while the rest departed on board the *Charles*. But before the two ships took leave of each other, Porter asked Captains Gardner and West to write down the names of all the American and British whaleships that they knew were in the Pacific. The list included twenty-three American and ten British ships, most of which could be found in the vicinity of the Galápagos Islands. Although the captains could recall the names of only ten British whaleships, they were confident that there were at least twenty in the area, and that their cargoes of oil would fetch more than $200,000 each in Britain. With this information, Porter crystallized his plan of action. He and his men would capture British whaleships and sell them and their precious cargoes at a profit. "If I should only succeed in driving the British from the ocean, and leaving it free for our own vessels," wrote Porter, "I conceive that I shall have rendered an essential service to my country, and that the effecting this object alone would be sufficient compensation for the hardships and dangers we have experienced, and be considered a justification for departing from the letter of my instructions." Porter knew that most of the British whaleships were armed and had a letter of marque on board from the British government, a legal document that gave them permission to prey on American commerce. But Porter dismissed this British whaling armada, boasting that "their whole force united would [not] be a match for the *Essex*." After painting the *Essex* to look like a Spanish merchant vessel, Porter continued on a course for the Galápagos.[11]

A few days out the *Essex* recaptured the *Barclay*, and both vessels continued sailing to the Galápagos, reaching the archipelago on March 29. There Porter dispatched his men to one of the islands to collect the letters at "Hathaways Post Office," which was nothing more than a box nailed to a tree in which whaling vessels deposited letters to communicate with one another or to send news home. The letters Porter's men found were out of date, but they confirmed that at least five British whaleships had visited the island the previous June and were likely still in the area. The proximity of such valuable prizes led Porter and his men to daydream about the "rich harvest" they would soon secure from the "enemy." But as the days turned into weeks, with no prizes in sight, the men's hopes dimmed, and Porter began fearing "the dread of a disappointment." Then with the dawn on April 29, the glorious cry "Sail ho! Sail ho!" roused Porter from his cot where he had spent another "sleepless and anxious night." It was the British whaleship *Montezuma*, with a bounty of fourteen hundred barrels of sperm whale oil, twenty-two men, and two guns on board. In what had become his signature ploy, Porter hauled aloft British colors. This placed the *Montezuma*'s captain at ease, and soon he was on board the *Essex* giving his fellow "Englishmen" information about other British whaleships in the vicinity. Having heard what he wanted, Porter imprisoned his guest and ordered the *Essex* to set sail, and in short order the *Essex* added the *Georgiana* and the *Policy*, armed with a combined total of sixteen guns, to its rapidly expanding fleet of British whaleships. Porter felt that the capture of these two ships, after a month of fruitless searching, provided a valuable lesson for his crew, some of whom had been bemoaning their lack of success. Eager to rally his men, Porter sent them another note:

SAILORS AND MARINES,

Fortune has at length smiled on us, because we deserved her smiles, and the first time she enabled us to display *free trade and sailor's rights*, assisted by your good conduct, she put in our possession nearly half a million of the enemy's property.

Continue to be zealous, enterprizing, and patient, and we will yet render the name of the *Essex* as terrible to the enemy as that of any other vessel, before we return to the United States.

The windfall provided by these last three ships was more than financial. On board each was a great store of supplies, which the *Essex* sorely needed, including "cordage, canvas, paints, tar, and every other article necessary for the ship."[12] There was also a small battalion of Galápagos tortoises in the holds of the ships. Ever since whalemen began frequenting the Galápagos Islands, they had gone ashore to capture these huge, long-lived, lumbering animals for food. Reaching up to six feet long and more than five hundred pounds, the tortoises had the virtue, at least from the whalemen's perspective, of being able to survive for months, if not years, on a ship without eating or drinking, and yet still retain enough meat to provide many meals. So esteemed were these tortoises as food that during the nineteenth century whalemen killed at least thirteen thousand of them, permanently devastating their population.[13] When Porter and his men found the tortoises, they knew they were in for a gustatory treat. "Hideous and disgusting as is their appearance," Porter wrote, "no animal can possibly afford a more wholesome, luscious, and delicate food than they do; the finest green turtle is no more to be compared to them, in point of excellence, than the coarsest beef is to the finest veal; and after once tasting the Galápagos tortoises, every other animal food fell greatly in our estimation."[14]

To expand his reach and increase his chances of success, Porter transformed the *Georgiana*, which he deemed "a noble ship," into a fully armed cruiser, adding the *Policy*'s ten guns to its six, and sent it off under the command of his trusted first lieutenant, John Downes, to capture more British whaleships. Meantime the *Essex*, the *Montezuma*, the *Policy*, and the *Barclay* continued their own search for prizes, spreading themselves out in a broad line, ready to come to one another's aid should an enemy sail be sighted. Many weeks went by, and then on May 29, after a day-and-a-half chase, the *Essex* had another ship in its sights. The British colors were raised, and Capt. Obadiah Wier of the British whaleship *Atlantic*, with twenty-four crewmembers and six guns, came aboard. Wier, a Nantucketer who still had a wife and family on the island, was excited to be welcomed on board what he supposed was a British man-of-war, and Porter, who had grown fond of such deception, let him talk. Wier told Porter where he could go to capture nine American whaleships, which were "in an unprotected and defence-less state," and he also said that rumor had it that the *Essex* had gone around the Cape of Good Hope. Porter listened intently, then asked Wier "how he reconciled it to himself to sail from England under the British flag, and in an armed ship, after hostilities had taken place between the two countries." Wier responded that it was not difficult at all, because "although he was born in America, he was an Englishman at heart." Porter was disgusted. "This man appeared a polished gentle-man in his manners," he observed, "but evidently possessed a corrupt heart, and, like all other renagadoes, was desirous of doing his native country all the injury in his power, with the hope of thereby ingratiat-ing himself with his new friends." Porter let the charade continue for a while longer before introducing Wier to the captains of the *Montezuma* and *Georgiana*, "who soon undeceived him with respect to our being an English frigate."[15]

Just after Porter took Wier to his cabin for their friendly chat, the men of the *Essex* spied another sail on the horizon, commenced the chase, and before long the British whaleship *Greenwich*, twenty-six men and ten guns, was added to Porter's fleet. The captain of the *Greenwich*, John Shuttleworth, was drunk when he was hauled on board the *Essex*, and he and Wier began insulting Porter's officers and expressing the fervent hope that soon British warships would "be sent to chastise" the *Essex* "for its temerity in venturing so far from home." When the two captains were ushered into a room for their confinement, their rants intensified. "They gave full vent to their anger," noted Porter, "and indulged in the most abusive language against our government, the ship and her officers, lavishing on me in particular the most scurrilous epithets. . . . They really appeared to have forgotten that they were prisoners and in my power."[16]

On June 24 Porter reunited with Downes, who had managed to assemble his own respectable fleet of British prizes, including the whale-ships *Hector*, *Rose*, and *Catherine*. Porter reviewed his miniarmada and took the opportunity to make some changes. Noting that the *Atlantic* was a "far superior" ship to the *Georgiana*, Porter had twenty guns mounted on the former and then transferred Lieutenant Downes and his crew to that ship, while the *Georgiana* was given another crew. To signal the *Atlantic*'s new position of preeminence in the fleet, it was renamed the *Essex Junior*. Porter also addressed two problems created by his success: namely, that he had too many prisoners and too many ships. He sent the prisoners ashore, and, evincing a deep faith in the power of honor among men, had them promise not to fight against the United States until they were exchanged for American prisoners of war. As for the ships, Porter sent Lieutenant Downes to Valparaiso, with the *Hector*, *Catherine*, *Policy*, *Montezuma*, and *Barclay* in tow, with instructions to leave the *Barclay* there and "sell the others to the best advantage." Bidding Downes good fortune, Porter, along with the *Greenwich* and the *Georgiana*, headed back to the Galápagos, where it wasn't long before Porter had captured three more heavily armed British whaleships—the *Charlton*, the *New Zealander*, and the *Seringa-patam*. Porter's capture of the latter gave him, he recalled, "more pleasure than that of any other which fell into my hands." The *Seringapatam* was not only a fine vessel but it had already captured one American whaleship, the *Edward* of Nantucket, and would, by Porter's estimation, have gone on to capture many others had it not been stopped. But Porter got the most satisfaction from stopping what he perceived to be a rogue operation. When Porter demanded that the *Seringapatam*'s captain produce his letter of marque, the captain responded, "with the utmost terror in his countenance," that he didn't have one. Attacking an American ship was bad enough when the attacker had a letter of marque, but to do so without such legal authorization was much worse, in Porter's eyes. As a result he branded the captain a "pirate" and had him thrown into irons.[17]

Once again Porter consolidated his fleet, filling the *Charlton* with prisoners and sending it to Rio de Janeiro, and dispatching the *Georgiana* along with one hundred thousand dollars' worth of sperm whale oil to the United States, where he hoped it would turn a nice profit. Then, after a frustrating and unsuccessful attempt to capture another British whaleship, Porter anchored in the middle of the Galápagos Islands, repaired and painted the ships, and gathered about fourteen tons of turtles. During this sojourn one of Porter's men was killed in a duel, and after burying the man, Porter decided to engage in a bit of deception. Suspended on a post that pointed to the grave, Porter left a note in a bottle, which told of the *Essex*'s arrival in the area and claimed that its crew had been devastated by "scurvy" and "ship-fever," which had killed forty-three men. The note added that "the *Essex* leaves this in a leaky state, her foremast rotten . . . her mainmast sprung . . . [and should any vessel arrive here and see this note] they would be doing an act of great humanity to transmit a copy of it to America, in order that our friends may know of our distressed and hopeless situation, and be prepared for worse tidings, if they should ever again hear from us."[18] Of course this was a total fabrication. The *Essex* was in fighting form, but there was no need for the enemy to know that.

On September 15, 1813, Porter gained his last prize, the *Sir Andrew Hammond*, a British whaleship whose decks were loaded with freshly cut blubber. On being told that the blubber "would make from 80 to 90 barrels," which would be worth "between two and three thousand dollars," Porter ordered his men to try out the blubber and store the oil. Soon thereafter the *Essex* and the *Essex Junior* rendezvoused. Lieutenant Downes brought with him valuable intelligence, including news of the 1812 reelection of James Madison and information about American naval successes. Porter also learned that the British frigate *Phoebe* and the sloop-of-war *Cherub* had been dispatched to seek out the *Essex* and put a halt to its depredations. As one might expect, when word of the *Essex*'s exploits finally filtered back to Britain, the British, who were used to ruling the seas, not being humiliated on them, reacted angrily and demanded retribution; the *Phoebe* and *Cherub* were sent to exact it. News that he was being chased did not demoralize Porter, it delighted him. These two formidable foes might finally give him the battle he had been looking for since the beginning of the war. Although Porter was proud of his accomplishments, he still "hoped," he wrote, "to signalize . . . [his] cruise by something more splendid before leaving" the Pacific Ocean. Attacking and overpowering whaleships that were armed only with small batteries of guns and lightly manned was not nearly so noble or dramatic or impressive as besting a British warship equipped with scores of cannons and manned by hundreds of sailors. Porter needed a battle for posterity, and he hoped that a meeting with the *Phoebe* or the *Cherub*, or both, would provide it.[19]

But first Porter needed to regroup and give his men a much-needed rest. So he sailed his fleet 2,500 miles to the southwest of the Galápagos, arriving at the Marquesas Islands in late October 1813. Porter's stay on the islands, which lasted a little over a month, was eventful to say the least. The Americans built a small fort, became embroiled in wars involving three local tribes, and Porter, in a fit of patriotic and imperialistic ardor, took possession of the Marquesas on behalf of the United States, renamed them Madison Islands in honor of the recently reelected president, and christened one of the islands' main harbors Massachusetts Bay (despite Porter's actions, the Marquesas later became French possessions). Then, just as Porter was planning to depart, he headed off a mutiny when some of his men, who had become particularly enamored of the native women, refused to leave. Finally, in early December, the *Essex* and the *Essex Junior* sailed for Chile, leaving the other ships behind.[20]

Unfortunately for Porter, his date with destiny was a debacle. On February 3, 1814, the *Essex* arrived in Valparaiso, and a few days later, so too did the *Phoebe* and the *Cherub*. The *Essex* tried to engage the *Phoebe* in one-on-one combat but was not able to get the British ship to take the bait. Then, when *Essex* made a run past the two British ships to the open ocean, disaster struck. A strong wind snapped the *Essex*'s main topmast, severely reducing the ship's speed and maneuverability. The *Phoebe* and the *Cherub*, taking advantage of the situation, quickly closed in and opened fire. Porter and his men fought valiantly, but they were severely outmatched. Late in the day on March 28, 1814, Porter surrendered, and the *Essex*'s career as an American naval ship ended.[21]

The legacy of Porter's cruise through the Pacific depends on who is doing the telling. In Porter's estimation it was a stunning success. "By our captures," he wrote, "we have completely broken up that important branch of British navigation, the whale-fishery of the coast of Chili and Peru." He claimed that such captures had "deprived the enemy of property to the amount of two and a half millions of dollars, and of the services of 360 seamen that I liberated on parole, not to serve against the United States until regularly exchanged." Porter added to this amount another $2.5 million, which he said was the value of American whaleships that, but for the *Essex*'s arrival in the Pacific, "would in all probability have been captured."[22] Theodore Roosevelt, in his sweeping history *The Naval War of 1812*, wrote that "it was an unprecedented thing for a small frigate to cruise a year and a half in enemy's waters, and to supply herself during that time, purely from captured vessels. . . . Porter's cruise was the very model of what such an expedition should be, harassing the enemy most effectually at no cost whatsoever."[23] Porter's old drinking partner, Washington Irving, claimed that Britain's "pride . . . was sorely incensed at beholding a single frigate lording it over the Pacific . . . in saucy defiance of their thousand ships . . . and almost banishing the British flag from those regions where it had so long waved predominant."[24] And a member of Parliament claimed that because of Porter's captures of British whaleships London "had burnt dark for a year."[25]

These accounts, however, are too glowing. Although Porter burned three of twelve whaleships he and his men captured, five others, along with much of their cargoes, were later retaken by the British. The ultimate fate of three of the captured ships is not clear, and only one ship is known to have been sold, that being the *Essex Junior*, which transported Porter and his crew to New York, where it was bought by the U.S. government for $25,000. And of course Porter also lost his greatest asset, the *Essex*, which was sent back to Britain, where it later served as a prison ship. Thus, while there is no doubt that Porter's exploits protected the largely defenseless American whaling fleet and damaged the British whale fishery, it is also true that Porter and his men could have done better. As Frances Diane Robotti and James Vescovi wrote in their history of the *Essex*, "Porter would have done more damage to the British Empire and etched his name a little deeper into the history books had he put a match to each of his prizes—and had he not returned to Valparaiso."[26]

WHEN PORTER HAD FIRST SAILED into Valparaiso, in March 1813, he was greeted by Joel R. Poinsett, the American consul general for Buenos Aires, Peru, and Chile, who, like Porter, would soon come to the aid of American whalemen in heroic fashion. Born in Charleston, South Carolina, in 1779, Poinsett had pursued a most unusual and dramatic path to Chile. After receiving a formal education in England, Scotland, and America, and bucking his family's wishes that he enter the medical or the legal profession, Poinsett set off on a tour of Europe in 1801. This was no vagabond excursion but rather a nearly ten-year sojourn during which a potent combination of family connections, personal charisma, and erudition enabled Poinsett to meet with the high and mighty, including Czar Alexander I of Russia and Napoleon. As Poinsett traveled through Europe, America was never far from his thoughts, and in 1809, when he concluded that the United States and Britain were marching irrevocably toward war, he returned to the States and offered to serve in the military, preferably as an assistant to a general. But his country decided that a man with his skills, including a flair for diplomacy and a proficiency in Spanish, would best be used on a special mission to southern South America. Thus, in August 1810, the secretary of state ordered Poinsett to go to that region to preach the benefits of creating strong commercial ties with the United States and subtly to encourage the Spanish colonies to seek their independence from Spain.[27]

Poinsett welcomed Porter with open arms, and the two got along well, attending parties together and discussing the war and the current political situation. A short while after Porter left Valparaiso, the Peruvians, who claimed allegiance to Britain, captured the Chilean port of Talcahuano, and along with it a large number of American whaleships anchored in the harbor, including the *Lyon, Sukey, Gardner, President, Perseverance, Atlas, Monticello, Chili, John and James, Mary Ann,* and the *Lima,* all of which hailed from Nantucket.[28] When Poinsett learned of this, and further, that the Peruvians planned to confiscate the ships and send the whalemen to Lima as prisoners, he devised a plan of attack. Using his close ties to the ruling junta in Chile, and his position as a trusted military adviser to the Chilean army, Poinsett, whom the Chileans referred to as *"el major chileno,"* helped to orchestrate an assault on Talcahuano, the dual goals of which were to free the port and the whalemen.[29] With four hundred handpicked men under his command, and only three pieces of artillery, Poinsett used the cover of darkness to overwhelm and beat back the fifteen hundred Peruvian defenders arrayed against him, after a pitched battle that lasted three hours. Once the fighting was over and the whalemen were freed, Poinsett resumed his diplomatic responsibilities by issuing consular certificates to those whaleships whose papers had been destroyed by the enemy. Not all the whaleships rescued that day made it back to Nantucket; a significant number of them were subsequently captured by the British. Still, that didn't diminish the impressiveness of Poinsett's actions in the eyes of Nantucketers. An article in the *Nantucket Inquirer* in August 1824 noted that "the benefits which resulted to this island from the enterprise are incalculable. Two hundred gallant seamen were released from imprisonment; a large amount of property was rescued from depredation; and this at a time of general distress in this place."[30]

WHILE PORTER AND POINSETT were giving aid to American whalemen in the Pacific, the whalemen back home were sinking deeper into depression. Even the most successful whaling merchants were devastated by the virtual cessation of their business, and the legions of men they had formerly employed wandered the countryside looking for alternate lines of work, usually finding none. Nantucket, of course, had the worst of it. In November 1812, with the war but a few months old, a group of Nantucketers sent a petition to President Madison, outlining their desperate situation and asking for assistance. It was a familiar refrain for those old enough to remember the Revolutionary War. "The island . . . is exposed to the ravages of an enemy . . . since the declaration of war, [the inhabitants] have been without employ, and thereby reduced to indigent circumstances . . . we have no choice, but that of respectfully [asking if] . . . any means can be devised to save our fleet of whale ships . . . and if any method can be adopted, whereby we may prosecute the cod and whale fisheries without the risk of capture by the enemy."[31]

The government was not in a position to help, and many Nantucketers chose to relocate, with a considerable portion of them heading for a Quaker enclave in Ohio. For those who remained the situation worsened, becoming especially dire in early 1814, when Britain, on the verge of vanquishing Napoleon, decided it could divert more of its navy to the United States to enforce a beefed-up blockade of the New England coast. Now, cut off from supplies on the mainland by a cordon of British cruisers, Nantucket was truly on its own. In this precarious state Nantucketers decided that their only alternative to further misery and possible starvation was negotiating with the enemy.

During the spring and summer of 1814, the Nantucketers and British commanders met on a number of occasions, with each group trying its best to gain concessions from the other. For their part the Nantucketers wanted permission to transport supplies from the mainland and to go whaling and cod fishing, without having to worry about being attacked. The British also had two goals: The first was to get Nantucket to declare itself neutral, an action that would drive a wedge between the island and the U.S. government. The second was to induce Nantucket whalemen to relocate their industry to British soil, preferably to Nova Scotia. In the end neither side was completely successful. Nantucket did declare itself neutral and, as a result, was awarded a number of passports that directed British ships and privateers not to interfere with the ships bearing passports as they visited certain ports on the mainland and brought back provisions and supplies. Nevertheless Nantucket was still in desperate straits because the number of vessels that received passports was too small to satisfy the island's needs, and some of those vessels refused to leave port for fear of being captured by British or American privateers, neither of whom respected the passports' authority. As for whaling, it was a stalemate. The Nantucketers showed no inclination to relocate, and the British showed no inclination to allow the Nantucketers to whale on any other terms.

In September 1814 the British commanders demanded that now-neutral Nantucket also refuse to pay any direct taxes or internal duties to the U.S. government. If the Nantucketers did not comply, they were warned that the passports would be withdrawn and the island would be forced to pay double taxes to His Majesty. Reluctant so clearly to sever their ties with the U.S. government, Nantucketers pursued a middle path—that of firing the town's tax collector, arguing that without a collector, no taxes could be collected or paid. When this logic proved unsatisfactory to the British commanders, the Nantucketers relented, and on September 28 voted to stop paying taxes and duties for as long as the war lasted. And there things sat for months as Nantucket entered another hard winter of want and isolation.[32] Where the negotiations between the Nantucketers and the British might have gone from this point will never be known, for on February 16, 1815, the islanders awoke to the glorious news that the Treaty of Ghent had been signed on December 24, and the war (save for the Battle of New Orleans two weeks later), was over. Immediately the whalemen of Nantucket, and their peers on the mainland, got to work. There were still whales in the ocean, and the Americans were determined to get them.

Chapter Thirteen

THE GOLDEN AGE

HERMAN MELVILLE IN 1861. HIS GREATEST BOOK,
MOBY-DICK, USED THE GOLDEN AGE OF AMERICAN WHALING
AS ITS BACKDROP. PHOTOGRAPH BY RODNEY DEWEY.

FROM THE CONCLUSION OF THE WAR OF 1812 THROUGH THE TWI-
light of the 1850s, the American whaling industry went through a
period of unparalleled growth, productivity, and profits. During this
golden age, U.S. whaling merchants, unburdened by international conflict and encouraged by the growing domestic and foreign demand,
built the largest whaling fleet in history, a veritable armada that peaked

at 735 ships in 1846, out of a total of 900 whaleships worldwide.[1] The tens of thousands of men who manned these ships traveled millions of miles in their ever-lengthening hunt for leviathans. They pursued and killed hundreds of thousands of sperm, right, bowhead, gray, and humpback whales in the Atlantic, Pacific, Indian, and Arctic Oceans, and in the process discovered new waters and new lands.[2] The value of the oil and bone brought back to port made whaling, by the middle of the nineteenth century, the third largest industry, after shoes and cotton, in Massachusetts, and according to one economic analysis, the fifth largest industry in the United States, leading U.S. senator William H. Seward to call whaling an important "source of national wealth."[3] At its height whaling provided a livelihood for seventy thousand people and represented a capital investment of $70 million, while whaleships accounted for roughly one-fifth of the nation's registered merchant tonnage.[4] In 1853, the industry's most profitable year, the fleet killed more than 8,000 whales to produce 103,000 barrels of sperm oil, 260,000 barrels of whale oil, and 5.7 million pounds of baleen, all of which generated sales of $11 million.[5]

The golden age is the lens through which people generally view America's whaling heritage. It is when New Bedford overtook Nantucket as the nation's whaling capital, and scores of coastal towns launched their own whaling enterprises hoping to cash in on this lucrative trade. It is when the maniacal Captain Ahab met his match and his destiny in the form of Moby-Dick. It is when the whaling industry spawned most of its greatest stories of human drive, perseverance, success, and failure, and when the American whalemen, harpoons in hand, attained mythic status.

On Nantucket the suffering and despondency brought on by the War of 1812 was quickly replaced with almost unbridled joy and optimism come war's end. The merchants who had managed to hold on through the long and desperate years now sprang to life, and the business of whaling, as Obed Macy observed, "commenced with alacrity."[6] Although the war had claimed half of the island's whaling fleet, twenty-three vessels still remained, and it seemed as if the entire town had but one goal—to get those vessels and others under construction off to sea. Before the end of 1815 twenty-five whaleships sailed from Nantucket. A contemporary article noted the departure of this small fleet and stated that the war-weary whalemen of New England "have at this moment as much cause of joy as any people under the sun. The produce of their labour is in high demand, and, literally speaking, with every fish they draw out of the sea, they draw up a *piece of silver.*"⁷ Sperm and whale oil found ready markets both here and abroad, and by 1819 Nantucket's whaling fleet had grown to sixty-one vessels. The next year that number rose to seventy-two, and a year later it was approaching ninety.⁸

One newspaper editorialist, noting Nantucket's smallness in size and population, and the great losses it suffered during the war, heaped praise on the island and its people. "We are struck with admiration at the invincible hardihood and enterprise of this little active, industrious and friendly community, whose harpoons have penetrated with success every nook and corner of every ocean."⁹ When Jared Sparks, who would later become president of Harvard University, arrived in Nantucket harbor in October 1826, he noted that there were "whale ships on every side and hardly a man to be seen on the wharves who had not circumnavigated the globe, and chased a whale, if not slain his victim, in the Broad Pacific." Although Sparks was impressed by the ten thousand sheep that grazed on the island, he had no doubt that "the absorbing business of Nantucket is the whale fishery. Many had made themselves rich by it, and it gives life to all."¹⁰

In September 1830, when the *Loper* returned from the Pacific brimming with 2,280 barrels of sperm oil after just fourteen and a half months at sea, the *Nantucket Inquirer* labeled it the "Greatest Voyage ever made."¹¹ While other voyages had brought back more oil, none had brought back so much in so little time. The *Inquirer's* editor mused that if the captain's "unparalleled success is the effect of superior *skill* in the art of whaling, would it not be proper for him to communicate it to others of the same profession, who are now *three* years in performing exploits for which he requires little more than *one*?"¹² The grateful owners of the *Loper* staged a sumptuous dinner for the captain and crew, preceded by a triumphant march through the streets of Nantucket. Instead of guns over their shoulders, the men had harpoons and lances as they stepped lively over the cobblestone streets in time with the musical accompaniment. At dinner, glasses were raised and toasts filled the air. To Capt. Obed Starbuck, "No man living has given so much real light to the world, in the same length of time." To the many whalemen who had died, "May they never want oil to smooth their ways;" and to whaling, "That war which causes no grief, the success of which produces no tears—war with the monsters of the deep."[13] The most interesting toasts of the evening were offered by Absalom Boston, a prominent black Nantucketer and fomer whaleman who shared with the *Loper's* nearly all-black crew his reflections on the dismal status of black America, and whose words were "recorded," as Nathaniel Philbrick notes, "in dubious dialect in the *Inquirer*."[14] To fellow people of color, Boston shouted out, "May de enemy of our celebration and of African freedom, hab 'ternal itch and no benefit of scratch so long as he lib," and to the iconic city of Boston, "Where seed of liberty come from—Washington plant him, Lafayette till him, may African reap him."[15] Boston's toasts were heartily cheered by all, and in particular by the black crewmen, who had the good fortune to be part of a community, given its strong Quaker influences, that had long since decided that black men were not pieces of property but human beings who had a right to all the benefits that entailed. The *Loper's* extraordinary voyage was not the only high point for the Nantucket whaling community in 1830. That is also when the *Sarah* returned after three years at sea, filled to overflowing with 3,497 barrels of sperm oil worth nearly ninety thousand dollars, the largest single voyage ever recorded on the island.[16]

Nantucket's whaling fleet built on its success throughout the 1830s and early 1840s, keeping the island's numerous oil and candle factories busy. William Comstock, writing in 1838, eloquently and in a rather racy manner captured the buoyant mood of the time and the island's intense connection to whaling. "In the present day, every energy, every thought, and every wish of the Nantucketman is engrossed by Sperm Oil and Candles. No man is entitled to respect among them, who has not struck a whale; or at least, killed a porpoise: and it is a necessary for a young man who would be a successful lover, to go on a voyage around Cape Horn, as it was for a young Knight, in the days of chivalry, to go on a tour of adventures, and soil his maiden arms with blood, before he could aspire to the snowy hand of his mistress, and enjoy the delights of 'ladye love.'"[17]

These good times, however, would prove ephemeral. Nantucket's fall from its lofty perch was the result of many factors, all of which conspired to dampen the hopes of the island's whaling aristocracy. First in line was the sandbar at the harbor's mouth. In the early years of Nantucket's rise as a whaling port, the bar posed no problem to navigation. Although it was a mere seven to eleven feet below the surface, depending on the tides, the bar was deep enough to let the relatively small whaling vessels of the day float over it. But the longer voyages of later years required larger ships, and larger ships, especially when laden with cargo, rode too low in the water to make the same passage. To overcome this obstacle, Nantucket's whaling merchants employed lighters, or small vessels, to ferry supplies and cargo over the bar, to and from whaleships anchored either beyond the harbor's mouth or at Edgartown on Martha's Vineyard, which was increasingly becoming Nantucket's alternative port. Lightering added time and expense to each voyage, and placed the Nantucketers at a competitive disadvantage with their whaling peers on the mainland, who could load and offload their vessels more efficiently while they were tied up at the wharves. For years, as frustration mounted, Nantucketers debated what to do about their predicament. By the early 1800s popular opinion coalesced around a plan for dredging a channel through the bar, but Nantucket's appeals to Congress to undertake the project were rejected, and the town's locally financed dredging effort failed. So, up through the early 1840s the sandbar problem persisted, much to the chagrin of Nantucket's whalemen. Then, in 1842, Peter Folger Ewer provided a solution.[18]

Borrowing from earlier Dutch designs, Ewer built two hollow wooden pontoons, connected by sturdy chains, to create a floating drydock that could ferry whaling vessels over the bar. The mechanics of these pontoons, which Ewer called "camels" because of their ability to hold great quantities of water and carry heavy loads, were relatively simple. Each pontoon, which was 135 feet long, 19 feet deep, and 29 feet wide, was flat on the top, the bottom, and the outer edge, but contoured on the inner edge to fit the curves of a vessel's hull. The camels used the same process to transport whaleships both into and out of the harbor. The pontoons would be flooded with seawater, causing them to sink. Once a whaleship was nestled between the pontoons, the camels' steam engines would then pump the water out of the pontoons, causing the camels and their cargo to float high enough to be towed over the bar. The camels would then be flooded again, thereby sinking and leaving the vessel free to make its way to the wharf or to begin its next voyage.

The camels' inaugural trial came on September 4, 1842. The guinea-pig vessel, the *Phebe*, was fully loaded and ready to begin its voyage.

The camels were maneuvered into place and the *Phebe* was lifted high in the water, but once the towing began the weight of the ship proved to be too great. In rapid succession all the chains broke, and as each one went asunder, it created a thunderous report like a cannon firing, which reverberated throughout the town, startling the locals. The *Phebe* sank back into the water and returned to the wharf for extensive repairs to her copper-sheathed hull, which was greatly damaged by the grating of the chains. This was hardly an auspicious debut, but Ewer forged ahead. He blamed himself for using regular ship's chains, rather than waiting for the ones designed specifically for the camels. And when those new chains arrived, shortly after the *Phebe* fiasco, Ewer convinced the owner of the whaleship *Constitution* to give the camels another try. This time they worked flawlessly, and on September 21, 1842, the *Constitution* floated over the bar into open water. Less than a month later, the camels passed an even more demanding test when they brought the *Peru*, laden with sperm whale oil from the Indian Ocean, over the bar. An errand boy living with Ewer's mother at the time wrote that "more than 1,000 people had assembled to view the novel scene, and someone cried out 'three cheers for Mr. Ewer.'" The *New Bedford Weekly Mercury* observed that, "The circumstance caused great rejoicing in Nantucket . . . the bells were rung, and a salute of 100 guns fired." Another newspaper report proclaimed that "the ultimate success of the Camels is now placed beyond a question. They will be the means of securing to Nantucket much business which has heretofore been done elsewhere."[19]

The camels provided a cost-effective alternative to lightering, and scores of whaleships hitched a ride over the bar. But in 1849, just seven years after their introduction, the camels made their last run. The much hoped for revitalization of whaling on Nantucket, which some thought that the camels might spark, failed to materialize. The camels could not overcome larger forces that were driving Nantucket's whaling fleet toward extinction. Nantucket's position within the industry was diminished, in part, because its whalemen failed to respond nimbly to changes in demand and to the availability of whales. While their competitors exploited the expanding markets for whale oil and baleen, and sought out new whaling grounds when the old ones had been depleted, Nantucket whalemen continued to hunt sperm whales almost exclusively, and to return to the same grounds year after year even though they were becoming less productive over time.[20] The Nantucket fleet's situation worsened in July 1846 when "the Great Fire" destroyed much of the town's waterfront, and with it a considerable part of the island's whaling infrastructure.[21] Then, two years later, California beckoned.

ON DECEMBER 5, 1848, President James K. Polk informed the nation that the fantastic rumors emanating from California were true. "The accounts of the abundance of gold in that territory," Polk said in his annual message to Congress, "are of such extraordinary character as would scarcely command belief were they not corroborated by authentic reports of officers in the public service."[22] Gold fever swept over the East Coast, and whalemen from Nantucket, New Bedford, Sag Harbor, New London, and other whaling ports sailed for the Golden Gate in San Francisco, drawn to California's rivers and streams by dreams of instant wealth.[23] Eastern whaling merchants could do little to stop this hemorrhaging of whaling talent. Even if their men were not leaving to pan for gold, they might still head to California to earn money as carpenters or laborers at rates many times what they could earn on a whaling cruise.[24]

San Francisco Harbor became a floating graveyard as scores if not hundreds of ships, including a great many whaleships, remained behind as their captains and crews set off for the interior. The interrupted voyage of the *Minerva*, out of New Bedford, offered evidence of how powerful the lure of gold could be. After whaling in the Pacific, the *Minerva*'s captain wrote to the ship's owners about a sudden change of plans. "I went to San Francisco to recruit . . . but the excitement there in relation to the discovery of gold made it impossible to prevent the crew from running away. Three of the crew in attempting to swim ashore were drowned, and the ship's company soon became too much reduced to continue the whaling voyage."[25]

Nantucket came down with a particularly severe case of gold fever. Hundreds of Nantucket whalemen and more than a dozen ships set sail for California.[26] The *Nantucket Inquirer* fed this fantasy by providing its readers with amazing visions. California "is likely to prove a perfect *El Dorado*," wrote the editor. "Portions of it are reputed to be almost paved with gold."[27] Although the Gold Rush quickly faded, the damage to

Nantucket's whaling fleet did not. Many of the whalemen and most of the whaleships that left for California never came back. In 1852 a Nantucket resident painted a depressing scene of the island's whaling business, noting that it "does not seem to flourish much in this seat of ancient glories. . . . The *Empire* which arrived here lately, has been sold at New Bedford. The *Daniel Webster* is to be sold next week. So they go. Only three whalers are at our wharves. . . . Of our thirty-two oil manufactories, only four are in operation. The Camels rot on the shore after costing $50,000. To crown all, our hotel is illuminated and perfumed with 'burning fluid'" (rather than the sperm whale oil that had made Nantucket famous).[28] Two years later oil took another hit when gaslight made its first appearance on the island. Throughout the 1850s and 1860s Nantucket's whaling fleet dwindled to the point where there were only a handful of voyages each year. The end came on November 16, 1869, when the *Oak*, Nantucket's last whaling vessel, sailed for the Pacific Ocean, never to return.[29]

NANTUCKET'S DECLINE as a whaling port coincided with New Bedford's rise. At the end of the War of 1812, New Bedford was, wrote historian Leonard Ellis, "in a sad condition. . . . The wheels of industry had long since ceased to move, and her fleet of vessels that had brought wealth and prosperity had been driven from the ocean. Her shops and shipyards were closed, the wharves were lined with dismasted vessels, the port was shut against every enterprise by the close blockade of the enemy, and the citizens wandered about the streets in enforced idleness."[30] But, like Nantucket, New Bedford sprang back quickly. Its whaling merchants expanded their operations by taking advantage of many of the factors that had originally brought Joseph Rotch to the area in 1765—the deep harbor, the heavily wooded forests, and the town's convenient location on the mainland. New Bedford's connection to the mushrooming network of railroads inserted the town directly into the stream of commerce, and gave it an efficient means of transporting supplies in and whaling products out. Capitalizing on the growing demand for sperm oil, whale oil, and baleen, New Bedford's whaling fleet grew at a phenomenal rate, eclipsing Nantucket's in the 1820s. From that point forward the gap between the two ports rapidly widened, and by 1850 Nantucket's fleet of 62 paled in comparison with

New Bedford's 288. New Bedford continued its climb until 1857, when it peaked at 329 whaleships, roughly half of the entire American whaling fleet. While New Bedford's geographical advantages were major factors in its meteoric rise, part of its success was due to the willingness of its whaling captains to hunt for all types of marketable whales wherever they might be, rather than focusing, as Nantucket had, largely on one species or locale.[31] Yet another reason for New Bedford's success had to do with the intensity with which it pursued whaling, bringing with it an extreme devotion to the industry that gave it a competitive edge. As Emerson observed, "New Bedford is not nearer to the whales than New London or Portland, yet they have all the equipment for a whaler ready, and they hug an oil-cask like a brother."[32]

America led the world in whaling, and during most of the golden age New Bedford was the nation's whaling capital. A forest of masts lined the harbor, silently witnessing the stream of ships exiting and entering the port. The waterfront was in a constant state of frenetic action, as armies of men loaded and unloaded the ships with seasoned familiarity, while crowds gathered to celebrate departing and returning whalemen. Shipyards built new ships and repaired those that were worn by the ravages of age. Riggers set thousands of square feet of sails, caulkers filled miles of seams with oakum, and carpenters hammered copper sheathing on the hulls to keep the ravenous and destructive marine boring worms from turning the ship's wooden skin into a pulpy, porous mass that would allow water to rush in at the slightest provocation.[33] The docks and quays were covered with enormous casks of oil and bundles of baleen arranged like sheaves of wheat drying in the sun. Nearly a score of chandlers pressed, molded, and packaged spermaceti candles for the well-to-do, and overflowing warehouses shipped whaling products throughout the United States and the world at large. The streets and alleys abutting the waterfront were lined with the shops of blacksmiths, coopers, and outfitters who supplied the whaling trade; the offices of shipping agents who hired the crews; and the counting rooms of the whaling merchants in which profits and losses were tallied. Farther up, on Johnny Cake Hill, toiled the insurance men who reduced the monetary risks of whaling, and the bankers who helped finance the voyages. Nearby was the Seaman's Bethel, where whalemen went to pray for forgiveness and protection before heading to sea. The spiritual comfort these men received was tempered by the words on the walls. There, at eye level and ringing the room, were marble cenotaphs that told the tragic tales of whalemen who had been lost at sea.

IN MEMORY OF

CAPT. WM. SWAIN

ASSOCIATE

MASTER OF THE CHRISTOPHER MITCHELL OF NANTUCKET

THIS WORTHY MAN, AFTER FASTNING TO A WHALE

WAS CARRIED OVERBOARD BY THE LINE, AND

DROWNED.

MAY 19TH 1844

IN THE 49TH YR. OF HIS AGE

BE YE ALSO READY: FOR IN SUCH AN HOUR AS YE THINK NOT THE SON OF MAN COMETH.[34]

In between their devotions, the men couldn't help but see these remembrances of the dead and wonder if they might be next.

Farther away from the waterfront stood the stately homes of the whaling captains and shipowners. "Nowhere in all America," wrote Melville, "will you find more patrician-like houses, parks, and gardens more opulent, than in New Bedford . . . all these brave houses and flowery gardens came from the Atlantic, Pacific, and Indian Oceans. One and all, they were harpooned and dragged up hither from the bottom of the sea."[35] Melville was not exaggerating. By midcentury New Bedford, whose population had swelled from three thousand in 1830 to more than twenty thousand in the 1850s, was arguably the richest city in the United States per capita.[36] Whaling fortunes made by the Rotches, the Russells, the Rodmans, the Morgans, the Delanos, and the Bournes reverberated through the economy, as the men whom the leviathan had made rich invested their wealth not only in whaling but in other businesses and philanthropies as well. And it was not only men who benefited financially from whaling. Hetty Green, who would become the richest woman in America at the beginning of the twentieth century (and be labeled the "Witch of Wall Street" by her detractors), got her start as the main heir to the great New Bedford whaling fortune created by the Howland family.[37] But there was also another side to New

Bedford—the grimy, dark, and mean streets where the men who manned the whaleships lived. These were what one historian referred to as the "squalid sections," such as the appropriately named "Hard-Dig," that housed "the saloons, where delirium and death were sold, [and] the boarding houses, the dance halls and houses where female harpies reigned and vice and violence were rampant." One of the most notorious destinations in the poorer part of town was the *Ark*, a whaleship that had been converted into a floating "brothel of the worst character," replete with a houselike superstructure and rooms to rent.[38]

With the hub of the rapidly expanding whaling industry in New Bedford, it is not surprising that the country's first and only newspaper devoted to whaling would be published there. The inaugural issue of the weekly *Whalemen's Shipping List and Merchant's Transcript* hit the streets on March 17, 1843. "It is our intention," the editors declared, "to present to our readers, a weekly report carefully corrected from the latest advices, of every vessel engaged in the Whaling business from ports of the United States, together with the prices current of our staple commodities, and interesting items of commercial intelligence." Now, rather than digging through traditional newspapers to glean valuable information about their trade, whalemen could find it all in one place. The *Whalemen's Shipping List* also provided a more personal service. "We have been led to believe," the editors continued, "that a paper of this kind would be interesting to . . . the parents and wives, the sisters, sweethearts and friends of that vast multitude of men, whose business is upon the mighty deep, and who are for years separated from those to whom they are dear."[39]

Although Nantucket and New Bedford were the largest whaling ports during the golden age, they were hardly the only ones. More than sixty other coastal communities pursued whaling at one time or another between the 1820s and the 1850s.[40] New London and Sag Harbor headed this list, and in their best years were home to between sixty and seventy whaleships.[41] At its height, in the late 1840s, New London's whaling fleet was second only to New Bedford's in size.[42] New London produced many well-known whaling captains, including the Smith brothers, all five of whom mastered their own ships, completing a combined total of at least thirty-five voyages and earning well over $1 million.[43] Perhaps the most famous New London whaling captain was James Monroe Buddington, the man who found the HMS *Resolute*.

In May 1845 renowned British explorer John Franklin led two ships to the Arctic on an expedition to discover the still-elusive Northwest Passage linking the Atlantic and the Pacific Oceans. Within a couple of months Franklin, his men, and his ships vanished. During one of the subsequent rescue missions, the *Resolute,* a six-hundred-ton bark, was trapped in the ice, and in May 1854, it was abandoned. Enter Captain Buddington. In May 1855, as master of the *George Henry,* Buddington left New London on a whaling cruise to the Davis Strait, and on September 10 he spied a vessel in the distance, listing severely to one side. It was the *Resolute,* and it had drifted in the ice pack more than one thousand miles in sixteen months. Buddington was well aware of the *Resolute*'s history, and he decided that salvaging it and returning it to port would be far more remunerative than whaling, so he and his men worked to make the *Resolute* seaworthy again, freeing it of ice and pumping out the water that filled its lower decks. This done, Buddington split his men between the *George Henry* and the *Resolute* and took command of the latter. For two months Buddington and his shorthanded crew sailed the battered and rickety *Resolute* through heavy gales and violent seas before arriving in New London.

The British government honored Buddington's heroics by announcing that it had waived its rights to the *Resolute,* and instead wanted to leave the ship to Buddington to dispose of as he saw fit. Congress, however, had a better idea. It purchased the *Resolute* from the owners of the *George Henry* for forty thousand dollars, and in a diplomatic effort to improve the United States' rocky relations with Britain, returned the ship to its original owners. When the *Resolute* arrived back in England in December 1856, Queen Victoria headed the welcoming party. On the *Resolute*'s main deck, Capt. Henry J. Hartstene of the U.S. Navy delivered a message from President Franklin Pierce and the American people, stating that the return of the ship was "evidence of a friendly feeling to your sovereignty, . . . [as well] as a token of love, admiration and respect to Your Majesty personally," to which the queen responded, "I thank you, sir."[44] While the story ended well for the Americans and the British, it was a bust for Buddington. Although he would forever be remembered as the savior of the *Resolute,* he claimed that he saw not a dime of the forty thousand dollars windfall the owners of the *George Henry* had received on account of his actions.[45]

Sag Harbor, which is situated on the southern tip of Long Island, reached its peak as a whaling center in 1847, when thirty-two ships brought back roughly four thousand barrels of sperm oil, sixty-four thousand barrels of whale oil, and six hundred thousand pounds of baleen.[46] James Fenimore Cooper was one of many men who caught whaling fever in Sag Harbor. During a visit to Shelter Island, New York, in 1818 Cooper met one of his wife's relatives, Charles T. Dering, who was also a shipping merchant. The two got to talking, and Cooper, with no other mode of employment in sight but with plenty of ready cash, joined forces with Dering and other investors to launch a whaling company. The venture not only promised the potential for success, given the whaling industry's growth in recent years, but it also allowed Cooper to maintain his connection to the sea. Over the next three years Cooper's whaling company sponsored three voyages out of Sag Harbor, all of which yielded poor returns. Given this track record it is doubtful that Cooper could have remained in the whaling business much longer, but, as it turned out, he didn't have to. While his ships were faring poorly at sea, Cooper was writing, and in 1821 he achieved his first commercial success, with the publication of *The Spy*. From that point forward literature became his sole vocation, and he created such classics as *The Last of the Mohicans* and *The Pioneers*. In one of his novels, *The Sea Lions*, published in 1849, Cooper wrote admiringly of Sag Harbor's whaling heritage, claiming that "Nantucket itself had not more . . . of the true whaling *esprit de corps*," than did this small Long Island community.[47]

Continuing down the list of whaling ports in the golden age, the number of vessels and voyages quickly diminishes. There were Fairhaven, Provincetown, and Westport, Massachusetts; Stonington, Connecticut; and Warren, Rhode Island—all of which, at their peaks, were home to between twenty-two and fifty whaling vessels each. Next came a raft of cities and towns, including Cold Spring, New York; Bucksport, Maine; Portsmouth, New Hampshire; Gloucester, Massachusetts; Mystic, Connecticut; Newark, New Jersey; Philadelphia, Pennsylvania; and Edenton, North Carolina—all of which had only a handful of vessels, and in some cases only one.[48] The driving force behind this great explosion up and down the coast was, of course, money. Some of the smaller ports even engaged in a public relations campaign to encourage whaling merchants to relocate. On May 4, 1833, the editors of the *Gloucester Telegraph*, jealous that Nantucket whalemen were thinking of migrating to Wiscasset, Maine, where the harbor was deep and rarely froze, wrote, "If it is really a fact that any of the good people of Nantucket intend to remove in search of better advantages that are to be found there, we would urge their stopping in at Gloucester. If ever a harbor was intended for extensive business, this is that one. It is comeatable [accessible] in all seasons and at all times; it is spacious and safe for vessels in storms . . . and, upon a moderate calculation, *one thousand whale ships* might ride at anchor as *slick as grease.*"[49]

Like Gloucester, Wilmington, Delaware, hoped to build a whaling fleet from the ground up.[50] In January 1832 a Wilmington merchant wrote a letter to the *Delaware Journal* in which he urged his peers to get into whaling because of its great profitability. "The eastern cities and towns have pursued whaling for about a century, and in no *one instance* when it has been undertaken, have they abandoned it—No— they have increased rapidly, and all those that are now pursuing it, are in a prosperous . . . condition."[51] By late 1833 the prowhaling forces in Wilmington had gained considerable strength, and on October 24 a large crowd of local residents met in city hall to discuss the possibility of establishing a whaling company, and they appointed a committee to further explore the matter. After just eleven days of review, the committee, confidently predicting that whaling in Wilmington would undoubtedly succeed, enthusiastically urged that the Wilmington Whaling Company be created. Wilmington's leading businessmen rushed to buy stock in the new venture, quickly giving it one hundred thousand dollars of working capital. As historian Kenneth R. Martin points out, to the somewhat naive and eager Wilmingtonians the whaling business seemed relatively straightforward. They would have to purchase a vessel or have one built, hire whaling captains and skeleton crews from one of the New England whaling communities, supplement those crews with eager and youthful men from Delaware, send the ships to the whaling grounds, and wait for the ships' triumphant and profitable return. And that is exactly what they set out to do.

The first vessel of Wilmington's fleet was the *Ceres*, an old and haggard ship out of New Bedford, yet one with some good years left. Along with the *Ceres* came Capt. Richard Weeden, a seasoned New Bedford whaling captain, and a few of his mates and boatsteerers. Much of the rest of the crew was comprised of wealthy Wilmingtonians, who had little firsthand knowledge of what a whaling voyage entailed, and rather viewed it as a grand adventure that would be great fun. They were what veteran whalemen called "green hands," landlubbers with no experience on board ship, a fact that became apparent as soon as they tried to leave port on May 6, 1834. Minutes after casting off the *Ceres*, its crew almost helpless against the tide, grounded in the mud, well within sight of much of the town, which had turned out to cheer on their men and say good-bye but now could only look on with a combination of amusement and concern. The *Ceres* remained mired for a couple of hours until a steamer pulled it free, and after one more grounding it finally began its cruise for sperm whales in the Pacific.

The trip was a failure, the ship returning in the fall of 1837 not even half full, with less than one thousand barrels of sperm oil on board. Just a few weeks from port, Captain Weeden began to fret about how the good people of Wilmington might react to this extremely poor showing, given that the voyage had began with such high expectations. Rather than let the people down right away, he decided to dupe them. He had his men fill more than one hundred casks with seawater to make the ship ride lower so that it would seem to be heavily laden with oil. That way, when the ship appeared on the horizon and came to dock, those on hand to welcome the whalemen might think that their prayers for a greasy voyage had been answered. Such duplicity prompted one of the crew to comment, "This looks rather blank, deceiving the people of Wilmington with the flattering hopes of our returning home in 30 months, with a full cargo."[52] If any were fooled by this rather silly ploy, they were soon disabused of that notion when they heard that the voyage had lost $5,228. The Wilmington youth who had so enthusiastically signed on to the *Ceres* were now much the wiser about the rigors and frequent disappointments of whaling, and most of them were just thankful to be home.

While the *Ceres* was away, the Wilmington Whaling Company had proceeded with its business plan, raising more funds and buying three additional ships, the *Lucy Ann*, the *Superior*, and the *North America*. Then, in 1839, the company added a fifth and final whaleship to its fleet, the *Jefferson*. Putting aside the *Ceres*'s first disastrous voyage, the Wilmington Whaling Company's fleet fared fairly well during the late 1830s, posting a number of profitable if not impressive voyages. But in the early 1840s, the company suffered an abrupt reversal. A major blow was landed when the *North America* foundered on a reef off Australia, losing its cargo and nearly the entire crew. This, combined with a couple of exceedingly poor voyages, low prices for whale oil, and the lingering effects of a nationwide depression, led the stockholders in 1842 to vote to liquidate the company's holdings, a task that was completed in 1846. Ironically most of Wilmington's whaleships were sold to northern whaling ports, whose success Wilmington had so earnestly hoped to emulate. Wilmington was not alone in its failure to capitalize on whaling. Many, though certainly not all, of the minor ports that went whaling during the heady days of the golden age were ultimately unsuccessful. Like Wilmington, these ports optimistically forged ahead only to discover that whaling was a hard and unforgiving business that required more skill than luck.

PART OF THE REASON that American whaling surged ahead during the golden age, notwithstanding the lackluster performance of many of the minor ports, was that American whalemen were simply the best at what they did. In 1843 the *Merchants' Magazine and Commercial Review* proudly proclaimed, "The enterprise and success of this fishery, as carried on in American ships, totally disables any other nation from competing with them."[53] And of all the nations that were thus disabled, none was more so than the British. The historic rivalry between Britain and America evaporated as the British whaling fleet, a major player in whaling between the Revolutionary War and the War of 1812, faded from view. British whaleships, which had larger crews, higher costs, and less whaling talent on board, failed to compete with their American counterparts. The Americans caught more whales in less time, undercut the British in world markets by offering the best prices, and did a better job of seeking out and exploiting new whaling grounds. And the British government's decision, in 1824, to end its long-standing policy of subsidizing the whaling fleet, only hastened, even if just by a little bit, the fleet's demise.[54] In a letter to the *London Times* in 1846, an Englishman who served nearly six years on board American whaleships pulled no punches in telling his fellow citizens exactly why the Americans were so much better at whaling than the British. "A few words will explain it,—the greater cost of fitting out whalers here, the drunkenness, incapacity, and want of energy of the masters and crews"—all of which were traits that he claimed the Americans didn't share. "I have little sympathy for the Americans," the writer continued, "for as a body, I do not believe you could well find a more dishonest people, but their energy in bringing the trade to the pitch it has arrived at, deserves the highest encomium."[55]

The explosive growth of the American whaling industry generated an equally explosive demand for labor. In the mid-1850s, New Bedford whaleships alone employed ten thousand seamen, with all the other ports accounting for another ten thousand. Supplying this quantity of bodies was no easy task. The captains and officers were usually hired directly by the shipowners or shipping agents, while the latter were responsible for recruiting the crews. To get men in the door, the agents advertised positions in newspapers, at public establishments, and on the streets. The pitch was always optimistic, like this one:

LANDSMEN WANTED!!

One thousand stout young men, Americans, wanted for the fleet of whaleships, now fitting out for the North and South Pacific fisheries. Extra chances given to Coopers, Carpenters, and Blacksmiths. None but industrious, young men with good recommendations, taken. Such will have superior chances for advancement. Outfits, to the amount of Seventy-Five Dollars furnished to each individual before proceeding to sea. Persons desirous to avail themselves of the present splendid opportunity of seeing the world and at the same time acquiring a profitable business, will do well to make early application to the undersigned.[56]

Exciting and encouraging words such as these camouflaged a less than "splendid" reality. Whaleship owners, so desperate for labor, rarely had the luxury of focusing on recommendations or the upstanding nature of the applicants. In the mid-1800s "industrious young men" had plenty of shoreside opportunities that were both less dangerous and more remunerative than becoming a whaleman. So the owners were often forced to take what they could get, which was usually green hands who were not infrequently some combination of penniless, delinquent, or drunk.[57] The quality of recruits, or more accurately the lack thereof, was a constant source of irritation in the industry, as an article from a Nantucket newspaper in 1836 makes clear: "Too many ungovernable lads, runaways from parental authority, or candidates for corrective treatment, too many vagabonds just from the clutches of the police of European and American cities—too many convicts . . . are suffered to enlist in this service. . . . The whale fishery shall not be converted into a mere engine for the repair of cracked reputations and the chastisement of those against the reception of whom even the jail doors revolt."[58] There were also, to be sure, whalemen who were, as one magazine called them, "hardy, intelligent sons of our soil," who came from fine families, had decent if not stellar educations, and simply chose to sign up believing it would be an adventure, a means of character building, or simply a potentially rewarding job, but they were a distinct minority.[59] The seventy-five-dollar signing bonus recruits received sounded generous until one realized that it was only an advance against wages, and from that amount the men would have to pay for clothes, food, and other supplies. As for seeing the world, if that meant gazing on seemingly endless stretches of ocean, then it was true enough that a whaleman would see a good portion of the world. But if by seeing the world one meant experiencing exciting stretches of terra firma, then a whaling voyage was the last place one wanted to be.

To ensnare recruits agents would usually echo the advertisements' message and focus on the positive attributes of whaling, even if these virtues where partially or wholly fictitious. "These shipping agents were," observed historian Elmo Paul Hohman, "marvels of suave deceit and shameless misrepresentation, if contemporary accounts of their methods may be credited. False promises and fluent mendacity were resorted to whenever it seemed advisable."[60] A whaleman in the late 1840s wrote of how "the runaway young man from the country is entrapped [by an agent]; stories are told him, which he, from his want of knowledge readily believes, and thus becomes an easy victim to the wiles of those heartless men who get their living by selling men for a term of years, uncertain in their number, at five dollars a head."[61] Samuel Eliot Morison told of a Boston agent who, after expounding on the "imaginary joys" of whaling to a Maine plowboy, "concluded confidentially: 'Now, Hiram, I'll be *honest* with yer. When yer out in the boats chasin' whales, yer git yer mince-pie *cold*!'"[62] A duplicitous agent out of New York devised a particularly ingenious scheme of recruiting. He hired a con artist to befriend young men new to the city and encourage them to go whaling with a compelling pitch. First the con artist would say that he was going on a whaling voyage out of New Bedford and that he was leaving the next day on a steamer headed for that port. The con artist would then plead with the newcomer to join him, so that they could share the adventure. Finally, to seal the deal, the con artist would assure his new best friend that there were great profits to be made in whaling—at least "a thousand dollars" for three years' work. Duly impressed, the newcomer would march down to the agent's office, accompanied by his new best friend, and sign on. Since agents only got paid if the men they signed actually showed up for duty, the New York agent had to make sure that his new recruit made it to his ship. The agent would, therefore, have the recruit spend the evening and the next morning with the con artist, all the while talking animatedly about the voyage to come. But when the new recruit finally got on board the steamer headed for New Bedford, he would soon discover that his putative friend had fast disappeared. Only then did the recruit realize that he "had been gulled."[63] The ploys used by agents to keep their recruits in line ranged from keeping them under close surveillance to, in extreme cases, forcibly delivering the men to the ship even if upon further reflection the men no longer wanted to ship out. Despite such tactics the agents didn't always get their men. Some recruits, sobered by the reality of their impending departure and, perhaps, clearer visions of the whaling life, failed to show up. Others were yanked away at the last minute by relatives who wanted to keep impetuous and wide-eyed young men from making a major life mistake.[64]

While the captains and mates, for the most part, were still pulled from the ranks of white Yankee stock, the men who served under them were a polyglot mixture of white and black Americans, Pacific islanders, Portuguese, Azoreans, Creoles, Cape Verdeans, Peruvians, New Zealanders, West Indians, Colombians, and a smattering of Europeans. According to one nineteenth-century observer, "A more heterogeneous group of men has never assembled in so small a space than is always found in the forecastle of a New Bedford sperm whaler."[65] Some of the crew were picked up en route to the whaling grounds, and in many instances this was part of the plan, with the captains stopping in foreign ports expressly to hire new hands. In other cases, however, the captains were forced to make such layovers because of the need to replenish their crew as result of desertions along the way or the loss of men due to injury or death. Many of the foreigners who were thus enlisted into whaling chose to settle in American ports rather than return to their homelands, creating cultural enclaves where English was a second language, if it was spoken at all.

A whaling voyage was a unique opportunity for black men. In a country that still condoned slavery, shipping out as a deckhand on a whaleship provided a black man with a rare measure of dignity and self-worth.[66] At sea the color of one's skin was less important than the skills one possessed and their contribution to the success of the trip. As one black seaman put it, "There is not that nice distinction made in whaling as there is in the naval and merchant services. A coloured man is only known and looked upon as a man, and is promoted in rank according to his ability and skill to perform the same duties as a white man."[67] Just as important to the black whaleman's sense of pride was the fact that he received equal pay for equal work.[68] This is not to suggest that whaleships were bastions of equality and brotherhood among men. There were still many whites who despised their black shipmates, even as they relied on them for their lives and livelihood. As one whaleman from Kentucky, who firmly believed in the rectitude of slavery, noted, "It was . . . particularly galling to my feelings to be compelled to live in the forecastle with a brutal negro, who, conscious that he was upon an equality with the sailors, presumed upon his equality to a degree that was insufferable."[69]

A few black men nonetheless became officers on whaleships, and some, such as Absalom Boston, the man who so heartily toasted the *Loper*'s black crew on their triumphant return to Nantucket in 1830, even became captains. Born on the island in 1785, Boston, a third-generation Nantucketer, was raised in the section of the island known as "New Guinea," a name that reflected the African roots of many who lived there.[70] His grandparents, who likely arrived on Nantucket in the mid-1700s, had been slaves who were later freed by their owner, and his uncle, Prince Boston, was the man who gained some measure of fame when William Rotch paid him, and not his alleged owner, directly for his work on the whaling sloop *Friendship*. Absalom Boston pursued the life of a laborer and a mariner, and in 1822, when he was thirty-seven, he took command of the *Industry*, a whaleship owned and crewed entirely by black men. This ship full of "coloured tars" was, as one of the crew commented, "quite strange."[71] The *Industry* fared miserably, at least as far as whaling went, returning to Nantucket within six months with a paltry seventy barrels of oil. This failure appears not to have bothered the crew much, and one of them even penned an admiring verse in honor of their leader.

> *Here is health to Captain Boston*
> *His officers and crew*
> *And if he gets another craft*
> *To sea with him I'll go.*[72]

Boston never did go to sea again, becoming instead a successful merchant and landowner, and one of the most respected and wealthy blacks on Nantucket.

There was also another side to the blacks' relationship with whaling. To some slaves, and possibly a considerable number, whaling was viewed as a means of escape. That was the case for John Thompson, who, around 1840, when questioned about his background by the captain of a whaling ship he was on, responded, "I am a fugitive slave from Maryland, and have a family in Philadelphia; but fearing to remain there any longer, I thought I would go a whaling voyage, as being [a] place where I stood least chance of being arrested by slave hunters."[73] To other slaves whaleships became prisons, as did the *Fame*, which left New London in 1844 on a routine whaling voyage to the Pacific. Two years later, after both the captain and the first mate died, the second mate, Anthony Marks, took command of the ship. While maintaining the outward appearance of a whaling cruise, Marks took the ship to the east coast of Africa, picked up 530 slaves, and delivered them in five months' time to Cape Frio, Brazil, collecting forty thousand dollars for his efforts.[74] Whaleships were particularly well suited for a barbarous conversion to slaving. Their cavernous holds had room for many people, and the tryworks provided a built-in galley, capable of cooking large amounts of food to feed the human cargo. Most convenient to those engaging in this even then reprehensible business was that a whaleship carrying slaves below decks looked like nothing more than what it purported to be. Faced with the potential of earning a windfall for such heinous work, a small number of whaling captains and owners turned their ships into "slavers in disguise," as historian Kevin Reilly has called them. While some of these men operated without interference, others were caught and successfully prosecuted for participating in this illegal trade.[75]

NO MATTER WHICH PORT they sailed from, the whaleships of the golden age shared many similarities. And there is no better example of a typical whaleship of the time than the 314-ton *Charles W. Morgan*, which was built in New Bedford and christened on July 21, 1841.[76] On the day of the ship's launching, the principal owner and namesake, Charles Waln Morgan, wrote in his diary of "his elegant new ship," and how "about half the town and a great show of ladies" had witnessed the event.[77] From the bluff bow to the squared-off stern the *Morgan* was about 105 feet long. It was broad of beam, measuring 28 feet wide, and had a draft of nearly 18 feet when fully loaded. A good part of its hull was constructed of live oak, a species that ranges from Virginia to Texas and was prized for its strength and reserved for use in the best ships of the day.[78] The *Morgan*'s three masts were shrouded in a dizzying array of ropes and studded with a phalanx of yards from which the white sails were suspended and held taut in the wind. The mainmast towered 100 feet above the deck and was topped by a fully exposed wooden platform with waist-high iron hoops, on which the men spent countless hours, totaling months on a long cruise, staring toward the horizon in search of spouting whales as far as eight miles away. On either side of the *Morgan*, beyond the main deck's rails, were a series of long, curved wooden arms, called davits, from which five whaleboats hung, clearly identifying the *Morgan* as a whaleship.

Below the main deck was the tween deck, which housed the captain's quarters, the officer's quarters and mess, the blubber room, and steerage—where the boatsteerers as well as the cooper, cook, steward, carpenter, sailmaker, and blacksmith slept. Within the curves of the bow was the cramped forecastle, or foc'sle as it was usually called, which had bunk beds for as many as twenty-four men and boys along its perimeter. Below the living quarters and the blubber room was the hold, where the food and water were stored as well as the casks of oil and the baleen, along with other supplies.[79] At maximum capacity the *Morgan* held roughly three thousand barrels, or about ninety thousand gallons of oil.

Most merchantmen viewed the wide-bodied, blunt-nosed, and

square-ended whaleships with disdain, condescendingly referring to them as "blubber hunters," "spouters," or "stinkers," and claiming that they were "built by the mile and cut off in lengths as you want 'em."[80] But this view entirely missed the point that whaleships, like the whaleboats they carried, were perfectly designed for the tasks they had to perform. "As a vessel," Hohman pointed out, the whaleship "was signally lacking in the grace, speed, and slender feminine beauty of the clipper; but in staunch seaworthiness, in bulldog battling with wind, wave, and whale, and in the range and seeming endlessness of her voyages she was the peer of any craft afloat."[81] Merchantmen also had few good things to say about whalemen. One such critic, on boarding a whaleship, noted that "Her captain was a slab-sided, shamble-legged Quaker, in a suit of brown, with a broad-brimmed hat, and sneaking about decks, like a sheep, with his head down; and the men looked more like fishermen and farmers than they did like sailors."[82] Here again the critique was too harsh. Where merchantmen often sailed set routes over and over again, and achieved success in part through familiarity, whalemen were forever shifting their course in the elusive search for whales. Although whaleships were not as fast as merchant ships, they still had to go true, and it took considerable skill to sail them for years at a time, in good weather and bad, with and against mighty currents, through uncharted seas, and over treacherous shoals and into tight harbors. While many of the crew on whaleships were a shabby lot, they quickly learned how to handle themselves ably aboard ship, and whaling captains and their mates were quite accomplished seamen, often more capable than the merchant sailors who derided them.

WHALING CAPTAINS LIKED to return to the whaling grounds where they had been successful in the past, but as the number of whaling voyages increased along with the number of whales killed, many of the historically productive areas were depleted. This boom-and-bust cycle, which was no stranger to the industry, forced whalemen to seek out new grounds. One of the first such discoveries during the Golden Age were the fabled offshore grounds, which lay one thousand miles from the Peruvian coast, and were found in 1818 by Capt. Edmund Gardner of the Nantucket whaleship *Globe*. Gardner's discovery was not an accident. After months of frustration cruising the "onshore" grounds off

South America, which had been hammered by whalemen for years, Gardner decided to sail west. His gamble paid off handsomely. The off-shore grounds were teeming with sperm whales, which for many years would provide whalemen with brilliant returns. When Gardner returned to Nantucket in 1820, with 2,090 barrels of sperm oil aboard, his fellow islanders were shocked and buoyed by his success, because just a year earlier, the *Independence* had returned from the "onshore" grounds with only 1,388 barrels of sperm oil, leading its captain, George Swain, to assert confidently that never again would a ship to the Pacific fill its hold with oil.[83] In subsequent years American whale-men discovered other productive whaling grounds, including ones off Japan (1820), Zanzibar (1828), Kodiak (1835), Kamchatka (1843), and in the Okhotsk Sea (1847).[84] The most important of all the new grounds, however, were those in the Arctic Ocean, and the first whal-ing captain to sail into this forbidding frozen region was Thomas Welcome Roys.

In 1847 Roys was given command of the *Superior*, a relatively small whaling vessel out of Sag Harbor. His instructions from the owners were to sail to the South Atlantic and hopefully return full within ten months, but Roys had other plans. In 1845, while laid up in a Siberian town, recuperating from a violent encounter with the fluke end of a right whale, Roys had heard from a Russian naval officer that the waters north of the Bering Strait were brimming with an unusual species of whale. Intrigued, Roys purchased some Russian naval charts, and when he returned to Sag Harbor he read accounts of Arctic explorers and found that they too had seen whales, which were referred to as "polar whales." Now, with the *Superior* under his command, Roys planned to find out if these tales were true. Roys hid his intentions from the owners of the *Superior*, for he knew that they would veto the idea, and while hunting for whales in the South Atlantic he didn't let on to his crew that their voyage would be anything other than routine. Finally, after the better part of a year, with little to show for his efforts, Roys decided to execute his plan. Stopping off in Hobart, Tasmania, Roys sent a letter to the owners, letting them know that he was sailing for the Bering Strait and, ultimately the Arctic Ocean, commenting that if they never heard from him again, at least "they would know where [he] went."[85]

When his crew finally figured out where they were headed, they panicked. No whaleship had ever sailed into the Arctic Ocean, and they didn't want to be the ones to blaze the trail. Faced with this unrest, Roys temporarily aborted his plan and had the *Superior* sail, instead, in the Bering Sea, south of the strait, looking for right whales. After a few weeks of this, Roys turned the bow of the *Superior* north again and sailed for the strait, the fears of his crew notwithstanding. Roys knew well the fate that might befall him if his gamble didn't pay out. "There is a heavy responsibility," he later wrote, "resting on the master who shall dare cruise different from the known grounds, as it will not only be his death stroke if he does not succeed, but the whole of his officers and crew will unite to put him down."[86]

Roys's courage and his faith in his abilities and intuition were hard won, and he was fast becoming a legendary figure in whaling circles. Only thirty-two at the time of the *Superior*'s voyage, Roys had already had a whaling career that spanned fifteen years and numerous voyages, each one a financial success. Then there was the oft-told and perhaps apocryphal tale of his ride on a whale's back. While chasing right whales in the northern Pacific, the story began, Roys was dragged overboard by a tangled line. No sooner had he gotten free of the line than a whale rose out of the water beneath him and he found himself straddling the whale's slippery back. He then jumped onto another whale's back, fell in the water, and was swatted by the flukes of yet a third whale, the impact of which sent Roys flying back into his boat, where he immediately grabbed his lance and killed all three of his tormentors.[87] A man who lived through that certainly wouldn't shy away from a challenge, especially when there was the potential for great profits.

The *Superior* entered the strait on July 15, 1848. When the first mate, Jim Eldredge, took his bearings, he assumed that his calculations were incorrect. They couldn't be that far north. Roys assured Eldredge that there was no mistake; they were indeed in the Arctic Ocean. "Great God," screamed Eldredge, "where are you going with the ship? I never heard of a whale ship in that latitude before! We shall all be lost!"[88] Overcome, Eldredge ran to his bunk and started sobbing. News of the ship's location quickly spread throughout the crew, all of whom begged Roys to turn around. Roys stood his ground, and soon he noticed a great number of whales about the ship. The officers labeled them humpbacks, which were not worth catching, but Roys disagreed.

These whales matched the description of the whales Roys had heard about, and he thought they might be polar whales, so he ordered the whaleboats lowered. Although his men were, according to Roys, "not inclined to meddle with the 'new fangled monster' as they called him," they overcame their trepidation and soon harpooned a whale, which immediately dived and "swam along the bottom for a full 50 minutes," long enough for Roys to begin wondering whether he "was fast to something that breathed water instead of air and might remain down a week if he liked."[89] The whale finally surfaced dead and was brought alongside the ship, with many of the crew members still insisting that it was a humpback. The cutting in and trying out, however, disabused them of that notion. The whale's baleen was twelve feet long and its blubber produced 120 barrels of oil. This was no humpback, nor was it a right whale, which it somewhat resembled. Roys's hunch was correct. It was a polar whale—actually a bowhead—and by killing it he and his men earned the distinction of becoming the first commercial whalemen to meet with success in the Arctic Ocean.[90]

Roys sailed the *Superior* 250 miles beyond the strait, "cruised from continent to continent," and then looped back through the strait on August 27. During that time he and his men, who were still expecting disaster to strike at any moment, took eleven whales and filled the hold to capacity with sixteen hundred barrels of oil. Since that far north the sun never fully sets in summer, the *Superior's* whaleboats operated around the clock, with the first whale being killed at midnight. So much blubber was brought on board that, once lit, the flames of the try-pots were not extinguished until the final whale was processed. While the whaling was phenomenally productive, it was not easy. Roys wrote, "On account of powerful currents, thick fogs, the near vicinity of land and ice, combined with the imperfection of charts, and want of information respecting this region, I found it both difficult and dangerous to get oil, although there are plenty of whales." And some of those whales were colossal, yielding upward of two hundred barrels of oil. Then there was the one that Roys didn't kill because it was *"too large"* and he didn't think that the *Superior* was big enough or had the equipment necessary to cut into it properly. This "King of the Arctic Ocean," was, the men reckoned, the largest whale any of them had ever seen, and they thought it would yield more than three hundred barrels of oil.[91]

When the *Superior* finally docked in Honolulu on October 4, 1848, word of its remarkable cruise spread quickly, and as whalemen have always done, they rushed to make their claim on the new whaling grounds. In the following year no fewer than fifty whaleships ventured north. Log entries for the *Ocmulgee*, out of Holmes Hole, Massachusetts, on Martha's Vineyard, provide a glimpse of the tremendous bounty shared by the Arctic fleet that year.

July 25	*"Plenty of whales in sight, but all hands too busy even to look at them."*
July 26	*"Blubber-logged and plenty of whales in sight."*
July 27	*"The same."*
July 28	*"Blubber-logged, but were obliged to cool down six hours for the want of casks. Whales aplenty."*
July 29	*"Blubber-logged and whales in every direction."*[92]

Part of the excitement resulted from the size of the bowheads. The biggest did, as Roys and his men had estimated, yield more than 300 barrels of oil, and the average was about 150, which still far outstripped sperms and rights, which averaged 25 and 60 barrels respectively.[93] And in each of the bowhead's mouths were thousands of pounds of long and valuable baleen.[94] In 1850 more than 130 whaleships were hunting on the Arctic grounds, but they didn't fare nearly as well as their predecessors. The whales were definitely becoming scarcer, prompting one "Polar Whale" to write a letter to the *Honolulu Friend*, pleading for restraint. The editors noted that they were "somewhat surprised that a member of the whale-family should condescend to make his appeal through our columns," but were nonetheless "honored by the compliment." The rather lengthy letter offered a particularly cogent if not self-serving argument, which was highly unusual, coming as it did in an era when few, if any, people spoke up against the ravages of whaling.

"The knowing old inhabitants of this sea have recently held a meeting," the letter began, "to consult respecting our safety, and in some way or another, if possible, to avert the doom that seems to await all of the whale Genus throughout the world." The Polar Whale had thought he and his peers were safe in the Arctic, far away from man, but still the whaleships came, and as a result, large numbers of polar whales had had been "murdered in 'cold' blood.'" His race, he continued, was no match for "the Nortons, the Tabers, the Coffins, the Coxs, the Smiths, the Halseys, and the other families of whale-killers," and he worried that, if the hunting did not stop, soon none of his kind would be left. "I write in behalf of my butchered and dying species," the letter concluded, and "I appeal to the friends of the whole race of whales. Must we all be murdered. . . . Must our race become extinct? Will no friends and allies arise and revenge our wrongs? . . . I am known among our enemies as the 'Bow-Head,' but I belong to the Old Greenland family. Yours till death, POLAR WHALE."[95]

Despite the Polar Whale's plea, whalemen did not stop their assaults on bowheads, or rights or spermacetis for that matter, and the numbers of whales continued to drop. Seeing the stocks dwindle, a few whalemen began to worry about the viability of their livelihood, with one writing, "The poor whale is doomed to utter extermination, or at least, so near to it that too few will remain to tempt the cupidity of man."[96] But whatever reservations whalemen might have had about the future, they kept on whaling with their characteristic drive and determination.

THE FARTHER WHALEMEN went in pursuit of whales, the longer the voyages became, to the point where the average trip lasted almost four years.[97] Some whalemen were able to joke about the length of their cruises. A popular story told of a California clipper ship passing near a whaleship off Cape Horn, whose crew appeared to be old, haggard men with wrinkled faces and shaggy beards. A man on board the clipper yelled, "How long from port?" to which one of the apparently geriatric whalemen responded, "we don't remember, but we were young men when we started!"[98] Humor notwithstanding, whalemen didn't like these long voyages, but they had no choice in the matter. Sailing halfway around the world, and then roaming about in search of the telltale spouts of an ever-diminishing population of whales took a huge amount of time, and most whaling captains chose to stay out longer rather than come home with a poor catch or, worse, a clean ship.[99] Capt. Leonard Gifford, of the whaleship *Hope*, typified this perspective, writing to his fiancée in 1853, after cruising the Pacific for two years, "If I am not fortunate I shall be shure to take another year for if I live to reach home no man shall be able to say by me thear goes a fellow that brought home a broken voyage." Unfortunately for Gifford and his fiancée, he was far too optimistic. Rather than one more year, Gifford took another three and a half years to make a good trip, not returning to New Bedford until April 1857. Gifford's desire to avoid a broken voyage was so strong because he knew that captains who failed to perform well were often forced to find another line of work, not only because the owners had lost faith in their abilities but also because crews didn't want to serve under captains who had earned a "bad name," and were thought to be unlucky or unskilled or both.[100]

One idea that would have shortened whaling voyages greatly never got off the ground: namely, to cut a canal across the Isthmus of Darien (modern-day Panama). Writing in November 1822, Samuel Haynes Jenks, the editor of the *Nantucket Inquirer*, noted that "the practicability of cutting a canal across the Isthmus of Darien, seems to be acquiring daily strength." Such a project would, Jenks noted, greatly benefit all whalemen. "The subduction of thousands of miles from the length of a voyage to the South Sea, merely by excavating a channel of perhaps only twenty miles, is a matter of the utmost moment to those concerned in the Whale Fishery—a saving of at least one half the time and expense of a voyage, and a total escape from the dangers which attend the doubling of Cape Horn, would be the results." Pointing out that other forms of commerce would likewise benefit from such a canal, Jenks urged that "every government on the globe" should unite behind this plan, and that the United States government, in particular, should begin the "topographical prerequisites" necessary to evaluate its feasibility.[101] But no action was taken, and the plan remained just that. Although Jenks and other supporters of the canal were disappointed, the editor of the *New Bedford Mercury* was not. He opposed the canal, fearing that it would increase the number of ships, which would in turn lead to a situation in which "there would soon be no whales in the Pacific."[102] Almost another hundred years would go by before there was a canal across Panama, coming far too late to be of much help to American whalemen.

Many whalemen spent more time at sea than they did at home, which led to an unusual sense of time, as evidenced by this apocryphal interchange between a whaling captain and his wife, which made the rounds on Nantucket.

"Dear Ezra:
        Where did you put the axe?
        Love, Martha."

Fourteen months later came the reply:

"Dear Martha:
        What did you want the axe for?
        Love, Ezra."

A year later came another letter:

"Dear Ezra:
        Never mind about the axe. What did you do with the hammer?
        Love, Martha."[103]

Nathaniel Hawthorne, in one of his "Twice-Told Tales," echoed this theme when he reflected on the odd married life of a whaling captain from Martha's Vineyard who hired a sculptor to carve a headstone for his dear departed wife. "So much of this storm-beaten widower's life," Hawthorne observed, "had been tossed away on distant seas, that out of twenty years of matrimony he had spent scarce three, and those at scattered intervals, beneath his own roof. Thus the wife of his youth, though she died in his and her declining age, retained the bridal dewdrops fresh around her memory."[104]

The long separations meant that the men on whaleships missed many of the important milestones of life, including the births and deaths of friends and relatives, and it was not unusual for a whaleman to return home only to be introduced to a son or daughter he had never seen. Whaling families were able to maintain some semblance of communication by sending letters, but like the fictional Martha and Ezra, the wait for replies, if they came at all, could be agonizingly long. Ironically letter writing often added to the stress and strain of being apart. Recipients opened letters with a combination of joyful expectation and dread. Good news and glad tidings would raise one's spirits and increase homesickness. Bad news, in contrast, not only pierced the heart, but it also caused the readers great frustration because they were not able to lend a hand, offer comforting words, or mourn, as the case may be.

If we are to judge from the lyrics of "The Nantucket Girls Song," written in 1855, perhaps being a whaling wife was not all that bad:

> *I have made up my mind now to be a sailor's wife,*
> *To have a purse full of money and a very easy life,*
> *For a clever sailor Husband, is so seldom at his home,*
> *That his Wife can spend the dollars, with a will thats all her own,*
> *Then I'll haste to wed a sailor, and send him off to sea,*
> *For a life of independence, is the pleasant life for me.*
> *. . . when he says; Good bye my love, I'm off across the sea*
> *First I cry for his departure; Then I laugh because I'm free, . . .*
> *For he's a loveing Husband, though he leads a roving life*
> *And well I know how good it is, to be a Sailor's wife.*[105]

These lyrics, however, cannot be taken at face value, for they were written, as historian Lisa Norling points out, somewhat tongue-in-cheek.[106] Few if any whaling wives viewed separation from their husbands as a blank check to freedom and good times. Instead, they were almost always quite pained at the prospect and the reality of being apart. One wife wrote to her absent husband that she was "very lonesome," and wondered if there might not be another way to live their lives. "Why should so much of our time be spent apart, why do we refuse the happiness that is within our reach? Is the acquisition of wealth an adequate compensation for the tedious hours of absence? To me it is not. . . . Thy absence grows more unsupportable than it used to be. I want for nothing but your company.[107]

It was not only the women who missed their men. In March 1860 Charles Pierce wrote to his wife, Eliza, "It is a dreadful thing for a man to be away from his wife for four long years, not knowing how she is."[108] It was because of such feelings that during the golden age an increasing number of whaling wives and husbands abandoned the married-but-apart arrangement, which had become the leitmotif for the whaling life. Whaling wives became "sister sailors," following their men to sea come hell or high water (at least one of which was usually guaranteed).[109] This privilege—if one were so bold as to call it that—of joining one's husband on board a whaleship was not afforded to all whaling wives but rather was exclusively reserved for captains' wives; due to rank, social status, and the fact that the captain's quarters were the only ones large enough to accommodate roommates of the opposite sex.

In her book *Petticoat Whalers* maritime historian and novelist Joan Druett documents the trials, tribulations, and joys of many of these resourceful, willful, and devoted women who lived on whaleships alongside their men. She points out that this form of oceangoing cohabitation—like the very notion of a woman living on a whaleship and, heaven forbid, participating in some of the routines of whaling life— was frowned upon when it first came into vogue in the 1820s, being perceived as most "unladylike."[110] A woman's place was in the home, society proclaimed, and that's where she should stay. One of the most compelling stories from those early years is provided by the indefatigable Abby Jane Morrell, of Stonington, Connecticut, who simply wouldn't take no for an answer.

When Abby's husband, Benjamin, was preparing to go to sea in 1829, she implored him to take her too, regardless of the hardships that the voyage would entail, because she would not "survive another separation." She swore that she was "willing to endure any privation—let my fare be that of the meanest creature on board, and I shall be happy, if I can see *you* in health and safety. . . . I would a thousand times rather share a watery grave with *you*, than to survive alone, deprived of my only friend and protector against the wrongs and insults of an unfeeling world."[111]

Benjamin worried about what the owners might say, and in particular that they would fear that he "would neglect his nautical duties," and focus more attention on Abby's needs than the ship's. Most of all Benjamin worried that bringing her along might lead "slanderous tongues" to damage his "professional character" and subsequent career. But nothing could dissuade Abby—not her husband's objections or her family's pleadings that she remain behind. And Benjamin, unable to withstand his wife's emotional assault or effectively to counter her assertions that all the obstacles he pointed out could be overcome, finally relented, and two days before the voyage was to leave, he said yes, whereupon Abby "threw herself upon my bosom," he later recalled, "and for some moments could only thank me with her tears."[112]

Over time these whaling wives, who often had children in tow, became less of a novelty and more of an accepted fact on board many whaleships, and by the middle of the nineteenth century it was not unusual to encounter so-called hen-frigates at sea. In 1858 the Honolulu-based Reverend Samuel C. Damon remarked, "A few years ago it was exceedingly rare for a Whaling Captain to be accompanied by his wife and children, but it is now very common." He added that there were at least forty-two such whaleships in the Pacific, and half of them were "now in Honolulu. The happy influence of this goodly number of ladies is apparent to the most careless observer."[113] Although whaling wives did not participate in the daily activities of shipboard life as they related to whaling, they did not have it easy. Just like the men on the ship they confronted nasty weather, worried when the whaling was poor, and had to deal with boredom and loneliness. "How would you feel," a whaling wife asked in a letter to her cousin, "to live more than seven months and not see a female face? ... I spend a great many hours in this little cabin alone during the whaling season, and if I were not fond of reading and sewing, I should be very lonely."[114] However, these wives also had a rare opportunity to escape the boundaries of domesticity and see the world and their husbands in a new light. "We are ... in a little kingdom of our own," wrote Mary Chipman Lawrence while on board the whaleship *Addison*, out of New Bedford, "of which Samuel is the ruler. I should never have known what a great man he was if I had not accompanied him."[115]

Many crews welcomed or at least tolerated having the captain's wife on board. These women sometimes cared for the men when they were sick and, just as important, gave them a glimpse of home, which could have a healing effect on a weary, weatherbeaten soul. And the children, with their antics and questions, provided a pleasant respite from the monotonous routine of shipboard life. But the captain's family, in particular the wife, was not always viewed as an asset to the voyage. Some crewmen believed that having a woman on board was bad luck, while others were frustrated that the captain had a woman to sleep with and they didn't. And more than a few disgruntled crewman saw the captain's wife as unwanted competition for a limited supply of food.

NOT ALL THE WOMEN on board whaleships were the wives or daughters of a captain. Some women joined the crew disguised as men.

Although it seems to strain credulity that a woman, no matter how androgynous or careful, could manage to work on a whaleship and inhabit the cramped forecastle for months on end without being discovered, such amazing feats of secrecy did, according to one estimate, occur on at least one out of every thousand whaling voyages, and that accounts only for the women whose cover was blown.[116] The best-documented case of such gender duplicity occurred on the Nantucket whaleship *Christopher Mitchell*, which left in December 1848 for the Pacific. Seven months later the *Christopher Mitchell* was on its way to the Galápagos Islands to continue its moderately successful cruise, when Capt. Thomas Sullivan abruptly turned the ship about and headed for Paita, Peru, arriving there on July 6, 1849. Sullivan changed course because of the startling discovery that green hand George Johnson was actually Ann Johnson, a nineteen-year-old woman whose father, the real George Johnson, lived in Rochester, New York. Deposited with the American consul in Paita, Ann soon thereafter was sent back to the States as a passenger, and a female one at that, on board a returning whaleship.

As to Ms. Johnson's background, why she signed on to the cruise, and how she managed to conceal her identity for seven months, there is no consensus. The most widely told, and least credible, account of Johnson's journey claims that she became a "whaleman" to track down the love of her life who had recently decided against marrying her and instead departed for the Pacific to hunt for whales.[117] With short-cropped hair, and using a homemade corset and loose-fitting clothes to hide her breasts, Johnson was able to fool the agent and get aboard the *Christopher Mitchell*, where she handled herself quite well and showed exceptional courage, in one case climbing the rigging and setting the sails during a violent storm off Cape Horn, while the rest of the crew were immobilized with fright. Of this deed the captain said, "No other man forward tried to do anything but hold on to save himself, except this one." Due to her pluck and bravery, Johnson was in such good graces with the captain and the officers that on at least two occasions they "checked some of the boys from causing him [Johnson] embarrassment by joking about his feminine appearance."

While the *Christopher Mitchell* was cruising the grounds of Peru, Johnson fell ill and took to her bunk. On the third day of Johnson's confinement, another crewman went below in the middle of the night to light his pipe using the forecastle's lamp. Johnson's shirt and make-shift corset had come undone, and the crewman, seeing Johnson literally in a whole new light, ran to the main deck shouting, "That young fellow who is sick is a woman!" The captain's sympathy for this poor young woman caused him to give her a spare stateroom and declare, "you are a sister of mine as long as [you are] on board this ship." In subsequent conversations the captain learned that Johnson came from a wealthy family and had been well schooled—a regular society girl—and when the captain asked her what she meant to do if she caught up with her erstwhile lover, Johnson replied, "I would kill him, like I would a venomous snake!"[118] The American consul's family welcomed Johnson with open arms. "She is a very fine young girl," the consul observed, "extremely well bred, and has not yet acquired any of the conversation so frequently practiced by sailors."[119]

Another version of the story, much shorter and devoid of colorful embellishments, gives Johnson's reason for shipping out as the pursuit of money rather than a lover who had jilted her, and it claims that she was a below-average whaleman, who "was so very awkward with an oar, that we took her out of the boats altogether."[120] Yet another account was provided by an article that appeared in the *New York Herald* on January 16, 1850, which told of a young woman "called 'Shorty,'" who was picked up by the local constable "on the Five Points [a particularly notorious and dangerous part of New York], flush of money, and spending the same very freely." She told the officers that about a year earlier she had gotten out of jail for prostitution, and not wanting to continue in that line of work, but still needing to support herself, she had dressed as a sailor and signed on to a Nantucket whaleship for a three-year cruise. After seven months at sea her true identity was accidentally discovered during a layover, and she was entrusted to the consul in Paita and dispatched to New York by ship, where a police officer witnessed her spending spree in the Five Points district and, assuming the money was stolen, brought her in for questioning. According to officials she had "a very good looking countenance, short stature, and broad built, her hair was cut short; she both chewed and smoked tobacco, and talked sailor lingo very fluently. . . . Her manner of walking and movements of her body would appear to the observer as if she was a young man dressed up in female clothing." The investigation proved that the sixty dollars on her person was in fact her share of the profits of the whaling voyage, and the magistrate set her free. From that point forward Ann Johnson, female whaleman, slips from the historians' gaze.[121]

THE WHALEMEN'S TRAVELS brought them to places where no other American, or any Westerner for that matter, had ever been. As nineteenth-century French historian Jules Michelet observed, whalemen were among the world's greatest explorers. "Who opened up to men the great distant navigation?" asked Michelet. "Who revealed the Sea, and tracked out its zones and highways? . . . who discovered the globe? . . . The Whale and the Whaler! And this, prior to the epoch of Columbus and the famous Gold-Hunters."[122] As many as two hundred islands were discovered by American whalemen as they sailed the globe, and the observations made by whaling captains and assiduously recorded in their logbooks corrected many mistakes and omissions on existing charts.[123]

The farther American whalemen ventured in their search for whales, the greater their need for assistance in avoiding navigational hazards, so they turned to the federal government for help. In 1828 the people of Nantucket pleaded their case in a petition sent to Congress, stating that the "extent of the voyages now pursued by the trading and whaleships into seas but little explored, and in parts of the world before unknown, has increased the cares, the dangers and the losses of our merchants and mariners." To remedy this the Nantucketers asked the legislators to outfit an expedition to "explore and survey the islands and coasts of the Pacific seas."[124] A similar request was forwarded by the people of New Bedford.[125] These entreaties came at a propitious time. Congress was already actively considering the expediency of launching such an exploring expedition, but while the interest was there, the follow-through wasn't. Not until ten years later did the expedition finally begin.

The U.S. Exploring Expedition of 1838–42, headed by Lt. Charles Wilkes, managed to establish one of the most impressive records of geographic, ethnographic, and scientific exploration ever achieved,[126] and throughout it all Wilkes never forgot that one of his primary charges had been to "render the dangerous path" of the whalemen "more safe."[127] In addition to filling in many of the blanks and correcting inaccuracies that existed on maps of the oceans, the expedition helped to clarify the intimate relationship between currents and the migration patterns of whales. In the fifth volume of his narrative of the expedition, Wilkes included an entire chapter on the nature of this relationship, replete with a detailed map showing where whales were likely to be found. He also lauded America's whaling industry: "Our whaling fleet may be said at this very day to whiten the Pacific Ocean with its canvass, and the proceeds of the fishery give comfort and happiness to many thousands of our citizens. The ramifications of the business extend to all branches of trade, are spread through the whole Union, and its direct or secondary influence would seem to recommend it to the especial protection and fostering care of the government."[128]

ONE PLACE WHERE AMERICAN whalemen were particularly in need of the protection and care of their government was Japan. For centuries this mysterious kingdom had been off limits to Westerners, with the exception of one or two Dutch ships per year, which were allowed in for the purposes of trade with the outside world. Any other ship that came too close to the Japanese coast, or which grounded on it, faced great danger. Many were the stories of shipwrecked mariners who were horribly treated, and in some cases tortured and killed, by the xenophobic Japanese. When American whalemen began hunting on the Japan grounds they too came into contact with the Japanese, and those contacts helped lay the foundation for Commodore Matthew Calbraith Perry's expedition to Japan in 1853–54, which led to a peace treaty that opened Japan to the West and assured the safety of American whalemen who happened on its shores. Although Melville placed too much emphasis on the whalemen's role in leading to this diplomatic triumph, he was not far off the mark when he wrote in 1851, "If that double-bolted land, Japan, is ever to become hospitable, it is the whale-ship alone to whom the credit will be due; for already she is on the threshold."[129]

One of the first whaleships to make contact with Japan was Sag Harbor's *Manhattan*, captained by Mercator Cooper, which sailed into the capital city of Edo (present-day Tokyo) in 1845.[130] When the *Manhattan* left Sag Harbor on November 8, 1843, it was headed for the Pacific in search of whales, and had not an inkling that its voyage would take it into the heart of Japan. But then in April 1845, Cooper anchored off St. Peter's Island, not far from the Japanese coast, and took a scouting party ashore to look for turtles. Walking along the beach the party found a strange wreck, and farther on they came on a few men who, seeing the Americans, dashed into the woods. Next the party stumbled on makeshift huts, out of which came eleven haggard and scared-looking men, who immediately threw themselves to the ground. After learning that they were Japanese sailors who had been shipwrecked months earlier, Cooper decided on a bold plan. He would take them to Edo, the very gates of the forbidden kingdom. Cooper was well aware of Japan's reputation, and he knew that no foreign ships, other than the Dutch, were allowed to enter Japanese waters. But Cooper did not think that repatriating the Japanese sailors was a fool's errand. Rather he saw it as a great opportunity. Not only would he be doing these eleven men a service, returning them to their homes, but he also hoped to impress on the Japanese, by virtue of his noble and kind act, that the Americans should not be feared but welcomed. Cooper's mission got an added boost a couple of days after leaving St. Peter's, when he sighted a Japanese junk that was slowly sinking. Cooper rescued the junk's eleven crewmembers and continued on to Edo.

The *Manhattan* touched the shore of Japan two different places north of Edo, each time dispatching a messenger from among the shipwrecked Japanese sailors to go to the capital and inform the emperor that Captain Cooper wished to enter the city and deliver his passengers. Before receiving a reply, the *Manhattan* sailed to the mouth of Uraga Bay, just a short distance from Edo, where it was greeted by a barge that had on board a high-ranking and richly dressed Japanese official who told Cooper that his messages had arrived and that the emperor had granted him permission to anchor off the city. The next four days were a whirlwind of activity. The shipwrecked sailors expressed their sincerest gratitude to their saviors and went ashore. The emperor, who thought "well" of Cooper's heart for having returned the sailors, commanded his men to give the *Manhattan* all it needed in the way of food and supplies, free of charge, and he sent Cooper his autograph as a token of "respect and consideration."[131] Numerous officials, including the local governor and emissaries from the emperor, visited the *Manhattan*, and through an interpreter, who was miserable at English but very good at signs and gestures, they were able to communicate with Cooper, who graciously answered questions and gave many tours of the ship.

The Japanese were interested in everything, but particularly the *Manhattan*'s eight black crewmembers, who were undoubtedly the first black men they had ever seen. And much to Cooper's surprise, his hosts were not as sheltered as he had thought. They "seem to have more knowledge of the world," Cooper later noted, "than we have of them, as the interpreter spoke to me of Washington, Bonapart, Wellington, & several other distinguished men."[132] The Japanese interpreter also translated the emperor's order that neither Cooper nor any of his men were to leave the ship at any time under any circumstances, and if they did they would be killed, a point underscored by a drawing of an unsheathed sword lying across a man's throat. To enforce the *Manahat-tan*'s isolation, the emperor placed a small detachment of guards on the whaleship, and then had it guarded by three concentric rings of more than a thousand Japanese boats, full of soldiers and bristling with weaponry. The only moment of tension occurred when one of the *Manhattan*'s crewmen started lowering a whaleboat. The Japanese guards immediately drew their swords, and the captain of the guard made it clear that if the crewman continued, he would be killed. Once Cooper explained, however, that the boat was being lowered for repairs and not as a means to get ashore, the Japanese guards, much relieved, sheathed their swords and let the work proceed.

Despite the relatively pleasant treatment afforded the *Manhattan*, the emperor made it clear that his hospitality was not a change in policy. Foreigners were still to be shunned by Japan, and Cooper was told never to come back, for if he did, "it would greatly displease the Emperor."[133] On the day the *Manhattan* was to depart, the winds did not cooperate, and Cooper could not sail his ship out of the bay. Not wanting the Americans to stay any longer, the Japanese quickly formed an armada of some five hundred small boats and towed the *Manhattan* twenty miles beyond the headlands of the bay into the sea. This massive train of Japanese boats, each propelled by several men operating a single stern-mounted oar, was to Cooper "a spectacle to the eyes . . . approaching the marvelous."[134] As the Japanese departed, Cooper headed the *Manhattan* toward Kamchatka and the northwest coast to continue its whaling cruise.

The guarded hospitality afforded the *Manhattan* contrasted sharply with the reception received by the men of the New Bedford whaleship *Lagoda* three years later. In June 1848 fifteen crewmen on the *Lagoda*, fed up with whaling and their abusive captain, stole three whaleboats and set out for the shores of Japan. What would quickly become apparent was they had traded one hell for another, the second being significantly worse. On landing in a small village, the deserters were quickly surrounded by sword-wielding soldiers who demanded that the whalemen return from whence they came. Instead the men fled, but were soon caught and placed under house arrest. For the next ten months the whalemen remained imprisoned, ultimately being transported to Nagasaki. Repeated escape attempts were made, but each time the men were recaptured and severely punished. Most of the time they were forced to live, barely clothed, in open-air cages and sleep on insect-infested mats. One of the crewmen hanged himself, and his body was left hanging for two days. Another crewman died a slow, agonizing death, with his throat blackening, his tongue swelling, and froth coming from his mouth—an odd series of symptoms that caused his shipmates to suspect the Japanese of poisoning him. At one point the men were told that they would be beheaded, only to have their execution mysteriously stayed, and another time they were forced to stomp on an image of the Virgin Mary and Child. Finally, on April 17, 1849, a single cannon shot rang through Nagasaki's harbor, announcing the arrival of the USS *Preble*, which had come to take the *Lagoda*'s crewmen home.[135]

The *Preble*, under the command of James Glynn, had been sent to Nagasaki after the Americans had learned of the whalemen's predicament from the Dutch. Glynn's orders were clear. He was to demand the release of all the American whalemen and conduct himself in a "conciliatory, but firm" manner. "The protection of our valuable whaling fleet and the encouragement of the whale fishery," the instructions continued, "are objects of deep interest to our government . . . be prompt to aid and promote these objects."[136] Negotiations between Glynn and the Japanese went on for more than a week, after which the *Preble* left with the whalemen and proceeded to Shanghai.[137] When news of the harsh treatment of the *Lagoda*'s men reached the United States, it created an uproar and helped to cement the government's plans, already under discussion, to send an expedition to Japan to open up the closed kingdom. As the official report of the *Preble*'s mission noted, "The narrative of the imprisonment of these unhappy mariners shows the cruelty of the Japanese government, and the necessity of making some arrangement with it, involving the better usage of those who are cast upon its shores."[138] Humane treatment of shipwrecked whalemen, however, was not the only reason for seeking improved relations with Japan. The U.S. government, eager to compete with the European powers, also desperately wanted permission to enter Japanese ports to obtain coal for its rapidly expanding fleet of steamships so that they wouldn't have to bring all their fuel from America on their trips to the Far East.

When Commodore Perry's squadron of ships arrived at Edo four years later, in July 1853, he delivered a letter to the emperor from President Millard Fillmore addressed to his "Great and Good Friend," which told of America's desire to establish commercial, diplomatic, and humanitarian links between the two countries.[139] In preparing for his mission Perry had communicated with various whalemen, including Cooper, to gather information about Japan, and he used this knowledge to his advantage in subsequent negotiations with the Japanese, which resulted in the Treaty of Kanagawa on March 31, 1854. This "Treaty of Peace, Amity, and Commerce" gave the Americans what they had wanted. Various ports were opened to visits by American ships for the purposes of replenishing food and supplies, including coal. Shipwrecked sailors were to be assisted by the Japanese and handed over to their countrymen. And while in Japan the sailors were to be "free as in other countries, and not subjected to confinement, but shall be amenable to just laws."[140]

THE U.S. EXPLORING EXPEDITION and the Perry expedition underscored the importance of the Pacific Ocean to the American whaling industry. With voyages lasting so long, whalemen began relying increasingly on Pacific ports as bases of operation. In this manner the picturesque islands of Hawaii, first visited by American whalemen in 1819, quickly became the foremost stopping-off point for whaleships in the region. By midcentury the ports of Honolulu and Lahaina were hosting many hundreds of whaleships annually, reaching a high of six hundred arrivals in 1846. Whaling captains used these ports to unload their cargoes and ship them back east, stock up on supplies, and hire thousands of Hawaiians, called Kanakas, as crewmembers.[141] The money that whalemen spent, both on themselves and for provisions, became the mainstay of the surging Hawaiian economy. But this financial bonanza also exacted a steep price. The waterfront areas whalemen frequented lost much of their local character and beauty, and instead grew to resemble the seedier parts of ports back home, with boardinghouses, gambling parlors, poolrooms, and grogshops in ample supply. Prostitution became widespread. "The truth is," wrote one contemporary observer, "the whole nation is rotten with licentiousness. Men hire out their wives & daughters without the least scruple, for the sake of money. It is computed by Dr——of Lahaina that at the port during the whaling season there are upwards of 400 instances of intercourse with sailors daily. . . . [One] establishment at that place is a perfect sink of iniquity. They are accustomed to have dances of naked girls for the entertainment of their customers the whalemen."[142] According to historian Ernest S. Dodge, the "whaling element" in Hawaii as well as elsewhere in the Pacific "was disastrous for the native population."[143] Sexually transmitted diseases, liquor, as well as a myriad of other foreign influences, decimated the local culture with increasing rapidity.

Neither the Hawaiians nor, more important, the missionaries who wielded great power on the islands, appreciated the bad behavior that so often coincided with the visits of American whaleships, and many local laws were designed specifically to keep whalemen in line.[144] "Halloing or making noise in the streets at night," for example, garnered a fine of between one dollar and five dollars; striking another in a fight or drunkenness would cost the perpetrator six dollars; "lewd, seductive, and lascivious behavior," would put a man back ten dollars; and rape was a fifty dollars offense.[145] Although there were many infractions over the years, nothing compared to what happened during the whalemen's riot in November 1852. On the night of the eighth, Henry Burns, a crewman from the New Bedford whaling barque *Emerald*, died while being held by local authorities in Honolulu's prison, after being detained for drunkenness and disturbing the peace. A coroner's jury called in on the matter concluded that Burns had been killed by a blow to the head landed by the constable on duty, although it was quick to point out that this blow had not been "given with malice aforethought, but rather from cowardice in quelling a disturbance." As word spread of Burns's death throughout the fleet of more than one hundred whaleships in the harbor and anchored just offshore, crowds of disgruntled whalemen began roaming the streets. Things remained somewhat under control until November 10, when Burns was buried in a local cemetery. After the service the angry whalemen marched to the saloons and started drinking. United States officials, including the consul, attempted to reason with the sailors and cool their rage, but failed, and the situation rapidly deteriorated. A mob of whalemen, estimated at four hundred to five hundred strong, ransacked police headquarters, terrorized the town, and torched waterfront buildings, just narrowly missing setting fire to the whaleships in the harbor. Only the combined efforts of the whaling captains and local authorities were able to quell the riot a few days after it had begun. Amazingly not a single life was lost.[146]

LIKE HONOLULU, SAN FRANCISCO was another port that came to prominence during the mid-nineteenth century. Whalemen went from there in search of sperm, right, and humpback whales in the Pacific and bowhead whales in the Arctic Ocean. They also initiated an especially bloody yet profitable form of whaling that focused on the pursuit of California gray whales, a species that produced oil and baleen far inferior to those of right and bowhead whales, but that was of good enough quality to be marketable. Of all those who hunted the California gray, Charles Melville Scammon was the most famous, and in the longer history of American whaling, among the most infamous.

A Mainer by birth, Scammon arrived in San Francisco in 1850 and spent much of the next seven years chasing whales and sea elephants, which, like whales, were also prized for their oily blubber.[147] Then, in 1857, as captain of the brig *Boston*, Scammon made a fateful decision. To improve the fortunes of a thus far unsuccessful whaling trip, he sailed to a long and shallow lagoon off the Sebastián Vizcaíno Bay, on the peninsula of Baja California, where he had heard there might be a large population of California gray whales. With great difficulty Scammon navigated the *Boston* and a smaller schooner into the lagoon and found himself in the middle of a whale nursery. Hundreds of white-splotched female gray whales and their newborn calves swam about. The boats were lowered, and two cows were quickly killed. But the next time the boats were lowered, disaster struck. The whales fought back, thrashing their massive flukes and smashing two boats in quick succession. The men went flying, and when a third boat retrieved them,

Scammon likened it to a "floating ambulance crowded with men—the uninjured supporting the helpless," some of whom had broken bones.[148] The ferocity of the whales was not totally unexpected. The California gray whale, which one whalemen claimed was a "cross 'tween a sea-serpent and an alligator," had already earned a reputation in whaling circles as the "devilfish."[149]

After a few days' rest, Scammon ordered the remaining boats lowered again, and their crews began rowing toward the whales. But when the boats got within harpooning range, most of the men on board were seized with fear and jumped into the water. "It was useless to attempt whaling," Scammon realized, "with men who were so completely panic stricken. . . . It was readily to be seen that it was impossible to capture the whales in the usual manner with our present company, and no others could be obtained before the season would be over." Rather than give up, Scammon brought out the heavy artillery. He had on board a number of bomb lances, a bazookalike weapon that propelled a missile nearly two feet long into the flanks of a whale. When the lance's time-delay fuse detonated, the bomb exploded, either killing the whale outright or mortally wounding it. Scammon had his men position the whaleboats in the shallow waters alongside the deeper channels that the whales traversed, and when a whale swam by, the men fired the lances. This new hunting technique worked effectively for the men, but not so for the whales, who were picked off with ease. "From that time," wrote Scammon, "whaling was prosecuted without serious interruption."[150]

Scammon's success brought many competitors, and within a few seasons the once-vibrant population of gray whales in what came to be known as "Scammon's Lagoon" was decimated. Other lagoon-nurseries for gray whales were exploited in subsequent years, but before long those too were depleted, and lagoon whaling faded into history. As for Scammon, he left whaling in the early 1860s to captain a revenue cutter out of San Francisco during the Civil War. Then in 1874, he published his one and only book—*The Marine Mammals of the North-Western Coast of North America*. In his chapter on the California gray whale, Scammon wrote that, "the large bays and lagoons, where these animals once congregated, brought forth and nurtured their young, are already nearly deserted. The mammoth bones of the California Gray lie bleaching on the shores of those silvery waters, and are scattered along the broken coasts, from Siberia to the Gulf of California; and ere long it may be questioned whether this mammal will not be numbered among the extinct species of the Pacific."[151] As historian Daniel Francis noted, "It is ironic that Charles Scammon should have written this epitaph for the gray whale, since he played such an important role in its near-extermination."[152]

Scammon's use of a bomb lance was unusual in part because it was a relatively new device, but more so because American whalemen tended to shy away from change when it came to the implements for killing whales. Since the beginning of American whaling and indeed, since the beginning of whaling in Europe, whalemen hunted almost exclusively with relatively simple harpoons propelled only by the strength of a man.[153] French whalemen once, hoping to kill whales more quickly, had embedded in the tips of their harpoons a vial of prussic acid that was designed to explode on impact, sending the lethal poison coursing through the whale's body. Apparently this worked well enough, but when the whalemen cut into the whale, they themselves were killed by coming into contact with the poison. At least one inventor proposed attaching a harpoon to a "magneto-electric rotation-machine" with a rubber-insulated copper wire, and then electrocuting the whale upon impact. This patented device was never used by commercial whalemen, who might have questioned the propriety of mixing water and electricity. Another idea fleetingly considered was that of heating the head of the harpoon before hurling it, the flawed theory being that this red-hot poker would cause the whale's blood to rise in temperature, if not to boil, killing the whale instantly. These and other creative ideas went nowhere, but when the more sophisticated and practical bomb lances and rocket harpoons were added to the whalemen's armamentarium in the mid-1800s, many whalemen, such as Scammon, used them with good results. Still, despite the awesome firepower of these new killing devices, a significant number of American whalemen stuck with the harpoon they had grown accustomed to. There was, however, one modification to the harpoon that was almost universally embraced, and it was provided courtesy of Lewis Temple, a nineteenth-century African American.

Not much is known of Temple's early years, other than that he was born in Richmond, Virginia, in 1800 and migrated north, perhaps in the late 1820s, settling in New Bedford, where he worked as a blacksmith.[154] Then, in 1848, he produced his first toggle harpoon. Unlike traditional harpoons, which had an immovable head, the single flue, or barb, on the end of Temple's harpoon swiveled on a pivot point up to ninety degrees. When a Temple toggle harpoon entered a whale, its barb, held in place by a wooden pin, was parallel to the harpoon's shank, thereby offering little resistance and enabling the harpoon to plant itself deep. But as soon as tension was placed on the line and the harpoon started to withdraw, the barb caught the blubber and swiveled into position, making a ninety-degree angle with the shank and shearing the wooden pin in the process. This swivel action dramatically increased the effectiveness of the harpoon by reducing the chances of it wrenching free. Temple was not the first to employ the toggle design. The basic principle had been used by native peoples in the Northwest and Eurasia for centuries, if not millennia. And soon after American whalemen began exploiting the Kodiak whaling grounds in 1835, and bringing back Eskimo spears with toggling heads, local blacksmiths realized the merit in the design and started copying it. But Temple's toggle harpoon proved to be the best, and it quickly became the industry standard or, as one historian argued, "the most important single invention in the whole history of whaling."[155] Unfortunately for Temple, he didn't patent his new harpoon, and therefore failed to cash in on its widespread adoption.

MANY HISTORICAL AGES INSPIRE artists to create works that capture the essence of the age, and the golden age of whaling is no exception. The finest literary example of this is of course Herman Melville's *Moby-Dick*, arguably the greatest novel in American history. Published in 1851, *Moby-Dick* has what one might call in modern parlance a split personality. A huge chunk of the novel offers a vivid in-depth history of cetology and whaling, in which Melville focuses most of his virtuosic descriptive ability on the golden age, taking liberally from his own experience aboard the whaleship *Acushnet* in the early 1840s. It is here that Melville creates an indelible image of what whaling was in the mid-nineteenth century, and why this industry was so emblematic of pre–Civil War America. Most of the rest of the book is a cautionary tale about Captain Ahab and his hatred of and obsession with the white whale, which in turn destroys him spiritually, emotionally, physically, and existentially.

When *Moby-Dick* was published, Melville was already a man of literary note, with a few well-received books to his credit, including *Typee* and *Omoo*. But contrary to Melville's hopes, *Moby-Dick* didn't add to his fame; rather it launched his long slide into obscurity. While some reviews were favorable, most were not. The *Boston Post* reviewer agreed with a London critic who called *Moby-Dick* "an ill-compounded mixture of romance and matter-of-fact," and added that it was "a crazy sort of affair, stuffed with conceits and oddities of all kinds."[156] The *United States Democratic Review* opined that Melville "had survived his reputation. . . . If there are any of our readers who wish to find examples of bad rhetoric, involved syntax, stilted sentiment and incoherent English, we will take the liberty of recommending to them" *Moby-Dick*.[157] Sales of the book were abysmal, and although Melville continued to publish, he was all but forgotten when he died in 1891, a fact underscored by his one-line obituary in *Harper's Magazine*.[158]

Looking back years later, at a time when Melville is widely considered one of America's most seminal writers, the public's repudiation of *Moby-Dick* seems strange—stranger still when one considers that when it was published the public was interested in, if not hungry for, tales of Yankee whaling, as evidenced by the wide array of whaling books and articles that appeared around this time.[159] Then again, *Moby-Dick* really wasn't the type of romanticized whaling yarn that many wanted to read. It was a demanding, dark, and, for the time, a wildly written book that used whaling as its anchor, but that was more than the readers of the era could or wanted to handle. Not until the early twentieth century, when the critics and the public rediscovered *Moby-Dick*, did Melville and his white whale get their due.

The golden age inspired painters, too, and none of them conveyed the beauty, the danger, and the brutal reality of whaling with as much grandeur and detail as did Benjamin Russell and Caleb Purrington, whose panorama, *A Whaling Voyage Round the World*, was dubbed by Morison as a "pictorial counterpart to . . . *Moby-Dick*."[160] The panorama covered an astounding 1,295 feet of canvas, although in advertising their creation Russell and Purrington claimed it was three miles long. The panorama had been Russell's idea. In the early 1840s, Russell, a member of one of New Bedford's foremost shipowning families, found himself in dire financial straits.[161] So in 1841 he shipped out on the whaleship *Kutusoff* as a cooper, leaving his wife, three children, and many unpaid bills behind. Although he earned a respectable $894.51, it was not enough to pay off his "unusually heavy 'dead horse' of prior debts," and he reportedly ended up with just one cent profit to show for his three years away.[162] Still intent on gleaning some profit from his voyage, Russell, a talented amateur artist who would later be famed for his whaling scenes, decided to use the sketches he had made on the *Kutusoff* as a basis for the panorama. To paint the panorama Russell turned to Purrington, a local housepainter who transferred Russell's sketches and ideas onto sheets of cotton canvas eight and a half feet wide, which were sewed together end to end and wrapped around two separate rollers.

Beginning in December 1848 Russell took the panorama on tour through American cities, charging adults twenty-five to fifty cents, and half price for children, to watch the story of whaling unfold before their eyes as the canvas was rolled off one roller and taken up by the other. Over the course of two hours, and at times accompanied by Russell's narration, the whaling panorama gave viewers a chance to experience the cruise of the *Kutusoff*. They saw it depart from the bustling port of New Bedford, survive a storm at sea, catch and process whales, discharge green hands, and sign on new crewmembers in the Azores, enter ports, and encounter native Pacific islanders, including scantily clad Tahitian girls who, in the imagination of the artists, were so eager to make the acquaintance of the whalemen that they swam to the ship. There were dramatic scenes of stove-in whaleboats, exotic landscapes with towering mountains, exploding volcanoes, lush green hillsides, and palm trees swaying in the wind. The panorama was greeted enthusiastically by the public and especially by former whalemen who, nostalgically smitten, found the images to be quite realistic. One Boston paper declared that the panorama was a "noble and elaborate work of art," while another claimed that it was "accurate in its delineation and beautiful in its execution."[163]

Viewed from afar—oblivious to the carnage it entailed—the golden age was indeed golden. The United States dominated the whaling industry, new hunting grounds were discovered, American oil illuminated the world, and profits soared. But on closer inspection the picture was far bleaker.

Chapter Fourteen

"AN ENORMOUS, FILTHY HUMBUG"

A Picture for Philanthropists, this nineteenth-century print shows the horrific and incredibly painful punishment of being whipped with the cat-o'-nine-tails, which left the recipient bloody but not always bowed.

During the golden age two images of the whaling life competed with each other. There were those who saw it as an exciting and even romantic enterprise, most often because they were considering it from the safety of their own homes and had neither experienced the rigors of whaling, nor knew anyone who had. Then there were others who had a decidedly darker image of the profession. The author of the following passage, written in 1835, clearly falls into the first camp. "'Tis high time you were aware that few voyages . . . can boast of greater attractions than a 'whaling cruise' offers to the nautical lounger, the novelty-monger, the devotee of exciting sports—the anything, or anybody, in short, who, like the Venetian Doges of yore, is in any degree 'wedded to the imperial sea.' "[1] Another contemporary writer saw whaling as a noble pursuit that could help men throw off the oppressive shackles of modern life, which forced them to earn their keep in menial jobs, and instead reinvigorate their character, satisfy their wild side, "gather wealth in the face of danger, and snatch subsistence from the impending jaws of death."[2]

The contrasting view, offered primarily by ex-whalemen, and in particular those who labored before the mast, painted whaling in far less glowing terms. To them whaling was a mean and singularly unprofitable line of work. After reflecting on four years at sea, whaleman William B. Whitecar, Jr., politely concluded "by advising all young men who can gain a livelihood ashore, to stay at home." Ben-Ezra Stiles Ely wrote to assure those who were contemplating a whaling cruise, "that a life on the ocean wave is generally one of many hardships, and of few bright prospects. It demoralizes most persons who devote themselves to it; and raises but a few to nautical eminence, honour and wealth. Generally they who live on the sea have but a short life; and nine hundred and ninety-nine out of a thousand of them are but poor Jack Tars at last." Charles Nordhoff was a little less genteel, stating succinctly that whaling was "an enormous, filthy humbug." And George Whitefield Bronson offered a particularly harsh assessment, observing that "whalemen, as a class, have been too long neglected. Too many ships that float are in reality prison-ships;—their crews-for the time being-perfect slaves. White slavery exists this side of Algiers. There are Legrees in spirit—and as far as power extends, in practice— north of the sugar fields of Louisiana. Uncle Tom has many nephews on the sea. We hope some gifted mind will soon faithfully and *fully* exhibit the interior of 'jack's' cabin."[3]

To determine which view is closer to the truth, one cannot simply split the difference. While whaling did have its thrilling moments, these were overshadowed by the inescapable fact that whaling was, during most of the golden age, a miserable pursuit, and the average whale-man's lot was depressing.

THE GREEN HAND'S TRIALS began as soon as his ship left port. The rocking motion, the salt air, and the uneasiness or outright fear of what was to come usually had him doubled over in fits of nausea and vomiting. Having left behind everything he knew on land, the green hand inevitably cursed his decision to become a whaleman and fervently wished that he could turn back time. One such green hand was nineteen-year old Robert Weir, who had dishonored his family by ruinous gambling and chose to punish himself by going on a whaling cruise. Leaving his hometown of Cold Spring, New York, for Mattapoisett, Massachusetts, Weir joined the crew of the *Clara Bell*, which left for a voyage to the Atlantic and Indian Oceans on August 20, 1855. His early journal entries are punctuated by the pain of a young man who clearly knows he has made a major mistake. On the second day out he was already bemoaning his situation. "Beginning to get seasick and disgusted. . . . We have to work like horses and live like pigs." The next day, while on watch, he saw large sharks circling the ship, and was "tempted" to throw himself "to them for food." And less than a week after he had lost sight of his "sweet Ameriky," Weir wrote that he was "absolutely sick and disgusted with living & everything."[4]

Regardless of his emotional or physical state, the green hand had to work, and if he didn't it was certain that one of the mates, with a barked order or a threat of more severe punishment, would quickly see to it that he was performing his duties, such as climbing high into the rigging and setting the sails, a task that was scary enough during the day but truly harrowing at night. In the weeks and months to come, the green hand would go through a trial of fire, as he tried to become a competent if not a respected seaman.

One of the most daunting tasks was becoming fluent in the language of the sea. Every part of the ship had a name. The green hand not only had to know where to find the bowsprit, the jib boom, the cat-heads, the lower deadeyes, the fore-topgallant mast, the spanker, the booby hatch, the lashing rail, the hawsepipe, and the mizzen yard, but also what they were for. Every one of the ropes in the rigging, which at first glance must have looked like a distressed spiderweb, had a name and a function, which had to be memorized, as did all the many sails the ship carried. The green hand also had to understand the language of command, so that when the officers issued orders, he could jump to. All this was difficult enough for native English speakers, but must have been abject hell for foreigners.

Even the rawest of recruits knew that the captain was in charge, but it wasn't until the captain called all the men forward to give his introductory speech, usually the first full day out, that the green hand realized the extent to which that was so. Every captain had his own style of delivery, but all of them had basically the same message, which was, I am the ultimate authority on this ship, and what I say goes. I will be fair, but any insubordination, any talking back, any failure to execute an order given by me or the other officers, will be met with immediate punishment. There will be no fighting or loafing. If you see a whale, sing out. It is our job to fill this ship with oil and return to port as soon as possible, and I expect that that is exactly what we will do. While most captains' speeches were extemporaneous affairs, a few captains, such as Edward S. Davoll, wrote theirs down and read it to his crew. Davoll's speech followed the basic plotline, but some of his specific directions to the foremast hands bear repeating. There was to be:

> No loud and noisy conversation . . . from sunrise til dark [to avoid scaring whales]. No singing or whistling. . . . No sneaking into the forecastle under the pretense of getting something when it is your watch on deck, because I know all about those things. [And] No sleeping in your watches. . . . If white water, sing out 'There She White Waters!' . . . if a spout, 'There She Blows!' . . . if flukes sing out 'There Goes Flukes!' . . . Always sing out at the top of your voices. There is music in it.

Davoll knew that the business of whaling often led to complaints, so he warned the crew, "Don't let yourselves be heard to grumble in any way. I and the officers can do all that. Grumblers and growlers won't go unpunished." Davoll had separate speeches for the steward, the cooks, the boatsteerers, and the officers. He took particular pains to clarify the boatsteerers' allegiance, for these men, although they lived and worked aft of the foremast, were only just above the foremast

Title page from the logbook of the whaleship *Edward Cary*, Perry Winslow, captain.

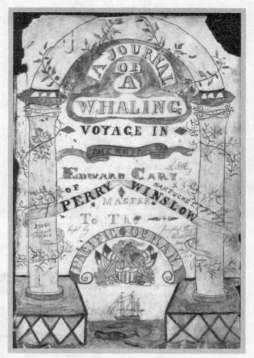

Many logbooks contained drawings and even paintings, but few rose to the level of artistry displayed by John F. Martin, who painted a right whale breaching in the logbook of the *Lucy Ann*, in the early 1840s.

A Right Whale Breaching

Print of a painting by Charles Sidney Raleigh, showing three whaleships gamming.

Scrimshaw jagging wheels, or pie crimpers.

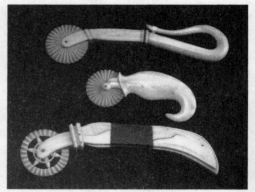

A fanciful view of what transpired when the kid was placed forward and the crewmen raced to be the first to the food.

Scrimshaw by Nantucketer Frederick Myrick, circa 1829. Generally
regarded as one of the best scrimshaw artists, Myrick is most famous
for the thirty or so teeth he carved while on board the *Susan*
(1826–29), which are referred to as *Susan*'s teeth, of which this is one.

One of the beautiful images from the *Russell-Purrington Panorama*,
showing whaleships stopping at the Azores for supplies and crewmen.

Men gone to find their fortune. One half of the *Forest of Masts Panorama*, which shows the gold rush fleet in San Francisco Harbor, early 1851.

Daguerreotype of Captain Edward S. Davoll, circa 1850.

Eighteen-year-old James McKenzie had this daguerreotype of himself made in 1856, after returning from his first whaling voyage. His luck wouldn't last. On another voyage, in 1862, he was washed overboard and lost.

New Bedford captains' wives, circa 1865.

MASTERS OF VESSELS!

And all others interested are hereby publicly cautioned against shipping the following officers of the "LANCASTER," of New Bedford, as it was through their ignorance, inefficiency and utter incompetency that the "Lancaster" was "SKUNKED!"

WILLIAM HENRY ROYCE,

SECOND OFFICER,

Was 3d mate and boatsteerer of the Bark "Black Eagle" for the season of '55, during which time he distinguished himself as an excellent DO-NOTHING, whilst as 2d officer of the "Lancaster" he won for himself the reputation of an extensive KNOW-NOTHING! Too ignorant to catch a bow-head, and afraid as death of a right whale. Would make a good deck walloper.

CHAS. BUSHNELL,

THIRD OFFICER,

Is equally incompetent and worthless. Was boatsteerer in the "Washington" when lost—no oil! Then 4th mate of the "Wm. Badger—no oil! Again 4th mate of the "Huntsville," brought no oil to the ship! And finally 3d dickey of the "Lancaster"—SKUNKED! Was fast six hours to a ripsack which drove him out of the head of the boat and from which he finally cut. Would make a good blubber room hand.

Of the mate we will say nothing, preferring to consign him to the tender mercies of Captain Carver.

Before shipping any of the above worthies, Masters of Vessels are requested to ascertain their true characters.

(Signed by the entire Crew.)

Truth in advertising, mid-nineteenth century.

Capt. Nelson Cole and
his wife, Charlotte
Brown Haley.

James Iredell Waddell
(*below, left*) and
Raphael Semmes (*right*).
Two Confederate naval
captains who caused
major problems for the
Northern whaling fleet
during the Civil War.

Advertisement in the *Whalemen's Shipping List and Merchants' Transcript*, in 1876, showing a few of the great range of high-powered devices available for killing whales.

The New Bedford waterfront, circa 1870, awash in casks of whale oil.

Coopers (*left*) tipping a full cask of whale oil so that it can be rolled.

HARPER'S WEEKLY.

A JOURNAL OF CIVILIZATION.

Vol. VI.—No. 263.]   NEW YORK, SATURDAY, JANUARY 11, 1862.   [SINGLE COPIES SIX CENTS.] [$2 50 PER YEAR IN ADVANCE.]

Entered according to Act of Congress, in the Year 1861, by Harper & Brothers, in the Clerk's Office of the District Court for the Southern District of New York.

SINKING THE STONE FLEET IN CHARLESTON HARBOR.—[See Page 31.]

Cover of *Harper's Weekly* showing the sinking of the Stone Fleet in Charleston Harbor.   COURTESY OF NEW BEDFORD WHALING MUSEUM

A sea of whalebone (baleen) drying in the sun in the yard of
the Pacific Steam Whaling Company in San Francisco.

OLD WHALERS AT NEW BEDFORD
BUILT ABOUT 1826.

Advertisements
for whaling-
related products.

The *Charles W. Morgan's* captain's cabin, 1925.

Carnival barker lures people to buy tickets to see the "Positivly Real Whale," displayed on a flatbed railroad car (note the harpoon imbedded in the whale's side). During the late nineteenth century a few promoters transported dead and reeking whale carcasses through the countryside to be viewed by paying customers. Painting by Richard Hook.

Beached pilot whales at Jetties Beach, Nantucket, 1918.

Part of the cast from the silent movie *Down to the Sea in Ships* in the forecastle of the *Charles W. Morgan*. The hero of the film, Thomas Allen Dexter, played by Raymond McKee, sits at the far right.

Whalemen in 1926, reminiscing about the past at Frank Brown's Gun shop, in New Bedford.

This massive British factory ship, the *Balaena*, hunting in the Antarctic in 1946, is representative of twentieth-century industrial whaling operations. A whale is being hauled aboard through the slipway, while two more whales float just beyond the ship, ready to be hauled in next.

hands in terms of rank, and the captain wanted to know where they stood in the event of trouble. "If you want to be respected by me," Davoll told the boatsteerers, "you do as I tell you. But in case you don't, you cannot inhabit the cabin. All who live aft I count on as my helpers, or officers. And now if you are not for me, say so, for if you are not for me you are certainly against me. . . . There is no such thing as hanging astride. Either keep aft or keep forward. Decide now and I shall know what ground I stand on." And to his officers Davoll counseled, "I do not want you should be tyrants and brutally treat men, but I do want you should make them know that what you say you mean, and mean what you say."[5]

A common saying among American whaling captains was, "This side of land [by which he meant Cape Horn] I have my owners and God Almighty. On the other side of land, I am God Almighty."[6] A whaleship truly was a "monarchy in miniature," in which the captain, often called the "old man," was king, and his officers were the generals.[7] For the most part, captains were reasonably benevolent despots, treating their men firmly but fairly, but there were also more than a few who were foul-mouthed, spiteful brutes who relied on intimidation rather than leadership to run their ships. While a captain's speech might have sounded harsh, especially to those who hadn't heard one before, that's how it had to be. Without rigid discipline the voyage would at best founder, and at worst descend into anarchy. The captain's most important ally in maintaining discipline was his own bearing and rank. If the men respected him, there would be scant possibility of trouble. However, if such respect wasn't forthcoming, or discipline broke down for some other reason, the captain possessed further tools to maintain order. The means of punishment ranged from a tonguelashing to extra duties to, in the extreme, being shackled, strung up by one's thumbs, or flogged. The last of these was feared the most. The cat-o'-nine-tails was nine strips of rope or leather with knots along their length, attached to a handle, which could quickly turn a man's back into a pulpy mass of bloodied flesh. Flogging on merchant ships was outlawed by the U.S. government in 1850, but before that time and after, it was employed by a relatively small number of whaling captains who believed that the cat was the ultimate means of keeping men in line.[8]

To those who felt that captains were too severe in their actions, a justification was invariably offered that the disputatious behavior of the wayward hands left the captains with no other recourse. To deal with the scurrilous behavior of these men, especially the green hands who often lacked an inherent respect for rank and discipline, captains, it was said, had to act and act quickly.[9] Nevertheless, there was a line between discipline and mistreatment, and some captains stepped over it. Such was the case with Benjamin Cushman, captain of the *Arab*, a Fairhaven whaleship that voyaged to the Indian Ocean in the late 1830s. On multiple occasions Cushman punished the steward, Michael Ryan, for supplying crew members with liquor, a substance that was prohibited on board. In one instance Cushman punched and kicked Ryan repeatedly, drawing blood, and thrashed him with a rope. Another time Cushman punched Ryan and then had him seized up in the rigging, stripped of his pants, and flogged fifteen times across his bare bottom and arms and legs, which not only inflicted hideous lacerations but also caused Ryan involuntarily to defecate on the deck. Not done yet, Cushman ordered Ryan to clean up his own waste with a shovel, and when the dazed and bleeding steward failed to do so quickly enough, he was flogged a second time, and then forced to stand naked at the masthead for two hours in a drizzling rain. On hearing this case on appeal, the Massachusetts Circuit Court upheld the lower court's ruling awarding Ryan $150 in damages, finding that "the punishment was . . . excessive in kind and degree," and "disproportionate to the offense." The judge added that "there was a gross indecency and impropriety in the character of the punishment, and in the mode of inflicting it."[10]

Beyond punishment, there were plenty of other potential discomforts on board, with accommodations ranking high on the list. The captain, of course, had the best lodgings, but they were hardly what one would consider elegant or spacious, and things quickly deteriorated from there, with the bunks becoming more cramped until one reached the worst accommodations on the ship, the forecastle, which seems almost universally to have earned the enmity of anyone who had ever had to dwell there. The best forecastles were bad, while the worst were truly vile. As many as twenty-five men had to fit into this cramped area, with low ceilings, no privacy, little or no natural light, and the grimy patina of whale oil coating everything. There they slept on uncomfortable straw or corn-husk-filled mattresses referred to as a "donkey's breakfast."[11] Worst was when the heat from the tryworks sent the rats and cockroaches scurrying toward the bow of the ship, where they would march, like armies from hell, over the fitfully sleeping men. One whaleman described the forecastle on his ship as "black and slimy with filth, very small, and as hot as an oven. It was filled with a compound of foul air, smoke, sea-chests, soapkegs, greasy pans, tainted meat, Portuguese ruffians, and sea-sick Americans." Later, he added, "It would seem like an exaggeration to say, that I have seen in Kentucky pig-sties not half so filthy, and in every respect preferable to this miserable hole; such, however, is the fact."[12]

The hierarchy of the ship was also reflected in the food. The captains and the officers, who were fed first, always got the best food and largest servings, while the quality and quantity diminished considerably as one moved on down the line. Shipboard food was designed for longevity, not for taste, and it was not particularly varied.[13] One captain told his new hands, only partly in jest, that the shipboard fare would consist of "beef and bread one day, and bread and beef the next for a change."[14] The food came in such predictable waves of the usual suspects that whalemen often could tell the day of the week by what was on the menu. There was salt horse, which was rarely horse and usually beef or pork salted for preservation to such an excruciating degree that if one soaked it in ocean water, the meat actually became *less* salty and more edible. Biscuits called hardtack were another staple; they were in fact hard as a rock, and any man who bit into one once never did so again. The only way to eat hardtack was either to shatter it and suck on one of the pieces, or immerse it in water or stew to soften it. The whalemen could also depend on getting rice, beans, potatoes, dried vegetables, water, and coffee, perhaps with a bit of molasses added for taste. There also were occasional "treats," often served on Sundays, such as lobscouse and duff; the former being a mixture of chopped meat, vegetables, and biscuits boiled with grease and spices, while the latter was a pudding of flour, lard, and yeast mixed with equal parts fresh and salt water.[15] For foremast hands mealtime was not meant to be an enjoyable occasion. The food was thrown into a wooden bucket, called a kid, and brought forward, whereupon the men attacked it on a first-come, first-served basis.

At the outset of the voyage the food, although not exactly inspired, was at least relatively fresh. As the weeks and months passed, however, the food began to spoil and the water became foul, a transition that was accelerated in hot climates. Everything, even the seemingly indestructible hardtack, became riddled with maggots and overrun by cock-roaches, all the while smelling like something that had begun to decay. The cooks made matters worse because often they were cooks in name only, and the results of their culinary adventures were not pretty to see or taste. Nordhoff noted that while the cook on his ship was a very respectable man, who kept his cooking stove exceptionally clean and shiny, he had not the least idea of how to perform his job. He was, said Nordhoff, simply an "abominable" cook. "His bean soup was an abortion—his rice, a tasteless jelly, and the duff—that potent breeder of heart-burns, indigestion, and dyspepsia, even in the iron bound stomach of a sailor—reached under his hands the acme of indigestibility."[16]

The whalemen's diets were greatly enhanced by the occasional catching of fish and periodic infusions of fresh meat and vegetables obtained during layovers. But the amount of fresh food brought on board varied considerably depending on the conscientiousness of the captain and the availability of friendly ports. Whalemen's journals are full of lively condemnations of shipboard cuisine. "Our duff this noon," wrote one whaleman, "heavy & watery was literally filled with dirt & cockroaches." Another found the meat "disgusting," the molasses to be no better than "tar," and the food in general to be not even good enough for "a swill pail."[17] And yet another complained that "our beef and pork in general would produce a stench from the stem to the stern of the vessel, whenever a barrel was opened."[18] The only thing worse than wretched food was not having enough to eat. More than a few captains, either following orders from frugal owners or deciding that the only way to cut costs was to cut rations, would serve their men such paltry fare as to skirt the edges of starvation. Whalemen were at least partially able to deaden their hunger pangs through the liberal use of tobacco. Morning, noon, and night, whalemen either lit up or chewed this addictive plant. According to one estimate, in 1844 nearly eighteen thousand American whalemen consumed just over half a million pounds of tobacco, which translates into a usage rate of almost thirty pounds per man.[19]

WHALEMEN ALSO HAD TO confront the ever-present possibility of getting sick or injured. The predominant malady was scurvy, a vitamin C deficiency caused by a lack of fresh vegetables and fruit. It led to sore gums, bleeding, extreme fatigue, and, if allowed to persist too long, death. Tropical fevers, dysentery, venereal disease, rheumatism, tetanus, tuberculosis, pneumonia, and run-of-the-mill colds invariably made appearances on board ship, as did depression, although not recognized as an illness at the time, which sometimes escalated to suicide, such as was the case for Capt. Thomas B. Peabody of the New Bedford whaleship *Morea*. At sea on June 3, 1854, Peabody asked some of his officers "if they thought a man would be punished in the other world for making away with himself if he had nothing to hope for or could see no prospect for happiness before him." The first mate, worried about the captain's mental state, kept an eye on him and noted that the next day he "seemed melancholy." In the late morning Peabody called the first mate into his cabin and told him "that he was going to meet his goal." Alarmed, the first mate called the two other officers to the captain's cabin, whereupon the officers asked Peabody if he had taken anything. Just "a spoonful of brandy," Peabody replied. Then, after thinking for a moment, he said that "he could not go with a lie for he had taken laudanum." The officers were gravely concerned, "but," as one of the wrote later, "we thought he had not taken enough to cause death [so] we let him bee." And indeed, the next day the captain appeared as usual on deck. But, the day after, while his men were preparing to chase a whale, they "heard the report of a gun and a musket ball came up through the deck." The officers rushed to Peabody's cabin and found him on the deck, "with his face blown off from his chin to his eyes . . . he breathed a few moments and was gone."[20]

In the annals of whaling one would be hard pressed to find a whaleship cursed more by illness and injury than the *Franklin*, which left Nantucket on June 27, 1831. From beginning to end, its Pacific voyage was a series of misfortunes so numerous as almost to defy belief. In 1831, for example, one man died of consumption, and two men fell from aloft, with one breaking both legs and the other receiving internal injuries that put him out of commission for two months. In 1832 the pace of calamity accelerated. Another man fell from aloft and died, three men got entangled in harpoon lines and were dragged under to their death, and another man caught malaria.[21] In 1833 a man who had strained himself earlier while carrying Galápagos tortoises back to ship died from those injuries, while five other men died from scurvy, including the captain. On July 3, 1833, the *Franklin* anchored in Maldonado harbor, at the mouth of the La Plata River, in Argentina. The remnants of the crew were so weak that they could not furl their sails, and that task was performed by some kindly French sailors. The same Frenchmen helped the *Franklin* travel north, to Montevideo, in Uruguay, where new crew members were signed. On August 12 the slightly rejuvenated crew of the *Franklin* departed for what they sincerely hoped would be the final leg of their journey home. But two months later the *Franklin* grounded on a reef off Brazil. Although the men and one-third of the cargo were saved, the ship broke apart within ten days, mercifully bringing a halt to the *Franklin*'s run of calamity.[22]

Sick or injured whalemen, however, were not left to their own devices. By law each whaleship had to have a medicine chest, and the captain served as the resident doctor.[23] The medicine chest came with a list of instructions, informing the captain which substances were to be used to treat various maladies; for example, castor oil for dysentery and cholic, opiates for pain and irritable bowel, and calomel for syphilis.[24]

Some captains ignored the medicine chest and instead relied on their own time-tested remedies. In this manner ocean sunfish oil was used to treat rheumatism, burying a man in the sand up to his neck for a couple of days or slathering his body with warm whale meat was seen as an antidote for scurvy, and Glauber's salts, which were used for horses on land, were believed by some "old school" practitioners to be the cure for just about anything.[25] When a man feigned illness to get out of work, a smart captain had a quick and effective response. One that was advocated by a Nantucket captain was to cut up a head of tobacco, soak it in blackfish oil, and administer it in the form of an enema, a treatment that was sure, swore the captain, to cure the patient![26]

The biggest test for the doctor-captain was the massive injury that demanded surgery. It took a tremendous amount of fortitude for a captain to cut into and try to repair one of his crew, and those are exactly the traits that Jim Hunting possessed. The captain of a Sag Harbor whaleship, Hunting was a giant of a man who stood six feet six and weighed 250 pounds, measurements even more remarkable in the nineteenth century. When one of his men got entangled in a line and was violently pulled from a whaleboat, having four of his fingers ripped from one hand and one foot nearly severed at the ankle, Hunting didn't flinch. While other men fainted, Hunting strapped the injured man to a plank and used his carving knife, a carpenter's saw, and a fishhook to amputate the foot and dress the mangled hand. This stabilized the patient long enough for the ship to make it to the Hawaiian Islands, where he was hospitalized.[27]

Some whaling captains were better prepared than Hunting, and had onboard surgical instruments that were provided with the medicine chest. Still, there was a big difference between having the instruments and having the will to use them. In many cases, rather than perform surgery, with or without surgical instruments, captains hoped that the men could hold on until a port was reached. That is what happened on the *Ploughboy* out of New Bedford. On March 4, 1849, the *Ploughboy* was cruising offshore grounds looking for sperms when one of its whaleboats approached a group of seven of them. The boatsteerer threw a couple of harpoons into the biggest one, which thrashed about and then dived. When the whale surfaced, Albert Wood, one of the mates, lanced him several times, whereupon the boatsteerer commented, "We have got an ugly customer." And so he was. The whale, spouting blood, clamped his jaw onto the boat and, spinning in the water, flipped it over. Wood ended up sitting astride the whale's jaw, pinned in place. Then the whale smashed his flukes down upon the boatsteerer, killing him instantly, and simultaneously let go of Wood, who grabbed onto the capsized boat. But the whale wasn't done, striking Wood a few more times with his jaw before backing off long enough for the injured sailor to be hauled aboard a whaleboat that had come to his rescue. Wood's injuries included a hole in his side, "with fat hanging out," an inner thigh cut to the bone, and a four-inch gash on his back. On seeing Wood's wounds, one of the crewmen wrote in his journal, I "am afraid he cannot live. His sufferings are terrible."[28] Wood managed to hang on for thirteen days, until the *Ploughboy* reached Tahiti, where he was treated by a French surgeon. As for the whale that nearly killed him, it made eighty barrels, and Wood saved one of its teeth as a keepsake.

Although Wood's encounter with a whale was harrowing to say the least, the chase in most instances provided whalemen with rare moments to experience exhilaration. Walt Whitman tried to capture this feeling in his poem, *Song of Joys*:

O the whaleman's joys! O I cruise my old cruise again!
I feel the ship's motion under me, I feel the Atlantic breezes fanning me,
I hear the cry again sent down from the mast-head, There—she
blows!
Again I spring up the rigging to look with the rest—we descend,
wild with excitement,
I leap in the lower'd boat, we row toward our prey where he lies,
We approach stealthy and silent, I see the mountainous mass, lethargic,
basking,
I see the harpooneer standing up, I see the weapon dart from his
vigorous arm; . . .[29]

Another writer contended that, "If we regard whaling merely as a manly *hunt* or chase, quite apart from its commercial aspects, we think it is far more exciting, and requires more nerve and more practiced skill, and calls into exertion more energy, more endurance, more stout-heartedness, than the capture of any other creature—not even excepting the lion, tiger, or elephant."[30] And when nineteenth-century journalist J. Ross Browne sailed aboard a whaleship in the early 1840s, he penned a stirring description of the chase. "Down went the boats with a splash. Each boat's crew sprang over the rail, and in an instant the larboard, starboard, and waist boats were manned," and they were off, with the oarsmen leaning into their work to gain the bragging rights of being the first whaleboat to strike a whale. "'Give way, my lads, give way!'" yelled the boatheader, "'A long, steady stroke! That's the way to tell it!' . . . 'Pull! pull like vengeance!' echoed the crew," as they "danced over the waves, scarcely seeming to touch them." More than two miles from the mother ship, the first whaleboat came within a quarter mile of a large bull sperm whale, and the boatheader redoubled his encouragements. "'On with the beef, chummies! Smash every oar! double 'em up, or break 'em! Every devil's imp of you, pull! No talking; lay back to it; now or never!'" But then the whale dived, surfacing nearly a mile off, and began swimming rapidly to windward. Despite the apparent hopelessness of the chase, the men "braced" themselves "for a grand and final effort." Battling nearly gale-force winds and choppy seas, the whaleboat maneuvered alongside the whale, and the boatsteerer "let fly the harpoon, and buried the iron." The whaleboat backed off as the whale thrashed its "tremendous flukes high in the air," showering the men "with a cloud of spray," and then disappeared beneath the waves. When the whale came up again, the men "dispatch[ed] him with lances." Weary from the chase, the victors laid upon their oars "a moment to witness [the whale's] . . . last throes, and, when he had turned his head toward the sun, a loud, simultaneous cheer burst from every lip."[31]

The only element missing from Browne's rendition is fear. A whalemen who claimed not to be afraid of battling against a sperm whale, or any whale for that matter, was either a damned fool or a liar. To row after a massive animal at least twice as long as your whaleboat, and then harpoon this animal, all the while knowing it could smash your boat or drag it under, was not something to be pursued without serious foreboding. Yet the whalemen had a job to do, and fear often acted as a catalyst. In fact the dangers of the chase were, as one whaleman said, "welcome visitors" because they provided a change of pace from the typical "wearisome" time at sea.[32]

The sense of achievement that whalemen felt at the end of a successful chase quickly disappeared. Then came the row back to the ship, and then the cutting in, described by one whaleman as "surgery, or dissection, on a gigantic scale."[33] First the whale was brought snug up to the starboard side of the ship, its tail facing forward and the head aft and secured in place by a sturdy chain looped around the flukes. A section of the bulwarks at the gangway was pulled away and the cutting stage—a wooden scaffolding comprising three narrow planks—was lowered over the carcass. The captain and the first and second mates walked out ten feet along either of the stage's perpendicular planks to the third plank, which connected the first two and provided a platform, replete with a handrail, on which they stood while cutting into the whale below. Armed with razor-sharp, steel-headed cutting spades mounted on sixteen-foot poles, the men began their operation. Typically the captain and the first mate separated the head from the body and secured it to the stern with a chain, to be dealt with later, while the second mate focused on stripping the blubber off of the whale. The second mate began his work by making a circular incision between the eye and the pectoral fin, into which was inserted a one-hundred-pound iron blubber hook that was attached by a chain to a block-and-tackle assembly on board. To get the hook into place, one of the boatsteerers, tethered about the waist to a man on board by the aptly named monkey rope, was slowly lowered onto the whale. This was not a job for the fainthearted. One errant swing of the blubber hook could fracture bones or kill a man, and maintaining one's footing on the wet, oily, and bloody carcass of a whale was difficult enough in calm weather and nigh impossible when the seas were up. Were the boatsteerer to slip and fall between the whale and the ship, and not be yanked clear by a tug on the monkey rope, he could be crushed against the hull; and if he fell into the water on the other side of the whale he would have to contend with the sharks, or sea wolves as they were called, that were gorging themselves on chunks of blubber.[34]

With the blubber hook inserted, the peeling commenced. As the men put their backs into turning the windlass, the block-and-tackle hanging from the mainmast creaked under the weight of the massive blanket of blubber that was slowly pulled and cut away from the whale. The cutting trajectory was always at an angle, "like the thread of a screw," so that the blubber could be stripped in one continuous ribbon, from head to tail, much in the manner that one would strip an entire apple without removing the blade from the fruit.[35] Slowly the four- to six-foot-wide strip of blubber ascended higher, as the whale, unraveling, rolled in the water. When the blubber rose twenty to thirty feet above the deck, the boatsteerer, two-foot boarding knife in hand, stepped up to the mountain of flesh and cut a hole in the center of the blanket strip, into which another massive hook and line was inserted, which would soon take up the task of peeling the next slab of blubber from the whale. On hearing the captain cry, "Board the blanket piece!" the boatsteerer stepped forward again, slicing the blubber just above the hole and severing the strip in two, sending the pendulous blanket piece careening across the deck, scattering the men out of the way lest they be knocked senseless or pitched overboard by the swaying mass.[36]

The blanket piece was then lowered through the main hatch to the blubber room, where one man, wielding a long pole with a hook on the end, called a gaff, tried to hold the blanket piece in place, while another man, perched upon the blubber, used a finely honed spade to chop it into "horse pieces" about one foot square. The blubber room was a treacherous place. Despite the gaffman's Herculean efforts, the massive blanket pieces would slosh across the floor every time the ship rolled, sliding on a slick of oil, blood, water, and dirt. The horse pieces were, in turn, pitched onto the main deck and sent to the "mincing-horse," where the mincer, using an extremely sharp two-handled knife, cut the blubber into narrow strips, leaving one end of them attached to the whale's skin. These flayed horse pieces were called books, and the strips of blubber were called "bible leaves" because of their resemblance to the fanned pages of a Bible. Mincing increased the surface area of the blubber and caused it to boil more efficiently once it was tossed, with a blubber fork, into the try-pots. The process of peeling, chopping, and mincing was repeated until the whale had been stripped of all its blubber, at which point what was left of the whale's carcass was released, making an excellent if not unexpected meal for the circling birds and the denizens of the deep.

Next the men turned their attention to the whale's head, which had been hanging off the stern and now was pulled up toward the gangway for processing. For baleen whales the head was hauled aboard or taken to the deck piece by piece. The whalebone was cut from the upper jaw, scraped clean, and set aside to dry before being bundled and stowed, while the whale's enormous, oil-laden tongue and lips were chopped up in preparation for the try-pots. For sperm whales, first the lower jaw was severed and set aside on the deck to rot until the teeth, still embedded in the gums, could be wrenched free from the jawbone and later extracted for use in scrimshawing or for trade. If the rest of the head wasn't too large, it would be hauled onto the deck so that the loss of the precious spermaceti could be kept to a minimum. If the head was too big for this maneuver, it was pulled as far out of the water as possible and lashed to the side of the ship. To get to the spermaceti the men cut a hole in the whale's head and began bailing the case. Usually this was accomplished by repeatedly plunging a bucket attached to a pole into the case to ladle out its contents. Sometimes, however, one of the crew would crawl into the case to do the ladling himself, in effect taking a spermaceti bath. Although this might seem to be a particularly gruesome task, whalemen rarely viewed it that way. Spermaceti was an excellent moisturizer, and the warmth of the liquid could be a welcome change from a cold, biting wind. Melville, in relating the experience of squeezing the lumps out of congealed spermaceti back into fluid, waxed poetic about the orgiastic joys of immersing one's hands in this most unusual substance:

A sweet and unctuous duty! No wonder that in old times this sperm was such a favorite cosmetic. Such a clearer! such a sweetener! such a softener! such a delicious molifier! After having my hands in it for only a few minutes, my fingers felt like eels, and began, as it were, to serpentine and spiralize. . . . Would that I could keep squeezing that sperm for ever! . . . In thoughts of the visions of the night, I saw long rows of angels in paradise, each with his hands in a jar of spermaceti.[37]

With the cutting in completed, the process of trying out began. For a large whale this could require as many as three days of nonstop activity, by multiple shifts of men periodically relieving one another. It was grueling and dirty work that caused one whaleman to call it "hell on a small scale."[38] Other whalemen offered more detailed and emotional descriptions. Browne observed that "a trying-out scene has something peculiarly wild and savage in it; a kind of indescribable uncouthness. . . . There is a murderous appearance about the blood-stained decks, and the huge masses of flesh and blubber lying here and there, and a ferocity in the looks of the men, heightened by the red, fierce glare of the fires, which inspire in the mind of the novice feelings of mingled disgust and awe. . . . I know of nothing to which this part of the whaling business can be more appropriately compared than to Dante's pictures of the infernal regions."[39] William Abbe, who shipped out on the Fairhaven whaleship *Atkins Adams* in 1858, provided a less ethereal and more pungent view of the proceedings. "To turn out at midnight & put on clothes soaked in oil—to go on deck & work for Eighteen hours among blubber—slipping—& stumbling on the sloppy decks— till you are covered from crown to heel with oil . . . to dream you are under piles of blubber that are heaping & falling upon you till you wake up with a suffocating sense of fear & agony . . . to be weary—dirty— oily—sleepy—sick—disgusted with yourself & everybody & everything . . . to go through such a scene, I confess the very thought turns my stomach."[40]

Toward the end of the trying-out process, the men mopped up in an attempt to glean every last bit of profit from the whale. The scraps of blubber and the oil on the deck, which was kept from oozing over the side by plugging the scuppers, was collected and thrown into the try-pots. The blubber encrusted with meat, which had been hewn from the horse pieces and tossed into casks, was brought forward. After days of decomposing these so-called fat-leans were a noisome mess. The men bent into this slurry of putridity, surrounded by the nauseating stench, and pulled out the "the slimy morsels which are not fit for the try kettles."[41] Those morsels were pitched into the sea, while the contents of the casks were fed to the pots. After the last bit of oil was wrung from the whale and placed in casks to cool, the men began cleaning the ship. The tryworks were attacked first, and here the whale gave its last measure of service. The ashes under the try-pots—the charred remains of burnt blubber and skin—contained lye, an excellent cleansing agent, which was mixed with water and used to clean the crew's grimy clothes, as well as the decks, until they were "white as chalk."[42] Once the oil had sufficiently cooled, the casks were lowered into the hold or the oil was funneled through a canvas or leather hose to the casks below. To keep the casks tight to avoid leakage, the men would douse them with water up to four times a week.

WHALING WAS A PROCESS of punctuated equilibrium, with the frenzied action of the chase, the cutting in, and the trying out being only a small part of the voyage. Given that it could take anywhere from three to five days to catch and process a whale, and that a good trip might kill on the order of twenty to seventy whales, depending on the species, whalemen were left with ample time on their hands over the course of an average four-year cruise. Not all of this in-between time, however, was free time. There were many activities to attend to, including sailing and cleaning the ship, readying the whaleboats, practicing lowering, sharpening lances and knives, looking out for whales, and doing shipboard repairs.

The length of the voyages, the separation from loved ones, the dangers of the profession, and the monotony of shipboard life made all whalemen pray for the return trip home. "God knows I shall be glad when this cruise is ended," wrote a whaleman in 1844. "I would not suffer again as I have the last 3 months for all the whales on the North West." The same year another whaleman moaned, "For the last three or four months I have looked for whales hard—pulled hard in the boats, worked hard on board—and have done next to nothing—which is very hard—and now I am very homesick and can't get home, which is harder yet. Oh! dear—Oh! Dear. Oh! Dear."[43]

How soon the men got to return home depended on a multiplicity of factors. Often the trip ended as soon as the hold was full, and the sooner this happened the shorter the voyage. But even a full hold didn't always mean a ticket home. Captains could offload their cargo at a port near the whaling grounds, and have it shipped back home on another vessel, while they soldiered on. And when the whaling was poor, the captain could decide to prolong the trip rather than return ignominiously with a barren ship to the icy stares of the owners. Whatever the reason, no whalemen wanted to be at sea any longer than absolutely necessary. When Richard Boyenton, for example, learned, on May 29, 1834, that his voyage on the Salem whaleship *Bengal* was being extended, he vented his anger in his journal. "I have heard today that our capt intends prolonging this voyage 16 months longer if that is the case I hope he will be obliged to drive a Snail through the Dismal swamp in dog dayes with hard peas in his shoes and suck a sponge for nourishment he had ought to have the tooth ache for amusement and a bawling child to rock him to sleepe."[44]

Even if a ship returned full, financial happiness was far from assured. Determining the ship's profits was a complicated bookkeeping exercise that required the owner to take the money earned by the sale of the cargo and subtract from that, among other charges, sales commissions, insurance premiums, and pilotage, wharfage, and shipping fees. Once the profits were known, they were further divided among the owners and the crew, with the former taking upward of 70 percent for themselves. The profits that remained went to the crew. While the lay system continued to give whalemen a direct stake in the success of the voyage, the gulf between the lays of the captains and officers and those of crewmen widenened over time. Thus a captain's lay of 1/15th or 1/18th in 1800, might, by midcentury, have risen to 1/12th or as high as 1/8th, and an officer's lay might have gone from 1/27th or 1/37th to 1/25th or 1/20th, while the lays for relatively green foremast hands during the same period could have dropped from 1/75th or 1/100th to 1/175th or 1/200th. The actual fluctuations depended on the ship, but the basic point held true—the men at the top were getting more, and the men at the bottom less.[45]

The lays, however, hardly determined the whalemen's earnings. This was merely the base amount from which a whole list of expenses was deducted. The advance received for signing on, which had been accruing interest ever since the ship left port, was subtracted first. Then came the five or ten dollars that the owner took to pay for loading and unloading the ship, along with a smaller fee to stock the medicine chest. Any purchases of clothes or personal items from the ship's slop chest, which was the equivalent of a floating general store, were added to the tally. This store, however, was quite different from most of those on land, because it had no competition, its patrons a captive market. Loans made by a captain to a crewman in port had to be repaid with often-exorbitant interest rates. There were other costs to consider as well. The often-overpriced outfitters, who sold supplies to whalemen at the beginning of the trip, and the equally rapacious infitters, who supplied the whalemen on their return, had their hands out, as did the boardinghouse keepers. And one could not forget the shipping agents, whose fee for recruiting crewmen was carved from the lay. Whalemen derisively referred to this menagerie of outfitters, infitters, boardinghouse keepers, and agents as "landsharks."

The net result was that many of the crewmen on whaleships made little if any money, averaging only about twenty cents per day, and a significant number of them returned in debt. "The lowest grade of landlubber could sell his untrained strength," Hohman observed, "for an amount two to three times as great as that obtained by the occupant of a whaling forecastle."[46] In contrast the captains and the officers fared much better, and according to one economic study, earned considerably more than their counterparts in the merchant marine.[47] And despite a high percentage of losing trips, owners profited the most during the golden age, often earning healthy double-digit returns on their investments. The *Lagoda* compiled a particularly enviable record between 1841 and 1860, earning an average of 98 percent profit on six voyages.[48] Even more lucrative was the *Envoy*'s trip to the northwest coast, which began in 1848. The year before, Capt. W. T. Walker had taken a great chance, purchasing the condemned *Envoy* for $325, and then investing $8,000 to fit it out for a voyage even though he was unable to persuade any agent to insure the trip. When the *Envoy* docked in San Francisco in 1851, Walker and his men had earned the right to gloat. In its three years at sea the *Envoy* had collected 5,300 barrels of whale oil and 43,500 pounds of baleen, which sold for $138,450. Then, as an additional bouns, Walker sold the *Envoy* for $6,000.[49]

Captains and officers, finding the work difficult but financially rewarding, and having few more attractive shoreside job possibilities, often became career whalemen. Not all of them, however, were pleased with a system that routinely rewarded owners so handsomely while often leaving those who generated the profits with relatively little to show for their efforts. On this point the perspective offered by a mate on the New Bedford whaleship *Kathleen*, in the 1850s, is telling.

> *For the owners at home a few words I will say*
> *We'll do all the work and they'll get all the pay*
> *You will say to yourself tis a curious note*
> *But don't growl for some day you may chance steer a boat*
>
> *When your fast to a whale running risk of your life*
> *Your shingling his houses and dressing his wife*
> *Your sending his daughter off to the high school*
> *When your up to your middle in grease you great fool.*[50]

As for the rest of the crew, and in particular the foremast hands, few of them were able to joke about their financial situation, as did Boyenton, who, after calculating that he had earned but a paltry six and a quarter cents per day during the first five months of his whaling voyage, mused about the charitable possibilities that this largess might afford. "I have not as yet concluded weather to give this as a donation to the sabath school union or to the education foreign mission or Temperance societies."[51] Rather than humor or resignation, the usual response after finding out that one had spent four years of his life and had little or nothing to show for it was to curse the captain, the officers, the owners, and the industry, and vow never to go whaling again. And indeed, few foremast hands shipped out on a whaleship for a second time, and those who did were usually in debt to the owner, mildly masochistic, unable to find any more satisfying line of work, or all of the above. The hugely discrepant financial rewards between owners, captains, and officers on the one hand and the rest of the crew on the other underscored the fact that whaling reflected class and social status as much as any industry in pre–Gilded Age America.

The miserable conditions on whaleships and the execrably low pay of the average whaleman spawned a new genre in mid-nineteenth-century publishing—the whaling exposé. Former whalemen, benefiting from the democratization of the press, published harsh and often scathing critiques of the whaling life, all of which complained about the conditions on board and the lack of personal profits. The most comprehensive and extreme attack on whaling came from Browne, who hoped, largely in vain as it turned out, that his representation of the horrors of whaling would generate public pressure to reform the whaling industry.[52] "While the laudable exertions of philanthropists have effected so much for the happiness of [merchant sailors, Browne observed] . . . It is a reproach to the American people that, in this age of moral reform, the protecting arm of the law has not reached [out to whalemen]. . . . History scarcely furnishes a parallel for the deeds of cruelty committed upon them during their long and perilous voyages."[53] Such whaling memoirs anticipated muckraking books like Upton Sinclair's *The Jungle* and Ida Tarbell's *The History of the Standard Oil Company* by at least half a century, yet they are hardly as well known. They clearly document, perhaps more than any other books of the period, the vast social disparities that would polarize the American work force in the century to come. And they provide a fascinating and historically significant glimpse of how the labor market would come increasingly to exploit the poor and dispossessed.

The sentiments of these whaling memoirs were echoed by many whalemen who, although not published, wrote down what they thought in their journals. Christopher Slocum, a seaman on board the *Obed Mitchell* out of New Bedford, addressed himself to the men and women who profited most from whaling. "You wealthy and respectable cityzins of New Bedford who have axquired their wealth by the whaleing business and are still endeveriring too augment their wealth by building and fiting more ships are but little awair how much abuse and hardships is suffered by those men who constitute the crews of their ships."[54]

Given such conditions it is no surprise that whalemen often literally jumped ship during a voyage. For much of the golden age it was almost unheard of for a whaleship to return to port with the same men it left with. Desertion rates often exceeded 50 percent, and at times the entire crew was replaced a few times over.[55] The United States consul in Paita, Peru, claimed that it was the "small pay and bad treatment" that led the many whalemen to become "disgusted, desert, and either from shame or moral corruption never return."[56] And when one combines desertions with discharges of crewman, often for unruly behavior, the turnover rate could skyrocket, as it did on the *Montreal*, which shipped thirty-nine men and during a five-year cruise racked up thirty desertions and seventy-nine discharges.[57]

Desertion was a dramatic step, especially when there was no assurance that the deserter's situation would improve once he left the ship. While many of these men ultimately returned home, sometimes as hands on another whaleship, others either settled where they landed, were killed by hostile natives, or simply disappeared.[58] A letter in *The Friend* in March 1846, told of three deserters from the New London whaleship *Morrison* who drowned in Gray's Harbor on the northwest coast while trying to reach the shore in a stolen whaleboat. The letter, which was signed, "A Friend to Whalemen," and was undoubtedly penned by a whaleship owner or captain, concluded with a stern lesson. "Would that this might serve as a warning to others when tempted to pursue a similar course, that they may avoid a similar fate, and be induced to continue faithfully discharging the duties of their calling however replete it may be with difficulties and trials."[59]

Neither this appeal nor any other plea had much, if any, effect. Desertions kept pace with the worsening conditions in the whaling industry. But no matter how bad whaling was, it offered employment and a salary, or least a semblance of it, to a growing number of impoverished men, both Native Americans and immigrants, who began crowding the city, creating desperate and growing pockets of urban poor, and reflecting a profound shift of America from an agrarian to an urban society.

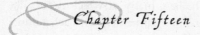

Chapter Fifteen

STORIES, SONGS, SEX, AND SCRIMSHAW

MEMORIES OF THINGS LEFT BEHIND. AN ARTISAN ON THE
WHALESHIP *CERES* CARVED THIS SPERM WHALE TOOTH.

IN BETWEEN SAILING, SLEEPING, EATING, AND HUNTING AND PROCESS-
ing whales, whalemen had to occupy themselves. Some used the respite
from the often monotonous shipboard routine to daydream or rest.
Others socialized, read, wrote, sang, scrimshawed, and when the
opportunity arose, drank and chased women. These forms of entertain-

ment helped to make whaling voyages if not pleasant, at least more bearable.

Tales of whaling and fond memories became an integral part of shipboard life. There were dramatic stories of brave men, tragic deaths, sea monsters, mutinies, even cannibalism, many of which raced, like rumors, from ship to ship, growing more fantastic with each telling. There were as well the recollections of the life the men had left behind, especially of the sweethearts, wives, and children that the whalemen longed to see again. The most exciting and anticipated social opportunity at sea emerged when two or more whaleships came within sight of each other, and the captains called for a gam, a gathering peculiar to whalemen.[1] After the ships drew close, the captains would repair to one ship, the first mates to the other, while the crewmen would mix between the two. Gams, or "deep-sea gossiping" sessions as one participant called them, could last for days and they gave the men a chance to spin "yarns that stretch to the 'crack of doom,'" tell jokes, swap reading materials, and barter for goods.[2] If the ships hailed from the same port, the gam became an opportunity to catch up with old acquaintances and share news from home, and when one of the ships was on a return voyage, it would be used to deliver letters back to the States.

The most consequential gam of all time occurred on the offshore grounds near the equator in the Pacific Ocean, and involved a green hand named Herman Melville. In December 1840, at the age of twenty-one, Melville, a former teacher, day laborer, and merchant sailor, signed on as an ordinary seaman aboard the whaleship *Acushnet* out of Fairhaven, for a 1/175th lay.[3] Seven months later, on July 23, 1841, the *Acushnet* encountered a Nantucket whaleship, the *Lima*, and they proceeded to "gam." On board the *Lima* Melville found himself face-to-face with William Henry Chase, the teenage son of Owen Chase, who had been first mate of the whaleship *Essex*. Like virtually every whaleman, and much of the American public, Melville knew the tragic story of the *Essex*—how, in November 1820, while on the Pacific grounds, the *Essex* had been rammed and sunk by an enraged sperm whale, and the captain, officers, and crew, sailing for three months and thousands of miles in their whaleboats, had resorted to eating the dead among them in order to survive.[4] These macabre events fascinated Melville, and he peppered Chase with questions about the *Essex* and the nightmare its men had endured. Chase and Melville continued their conversation the next morning, for their captains had decided to cruise together for a couple of days, and that is when Chase dug out of his sea chest a copy of his father's book, *Narrative of the Wreck of the Whaleship* Essex, and loaned it to Melville. "This was the first printed account of . . . [the disaster] I had ever seen," Melville later wrote. "The reading of this wondrous story upon the landless sea & close to the very latitude of the shipwreck had a surprising effect upon me."[5] Melville's fascination with the *Essex* never waned, and when he wrote *Moby-Dick*, he used the ramming of the ship as the basis for the book's unforgettable ending, when the seemingly possessed white whale sinks the *Pequod*, vanquishes Ahab, and leaves behind a sole survivor to tell the tale.

ANOTHER FORM OF SHIPBOARD entertainment was whaling songs. These were not the rhythmic shanties that the men sang in unison to coordinate their work and keep time, but rather they were full-throated ballads that sentimentalized, vilified, or mocked the whaling life, and that were, on occasion, accompanied by music. "Blow Ye Winds," one of the most widely known whaling songs, offered an unusually comprehensive description of the whalemen's lot. Over the course of twenty-one stanzas, this ballad runs the gamut from the recruiting of green hands and the fitting out of a whaleship to the hunting and processing of the whale, and the return voyage. It ends with a high-spirited condemnation of the captain, the officers, and the profession itself.

> *Here's to all the skippers and all mates*
> *I wish you may all do well*
> *And when you die may the devil*
> *Kick you all into hell*
>
> *Now we got home our ship made fast*
> *And we got through our sailing*
> *A winding glass around we'll pass*
> *And damn this blubber whaling.*[6]

Whalemen often wrote down these songs in their journals, where the verses shared space with whatever other musings might seem worthy. These journals gave the men a pleasurable means of passing the time, as Edwin Pulver, a third mate on board the *Columbus*, made clear in his journal's final entry.

> *Farewell old journal I love you well*
> *Because of by gone days you tell*
> *And I love you for other reasons too*
> *One is because you allways gave me something to do.*[7]

Another option for some whalemen was reading, a predominant form of nineteenth-century entertainment. A few whaleships boasted libraries stocked with hundreds of volumes, but far more contained just a few well-worn titles.[8] Religious and temperance groups often provided whaleships with Bibles or other texts, intended to transform whalemen sinners into saints. A whaleman on the *Mt. Wollaston* viewed books in a much more practical manner, writing that he had "read Shakespeare's *Twelfth Night*. I find great pleasure in the few books which I have with me. They serve to drive away the *blues*."[9]

Other whalemen often whiled away the hours doing scrimshaw, or "skrimshander," as it was sometimes called, the art of carving images into whalebones, baleen, and teeth. Many claim that scrimshaw is an indigenous American art form, but that is not true. European whalemen were carving whalebones and baleen well before the Americans, and when it comes to working with sperm whale teeth, the most storied and collected form of scrimshaw, it appears that the British were first, but only by a few years. Regardless of which country's whalemen were first, however, it is the Americans who took scrimshaw to its greatest heights, producing the largest number of pieces.[10]

Scrimshawing sperm whale teeth was a time-consuming, laborious, and—when done well—highly rewarding process. In their raw form the teeth are rough and furrowed, so the first task was sanding and polishing them to a smooth finish with a file, rasp, or dried sharkskin, thereby allowing the image to be evenly applied. Some whalemen softened the tooth's hard outer layer with a saltwater bath before carving, while others dived right in. The jackknife was the most ubiquitous carving tool, but any sharp instrument would do. Accomplished scrimshaw artists often brought along specialized carving kits with a range of "dentistical-looking implements," as Melville called them, which were capable of cutting an impressive range of lines and shapes. The artist scratched the tooth lightly to outline the image, and then, once he was satisfied with its appearance, he dug deeper with each stroke, slowly bringing his vision to life. Those who were less creative or less skilled could avoid freehand carving and use the pinprick method instead, which required them to place a picture from a newspaper or magazine on top of the tooth, jab the pin through the picture to transfer its outline, and then use the outline as a guide for carving. When the carving was completed, the artist rubbed India ink, charcoal, soot from a lamp or the tryworks, or some colored dye over the tooth, wiped away the excess, and buffed the tooth until it shone.

Scrimshaw was rarely done for sale, but produced as gifts for loved ones back home or as trinkets.[11] Although pictorialized sperm whale teeth are the most recognizable form of scrimshaw, whalemen made other objects, including jagging wheels for crimping the edges of pies, corset stays or busks, and yarn swifts. Images portrayed on scrimshaw included ships, famous personages, domestic scenes, and in at least a few instances, sexual intercourse. Many pieces of scrimshaw also included phrases, as do most of the teeth that Nantucketer Frederick Myrick carved on board the *Susan*, which are inscribed with a common whaling motto of the time:

DEATH TO THE LIVING
LONG LIFE TO THE KILLERS
SUCCESS TO SAILOR'S WIVES
& GREASY LUCK TO WHALERS.[12]

THE MOST PLEASURABLE PART of any whaling voyage was when the ship went into port. Usually the first thing that the whalemen wanted upon setting foot on land was, of course, sex. Other than some captains who had their wives along, and other men who engaged in homosexuality, masturbation provided the only recourse for whalemen to release sexual tension while at sea. Understandably, given the cramped conditions on board and the severe punishment usually meted for homosexual acts, it was hard for any crew member to express sexual urges. No wonder, then, whalemen inevitably looked for sex upon entering port. In the major ports, men often hired prostitutes—Honolulu, like other major ports, even had a special area where the sex trade flourished called, appropriately enough, Cape Horn—while in minor ports and on many of the smaller tropical islands, there was no need to pay for sex because it was frequently freely offered by the native women, and the whalemen rarely said no.[13]

The journal of the *Samuel Robertson* provides a glimpse of the kind of reception afforded many whaleships in the Pacific. After pulling into Nuku Hiva, one of the Marquesas Islands, in 1843, the *Samuel Robertson*'s crew "were surprised to see about 30 to 40 girls all standing on the beach with their white tappa or cloth in their hands or thrown round their necks perfectly naked . . . [inquiring] if we were after girls." The same journal noted that "it is the fashion for 2/3 of our whaleships when they cruise round these, or any other islands, where they can to run in to land at night [to] send 2 boats or 3 on shore and fetch of girls 1 to a man for and aft Cabin boy and all included and after a nights debauchery put them on shore and repeat the same night after night as long as they stop round here. . . . Plenty of young men are ruined by this and catch a disorder [of the blood] which . . . makes old men of them."[14]

Victorian shame-suffused attitudes toward sex—in both Europe and America—diverged, often radically, from the sexual mores of so-called primitive islanders. As historian Briton Cooper Busch notes in his history of nineteenth-century whaling, "the sexual 'favors' from attractive islanders that Western commentators found so astonishing were not so significantly regarded in island societies. Promiscuity, it may be said, was common, though payment for sex was not."[15]

Alcohol frequently commingled with sex while men were on shore. In the 1700s and early 1800s it was a rare whaling captain who didn't have a good supply of liquor on board. But by the 1830s, as the temperance movement made significant inroads into American life, an increasing number of whaleships became dry, another cogent example of how the whaling industry keenly mirrored the society at large. Although the temperance advocates welcomed this change, it is hardly surprising that most whalemen did not. The pleasures of whaling were too few to begin with. The elimination of drink at sea only seemed to whet the men's desire for drink on land. When the Reverend Daniel Wheeler, for example, observed whalemen arriving in Tahiti in 1835 on what he had been told were "temperance ships," he was shocked and dismayed to learn that "the word temperance applies only to the ships," and while the men were forbidden from drinking on board, they drank heartily once on shore.[16]

In fairness, it must noted that not all whalemen got soused or "laid," either on or off their ships. As Busch notes, "Many were clean-living and God-fearing men."[17] Still, the Melville-era stereotype of the American whaleman as a hard-drinking and sex-crazed reprobate is not without justification.

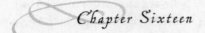

Chapter Sixteen

MUTINIES, MURDERS, MAYHEM, AND MALEVOLENT WHALES

SPERM WHALING IN THE PACIFIC OCEAN. 1834 PRINT
BASED ON A PAINTING BY WILLIAM JOHN HUGGINS.

WITH THE LENGTHENING OF VOYAGES, MANY CAPTAINS AND THEIR
officers found it difficult to maintain order on board, especially given
the degraded character of the crews. In the worst cases, usually when
cruel and vindictive officers butted heads with strong-willed and unsa-
vory crewmen, mutinies resulted. Near the end of whaling's golden
age, as the United States marched inexorably toward civil war, these
uprisings occurred with surprising regularity and a few became media
sensations. Such was the case of the whaleship *Junior*, which departed

from New Bedford on July 21, 1857, bound for the Sea of Okhotsk. The voyage began with high expectations. The *Junior* had recently returned from a profitable four-year cruise to the North Pacific, and the owners were hoping for a repeat performance.

The owners entrusted the *Junior* to a callow first-time captain, the twenty-seven-year-old Archibald Mellen, Jr., of Nantucket, a very poor choice indeed. Mellen, who was immediately overwhelmed by his new position, proved to be a woefully lacking leader. Rather than exert his authority, he often wavered in his decision making, projecting weakness to the crew. He made matters worse by turning to his first mate, Nelson Provost, for advice and giving him wide latitude in administering discipline. Provost, a malicious and vindictive officer, looked down on the crew and chose to put them in their place with tonguelashings and repeated corporal abuse. He rarely referred to the men by their names but rather called them "damned Mickey," "damned Indian," "black Arab," or the like, and on one occasion beat a man into unconsciousness with a club, while on another threatened to shoot half the crew before the voyage was over.[1]

Beyond this litany of abuse, the men had to put up with horrible food. The owners, seeking to economize, had left on board three casks of salt beef that had been on the *Junior*'s prior cruise. The meat stank and was so rotten than when cooked it simply fell apart, leaving behind a foul slurry that the men could hardly bear to eat. Other provisions, including rock-hard vegetables and wormy bread, were equally inedible. In addition the voyage was, during its first six months, an utter failure. While many whales were seen, not a single one was struck. This dismal record led the officers and the crewmen to accuse one another of incompetence, while the captain drove the men harder and chose to limit their time and freedoms in port. With each passing day the crew became increasingly disgruntled, so much so that all they needed was a spark to set them off, which was provided by a twenty-four-year-old harpooner named Cyrus Plumer.

On his two prior whaling cruises Plumer had distinguished himself not as an experienced whaleman but as an inveterate troublemaker. In December 1854 Plumer had been discharged from the *Daniel Wood* at Honolulu by "mutual consent," according to captain Joseph Tallman. Later Tallman remarked that Plumer was "of a very restless, roving and discontented disposition, always wanting to get away from the ship, and a bad and dangerous man to have on ship-board."[2] Then, in 1855, Plumer joined the crew of the New Bedford whaleship *Golconda*, captained by Philip Howland. The following year Plumer and six others deserted the ship off the coast of Chile. After the deserters left the *Golconda*, Howland learned that things could have turned out much worse, when one of the boatsteerers said that Plumer had tried to induce him to join in a plot to jettison the captain and take control of the ship. Failing to get enough support, Plumer deserted instead. Given this miserable record, it is a small wonder that Plumer was able to get hired again. That he accomplished this provides yet another example of his duplicity. When Plumer applied for a spot on the *Junior*, he presented the agent with a beautifully written—and forged—recommendation from Captain Howland. Even if the outfitter had had doubts about the authenticity of the document, he did not have the option of verifying it because Howland was still at sea on the *Golconda*, which Plumer had seen fit to abandon.[3]

Given the widespread discontent on the *Junior*, Plumer had no problem finding other crewmen with whom to conspire, and before long he, William Cartha, Charles Fifield, Charles Stanley, William Herbert, and John Hall were plotting among themselves. Their first impulse was to desert, but when they tried to leave the ship off the Azores, barely six weeks into the voyage, they found their way blocked by the officers, who were ready for such an attempt. Subsequently Plumer convinced his compatriots that mutiny was the only alternative. The plan was to lure the second mate, Nelson Lord, to the main deck to check a damaged sail, whereupon Fifield would knock him unconscious while the other mutineers, hiding in the shadows, would go below to subdue the captain and the other officers. But when Lord fell for the bait, and climbed onto the bowsprit to fix the sail, Fifield lost his nerve. Striking Lord at that point would have sent him plummeting into the ocean, and although Fifield was willing to mutiny, he was not, he later recalled, willing to kill a man.[4] This close call caused the mutineers to lose some of their ardor, and for a couple of months they stayed their hands. Then, on Christmas, while spirits sagged and the *Junior* was sailing in a northeasterly direction five hundred miles off the southeastern tip of Australia, Plumer roused them to action.

Early in the evening Captain Mellen honored the holiday, giving each of the crew a shot of brandy, while he retired to his stateroom. A short while later Lord gave them a bottle of gin as a "treat," and then he too went below.[5] The liquor loosened the men's tongues, and soon they were complaining bitterly about the voyage, their bad luck, and their treatment at the hands of the officers, in particular Provost. Just after midnight Plumer turned to the small group huddled around the deck pot and barked angrily, "By God, this thing must be done tonight!" When one of the men asked what thing he was talking about, Plumer responded, "We must take the ship."[6] Plumer then passed around a coconut shell full of gin and urged his coconspirators to take a deep draft and prepare for action.

While Fifield and Stanley stood guard on the main deck, Plumer, Cartha, Herbert, Hall, and Cornelius Burns went below and armed themselves with thirty-five-pound whaling guns, boarding knives, cutting spades, and pistols. As the others stood silently outside the officers' cabins, Plumer crept into the captain's cabin, leveled the muzzle of a whaling gun, yelled "Fire!" and pulled the trigger.[7] Three large balls tore through Mellen's chest and embedded themselves in the side of the ship.

"My God! What is this?" Mellen yelled as jumped up from his bed. "God damn you, it's me!," Plumer screamed, as he grabbed Mellen by the hair, yanked back his head, and began hacking away at him with a hatchet, slicing open his chest and administering a lethal blow that nearly severed his head.[8] The firing of the gun woke the men in steerage and the forecastle, but when they came aft to see what was the matter, one of the mutineers shouted, "Go back, or I will cut you down!"[9]

The violence quickly escalated. Following Plumer's lead, Hall shot the third mate, Smith, with a whaling gun, then Burns skewered him with a boarding knife to make sure that he was dead. Cartha shot Lord in the chest, and Provost was shot in the shoulder with a whaling gun, the impact of which flung him back into his bed; the shot also ignited the bedding. As smoke filled the lower deck, the mutineers and the others below, including Lord, who had survived his injuries, climbed onto the main deck. When Provost came to moments later, he moved through the smoked-filled cabins, opened the captain's sea chest, took out his revolver, and loaded it with three shots. Plumer yelled down to Provost to come up. "I shan't come up there," Provost replied. "And if any of you shows himself below the hatch he is a dead man. I have a revolver, and I will shoot."[10] Bleeding badly and choking on the smoke, Provost retreated to the lower hold to hide.

The mutineers controlled the ship, and Plumer took command. "I want you all to understand," he said to the men on the deck, "that I am captain of this ship now. If you behave yourselves and obey orders, you will be well treated; if not, look out for squalls."[11] His first order was to extinguish the fire, and the men responded by dousing it with water. By the time the sun rose on December 26 the fire was out, and Plumer proceeded to consolidate his position. All the men who did not participate in the mutiny were made to hand over their sheath knives and any other potential weapons. These, along with all the harpoons, spades, and knives, were thrown overboard. Now only the six mutineers were armed, and they kept a close watch on the rest of the men. The next step was to dispose of the bodies. Plumer refused to participate, claiming that "he could kill a man, but couldn't handle the corpse," and instead he sent three men below for this gruesome task.[12]

The captain was hauled up first, and his body was weighted with a chain and thrown overboard. "Go down to hell," yelled Plumer, "and tell the devil I sent you there!"[13] The third mate was then brought up and tied to a grindstone before being pitched over the side. A little while later, thinking that Provost might have succumbed to his wounds, Plumer sent Dutch crewman Anton Ludwig below to find the first mate. While Ludwig groped around in the sooty darkness, he bumped into something and yelled, "Another body hard fast to a rope!" Plumer inquired, "Large or small whiskers?" and Ludwig responded, "Small whiskers." Plumer yelled back for Ludwig to haul up the body, but when he climbed out of the cabin and into the light, the men started laughing and poking "fun at the Dutchman," because the body that Ludwig had in tow was not Provost's, but that of the captain's dog, which had died from smoke inhalation.[14]

Plumer had been in this part of the world before, and he knew not only of Australia's vast size but also of its gold mines. If he and the other men could get ashore, Plumer thought that they could disappear and ultimately find their fortune. But first he had to get ashore, and that, he quickly realized, was going to be a real problem. They were five hundred miles from the coast, and none of the mutineers knew how navigate the ship. If they headed in the wrong direction, it could be weeks or months before they hit land. The only navigator on board was Provost, so Plumer demanded that he be found. Repeated searches turned up nothing, leading some of the mutineers to fear that Provost had gone over the side. But then, on the fifth day after the mutiny, Provost's hiding place was discovered. Unable to stand and teetering on the edge of death, Provost passed up his revolver and was hauled to the main deck. He "presented a shocking and pitiable appearance," according to one witness, his body caked in dried, blackened blood, his greasy hair standing on end, his eyes sunken into their sockets.[15] To gain Provost's assistance, Plumer promised to spare his life and give him control of the ship as long as he sailed the *Junior* to Cape Howe so that Plumer and the other mutineers could make their escape. Provost agreed, and by January 4 they were in sight of land.

In preparing to depart the five mutineers, with five other crewmen, some who had been conscripted, loaded two whaleboats with provisions, valuables, and firearms.[16] Plumer, knowing that Provost was a religious man, had him swear on a Bible that he would take the *Junior* to New Zealand, thereby giving the mutineers a head start on their new life. Provost, in turn, concerned that he and the other men left behind might be implicated in the mutiny without evidence to the contrary, asked Plumer to provide written proof of their innocence. Plumer obliged by dictating a confession, which was written into the ship's log by Herbert, and signed by the mutineers. It surely ranks as one of the most unusual and fascinating documents in all of whaling:

This is to testify that we, Cyrus Plumer, John Hall, Richard Cartha, Cornelius Burns, and William Herbert did on the night of the 25th of December last take the Ship *Junior* and that all others in the ship are quite innocent of the deed. . . .

We agreed to leave [Provost] . . . the greater part of the crew and we have put him under oath not to attempt to follow us; but to go straight away and not molest us. We shall watch around here for some time and if he attempts to follow us or stay around here we shall come aboard and sink the ship. . . .[17]

When the whaleboats departed with the mutineers on January 4, Provost headed the ship on a course towards New Zealand, as he had sworn to do, but as soon as the whaleboats were out of sight, he turned the *Junior* around and sailed for Sydney. Oath or no oath, Provost didn't feel bound by promises made to murderers. The *Junior* arrived in Sydney on January 10, and two days later Provost dictated a letter to the ship's owners, apprising them of the situation.[18]

As soon as the *Junior* sank below the horizon, the mutineers headed for land, only twenty miles away. Plumer's boat, with four men on board, took the lead, sailing through the rough seas at a good clip, while the six men in the second boat, which was leaking and heavily weighted down with supplies, quickly fell behind. As night approached, Plumer, wanting to keep the group together, waited for the second boat to catch up, and the two boats floated together until dawn on the rough, open ocean. During the night Alonzo D. Sampson, fearing that his second boat would swamp unless lightened, convinced Plumer to allow him to discard all of the items on board, save a "keg of powder and a little hard bread."[19]

At first light, the two whaleboats set off again, and soon Plumer's was way out in front. According to Sampson, this is when he and one of the other men on his boat, Joseph Brooks, neither of whom had participated in the mutiny, decided they didn't want to continue following Plumer, preferring instead to set out on their own. Before they could make a break for it, however, they had to get the four other men on board, Herbert, Burns, Hall, and Adam Canel, to accept the wisdom of their plan. "We soon convinced them," Sampson later recalled, "that Plumer had plotted to drown them," by placing them on the least seaworthy boat, and that their only chance was to get to shore as quickly as possible. And with that agreement, the men on the second boat rowed to shore, landing after a short, drenching, and damaging ride through the churning surf a little to the south of Cape Howe.[20]

Plumer, who soon realized that he had lost his consort, turned his boat around to see what had happened. When Plumer sighted the six men and their boat pulled up on the shore, he demanded to know what was the matter, and why in the "Devil's name" they had landed.[21] Sampson replied that they did so to avoid sinking, an answer that didn't sit well with Plumer, who began waving his hands, claiming that if he could get to shore he would "shoot" them. But with the surf even worse than when the men had landed, Plumer decided not to try, and he reluctantly continued sailing until he reached Twofold Bay, some 50 to 75 miles north of where Sampson and the others had come ashore.

On shore Plumer's hapless group, which included Stanley, Cartha, and Jacob Rike, wandered into a nearby town and tried to pass themselves off as Americans in the middle of a trip from Melbourne to Sydney. "But," as the *Sydney Morning Herald* reported, "the singularity of such a voyage being taken in a whaleboat, their arms and the nature and value of the property they had with them, excited suspicions." The local authorities were suspicious enough to arrest the four, only to release them soon after for lack of evidence. Although they were still not quite sure what to make of this motley band of visitors, the locals let them be for a while, during which time the men settled into a rather comfortable lifestyle, donning fine clothes and spending a considerable amount of money in drinking establishments. Plumer, who referred to himself as Captain Wilson, amused the locals with wild stories of daring on the high seas, and apparently was quite a ladies' man, with one rumor circulating that he had become engaged to a local girl.[22] But when the news of the mutiny reached this outpost, the mutineers were captured in early February and brought to Sydney.

The other six men had an even more interesting fling with freedom. After spending seven days walking under the blazing sun along the endless beach, finding water scarce and food scarcer, they were on the verge of starvation when they saw a man in the distance, at a river's edge. "Boys," Sampson shouted, "yonder is an Indian, or something in human shape. Let us go to him. It is the best we can do. Our condition can't be made any worse than it is already." When they approached the native, he took fright and ran off, and the men followed, soon coming to a village which lay on the stream's opposite bank. The natives (Aborigines), who spoke no English, motioned for the men to cross the river, and then sent a canoe to get them. One at a time the men were ferried over, and on landing they were stripped of most of their belongings. "When they had robbed us to their heart's content," Sampson said, "they took us before their chief, whom we found in the principal hut, which would have made a tolerable pig-sty in good weather." Despite being nearly blind, the gray-haired chief inspected the men very closely, looking them up and down and even examining the insides of their mouths, and every once in while saying something that caused peals of laughter to erupt from the other Aborigines. Once the inspection was over, the men were ushered into an empty hut and given fresh fish to eat.

Fearing that the Aborigines were cannibals, the men "stood watches in order to guard against being massacred by stealth," and looked for an opportunity to escape, which came about a week after they had arrived. As soon as their guards had fallen asleep, the men crawled out of the hut and down to the river. They decided to swim from bank to bank while slowly making their way upstream, hoping that the frequent immersions would throw off any pursuers. After swimming the river twelve times, however, they were too exhausted to continue and headed into the bush.

The next day they came upon another group of natives, one of whom spoke broken English and told them that two white herdsmen lived nearby, and that he would guide the men to the herdsmen in return for a shirt. The deal struck, the men and their guide set out. Within a day they found the two herdsmen, who fed them and told them of another settlement which the men went to next. It was there that the group split up, with Burns and Hall going one way and the other four men—Sampson, Brooks, Herbert, and Canel—going another. The group of four hired themselves out at the end of January 1858, to an Irishman who ran a pub house near Port Albert in southern Victoria. They stayed there about a month and then continued on their way, stopping to hire themselves out again, this time as lumbermen, but before they could settle in to this new job, the law caught up with them. According to Sampson, one day while walking down a dirt road, a couple of policemen on horseback approached the men and inquired what they were about.

"We are going to work for Mr. Smith," Sampson replied.

"You are, eh?"

"Yes, that is the calculation."

"What are your names?"

The men told them.

"Did you sail on the ship *Junior*?"

Inexplicably, they said yes.

"Just the men we want," and with that the policemen drew their revolvers.

Sampson, laughing nervously, asked them what they planned on doing with their guns, to which the policeman replied, "Nothing, but we are going to put you in irons."[23] Back at the station, the policemen asked where Burns and Hall were, but Sampson and the others told the police they had no idea. Indeed, Burns and Hall were never found or heard from again, causing one to wonder whether they were killed by Aborigines or were assimilated into the local population.[24] Soon after their capture Sampson, Brooks, Herbert, and Canel were duly shipped off to Sydney, where they joined Plumer and the others in Darlinghurst jail in early March.[25]

After a hearing that conferred legal jurisdiction on the American courts, the mutineers were shipped back to New Bedford, ironically aboard none other than the *Junior*. The American consul in Sydney, understandably eager to avoid escape attempts, had the *Junior* fitted out with eight specially constructed prison cells, which measured six feet square apiece, had thick wooden bars reinforced with iron, and were bolted to the deck. Provost and Lord had to be sent home on another ship, for the *Junior*'s crew, or what was left of it, categorically refused to sail with their former officers. The *Junior*'s return voyage proved uneventful, with one exception. Herbert wrote a note and managed to get it to Plumer through a chink in the cells. Plumer read it, tore off a piece that had his name written on it, and attempted to pass the remaining portion of the note to Richard Cartha, by way of one of the guards. Plumer had hoped that by wrapping the note in a lock of his hair the guard might not take notice, but simply pass it along. The guard, whose curiosity was piqued by this curious package, immediately gave it to Captain Gardner, who upon reading it discovered that the mutineers had hoped to bribe one of the guards into letting them out so that they could attempt to take over the ship. With the plot uncovered, Gardner ordered further reinforcements for Plumer, Herbert, and Cartha's cells.[26]

At the New Bedford dock, the manacled mutineers were greeted on their arrival by throngs of curious and angry onlookers, who had been avidly reading about the mutiny for weeks. Thousands of people came to see the *Junior* and inspect its holding cells, and many made their way to the large window of a local insurance company where daguerreotypes of eight mutineers were displayed. Reflecting on this unfolding spectacle, worthy of a scene in a Dickens novel, the *New Bedford Mercury* wrote, "No whaler that ever belonged to this port has been an object of so much interest as the *Junior*."[27] On viewing the daguerreotypes a writer for another local paper quipped, "The prisoners were pronounced on all hands to be a 'desperate looking set of fellows.' We don't think they look half as badly as they acted."[28]

The trial, held in U.S. District Court in Boston, lasted three weeks and included passionate speeches from the prosecution and the defense, accusations of guilt from various officers and crew members, proclamations of innocence from the accused, and charges and countercharges about what transpired on the *Junior*. Papers in Boston, New York, New Bedford, and Nantucket followed the proceedings with a tabloid intensity that was surpassed only by their readers' appetite for news about the case. On November 9, 1858, the first day of the trial, one of the lawyers for the government stated, "The case to be presented and proved was not one of manslaughter, or any minor degree of crime, but one of downright, absolute *murder*, and if the government does not prove this in its fullest degree, it will prove nothing."[29] By this measure the government failed. While the jury found Plumer guilty of murder, his three accomplices—Cartha, Herbert, and Stanley—were found guilty of the lesser charge of manslaughter.[30] The other four men were not implicated in the murders and were not found guilty of any crimes.

Almost five months later, on April 21, 1859, the mutineers were back in the courtroom for sentencing. The room was filled to capacity, and every available standing place was taken, with the overflow crowd spilling into the entryway. According to one local paper, "Plumer received the announcement of the sentence calmly, but with a sad expression upon his countenance; Cartha manifested extreme indifference; while Herbert and Stanley smiled."[31] Justice Nathan Clifford, one of the two judges who had heard the case, asked Plumer if he had anything to say as to "why the sentence of death should not be pronounced upon him." Plumer responded, "I have very much to say," and he asked the clerk to read his written statement to a hushed courtroom.

> I object to the sentence of death being passed upon me: 1st because I am not guilty of the death of Captain Archibald Mellen. His blood does not rest on my hands. . . . the death of Captain Mellen was caused by wounds inflicted with a hatchet in the hands of another person, who went into the Captain's stateroom, and who afterwards coming on deck, stated to another person that I "missed the captain, but that he did not miss him," and boastingly showed the blood on his Gurnsey frock, saying "it was the Captain's blood, and that he was the butcher."

That man is Charles L. Fifield, whom I generously, but unwisely, screened from suspicion, assuming his crime, that he might remain in the ship, because he came to me in tears and told me he dared not go on shore with the other men with whom he had quarreled, and who abhorred him and his conduct. I have been convicted by the perjury of that man.

Plumer's statement further maintained that the "real culprit" was none other than one of the officers on the ship, Nelson Provost, "whose contriving and intriguing heart were the instigating cause of the conspiracy and mutiny." Plumer's third reason for objecting to the sentence was that he was "guiltless of taking life," and, in fact, had tried to preserve life by sparing Lord and Provost.

In view of these facts I maintain what I know to by my real character, that I am *not* the bloodthirsty man that the law would make me out to be, and that the ends of justice and the security of life and property in the commercial marine under similar circumstances, would not be promoted, but jeopardized by passing and executing sentence of death upon me.[32]

The judges were unmoved by Plumer's plea, his claim to be "a humble and penitent believer in the Lord Jesus Christ," as well as the numerous affidavits he laid before the court, attesting to his character and his version of the story. Judge Clifford delivered Plumer's sentence: "It is considered by the court that you be deemed guilty of felony and that you be taken [back to prison until June 24, 1859, when you will be taken to your place of execution] . . . and there you be hanged by the neck until you are dead; may God have mercy on your soul."[33]

Next Clifford sentenced Plumer's accomplices to jail time and fines. One of the reporters noted that tears welled up in Plumer's eyes while listening to the judge's statement. The *New Bedford Mercury*, however, had scant sympathy for Plumer's plight, and ran an editorial that described him as a symbol of abject failure.

Cyrus Plumer's case reads a sad, impressive and terrible lesson to the youth who embark on our ships and sail to distant seas for a long period of difficult duty. The experience of this man shows the need of full and firm conviction that duty must be done and discipline must be maintained. The constraint of the voyage, the perils, the tedium, and the confinement demand cheerful spirits and repression of all dark and evil thoughts. Cyrus Plumer did not, in the hour of temptation, come up to the required demands.[34]

The *Mercury's* harsh assessment was shared by virtually all of the other papers as well as the people of New Bedford. The more frequent these mutinies became, the greater the threat to the livelihoods of whaleship owners, captains, crews, and those who depended on them, and, therefore, the greater the threat to New Bedford's economic well-being. Not surprisingly New Bedford's residents cheered Plumer's sentence and hoped that it would serve as a warning to those who might contemplate a similar crime.

Ultimately the court of public opinion proved more powerful than the court of law. While Plumer languished in jail and his lawyers sought to overturn his sentence, he actually became an object of compassion and an unlikely cause célèbre, his case taken up by the swelling ranks of Northern evangelicals, many of whom detested capital punishment.[35] New witnesses were duly trotted out, whose recollections, it was argued, proved Plumer's innocence, and new "facts" were uncovered that purportedly did the same.[36] Petitions were circulated on Plumer's behalf, and one such effort generated 21,146 signatures—including Ralph Waldo Emerson's—mostly from the Boston area, with only a very few from New Bedford.[37] Plumer aided his own cause, either out of conviction or calculation, by aligning himself with God and taking baptism in his cell from the prison's chaplain on the eve of his scheduled rendezvous with the hangman's noose. Editorialists took sides on the issue of whether Plumer should live or die. The *Boston Courier* and the *Boston Journal* sniped at each other in one of the harsher interchanges recorded during this time.

The *Boston Courier* opined:

The murders of the officers on the whaleship *Junior* were as atrocious as any we have ever heard of. Does the fact that Plumer saved the lives of two officers blot out the guilt of his taking the lives of Captain Mellen and Mate Smith? We cannot find the shadow of a trace of palliation in this case or this crime and must reserve our sympathies for a better cause. Let others indulge their own.

The *Boston Journal*, eager to appeal to its own audience of more sympathetic readers, shot back:

> The *Boston Courier* seems to be thirsting for the blood of Cyrus Plumer and descends to the contemptible artifice of sneering at those acting in his behalf.... It appears as though the *Courier* man would be glad to volunteer to kick the fatal drop from beneath the convict's feet and hurry him into eternity.... Let the *Courier* and its malignant hatred of whatever is generous and human pass. It is hoped that the President will grant Plumer a reprieve.[38]

President James Buchanan, woefully inept at dealing with the regional divisions that were leading the country toward civil war, found time to focus on the case, and succumbed to the coordinated public campaign on Plumer's behalf, commuting his sentence to life in prison. In his letter of commutation Buchanan noted that "ten of the jurors who tried the cause have earnestly besought me to commute the punishment," and that even "the District Attorney who conducted the prosecution against Plumer on the part of the United States, has in an official communication 'cheerfully' borne the testimony of his opinion 'that there are considerations connected with the conduct of Plumer which address themselves to the execution of clemency.' " On learning that his life would be spared, Plumer wrote a note in which he expressed his "thanks to all the friends and editors of public journals who have been active in my behalf—to all the signers of petitions in my favor—to many friends at Washington—to members of the cabinet, and especially to the President of the United States." He assured them that his "future conduct shall show that interest has not been felt or mercy shown to a bad or unworthy man."

Not surprisingly Buchanan's commutation precipitated another heated debate in the press, with observers either applauding or decrying the president's action. Whaleship owners, in particular, were outraged that a convicted murderer would be let off, fearing that such a precedent would make subsequent mutinies more likely. "Whaling masters in these days must go well-armed," wrote the editors of the *Whalemen's Shipping List* upon hearing of the commutation, "and, expecting no favors from home, must exercise their judgment for the maintenance of order, the preservation of peace, and protection of life."[39]

But that was not the end of the story. Plumer's lawyer, Benjamin F. Butler, who went on to become a highly controversial general under Ulysses S. Grant, was elected after the war to Congress representing Massachusetts. He had not forgotten about Plumer all those years, and when Grant became president, Butler pleaded his former client's case to his old commander, aided by testimonials from various Massachusetts politicians and the warden in the prison where Plumer was being held. Grant, in turn, pardoned Plumer—nearly fifteen years after the trial.[40]

ATTACKS FROM WITHIN WERE not the only ones that whaling captains feared. Hostile natives sometimes posed a serious threat to a whaleship's command, and a smart captain was always prepared for the worst, especially when sailing near Pacific islands with dangerous reputations. In one instance, on October 5, 1835, the *Awashonks*, out of Falmouth, Massachusetts, anchored off the island of Namorik (Baring's Island), in the Pacific Ocean, to get supplies. Shortly before noon, about a dozen natives paddled to the ship in three canoes loaded with coconuts and plantains, unarmed and seemingly intent on bartering with the crew for metal and sperm whale's teeth. Capt. Prince Coffin, looking upon this as a good opportunity to stock up, let the natives, who were noted to be "well-formed, muscular men," come aboard.[41] Nothing seemed amiss, as additional canoes came from the island, and the number of natives on the ship swelled to a band of almost thirty. A small group of them clustered about the middle of the ship where the harpoons, spades, and lances were stored. Coffin, seeing that the natives were fascinated by the iron and steel instruments, grabbed a spade and wielded it as if cutting into blubber, then put it back on the rack. This display generated quite a bit of animated conversation among the natives. Then the third mate, Silas Jones, called out to Coffin that one of the natives was coming up the gangway with a war club in his hands.

Coffin, sensing danger, ordered the first mate immediately to clear the natives from the deck. Jones struggled with the man coming up the gangway, wrenched the war club free, and threw it over the side. But no sooner had he done so than another native, also clutching a war club, tried to get over the railing. As Jones went to deal with that native he heard a commotion behind him, and turned to see that the other natives had rushed forward, snatched the spades, and then turned on the surprised and largely defenseless crew. With a single swipe of a spade, one of the natives cut off Coffin's head. The second mate and two crewmen jumped overboard where "they were soon destroyed," while the rest of the crew ran for their lives, with some climbing the rigging and others jumping through the hatch. Within minutes the natives had control of the deserted main deck. Below decks Jones and four other seamen gathered to assess the situation. Lying before them was the first mate, who had been fatally stabbed as he leaped down the hatchway. "Oh, dear Mr. Jones," the first mate was reported to have said with his dying breath. "What shall we do? Our captain is killed and the ship is gone!"

Jones and the other men found and loaded a couple of muskets. Meantime the natives had gathered at the head of the gangway, but before they could descend to dispatch the crew, Jones aimed and fired into their midst. "If they had all been struck by lightning from heaven," Jones later wrote, "they could not have ceased their noise quicker than they did." The stunned natives began throwing their weapons toward Jones and the other men, who continued firing back. Suddenly the crew was faced with an even greater concern. The natives were attempting to steer the *Awashonks* toward land. Were they to succeed, the ship would surely founder against the rocks and the remaining crew would have no chance of survival, because instead of dealing with a small band of natives on board they would have to face all the inhabitants of the island. Jones and one other crewman fired their muskets repeatedly through the planking in the vicinity of the helm, and all went quiet. Not knowing what was happening above them, Jones and his men thought that their only chance lay in attacking the natives head-on. As the men made their way up the companionway, they heard the rush of footsteps on the main deck, and before Jones could get his head above the level of the deck, the muzzle of his musket was grabbed. Jones's momentary shock was immediately replaced with joy. The hand on the muzzle belonged to one of the crewmembers who had earlier climbed aloft, and who now exclaimed, "Oh, Mr. Jones, I did not know you were alive. They are all gone. They are all gone." When Jones had shot through the planking, he had killed the chief. Their leader lost, the remaining natives jumped over the side and paddled for shore. Fearful of another attack, Mr. Jones, now Captain Jones, and the crew got the ship under way. Six weeks later the *Awashonks* sailed into Honolulu. The final toll—six dead and seven wounded.[42]

The *Charles W. Morgan* had a very different kind of encounter with hostile natives.[43] In 1850, Capt. John D. Samson spied a raft of canoes coming from the Central Pacific island of Sydenham and paddling quickly toward the *Morgan*. He ordered his men to bring up the firearms and pull in all the ropes that could be used to climb aboard. Samson would much have preferred simply to sail away, but there was no wind, and the ocean current was bringing the *Morgan* ever closer to the reef surrounding the island, where the natives appeared to be anything but a welcoming party. As the canoes got closer, Samson moved his men into position along the rails, each one armed with a spade or lance, ready to repel any boarding attempt but not kill the natives if it could be helped.

The first canoes to arrive came right up to the ship, but as the natives tried to grab the hull, the men above swung and jabbed their weapons, causing the attackers "to shove off with shouts of fear and eyes sticking out like crabs'." For an hour or more, canoes kept arriving until the *Morgan* was surrounded by "a cluster twice the length of the ship and at least five or six deep." The five hundred or so natives in this war party were "jabbering and gesticulating with a din and uproar that made things hum." Their most heated gestures were directed at Samson, who was armed with a musket and walking calmly back and forth on the poop deck, surveying the scene, and giving occasional orders to his men. Despite his apparent nonchalance Samson was increasingly worried. The ship was continuing to drift toward the reef, which was now only three-quarters of a mile off the bow. He and his men knew that if the ship grounded on the reef or managed to clear the reef and grounded near the beach, they would be done for. The option of lowering the whaleboats and using ropes to tow the *Morgan* clear of these obstacles was foreclosed by the natives, who would certainly kill any whalemen foolish enough to leave the ship.

The natives, apparently concerned that the currents might allow their prize to slip away, rushed at the ship from both sides, whooping and hollering insults, and then retreated at the first sign of resistance. With considerable glee they showed their rumps to the whalemen, a move that finally got the better of Samson, who asked for the shotgun. When a "large dignified-looking chap" repeated this gesture, amplifying the effect by placing one hand on either side of his rear end, Samson hit the "shining mark" with a load of shot, propelling the offending native headlong into the water. This quieted the natives for only a moment, and then they resumed their attacks more furiously than before, this time coming at the ship simultaneously with many canoes from different angles, and trying desperately to grab onto "the chain plates and moldings with their fingers" in order to climb up the sides, "which were bristling with steel fore and aft." Many of them cut and bloodied, the natives fell back into their canoes. Having failed in so many attempts, they did not attack again but waited to see if the ship would come to them.

The *Morgan* slowly drifted to the edge of the reef, and the men could clearly see the coral just beneath the surface on both sides of the ship. When the copper-sheathed hull gently grazed a coral head, breaking off some fronds, the natives began jumping up and down and swinging their clubs. As boatsteerer Nelson Cole Haley observed, there was no mistaking this display, it clearly "meant they would soon be beating out our brains." The *Morgan* was eerily silent. All the men could do was watch and pray that the ship would skirt the reef. At the same time the nearby beach was lined with natives who were hoping for a very different denouement. After nearly a half hour of mounting tension, the mate gave all on board a fright, calling out that there was "a patch of coral right across our bows just under water," which the ship would could not clear. The natives, sensing that the final act was near, "began dancing up and down with delight." But then, slowly, the *Morgan*'s course shifted. The current gently turned the ship's bow until it was almost ninety degrees from the collision course it had been on just a few moments before. In ten minutes the *Morgan* was miraculously well past the reef and in deep water, slowly drifting away from danger. Now it was time for the whalemen to celebrate, firing all their guns and letting out "three cheers" as the severely disappointed natives paddled back to shore.

There are many other stories of bellicose natives attacking whaleships and, in some cases, enslaving and even eating the men they captured. Some of these attacks, like those on the *Awashonks* and the *Morgan*, were unprovoked. But it is equally true that in many instances the natives had profound reason to be angry, if not murderous. Some whaling captains were guilty of what was called "paying with the fore-top-sail," which essentially meant telling the natives that they would be paid for the proffered supplies the following day, then sailing off. Little wonder then that when the next whaling vessel stopped by this island, the chief would believe that white men lacked honor. There was, unfortunately, a good deal of truth to J. Ross Browne's claim that "there has been more done to destroy the friendly feelings of the inhabitants of the islands of the Indian and Pacific Oceans toward Americans by the meanness and rascality of whaling captains than all the missionaries and embassies from the United States can ever atone for."[44]

WHALESHIPS WERE NOT ONLY vulnerable to mutineers and hostile natives but also to whales.[45] At about ten o'clock on the evening of September 29, 1807, the *Union* out of Nantucket was cruising at a good clip off Patagonia when it plowed into a large sperm whale, a collision that caused the ship to shudder and left a gaping hole in the hull.[46] Capt. Edward Gardner, realizing that the pumps were no match for the torrent of sea water rushing into the hold, called for the men to abandon ship. Within a couple of hours the *Union* sank and Gardner and his crew of sixteen were left bobbing on the open ocean in the middle of the night in three whaleboats loaded with food, navigational instruments, water, books, and fireworks. "Our trust," Gardner later recalled, "was on Divine Providence to bear us up and protect us from harm. Never was it more fully brought to my view than at this time, [that] 'they that go down to the sea, and do business on the great waters, these see the wonders of the Lord in the mighty deep.'"[47] Gardner set a course for the Azores, and after eight days and six hundred miles of sailing, they landed on Flores Island, from which they were later rescued.

Whereas the *Union*'s encounter with a whale was most likely an accident, the *Essex*'s was most definitely not. On November 20, 1820, the *Essex* was sailing near the equator, on the offshore grounds of the Pacific, when the lookout cried, "There she blows!"[48] Capt. George Pollard, Jr., ordered whaleboats lowered and soon two of them were fast to whales. As the *Essex* sailed to meet these boats, Thomas Nickerson, a boy of fifteen who had been left to tend the wheel, saw a large whale, perhaps as much as eighty-five feet long, not more than one hundred yards from the port bow, quite still in the water and facing the ship. After diving briefly the whale surfaced again about thirty yards away. "His appearance and attitude," wrote Nickerson, "gave us at first no alarm."[49] Then the whale began moving forward, powerfully thrusting its mighty flukes, reaching a speed of three knots, which equaled the speed of the ship that was heading toward it. Before the men on board could take evasive action, the whale struck, as first mate Owen Chase recalled, "just forward of the fore chains," stopping the ship "as suddenly and violently as if she had struck a rock," and nearly throwing "us all on our faces." Water poured into the hold, and the whale continued under the ship, "grazing" the keel, and surfacing on the other side, about six hundred yards away, where it snapped its jaws open and shut and thrashed about in the water "as if distracted with rage and fury." While the men manned the pumps, the whale once again made for the ship, coming twice as fast as before, "with," Chase said, "tenfold fury and vengeance in his aspect," and its head "about half out of the water."[50] The whale smashed the port bow and was moving with such velocity and continuing to pump its flukes with such strength that the *Essex*, a ship of nearly 240 tons, was pushed backward.[51] The *Essex*'s tormentor, perhaps satisfied that his work was done, left the scene, and soon the ship listed sharply to port, giving the men just enough time to cut loose the whaleboats, get in, and pull away from the sinking hulk.

At the time of the ramming the *Essex*'s two whaleboats were miles from the ship, including one headed by Captain Pollard. When the whaleboats' crews noticed that the ship was slowly disappearing from view, they became puzzled and deeply concerned, and quickly rowed back to investigate. On coming within hailing distance of Chase's whaleboat, Pollard, dumbfounded, called out, "My God, Mr. Chase, what is the matter?" Chase, still scarcely able to believe what had happened, responded, "We have been stove by a whale."[52] The sinking of the *Essex* provided Herman Melville with the material he needed for the perfect climax to *Moby-Dick*. Had he waited just a while longer before penning his magnum opus, he would have had another example to draw on—that of the *Ann Alexander*.[53]

The *Ann Alexander* sailed from New Bedford on Saturday, June 1, 1850, thirty years after the *Essex* disaster. The beginning part of the cruise was successful, with the *Ann Alexander* capturing a number of good-size whales off Brazil, and then, in March 1851, heading round the Horn to the Pacific. The *Ann Alexander* reached the offshore grounds in August, and on the twentieth of that month, Capt. John Scott DeBlois saw sperm whales swimming in the distance. Three hours later one of the whaleboats harpooned a large bull, deemed to be "a noble fellow," and DeBlois sang out, "Boys, pull for your dear lives! Get that whale and your voyage will be five months shorter." But no sooner had the men fastened on than the whale turned, swam directly at its tormentors, and shattered the whaleboat between its jaws, sending the startled crew into the water. The whale "rushed through the wrecked boat two or three times, crushing the largest pieces left, in the wildest fury. The men were thrown hither and thither into the water, and climbing on the broken boat, were again dashed from it."[54] Two other whaleboats quickly rescued their soaked mates and set out after the offending whale. The chase had hardly commenced, however, when the whale turned again and repeated its earlier performance, "knocking" the second boat "all to pieces" and sending its crew overboard.[55] DeBlois, shorn of confidence and fearful of the whale's third act, had had enough. After collecting the second crew from the water, he turned the remaining whaleboat around and ordered the men to pull for the *Ann Alexander*, which lay seven miles away.

It was a hard row with "a heavy sea on," and with eighteen men weighing down the boat, "every now and then," a few of them "would have to jump overboard" while the rest bailed to keep the boat afloat. DeBlois thought the worst might be over, because the first few times he looked over his shoulder he saw the whale about a quarter to a half a mile off, floating at the surface. But the next time he looked the whale had disappeared. Then, "suddenly I heard under the boat a noise as of coach whips," DeBlois remembered, "and I caught a glimpse of the whale coming for me. But he just missed the boat, and turning on his side, he looked at us, apparently filled with rage at having missed his prey. Had he struck us, not a soul of us could have escaped; for the ship knew nothing of our peril, and we were too far away to have reached it by swimming. It was indeed a narrow escape."

Once the men made it back to the *Ann Alexander*, the whale reappeared about two miles off, and DeBlois, no doubt feeling less humble from his commanding perch aboard a massive ship, began sailing toward the whale, harpoon in hand, ready to launch his weapon should the gap be closed. "My blood was up," DeBlois said, "and I was fully determined to have that whale cost what it might." When the whale was within range, DeBlois threw a lance at its head, and at the same instant the whale hit the ship "with a dull thud," knocking DeBlois "off the bow clean on the deck." DeBlois commanded his men to lower a whaleboat and renew the chase at close quarters, but the crew was petrified into inaction. "If I was as big as you, and you, and you," DeBlois screamed, pointing to his men, "I could eat that whale up!" but still they wouldn't budge.

With the sun setting on the horizon, DeBlois could see the whale a half mile off, and he assumed that the battle was over. Then the whale started barreling toward the ship at an alarming rate. The *Ann Alexander* shuddered "from stem to stern" on impact, and the men were thrown to the deck. Water rushed in through the breach in the hull, and DeBlois ordered his men to cut the anchors and throw over the chains to lighten the ship in the hope of keeping it afloat. DeBlois then ran to his cabin to grab navigational equipment. Back on deck, sextant and chronometer in hand, DeBlois ordered the men into the two whaleboats, while he returned to his cabin to retrieve an almanac and some charts. Soon after DeBlois descended, a tremendous sea hit the ship, and the cabin filled with water. DeBlois swam for his life, and when he reached the upper deck he was "astonished" to discover that he had "been left alone on the doomed craft." He called to his men, pleading with them to pick him up, but they ignored him. "You don't know how quick this ship may sink," screamed DeBlois over the waves, and then to his "great relief," one of the boats came back for him.

The men spent a horrific night aboard the whaleboats near the wreck. Some of them accused the captain of getting them into this mess, to which DeBlois responded, "For God's sake, don't find fault with me! You were as anxious as I to catch that whale. I hadn't the least idea that anything like this would happen." DeBlois tried to comfort his men, but there little he could do or say to make them feel better about their plight. "Here were crowded into a small, weak boat a band of hungry sailors," recalled DeBlois, "without a drop of water or a morsel of bread. The sea was running heavily, and the boat was leaking a good deal," and they were two thousand miles from the nearest land. For the rest of the night, until dawn, the sounds of men sobbing and pleading for their lives punctuated the long hours of silence and fitful sleep.[56]

At first light DeBlois swam to the *Ann Alexander*, which was on its side, and using a hatchet, he cut away some of the masts, whereupon the ship righted slightly. Now men from the whaleboats scampered aboard and cut the other anchor free from the foremast, causing the ship to right further, giving them a chance to cut holes in the deck to search for stores below. The only items retrieved were two quarts of dried corn, six quarts of vinegar, a little barley, and a bushel of bread. Before leaving the wreck DeBlois scratched a message in the taffrail with a nail. "Save us; we poor souls have gone in two boats to the north on the wind." All the men were familiar with the fate of the *Essex*, and they knew that unless something dramatic happened, they too might be forced to draw lots to see which of them would be eaten first. Fortunately, however, it didn't come to that. After just two days at sea the men sighted a sail on the horizon and soon boarded the whaleship *Nantucket*.[57] As for the whale, his tale had a sadder ending, being killed five months later by the men of the New Bedford whaleship *Rebecca Sims*. Identifying the whale, which yielded nearly eighty barrels of oil, was easy; two harpoons from the *Ann Alexander* and some wood from its hull were still embedded in its flesh.[58]

Just as *Moby-Dick* was about to be published, in 1851, Melville learned of the *Ann Alexander's* misfortune. So carried away was he with the power of his own story that in a letter to a friend, commenting on the fate of the whaleship, Melville mingled fact with fiction. "I make no doubt," wrote Melville, "it *is* Moby Dick himself, for there is no account of his capture after the sad fate of the *Pequod* about fourteen years ago.—Ye Gods! What a Commentator is this *Ann Alexander* whale. What he has to say is short & pithy & very much to the point. I wonder if my evil art has raised this monster."[59]

The *Ann Alexander's* tale made a considerable splash in the press. Whaling stories were in vogue, and a story about a whale sinking a ship was simply too good to ignore. Not every news outlet, however, took it seriously. The *Utica Daily Gazette* argued that the *Ann Alexander's* story was too fantastic to be believed, especially the parts dealing with the escape of the men from the sinking ship and their subsequent efforts to salvage what they could. The editorialist claimed, in fact, that feats such as cutting away masts and parting anchor chains surpassed those of "Jack the Giant Killer or Saladin." The *Gazette*'s incredulity brought a quick and sharp response from the *Whalemen's Shipping List*, whose editors questioned why a newspaper located in the center of New York State, far from the ocean, should think itself knowledgeable enough to offer any commentary on the subject. The writer for the *Gazette* "may be remarkably well posted upon the navigation of mill-ponds," wrote the *Shipping List*'s editors, "and the stormy terrors of the *'raging canawl,'* but we opine that he gets altogether out of his depth when he undertakes the task of throwing doubt upon the account given by Capt. DeBlois of the loss of his ship."[60]

Mutinous men, murderous natives, and seemingly vengeful whales were some of the most merciless foes that the whalemen ever faced. But as whaling entered the twilight of the golden age, there were new enemies on the horizon that would be much more relentless and damaging than any the industry had faced before, and that would ultimately defeat the American whalemen.

Part Three

DISASTER *and*

DECAY

1861 — 1924

Chapter Seventeen

STONES IN THE HARBOR
AND FIRE ON THE WATER

THE CAPTAINS OF THE STONE FLEET GATHER IN 1861 TO
RECORD THEIR INVOLVEMENT IN THE SINKING OF STONE-FREIGHTED
WHALESHIPS IN CHARLESTON HARBOR, SOUTH CAROLINA.
PHOTOGRAPH BY THE BIERSTADT BROTHERS.

TOWARD THE END OF THE 1850S, EVEN AS WHALESHIP OWNERS
were still counting their profits, many of them looked with foreboding
to the future and the increasingly inevitable conflict between the North
and the South, which would be ignited in 1861 and engulf the nation
for four and a half long and exceptionally bloody years. Like the Revolutionary War and the War of 1812, the Civil War had a crippling
effect on American whaling. Many whaleship owners, faced with the

increasing difficulty of obtaining insurance for whaling voyages, idled their ships and sought land-based outlets for their capital. Others took "flight from the flag" and registered their ships with foreign nations in an effort to skirt the war. The demand for whale oil in the North plummeted, as kerosene became the illuminant of choice, while the pipeline of whale oil flowing to the South was completely cut off. In fact, during the course of the war, the American whaling fleet contracted by roughly 50 percent.[1]

From the outset of the war the Union sought to place a stranglehold on Confederate commerce to prevent the flow of supplies. The Union also hoped to keep the South from sending privateers to attack Union shipping. Capitalizing on its vast naval superiority, the Union planned to seize commercial and military vessels traveling to and from the South. But there was, Union military strategists thought, another way to choke the Confederacy: Why not sink a large number of ships in the channel leading to Savannah's harbor, making it impassable? Deciding to pursue this course in the fall of 1861, Gideon Welles, the secretary of the Union navy, instructed a team of purchasing agents to obtain "twenty-five old vessels of not less than 250 tons each for" this purpose. The ships were to be loaded with blocks of granite to weigh them down, and in each vessel's hull there was to be placed a "pipe and valve" so that on anchoring, the valve could be opened and the ship scuttled.[2] The purchasing agents located the readiest source of old ships available for a good price—the fleet of Northern whaleships. Whaleship owners, already experiencing a dramatic decrease in demand for whaling products, were more than willing to sell their ships for both economic and patriotic reasons. At the bargain price of about ten dollars per ton, the purchasing agents quickly obtained the twenty-five vessels, twenty-four of which were whaleships, with fourteen coming from New Bedford and Fairhaven, five from New London, two from Mystic, and one each from Nantucket, Edgartown, and Sag Harbor. The final vessel was a New York merchant ship. The whaleships ranged from around 250 to 600 tons, and while some had recently returned from whaling voyages, others were quite old, with two of them approaching one hundred, and all of them had seen better days. This most unusual group of ships—sacrificial lambs for the Union cause—was dubbed the Stone Fleet in honor of its intended cargo.[3]

Everything of value was stripped from the ships and sold at auction. Although the navy had requested that the ships be filled with granite blocks, the granite was not as readily available as fieldstone, and soon farmers, getting fifty cents per ton, were doing a brisk business dismantling their rock walls and carting them to the docks. Cobblestones, too, were ripped from the streets until 7,500 tons of stone were collected and placed in the ships' holds.[4] The Stone Fleet's captains, many of them former whaling masters, and their skeleton crews, were ordered to proceed directly to Savannah, where they were to deliver their ships "to the commanding officer of the blockading fleet."[5] Originally conceived as a clandestine operation, the outfitting of the Stone Fleet was so massive that it became an open secret among New Englanders who were eager to do their part to support the war and weaken the Confederacy. The Stone Fleet's departure from New Bedford, on November 20, 1861, was the occasion of a public celebration, with the revenue cutter *Varina* leading the fleet into the bay, while thousands of spectators cheered and loud blasts from signal guns and a thirty-four-gun salute from Fort Taber heralded the procession.[6] The *New Bedford Mercury* noted that blocking harbors in this manner was "an exceedingly pacific mode of carrying on the war, [and that] all of our citizens will join in wishing it success."[7] On November 22 the *New York Times* declared, with characteristic nineteenth-century bluster, "The rebels cannot but regard our proceedings with terror and dismay. They cannot lift a finger in resistance, or to prevent the cities through which their commerce has been carried on from becoming desolate wastes. They have tasted many a bitter cup since the rebellion broke out, but this last one is the most fatal chalice yet commended to their lips."[8]

The stormy voyage from New Bedford to Savannah was difficult for the old fleet, which finally began arriving in early December. The commanding officer for the Savannah blockade, J. S. Misroon, complained to his superior, Flag Officer Samuel F. DuPont, that there were "few good vessels among them and all badly found in every respect," noting that "several had arrived in sinking condition."[9] Whether the fleet was sinking or not, its arrival had a terrifying effect on the Confederate forces, who thought that it signaled the beginning of a Union invasion. It was a natural mistake. Some of the whaleships had false gun ports painted on their sides, called "Fiji ports," which had been placed there years before to fool would-be attackers into thinking that the whaleships were warships bristling with cannons, and therefore should not be trifled with.[10] It certainly confused the Confederates, who, fearing a major assault by a superior Union force, torched a lighthouse, fled some of their defensive positions, and reinforced Fort Pulaski, near the mouth of the Savannah River. The Confederates, however, weren't fooled for long. Soon after arriving the Stone Fleet literally began to fall apart. The *Meteor* and the *Lewis* grounded, and the *Phoenix*, "leaking badly," was intentionally sunk near shore along with three other ships, the *Cossack*, the *South American*, and the *Peter Demill*, all of which were used to create a "breakwater and bridge" to land supplies and Union troops on Tybee Island.[11]

As it turned out, the Stone Fleet's services weren't needed. The Confederates beat the Union forces to the punch by sinking a few old vessels in the channel leading to Savannah to keep the Yankee fleet out. This strategic maneuver played right into the hands of the Union and provided DuPont with an opportunity to poke fun at the enemy. In a letter to Gustavus V. Fox, the assistant secretary of the Union navy, DuPont observed that Confederate naval captain Josiah Tattnall "is doing all the work for us . . . I sent word to Misroon to get [Tattnall] . . . word if he could, that we would supply him with half a dozen vessels to help his obstruction of Pulaski."[12] The Confederate blockade of Savannah allowed what was left of the Stone Fleet to be redirected to a second target, Charleston, another critical Southern port, where Capt. Charles Henry Davis, the chief of staff under DuPont, was waiting to take charge. Davis, who was an expert on navigation and the effects of tides and currents, did not welcome this assignment. "The pet idea of Mr. Fox has been to stop up some of the southern harbors," Davis observed. "I had . . . a special disgust for this business. . . . I always considered this mode of interrupting commerce as liable to great objections and of doubtful success." Another time Davis called Fox's preoccupation with placing obstacles in Southern harbors a "maggot in his brain."[13]

Despite these misgivings Davis carried out his job and oversaw the sinking of sixteen ships of the Stone Fleet across the mouth of Charleston's main shipping channel, a task that was completed by December 20 (the few remaining ships of the first twenty-five were converted to use as storage and coaling vessels for Union forces). Davis laid the ships out in what DuPont referred to as "checkerboard or indented form, lying as much as possible across the direction of the channel," the hope being that this design would facilitate the shoaling of sand around the hulks and thereby form an impenetrable barrier to navigation.[14] Once the ships were in place their crews stripped them of valuable cordage and supplies that could be used by the enemy, cut away their masts, and then scuttled them by opening the valves on the pipes inserted into the hulls. All the ships sank under the waves, with one exception, the *Robin Hood*, which had settled on a sandbar with its main deck still well above the water. The men took advantage of this during their operation, piling the *Robin Hood*'s deck high with materials taken from the other ships, such as damaged sails, frayed lines, and worn-out blocks. But they couldn't leave the *Robin Hood* in this exposed position for fear that it might be used by Confederate ships as a landmark to guide them into port. So at dusk the *Robin Hood* was set ablaze. The Union commanders had hoped to create a conflagration of epic proportions that would light up the sky with a dazzling display and strike fear into the hearts of the Confederate onlookers, but the fire burned only fitfully, with more smoke than flames, and it was many hours before the ship burned down to the waterline and the fire was extinguished.

Shortly after the first twenty-five vessels were purchased, Welles ordered that another twenty be obtained, which was easier said than done. The first buying spree had stripped many of the whaling ports of their oldest, least seaworthy, and cheapest ships, forcing the purchasing agents to look farther afield and, in many instances, pay higher prices to get the additional ships—fourteen whaleships and six merchantmen.[15] This second Stone Fleet was prepared for scuttling and sent south toward the end of December 1861, in the same manner as the first, with Charleston as its ultimate destination. There, on January 25–26, 1862, most of the fleet was sunk across Maffitt's Channel, in the signature checkerboard fashion.

A reporter for the *New York Times*, watching the sinking of the Stone Fleet's first squadron, grew nostalgic and wistful.

Who could help feeling melancholy at the reflection that the poor old vessels, which had traversed so many thousands of miles of ocean, safely carrying human beings amid Pacific calms and Arctic colds through long years of dreary, tedious whaling voyages, were to be relentlessly destroyed? . . . Short, broad, square-sterned, bluff-bowed.... Queer old tubs with queer fittings-up, and quaint names set in elaborate beds of quaint carved work. Yet many of these fossil vessels were celebrated in their time. The fortunes of the Tabers, the Howlands, the Sims', Swifts, Coffins, Starbucks and many other New England families have been created from their voyages.[16]

While the sinking of the Stone Fleets created a psychological boost for the North, it was viewed in the South as yet another example of the Union's perfidy.[17] Gen. Robert E. Lee called "this achievement, so unworthy [of] any nation . . . the abortive expression of the malice and revenge of a people."[18] Many observers in Britain and France joined in the chorus of condemnation. *The Times* of London kept up a particularly biting line of attack, writing in several issues, "Among the crimes which have disgraced the history of mankind it would be difficult to find one more atrocious than this"; "No belligerent has the right to resort to such a warfare"; and "People who would do an act like this would pluck the sun out of the heavens, to put their enemies in darkness, or dry up the rivers, that no grass might for ever grow on the soil where they had been offended."[19] Even foreigners who strongly supported the Union had little good to say about the Stone Fleet, as evidenced by a letter from a British manufacturer, John Cobden, to Massachusetts senator Charles Sumner.

I am not pleased with your project of sinking stones to block up ports! That is barbarism. It is quite natural that, smarting as you do under an unprovoked aggression from slave-owners, you should even be willing to smother them like hornets in their nest. But don't forget the outside world, and especially don't forget that the millions in Europe are more interested even than their princes in preserving the future commerce with the vast region of the Confederate States.[20]

Given the extent of the hostility registered from overseas, compounded by the fear that such outrage might induce Britain to break the blockade, possibly precipitating another war, the Union could not simply ignore the criticism. Thus William H. Seward, the Union secretary of state, let it be known through official diplomatic channels that the sinking of the Stone Fleet was never "meant to destroy the harbor permanently. It was only a temporary measure to aid the blockade, and it was well understood that the United States would remove the obstructions after the war was over."[21] And to allay any lingering concerns that sinking stone-laden vessels in Southern harbors was an ongoing policy, Seward added that there were no plans to employ this tactic again.

All the acrimony was for naught. If the Stone Fleet impeded traffic at all, it was only for a very short while, and certainly not long enough to have any measurable impact on the outcome of the war, except perhaps to inflame the passions of the Confederacy. Powerful currents coursed around the wrecks and scoured out new channels. Swarms of marine worms soon riddled the ships with holes. As the ships' already elderly skeletons weakened, pieces of planking and ribbing broke free and washed up on nearby shores. And all the while these heavy hulks, weighted down by tons of stone, sank into the mud and sand. A coastal survey in May 1862 found that parts of Charleston's main channel were deeper than they had been before the Stone Fleet arrived, and when another survey was conducted the following year, all evidence of the fleet had simply disappeared.[22] The final requiem for the Stone Fleet came from Melville's pen, in the form of a poem he published in 1866, which he called, "The Stone Fleet, An Old Sailor's Lament."

> *I have a feeling for those ships,*
> *Each worn and ancient one,*
> *With great bluff bows, and broad in the beam:*
> *Ay, it was unkindly done.*
> *But so they serve the Obsolete—*
> *Even so, Stone Fleet!*
> *You'll say I'm doting; do but think*
> *I scudded round the Horn in one—*
> *The* Tenedos, *a glorious*
> *Good old craft as ever run—*
> *Sunk (how all unmeet!)*
> *With the old Stone Fleet.*
> . . . .
> *And all for naught. The waters pass—*
> *Currents will have their way;*

Nature is nobody's ally; 'tis well;
  The harbor is bettered—will stay.
    A failure, and complete,
    Was your Old Stone Fleet.[23]

THE SOUTH ALSO WANTED to sink Northern whaleships, but not in the manner of the Stone Fleet. Instead the Confederacy's goal was to seek out and destroy whaleships as part of a much larger naval strategy aimed at crippling the Northern economy and forcing Union warships to shift from blockading Southern ports to protecting the Union's assets at sea. But to implement this strategy, the confederacy needed ships they didn't have. When the war broke out the Union seized almost all of the United States Navy, as well as a massive merchant fleet, and the South was left in the unenviable position of having to build a navy of its own, largely from scratch. Although the South had plenty of wood, it lacked the other critical resources necessary for building and fitting out warships, including iron, ammunition, and the skilled workmen to do the job; reflecting the fact that the North had greatly industrialized over the previous decades while the South remained agrarian, its economy based to a large degree on slave labor.

Even if the resources and workmen had been available, there were no facilities to build the ships. There was only one manufacturer in the entire Confederacy capable of building a "first-class marine engine," and the South's main shipyard, at Norfolk, had been greatly damaged by Northern forces.[24] If the South was to rebuild at Norfolk and launch new warships, it would still have to run the gauntlet through the powerful Union blockade, a virtual impossibility given how many guns were trained on Norfolk's exit to the sea. Rather than give up on its desire for a navy, the Confederacy looked across the ocean for assistance, and Confederate president Jefferson Davis and his secretary of the navy, Stephen R. Mallory, sent special agents to Europe to arrange for the building of warships. One of those agents was James D. Bulloch, and of the twelve vessels he obtained for the South, none were more feared by whalemen than the *Alabama* and the *Shenandoah*.

Bulloch, a native of Georgia who had spent many years in the U.S. Navy and then the merchant service, was by all accounts shrewd, diplomatic, decisive, and thoroughly knowledgeable in naval affairs, and his role as agent for the Confederacy required that he use all his talents to their utmost.[25] Bulloch arrived in England in the summer of 1861 and immediately began commissioning ships for the Confederate navy, but he had to be extremely careful to conceal their true purpose. Britain had declared itself neutral during the Civil War, and the Foreign Enlistment Act of 1819 forbade any British subject from arming or outfitting any vessel for use by a belligerent power. Thus if the British authorities determined that a shipyard was engaged in supplying a warship for the Confederacy, it would be violating the act and its operations would be shut down and the ship confiscated. Bulloch avoided this outcome by exploiting a loophole in the law. Although it was clearly illegal for a British shipyard single-handedly to build, arm, and outfit a warship for a belligerent, it was perfectly legal, according to the lawyers Bulloch consulted, to have all these acts be performed by different vendors; the key was keeping the elements of the enterprise separate from one another, and that is exactly what Bulloch did. So well, in fact, that even though the North soon caught on to Bulloch's ploy and pleaded with the British government to confiscate the ships he was building, the government said that it couldn't because Bulloch wasn't violating the law. In this manner the CSS *Alabama* was launched from Birkenhead Ironworks in Liverpool on July 29, 1862.

At 210 feet long the *Alabama* was a beautiful, sleek, and fast ship. "Her model was of the most perfect symmetry," observed Capt. Raphael Semmes of his new command, "and she sat upon the water with the lightness and grace of a swan."[26] With auxiliary steam power the *Alabama* had the luxury of running down prizes and escaping from enemies in dead calms, when sail-driven ships could only drift. After departing from Liverpool the *Alabama* sailed to the Azores, where it was armed and provisioned by a supply ship sent by Bulloch. Now the *Alabama* was ready to seek out and destroy Union shipping wherever it could be found, and Semmes, "following Porter's example in the Pacific . . . resolved to strike a blow at the enemy's whale fishery off the Azores."[27]

On September 5, seeing a ship in the distance, the *Alabama* raised a U.S. flag and went to investigate. It was the *Ocmulgee*, a whaleship out of Edgartown, and it was so busily engaged in the process of cutting into a large sperm whale that it took little notice of the *Alabama* and, seeing the Union colors flying on its mast, had no reason to be concerned. Indeed Semmes learned later that the *Ocmulgee*'s master had thought the *Alabama* to be a military ship sent by Union navy secretary Welles, to protect the American whaling fleet from attack. "The surprise was," Semmes wrote, "perfect and complete. . . . [the *Ocmulgee*'s master, Abraham Osborne] was a genuine specimen of the Yankee whaling skipper; long and lean, and as elastic, apparently, as the whalebone he dealt in. Nothing could exceed the blank stare of astonishment that sat on his face as the change of flags took place on board the *Alabama*."[28] Osborne was not merely astonished, he was furious. "This is a disgraceful act," Osborne told Semmes, "you flying the United States colours until you come right alongside my ship and only then exchanging them for your Confederate flag." Semmes saw things a little differently, telling Osborne, "I see your point, but this is war and my tactics were quite legitimate."[29]

Osborne was ordered to bring his ship's papers and chronometer to Semmes's cabin. Semmes perused the papers, then looked up at the captain. "So you're from Edgartown," Semmes purportedly said. "I thought so. You're the kind we are looking for. Anything from that blackhearted Republican town we must burn if it comes within reach."[30] As Semmes was saying this, Osborne observed him carefully. He thought Semmes looked familiar, and then it came to him. Before the war Semmes, then a U.S. naval officer, had visited Edgartown to purchase whale oil for government use, and Osborne's parents had had him over for dinner. Osborne mentioned this, but his family's prewar hospitality meant nothing to Semmes now. Northerners were the enemy, and he had his orders. Semmes proceeded to transfer the thirty-seven whalemen, along with provisions, to the *Alabama*, and then burned the *Ocmulgee*. He had no intention of harming the whalemen, who were noncombatants, and after paroling them he let them row their whaleboats to a nearby island, from which they were later rescued.

Over the next two weeks, as the whaling season off the Azores wound down, the *Alabama* captured and burned eight more whaleships. Reflecting on the ease with which he bagged these prizes, Semmes wrote, "It was indeed remarkable, that no protection should have been given to these men, by their Government. Unlike ships of commerce, the whalers are obliged to congregate within small well-known spaces of the ocean, and remain there for weeks at a time, whilst the whaling season lasts." One of Semmes's prizes was the *Ocean Rover*, a New Bedford whaleship that had been out for more than three years in the Indian and Atlantic Oceans, whose captain had decided to stop off in the Azores on the way home to top off his voyage with the oil of a few more whales. Soon after the *Ocean Rover* was captured, its captain asked Semmes if he and his men could be accorded the same opportunity as the men of the *Ocmulgee*, to row ashore. Semmes, noting that the *Alabama* was four or five miles from land, wondered aloud whether the captain really wanted to row that far. "Oh! That is nothing," the captain replied. "We whalers sometimes chase a whale on the broad sea, until our ships are hull-down and think nothing of it. It will relieve you of us sooner and be of some service to us besides." Semmes consented and gave the whalemen time to return to the *Ocean Rover* and load six whaleboats with their belongings and provisions. When the whaleboats returned, overflowing with "plunder," Semmes, somewhat amused by the scene, said, "Captain, your boats appear to me to be rather deeply laden; are you not afraid to trust them?" The cheery captain replied, "Oh! No, they are as buoyant as ducks, and we shall not ship a drop of water." And with that Semmes, who possessed a literary flair even Melville might have admired, watched as the whalemen departed under the moonlit sky. "That night landing of this whaler's crew was," Semmes wrote, "a beautiful spectacle. . . . The boats moving swiftly and mysteriously toward the shore might have been mistaken, when they had gotten a little distance from us, for Venetian gondolas with their peaked bows and sterns."

In later reports the Northern press would claim that Semmes intentionally burned the whaleships at night, using the flaming beacons as bait to draw in other victims, relying on sailors' natural and honorable impulse to aid fellow sailors in distress. Such reports greatly offended Union sensibilities, but they reflected Northern propaganda and simply weren't true. Semmes was much smarter than that: "A bonfire by night," he knew, "would flush the remainder of the game . . . in the vicinity; and I had become too old a hunter to commit such an indiscretion. With a little management and caution, I might hope to uncover the birds no faster than I could bag them." The Northern press also demonized Semmes, labeling him no better than a pirate. However, from where Semmes sat, his actions seemed quite reasonable. His beloved South was at war, and it was his responsibility to strike at the enemy however he could. When captains pleaded with Semmes not to set fire to their ships, he responded, "Every whale you strike will put money into the Federal treasury, and strengthen the hands of your people to carry on the war. I am afraid I must burn your ship."[31] Semmes commented later that, "The New England wolf was still howling for Southern blood, and the least return we could make for the howl, was to spill a little 'ile.'"[32] Semmes's officers shared his contempt for the North, and shortly after President Abraham Lincoln issued the Emancipation Proclamation on January 1, 1863, a couple of them left a two-by-four-foot carved wooden tombstone on an island the *Alabama* visited, which read, in part, "In memory of Abraham Lincoln, President of the late United States, who died of Nigger on the brain. 1st January 1863."[33]

For nearly two years the *Alabama* pursued its mission of destruction, in the end capturing or burning nearly 70 Union vessels, fourteen of them whaleships. The end came on June 19, 1864, when the *Alabama*, which had pulled into Cherbourg, France, for much-needed repairs, left the port to engage the USS *Kearsarge*, which had been sent to hunt it down. The battle, which was witnessed by throngs of observers from the shore, ended when the hull and rudder of the outmatched *Alabama* was shattered by a cannon-ball strike just beneath the waterline, causing the ship to sink.[34] Within weeks of the *Alabama*'s demise, Confederate leaders, desperate to grab onto any scheme that might turn the tide of the war in their direction, asked Bulloch if there was another vessel that could replace the *Alabama* in order to continue to attack Union shipping. Bulloch responded in late summer by purchasing the *Sea King*, an East India merchantman docked in England that was quite similar to the *Alabama*, being about the same size and with auxiliary steam power, but the *Sea King* was the faster of the two, having traveled on one occasion 330 miles in twenty-four hours.[35] Using the same secrecy and deception that had become his hallmark, Bulloch completed his preparation of the new Confederate raider before Union representatives, fearing that the *Sea King* was to be another *Alabama*, could induce the British government to halt its departure. When the *Sea King* left the Port of London on October 8, 1864, its manifest claimed that it was nothing more than a merchant ship heading to Bombay, but British India was most definitely not on its itinerary.

In a little more than a week the *Sea King* made it to Madeira, off the coast of northwestern Morocco, where it rendezvoused with the *Laurel*, a Bulloch-sponsored steamer full of the cargo necessary to outfit and arm the raider. Also on board the *Laurel* was Capt. James I. Waddell, who would soon have the *Sea King* under his command. Waddell, who walked with a limp courtesy of a dueling injury, had been born in North Carolina. In the years prior to the Civil War he had achieved considerable success in the U.S. Navy, rising to the rank of lieutenant, but when his beloved North Carolina seceded, Waddell left the navy to serve the Confederacy, writing in his letter of resignation that, "I wish it to be understood that no doctrine of the right of secession, no wish for disunion of the States impels me, but simply because, my home is the home of my people in the South, and I cannot bear arms against it or them." After most of the *Laurel*'s cargo had been transferred to the *Sea King*, Waddell came on deck dressed in his Confederate navy uniform and informed the assembled crews of the *Laurel* and the *Sea King* that the latter had been purchased by the South and was now the CSS *Shenandoah*. Before the dumbfounded men could fully absorb this revelation, Waddell "asked them," as he later recalled, "to join the service of the Confederate states and assist an oppressed and brave people in their resistance to a powerful and arrogant northern government."[36]

Waddell had brought with him, on the *Laurel*, only eighteen hand-picked officers and crew. While they were good and dependable men, a few of whom had seen duty on the *Alabama*, there simply weren't enough of them effectively to man the *Shenandoah*. So convinced were Bulloch and Waddell of their cause, that they had hoped at least sixty out of the eighty crew members of the *Laurel* and the former *Sea King* would sign on to the *Shenandoah*, but only twenty-three did, bringing the *Shenandoah*'s total complement to a paltry forty-two, still far fewer than the 150 men who would be wanted for a warship of its size.[37] Waddell, although severely disappointed, accepted this outcome with steely composure and told those who rejected his offer to board the *Laurel*, which would take them back to England. Then Waddell ordered his men to get under way, but that proved easier said than done. There were not enough crew members to haul up the anchor, forcing Waddell and his officers to shed their coats and give the men a hand. With the anchor secured, the *Shenandoah*'s career as a Confederate raider began.

Waddell's orders were clear. "You are about to proceed upon a cruise in the far-distant Pacific," read the letter from Bulloch, "into seas and among the islands frequented by the great American whaling fleet, a source of abundant wealth to our enemies and a nursery for their seamen. It is hoped you may be able to greatly damage and disperse that fleet, even if you do not succeed in utterly destroying it."[38] Although the ultimate goal of the cruise was to damage the whaling fleet, the *Shenandoah* did not pass up the chance to gain other prizes when such opportunities arose, and within six weeks of leaving Madeira, Waddell and his men had captured six merchant vessels, scuttling or burning all but one of them, which was used to transport prisoners to Brazil.

On December 4, 1864, not long after Union general William Tecumseh Sherman began his infamous March to the Sea through Georgia and the Carolinas, the *Shenandoah* encountered its first whaleship, the *Edward* of New Bedford, just fifty miles from the island of Tristan da Cunha in the South Atlantic Ocean. The men of the *Edward Carey* were so busy cutting into a right whale that they did not notice the *Shenandoah* until it was within close range.[39] The *Edward Carey* was well provisioned, and the *Shenandoah* stood by it for two days, stripping it of much needed supplies, including cotton canvas, blocks, one hundred casks of beef and pork, and thousands of pounds of hardtack, which was, according to Waddell, "the best we had ever eaten." The *Edward Carey* was then set ablaze. Waddell didn't enjoy burning his prizes; it was simply the most effective and efficient way to dispose of them.

The captain and crew of the *Edward Carey* were taken to Tristan da Cunha, an island that had been used since the early 1800s by whalemen and sealers as a stopping-off point, and which now had a population of about forty, most of whom were of either American or British lineage.[40] On nearing the island, the *Shenandoah* was greeted by locals in a canoe who wanted to barter for supplies. When one of the islanders looked to the masthead and saw the Confederate flag, he asked what it was. When they were informed that the *Shenandoah* was a Confederate cruiser and that there were prisoners on board whom the Confederates planned to leave on the island, the islander responded:

"And where the devil did you get your prisoners?"

"From a whaler not far from here, " replied one of the *Shenandoah*'s officers.

"Just so, to be sure; and what became of the whaler?"

"We burned her up."

"Whew! Is that the way you dispose of what vessels you fall in with?"

"If they belong to the United States; not otherwise."

"Well, my hearty, you know your own business, but my notion is that these sorts of pranks will get you into the devil's own muss before you are through with it. What your quarrel with the United States is I don't know, but I swear I don't believe they'll stand this kind of work."[41]

Their concern for the Confederates notwithstanding, the islanders, whose governor was a Yankee no less, agreed to take the prisoners, who stayed on the island for three weeks until they were rescued by the USS *Iroquois*, which had been sent to pursue the *Shenandoah*.[42]

Soon after the *Shenandoah* left Tristan da Cunha, one of the crewmembers discovered a cracked coupling band on the propeller shaft. Instead of going to Cape Town, the closest port where the needed repairs could be made, Waddell took a risk and continued on his intended course to Melbourne, Australia, under sail. When the *Shenandoah* arrived, it was an instant sensation. According to Cornelius Hunt, acting master's mate on the *Shenandoah*, "Crowds of people were rushing hither and thither, seeking authentic information concerning the stranger, and ere we had been an hour at anchor, a perfect fleet of boats was pulling toward us from every direction."[43] Waddell officially requested the local governor's permission to make repairs to the *Shenandoah* as quickly as possible and take on a load of coal for its subsequent voyage. The governor, nervous about hosting a Confederate raider and mindful of Britain's official stance of neutrality, ultimately consented, and thus began the *Shenandoah*'s nearly four-week stay in Melbourne. After Waddell agreed to allow visitors, "the news spread like wildfire," wrote Hunt. Thousands of people, "all eager to say that they had visited the famous 'rebel pirate,'" came aboard.[44] The U.S. consul in Melbourne had a much dimmer view of the proceedings. Incensed about the courtesy afforded the *Shenandoah*, he repeatedly urged the governor to seize it, but to no avail.

Its repairs complete and its coal hoppers full, the *Shenandoah* left Melbourne on February 18, 1865, the day on which Fort Sumter was recaptured by Union forces. While in Melbourne, hundreds of Australians, sympathetic to the Confederate cause, asked to ship out on the *Shenandoah*, but Waddell and his officers had politely refused them, not wanting to run afoul of Britain's Foreign Enlistment Act. It was a bitter pill to swallow because seventeen men had deserted the already undermanned *Shenandoah* while it was being repaired, apparently induced to do so, Waddell claimed, by one-hundred-dollar bribes from the U.S. consul.[45] But no sooner had the *Shenandoah* gotten under way than men literally began to crawl out of the woodwork. All told, forty-five new recruits had smuggled themselves on board, most likely the night before departure. They had been hiding in the hollow bowsprit, the empty water tanks, and the lower hold. "How such a number of men could have gained our decks unseen was a mystery to me," said Hunt, "but there they were, and the question now was, how to dispose of them."[46] Despite Hunt's surprise, the stowaways, all of whom claimed to be "natives of the Southern Confederacy," were undoubtedly helped on board, as one midshipman argued, "with the knowledge and connivance of the crew."[47] Knowing full well that he desperately needed these men, Waddell decided that what was done was done, and the stowaways could stay.

The *Shenandoah* sailed next to the Caroline Islands, where it captured four whaleships. Rather than burn these prizes, Waddell had them run aground to allow the natives to strip them of whatever they wanted, and in return for this indulgence the native king agreed to take 130 whalemen off Waddell's hands and host them until another U.S. ship happened by. These whaleships provided an unexpected windfall in the form of charts the whalemen used in hunting whales. "With such charts," observed Waddell, "I not only held a key to the navigation of all the Pacific Islands, the Okhotsk and Bering Seas, and the Arctic Ocean, but the most probable localities for finding the great Arctic whaling fleet of New England, without a tiresome search."[48] Thus armed and eager to engage that fleet, the *Shenandoah* headed north, battling through typhoons and gales, and arriving off the Kamchatka Peninsula in late May, where it captured and burned the New Bedford whaleship *Abigail*.[49]

Nobody was more surprised by this turn of events than the *Abigail*'s captain, Ebenezer Nye. He had pegged the *Shenandoah* as a Russian vessel, and was amazed to discover its true identity. When Nye asked what a raider was doing in those waters, he was informed by one of the

Shenandoah's officers that, "the fact of the business is, Captain . . . we have entered into a treaty offensive and defensive with the whales, and we are up here by special agreement to disperse their mortal enemies." Nye, reflecting on the relatively poor success of his trip thus far, responded, "The whales needn't owe me much of a grudge, for the Lord knows I haven't disturbed them this voyage, though I've done my part at blubber hunting in years gone by."[50] But Nye was far unluckier than that. This was not his first experience with a Confederate raider. He had been on one of the whaleships captured and burned by the *Alabama*, leading one of his forlorn crew to exclaim, "You are more fortunate in picking up Confederate cruisers than whales. I will never again go with you, for if there is a cruiser out, you will find her."[51] Nye may have been unlucky, but he didn't lack courage. While watching his ship go up in flames, Nye told Waddell, "You have not ruined me yet; I have ten thousand dollars at home, and before I left I lent it to the government to help fight such fellows as you."[52]

As he had done with all his earlier captures, Waddell asked the *Abigail*'s crew if any of them wanted to join the *Shenandoah* and help fight for the Southern cause. One who did was the second mate, Thomas S. Manning, a native of Baltimore who, through mendacity and obnoxiousness, soon managed to become thoroughly despised by the *Shenandoah*'s crew.[53] The addition of Manning, however, was not a total loss. He provided a valuable service, using his knowledge of the Northern whaling fleet's movements to guide the *Shenandoah* to its prey. On June 21, off Cape Navarin in the Bering Sea, the *Shenandoah* picked up the trail, encountering blubber floating in the water, indicating that there were whaleships nearby. Two sails were soon sighted, and before long the *Shenandoah* captured and burned the whaleships *William Thompson* and the *Euphrates*, both from New Bedford. The next day the *Shenandoah* captured three more New Bedford whaleships, the *Milo*, the *Sophia Thornton*, and the *Jireh Swift*. The last of two of these provided the *Shenandoah* with a bit of excitement. Unlike the other whaleships the *Shenandoah* had captured, the *Sophia Thornton* and the *Jireh Swift*, both of whom had watched the *Shenandoah* overhaul the *Milo*, made a run for it, lowering their sails and heading into the ice fields.[54] The *Shenandoah*, with its steam engine pumping, set off after the two, drawing close to the *Sophia Thornton* first. A couple of warning shots from the *Shenandoah*'s thirty-two-pound Whitworth rifle, one of which tore through the *Sophia Thornton*'s topsail, convinced her captain to surrender. Meantime the much faster *Jireh Swift* sailed free of ice and was heading for the Siberian coast. Using both steam and sail power, the *Shenandoah* pursued it, moving through the water at eleven-plus knots, but even at that impressive speed it took three hours before the *Shenandoah* was able to get within shelling range, at which point, Waddell observed, "Captain Williams, who made every effort to save his bark, saw the folly of exposing her crew to the destructive fire and yielded to his misfortune with a manly and becoming dignity."[55]

Waddell's success was creating a problem. With each ship captured, the number of prisoners increased, to the point where they couldn't safely be held on board the *Shenandoah*, and since Waddell didn't want to leave the men among the ice floes, an almost certain death sentence, he had to come up with another plan. So he ransomed one of the ships. Waddell invited the *Milo*'s captain, Jonathan C. Hawes, onto the *Shenandoah* and offered him a deal: Waddell would spare the *Milo* if Hawes agreed to give a bond of $46,000 and take all the prisoners to San Francisco.[56] The bond, which was equal to the value of the ship and its contents, was intended to serve as an IOU that would be paid by the *Milo*'s owners to the Confederacy at the end of the war. Hawes quickly consented, and the *Milo*, with its human cargo, sailed south, leaving behind the *Sophia Thornton* and the *Jireh Swift*, both of which were burned. As for the bond, it was never paid, a fact that still rankled Hunt years later when he wrote a book about his time on the *Shenandoah*.

> This and a number of similar vouchers taken by us during our cruise, have not yet been paid, and if they ever intend to take up these obligations, no better time than the present will ever offer. To be sure the war terminated disastrously to our cause, but we are, therefore, so much the more in need of any trifling sums that may be owing to us. The above amounts, therefore, may be sent to me, care of my publisher, who is hereby authorized for receipt for the same.[57]

Ever since leaving Australia the *Shenandoah* had been virtually cut off from the outside world, leaving Waddell and his men to wonder and worry about the progress of the war. Thus, before the *Milo* departed, Waddell asked Captain Hawes the same question that he posed to all the captains whose ships he had captured—did he have any news from the States? Hawes's response, that the war was over, agitated Waddell. Unwilling to accept the captain's word at face value, Waddell asked him for proof, and when the captain couldn't provide such evidence, Waddell relaxed, assuming that the captain's intelligence was incorrect. But Waddell's confidence would soon be shaken. Two days later the *Shenandoah* captured and burned the *Susan Abigail*, a trader recently sailed from San Francisco. On board the *Abigail* were California newspapers that contained dire news about the South, reporting on Grant's victory at Richmond, Lee's surrender at Appomattox, and the removal of President Jefferson Davis and the rest of the Confederate government to Danville, Virginia. Waddell also read with keen interest news of Lincoln's assassination and a proclamation issued by Davis, in which he urged Southerners to carry on the war "with renewed vigor, and exhorting the people of the South to bear up heroically under their calamities."

Waddell then asked the *Susan Abigail*'s captain what Californians thought about the likely outcome of the war. "Opinion is divided," he said. "For the present the North has the advantage, but how it will all end no one can know, and as to the newspapers they are not reliable."[58] That was exactly what Waddell wanted to hear. He couldn't bear the thought the South had lost, and he took this man's opinion, along with Davis's proclamation and the fact that a couple of the *Susan Abigail*'s crew voluntarily joined the *Shenandoah*, as proof that the war was not over. Of course the newspapers on the *Susan Abigail* were three months out of date, as was the captain's information. Still, without solid proof that the war had ended, and no matter the misgivings Waddell likely had about the prudence of continuing on his present course, he did so with the same grim and unfaltering determination that had gotten him that far. And that proved to be disastrous for the Arctic whaling fleet.

The *Shenandoah* sailed North, and on June 25, 1865, burned the *General Williams* of New London. Two days later, on a beautiful and serene day, the *Shenandoah* made good use of its steam power to capture three more whaleships, the *William C. Nye*, the *Nimrod*, and the *Catherine*, all of which were essentially immobilized due to the lack of wind. Like Ebenezer Nye of the *Abigail*, Capt. James M. Clark of the *Nimrod* was no stranger to Confederate cruisers. Two years earlier, when he was captain of the *Ocean Rover*, his ship had been captured and burned by the *Alabama*. At that time the first Confederate officer to board his ship was Lt. S. Smith Lee, and now the first person from the *Shenandoah* to board the *Nimrod* was the very same Lieutenant Lee, who seemed to regard the coincidence as "an excellent joke," a sentiment most definitely not shared by Clark.[59]

There was now "a much larger delegation of Yankees than we cared to have on board," according to Hunt, "with nothing to do but plot mischief." So 150 of the whalemen were placed in whaleboats that were strung off the back of the *Shenandoah*. No sooner had Waddell's men set fire to their last three captures than the man at the mast spotted five more ships in the distance. "It was a singular scene upon which we now looked out," remembered Hunt. "Behind us were three blazing ships, wildly drifting amid gigantic fragments of ice; close astern were the twelve whale-boats with their living freight; and ahead of us the five other vessels, now evidently aware of their danger, but seeing no avenue of escape." Dodging the ice floes, the *Shenandoah* closed in on the five helpless vessels. Waddell was careful to avoid one of them, which was rumored to have men on board stricken with smallpox, but the other four were fair game, and the *Shenandoah* managed to catch three of them—the *Gypsy*, the *Isabella*, and the *General Pike*. The *Gypsy's* captain was visibly shaken on capture, and according to Hunt, "could scarcely return an articulate answer to any question addressed to him. He evidently imagined he was to be burned with his ship, or at best run up to the yardarm, and could scarcely believe it when I assured him that no personal injury or indignity would come to him."[60] After burning the *Gypsy* and the *Isabella*, Waddell ransomed the *General Pike* for $45,000 to take the *Shenandoah's* 222 prisoners back to the States. When the captain of the *General Pike* wondered aloud how he was going to feed all these prisoners, along with his crew of thirty, during the long voyage back to San Francisco, Waddell told him he could "cook the Kanakas" or Hawaiians, since there were "plenty of them."[61]

On June 27 the *Shenandoah* sighted yet another eleven whaleships in the distance. Waddell wanted to capture all of them, but caution was necessary. The wind had picked up, and if any of those vessels were to become alarmed by the *Shenandoah's* arrival, they would undoubtedly attempt to flee, greatly reducing the *Shenandoah's* chances of success. So Waddell decided to be patient. The steam engines' fires were banked, the smokestack was lowered, and the propeller lifted, as the *Shenandoah* sailed far back from the pack so as not arouse suspicion. Waddell did not have to wait long. The next day the winds died, and the *Shenandoah*'s steam engine kicked into gear. At ten A.M. the *Shenandoah* picked off the *Waverly*, a whaleship out of New Bedford, which was trailing well behind the others, and after transferring the prisoners, burned it. By 1:30 the *Shenandoah* caught up to the other ten. As Waddell recalled, "The game were collected in East Cape Bay, and the *Shenandoah* entered the bay under the American flag with a fine pressure of steam on. Every vessel present hoisted the American flag." The whaleships were gathered closely together because they were trying to render assistance to one of their number, the *Brunswick*, which had just a few hours before been stove in by a large chunk of ice and was now listing badly, having taken on a considerable amount of water. Soon after the *Shenandoah* arrived in the bay, a boat from the *Brunswick* came alongside, ignorant of the *Shenandoah*'s true identity, and asked for help. Waddell replied, "We are very busy now, but in a little while we will attend to you," and that they would.[62]

Once Waddell had the *Shenandoah* in a good strategic position, he hoisted the Confederate flag and shot off a blank cartridge to announce formally the turn of events. "All was now consternation," wrote Hunt. "On every deck we could see excited groups gathering, gazing anxiously at the perfidious stranger, and then glancing wistfully aloft where their sails hung idly in the still air. But look where they would, there was no avenue of escape. The wind, so long their faithful coadjutor, had turned traitor, and left them, like stranded whales, to the mercy of the first enemy."[63] All the whaleships lowered their colors and immediately surrendered, with one exception. The *Favorite* of Fairhaven kept its flag flying, and when one of the *Shenandoah*'s boats got near, it was clear why. There, standing on the deck, armed with whaling gun and a revolver, was the *Favorite*'s captain, Thomas G. Young, along with a couple of crew members, who were also armed. Young's courage, although not his wisdom, apparently had been amplified by a heavy dose of liquor. When the *Shenandoah*'s boat came alongside, Young yelled, with an odd questioning tone, "Boat ahoy?"

"Ahoy!"

"Who are you, and what do you want?"

"We come to inform you that your vessel is a prize to the Confederate Steamer *Shenandoah*."

"I'll be damned if she is, at least just yet, and now keep off or I'll fire into you." [64]

The *Shenandoah*'s boarding party reported to Waddell what had transpired, and he called them back to the ship. Young would have to deal directly with Waddell, who ordered his men to steam toward the *Favorite*. In the meantime Young's crew, who had begun to "get shaky in the knees" at the prospect of tangling with the *Shenandoah*, removed the firing caps from the captain's guns and took all his ammunition, and then lowered themselves and the whaleboats into the water, leaving Young alone on the ship. As Young, who was more than sixty years old, watched the *Shenandoah* approach, he became stoic about the possibility of literally going down with his ship. "I have only four or five years to live anyway," he thought to himself, "and I might as well die now as any time, especially as all I have is invested in my vessel, and if I lose that I will have to go home penniless and die a pauper." [65] When the *Shenandoah* had come within hailing range of the *Favorite*, the officer of the deck called to Young, "Haul down your flag!"

"Haul it down yourself! God Damn you! If you think it will be good for your constitution."

"If you don't haul it down we'll blow you out of the water in five minutes."

"Blow away, my buck, but may I be eternally blasted if I haul down that flag for any cussed Confederate pirate that ever floated." [66]

This display of bravado amused Waddell, and with grudging respect for Young's sheer audacity, he sent an armed contingent onto the *Favorite* to capture Young, rather than fire on the ship at close range. As the Confederate boarding party made its approach, Young attempted to fire the whaling gun, and when he discovered that its caps were missing, he lowered his weapon and surrendered. When Young boarded the *Shenandoah*, recalled Hunt, "it was evident that he had been seeking spirituous consolation, indeed to be plain about it, he was at least three sheets to the wind, but by general consent he was voted to be the bravest and most resolute man we captured during our cruise."[67]

Of the ten vessels cornered in East Cape Bay, eight were burned, including the *Hillman, Nassau, Isaac Howland, Brunswick, Martha 2d, Congress 2d, Favorite,* and the *Covington.* This blaze created a scene that Hunt described as one "never to be forgotten by any who beheld it. The red glare from the . . . vessels shone far and wide over the drifting ice of those savage seas; the crackling of the fire as it made its devouring way through each doomed ship, fell on the still air like upbraiding voices."[68] The remaining vessels, the *Nile* and the *James Maury,* were ransomed and sent to San Francisco with all the prisoners on board. There was, however, one passenger on the *James Maury* who technically didn't qualify as a prisoner. Before the *Shenandoah* had appeared, the captain of the *James Maury,* who had brought along his wife and three children, died. Rather than bury her husband at sea, the wife had him preserved in a whiskey cask for the journey home.

WADDELL NOW HEADED NORTH through the Bering Strait. He knew there were more whaleships in that direction, and he wanted to catch them if possible. But in less than a day of sailing Waddell turned around and headed south. There were, he later wrote, two reasons for this about-face. First, because it was getting colder and there were so many ice floes, he worried about "the danger of being shut up in the Arctic Ocean for several months." He was also concerned that, if word had gotten out about his exploits, enemy warships would soon be coming for him, and "it would have been easy for them to blockade the *Shenandoah* and force her into action."[69] According to whaling historian John Bockstoce, "neither of these . . . [reasons] is convincing."[70] Instead he argues that the newspapers that Waddell captured from his prizes were actually of more recent vintage than he had admitted in his diary of the events, and that, as a result, Waddell knew that the war was virtually over. Thus his decision to head south had less to do with escaping the elements or enemy cruisers than it did with wanting to learn more about the status of the war. Whichever explanation is closer to the truth, by August 2 the *Shenandoah* was off the coast of California, when it spotted a ship in the distance and gave chase.

It was the British bark *Barracouta*, on its way to Liverpool from San Francisco. Waddell dispatched a boat to inquire about the news, and when it returned, the news couldn't have been worse. The Union had indisputably won. "The Southern cause," wrote Hunt, "was lost,— hopelessly—irretrievably—and the war ended. Our gallant generals, one after another, had been forced to surrender the armies they had so often led to victory. State after State had been overrun and occupied by the countless myriads of our enemies, until star by star the galaxy of our flag had faded, and the Southern Confederacy had ceased to exist."[71] Waddell was stunned. "My life had been checkered from the dawn of my naval career," he wrote, "and I had believed myself schooled to every sort of disappointment, but the dreadful issue of that sanguinary struggle was the bitterest blow."[72]

The *Shenandoah's* career as a Confederate raider was over. Waddell and his men had captured thirty-eight ships and 1,053 prisoners. The thirty-two ships that the *Shenandoah* destroyed were valued at nearly $1.4 million; and of those thirty-two, twenty-five were whaleships. But it was all for naught. The *Shenandoah's* actions had absolutely no impact, other than psychological, on the course of the war, which had ended well before the most destructive phase of the *Shenandoah's* cruise had even begun. Now Waddell had to decide what to do. From the *Barracouta* he had learned not only that the South had lost but also that he and his men had been branded pirates and traitors by President Andrew Johnson's administration and that U.S. Navy warships had been sent to hunt him down. Rather than submit to what he knew would be particularly harsh treatment should the *Shenandoah* run into an American port, Waddell set a course for England, where he assumed, as Bulloch later wrote, that he would "receive impartial consideration and a fair, equitable hearing" from the government and the courts.[73] So as to avoid arousing suspicion during the *Shenandoah's* long journey, Waddell stripped the decks and the crew of arms, placing them below, planked over the gun ports, and lowered the steam engine's stack, trying as best he could to make the *Shenandoah* look like nothing more than a fine merchant ship going about its business.[74]

Meanwhile word of the tragedy that befell the Northern fleet had begun to spread.[75] Bold headlines in Northern newspapers and first-hand accounts from the *Shenandoah's* prisoners heralded the calamity:

THE PIRATE SHENANDOAH
HER CRUISE IN THE ARCTIC SEAS—
WHOLESALE DESTRUCTION
OF AMERICAN WHALERS[76]

The greatest outcry and the deepest grief emanated from the staunch Yankee port of New Bedford, from which most of the burned vessels hailed. The editors of one of the local papers, the *Republican Standard*, bemoaned the failure of the American government to come to the aid of the whaling fleet at this time of its direst need. "It seems," the editors complained, "that there has been gross negligence on the part of the government, in leaving so important of a branch of national industry and so much property without adequate protection. One or two powerful steamers should have been cruising in the North Pacific ever since we had reason to apprehend the depredations by Confederate cruisers."[77]

After traveling seventeen thousand miles without a single stop for provisions, the *Shenandoah* arrived in England on November 5, to an extremely chilly reception. As one London paper put it, "The reappearance of the *Shenandoah* in British waters is an untoward and unwelcome event. When we last heard of this notorious cruiser she was engaged in a pitiless raid upon American whalers in the North Pacific. . . . It is much to be regretted . . . that no federal man-of-war succeeded in capturing the *Shenandoah* before she cast herself, as it were, upon our mercy."[78] The *Shenandoah*'s return fanned the flames of American anger over Britain's duplicitous role in building and outfitting Confederate raiders, while at the same time it mortified the British politicians and their constituents, who knew that America's anger was partly, if not wholly, justified. There followed a few tense days of detention during which the men of the *Shenandoah* waited to hear news of their fate. Then, much to their surprise and great relief, they were set free. The British government had concluded that it had neither the grounds nor the desire for pursuing any form of prosecution. The *Shenandoah* was handed over to the U.S. consul, and the men who had sailed her went their separate ways. The surrender of the *Shenandoah*, however, was not the end of the story. Instead of forgetting about Britain's role in the launching of the *Alabama*, the *Shenandoah*, and a third raider, the

Florida, the American government demanded that Britain pay reparations for the damages that these ships inflicted on Northern shipping during and after the war. An international tribunal ultimately arbitrated these "*Alabama* claims," and the United States was awarded $15.5 million in gold.[79]

As for Waddell, he stayed ten years in England and then moved to Hawaii to take command of a mail ship that ran between Yokohama and San Francisco, finally settling in Annapolis, where, after a brief stint as an oyster warden, he died in 1886.[80] Until the end Waddell never wavered from his conviction that the *Shenandoah* had pursued a noble cause in a noble fashion. As he wrote in his memoir, "She was the only vessel which carried the flag of the South around the world. . . . The last gun in defense of the South was fired from her deck. . . . She ran a distance of 58,000 miles and met with no serious injury during a cruise of thirteen months. . . . Her anchors were on her bows for eight months. She never abandoned a chase and was second to no other cruiser, not excepting the celebrated *Alabama*. I claim for her officers and men a triumph over their enemies and over every other obstacle which they encountered."[81]

The *Shenandoah*'s return to England brought to a close one of the most dramatic chapters in the history of American whaling. The sinking of the Stone Fleet and the depredations of Confederate raiders combined to destroy more than eighty whaleships, and the war itself had caused a serious disruption and hobbled the industry. If history repeated itself, then whaling would rise again, as it had after the Revolutionary War and the War of 1812, when American whalemen rebounded from near destruction to grow again into a major national and international commercial force. But the Industrial Revolution had changed the American landscape so profoundly and irrevocably that history no longer served as a useful guide. The dissolution of the American whaling industry would be further accelerated by a competing source of energy that would soon render the Yankee whaleship a historical relic.

Chapter Eighteen

FROM THE EARTH

DETAIL OF A *VANITY FAIR* CARTOON (APRIL 1861)—
*GRAND BALL GIVEN BY THE WHALES IN HONOR OF THE
DISCOVERY OF THE OIL WELLS IN PENNSYLVANIA.*

A CARTOON IN *VANITY FAIR* IN 1861 DEPICTS A ROOM FULL OF
well-dressed whales at a grand ball, dancing, drinking, and looking
exceptionally happy. The banners hanging in the background offer
clues to their merriment. One proclaims, "The Oil Wells of Our Native
Land, May They Never Secede," while another reads, "We Wail No
More For Our Blubber." The whales were giddily celebrating the
recent discovery of oil in Pennsylvania, an event that presaged the
whale industry's rapid decline. Before the petroleum revolution, whale

oils had been used extensively in various manufacturing processes. During that time, whale oil merchants held their own against a wide range of competitors. But the viscous black oil that gushed out of the earth provided a challenge that could not be circumvented, becoming so plentiful, so versatile, and so cheap that it quickly replaced whale oil in many of its applications. It is hardly a wonder then that the whales in the cartoon were so joyful.

Even by the 1840s whale oil's dominance in lighting had already come under sustained attack. Refinements in production and improvements in lamp designs made lard oil, boiled from the fat of hogs, an increasingly attractive lighting source, especially for those who lived far from the ocean and were surrounded by farms with large numbers of hogs, or "prairie whales" as they were called.[1] And an entirely new form of illuminant called camphene, a distillate of turpentine mixed with alcohol, had come on the scene, quickly proving to be another potent threat to whale oil's market position. The rise of these and other competitors led many in the press to proclaim that whale oil's days were numbered. An article that appeared in the *New York Journal of Commerce* in 1842 is typical of the times:

This spring there has been almost no demand from the interior for sperm oil, and very little from the city. Camphine and lard oil have supplied the demand at a cheaper rate. Crude sperm has fallen one third in price, and yet remains neglected. The hogs have fairly run the whales out of the market, and are likely to hold their ground, unless some new process of cheapening can be contrived on the other side. The woods of the West are more full of the quadruped than any ocean is of the finny whale, and the quadruped is much more easily taken.[2]

Such pieces engendered a lively and often humorous response from whalemen and their communities, whose financial health depended on them.[3] The *Nantucket Inquirer* warned its readers in 1843 against believing the rumors of the whale oil industry's imminent demise.

Great noise is made by many of the newspapers and thousands of the traders in the country about Lard Oil, Chemical Oil, Camphene Oil, and a half dozen other luminous humbugs; and it has been confidently predicted by more than one astute prophet that the Sperm Oil trade would soon come to an end, and the whales be left in undisturbed possession of their abode ... it has even been said, *horribile dictu,* that Nantucket must soon be reduced from its present elevated position among the isles of the sea and the habitations of the earth, to a poor, miserable spot capable only of nourishing sand-lice and horse-shoes, and compelled to live on its accumulated stock of Sperm oil and candles! But let not our envious, and—in view of the Lard oil mania—we had well nigh said, *hog*-gish opponents, indulge themselves in any such dreams.[4]

Whalemen and their supporters were quick to highlight the disadvantages of their competitors. Many respondents, for example, chose to lampoon lard oil by pointing out that while hogs were fine to eat, the oil they produced would never do because it congealed when cold, smelled when burned, and didn't produce a strong, clean light.[5] As for camphene, while whaling merchants grudgingly had to admit that it was cheaper than whale oil and burned quite brightly, they didn't let anyone forget that this new burning fluid was extremely volatile. Reports of exploding camphene lamps were received in whaling communities with unrestrained glee, sprinkled with more than a touch of I-told-you-so.[6] The *Nantucket Inquirer,* after noting one such explosion at a Philadelphia hotel, observed rather harshly, "How hard people are to learn! If they will use such articles, they deserve to be 'blown up.'"[7] The *Whalemen's Shipping List* recommended that the government take steps to protect the people from this dangerous substance.[8] Many commentators argued that the apparent economy of camphene evaporated if one factored in the true costs of using it. Besides being so combustible, camphene burned faster than whale oil, and if it were not liberally supplied with oxygen, it created a considerable amount of soot. What good were camphene and other chemical burning fluids, wrote the editor of the *Nantucket Inquirer,* "if a man save sixpence or a shilling on a gallon of illuminating fluid, if at the same time his shirt collar is begrimed with particles of lampblack, and the saved shilling thereby be demanded for soap; or his lungs exsiccated by reason of the undue absorption of those atmospherical dregs which are only left for him to breathe ... [or] his eyes put out, or his children burnt to death by the explosion of a quantity of cheap 'portable gas.' "[9]

Whale oil merchants could dismiss or mock lard oil and camphene, but that still didn't alter the fact that these and other competitors were eating into the merchants' profits. One of the factors that helped those merchants hold on in the face of such intense competition was the dramatic urban population growth in the United States, which caused the demand for all types of lighting to rise. Nevertheless, at midcentury the situation for whale oil merchants had already worsened as the competition improved. Hydrogen gas, for example, derived from coal had been used for decades in a small number of American cities as a lighting source, but only to a very limited extent because of the high cost of producing the gas and the lack of piping necessary for distribution.[10] By the 1850s, however, with the price of production on the decline and distribution networks becoming more extensive, the use of coal gas, or "town gas" as it was often called, expanded dramatically. Even in New Bedford, where one might assume that anything that threatened whale oil's dominance would be shunned, gas came into use, much to the chagrin of the editors of the *Whalemen's Shipping List*, who noted in June 1852 that "we have lived to witness ... *the introduction of Gas into New Bedford*—that ancient city of the whale! ... As we reflect upon these humiliating vicissitudes, we seem to hear the laugh of the whales. ... Mr. SPERMACETI may even now be ponderously nudging half a dozen of his wives, and whispering 'Spout in peace hereafter, my dears! Enjoy hereafter the savory squid! No more harpooning, no more cutting and running, no more *trying* circumstances! They have got up gas in that Golgotha of New Bedford! I don't know what gas is—all I know is that it ain't blubber."[11]

The first gas plant in New Bedford began operating one year later, in 1853, and quickly earned converts, including William How, who wrote in his diary on February 5, 1853, that, "Today marks an epoch in this City's history, by the introduction, for the 1st time, of gas in lanterns and stores. Quite a crowd followed the 'Lamplighters' on their tour. The streets presented a brilliant appearance, and the stores were very much lighter than under the 'old dispensation.' The streets were crowded to see the effect of the new burning fluid, and all seem to be pleased. May it be a long time before the inhabitants shall consent to go back to the old [whale] oil lamps, and wander through the streets in doubt as to the way they may be going."[12]

Kerosene proved to be an even greater threat to whale oils. First refined in the late 1840s by Canadian geologist Dr. Abraham Gesner, kerosene, a distillate of bituminous tar or "asphalte rock," burned cleanly and much more brightly than any other illuminant on the market, and produced its brilliant light at a far lower cost per unit of light.[13] Within a decade, it was well on its way to illuminating millions of American homes. By the end of the 1850s there were thirty-three kerosene plants in the United States, and people found it easy to switch to this new lighting source by simply replacing the whale-oil burners in their lamps with new ones designed to burn kerosene.[14]

To compound these difficulties, the price of whale oils, especially sperm, rose dramatically in the 1850s, in part because whalemen had to spend more money and time, traveling farther to chase an ever-dwindling number of whales. The average price for a gallon of sperm oil, which was $1.00 in 1848, reached a high of $1.77 only seven years later. Similarly, whale oil, which stood at thirty-three cents in 1848, had more than doubled to seventy-nine cents in 1856.[15] Just when the whale oil industry needed to be at its most competitive, it was slowly pricing itself out the market, and its competitors swooped in to take advantage of the situation. An article in a March 1858 issue of the *New York Evening Post* highlighted the problem. After noting that prices for crude sperm oil appeared to be rising once again, the paper said, "Our sagacious Yankee friends at the east think this is smartness; well, admitting so, will they not concede that the more they advance the price of the crude article the more they cut into the interest of the manufacturer; and finally into their own in the end; as it is notorious that year by year Lard oil and other substitutes are being used in its stead, on account of its higher cost."[16]

By the end of the 1850s Americans were already spending much more on both gas and kerosene than they were on whale oil.[17] The most devastating blow came in 1859 when "Colonel" Edwin L. Drake drilled a well seventy feet into the ground in the small town of Titusville, Pennsylvania, and struck oil. Soon thereafter the whale oil industry was sent reeling.[18]

The discovery of crude oil proved especially disastrous to whale oil interests because it provided a new and much more plentiful raw material for the production of kerosene.[19] Before Drake's discovery, kerosene was primarily derived from coal. While the coal-to-kerosene process worked well enough, the kerosene plants in operation could supply only a limited amount of product, far less than consumer demand for lighting could bear. After Drake's discovery the supply problem was solved. The amount of Pennsylvanian crude oil being taken out of the ground rose from roughly half a million barrels in 1860 to three million barrels by 1862, and much of that oil was refined into a veritable flood of cheap kerosene, which surged throughout the country, largely displacing whale oil as well as other illuminants.[20] The new petroleum industry not only marginalized whale oil's use in lighting, but it also loosened whale oil's traditional hold on the market for lubrication because many of the products refined from oil, including kerosene, turned out to be excellent lubricants and were soon in great demand in the increasingly industrialized American economy.

The whaling industry had no illusions about how this would affect its business. The numbers were simply too great to ignore. During 1847, its most productive year for oil production, the American whaling industry processed just over 430,000 barrels of sperm and whale oil combined, a mark that petroleum beat in 1860, its first full year of production. Just two years later, when Pennsylvania's wells produced three million barrels, the entire American whaling fleet produced a comparatively paltry 155,000 barrels, and in subsequent years the gap widened at an astonishing rate, as new oil deposits were discovered and new wells sunk.[21] In 1860 Capt. Willis Howes of the whaling vessel *Nimrod* commented in his journal on the reality confronting whalemen at the dawn of this new age. "Capt. Low . . . came on board," wrote Howes, "Talking about pumping up oil at the rate of 90 . . . [barrels] per day. In fact coal and its offspring oil was the all absorbing exciting topic of the day and was likely to become one of the planks in each political platform of the various presidential nominees. In a word this infernal pursuit of extracting oil from the bowels of the earth was second only to California in its palmiest days."[22] And it wasn't only miners that were heading for the oil fields. Many whalemen abandoned their ships and journeyed to Pennsylvania, happy to leave an industry with declining fortunes for one that was on the rise. One writer called the "number of whale-catchers and former dealers in whale-oil now engaged in the petroleum business . . . somewhat remarkable."[23]

Throughout the early 1860s whale oil merchants fought a losing battle against the rise of petroleum and other whale oil substitutes. But when the Civil War ended in 1865, and a nation at peace sought to revitalize its ravaged economy, the demand for spermaceti and whale oil, which was in relatively short supply, spiked, sending the price of the former to an all-time high of $2.55, and the latter to $1.45.[24] Then, as quickly as they had risen, the prices began falling again, and little by little whale oil merchants continued to lose market share. When the editors of the *Whalemen's Shipping List* published their annual trade review in 1870, all they could offer their readers was depressing news: "Because of the poor results and low prices, combined with the high cost of outfits, many were deterred from fitting out their ships again, and the fleet at home ports on the New Year, was largely in excess of former years. Our merchants do not look upon the future of whaling with encouragement, and seem disposed to distrust it as to its pecuniary results."[25] Not long after these words were written, the whaling industry was jolted by not just depressing but tragic news, and it came from the Far North.

Chapter Nineteen

ICE CRUSH

THIS PRINT, BASED ON A PAINTING BY BENJAMIN RUSSELL AND TITLED
ABANDONMENT OF THE WHALERS IN THE ARCTIC OCEAN, SHOWS THE
HEAVILY LOADED WHALEBOATS BATTLING THROUGH THE WAVES JUST
SOUTH OF ICY CAPE, TRYING TO GET TO THE WHALESHIPS WAITING
TO RESCUE THEM, IN SEPTEMBER 1871.

THE 1871 BOWHEAD HUNTING SEASON STARTED OFF IN THE USUAL
fashion. Forty whaleships headed north in the early spring on their
way to the frigid waters off Point Barrow in the Arctic Ocean. The captains of those ships, most of them seasoned veterans of Arctic cruises,
knew that many potential dangers lay ahead. Whaling was difficult and
harsh work no matter where it was conducted, but whaling in the far
north was the most unforgiving of all. It wasn't the whales that caused
most of the problems; bowheads were far less aggressive than sperm or

even right whales, although they did their fair share of damage. Rather, it was the Arctic weather that whalemen feared the most. Between the ice floes, the bitter temperatures, the freezing water, and the unpredictable and often violent gales, the margin between life and death was hair-raisingly thin. Each season the captains had to balance the desire to catch more whales with the need to respect the elements and turn back before it was too late. In 1871, as the northern fleet slowly edged northward, troubling signs abounded, yet the captains pressed on. They decided to gamble against the weather and they lost, leading to the greatest single disaster in the history of American whaling.

Ever since Capt. Thomas Welcome Roys led his frightened crew through the Bering Strait in 1848, whaleships had ventured to the Far North in search of bowheads. The first few years were a tease. The weather was relatively mild and the catches were phenomenal, leading a Honolulu newspaper in 1850 to paint a most flattering picture of whaling in the Arctic. "We doubt so much oil was ever taken in the same period, by the same number of ships and attended with so few casualties. In fact, a cruise in the Arctic Ocean has got to be but a summer pastime, as is proved by the fact that the wives of some half dozen of the captains accompanied their husbands in the last cruise, with the same willingness that they would have gone to Saratoga or Newport."[1] But this image was shattered the next year, when catches plummeted and inclement weather and heavy ice conspired to destroy seven ships. Never again would anyone, and certainly no self-respecting whaleman, view whaling in the Arctic with such insouciance. One New Bedford whaling captain in 1852 went so far as to wonder whether men should whale there at all, writing, "I felt as I gazed upon the great frozen ice-fields stretching far down to the horizon that they were barriers placed there by Him to rebuke our anxious and overweening pursuit of wealth."[2] Despite the potentially lethal weather, or even the possibility of displeasing God in their search for lucre, whaleships returned to the Arctic each year. And in 1871 dozens of whaleships of the northern fleet, bound by this tradition, began their journeys hopeful that this season would be a good one.

The fleet made it to the lower reaches of the Bering Sea in early May, and finding the ice tightly packed and more southerly than they had expected, hunted for right whales. Slowly the fleet inched north and by June, they were off Cape Navarin on the Siberian coast, where six whales were taken. Shifting currents, strong winds, and dense fogs, however, made navigating through the large and very mobile ice floes exceptionally difficult, and the captains and their crews had to be on guard constantly to avoid collisions. But no matter how vigilant they were, collisions did happen, as the men on the *Oriole* learned. Toward the end of June, their ship was stove in by ice, and when the captain ordered the pumps manned, it quickly became apparent that the wounded ship was beyond repair. The pumps were no match for the flood of freezing ocean water rushing in below the waterline. The men were barely able to keep the *Oriole* afloat until it could be brought into Plover Bay, where it was sold for parts to the captain of the *Emily Morgan*. The northern whaling season of 1871 already had its first victim.

Shortly thereafter the ice retreated farther north, allowing the fleet to pass through the Bering Strait, with all the ships arriving in the Arctic Ocean by the beginning of July. Faced with an impenetrable wall of ice ahead of them, and the bulk of the whales still many hundreds of miles away, the men began walrus hunting. This was not an idle pastime but an alternative way of making money. Walrus oil was as valuable as whale oil, and sometimes even a bit more remunerative, and the ivory tusks were prized as well. So, year after year, while waiting for the ice to recede and the serious whaling to commence, the whalemen turned to harpooning and shooting walruses. The tusked pinnipeds didn't have a chance. Docile to begin with and easily approached, both on the ice and in the water, the walruses were killed by the tens of thousands. A whaling captain, even in an age which countenanced animal cruelty with barely a thought, called the walrus hunt "one of the most cruel occupations that I know of," and claimed that "many a humane whaleman has felt guilty and turned aside as he did it." While the bounty of walrus oil and ivory was good news for the whalemen, it was devastating to the local natives, who depended on walrus meat and blubber for sustenance. The whalemen were literally taking food out of the Eskimos' mouths and forcing them to travel in ever widening arcs to hunt for walrus or risk starvation. Many whalemen knew that this was happening, but only a few spoke out against it. "I wish to say to the ship agents and owners in New Bedford and elsewhere," began one whaling captain's epistle, "that the wholesale butchery of the walrus pursued by nearly all their ships during the early part of each season will surely end in the extermination of this race of natives. . . . If this is continued much longer, their fate is inevitable, as already this cruel persecution had been felt along their entire coast."[3] During the 1871 season the walrus hunt, while not as good as in years past, went well enough. The *Monticello*'s four whaleboats, for example, killed five hundred walrus in less than a month, which yielded three hundred barrels of oil and many hundreds of pounds of ivory.[4]

At the end of July favorable winds drove the ice away from the Alaskan shore, and the whaling fleet took advantage of this opportunity and began sailing toward Point Barrow, which lies just above the seventieth parallel and is the northernmost spot in Alaska. In the early years of the Arctic fishery, when Roys and his peers were active, whalemen didn't have to travel that far because there were more bowheads, and they could be found in and around the Bering Strait and even farther south. But over the next couple of decades, as the bowhead population dwindled, the whalemen were forced to travel ever northwards in search of large concentrations of whales. Now that the conditions were right, the northern fleet crept up the coast, following a narrow ribbon of water just a few miles wide, with the land hard on their right flank and a massive shield of pack ice on their left, whaling when they could and doing their best to keep from grounding on the shoals. On August 11 the winds shifted, pushing the pack ice toward the shore, causing many of the ships to scramble to avoid being caught or crushed. Whaleboats that were on the hunt were suddenly marooned in the ice or stove in, and their crews had to haul their boats many miles to their ships over the jagged and bobbing ice floes. On August 13 the ice pack ground to a halt and the wind died down, but a couple of days later another strong wind took its place and the ice was driven closer to the shore. The fleet was pinned down in the vicinity of Point Belcher, spread out along a twenty-mile sliver of open water that was less than a mile wide in places, and only fourteen to twenty-four feet deep.

Although the situation was increasingly precarious, none of the whalemen panicked. In seasons past strong northeast winds had usually come to their rescue, pushing the pack ice offshore and allowing them to finish hunting and leave the Arctic before ice swallowed up all the open water and cut off their escape route. The men expected that this would happen again, and in the meantime whaling continued, with a twist. Hemmed in by the shoal water and ice, the whaleships could not get to the whales, so the whaleboats were sent out on hunting expeditions. Provided with food and all the implements for whaling, the whaleboat crews sailed off in search of prey, traveling many miles from their ships, and setting up temporary base camps on the ice floes. When they harpooned a whale they would tow it back to the camp and start cutting in, turning the edge of the ice floe into a cutting stage. While one whaleboat towed the severed slabs of floating blubber back to the ship for processing, the other whaleboats kept hunting. The men continued this bone-wearying task for days at a time, sleeping fitfully on the ice floes and using their propped-up sails for protection from the cold and wind.[5]

Every day the men prayed for wind from the northeast. On August 25 it came. The men's spirits lifted as they watched the ice move four to eight miles offshore. In short order they were back to traditional whaling, and the whaling was good. Perhaps this would be a saving season after all. The only hint of doubt came from the Eskimos, who visited the ships to trade for goods. They told the whalemen that they should leave, and soon, because this was going to be a bad winter, and when the ice came back the ships would be stuck. The whalemen, generally lacking respect for the wisdom and knowledge of the natives, disregarded this advice. They had been sailing these waters for years and were confident that the worst was past. They would not let the warnings send them packing, especially now that the whales were plentiful and the weather so fine.[6]

The whalemen's confidence, however, quickly faded. On August 29 the weather changed precipitously. With the wind blowing from the southwest, it started snowing, and the ice crept closer to the shore. Open water was vanishing fast, and many of the whaleships had to work hard to keep from being crushed or run aground, and a few of them had to slip their cables to get out of the way of the oncoming ice. On August 31 Timothy Packard, the captain of the *Henry Taber*, took in the ominous scene and wrote in his journal, "Oh how many of this ship's company will live to see the last day of next August? God only knows. I will trust to his all wise hand."[7] The following day the mate of the *Eugenia* observed, "some twenty-six sail in sight. All jammed in the ice close into the beach. Things look bad at present."[8]

While the men of the *Roman* were busy cutting into a whale on the first day of September, the ship got trapped between ground ice and a massive floe that descended on it from offshore. The floe crushed the

Roman's hull "like an egg-shell" and lifted the ship partway out of the water.[9] As the sound of cracking timbers filled the air, the *Roman's* crew managed to lower three whaleboats and pull them a safe distance away from the ship, where the petrified men watched as the ice relaxed and then tightened its grip three times, turning their once-proud ship into a splintered wreck. Within forty-eight minutes the *Roman*, or what was left of it, sank out of sight. The orphaned men walked and then sailed until they reached other ships in the fleet, which welcomed them on board. The next day a similar scene unfolded, but this time it was the *Comet's* turn to be crushed and its crew orphaned. Amazingly, even after these two disasters, many of the whaleships continued whaling. The captains still believed that the weather would turn and release them from its icy grip. Then, on September 8, the *Awashonks* succumbed to the ice, and yet another crew had to be rescued. Now survival, not whaling, became the major concern.[10]

On September 9 the captains met to consider their options. The situation was bleak. Winds from the southeast and southwest continued to push the ice toward the shore, slowly closing the already narrow open-water channel that provided the ships with their only refuge. "Offshore is one vast expanse of ice," wrote William Earle, a mate on the *Emily Morgan.* "Not a speck of water to be seen in that direction. All but three of the northern fleet have come down and anchored near us. There are twenty ships of us lying close together. There seems to be but little hope of our saving the ship or any of the other ships being saved."[11] The weight upon the captains' shoulders was immense. Their deliberations would determine the fate of their ships and their men. "We felt keenly our responsibility," wrote Capt. William H. Kelley of the *Gay Head,* "with three million dollars worth of property and 1,200 lives at stake. Young ice formed nearly every night and the land was covered with snow. There was every indication that winter had set in."[12]

The captains knew that they and their men could not survive the winter. There were just a couple of months' worth of supplies on board. Their only hope lay in contacting the whaleships that they thought might still be farther south beyond the ice in open water. To do this, the captains ordered the smallest ships of the fleet, the *Kohola* and the *Victoria,* to be lightened as much as possible, believing that they might then draw so little water that they could snake their way down the coast and reach the whaleships. But even after every conceivable item was removed from the ships, they still did not ride high enough to make it over the nearby shoals. Fortunately there was a backup plan. At about the same time that the ships were lightened, three whaleboats, under the command of Capt. D. R. Frazer of the *Florida*, headed south, and on September 12, after a round trip of 141 miles, this expeditionary force returned with good news. Seven whaleships were still south of Icy Cape, and they were ready to remain there to assist in the rescue. "Tell them all," said Capt. James Dowden of the *Progress*, in a flourish that would become legendary, "I will wait for them as long as I have an anchor left or a spar to carry a sail."[13]

When Frazer shared this intelligence with the other captains, they decided that the time had come to abandon their ships and head south. To defend their decision to others who might question it, the captains drafted a letter on September 12: "Know all men . . . that we, the undersigned, masters of whale-ships now lying at Point Belcher . . . have all come to the conclusion that our ships cannot be got out this year, . . . and not having provisions enough . . . and being in a barren country, where there is neither food nor fuel to be obtained, we feel ourselves under the painful necessity of abandoning our vessels, and trying to work our way south with our boats, and, if possible, get on board of ships that are south of the ice." The masters briefly recounted the recent destruction of the whaleships, and claimed that if the members of the fleet were forced to overwinter, "Nine out of ten would die of starvation or scurvy before the opening of spring."[14]

Even before Frazer returned, the captains had begun dispatching whaleboats to place provisions along the escape route, and this process quickly sped up. The captains also sent a whaleboat with a letter to deliver to the "masters of the ships in clear water south of Icy Cape," which informed them of the decision to abandon the ships and head south. The letter implored those masters "to abandon your whaling, sacrifice your personal interest as well as that of your owners and put yourselves in condition to receive on board ourselves and crews for transit to some civilized port."[15]

Finally, on September 14, the signal was given for the mass exodus to begin, and by four in the afternoon more than one-hundred whaleboats, weighted down with people and supplies, were, in what must have been one of the most dramatic tableaus in whaling history, heading south. "At twelve noon," wrote Earle, we "paid out all the chain on both anchors and at 1:30 P.M., with sad hearts, ordered all the men into the boats and with a last look over the decks, abandoned ship to the mercy of the elements. And so ends this day, the writer having done his duty and believes every man to have done the same."[16]

Some members of the whaleboat armada chose to camp on the shore that night, while others continued sailing, frequently checking the water's depth so as not to ground, and straining their eyes in the darkness to avoid ice floes. Either way they had a miserable time, with the wind howling and a cold rain falling. The next day most of the whaleboats reached Icy Cape, where they could see the rescue ships lying offshore. Getting to them, however, was not going to be easy. Wind was whipping across the water, white-capped waves were breaking against the ice pack "masthead high," and three of the rescue ships had already lost anchors trying to maintain their position against the surging ocean.[17] The men on shore, however, could not wait for the seas to subside, for if they did their only opportunity for salvation might be lost. They launched the heavily laden and low-riding whaleboats into open water and, as one whaling captains later recalled, "encountered the full force of a tremendous southwest gale and a sea that would have made the stoutest ship tremble." The whaleboats were pummeled by every wave, and "tossed about like pieces of cork . . . requiring the utmost of diligence of all hands to keep them afloat."[18] First they bailed, then they began throwing over their prized belongings to keep the whaleboats from being swamped, and finally they made it to the ships, where, battered, and coated with a thin layer of ice, they were taken aboard. By September 16 all the whaleboats had run the same gauntlet, and a total of 1,219 passengers, including a small number of women and children, had been safely taken aboard and spread out among the seven now-very-crowded rescue ships, which hauled their anchors and promptly headed to Honolulu, arriving there in late October. "The sudden arrival of from a thousand to twelve hundred wrecked seamen in the course of a day," reported the *Honolulu Gazette* on October 24, "has had the effect to make the town look lively." But when one considered that this great influx of humanity had just passed through the most horrific of trials, and that all of the men had just lost their ships and their livelihood, the scene took on a thoroughly depressing cast, which was reinforced by the great sadness evident on every survivor's face.[19]

In the States the news of the Arctic disaster—which claimed 33 ships, valued at about $1.6 million, but not a single life—was viewed as both a tragedy and a miracle. New Bedford, which was home port for twenty-two out of the thirty-three ships, was hardest hit.[20] The *New York Times* wrote, "It is reported from that city that the disaster is really almost as severe a blow to it as was the great fire to Chicago; it has prostrated its main business—that of whaling—and has seriously damaged, if not crippled, its leading insurance offices."[21] The owners, captains and crews, and insurers of the lost ships were not the only ones who suffered financially. The members of the rescue fleet gave up some of their whaling season to ferry their unexpected passengers to safety. Five of those ships were American, and to get back some of their forgone profits, the owners petitioned the U.S. government for compensation. It took Congress twenty years to respond, ultimately paying the owners roughly $140 for each American citizen they had rescued.[22]

Soon after the rescue fleet left the Arctic in mid-September 1871, the Eskimos descended on the abandoned ships, stripping them of everything of value, including spars, cordage, whalebone, nails, guns, and tools. The Eskimos searched for liquor but found none, because before leaving the ships, the whalemen had dumped all the liquor that was on board "so that the natives would not get to carousing and wantonly destroy the ships."[23] The whalemen forgot, however, to empty the medicine chests, and when the Eskimos opened these and began drinking the contents, they got violently ill, and a few of them were said to have died. In late September a strong gale, the type for which the whalemen had so fervently prayed, bore down from the northeast, pushing the pack ice offshore. Although some who learned of this in later years argued that it was proof that the captains should have held on and thereby escaped with their ships, it is far from certain what the outcome might have been had they pursued this strategy. And as historian Everett S. Allen points out, "In any event, soon thereafter, a second gale stormed out of the north and rendered any alternatives academic."[24]

THE ARCTIC DISASTER of 1871 did not put a halt to Arctic whaling, and the very next year another fleet, though slightly smaller than the one that sailed in 1871, headed north, along with a couple of salvage ships sent to see if they could find any valuable items among the wrecks. There wasn't much left to recover. Crushed and mangled ships lined the coast, which was littered with debris, and a few of the ships had been torched by the Eskimos, apparently in retribution for being made sick by the contents of the medicine chests. Only one ship from the abandoned fleet, the *Minerva*, was brought back to the States, along with a relatively small quantity of oil and whalebone.[25] There was, however, another most unusual discovery made during the Arctic whaling season of 1872. As it turned out the abandonment of the fleet in September 1871 was not complete. One whaleman had stayed behind, hoping to be the first salvager on the scene, gathering whalebone from the wrecks and stockpiling it over the winter to sell the next year when the whaleships returned. Things didn't work out the way he had planned. He sought refuge on board the *Massachusetts*, and had, according to his own account, managed to collect quite a bit of whalebone before the Eskimos stole it from him. Then, he claimed, "They set out to kill me, but the women saved me and afterward, the old chief took care of me. A hundred and fifty thousand dollars would not tempt me to try another winter in the Arctic."[26]

In the following years whalemen continued heading to the Arctic. Although they could not help but recall the disaster of 1871, they viewed it as a fluke and were willing to write it off to peculiar circumstances. According to two whaling captains who were interviewed in November 1871, "the disaster was merely one of those deviations from natural laws against which all precautions are futile. Such an event would not probably occur again in a lifetime."[27] The captains were at least partly correct. The summer of 1871 was an anomalous season, or a "deviation from natural law," if you will, when the air over the Arctic was unusually cold, the ice pack thicker than normal, and the prevailing winds such that instead of pushing the ice offshore, as most often happens, they pushed it toward the coast.[28] But as for the prediction that another lifetime would pass before there was a similar event, they were unfortunately wrong. In 1876, history repeated itself, but with a more tragic outcome. Once again, whaling captains bet against the ice and lost.[29] The oversize headline of a *Boston Globe* article on the disaster undoubtedly dredged up a whole range of sad memories for its readers, especially those in the whaling trade.

CAUGHT IN THE ICE
A WHALING FLEET DESTROYED IN THE ARCTIC SEAS
A TERRIBLE EXPERIENCE
SOME OF THE CREW FROZEN TO DEATH . . .

As the disaster played out, part of the northern fleet was whaling in the vicinity of Point Barrow at the end of August 1876, when it became trapped in the pack ice. On August 29, after drifting quite some distance and fearing that there would be no break in the weather, the captains concluded that "there was no further hope of saving the ships," and they decided to abandon them. Not all the crewman were convinced that this was the best course, and more than fifty of them chose to remain behind, perhaps thinking that the weather would turn or, if not, that they could survive the winter and salvage valuable items from the ships. So, on September 5, almost precisely five years after the last such exodus, three hundred men left the ships and began the twenty-mile trek to the shore, over the crumpled ice floes, pulling their whaleboats behind. The next day they reached a narrow strip of open water and sailed to Point Barrow, reaching there on September 9 only to find the whaleships *Three Brothers* and the *Rainbow* stuck fast in the ice. After building sleds to continue their journey, the men set out again, and in a couple of days sighted the whaleship *Florence*, itself pinned in the ice. The captains decided that to press on "would be madness," and instead they began preparations for overwintering. But then on September 13 the ice began to move, and within a day's time the *Florence* was floating free. All the men got on board, and the *Florence* began sailing south, its captain carefully dodging ice floes along the way. Soon the *Florence* was joined by the *Three Brothers* and the *Rainbow*, both of which had also broken free of the ice. While the *Rainbow*'s captain decided to continue whaling, the other two captains had had their fill of the Arctic for one year, and, dividing the displaced whalemen between them, they sailed back to port.[50] All told, twelve whaleships were lost during the Arctic disaster of 1876, at a devastating cost of roughly $1 million. When whalemen returned to the Arctic the following season they found only three survivors—the rest had simply disappeared.

Chapter Twenty

FADING AWAY

PAINTING BY JOHN BERTONCCINI, SHOWING THE ARCTIC FLEET WINTERING
OVER AT PAULINE COVE OFF HERSCHEL ISLAND, CANADA. THE SEVEN
STEAM-POWERED WHALESHIPS ARE BANKED IN SNOW, AND THE CREWS ARE
PLAYING SOCCER AND BASEBALL IN THE FOREGROUND.

PROUD AND VIBRANT AT MIDCENTURY, WHALING WAS BY THE LATE
1870s already becoming a relic of bygone glory and even a subject for
nostalgic reminiscences. The dramatic rise of petroleum, the blazes lit
by Confederate cruisers, the ineffectual sinking of the Stone Fleet, the
crushing disasters in the Arctic, and the growing scarcity of the oceans
great leviathans all combined to severely diminish the American

whaling industry. A contemporary writer observed that, "Twenty or thirty years ago, on visiting the large whaling ports down east . . . the wharves were literally alive with business in discharging the arrivals of whale ships. . . . Visit those places now and you will find them almost utterly deserted."[1] The whaling fleet, which had once numbered more than seven hundred strong, now shrank to fewer than two hundred.[2] Of the more than sixty ports that had sent whaleships to sea, only about a dozen remained, and many of them were just barely surviving. The whaling aristocracy—the men whose wealth was built by oil, baleen, and precious lumps of ambergris—increasingly found more productive ways to invest their money. The pages of the *Whalemen's Shipping News*, once replete with stirring stories of great catches and new whaling grounds, now offered its readers a litany of pessimistic predictions for the future. But it was not yet time to pen the obituary of the industry. Another half century would elapse before the last wooden whaleship left an American port.

With every revolution of an oil well pump and every mile of gas line laid, whale oil's days as a major illuminant faded further into the past. By the end of the nineteenth century, whale oil still burned primarily in lighthouses and churches, where spermaceti candles could be found adorning the altars. This left the lubrication of some machinery, the manufacture of a few textiles, and other niche applications as the last markets of any consequence where whale oil was of service. Declining whale oil prices exacerbated the industry's predicament. The halcyon days of the mid-1850s, when American sperm oil commanded nearly two dollars per gallon and whale oil approached eighty cents were long past. In 1888 sperm oil sank to sixty-two cents per gallon, and then in 1896 it tumbled to a low of forty cents, and stayed below sixty-three cents until the outbreak of World War I, when it experienced a slight rise in price.[3]

Nevertheless, with each uptick in the price for oil, no matter how slight, whaling merchants tried to delude themselves that the worst was over and the industry was set for a rebound, but prices invariably slipped, and each year more whaling owners decided to abandon this obsolescent industry. Given how successfully they had been hunted in previous decades, whales were now harder to find, forcing whalemen to take longer, more expensive cruises to get a good catch. Finding insur-

ance for whaling trips proved very difficult, and while it was one thing
to send a ship on a multiyear journey in search of uncertain profits
with the confidence that should something terrible happen the insurance policy would kick in, it was quite another to send forth a ship with
no insurance policy at all. As insurers became less willing to bet on the
whaling industry, whaling owners became less willing to bet on themselves. All this was compounded by the reality that the whaling fleet
had become decrepit, in need of extensive repairs. It is no wonder, then,
that many whaling owners opted out of the industry and turned their
entrepreneurial attention to other business pursuits. As early as 1873
the *Whalemen's Shipping List* commented on this phenomenon: "The
continued purpose to sell whalers," wrote the editors, "shows the judgment of those who have long and successfully been engaged in the
business . . . that it has become too hazardous, and its results too uncertain to continue it, when capital is promised as safer employment, and
surer rewards in enterprises on the land, and in our own city where the
products of two large cotton mills equal very nearly the aggregate
value of the imports of the [whale] fishery yearly."[4] Merchants who
continued whaling cut costs to the bone in order to remain solvent, even
if only marginally so.

Ironically, in 1911, at the moment when the whale oil market was
on its shaky last legs, John D. Rockefeller's Standard Oil Company was
actually propping it up.[5] In prior years, Standard Oil had purchased the
entire sperm whale oil catch from the whaleships operating out of San
Francisco. When the whaleships returned to port after the 1911 season,
they had expected that the agents for Standard Oil would offer the cus-
tomary fifty cents per gallon. This time, however, the agents, offered
only thirty cents per gallon. The shipowners, shocked and angry,
refused to sell, and they complained that such a meager price would not
even cover the costs of their voyages, much less earn a profit. Take it or
leave it, was the agents' reply. And so the whalemen left it and moored
their loaded ships in a nearby estuary, vainly hoping for a change of
heart on the part of Standard Oil or the appearance of another purchaser. After a while some of the shipowners began selling their oil to
businesses and housewives in the area. Thus the great sperm whale
fishery, which had once lit the world, was reduced to a door-to-door
retail operation begging for buyers.

WHILE SPERM AND WHALE OIL were losing their commercial appeal, however, baleen had suddenly come into vogue again. This versatile material was used in a great variety of products, including "whips, parasols, umbrellas, ... caps, hats, suspenders, neck stocks, canes, rosettes, cushions to billiard tables, fishing-rods, divining-rods ... tongue scrapers, pen-holders, paper folders and cutters, graining-combs for painters, boot-shanks, shoe-horns, brushes, mattresses," and even as practice bayonets for cadets at West Point.[6] But none of these uses accounted for baleen's rise in the marketplace. Rather it was the vagaries of the women's fashion industry that suddenly made baleen such a prized commodity. During the latter half of the nineteenth century, the hourglass figure made a resplendent, if rather painful, comeback. Baleen had long given corset manufacturers the perfect blend of pliability and rigidity necessary to mold women's bodies into the unnatural shapes demanded by the dictates of contemporary beauty. Now that the trendsetters of the age were telling women that impossibly pinched waists and uplifted bosoms were the in thing, demand for baleen skyrocketed. This generated a gold rush of sorts in the Arctic, as whaleships headed north in search of bowheads, whose mouths had the longest and most valuable baleen of all.

When the first whalemen hunted bowheads in the mid-nineteenth century, huge amounts of baleen were brought back to port, and although sales were brisk, prices stayed relatively low. Sometimes whalemen even ignored the baleen, letting it sink with the carcass, focusing instead on boiling oil from the blubber. Just a few decades later, however, the situation was reversed. Baleen was the prize, and oftentimes, after the baleen was secured, it was the carcass, blubber and all, that was let go. In 1870 baleen fetched 85 cents per pound; a decade later it had risen to $2.00. Then in 1891 it shot up to $5.38 per pound, and in 1904 it reached an all-time high of $5.80.[7] Adding to baleen's meteoric rise was the inescapable fact that bowheads, owing to excessive hunting, were on a crash course toward extinction. As the *Boston Globe* reported in 1889, whalebone was "becoming so rare and costly that the old whalemen are being drawn away from their firesides once more in the hope of making big money quickly in taking it. A quantity of bone that would not fill an ox-cart was sold last week for $1,800."[8]

Whaling voyages were now being dubbed whalebone cruises, and with a large bowhead capable of providing upward of three thousand pounds of baleen, the profits for a really successful cruise were simply astounding, as was the case in 1898, when four whaleships returned with whalebone that sold for $750,000.[9]

The baleen frenzy forced whalemen to become more creative hunters. To kill bowheads one had to find them, which was increasingly problematic. By the end of the nineteenth century, whaleships were routinely traveling well to the east of Point Barrow, to the Beaufort Sea, in their search for new grounds. To go so far north and east, and then return south before the ice locked them in, was an almost impossible task for sail-powered whaleships. To solve this dilemma whalemen relied in part on auxiliary steam engines. With these coal-eating, smoke-belching workhorses on board, whalemen didn't have to wait for favorable winds to get moving. They could go where they wanted and when they wanted, making it possible for them to find and kill whales and leave the Arctic quickly with time to spare. Ice floes and strong currents that had once been impenetrable obstacles to traditional whaleships were less of a problem for steam-powered vessels. Whalemen also used time as an ally in the search for bowheads. Since the problem was getting to and from the whaling grounds in a single season, then why not just stay in the Arctic over the winter and resume whaling when the ice broke up the following summer? This was not a new idea. Since the early 1860s American whalemen had been overwintering in Hudson's Bay, and now the Arctic whalemen followed suit.[10]

Staying in the Arctic through the winter remained a major undertaking. Before leaving port, the ships were loaded with food and supplies, including coal and all of the materials that might be needed to make shipboard repairs. On the way to their final destination, the whalemen traded with Eskimos for fur-pelt clothing and often hired them as crew for the whaling season. Once they arrived on the grounds, hunting proceeded around the clock as long as the weather was good, and when the temperature dropped and the ice started its inexorable creep toward the shore, the whalemen hunkered down. One of the most important tasks was readying the ship and carefully positioning it in the ice to keep it from being crushed. The bow was pointed into the prevailing winds, many of the sails and yards were taken down, seams were caulked, water pipes emptied, and a stove set up in the engine room or one of the cabins for heat. A thick ridge of snow was tightly packed around the ship's hull to push down the ice and cradle the ship so that it would rise when the ice expanded. The whalemen built enclosures on the deck for protection from the elements, gathered wood, and cut blocks of ice from inland ponds, which would be melted later for drinking water. They bought caribou, moose, polar bear, duck, and other game from the Eskimos, or hunted for it themselves. To feed the huskies, which were brought along as work dogs, the whalemen hauled whale carcasses onto the ice and hacked frozen steaks from them as needed.[11]

Overwintering Arctic whalemen, along with a smattering of captain's wives and children, established active communities, replicating many of the amenities of home. They played soccer and baseball, paid social visits to one another, held formal dances and dinners, and even staged plays. One wife who had recently returned from the Arctic said that she had, in classic Victorian parlance, "a delightful trip. The ship was comfortable, and we had a really splendid crew. Officers and men were kind and considerate of each other's happiness, and the ship was like the home of a big family."[12] But problems persisted. During the long, cold, dark months of winter, boredom and loneliness took a terrible toll, sometimes leading to depression or suicide. Many whalemen and Eskimos got drunk and rowdy, a situation that precipitated fights and in a few instances led to murder. Whalemen who wandered away from the ship, either to explore or desert, often paid for their trip with frostbite or their lives. And just as whalemen in the Pacific had had sexual relations with the natives, so too did the whalemen in the Arctic, with some taking mistresses and others leaving mixed-race children behind.

The rise of steam whaling and overwintering in the Arctic coincided with another dramatic shift in the whaling industry. This was when San Francisco eclipsed Hawaii as the premier whaling port in the Pacific, a turn of events that no doubt made Mark Twain very happy. In 1866, on assignment in Honolulu for the *Sacramento Union*, the thirty-year-old Twain, who had yet to achieve any significant literary fame, cabled back a piece in which he urged the San Francisco Chamber of Commerce to "make an effort to divert the whaling trade [from Honolulu] to her city." Pointing out that Honolulu "fits out and provisions a majority out of ninety-six whalers this year, and receives a very respectable amount of money for it," Twain argued that "San Francisco might manage to get several hundred thousands a year out of the whaling trade if she could get it into her hands, or a million or so, should whaling again reach its former high prosperity."[13]

Before writing the article, Twain spent a couple of weeks reading statistics and talking to people, all the while trying to figure out why it was "that this remote port, in a foreign country, is made the rendezvous of the whaling fleet, instead of the seemingly more eligible one of San Francisco, on our own soil?" The complaints he heard were many. It was harder to get crews in San Francisco; men could desert more easily on the mainland than they could on an island; the harbor was too small to host the fleet without the ships knocking into one another; in Hawaii the whaleman was "the biggest frog in the pond"; and that everyone who came into contact with the whalemen in San Francisco tried to fleece them. But of all the reasons, the one cited most often was legal. "And they say," Twain quipped, "finally (and then the old sea dogs gnash their teeth and swear till the air turns blue around them), that 'there's more land-sharks (lawyers) in 'Frisco than there's fiddlers in hell, I tell you; and you'll get 'pulled' [snatched up] before your anchor's down!' If there is a main, central count in the indictment against San Francisco that is it."

Twain countered with arguments of his own as to why San Francisco should prevail. The main reason was the cost of labor. Normally whaling captains stopped at Hawaii not only to stock up on supplies but also to sign on local men to fill out the crew. As the sugar economy took off at midcentury and the Hawaiian plantation owners needed more laborers, they and other Hawaiians interested in spurring the local economy cast a covetous eye in the whalemen's direction. Shouldn't the Hawaiians who were manning the whaleships stay home instead to pick sugar cane? To encourage labor to flow in that direction, the plantation owners and their supporters persuaded the Hawaiian government to require whalemen to post bonds to gain the right to take Hawaiian crew members aboard. As Twain noted, these bonds, which had started at one hundred dollars, had reached three hundred dollars, and when one added other charges levied by Hawaiian ports, the cost per man reached six hundred dollars. Since a crew might ship as many as twenty or more Hawaiians, that could be a substantial added expense.[14]

Three years after Twain wrote his article, San Francisco's claim became much stronger. On May 10, 1869, the final spike of the transcontinental railroad was driven at Promontory Point, Utah, creating a most effective conduit for trade between the West and East Coasts. From that point forward, whaling owners had the option of shipping their oil and baleen across the country in train cars, getting it there much faster and more cheaply than the traditional route of sailing around Cape Horn or transporting it via rail over the Isthmus of Panama.[15] By the late 1860s whaling owners therefore began shifting their ships to San Francisco, and within a couple of decades this California port became, as one historian dubbed it, "the New Bedford of the Pacific."[16]

DESPITE THE BALEEN FRENZY and the emergence of San Francisco as a major whaling entrepôt, the whaling industry continued on its downward spiral as the nineteenth century drew to a close. Contemporary articles mixed romantic images of the industry's past success with dismal accounts of its current state.[17] Nobody was building new whaleships. Instead these old workhorses were increasingly converted to different uses, left to rot at the docks, or broken up. One entrepreneurial outfit managed to benefit from whaling's misfortunes by selling the "planking" of old whaleships as "driftwood for open fireplaces." The wood was taken only from ships whose hulls had been sheathed in copper, for each piece was guaranteed to be "completely impregnated with copper through the action of . . . salt water." As a result of the copper, when the wood burned it would "delight the eye" with a "brilliant" display of "changing colors . . . that breathes out beauty, witchery, mystery, all in one."[18]

Still, even as the whaling industry was disappearing, there remained occasional hope that things would turn around. On September 14, 1902, the *New York Times* published an article titled, "Whaling Enjoys a New Life," which painted a rather optimistic picture for the future of the industry, based on an upturn in the prices for sperm oil and the continued strength in the sales of baleen. "The market conditions now favor the whaling business," the *Times* noted. "After it had seemed on the eve of extinction, it is again profitable and likely to be continued as a paying industry for many years, if not indeed to undergo something of a boom. . . . So long as large profits can be made whalers will continue to be built and sent to sea, thereby preserving perhaps the most romantic occupation to which the sea has given rise since pirates went out of business."[19] Three months later, as if to underscore the newspaper's prediction, the whaleship *Canton* returned to New Bedford with 2,200 barrels of sperm whale oil valued at $44,000. But neither the predictions of newspapers nor the *Canton*'s profitable trip cajoled whalemen into thinking that the worst was past, and that their industry was set for a sustained rebound. As the *Boston Globe* reported on the *Canton*'s triumphant return, "This, and an occasional voyage, are exceptional, but they are not regarded . . . [in New Bedford] as of greater significance than the occasional flare from the dying embers in a fireplace."[20] And indeed, the boom that the *Times* had predicted became a bust as oil prices dropped again, and, more important, the market for baleen evaporated.

Baleen's fall from grace actually had begun many years before. The high prices for baleen toward the end of the 1800s had created an incentive to find cheaper materials for corset stays, and soon steel bands, celluloid, and other substitutes began to take over the task of reshaping women's bodies. But while these substitutes were deemed good enough for inexpensive corsets, they simply would not do for those worn by well-bred women, whose corsets continued to be made with baleen supports, and whose purchases kept the demand for and price of baleen high.[21] It was not just the availability of substitute materials that was eroding the market for baleen stays; medical concerns also played a role. For many decades, doctors had been warning women about the dangers of corsets. In 1868 the British medical journal *The Lancet* argued that "it is certainly much to be regretted that any Englishwoman would torture herself or her children by employing tight or unyielding [corset] stays or belts."[22] As the Edwardian age loomed, efforts were even made to outlaw corsets. In 1902, for example, a Parisian doctor urged his countrymen to pass a law that would make it illegal for women under the age of thirty to wear corsets, thereby keeping them from ruining their bodies. This doctor was, as an American newspaper article noted, "a bold man" who had the "courage of his convictions," for "Paris is the stronghold of the corset; all the good ones come from there."[23]

Although doctors' efforts persuaded some affluent women to cast aside their "whalebone prisons" and allow their bodies to regain a more natural form, it took a much more powerful force to get those women to take off their corsets en masse.[24] Around 1907 Parisian designer Paul Poiret "introduced," as fashion historian Elizabeth Ewing points out, "a slim, up-and-down fashion line, banishing at a stroke the curved 'S'-shaped figure and its accompanying melee of elaborate underwear."[25] And with that, women all over the world literally breathed a sigh of relief. Whales, too, got a reprieve, for although the fashion trend Poiret initiated did not cause corsets to disappear, it did reduce their use dramatically enough to virtually eliminate the need for baleen stays. Whaling merchants watched these developments with alarm, and as baleen began its dramatic fall in value, a group of them banded together to create the "whalebone trust," their goal being to purchase all the supplies of whalebone and then control its sale so as to drive prices up. This last ditch effort, however, ultimately failed. By 1913, the trust had disbanded and the remainder of America's once mighty whalebone industry lay wrapped tight in neat bundles in warehouses in New Bedford waiting for a market that never resurfaced.[26]

The surest sign that the American whaling industry had nearly run its course came six months after the outbreak of World War I in Europe, on December 29, 1914, when the *Whalemen's Shipping List* published its final issue. "And a good journal," wrote the editors in their farewell column, "goes the way of many a staunch old whaling bark. It has outlived its usefulness, there is no demand for it: its subscription list has fallen off and it is not self-sustaining. So then . . . [the] Journal is to be hauled out on the beach. Its activities at an end."[27] The *Shipping List*, first published in 1843, had given a keen and occasionally literary voice to the American whalemen for seventy-two years. The newspaper, which one writer has appropriately dubbed "the *Wall Street Journal* of the whaling market," had witnessed the dramatic rise and fall of the industry.[28] It had chronicled the heady days of the golden age and watched as port after port entered the industry hoping to cash in, and then fell by the wayside. The *Shipping List* had reported on the rise of petroleum, the horrors of the Civil War, the dangers of the Arctic, and the industry's struggle to survive in a modernizing world. It had seen the American whaling fleet grow from 675 to a high of 735 in 1854, and then begin its long decline, shrinking to 321 in 1870, 178 in 1880, 97 in 1890, 48 in 1900, and just 32 whaleships on the eve of its last issue.[29] In its early years the paper's pages were full of information and advertisements related to the whaling industry, and little else; as the industry shrank so too did the portions of the paper that covered it. By the late 1800s the *Shipping List* regularly included filler pieces reprinted from other publications that had absolutely nothing to do with whaling, and during the paper's last few decades such pieces often made up the bulk of the copy. A reader of the *Shipping List* in 1912 and 1913, for example, would have found articles on the dangers of guzzling liquor, African ants, and the National Civic Federation's plans to encourage working women to take more vacations.[30] Given this trend, it is perhaps fitting that the swan song issue of the *Shipping List* offered not only its own requiem but also an entire column of jokes. Thus, after the reader had become thoroughly depressed by the issue's miserable whaling news, he could simply turn the page for some levity.

AS AMERICAN WHALING sailed into oblivion, the whaling industry was acutally flourishing overseas, with Norway leading the way. While the Americans relied heavily on traditional hunting techniques— sailpower, whaleboats, and hand-propelled harpoons—to pursue an ever-dwindling number of right, humpback, and sperm whales, the Norwegians took full advantage of innovations in whaling to hunt not only those species but also the still relatively plentiful blue and fin whales, and other rorquals, which the Americans had largely avoided because they were considered too fast and too strong to capture. Foremost among the innovations the Norwegians adopted was the whaling cannon, which had been perfected in the 1860s by their countryman Svend Foyn. This fearsome weapon shot a massive four-pronged harpoon that was connected to a thick wire cable and tipped with a bomb that exploded on impact. By mounting such cannons on the bows of highly maneuverable, steam-powered chaser boats, the Norwegians could easily track down the fast-swimming rorquals. And if the harpooner aimed true he could kill even the largest of whales with a single shot. For those whales that were not dispatched immediately, the Norwegians had a backup plan to make sure that the whale didn't wrench itself free of the harpoon with one strong tug and escape or, worse, sink to the bottom as rorquals had a tendency to do. Using a system of pulleys and springs on the chaser ship, to which the harpoon's thick and strong cable was attached, the Norwegians were able to minimize the strain on the cable, letting out wire when needed and reeling it back in as the whale tired. To overcome the problem of sinking, the Norwegians relied on powerful winches attached to the cables, as well as lances that injected air into the carcasses to make them more buoyant.

Beyond capitalizing on hunting abundant whales, the Norwegians also processed whales more efficiently than the Americans. While the latter focused on rendering oil from blubber, the Norwegians used industrial-size boilers to extract oil from the entire whale—blubber, meat, and bones—and then, rather than discard the carcass, they used it for meat and ground what was left it into fertilizer, bonemeal, and feed for livestock. The resourceful Norwegians also used whales to produce glue, vitamins, and the strings for tennis rackets. And with the introduction of hydrogenation in the early 1900s, which minimized the pungent smell and taste of whale oil and solidified it into fat, the Norwegians found yet another outlet for their whale oil in the production of high-quality soap and margarine, the latter of which in particular was in great demand elsewhere in Europe.[31]

Norway was not the only country to take up where the Americans left off. In the early twentieth century Japan and Russia came into their own as whaling powers, and as the century progressed, these and other countries, including Germany, Holland, and Britain, forged a new path for the whaling industry to follow, one that would foster the growth of enormous fleets of efficient factory whaleships that would in a single year kill more whales than the Americans, at the height of the golden age, had been able to kill in nearly a decade.[32]

World War I provided a short respite for the fast-disappearing American whalemen. War-induced shortages of raw materials along with the fact that spermaceti was the highest-quality lubricant for battleship engines because of its ability to withstand intense heat and pressure, caused the price of sperm whale oil suddenly to climb. The small American whaling fleet took advantage of this shift in demand, and posted a few highly profitable cruises. The *Viola* of New Bedford, for example, returned from the South Atlantic with 1,300 barrels of sperm oil worth about 85 cents per gallon, for a total of $35,000. The *Viola* had been doubly lucky because in addition to the oil, it also brought back one-hundred-twenty-one pounds of ambergris, worth $37,000.[33] Success such as this led some to talk of a turnaround in the whaling industry. "If the whales all aren't blown out of the water on account of being mistaken for submarines," wrote the editor of the *Newark News*, "it is likely that a revival of the old-time whaling industry may follow the war, or even be witnessed before the war ends."[34]

Although American whalemen might have been buoyed by such predictions, they were also very nervous every time they left port. Enemy submarines didn't pose much of a threat to whales, but they most definitely were a serious threat to American whaleships, two of which returned to New Bedford in early July 1918, just four months before the war's armistice, after a close call in the Atlantic Ocean off Cape Hatteras. According to Capt. J. T. Gonsalves, a submarine surfaced near his whaleship, the *A. M. Nicholson*, on June 5, and fired a shot across his bow. Believing it to be an American submarine, Gonsalves raised the Stars and Stripes, whereupon the submarine submerged. When the submarine resurfaced a short while later, Gonsalves raised his flag again, and this time the submarine raised one, too—only it was German. An officer on the deck of the submarine ordered Gonsalves to "heave to" and to place his men, twenty-five in all, in the *Nicholson*'s whaleboats and come alongside the submarine, which he did.

"What is your vessel doing?" yelled the German officer.
"Catching sperm whales," Gonsalves replied.
"Catching any other fish?" the German asked.

After assuring the German that he was not, Gonsalves pleaded, "For God's sake . . . don't sink this vessel. I am a poor man and it will ruin me, as I am a big owner in her." The German laughed and reported his conversation to the captain, who soon came topside and called to Gonsalves, "Don't you know that it is a poor time to buy vessel property when people are at war?" As Gonsalves was telling the German that he had bought the ship "before the war started," another New Bedford whaleship, the *Ellen A. Swift*, came into view, and the German asked Gonsalves if he knew what ship it was and what it was doing. When Gonsalves identified it as a fellow American whaleship, the German, apparently satisfied, waved his hand dismissively and said, "You get aboard your vessel, and get home as quick as you can, and tell the other vessel to go in with you, and don't let me catch you out this way again."[35] With that both whaleships cut short their season and headed back to port, cursing their bad luck but thankful that the Germans hadn't blown them out of the water.

The war also framed whale meat in a new light. A nation that had never considered the possibility of eating such meat was asked to do so now. Shortages of beef, pork, and mutton led the government to advocate the virtues of whale meat, claiming that by eating it we could help win the war.[36] In February 1918, New York City's American Museum of Natural History held a "conservation luncheon," during which whale meat was prepared by the head chef of Delmonico's Restaurant, and served to individuals "prominent in scientific, business, and professional spheres." The menu featured "Whale pot au feu," and "planked whale steak, a la Vancouver." As for taste, Federal food administrator Arthur Williams pronounced the whale meat, which many of the guests compared to venison or roast beef, to be "about as 'delicious a morsel' as the most aesthetic or sophisticated palate could possibly yearn for." The reporter claimed that the speakers at the luncheon "were almost unanimously in favor of having whale meat substituted for beef-steak and urged its immediate adoption as a feature of the national war diet."[37] In addition to eating whale meat to benefit the war effort, some were championing whale meat as a means to end hunger. After returning from a trip to Japan where he learned that the Japanese ate large quantities of whale meat, famed naturalist Roy Chapman Andrews urged Westerners to do the same. "If," Andrews wrote, "the American and European people could be educated to the point of eating canned flesh of animals which individually yield as much as 80,000 pounds of whale meat, what a wonderful food supply would be within reach of the poor of our great cities."[38] Despite such varied pleas, and assurances as to the excellent taste of whale meat, Americans didn't rush to trade in their beef, mutton, or pork for whale steaks.[39]

The end of the war also brought an end to any talk of a comeback of the American whaling industry. New Bedford was by this time America's only remaining whaling port, boasting fewer than a dozen whaleships, which made occasional and relatively brief forays into the Atlantic Ocean.[40] The profits were slim, and as the price of oil fell from wartime highs, one by one the old whaleships ceased whaling. Long called the Whaling City, New Bedford no longer lived up to its name. The wharves to which thousands of whaleships had once tied up now stood forlorn, as were the docks and quays where thousands of casks brimming with oil and forests of baleen once blanketed nearly every inch of available space. The coopers, the caulkers, the blacksmiths, and the outfitters were now nearly all gone. And then, for a brief moment, as if part of a mirage, the great days of whaling in New Bedford returned—on the silver screen.

On September 25, 1922, New Bedford's Olympia Theater hosted the world premiere of Elmer Clifton's silent movie, *Down to the Sea in Ships*, a love story that was played out against the backdrop of the golden age of whaling circa 1850.[41] The movie begins with New Bedford Quaker and whaleship owner Charles W. Morgan mourning the loss of his only son, who had died at sea. In his grief, Morgan turns to his daughter, Patience, and makes her promise that she "will never be any but a whaleman's wife!" At the same time that this promise is being exacted, Jake Finner, the mate on Morgan's prize ship, the *Charles W. Morgan*, and his "partner in nefarious schemes," Samuel Siggs, hatch a plan whereby Finner will take over the ship and sail it to the California goldfields, while Siggs, melodramatically in the finest tradition of the silents, courts the beautiful Patience and makes her his wife. Claiming that he is a Quaker and using false letters of introduction that said he had entered the whalemen's fraternity by harpooning a whale, Siggs gets hired in Morgan's counting room and soon asks Morgan for permission to call on his daughter. Morgan consents, but when Siggs asks Patience for her hand, she demurs, and then, before Siggs can continue the pursuit of his prize, the "boy next door," Thomas Allen Dexter, whom Patience had adored as a child, returns from college and their relationship rekindles.

Not wanting Patience to wed Dexter, Finner and Siggs kidnap him and throw him into the hold of the *Morgan*, and by the time he awakens and is untied, the *Morgan* is well out to sea. The situation on the *Morgan* quickly deteriorates as Finner takes over the ship, then tells the stunned crew that they are heading to California. The crew divides in two, with half of them wanting to go home and the other half wanting to follow Finner. With Dexter in the lead, the men who long for home gain control of the ship. Before heading back to New Bedford, however, the men decide to go whaling, and that is when Dexter, who has been promoted to boatsteerer, becomes a true whaleman by harpooning a sperm whale.

Meantime, back in New Bedford, crestfallen that the love of her life has suddenly left, Patience finally gives her consent to marry Siggs. On the appointed day Patience and Siggs enter the Quaker meeting house to present themselves to the congregation. But just as the supremely sad-looking Patience is about to conclude her oath of marriage, Dexter, whose ship has literally and figuratively just come in, breaks through the meeting house window, pummels Siggs, and reunites with his love in a warm embrace. The movie concludes with a scene showing Patience and Dexter playing with their newborn son, while old man Morgan beams down at them with pride.

The audience at the premiere of *Down to the Sea in Ships* couldn't have been more pleased with the movie, especially since many of them had played an integral part in its production. When director Elmer Clifton decided to make the movie, he knew it had to be filmed on location. And when he approached the city of New Bedford, its citizens, foremost among them the descendants of the "whaling aristocracy," not only formed the Whaling Film Corporation to help finance the venture, but many of them also acted in the film and shared their period homes and clothes to give the film more authenticity. "Their purpose in acting in and partially underwriting the film was," as one contemporary reporter wrote, "for the honor of old New Bedford, and that the present generation might see the romance and glamour of the past."[42]

In addition to actors and historic homes and clothes, the movie also needed whaleships and whalemen. And here, too, the city came through. Two New Bedford whaleships, the *Charles W. Morgan* and the *Wanderer*, were hired for duty, with the former being used to shoot deck and interior ship scenes, and the latter for sailing scenes on Buzzard's Bay.[43] These two ships, however, were not enough. A movie that depended so heavily on the theme of whaling had to show a whaleship hunting and processing whales. That role went to the fishing schooner *Gaspe*, which was chartered in Gloucester, and brought to New Bedford where it was fitted out as a whaleship, replete with newly added davits from which to hang the whaleboats. Veteran whaling captain Fred Tilton mastered the *Gaspe* on its cruise to the coast of Haiti, with a crew comprising mainly of "husky New Bedford youths," none of whom had been on a whaleship before, and all of whom, according to Tilton quickly became "exceptional whalemen."[44]

On the way to Haiti, Captain Tilton taught Raymond McKee, the actor who played Dexter, how to throw a harpoon by practicing on a school of porpoises, and by the time they arrived on the whaling grounds, McKee was good enough so that he didn't need a double to do his harpooning for him. The whales were plentiful, and the men of the *Gaspe* soon killed and acutally processed a hundred-barrel sperm, which Tilton claimed to be the largest sperm whale he had ever seen.[45]

At the beginning of the movie, words appeared on the screen informing the audience that "Whalers continue to go out from New Bedford on similar voyages to the one portrayed in this picture. The brawny boatsteerer still throws the hand harpoon." While this was true at the time, many of the New Bedforders sitting in the darkened Olympia Theater undoubtedly were thinking as they read those words, Not for long. They knew that the movie they were about to see was more of an epitaph for a virtually extinct industry, enlivened by artistic license, than it was a reflection of present-day realities.

Epilogue

FIN OUT

PEOPLE GATHER ON THE SHORE OF CUTTYHUNK ISLAND
TO SEE THE *WANDERER*, WRECKED IN THE SHALLOWS.
PHOTOGRAPH BY WILLIAM H. TRIPP.

AFTER APPEARING IN *DOWN TO THE SEA IN SHIPS*, THE *WANDERER* remained tied to the dock until its owners decided to attempt another voyage. Thus it was that on Sunday, August 24, 1924, hundreds of people gathered at the edge of New Bedford harbor to send the *Wanderer* on its way.[1] They crowded onto the pier and the *Wanderer*'s main deck. Some of the more nimble among them climbed into the rigging to get a good view of the proceedings. Following a long-held tradition of send-ing off whalemen with the blessings of their Maker, Chaplain Charles S. Thurber of the Seamen's Bethel used the twenty-sixth verse of the 104th Psalm—"There go the ships; there is that Leviathan whom thou hast made to play therein"—as the basis for his sermon. "While these men are absent," Thurber intoned, "we will pray God to preserve and keep them, in the hour of danger as well as in the hour of joy."[2] The Bethel's organist, Miss Henrietta Humphrey, whose instrument had been brought down to the pier in a wheelbarrow, played familiar hymns such as "Throw Out the Lifeline," "Pull for the Shore," and "The Lifeboat at Sea," while those in attendance, adorned in their Sunday New England finery, sang along.

It was a solemn and historic occasion. Capt. Antone T. Edwards had announced that this would be the *Wanderer*'s final voyage, and that he did not believe that New Bedford would ever send another whaleship to sea. Thus, many of the people on the pier, including a large contingent of sightseers, thought that they were witnessing not merely the begin-ning of the *Wanderer*'s last trip, but also the end of an entire era. As the *New York Herald Tribune* noted, "The departure of a whaleship has already become . . . one of the rarest of events; and when a year or so from the present the *Wanderer*'s topsails are again sighted coming up Buzzard's Bay it will very probably be the closing page of one of the greatest chapters in that kind of American history which is so inade-quately written."[3] The *Wanderer* was oddly being viewed not so much as a ship but as "a bit of the past," as the *New Bedford Mercury* noted, "a left-over that seems out of place at the present time."[4]

The *Wanderer*, built in 1878, in Mattapoisett, Massachusetts, boasted an impressive whaling résumé. It had hunted in three oceans, with one trip yielding an astonishing 6,200 barrels of whale oil.[5] At forty-six the *Wanderer*, well beyond middle age, was still in good shape. Some people claimed whaleships lasted so long because oil, which sloshed around on their decks, preserved the wood and made them more resistant to the ravages of age. If this was true, then all of the *Wanderer*'s well-lubricated trips had added to its longevity. And now, having been refit-ted, repaired, and restocked in anticipation of its final cruise, the *Wanderer* was ready to go.

On Monday morning the tugboat *J.T. Sherman* towed the *Wanderer* out of New Bedford harbor. Given the unfavorable winds and the imperative to recruit men to add to his understaffed crew, Edwards anchored the *Wanderer* off Dumpling Rocks in Buzzard's Bay, and returned to New Bedford on the *Sherman*, leaving his first mate, Joseph A. Gomes, in charge of the ship. The winds shifted and dramatically increased that night as a northeasterly gale bore down on the Atlantic coast, catching the region off guard. By the next day the *Wanderer* was being lashed by eighty-mile-per-hour winds and tossed about in a raging sea. In the face of this tempest, the ship began moving, dragging its massive anchor along the bottom. No sooner had Gomes let out a second anchor to arrest the *Wanderer*'s advance then the first anchor's chain broke, and the ship continued to be pushed into open water and across the bay. Gomes attempted to get the *Wanderer* under way, but failed, as the wind ripped through the sails and "the rudder head snapped clean off" under the strain.[6] Gomes and the fifteen others on board abandoned ship in two whaleboats and, after a harrowing time at sea, finally made it to shore. A short while later the hapless whaleship crashed into the Middle Ground Shoal, just over a mile from the western tip of Cuttyhunk Island, and with the winds and waves beating down on it, it bounced along the sand and rocks, ultimately coming to rest about one hundred feet from the beach.[7]

As soon as he awoke on Tuesday morning and saw the storm raging, Captain Edwards sought to return to the *Wanderer*, but the *Sherman*, the tug he relied on, was not able to leave the harbor until late in the afternoon, and by the time it reached Cuttyhunk, "the spray was so thick where the surf was breaking on the reefs," wrote a local reporter, "that it looked like black smoke." Edwards and all the others on board could discern through the storm that the *Wanderer* was wrecked.[8] Realizing that he could do nothing else, Edwards headed back to New Bedford for the night and then returned to Cuttyhunk the next morning to assess the damage. It was nearly a total loss. The keel was crushed and the bow crumpled. The rudder had been ripped free and was found a quarter of a mile down the beach. As Edwards stood there, looking at his crippled ship, Gomes ran up to him crying, "Capt'n, I couldn't save the ship if I went to hell!" Despite Gomes's protestations, there were some who faulted him and his relatively inexperienced crew for the disaster, but most knowledgeable observers thought that the men had done all they could under the circumstances and should not be blamed. One New York reporter cheekily declared that the ship's demise was "a plain case of ship suicide. The *Wanderer* plunged to her death, the victim of a broken heart!"[9]

Over the next few days, under a clear blue sky, the crew and a smattering of Cuttyhunk residents salvaged what they could from ship.[10] The lower decks were awash in floating debris, and one man who ventured into the hold found himself "waist deep in spaghetti."[11] Casks of beef, belaying pins, flags, whaleboats, harpoons, and other whaling implements were brought to shore, as crowds of curious onlookers visited the site and watched the men, as if part of a maritime dirge, perform their depressing task.

A poignant story resulting from the *Wanderer*'s ignominious end involved one of its Cape Verdean crew members. For months he had been scrimping and saving his money, planning to take it back to his family when the *Wanderer* docked in the Azores to drop off a few passengers and pick up supplies and crew before continuing on its way to Argentina for the whaling season. But he and the other men abandoned ship so quickly that they didn't have time to gather any of their belongings, jumping into the whaleboats with little more than the clothes on their backs. So when the ship crashed, all of that crewman's hard work and his hopes of making the lives of his relatives a little better literally washed away. Although this crewman lost everything, at least one person profited from the disaster. While people were busy salvaging the wreck, the ship's whaling guns were retrieved. They made it to shore, but then they simply disappeared.[12]

It's ironic that the *Wanderer*, in the end, didn't wander very far. There would have been some poetic justice had it, with its star-crossed name, been the very last of America's wooden whaleships to head, symbolically as it were, out to sea on a whaling cruise. But, still, the *Wanderer*, slowly disintegrating in the surf, provided a fitting final image for the great era of American whaling, which had now become part of America's mythic past.[13]

Notes

Abbreviations used in the Notes

BLHBS   Baker Library, Harvard Business School
KWM   Kendall Whaling Museum (part of NBWM)
MHS   Massachusetts Historical Society
MSM   Mystic Seaport Museum, G. W. Blunt White Library
NA   Nantucket Atheneum
NBFPL   New Bedford Free Public Library
NHA   Nantucket Historical Association
NBWM   New Bedford Whaling Museum
ODHS   Old Dartmouth Historical Association
            (parent organization of NBWM)
PEM   Peabody Essex Museum
PPL   Providence Public Library

INTRODUCTION

1. Herman Melville, *Moby-Dick* (1851; reprint, New York: Bantam Books, 1986), 419. "Comparable only to the prairie schooner," President Franklin Delano Roosevelt once remarked, "the whaleship will always remain an American epic symbol." Franklin D. Roosevelt, introduction to Clifford W. Ashley, *Whaleships of New Bedford* (Boston: Houghton Mifflin Company, 1929), vi.

CHAPTER ONE: John Smith Goes Whaling

1. John Smith, *The Complete Works of Captain John Smith (1580–1631)*, vol. 1, edited by Philip L. Barbour (Chapel Hill: University of North Carolina Press, 1986), lv–lx; John A. Garraty, *The American Nation: A History of the United States* (New York: Harper & Row, 1966), 25; Bradford Smith, *Captain John Smith, His Life & Legend* (Philadelphia: J. B. Lippincott Company, 1953), 46, 48, 52–53, 58, 61–64, 115–16; E. Keble Chatterton, *Captain John Smith* (New York: Harper & Brothers Publishers, 1927), 16–17, 35–38, 65. 141–48; Thomas Hutchinson, *The History of the Colony and Province of Massachusetts-Bay*, vol. 1, edited by Lawrence Shaw Mayo, 2nd ed. (1765; reprint, Cambridge: Harvard University Press, 1936), 2; Harry M. Ward, *Colonial America 1607–1763* (Engelwood Cliffs, NJ: Prentice Hall, 1991), 20. John Smith is one of those outsize personalities of history that compels large numbers of authors to write about them. Smith's many biographers have painted so many images of the man that it is impossible to divine which is closest to the truth. As Bradford Smith wrote, "No figure in American history has raised such a ruckus among scholars as Captain John Smith." Smith, *Captain John Smith*, 11.

2. John Smith, *The General Historie of Virginia, New-England, and the Summer Isles*, in John Smith, *The Complete Works of Captain John Smith (1580–1631)*, vol. 2, edited by Philip L. Barbour (Chapel Hill: University of North Carolina Press, 1986), 400.

3. John Smith, *A Description of New England*, in Smith, *The Complete Works of Captain John Smith*, vol. 1, 324. It is often mentioned that Roydon might actually have been spelled "Rawdon." Ibid., John Smith, 323 n1.

4. Smith, *The General Historie of Virginia, New-England, and the Summer Isles*, in Smith, *The Complete Works of Captain John Smith*, vol. 2, 403.

5. Benjamin F. DeCosta, "Norumbega and Its English Explorers," in *Narrative and Critical History of America*, edited by Justin Winsor, vol. 3 (Boston: Houghton, Mifflin and Company, 1884), 180–81; Neal Salisbury, *Manitou and Providence, Indians, Europeans, and the Making of New England, 1500–1643* (New York: Oxford University Press, 1982), 95; and Smith, *The Complete Works of Captain John Smith*, vol. 1, 293–95.

6. Smith, *A Description of New England*, in Smith, *The Complete Works of Captain John Smith*, vol. 1, 323. Smith had another reason to doubt the claims of gold. The charter for Virginia had given the settlers the right to dig for this and other precious metals, but despite searching, they found none. Garraty, *The American Nation*, 24–25.

7. John Brereton, *Discoverie of the North Part of Virginia*, March of American Facsimile Series 16 (1602; reprint, Ann Arbor, MI: University Microfilms, Inc., 1966), 15; Henry C. Kittredge, *Cape Cod: Its People and Their History* (1930; reprint, Boston: Houghton Mifflin Company, 1968), 14.

8. Brereton, *Discoverie of the North Part of Virginia*, 6.

9. James Rosier, *Prosperous Voyage*, March of America Facsimile Series 17 (1605; reprint, Ann Arbor, MI: University Microfilms, 1966).

10. Brereton, *Discoverie of the North Part of Virginia*, 13; and Rosier, *Prosperous Voyage*.

11. Smith's familiarity would have come both from reading these accounts as well as his conversations with some of the men who had participated in, and, in some instances, written about the voyages these accounts were based on, such as Bartholomew Gosnold. Warner F. Gookin, *Bartholomew Gosnold Discoverer and Planter* (Hamden, CT: Archon Books, 1963), 51. See also Charles Knowles Bolton, *The Real Founders of New England, Stories of Their Life Along the Coast, 1602–1628* (Boston: F. W. Faxon Company, 1929), 7–8; and William P. Cumming, "The Colonial Charting of the Masschusetts Coast," in *Seafaring in Colonial Massachusetts* (Boston: Colonial Society of Massachusetts, distributed by University Press of Virginia, 1980), 79.

12. At the time that Smith set sail, "Monhegan was a familiar anchorage for English sailors since as many as two hundred ships might touch there during a fishing season." Smith, *Captain John Smith*, 191. According to Morison the only record that those fishermen left was "a fierce resentment in the breast of some wronged savage." Samuel Eliot Morison, *Builders of the Bay Colony* (Boston: Houghton Mifflin Company, 1930), 6. According to Barck and Lefler, "At least by 1500, fisherman from all countries of Western Europe were found off the Grand Banks of Newfoundland, gathering huge hauls from the large schools of fish in that area." Oscar Theodore Barck, Jr., and Hugh Talmage Lefler, *Colonial America*, 2nd ed. (London: Macmillan Company, 1969), 356. See also Donald S. John-

son, *Charting the Sea of Darkness: The Four Voyages of Henry Hudson* (New York: Kodansha International, 1993), 140–41.

13. Gordon Jackson, *The British Whaling Trade* (Hamden, CT: Archon Books, 1978), 3. According to Browne, "I have found it extremely difficult to obtain any definite and authentic facts in relation to the origin of the whale fishery. The works which I have before me, containing the earliest records on this subject, are of so conflicting a character, that, after wading through volumes embracing a great variety of other topics, I am puzzled upon which to place the most reliance." J. Ross Browne, *Etchings of a Whaling Cruise*, edited by John Seelye (1846; reprint, Cambridge: Belknap Press of Harvard University Press, 1968), 511.

14. Mark Kurlansky, *The Basque History of the World* (New York: Penguin, 1999), 48–50; Richard Ellis, *Men and Whales* (New York: Alfred A. Knopf, 1991), 42; and Ronald M. Lockley, *Whales, Dolphins & Porpoises* (New York: W. W. Norton & Co. Inc., 1979), 107. The right whale has been known by many names. It has been called the Biscayan right whale, with a nod to the Basques and the first locale in which it was hunted; the black right whale, due it its coloration; and the Northern and Southern right whale by people who split the species into distinct populations and/or subspecies, and the Nordkaper. A. B. C. Whipple, *The Whalers* (Alexandria, VA: Time-Life Books, 1979), 43; F. D. Ommanney, *Lost Leviathan* (New York: Dodd, Mead & Company, 1971), 70–71; William A. Douglass and Jon Bilbao, *Amerikanuak: Basques in the New World* (Reno: University of Nevada Press, 1975), 51–52; Richard Ellis, *The Book of Whales* (New York: Alfred A. Knopf, 1980), 70, 73; and Ellis, *Men and Whales*, 7.

15. Phil Clapham, *Whales of the World* (Stillwater, MN: Voyageur Press, 1997), 73; Ellis, *Men and Whales*, 4–5; and L. Harrison Mathews, *The Natural History of the Whale* (New York: Columbia University Press, 1978), 43. An English writer who observed a right whale stranded near the river Thames in 1658, marveled at the whale's tremendous maw. It has, he wrote, "a mouth so wide, that divers men might have stood upright in it." Quoted in *The Whale* (New York: Simon & Schuster, 1968), 35, 38. The right whale's feeding habits weren't always so well known, and have at times provoked wild speculation. A thirteenth-century Icelandic tract claimed that the right whale "does not eat any food except darkness and the rain which falls on the sea. And when it is caught and its intestines opened, nothing unclean is found in its stomach as would be in other fish that eat food, because its stomach is clean and empty. It cannot open its mouth easily, because the baleen that grows there rise up in the mouth when it is opened, and often causes its death because it cannot shut its mouth." Quoted in Ellis, *Men and Whales*, 39–40.

16. Melville, *Moby-Dick*, 258.

17. John R. Spears, *The Story of New England Whalers* (New York: Macmillan Company, 1922), 22–23. Rudyard Kipling offered a fanciful reason why the whale's throat is so narrow. In one of his *Just So Stories*, titled "How the Whale Got His Tiny Throat," Kipling says that the credit or blame for this anatomical feature should go to a shipwrecked mariner who was sitting on a raft in the middle of the ocean, minding his own business, with nothing on his person other than a pair of blue pants, a pair of suspenders, and a jackknife. The tale begins with a ravenous whale that devoured all the fish in the sea save a lone 'Stute Fish. As the whale was about to munch on the 'Stute Fish, the latter inquired, "Noble and generous Cetacean, have you ever tasted Man?" The whale said no, and asked

what a man tasted like? The 'Stute Fish, seeing an opportunity to avoid his own demise, eagerly told the whale that a man makes a "Nice but nubbly" meal, and further that if the whale wanted one he should swim to the shipwrecked mariner and give him a try. The 'Stute Fish, to be fair to the whale, and in the spirit of full disclosure, also warned him that the mariner should be approached cautiously because he was "a man of infinite—resource—and—sagacity." Not one to be easily dissuaded, the whale, guided by his insatiable hunger and the 'Stute Fish's excellent directions, swam to the mariner and ate him and his raft in one big gulp. Finding himself in the belly of the whale, the mariner raised a ruckus, dancing, stomping, and thumping to the point that the whale got a nasty case of the hiccups. The greatly distressed whale asked the 'Stute Fish what he should do. "Tell him to come out," said the fish, which the whale did. But the mariner ignored this request, and instead demanded that the whale take him back to his "natal—shore . . . the white—cliffs—of—Albion, and [then] I'll think about it." As soon as the dancing resumed, the whale started swimming furiously toward the mariner's home. On arriving there and temporarily beaching himself, the whale opened his mouth and asked the mariner to be so kind as to hop out. But it wasn't going to be that easy. The mariner had made good use of his time in captivity, cutting his raft into strips and using his suspenders to tie the strips together, creating a canvas grate. And before he hopped out, the mariner lodged that grate in the whale's throat, and then said good-bye with these parting words, "By means of a grating, I have stopped your ating." From that point forward, according to Kipling, whales could eat only "very, very small fish." Rudyard Kipling, "How the Whale Got His Tiny Throat," in *Just So Stories* (1902; reprint, New York: Airmont Books, 1966), 11–15.

18. E. J. Slijper, *Whales* (New York: Basic Books, Inc., 1962), 18; Charles Sumner, *The Works of Charles Sumner*, vol. 11 (Boston: Lee and Shepard, 1877), 332–33; Paul Schneider, *The Enduring Shore* (New York: Henry Holt and Company, 2000), 162; and John Steele Gordon, *Empire of Wealth: The Epic History of American Economic Power* (New York: HarperCollins, 2005), 168.

19. Randall R. Reeves and Robert D. Kenney, "Baleen Whales: Right Whales and Allies," in *Wild Mammals of North America*, 2nd ed., edited by George A. Feldhamer, Bruce C. Thompson, and Joseph A. Chapman (Baltimore: Johns Hopkins University Press, 2003), 425; Alexander Hyde, A. C. Baldwin, and W. L. Gage, *The Frozen Zone and Its Explorers* (Hartford: Columbian Book Company, 1876), 122; Francis T. Buckland, *Curiosities of Natural History*, 2nd series (New York: Rudd & Carleton, 1860), 397; Melville, *Moby-Dick*, 131; and personal communication with Michael P. Dyer, librarian and maritime historian, NBWM, Mar. 3, 2006. It should also be pointed out that the appellation "true" whale has also been accorded to the bowhead. John Leslie, Robert Jameson, and Hugh Murray, *Narrative of Discovery and Adventure in the Polar Seas and Regions* (New York: Harper & Brothers, 1836), 298.

20. "Each year," wrote a Venetian historian more than five hundred years ago, "many die in these battles because [of] the resistance that the beast opposes. . . . The monster, feeling the blow [from the whalemen], makes a great to-do, rushing toward the boats and striking them with its tail." Quoted in Whipple, *The Whalers*, 43–44.

21. Kurlansky, *The Basque History*, 48–49, and Jean-Pierre Proulx, *Whaling in the North Atlantic From the Earliest Times to the Mid-19th Century* (Ottawa: Parks Canada, 1986), 16.

22. William Scoresby, *An Account of the Arctic Regions with a Description of the Northern Whale Fishery, The Whale-Fishery*, vol. 2 (1820; reprint, Devon, England: David & Charles Reprints, 1969), 14; Proulx, *Whaling in the North Atlantic*, 16; Kurlansky, *The Basque History*, 49; Selma Huxley Barkham, "The Basque Whaling Establishments in Labrador 1536–1632—A Summary," *Arctic* 37 (Dec. 1984), 518; Jackson, *The British Whaling Trade*, 55–56; and Paul LaCroix and Sir Robert Naunton, *Manners, Custom and Dress During the Middle Ages and During the Renaisance Period* (Whitefish, MT: Kessinger Publishing, 2004), 96. The importance of whaling to the Basques is reflected in the imagery they used to represent their towns. The coats-of-arms of many Basque ports display a whaling scene. Lequeitio's emblem, for example, is inscribed with a boast that the men of that town proved true time and again—*Horrenda cette sujecit*, or "Dominated the horrible cetacean." Quoted in Douglass and Bilbao, *Amerikanuak*, 53.

23. Scoresby, *An Account of the Arctic Regions*, vol. 2, 11–16. The most famous story of whaling during medieval times is of a voyage taken by the Flemish explorer Othere in 890, which was written down by England's King Alfred the Great, who heard it from the explorer himself. According to this account Othere sailed north along the Norwegian coast into the White Sea, going "as far north," he related, "as commonly the whale-hunters used to travel." There he pursued "horse-whales," or walruses, which were in great demand for their tusks as well as for their skins, which were dried and used for ships' cables. But Othere also went after much larger animals, which unlike the erroneously named "horse-whales" actually *were* whales. Othere pegged the size of these whales at forty-eight to fifty ells, and claimed that he and six of his men killed sixty of them in two days.

Many historians have wondered what to make of this account, and the main sources of puzzlement revolve around the definition of an ell and the magnitude of the carnage. There is no agreement on the length of an ell, and therefore no agreement as to the size of Othere's whales. Twelve inches, twenty-seven inches, and forty-five inches per ell are three measures that have been cited. Application of the largest number results in a whale that is 187 feet long, clearly an impossibility, unless one is willing to enter the realm of fantasy or admit to the existence of a long-lost, ancestral megawhale. The next number down, twenty-seven inches, makes for a whale that is more than 110 feet long, and the only whale that could conceivably fit that description is a blue whale, and a truly gigantic one at that. This is implausible, however, for not only are blue whales too fast and powerful for Othere and his men to have pursued, but they also have the unfortunate trait, at least from a whaleman's point of view, of sinking after dying, removing the possibility of Othere's crew being able to tow the dead whales to shore, assuming they had been able to kill them in the first place. At twelve inches per ell, Othere's whales are of a more reasonable size, on the order of 50 feet, roughly the same size as a right whale or a bowhead, species that Othere certainly could have encountered. Even if one assumes that Othere was talking about such whales, that still leaves a rather considerable problem. He claimed that he and his men killed sixty whales in two days. That would be an amazing feat for modern whale hunters equipped with motorized factory boats and harpoon guns, and certainly not something that a band of ninth-century men in a relatively small vessel, with hand-propelled harpoons, could have achieved. Some have resolved this apparent anomaly by asserting that translations of Alfred's story incorrectly assumed he wrote sixty, when in reality he wrote six; still a sizable haul of whales, but at least one that is closer to the realm of possibility. Others who have pondered Othere's claims believe that he must have been talking about pilot whales or dolphins, relatively small species of whale that might have been captured in such large numbers. But this solution still leaves one scratching his head about the size of the whales, for even at twelve inches per ell, a large pilot whale would rate only about twenty ells, not the forty-eight to fifty ells that Othere claimed. Scoresby, *An Account of the Arctic Regions*, vol. 2, 8–16; Proulx, *Whaling in the North Atlantic*, 11–12; and Ellis, *Men and Whales*, 39.

Another medieval account of whaling comes from Marco Polo, the Venetian trader who gained fame through his travels to China and his work as an agent for the Chinese ruler, Khubilai Khan, all of which was recounted in his book, *A Description of the World*, written at the end of the thirteenth century. In it Polo describes whaling operations in the Arabian Sea. "We shall tell you how whales are caught in these parts," Polo began. "The whale fishers have a lot of tunny fish, which they catch only for this purpose. These fish, which are very fat, they chop up small and put in big jars or pots, to which they add salt, making a plentiful supply of pickle." The whale fishermen then soaked rags in the pickle and at sea they tied them to a line and threw them overboard. The rags left a pungent slick on the water that was so delectable and enticing that once a whale caught the scent, he would chase the ship for up to one hundred miles, "so greedy is he to get at the tunny." When the whale approached the ship, the men lured him closer still by tossing morsels of tunny into the water, which the whale would eat, becoming "intoxicated, as a man is with wine." Just as the whale settled into a state of inebriated bliss, the men would leap onto its back and thrust a harpoon into its flesh, driving it deep with a whack from a "wooden mallet." One might think that a whale thus maltreated might rapidly depart the scene or, at least, thrash about violently. The whale's "drunken stupor," however, was so profound, Polo said, that the whale "scarcely feels the men on his back, so that they can do what they like." When the whale finally realized the gravity of its situation, it would swim away, leaving the men floundering in the water, only to be picked up by the nearby ship. But the whale wouldn't get too far. Attached to the harpoon was a rope, which was tied onto the ship, and attached to the rope were empty casks and planks of wood that served to slow the whale's escape. If the whale pulled the rope "downward too strongly," casks were added to give the line more buoyancy. When the whale succumbed to its wounds, the ship would tow the carcass ashore and sell it, making a profit of as much as "1,000 livres. This, then," said Polo, "is how they catch them." Polo claims in the prologue to his book that it is "an accurate record that "contains nothing but the truth." But this tale of whaling is too fantastic to be believed, and there are good reasons not to accept it at face value. The book was coauthored by Rustichello of Pisa, a romance writer with more of a flair for drama than history, and when the book was published many doubted its veracity. Marco Polo and Rustichello of Pisa, *The Travels of Marco Polo*, translated and with an introduction by Ronald Latham (New York: Penguin Books, 1958), 33, 296–97; Manuel Komroff, *Marco Polo* (New York: Julian Messner, Inc., 1952), 164; Richard Humble, *Marco Polo* (New York: G.P. Putnam's Sons, 1975), 7; and Frances Wood, *Did Marco Polo Go to China?* (Boulder, CO: Westview Press, 1995).

24. Many have speculated on the forces that led the Basques to cross the Atlantic in search of whales. Some have argued that the Basques abandoned the Bay of Biscay because the local population of right whales had been depleted through

hunting, or had simply moved farther offshore or to different grounds to escape the whalemen's attacks. As the whales departed local waters, the argument continues, the Basques began whaling farther and farther to the north and then slowly hunted their way across the Atlantic, ultimately reaching North America. Historians that have looked most closely at the record, however, disagree with these assumptions. Instead it appears that the whales in the Bay of Biscay were not hunted to local extinction, and that shore-based whaling continued there until well into the seventeenth century. And rather than leapfrog from one whaling ground to the next, across the Atlantic, the Basques most likely ventured directly to North America, lured there by the reports of Basque cod fishermen who had seen vast numbers of whales. Selma Barkham, "The Basques: Filling a Gap in Our History Between Jacques Cartier and Champlain," *Canadian Geographic* 96 (Feb.–Mar. 1978), 8; Barkham, "The Basque Whaling Establishments in Labrador," 515; Stephen L. Cumbaa, "Archaeological Evidence of the 16th Century Basque Right Whale Fishery in Labrador," in *Right Whales: Past and Present Status*, edited by Robert L. Brownell, Jr., Peter B. Best, and John H. Prescott, Reports of the International Whaling Commission, Special Issue 10 (Cambridge, England: International Whaling Commission, 1986), 187–90; and James A. Tuck, "The World's First Oil Boom," *Archaeology* 40 (Jan.–Feb., 1987), 50–55. Prior to the mid-1970s, the evidence for Basque whaling operations in North America was sparse and based entirely on written accounts. In 1587, for example, English explorer John Davis reported meeting a ship off the Grand Bank of Newfoundland that, "as farre as wee could judge ... was a Biskaine: wee thought she went a fishing for Whales, for in 52 degrees or thereabout, we saw very many." In 1594 the English whaleship *Grace of Bristoll* reported finding in the Bay of St. George, on the coast of Newfoundland, "the wrackes of 2 great Biskaine ships, which had bene cast away three yeres before: where we had some seven or eight hundred whale finnes, and some yron bolts and chains of their mayne shrouds & fore shroudes: al their traine [whale oil] was beaten out with the weather but the caske remained still." Frederick W. True, *The Whalebone Whales of the Western North Atlantic* (1904; reprint, Washington, DC: Smithsonian Institution Press, 1983), 15–16. And on May 14, 1602, Gosnold and his men were greeted with a most curious sight soon after coming to anchor somewhere off the coast of southern Maine. At about midday, "Six indians in a Basque shallop [small whaleboat] with mast and sail, an iron grapple and a kettle of copper, came boldly aboard us," wrote John Brereton in his firsthand account of the voyage. "One of [the Indians was] appareled with a waistcoat and breeches of black serge, made after our sea fashion, hose and shoes on his feet; all the rest (saving one that had a paire of breeches of blue cloth) were all naked." See Brereton, *A Briefe and True Relation*, 4.

The most detailed contemporary account of Basque whalemen in North America comes from Samuel de Champlain, the great French explorer who visited the continent numerous times during the early seventeenth century in an effort to solidify his country's claims to eastern Canada, which at the time was called New France. During his visits to the region Champlain witnessed Basque whaling operations with considerable interest, and in his narrative of his voyages and explorations from 1603 to 1616 he recounted what he saw in order to correct an apparently common misconception: "It has seemed to me," Champlain wrote, "not inappropriate to give here a short description of whale fishing [in New France], which many people have not seen and believe to be done by cannon shots, since there are bold liars who affirm as much to those who know nothing of it. Many have obstinately maintained it to me, on account of these false reports." To put to rest this notion Champlain described how the Basques, whom he called the "most skillful in this fishery," actually hunted whales. "They have in each shallop a harpooner, who is the most agile and adroit man among them and draws the biggest wages next to the masters, inasmuch as his is the most dangerous position ... as soon as the harpooner sees his opportunity he throws his harpoon at the whale and strikes him well in the front, and, at once, when he feels the wound, he goes to the bottom. And if by chance, in turning, he strikes sometimes the shallop with his tail, or the men, he breaks them like glass." If the whale did not sound, but rather swam along the surface, it could "drag the shallop more than eight or nine leagues, going as fast as a horse," sometimes forcing the men to cut the line or be dragged under water. When the whale was within reach, the shallops surrounded it and gave "him several blows," and if the whale dived, the men would wait for it to surface and then renew the attack until the whale died. They then used ropes to tow the whale ashore, where the blubber was hacked off and melted into oil. "This is the way," protested Champlain, "in which they are caught, and not by cannon shots, as many think." Samuel de Champlain, *Algonquians, Hurons and Iroquois Champlain Explores America 1603–1616* (Dartmouth, Nova Scotia: Brook House Press, 2000), 111–12. Champlain had his own unusual run-in with a whale. On August 18, 1610, as he was sailing out of the mouth of the St. Lawrence River, his ship "encountered a whale, which was asleep. The vessel, passing over him, awakening him betimes, made a great hole in him near the tail, without damaging our vessel; but he threw out an abundance of blood." Quoted in George Francis Dow, *Whale Ships and Whaling, A Pictorial History* (New York: Dover Publications, 1985), 3.

25. Scoresby, *An Account of the Arctic Regions*, vol. 2, 18.

26. Russell Shorto, *The Island at the Center of the World* (New York: Doubleday, 2004), 21; and Johnson, *Charting the Sea of Darkness*, 34–36.

27. Rights and bowheads share many of the same characteristics, and they appear so similar in form that many have argued that they are one and the same. Even Melville, who had a very discriminating eye when it came to describing the world around him, scoffed at those who saw two species instead of one. "Some pretend to see a difference between" these two whales, he wrote, "but they precisely agree in all their grand features; nor has there yet been presented a single determinate fact upon which to ground a radical distinction. It is by endless subdivisions based upon the most inconclusive differences, that some departments of natural history become so repellingly intricate." Scientists disagree with Melville's assessment. Melville, *Moby-Dick*, 131–32.

28. The bowhead whale has gone by many names, including the Arctic right whale, the great polar whale, and the Greenland whale. Stanley M. Minasian, Kenneth C. Balcomb III, and Larry Foster, *The World's Whales: The Complete Illustrated Guide* (Washington, DC: Smithsonian Books, 1984), 76; and Ellis, *The Book of Whales*, 80. According to Scoresby, "This valuable and interesting animal [the bowhead], generally called *The Whale* by way of eminence, is the object of our most important commerce to the Polar Seas,—is productive of more oil than any other of the Cetacea, and being less active, slower in its motion, and more timid than any other of the kind, of similar or nearly similar magnitude, is more easily captured." Scoresby, *An Account of the Arctic Regions*, vol. 1, 449–50.

29. Jackson, *The British Whaling Trade*, 7, 11–14; Scoresby, *An Account of the Arctic Regions*, vol. 2, 20–25; J. T. Jenkins, *A History of the Whale Fisheries* (1921; reprint, Port Washington, NY: Kennikat Press, 1971), 79. The Muscovy Company gave its whaling captains an impressively lengthy list of whales and their characteristics so that they and their men might be able to "choose the good [to strike], and leave the bad." On the good side of the ledger, at the top of the list was the "bearded whale," or bowhead, which was said to yield "usually four hundred, and some five hundred finnes, and between one hundred and one hundred and twenty hogsheads of oyle," a hogshead being two barrels' worth. Not far behind was the "Sarda," or right whale, and the "Trumpa," or sperm whale. Other whales on the list included the "Sewira," or beluga (white) whale, as well as species called "Sedeva," "Sedeva Negro," and "Otta Sotta," whose identities are not clear based on their descriptions. While the mysterious Otta Sotta was claimed to yield the finest oil, all the others were found to be very deficient in or totally devoid of oil and whalebone and therefore were not to be pursued. Quoted in Jenkins, *A History of the Whale Fisheries*, 83–86.

30. Scoresby, *An Account of the Arctic Regions*, vol. 2, 25–29; Daniel Francis, *A History of World Whaling* (New York: Viking, 1990), 29; and Jackson, *The British Whaling Trade*, 14.

31. Smith, *A Description of New England*, in Smith, *The Complete Works of Captain John Smith*, vol. 1, 323; and Smith, *The General Historie of Virginia, New-England, and the Summer Isles*, in Smith, *The Complete Works of Captain John Smith*, vol. 2, 400.

32. True, *The Whalebone Whales*, 46; and Scoresby, *An Account of the Arctic Regions*, vol. 1, 484.

33. Slijper, *Whales*, 112; and Ellis, *Men and Whales*, 21.

34. The profits of the trip amounted to 1,500 pounds. Smith, *A Description of New England*, in Smith, *The Complete Works of Captain John Smith*, vol. 1, 323–24.

35. Smith, *The General Historie of Virginia, New-England, and the Summer Isles*, in Smith, *The Complete Works of Captain John Smith*, vol. 2, 400–401.

36. Smith, *A Description of New England*, in Smith, *The Complete Works of Captain John Smith*, vol. 1, 340.

37. Smith, *New England Trials* (1622), in Smith, *The Complete Works of Captain John Smith*, vol. 1, 425. In 1631, during the last year of his life, Smith published a book that recounted his adventures in Virginia and New England, in which he reiterated this claim, writing, "Had the fishing for Whale proved as we expected ... [I would have] stayed in the Country." Smith, *Advertisements for the Unexperienced Planters of New England, or Any Where*, in John Smith, *The Complete Works of Captain John Smith (1580–1631)*, vol. 3, edited by Philip L. Barbour (Chapel Hill: University of North Carolina Press, 1986), 278.

38. Smith, *A Description of New England*, in Smith, *The Complete Works of Captain John Smith*, vol. 1, 330.

39. Noel B. Gerson, *The Glorious Scoundrel, A Biography of Captain John Smith* (New York: Dodd, Mead & Company, 1978), 194–97; and *Sir Ferdinando Gorges and His Province of Maine*, vol. 1 edited by James Phinney Baxter (Boston: Prince Society, 1890), 96–99.

40. Smith, *A Description of New England*, in Smith, *The Complete Works of Captain John Smith*, vol. 1, 357.

41. Gerson, *The Glorious Scoundrel*, 198–203.

42. Commenting on the six or seven maps he had brought along on the trip, Smith

said that they were "so unlike each other, and most so differing from any true proportion or resemblance of the Countrey, as they did mee no more good then so much waste paper, though they cost me more." Quoted in Chatterton, *Captain John Smith*, 240. According to Lemay, the image of Smith on the map is "the only good source for his physical appearance." J. A. Leo Lemay, *The American Dream of Captain John Smith* (Charlottesville: University of Virginia Press, 1991), 47.

43. Smith, *The General Historie of Virginia, New-England, and the Summer Isles*, in Smith, *The Complete Works of Captain John Smith*, vol. 2, 401–2; and Smith, *A Description of New England*, in Smith, *The Complete Works of Captain John Smith*, vol. 1, 319.

44. Samuel Eliot Morison, *The Story of the "Old Colony" of New Plymouth* [1620–1692] (New York: Alfred A. Knopf, 1960), 4, 8–9, 14.

45. Gerson, *The Glorious Scoundrel*, 220; and *A Journal of the Pilgrims at Plymouth, Mourt's Relation*, with an introduction and notes by Dwight B. Heath (1622; reprint, New York: Corinth Books, 1963), xxiii.

46. In writing about the Puritans' expedition, Morison writes, "No more desperate colonial venture was ever launched from English shores." Morison, *The Story of the "Old Colony,"* 24.

47. Smith, *The True Travels, Adventures, and Observations of Captaine John Smith*, in Smith, *The Complete Works of Captain John Smith*, vol. 3, 221. Other writers, however, have offered different reasons for Smith not getting the job, including his overbearing personality and his perspective on the new colony's organization, which might have been at odds with the aspirations of the Pilgrims. Bradford, *Captain John Smith*, 244; Gerson, *The Glorious Scoundrel*, 221; Morison, *The Story of the "Old Colony,"* 22. Smith never did make it back to New England, although he remained an ardent booster of colonization until his death in 1631. Henry F. Howe, *Prologue to New England* (New York: Farrar & Rinehart, 1943), 236.

48. Of the 102 passengers on board the *Mayflower*, about half were true Pilgrims; the rest were non-Pilgrims or "strangers," as they were called.

CHAPTER TWO: "The King of Waters, The Sea-Shouldering Whales"

1. *The Journal of the Pilgrims at Plymouth, in New England, in 1620: Reprinted from the Original Volume*, compiled by George B. Cheever (New York: John Wiley, 1848), 29, 30–31.

2. Ibid., 30, 40.

3. In the early 1300s King Edward II of England issued decrees that made all whales taken within the realm, either cast on the shores or caught at sea, the property of the king, and from that point forward whales became known as the "Royal fish"— and "fish" was the operative word. Although Aristotle pointed out a thousand years earlier that whales had many features that clearly separated them from fish, such as breathing air, bearing live young, and being warm blooded, and Carolus Linnaeus formally classified whales as mammals, not fish, in 1758, this important phylogenetic distinction was not widely accepted until the early nineteenth century. Before then, most people, including whalemen, thought whales were fish and referred to them that way. Scoresby, *An Account of the Arctic Regions*, vol. 2, 15; Ephraim Chambers, *Chambers' Cyclopædia* (Philadelphia: J. B. Lippincott & Co., 1870), 154; Melville, *Moby-Dick*, 6, 371; Ernst Mayr, *The Growth of Biological Thought* (Cambridge: Belknap Press of Harvard University Press, 1982), 152; and Wilfrid Blunt, *The Compleat Naturalist* (New York: Viking Press, 1971), 219.

Ironically, if whales were fish, there never would have been a whaling industry. For men to attack and kill whales they first had to get close enough to them to launch a harpoon and have it strike deep. The only reason that men in their wooden boats could do that is because the whales, by virtue of their terrestrial and mammalian ancestry, had to come to the surface to breathe, giving away their location by spouting vaporous clouds of mist into the air. If whales were fish and had gills, they wouldn't need to surface, and whalemen wouldn't have seen them, much less been able to hunt them down. And if whales were not warm blooded like other mammals, they wouldn't have needed such thick layers of blubber to maintain their body temperature in the cold ocean waters, and without that blubber their value to men would have been dramatically reduced. Thus, while whalemen could refer to whales as fish all they wanted, had that indeed been the case, those whalemen would have been forced to find another line of work.

For those interested in exploring this issue further, within the context of whaling, a fascinating case was heard in New York City in 1818, which explored the following question: "Is a Whale a Fish?" The case hinged on whether a Mr. Judd owed a Mr. Maurice money as a penalty for not complying with the state law that required that all fish oil had to be inspected, certified, and gauged by an oil inspector, to make sure that the fish oil was just that and not adulterated with some other substance, such as water. Under the law the oil inspector received a twenty-five-cent fee for each cask of oil he inspected, but if someone failed to get his oil inspected, the penalty was twenty-five dollars per cask. Judd had bought three casks of sperm whale oil from a Mr. Russell. The casks were not inspected, certified, or gauged. This miffed Maurice, the local oil inspector, and he brought Judd to court, claiming that Judd owed him seventy-five dollars because sperm whales were fish, sperm whale oil was a type of fish oil, and therefore Judd had failed to do what the law required—have his casks inspected. Numerous experts were brought in by the prosecution and the defense, and in the end the jury deliberated just fifteen minutes before declaring that whales were indeed fish, and that Maurice was due the seventy-five dollars. The case was appealed, but before it could be heard the legislature changed the law so that it applied only to "liver oil, commonly called fish oil." Whales, the legislature had decided, are not fish, or at least their oil should not be treated like fish oil. William Sampson, *Is a Whale a Fish?, An Accurate Report of the Case of James Maurice Against Samuel Judd Tried in The Mayor's Court of the City of New York on December 30th and 31st of December, 1818, Wherein the Above Problem is Discussed Theologically, Scholastically, and Historically* (New York: C.S. Van Winkle, 1819); and Charles Boardman Hawes, *Whaling* (Garden City, NY: Doubleday, Page & Company, 1924), 120–26.

4.   *The Journal of the Pilgrims at Plymouth*, 30.
5.   At this time Spitsbergen was considered to be part of Greenland, and the two names were often used interchangeably. John Monck, *An Account of a Most Dangerous Voyage Performed by the Famous Capt. John Monck in the years 1619 and 1620* (Frankfurt, 1650), 564.
6.   *The Journal of the Pilgrims at Plymouth*, 30, 40–42.
7.   Ibid., 43.
8.   John Braginton-Smith and Duncan Oliver, *Cape Cod Shore Whaling, America's First Whalemen* (Yarmouth, MA: Historical Society of Old Yarmouth, 2004), 23; and Paula A. Olson and Stephen B. Reilly, "Pilot Whales," in the *Encyclopedia of Marine Mammals*, edited by William F. Perrin, Bernd Würsig, and

J. G. M. Thewissen (Burlington, MA: Academic Press, 2002), 898. There are two species of pilot whales found in the western Atlantic—short-finned (*Globicephala macrorhynchus*) and long-finned (*Globicephala melas*). The ones that the Pilgrims most likely encountered were long-finned pilot whales, for short-finned pilot whales are generally found off the coast of New Jersey and farther south. Although the Pilgrims used "Grampus" to identify the pilot whales, the same word has been used as another name for killer whales. Ommanney, *Lost Leviathan*, 481; and Frederick D. Bennett, *Narrative of a Whaling Voyage Round the Globe From the Year 1833–1836*, vol. 2 (New York: Da Capo Press, 1970), 238–39.

9. Henry David Thoreau, *Cape Cod* (1864; reprint, Orleans, MA: Parnassus Imprints, Inc., 1984), 166.

10. Bennett, *Narrative of a Whaling Voyage*, vol. 2, 233. Although Bennett is referring to the southern species, the short-finned pilot whale, the same can be said for the northern species, the long-finned pilot whale.

11. *The Journal of the Pilgrims at Plymouth*, 43.

12. These events are noteworthy enough when just a couple of whales beach themselves, but when scores of individuals are found wallowing or dead in the shallows, then the occurrence takes on tragic proportions, such as was the case in 1982, when fifty-nine pilot whales stranded on the beaches of the Cape Cod town of Wellfleet, and, more recently, in January 2005, when a little over thirty pilot whales washed ashore on a five-mile-long stretch of beach on North Carolina's Outer Banks. *Associated Press*, "Scientists Hoping Beached Whales Give Clues to Deaths," *Wilmington Morning Star*, Jan. 19, 2005; and Peter Tyack, "Stranded on the Cape," *New York Times*, Aug. 3, 2002.

13. Tyack, "Stranded on the Cape"; Olson, "Pilot Whales;" Clapham, *Whales of the World*, 33; Johann Sigurjonsson and Gisli Vikingsson, "Mass Strandings of Pilot Whales (*Globicephala melas*) on the Coast of Iceland," in *Biology of Northern Hemisphere Pilot Whales, Report of the International Whaling Commission*, special issue 14, edited by G. P. Donovan, C. H. Lockyer, and A. R. Martin (Cambridge, England: International Whaling Commission, 1993), 407; and Ommanney, *Lost Leviathan*, 248–49.

14. *The Journal of the Pilgrims at Plymouth*, 43.

15. Ibid., 46–47. According to Morison, the Thievish Harbor that Coppin had in mind was probably Gloucester Harbor on Cape Ann, which is quite a distance north of Plymouth. Morison, *The Story of the "Old Colony,"* 50.

16. There is some evidence that colonists at the Pemaquid settlement, in Maine, were involved in shore whaling, possibly as early as 1625. According to Kenneth Martin, the unearthing of whalebone fragments would seem to indicate that people were engaged in that activity, possibly that early. See Kenneth R. Martin, *Whalemen and Whaleships of Maine* (Brunswick, ME: Harpswell Press, 1975), 13–14.

17. Reverend Francis Higginson, *New-England's Plantation, with The Sea Journal and Other Writings* (1608; reprint, Salem: Essex Book and Print Club, 1908), 102–3. See also Carl Bridenbaugh, *Cities in the Wilderness, The First Century of Urban Life in America, 1625–1742* (London: Oxford University Press, 1938), 12; and Alice Morse Earle, *Home Life in Colonial Days* (1898; reprint, Middle Village, NY: Jonathan David Publishers, 1975), 32.

18. John Josselyn, *Colonial Traveler, A Critical Edition of Two Voyages to New England*,

edited by Paul J. Lindholdt (1674; reprint, Hanover, NH: University Press of New England, 1988), 48.

19. Arthur H. Hayward, *Colonial and Early American Lighting* (New York: Dover Publications, 1962), 3, 11, 15; F. W. Robbins, *The Story of the Lamp (and the Candle)* (London: Oxford University Press, 1939), 91; and Francis Russell Hart, *The New England Whale-Fisheries* (Cambridge, England: John Wilson and Son, University Press, 1924), 66–67. According to Higginson, "Though New England haue no Tallow to make Candles of, yet by aboundance of the Fish thereof, it can afford Oyle for Lampes." Higginson, *New-England's Plantation*, 102–3.

20. John Winthrop, *The Journal of John Winthrop, 1630–1649*, edited by Richard S. Dunn, James Savage, and Laetitia Yeandle (Cambridge: Belknap Press of Harvard University Press, 1996), 143.

21. Council for New England, *A Brief Relation of the Discovery and Plantation of New England: And of Sundry Accidents Therein occurring, from the Year of our Lord M.D.C.VII to the present M.D.C.XXII* (London: John Haviland, 1622), in *Collections of the MHS*, vol. 9 of the second series (Boston, 1832), 1, 20; Herbert L. Osgood, *The American Colonies in the Seventeenth Century*, vol. 1 (1904; reprint, Gloucester, MA: Peter Smith, 1957), 103; and Ida Sedgwick Proper, *Monhegan: The Cradle of New England* (Portland, ME: Southworth Press, 1930), 148–49.

22. *Select Charters and Other Documents Illustrative of American History, 1606–1775*, edited, with notes, by William Macdonald (London: Macmillan & Co., 1904), 39.

23. Elizabeth A. Little, *Indian Whalemen of Nantucket: The Documentary Evidence, Nantucket Algonquian Study #13* (Nantucket: NHA, 1992), 1. Indian use of whales continued after the colonists arrived. As Roger Williams, one of Rhode Island's colonial governors, noted, "The *natives* cut them [whales] out in severall parcells, and give them and send farre and noere, for an acceptable present, or dish." Roger Williams, *A Key into the Language of America* (London: George Dexter, 1643), 115.

24. See, for example, Charles Henry Robbins, *The Gam: Being a Group of Whaling Stories* (Salem, MA: Newcomb & Gauss, 1913), xii; Robert Coarse, *The Seafarers: A History of Maritime America 1620–1820* (New York: Harper & Row, 1964), 31; Everett J. Edwards and Jeannette Edwards Rattray, *"Whale Off!" The Story of American Shore Whaling* (New York: Coward McCann, Inc., 1932), 195–96; Ommanney, *Lost Leviathan*, 80; Foster Rhea Dulles, *Lowered Boats: A Chronicle of American Whaling* (New York: Harcourt, Brace and Company, 1933), 29; Douglas Liversidge, *The Whale Killers* (Chicago: Rand McNally & Company, 1963), 76; Howard S. Russell, *Indian New England Before the Mayflower* (Hanover, NH: University of New England Press, 1980), 124; and Charles Edward Banks, *The History of Martha's Vineyard Dukes County Massachusetts, General History*, vol. 1 (Edgartown: Dukes County Historical Society, 1966), 430.

25. Spears, *The Story of the New England Whalers*, 20.

26. Thomas Beale, *The Natural History of the Sperm Whale* (1839; reprint, London: New Holland Press, 1973), 138.

27. Little, *Indian Whalemen of Nantucket*, 2.

28. William S. Fowler, "Contributions to the Advance of New England Archaeology," *Bulletin of the Massachusetts Archaeological Society* 25 (1964), 60–61; and Little, *Indian Whalemen of Nantucket*, 1.

29. Quoted in True, *Whalebone Whales*, 27, 44.

30. Marianne S. V. Douglas, John P. Smol, James M. Savelle, and Jules M. Blais,

"Prehistoric Inuit Whalers Affected Arctic Freshwater Ecosystems," in *Proceedings of the National Academy of Science* 101 (Feb. 10, 2004): 1613.

31. Rosier, *Prosperous Voyage.*

32. Kugler argues that with the exception of the Rosier paragraph, from the Waymouth expedition, "there is no other documentary or archaeological evidence to sustain the assertion of an independent whaling tradition by Native Americans. Without such confirmation, the Waymouth account should be treated with care." Richard C. Kugler, "The Whale Oil Trade, 1750–1775," in *Seafaring in Colonial Massachusetts,* 156n.

33. Much of the information for this section on early Dutch whaling in Delaware comes from two sources: Edwards and Rattray, *"Whale Off!"* 185–90; and Charles McKew Parr, *The Voyages of David de Vries, Navigator and Adventurer* (New York, Thomas Y. Crowell Company, 1969).

34. Quoted in Edwards and Rattray, *"Whale Off!"*189.

35. Quoted in Thomas Wentworth Higginson, *Life of Francis Higginson, First Minister in the Massachusetts Bay Colony, and Author of "New England's Plantation" (1630)* (New York: Dodd, Mead & Company, 1891), 62–63.

36. Higginson, *New-England's Plantation,* 19.

37. Richard Mather, *The Journal of Richard Mather, 1635; His Life and Death, 1670* (Boston: David Clapp, 1850), 21.

38. William Morell, "Morell's Poem on New-England," *Collections of the MHS for the Year 1792,* vol. 1 (Boston: MHS, 1895), 125; and Bolton, *The Real Founders,* 3.

39. Morell, "Morell's Poem," 130.

40. William Wood, *New England's Prospect,* edited by Alden T. Vaughan (Amherst: University of Massachusetts Press, 1977), 53–57.

CHAPTER THREE: All Along the Coast

1. Braginton-Smith and Oliver, *Cape Cod Shore Whaling,* 58.

2. *The Laws and Liberties of Massachusetts, 1641–1691: A Facsimile Edition, Containing Also Council Orders and Executive Proclamations,* vol. 1, compiled and with an introduction by John D. Cushing (Wilmington, DE: Scholarly Resources, Inc., 1976), 61.

3. Quoted in William R. Palmer, *The Whaling Port of Sag Harbor* (PhD diss. Columbia University, 1959), 5–6.

4. Edwards and Rattray, *"Whale Off!"* 193–94, 204; Alexander Starbuck, *History of the American Whale Fishery* (1878; reprint, Secaucus, NJ: Castle Books), 9; James Truslow Adams, *History of the Town of Southampton* (1918; reprint, Port Washington, NY: Ira J. Friedman, Inc., 1962), 229; and Jacqueline Overton, *Long Island's Story* (Garden City, NY: Doubleday Doran & Company, 1929), 1.

5. In the early 1650s Martha's Vineyard employed both approaches. In 1652 the town appointed William Weeks and Thomas Daggett whale "cutters." The next year the town issued an edict that set up a rotational system. "Ordered by the town, that the whale is to be cut freely, four men at one time and four men at another; and so every whale, beginning at the east end of the town." Banks, *The History of Martha's Vineyard,* vol. 1, 431.

6. Quoted in Edwards and Rattray, *"Whale Off!"* 205–6.

7. Adams, *History of the Town of Southampton,* 229; Braginton-Smith and Oliver, *Cape Cod Shore Whaling,* 64; and H. Roger King, *Cape Cod and Plymouth Colony in the Seventeenth Century* (Lanham, MD: University Press of America, 1994), 206.

The processing of a drift whale was a particularly welcome event for poorer areas, as Thomas Hinckley made clear in his letter to King James II in 1687. "There are also some small whales, or part of them, sometimes in some winters cast on our shore,—some whereof making, with much labor, seven or eight barrels of oil, and some between that and twenty,—which have been some help to the poor of those poor towns planted on the Cape, being the barrenest part of the country." "Address and Petition from the Colony of New Plymouth to King James II," October 1687, in *The Hinckley Papers; Being Letters and Papers of Thomas Hinckley, Governor of the Colony of New Plymouth, 1676–1699, Collections of the MHS, vol. 5, fourth series* (Boston: Printed for the Society, 1861), 178.

8. For example, on Long Island, in 1659, the sachem "Wyandanch and his son sold to Lyon Gardiner 'all the bodys and bones of all the whales that shall come upon the land or come ashore from the place called Kitchaminfchock unto the place called Enoughquanck, only the fins and tayles of all, we reserve for ourselves and Indians for the space of 21 years.'" Quoted in Adams, *History of Southampton*, 230.

9. Quoted in Banks, *History of Martha's Vineyard*, vol. 1, 432.

10. King, *Cape Cod and Plymouth Colony*, 206.

11. *Records of the Colony of New Plymouth in New England*, vol. 9, *Laws 1623–1682*, edited by David Pulsifer (Boston: Press of William White, 1861), 114–15; and Braginton-Smith and Oliver, *Cape Cod Shore Whaling*, 77.

12. *Records of the Colony of New Plymouth in New England, Laws 1623–1682*, 139; and King, *Cape Cod and Plymouth Colony*, 207–8. The full text of the letter from Southworth reads as follows:

    OCT. 1, 1661.—LOUEING FRINDS: Whereas the Generall Court was pleased to make some proposition to you respecting the drift fish or whales; in case you should refuse theire proffer, they impowered mee, though vnfitt, to farme out what should belonge vnto them on that account; and seeing the time is expired, and it fales into my hands to dispose of, I doe therefore, with the advice of the Court, in answare to youer remonstrance, say, that if you will duely and trewly pay to the countrey for euery whale that shall come one hogshead of oyle att Boston, where I shall appoint, and that current and marchantable, without any charge or trouble to the countrey,—I say, for peace and quietnes sake you shall haue it for this present season, leaueing you and the Election Court to settle it soe as it may bee to satisfaction on both sides; and in case you accept not of this tender, to send it within fourteen dayes after the date heerof and if I heare not from you, I shall take it for graunted that you will accept of it, and shall expect the accomplishment of the same. Youers to vse, CONSTANT SOUTHWORTH TREASU.

    Records of the Colony of New Plymouth in New England, Court Orders, vol. 4, *1661–1668*, edited by Nathaniel B. Shurtleff (Boston: Press of William White, 1855), 6–7.

13. *Records of the Colony of New Plymouth in New England*, vol. 9, *Laws 1623–1682*, 139. Many decades later a few other Cape Cod towns, including Yarmouth and Sandwich, followed Eastham's lead and similarly provided for their ministers. See Braginton-Smith and Oliver, *Cape Cod Shore Whaling*, 77–79. In 1702, for example, Reverend John Cotton of Yarmouth was paid roughly forty pounds out of the profits of drift whales thrown up on the beach. Glover M. Allen, "Whales and Whaling in New England," *Scientific Monthly* 27 (Oct. 1928), 340.

14. Thoreau, *Cape Cod*, 51–52.

15. Bernard Bailyn, *The New England Merchants in the Seventeenth Century* (Cambridge: Harvard University Press, 1955), 83; and Bolton, *The Real Founders*, 129. According to a history of Ipswich, Massachusetts, around this time the "wealthier people" of that town burned whale oil "occasionally, if not frequently." Shops often had whalebone on hand for their customers, as did Joseph Weld of Roxbury, who listed among his store's inventory on February 4, 1646, twenty pounds of whalebone valued at ten and three-quarter pence. Joseph B. Felt, *History of Ipswich, Essex, and Hamilton* (1834; reprint, Ipswich: Clamshell Press, 1966), 26; and George Francis Dow, *Every Day Life in the Massachusetts Bay Colony* (Boston: Society for the Preservation of New England Antiquities, 1935), 242.

16. When shore whalemen took to their boats, they had a fairly good idea of what they would be chasing. But at least one time this apparently was not the case. On September 28, 1719, Benjamin Franklin, uncle to the more famous Benjamin Franklin, penned the following in his diary: "On the 17 instant there appear'd in Cape Cod harbour [Provincetown Harbor] a strange creature, His head like a lyons, with very large teeth, ears hanging down, a large beard, a long beard, with curling hair on his head, his body about 16 foot long, a round buttock, with a shore tayle of a yellowish colour, the whale boats gave him chase, he was very fierce and gnashed his teeth with great rage when they attack him, he was shot at 3 times and wounded, when he rose out of the water he always faced the boats in that angry manner, the Harpaniers struck at him, but in vaine, for after 5 hours chase, he took to sea again. None of the people ever saw his like befor." And none have since! Benjamin Franklin, "The Provincetown Sea Monster," quoted in *Cape Cod Stories*, edited by John Miller and Tim Smith (San Francisco: Chronicle Books, 1996), 147–48.

17. One brief account claims that William Hamilton was the first person to kill a whale off of Cape Cod, and that he did so in 1643. This would certainly qualify him as the first colonist known to have killed a whale. But the only evidence for his distinction comes from a brief obituary for the man (his age, 103); without any more solid leads, the reliability of this claim is highly dubious. "Longevity," *New Bedford Daily Mercury*, June 12, 1831; and Starbuck, *History of the American Whale Fishery*, 7–8.

18. The original language for this resolve is, "In 1647 (May 25) at a meeting of the general court held at Hartford, Conn., the following resolve was passed: 'Yf Mr. Whiting, wth any others shall make tryall and p^rsecute a designe for the takeing of whale wth in these libertyes, and if vppon tryall wth in the terme of two yeares, they shall like to goe on, noe others shalbe suffered to interrupt the, for the tearme of seauen yeares.'" Quoted in Starbuck, *History of the American Whale Fishery*, 9.

19. Quoted in Palmer, *The Whaling Port of Sag Harbor*, 6.

20. Quoted in Adams, *History of Southampton*, 231.

21. Henry P. Hedges, *A History of the Town of East Hampton, N.Y.* (Sag Harbor, NY: J. H. Hunt, 1897), 11; and Frederick P. Schmitt, *Mark Well the Whale* (Cold Spring Harbor, NY: Whaling Museum Society, Inc., 1971), 8. Although shore whaling, like the deep-sea whaling that would follow, was an industry almost exclusively run by men, at least one woman headed up her own whaling operation. This was not a role that Martha Tunstall Smith had expected to fill. It was her husband, after all, Col. William Smith, who had started a whaling company on Long Island around 1700. But after he died Martha carried on. Her boats were manned by Indians, and for a number of years her crews brought in twenty whales each winter, with the resulting oil and whalebone being shipped to Eng-

land. Martha's logbooks provide a running account of the business. On January 16, 1707, for example, she wrote, "My company killed a yearling whale, made 27 barrels." On February 4 of the same year, she noted, "Indian Harry with his boat, struck a stunt whale [2-year-old right whale] and could not kill it—called for my boat to help him. I had but a third, which was 4 barrels." Quoted in Edwards and Rattray, *"Whale Off!"* 232–33.

22. According to Kugler, "Contrary to popular belief, the Indians brought to whaling no traditions or prior experience of their own. They were taught to whale, they learned well, and were esteemed, not only for their prowess but for the cheapness for which they could be hired." Kugler, "The Whale Oil Trade," 156.

23. T. H. Breen, *Imagining the Past* (Reading, MA: Addison-Wesley Publishing, 1989), 168.

24. *An Act for the Encouragement of Whaling, Acts Passed by the General Assembly of the Colony of New-York, in September and October, anno. Dom. 1708, being the 7th year of Her Majesties reign* (New York: William Bradford, 1708).

25. Quoted in Edwards and Rattray, *"Whale Off!"* 199.

26. Quoted in Palmer, *The Whaling Port of Sag Harbor*, 8.

27. The terms of such economic servitude were usually spelled out in the labor contracts that the Indians signed. One such contract, executed on January 6, 1681, states that, "I, Harry, alias Quauquaheid, Indian of Montauk, do firmly bind and engage myself to John Streton, Sr., of East Hampton, upon consideration that I am much indebted to him upon former accounts and his present supply of my present necessity do, I say, bind and engage myself to go sea awhaling." Quoted in Breen, *Imagining the Past*, 175.

28. Thomas G. Lytle, *Harpoons and Other Whalecraft* (New Bedford: Old Dartmouth Historical Society Whaling Museum, 1984), 5. According to Lytle a harpoon had to have a tensile strength of roughly six thousand pounds. Lytle, ibid., 7.

29. The origins of this term—"Nantucket Sleigh Ride"—are murky at best. The earliest known reference to this term can be found on page 311 of Francis Warriner's *Cruise of the United States Frigate Potomac Round the World, During the Years 1831–34, Embracing the Attack on Quallah Battoo, with Notices of Scenes, Manners, etc., in Different parts of Asia, South America, and the Islands of the Pacific* (New York: Leavitt, Lord & Co.; Boston: Crocker & Brewster, 1835). Personal communication with Klaus Barthelmess, Whaling Research Project, Cologne, Germany, September 20, 2007.

30. Clifford W. Ashley, *The Yankee Whaler* (1926; reprint, New York: Dover Publications, 1991), 87. Whalemen also referred to this bloody moment as "tapping the claret."

31. Paul Dudley, "An Essay Upon the Natural History of Whales, with a Particular Account of the Ambergris Found in the Sperma Ceti Whale, in a Letter to the Publisher, from the Honourable Paul Dudley, Esq; F. R. S.," *Philisophical Transactions* 33 (1683–1775), 263. One of the earliest and most fascinating descriptions of shore whaling in America comes to us from Dr. Felix Christian Spörri, a Dutchman who, in March 1662, witnessed a small contingent of Rhode Island men launch an attack on a right whale near the mouth of Narragansett Bay:

> There were two small fishing-boats, each containing six or seven men. These followed closely in the fish's wake; when it raised its head . . . they moved up beside it and hurled a harpoon into its body. . . . To the harpoon was fastened a rope a finger-breadth in thickness, which the whale drew out. But when they had let out forty or fifty fathoms of rope after him, they held fast, while he dove toward the bottom to break off the harpoon.

As this was impossible he rose again, which fact they noticed by the slack in the line and they drew it in again quickly. The other shallop moved up with another harpoon. As soon as he appeared, they cast it into his body. When he felt this new wound, he turned his head down and raised his tail out of the water and beat about with such violence that it was terrible to behold. The fishermen had enough to do to avoid him. When this was of no avail, he began to swim off and shot away with the two shallops so rapidly that the water was cast over them in a spray. He did not continue this for long, for he was already quite weakened and he soon rose again. The fishermen moved closer with long lances or spears and inflicted innumerable wounds until he grew weaker still and began to spew up blood instead of water. This elated the fishermen, who yelled with joy, for it was a sure sign that the fish was dying. They towed him ashore, greatly pleased, for they had earned more than a whole farm would bring us in an entire year. This fish was fifty-five feet long and sixteen feet high.... Its blubber was two feet thick.

Quoted in Carl Bridenbaugh, *Fat Mutton and Liberty of Conscience* (Providence: Brown University Press, 1974), 144–45.

Sometimes, even after the whale appeared to be dead, it wasn't. And at least a few whaleboats, in the process of towing a "dead" whale in, were mightily surprised when the listless whale sprang to life and, in thrashing about, managed to damage or sink the boat. To avoid this unpleasant situation, whalemen often jabbed a hand lance into the whale's eye. If the whale didn't move, it was almost certainly dead. James Templeman Brown, "The Whalemen, Vessels and Boats, Apparatus, and Methods of the Whale Fishery," in George Brown Goode, *The Fisheries and Fishery Industries of the United States, Section V, History and Methods of the Fisheries* (Washington, DC: Government Printing Office, 1887), 269.

32. Kathleen J. Bragdon, *Native People of Southern New England, 1500–1650* (Norman: University of Oklahoma Press, 1996), 122. Dulles claims that a single whale could be butchered into 120,000 steaks. Dulles, *Lowered Boats*, 12. For a good review of the literature on eating whale meat in America, see Nancy Shoemaker, "Whale Meat in American History," *Environmental History*, 10 (Apr. 2005), 269–94.

33. According to Scoresby the flesh of a young bowhead whale "is of red colour; and when cleared of fat, broiled, and seasoned with pepper and salt, does not eat unlike coarse beef. . . . The old whale approaches to black and is exceedingly coarse." Scoresby, *An Account of the Arctic*, vol. 1, 463. In America the brains of pilot whales were sometimes made into "dainty cakes," and the livers were also often eaten. Braginton-Smith and Oliver, *Cape Cod Shore Whaling*, 23. Bennett said that "the flesh of the infant animal [humpback] is a delicate food, not to be distinquished from veal." Bennett, *Narrative of a Whaling Voyage Round the Globe from the Year 1833–1836*, vol. 2, 232. According to Brandt, "While the meat of sperm whales and beaked whales is considered inedible, porpoises have been eaten by crews of sailing ships for centuries. The meat of all baleen whales is edible. Its taste closely resembles that of beef, but the texture is coarser." Karl Brandt, *Whale Oil, An Economic Analysis* (Palo Alto, CA: Food Research Institute at Stanford University, 1940), 30. When Meriwether Lewis and William Clark made it to the Oregon coast on their expedition of discovery, they ate part of a whale that was washed ashore and cut up by the local Indians. Lewis wrote that the "blubber ... was white & not unlike the fat of Poark, tho' the texture was

more spongey and somewhat coarser. I had a part of it cooked and found it very pallitable and tender, it resembled the beaver or the dog in flavour" Journal entry for "Sunday January 5th 1806," *The Journals of the Lewis and Clark Expedition*, compiled by Gary E. Moulton, University of Nebraska, accessed on April 8, 2006, via the Web site http://lewisandclarkjournals.unl.edu/index.html. See also Sandra L. Oliver, *Saltwater Foodways* (Mystic, CT: MSM, 1995), 180.

34. Scoresby, *An Account of the Arctic*, vol. 1, 475.

35. The description of Houghton's plan is based entirely on *The Acts and Resolves, Public and Private of the Province of Massachusetts Bay*, vol. 8, *Resolves, Etc., 1703–1707* (Boston: Wright & Potter Printing Company, 1895), 658–60.

36. Today there is hardly any evidence of the shore-whaling operations that once dotted the coast. The try-houses, storage sheds, and whalemens' quarters, often relatively insubstantial structures, were not viewed as things worth preserving once their usefulness was through. They were either torn down by man or beaten down by the elements. But traces still remain. Some of the most fascinating come from the Whaler's Tavern on Great Island in Wellfleet, Massachusetts. Unearthed by archaeologists in the latter half of the twentieth century, the remains of the tavern show that it was a large, clapboard building, likely two stories high, with windows, multiple rooms, a chimney, and two cellars. The structure appears to have been built sometime in the late seventeenth century. Twenty-four thousand artifacts have been recovered, and the ones that point to the tavern's whaling history were found in the cellars. There the archaeologists discovered the remains of a shaft of a harpoon or lance; a whale vertebra, with marks indicating its use as a cutting board; and many other whalebones. It seems that the building was used by shore whalers as a place to eat, drink, socialize, and sleep. James Deetz and Patricia Scott Deetz, *The Times of Their Lives: Life, Love, and Death in the Plymouth Colony* (New York: W. H. Freeman and Company), 249–52.

37. "Starting the process of trying-out blubber is much like trying pork fat," according to Edwards and Rattray.

> You put in only a little at first; adding to it slowly. The scrap is skimmed off before fresh blubber is put in. When the scrap is about ready for skimming, it will be so dry in the hot oil that it rattles when stirred; then the fire is slacked up. The heat of the oil is tested by spitting in it; if the oil crackles when the spittle hits it, the heat is right for more blubber. It takes a good tobacco-chewer to do the testing. If the oil is too hot when the green blubber is put in, the water in it will make the kettle boil over. ...It must not be barrelled over blood-warm, or the barrels will shrink up and leak.

Quoted in Edwards and Rattray, *"Whale Off!"* 95. Tryworks were greedy consumers of fuel wood, contributing to the deforestation of coastal areas. Some towns attempted to protect their trees from being recklessly used in this manner by requiring whalemen to pay for the privilege of obtaining fuel wood. The main targets of these measures were the bands of whalemen who roamed the shore and set up their whaling operations on the common lands of towns other than their own. It was bad enough when a resident abused the town common, but much worse when a stranger did so, for then most or all of the profits gained thereby would leave the area. The use of fees to regulate wood-cutting activities of whalemen was particularly common on Cape Cod, where trees were critical to keeping the sandy soil in place, and the locals worried that without those trees the sand would blow away, including into the water, where it could create navigational hazards. In 1711, for example, the town of Barnstable decided that it had had enough of outside whalemen setting up tryworks in the area and then cutting down large swaths of trees to feed their fires. To that end the town passed an ordinance that required "every stranger, both English and Indian yt shall come and settle at Sand Neck to goẹ on whaling voiages ... shall pay for their fire wood each person three shillings at entry." Quoted in Braginton-Smith and Oliver, *Cape Cod Shore Whaling*, 126–30; and Kittredge, *Cape Cod*, 170.

38. Properly tending the pots required vigilance. Blubber had to be fed at regular intervals, and the pot had to be hot enough to melt the blubber but not so hot that the oil boiled over. Care was taken to avoid getting sand or water into the try-pots, for the former could discolor and devalue the oil, while the latter could cause the oil to bubble violently. Getting splashed with burning oil was an ever-present danger. One poor man in Truro, who fainted while tending a pot, got much more than a splash. According to a contemporary account, the man fell into "a large Vessel of boiling hot Oyl, and was scalded in a most miserable manner." "Truro," July 14, *Boston News-Letter*, July 16–23, 1741.

39. "Lord Cornbury to the Board of Trade," in *Documents Relative to the Colonial History of the State of New York*, vol. 5, edited by E. B. O'Callaghan (Albany: Weed, Parsons and Company, 1855), 60.

40. "Whereas the trying of oyle so near the street and houses," the order read, "is soe extreme noysome to all passers by, especially those not accustomed to the sent thereof, and is considered hurtful to the health of the people, and is very dangerous (if oyle should fire) for firing houses or haystacks, the court doth order that noe person after this present yeare shall try any oyle in this towne nearer than 25 poles from Main Street, under penalty of paying five pounds fine." Quoted in Edwards and Rattray, *"Whale Off!"* 207.

41. Ibid.

42. Palmer, *The Whaling Port of Sag Harbor*, 9.

43. Letter from John Thacher to Governor William Stoughton, December 22, 1694, in MHS, *Proceedings, October 1909–June 1910*, vol. 43 (Boston: MHS, 1910), 507–8.

44. Randall R. Reeves and Edward Mitchell, "The Long Island, New York, Right Whale Fishery: 1650–1924," in *Right Whales: Past and Present Status, in the Proceedings of the Workshop on the Status of Right Whales, New England Aquarium, June 15–23, 1983, International Whaling Commission, Special Report 10*, edited by Robert L. Brownell, Jr., Peter B. Best, and John H. Prescott (Cambridge, England: International Whaling Commission, 1986), 201; and "Lord Cornbury to the Board of Trade," in *Documents Relative to the Colonial History of the State of New York*, vol. 5, 59.

45. Quoted in John F. Watson, *Annals of Philadelphia and Pennsylvania in the Olden Time*, vol. 2 (Philadelphia: J. B. Lippincott & Co., 1870), 428.

46. Quoted in Dow, *Whale Ships and Whaling*, 16–17.

47. Quoted in Joseph B. Felt, *Annals of Salem*, vol. 2, second edition (Salem: W. & S. B. Ives, 1849), 223. Randolph's reference to the disappearing trade in beaver pelts provides a fascinating juxtaposition. Years of hunting beavers had made them scarce in the colonies. With the same ruthless logic, the many years of shore whaling that would follow Randolph's comment would serve to make whales scarcer in coastal waters, thereby pushing the whaling industry offshore.

It is ironic, then, that Randolph would set his sights on whales as a partial replacement for the diminished trade in beaver pelts, because the whales would one day succumb to the same fate as their furrier counterparts.

48. For the purposes of this book the Dutch dominance in whaling, especially during the mid- to late 1600s, is not of central concern, and that is why it is mentioned only as a means of highlighting how the colonial whale fishery benefited from the ascendance of Dutch and the decline of English whaling. Readers who are interested in learning more about the extensive reach of the Dutch whale fishery during the seventeenth and eighteenth centuries should explore the following sources: Scoresby, *An Account of the Arctic Regions with a Description of the Northern Whale-Fishery*, vol. 2, 138–60; and Ivan T. Sanderson, *A History of Whaling* (New York: Barnes & Noble Books, 1993), 157–72.

49. Jackson, *The British Whaling Trade*, 51.

50. Cotton Mather, *Magnalia Christi Americana*, books 1 and 2, edited by Kenneth B. Murdock (1702; reprint, Cambridge: Belknap Press of Harvard University Press, 1977), 141–42.

51. Cotton Mather, *Diary of Cotton Mather*, vol. 2, 1709–1724 (New York: Frederick Ungar Publishing Co., 1957), 379.

52. Cotton Mather, *The Thankful Christian* (Boston: B. Green for Samuel Gerrish, 1717), 25, 31, 35, 42–43. Certainly other sermons were directed at whalemen, though how many is not known. One other was offered by Pastor Nathaniel Stone, on "Feb. 10, 1719, 20," to his congregation in Harwich. Nathaniel Stone, *A Lecture Sermon Asserting GOD's Right Sovereignly to dispose of his own Gifts and Favours Both preached (Feb. 10, 1719, 20) and printed, at the Desire, and for the Use of the People of Harwich; WHO go on the Whaling Employment in the Winter Season* (Boston: James Franklin, 1720).

53. A letter written on March 18, 1691, by John Higginson and Timothy Lindall, of Salem, to a lawyer on Cape Cod, provides an interesting example of this:

> Sir: We have been jointly concerned in several whale voyages at Cape Cod and have sustained great wrong and injury by the unjust dealing of the inhabitants of those parts, especially in two instances: ye first was when Woodbury and Company in our boats in the winter of 1690 killed a large whale in Cape Cod harbor. She sank and after rose, went to sea with a harpoon, warp, etc. of ours, which have been found in the hands of Nicholas Eldridge. The second case is this last winter, 1691. William Edds and Company in one of our boats, struck a whale, which came ashore dead, and by ye evidence of the people of Cape Cod, was the very whale they killed. The whale was taken away by Thomas Smith of Eastham and unjustly detained.

Quoted in Frances Diane Robotti, *Whaling and Old Salem* (New York: Bonanza Books, 1962), 16.

54. Quoted in Starbuck, *History of the American Whale Fishery*, 8.

55. *Records of the Colony of New Plymouth in New England, Court Orders*, vol. 6, *1678–1691*, edited by Nathaniel B. Shurtleff (Boston: Press of William White, 1856), 251–53. When the dispute over a whale could not be settled by the whale inspector, in some locales the disputants could turn to the Court of Admiralty for satisfaction or frustration, whichever the case might be. On February 1, 1706, Governor Dudley of Massachusetts wrote to the Board of Trade with news about his decision to apply this form of adjudication. "I have directed the judge of the admiralty at all time to receive and decide tryalls between the fish-

ermen, which must often happen, because the wounded whales often break loose and there are disputes as to whom they belong." Local newspapers were employed to let the public know when a wounded whale had washed ashore so that potential claimants could make their case. Thus it was that on September 3, 1722, a Boston newspaper ran the following notice:

> Whereas a Whale, much Decayed and Wasted, was found floating near the Brewster, and towed on shoar last Month, in which was found by the Cutters up, a Ball [indicating that the whale had been shot]. If any Person can lay Claim to said Whale, so as to make out a Property; These are to Notefy such person to appear at the Court of the Admiralty, to Holden in Boston, on the last Wednesday in this Month, at three o'clock in the Afternoon, to make out his Claim, otherwise the said Whale (or the neat Produce thereof) will be deem'd as a Perquisite of Admiralty.

Charles M. Andrews, *The Colonial Period of American History, England's Commercial and Colonial Policy*, vol. 4 (New Haven: Yale University Press, 1938), 234n; "Advertisements," *Boston News-Letter* (Aug. 27–Sept. 3, 1722); and Albert Bushnell Hart, *Commonwealth History of Massachusetts*, vol. 2 (New York: States History Company, 1928), 230–31.

56.   Marcus B. Simpson, Jr., and Sallie W. Simpson, *Whaling on the North Carolina Coast* (Raleigh: Division of Archives and History, North Carolina Department of Cultural Resources, 1990), 6; Palmer, *The Whaling Port of Sag Harbor*, 12–13; and Barbara Lipton, "Whaling Days in New Jersey," *Newark Museum Quarterly* (Spring/Summer 1975), 5.

57.   Breen, *Imagining the Past*, 187; Starbuck, *History of the American Whale Fishery*, 14; and Edwards and Rattray, *"Whale Off!"* 213.

58.   Edwards and Rattray, *"Whale Off!"* 217; and Breen, *Imagining the Past*, 191–93. Lord Cornbury didn't only pick on Long Island's whalemen. In 1704 he granted a license to the Lawrence family of New Jersey (which he also governed), with the proviso that he and the Crown receive one-twentieth of the oil and bone. But just three years later Cornbury had changed his mind. On April 11, 1707, the Lawrences were granted another whaling license, but now Cornbury's price was half the proceeds. Cornbury wasn't completely heartless; he did let the family deduct the cost for obtaining the oil and bone before paying him his share. Lipton, *Whaling Days in New Jersey*, 21.

59.   Benjamin F. Thompson, *The History of Long Island from its Discovery and Settlement to the Present Time*, vol. 1 (New York: Gould, Banks & Co., 1843), 174.

60.   "Lord Cornbury to the Lords of Trade," in *Documents Relative to the Colonial History of the State of New York*, vol. 4, 1058.

61.   The year Samuel was born, his father, John, was appointed to the Southampton whale commission and placed in charge of one of the wards whose responsibility it was to keep a lookout for drift whales. In 1648 John moved his family to East Hampton, a town that he helped found. *Lineal Ancestors of Susan (Mulford) Cory, Wife of Captain James Cory, Genealogical Historical and Biographical*, vol. 3, part 1 (1937), 4, 14–18, 47, 51, 73–75. See also David E. Mulford, "The Captain and the King," in *Awakening the Past, The East Hampton 350th Anniversary Lecture Series, 1998* (New York: Newmarket Press, 1999), 83; Robert C. Ritchie, "East Hampton versus New York, A Very Old Story," in *Awakening the Past*, 168; Breen, *Imagining the Past*, 189–90; and Noel Gish, "Pirates," in *Awakening the Past*, 254.

62.   Ritchie, "East Hampton versus New York," 169.

63. Quoted in Edwards and Rattray, *"Whale Off!"* 217.

64. Starbuck, *History of the American Whale Fishery*, 27–28; and Edwards and Rattray, *"Whale Off!"* 224.

65. "Governor Hunter to the Lords of Trade," in *Documents Relative to the Colonial History of the State of New York*, vol. 5, 499.

66. Palmer, *The Whaling Port of Sag Harbor*, 19; Starbuck, *History of the American Whale Fishery*, 28; and Breen, *Imagining the Past*, 195.

67. "The Humble Address of the General Assembly of New-York," in Samuel Mulford, *An Information, Samuel Mulford's Defence for his Whale-Fishing* (New York: William Bradford, 1716).

68. Breen, *Imagining the Past*, 197.

69. Quoted in *Lineal Ancestors of Susan (Mulford) Cory*, 76–77. See also Mulford, "The Captain and the King," 85.

70. Quoted in Starbuck, *History of the American Whale Fishery*, 26–27.

71. "Governor Hunter to Secretary Popple, November 22, 1717," in *Documents Relative to the Colonial History of the State of New York*, vol. 5, 494; and "Governor Hunter to the Lords of Trade," in ibid. 498.

72. "Governor Hunter to the Lords of Trade," in ibid.

73. Quoted in Starbuck, *History of the American Whale Fishery*, 29.

74. Breen, *Imagining the Past*, 196.

75. "Lords of Trade to Governor Hunter, February 25, 1718," in *Documents Relative to the Colonial History of the State of New York*, vol. 5, 501.

76. Quoted in Breen, *Imagining the Past*, 197.

77. "Governor Burnet to the Lords of Trade, November 26, 1720," in *Documents Relative to the Colonial History of the State of New York*, vol. 5, 576.

CHAPTER FOUR: Nantucket, the "Faraway Land"

1. Nathaniel Philbrick, *Away Off Shore, Nantucket Island and Its People, 1602–1890* (Nantucket: Mill Hill Press, 1994), 13; Nathaniel Philbrick, *Abram's Eyes: The Native American Legacy of Nantucket Island* (Nantucket: Mill Hill Press, 1998), 15; and R. A. Douglas-Lithgow, *Nantucket: A History* (New York: G.P. Putnam & Sons, 1914), 25.

2. Melville, *Moby-Dick*, 66.

3. Douglas-Lithgow, *Nantucket: A History*, 17.

4. Robert N. Oldale, *Cape Cod and the Islands: The Geologic Story* (East Orleans, MA: Parnassus Imprints, 1992), 37–41; and Beth Schwarzman, *The Nature of Cape Cod* (Hanover, NH: University Press of New England, 2002), 7–16.

5. Edward Byers, *The Nation of Nantucket: Society and Politics in an Early American Commercial Center, 1660–1820* (Boston: Northeastern University Press, 1987), 34–36.

6. Lydia S. Hinchman, *Early Settlers of Nantucket* (1896; reprint, Rutland, VT: Charles E. Tuttle Company, 1980, 5; and *Nantucket in a Nutshell* (Nantucket: Inquirer and Mirror Steam Press, 1889), 9.

7. Obed Macy, *The History of Nantucket* (1835; reprint, Clifton, NJ: Augustus M. Kelley, 1972, 27–30; and Hinchman, *Early Settlers of Nantucket*, 17.

8. Philbrick, *Away Off Shore*, 21–22.

9. William F. Macy, *The Nantucket Scrap Basket* (Boston: Houghton Mifflin Company, 1916), 6. There is some confusion here about Macy's supposed command to his wife to "go below." As William F. Macy points out, there is general agree-

ment that the boat that Thomas Macy and his fellow travelers used was an "open boat," and therefore it had no "below" to go to. According to William Macy the phrase "go below" might have been a figurative expression only. William F. Macy, *The Story of Old Nantucket* (Boston: Houghton Mifflin Company, 1915), 27.

10. Elizabeth A. Little, "Drift Whales at Nantucket: The Kindness of Moshup," *Man in the Northeast*, 23 (1982), 17–18; Philbrick, *Abram's Eyes*, 62–63; and Little, *Indian Whalemen of Nantucket*, 2.

11. Philbrick claims that it was an Atlantic gray whale. Ellis points out that "scrag whale" is a name for a "thin or undernourished" right whale. Philbrick, *Away Off Shore*, 68; and Ellis, *The Book of Whales*, 70.

12. Macy, *The History of Nantucket*, 41.

13. Loper is also spelled "Lopar" by some sources. I have gone with "Loper" because that is the way most authors appear to spell it. See, for example, Philbrick, *Abram's Eyes*, 144; Starbuck, *A History of the American Whale Fishery*, 16; Byers, *The Nation of Nantucket*, 43; and Daniel Vickers, "The First Whalemen of Nantucket," *William and Mary Quarterly* 40 (1983), 562.

14. Breen, *Imagining the Past*, 158–59; and Edwards and Rattray, *"Whale Off!"* 177–78.

15. Macy, *The History of Nantucket*, 41.

16. Quoted in Alexander Starbuck, *The History of Nantucket, County, Island and Town* (Boston: C. E. Goodspeed, 1924), 19; and Byers, *The Nation of Nantucket*, 29.

17. Macy, *The History of Nantucket*, 42.

18. Ibid., 45.

19. Ruth Whipple Kapphahn and James Grafton Carter, *Genealogy of Whipple, Paddock, Bull Families in America 1620–1970* (Columbus, OH: self-published, 1969), 28–29; and Philbrick, *Away Off Shore*, 65.

20. This telling of the legend of Ichabod Paddock is based on two accounts of the story. Jeremiah Digges, *Cape Cod Pilot* (Provincetown: Modern Pilgrim Press, 1937), 81–84; and Philbrick, *Away Off Shore*, 66–68. At least one children's book on the story has also been written, based on the Digges account. Anne Malcolmson, *Captain Ichabod Paddock, Whaler of Nantucket* (New York: Walker and Company, 1970).

21. Digges, *Cape Cod Pilot*, 81, 82, 84.

22. Philbrick, *Away Off Shore*, 70.

23. Quoted in Elizabeth A. Little, *Nantucket Algonquian Studies #6, Essay on Nantucket Timber* (Nantucket, MA: NHA, 1981), 6; and Edouard A. Stackpole, *The Sea-Hunters* (Philadelphia: J. B. Lippincott Company, 1953), 21.

24. Philbrick, *Abram's Eyes*, 151.

25. Winthrop, *The Journal of John Winthrop*, 133.

26. Macy, *The History of Nantucket*, 42–43.

27. Vickers, "The First Whalemen of Nantucket." 569.

28. Philbrick, *Abram's Eyes*, 151.

29. Zaccheus Macy, "A Short Journal of the First Settlement of the Island of Nantucket, With Some of the Most Remarkable Things That Have Happened Since, to the Present Time (May 15, 1792)," in *Collections of the MHS for the Year 1794*, vol. 3 (Boston: Johnson Reprint Corporation, 1968), 157.

30. Philbrick, *Abram's Eyes*, 163–64.

31. Philbrick, *Away Off Shore*, 72.

32. Vickers, "The First Whalemen of Nantucket," 564.

33. *The Boston News-Letter*, Oct. 4, 1744.

34. Macy, *The History of Nantucket*, 44.

35. Ibid, 48,

36. Little, *Indian Whalemen of Nantucket*, 5–6.

37. Ellis, *Men and Whales*, 141.

38. Thomas Jefferson offers a hint that the Americans discovery of sperm whaling might have happened in a different fashion. In his report on the fisheries he says, "In 1715 the Americans began their whale fishery. . . . As the whale, being infested, retired from the Coast, they followed him farther and farther into the Ocean. . . . Having extended their pursuit to the Western Islands [Azores], they fell in accidentally with the Spermaceti whale." Thomas Jefferson, "Report on the Fisheries, February 1, 1791," in Thomas Jefferson, *The Papers of Thomas Jefferson*, vol. 19, edited by Julian P. Boyd (Princeton: Princeton University Press, 1974), 212.

39. Nantucketers weren't the only colonists to encounter a sperm whale dead on the beach. There were occasional strandings along the coast. In 1666 the Royal Society of London received a report of a sperm whale washing ashore in New England, which the local inhabitants called "Trumpo, having Teeth resembling those of a Mill, and its mouth at a good distance from, and under the Nose or Trunk." In 1668 a sperm whale grounded on the coast of northern New Jersey, forever labeling the location where it was found "Spermaceti Cove." That same year, while visiting his brother in Maine, the writer and scientist John Josselyn noted that a sperm whale "was thrown up on the shore between Winter-harbour and Cape-porpus, about eight mile from the place where I lived, that was five and fifty foot long." *A Further Relation of the Whale-Fishing about the Bermudas, and on the Coast of New-England and New-Netherland, Philosophical Transactions* 1 (1665–1666), 132; Harry B. Weiss, *Whaling in New Jersey* (Trenton: New Jersey Agricultural Society, 1974), 103; and Josselyn, *Colonial Traveler*, 75.

40. Macy, *The History of Nantucket*, 44–45.

41. Obed Macy, *A Short Memorial of Richard Macy, Grandfather of Obed Macy*. The Diary of Obed Macy When an Old Man, NHA, NHARL MS 96 (Macy Family Papers, 1729–1959), Folder 20, 21, 23.

42. Macy, *The History of Nantucket*, 45.

43. Ommanney, *Lost Leviathan*, 70.

44. Polo and Rustichello of Pisa, *The Travels of Marco Polo*, 299.

45. Jenkins, *A History of the Whale Fisheries*, 83–86.

CHAPTER FIVE: The Whale's Whale

1. Jonathan Gordon, *Sperm Whales* (Stillwater, MN: Voyageur Press, 1998), 7, 14, 29; Hal Whitehead, "Sperm Whale," in the *Encyclopedia of Marine Mammals*, 1165; Ellis, *Book of Whales*, 114; Lockley, *Whales, Dolphins and Porpoises*, 60; Melville, *Moby-Dick*, 347; and Roger S. Payne and Scott McVay, "Songs of the Humpback Whales," *Science* 173 (Aug. 13, 1971), 585.

2. A. A. Berzin, *The Sperm Whale* (Washington, DC: National Marine Fisheries Service, 1971), 7–10; Bennett, *Narrative of a Whaling Voyage*, vol. 2, 153; Ellis, *Men and Whales*, 100–101; Whitehead, "Sperm Whale" and Bennett, *Narrative of a Whaling Voyage*, vol. 2, 153.

3. Beale, *The Natural History of the Sperm Whale*, 25.

4. Dale W. Rice, "Spermaceti," in the *Encyclopedia of Marine Mammals*, 1163;

Ommanney, *Lost Leviathan*, 46; and William M. Davis, *Nimrod of the Sea or the American Whaleman* (1874; reprint, North Quincy: Christopher Publishing House, 1972), 86.

5. Berzin, *The Sperm Whale*, 112–13. The junk earned its "dismissive" name from whalemen who viewed it as being less valuable than the spermaceti organ, which it in fact was. Gordon, *Sperm Whales*, 50.

6. Smith, *The True Travels*, in Smith, *The Complete Works of Captain John Smith*, vol. 3, 219.

7. Berzin, *The Sperm Whale*, 113–15; Ellis, *Book of Whales*, 113; and Adam Summers, "Fat Heads Sink Ships," *Natural History* 3 (Sept. 2002), 40. One recent scientific study shows that, contrary to a long-held belief, sperm whales do in fact suffer, at least to some extent, from the bends. Michael J. Moore and Greg A. Early, "Cumulative Sperm Whale Bone Damage and the Bends," *Science* 306 (Dec. 24, 2004), 2215.

8. Roger Payne, *Among Whales* (New York: Delta, 1995), 21; and Melville, *Moby-Dick*, 128.

9. Berzin, *The Sperm Whale*, 45; and Ellis, *Book of Whales*, 114.

10. Bennett, *Narrative of a Whaling Voyage*, vol. 2, 163; Gordon, *Sperm Whales*, 11; and N. S. Shaler, "Notes on the Right and Sperm Whales," *American Naturalist* 7 (Jan. 1873), 2. Any animal with teeth is susceptible to toothaches, and sperm whales are no exception to the rule. On occasion whalemen have witnessed sperm whales acting very agitated, only to find out later that they were thus afflicted. In 1852 a whaleship approached and killed a bull sperm whale they had seen thrashing about in the water, and jumping out of the water repeatedly. When they extracted his teeth, they discovered the reason for this odd behavior. "The cavities in several [of the teeth] contained a large number of worms, an eighth of an inch in length." While the outside of the teeth looked fine, the insides were eaten away. "Extract from a Whaleman's Journal," *Whalemen's Shipping List and Merchants' Transcript*, Sept. 28, 1852.

11. Berzin, *The Sperm Whale*, 37–44.

12. Davis, *Nimrod of the Sea*, 182. The best way to appreciate the tail's grandeur is to watch a sperm whale begin a dive. Preparing to descend, the whale will lift its head slightly, then pitch forward and raise its tail straight up out of the water, to a height of twenty feet or more, a sight that prompted whalemen to cry out, "There goes flukes!" and in short order the whale begins its journey to the depths, given, as it were, an initial shove by its weighty tail. If one could freeze the dive at its inception, and gaze closely at the scene, the most arresting feature, beyond the majestic flukes, would be the massive, sinewy cables of muscle supporting the tail. An idea of the great power of these muscles can be gleaned from entries in the logbook of the British whaleship *Royal Bounty*, which battled a sperm whale in May 1817. The first round of the battle lasted sixteen hours, during which time the whale, pierced by numerous harpoons and trailing sixteen hundred fathoms of line, towed six whaleboats at a fast clip bouncing over the waves. The second round commenced when the *Royal Bounty*, which had been able to keep pace with the whaleboats, took aboard one of the lines, hoping to use its great bulk to halt the whale's advance. But the harpoon attached to that line didn't hold, and the whale continued dragging the whaleboats, and their exhausted and petrified crews, for another twenty hours. In round three the *Royal Bounty* took aboard two lines, which held fast. Yet the hunt was not over. For another hour and a half the whale pulled the *Royal Bounty* and its

whaleboats into the wind at a speed of two knots. Finally, early in the evening of the second day of the chase, forty hours after it had begun, this "formidable and astonishingly vigorous" whale, spent by its "almost incessant, and for the most part fruitless exertion," was killed. Scoresby, *An Account of the Arctic Regions*, vol. 2, 289–92.

13. Ellis, *Men and Whales*, 39.

14. MSNBC, "Thar she blows! Dead whale explodes," MSNBC News (Jan. 29, 2004), accessed from the following Web site on February 4, 2005: http://www .msnbc.msn.com/id/4096586/; Jason Pan, "Sperm Whale Explodes in Tainan City," *Taiwan News*, Jan. 27, 2004; and *Taipei Times*, "Taiwan Quick Takes," Jan. 29, 2004.

15. Melville, *Moby-Dick*, 387–88.

16. Ibid., 174; and Ellis, *Book of Whales*, 101.

17. J. N. Reynolds, "Mocha Dick: or the White Whale of the Pacific: A Leaf from a Manuscript Journal," *Knickerbocker* 13 (May 1839), 379, 390; and Frank B. Goodrich, *Man Upon the Sea: Or, A History of Maritime Adventure, Exploration, and Discovery, From the Earliest Ages to the Present Time* (Philadelphia: J. B. Lippincott & Co., 1858), 504.

18. Quoted in A. B. C. Whipple, *Yankee Whalers in the South Seas* (Rutland, VT: Charles E. Tuttle Co., 1973), 61.

19. Gordon, *Sperm Whales*, 17; Ellis, *Book of Whales*, 105; and Beale, *The Natural History of the Sperm Whale*, 51.

20. Bennett, *Narrative of a Whaling Voyage*, vol. 2, 173.

21. Gordon, *Sperm Whales*, 12, 18, 45. It might have been such communication that caused the following behavior observed by Bennett: "It is a confirmed fact, and one often noticed with surprise by southern whalers, that upon a Cachalot being struck from a boat, others, many miles distant from the spot, will almost instantaneously express by their actions, an apparent consciousness of what has occurred, or at least some untoward event, and either make off in alarm, or come down to the assistance of their injured companion." Bennett, *Narrative of a Whaling Voyage*, vol. 2, 178.

22. Charles Darwin, *Charles Darwin's Diary of the Voyage of the H.M.S. "Beagle,"* edited from the manuscript by Nora Barlow (New York: Macmillan Company, 1933), 211. When people think of whales breaching, it is almost always in association with humpback whales, which are known to put on spectacular leaping displays that have been witnessed by numerous fortunate whale watchers. But humpbacks and sperms are not the only great whales known to breach. For example, when Sir Arthur Conan Doyle, who would later gain fame for creating the character Sherlock Holmes, went whaling in the Arctic in 1880, he witnessed a right whale breaching. "I shall never forget my own first sight of a right whale," Doyle wrote. "It had been seen by the look-out on the other side of a small ice-field, but had sunk as we all rushed on deck. For ten minutes we awaited its reappearance, and I had taken my eyes from the place, when a general gasp of astonishment made me glance up, and there was the whale *in the air*. Its tail was curved just as a trout's is in jumping, and every bit of its glistening lead-coloured body was clear of the water. It was little wonder that I should be astonished, for the captain, after thirty voyages, had never seen such a sight." Sir Arthur Conan Doyle, *Memories and Adventures* (Boston: Little, Brown and Company, 1924), 40.

23. Ellis, *The Book of Whales*, 111.

24. Davis, *Nimrod of the Sea*, 187.

25. Ellis, *Book of Whales*, 109.

26. Frank T. Bullen, *The Cruise of the Cachalot* (New York: D. Appleton and Company, 1899), 143–44.

27. Mathews, *The Natural History of the Whale*, 70.

28. Gordon, *Sperm Whales*, 37; Beale, *The Natural History of the Sperm Whale*, 35; Ellis, *Book of Whales*, 109; and Shaler, "Notes on the Right and Sperm Whales," 3.

29. Berzin, *The Sperm Whale*, 207–8.

30. Ommanney, *Lost Leviathan*, 70; and Thomas Beale, *The Natural History of the Sperm Whale*, 7. In contrast to the sperm whale's gullet, the blue whale's is downright diminutive, measuring no more than four or five inches in diameter. "Sea Secrets," *Sea Frontiers*, 32 (Mar.–Apr. 1986), 139.

31. William Kastner, "Man in Whale," *Natural History* 56 (Apr. 1947), 145.

32. Robert Cushman Murphy, *Logbook for Grace* (New York: Time Incorporated, 1947).

33. Robert Cushman Murphy, "Response to Kastner, Man in Whale," *Natural History* 56 (Apr. 1947), 190. See also, "Was James Bartley Swallowed by a Whale?," *Mariner's Mirror* 79 (Feb. 1993), 87–88. That wasn't the end of the matter, however. The original letter and Murphy's response spurred Dr. Egerton Y. Davis, Jr., to write a letter of his own, in which he recounted his experience as the surgeon on a ship that was hunting seals off the coast of Newfoundland in the mid-1890s. Davis claimed that while chasing seals, one of the men got separated from his fellows, and floated away on a small ice floe. As the others watched, the man slipped off the ice into the water and was promptly swallowed by a very large sperm whale. The whale then set a course for a nearby sealing ship, apparently intent on ramming it. A good shot from a shipboard cannon delivered a mortal blow, and the whale was found the next day, belly up, floating nearby. The men, eager to see what had become of their swallowed mate, began hacking away at the whale's belly. After a couple hours of hard labor, they were able to extract the whale's "upper stomach" which was brought back to Dr. Davis, who cut it open, unleashing "an overpowering stench," and exposing "a fearsome sight." The dead man's chest was badly crushed, no doubt by the whale's jaws, and "the whale's gastric mucosa had encased his body . . . like the foot of a huge snail." Once this covering was peeled away, the man was shown to be "badly macerated and partly digested." For his final observation Davis noted that, "curiously enough some lice on his head appeared still to be alive." Davis's account is certainly more believable than the one starring Bartley, but its ultimate veracity must be left to the reader to decide. Egerton Y. Davis, Jr., "Man in Whale," *Natural History* 56 (June 1947), 241.

34. William Shakespeare, *The Works of William Shakespeare*, vol. 5 (Boston: Little Brown and Company, 1892), 293.

35. Ephraim Chambers, *Cyclopædia, or an Universal Dictionary of Arts and Sciences Containing the Definitions of the Terms and Accounts of the Things signify'd thereby, in the Several Arts both Liberal and Mences Human and Divine . . . Compiled from the best Authors, Dictionaries, Journals, Memoirs, Transactions, Ephemerides &c. in Several Languages . . . by E. Chambers Gent. . . . vol. the Second, MDCCXXVIII* (London: J. and J. Knapton, 1728), 106. It appears that "spermaceti" was also valued for easing the physical difficulties of aging. According to Mawer, George Ripley's *Compound of Alchemy*, written in 1471, recommended the use of "Sperma

cete ana redd Wyne when ye wax old." Quoted in Granville Allen Mawer, *Ahab's Trade, The Saga of South Seas Whaling* (New York: St. Martin's Press, 1999), 6.

36. Clapham, *Whales of the World*, 98.
37. Howard Clark, "The Whale-Fishery, History and Present Condition of the Fishery," in George Brown Goode, *The Fisheries and Fishery Industries of the United States, Section V, History and Methods of the Fisheries* (Washington, DC: Government Printing Office, 1887), 5.
38. Ommanney, *Lost Leviathan*, 65; and Andrew Dalby, *Dangerous Tastes* (Berkeley: University of California Press, 2000), 68.
39. Thomas Babington Macaulay, *The Works of Lord Macaulay Complete*, edited by Hannah More Macaulay Trevelyan, vol. 1 (London: Longmans, Green, and Company, 1866), 345; Dalby, *Dangerous Tastes*, 68, 146; and Melville, *Moby-Dick*, 378.
40. Karl H. Dannenfeldt, "Ambergris: The Search for Its Origin," *Isis* 73 (Sept. 1982), 392.
41. Quoted in Beale, *The Natural History of the Sperm Whale*, 130.
42. M. I., "An Account of a Strange Sort of Bees in the West-Indies, Communicated by M.I.," *Philosophical Transactions* 15 (1683–1775), 1030–31.
43. Charles Gould, *Mythical Monsters* (London: W. H. Allen & Co., 1886), 306–7.
44. Polo and Rustichello of Pisa, *The Travels of Marco Polo*, 296–97.
45. Quoted in Jenkins, *A History of the Whale Fisheries*, 83–85.
46. Dr. Boyslton, "Ambergris Found in Whales. Communicated by Dr. Boylston of Boston in New-England," *Philosophical Transactions* 33 (1683–1775), 193. In the same issue of *Philosophical Transactions* there came another communication from an American, Paul Dudley, also on the topic of ambergris and its association with sperm whales. After arguing that the sperm whale should henceforth be known as the "Ambergris Whale," Dudley presented a description of ambergris's origin, which though it included many errors, was both thorough and thoughtful. Rather than simply discuss the source of ambergris, as Boylston had done, Dudley decided to lay a claim for the home team. "But truth," he said, "is the daughter of time; it is now at length found out, that this *Occultum Natura* is an animal production, and bred in the body of the Sperma Ceti whale. . . . I doubt not but that, in process of time some further particulars may be procured with respect to ambergris, and I shall be proud to transmit them; in the mean time I hope the Society will accept of this first essay, and allow my poor country the honour of discovering, or at least ascertaining, the origin and nature of ambergris." Dudley's patriotic ardor notwithstanding, he was, as has been shown, a little late with that claim. Paul Dudley, "An Essay Upon the Natural History of Whales," 266, 269.
47. Dr. Schwediawer and Joseph Banks, "An Account of Ambergrise, by Dr. Schwediawer; Presented by Sir Joseph Banks, P.R.S.," *Philisophical Transactions of the Royal Society of London* 73 (1783), 226–41.
48. Starbuck, *History of the American Whale Fishery*, 148.
49. Thomas Jefferson, "Observations on the Whale Fishery" (1788), in Merrill D. Peterson, ed., *Thomas Jefferson's Writings* (New York: Library of America, 1984), 388.
50. Quoted in Gordon, *Sperm Whales*, 18.
51. Frederick D. Bennett, *Narrative of a Whaling Voyage*, 217.

CHAPTER SIX: Into "Ye Deep"

1. Macy, "A Short Journal of the First Settlement of the Island of Nantucket," 161.
2. Walter Folger, "A Topographical Description of Nantucket, May 21, 1791," in *Collections of the MHS, for the Year 1794*, vol. 3 (New York: Johnson Reprint Corporation, 1968), 154.
3. Melville, *Moby-Dick*, 76.
4. Thomas Chalkley, *Journal or Historical Account of the Life, Travels, and Christian Experiences, of that Antient Faithful Servant of Jesus Christ, Thomas Chalkley*, 3rd ed. (London: Luke Hind, 1751), 294. For a modern paraphrase of this quote, see also William Root Bliss, *Quaint Nantucket* (Boston: Houghton Mifflin and Company, 1897), 98.
5. Nathaniel Philbrick, "'Every Wave Is a Fortune': Nantucket Island and the Making of an American Icon," *New England Quarterly* 66 (Sept. 1993), 442–43.
6. Melville, *Moby-Dick*, 77.
7. Folger, "A Topographical Description of Nantucket," 154. An oft-told story has a young boy tying one end of his mother's ball of "darning cotton" to his fork in an attempt to harpoon the cat. Just as the tormented animal was making its hasty retreat, the boy's mother walked in to see what all the fuss was about. With his only thoughts on fastening to the "whale," the boy yelled, "Pay out, mother! Pay out!! There she 'sounds' through the window!" Macy, *Nantucket Scrap Basket*, 23.
8. J. Hector St. John de Crèvecoeur, *Letters from an American Farmer* (1782; reprint, New York: E.P. Dutton & Company, 1957), 109–10.
9. For example, in 1737 a Cape Cod Indian by the name of Robin Mesrick struck a deal with one of his creditors, Gideon Holway, to whom he owed nine pounds. To pay off Holway, Mesrick agreed to "worke on Shoar and Whale for him Three years." Holway, for his part of the bargain, agreed to pay Mesrick eleven shillings a month on "Shoar," and "when he Goes on the Spring [deep-sea] Whaleing to find him a suitable Berth . . . [and] allow him half an Eighteenth of what is Obtained On Each of" the voyages, after deducting the vessel's share and the cost of food and liquor. When Mesrick went shore whaling, he was entitled to "a whole Eighth Clear" if he provided his own food, lodging, and wood; If Holway provided these things, then Mesrick would "Draw but Half an Eighth as according to custom." Were Mesrick lucky enough to repay the debt before three years elapsed, he would regain his freedom. Quoted in Vickers, "The First Whalemen of Nantucket," 579.
10. Elizabeth A. Little, "Nantucket Whaling in the Early 18th Century," in *Papers of the Nineteenth Algonquian Conference*, edited by William Cowan (Ottawa: Carleton University, 1988), 116.
11. Quoted in Starbuck, *History of the American Whale Fishery*, 31.
12. Patricia C. McKissack and Frederick L. McKissack, *Black Hands, White Sails: The Story of African-American Whalers* (New York: Scholastic Press, 1999), 2–16.
13. "Advertisements," *Boston News-Letter* (Nov. 29 to Dec. 5, 1723).
14. Quoted in Durand Echeverria, *A History of Billingsgate* (Wellfleet: Wellfleet Historical Society, 1991), 94–95.
15. Felt, *Annals of Salem*, vol. 2, 224–25. Dudley observed that whaleboats "are made of Cedar Clapboards, and so very light, that two men can conveniently carry them, and yet they are twenty Feet long, and carry six men, viz. The Harpooner

in the Fore-part of the Boat, four Oarsmen, and the Steersmen. These boats run very swift, and by reason of their lightness can be brought on and off, and so kept out of Danger." Dudley, "An Essay Upon the Natural History of Whales," 262–63.

16. There is some disagreement over when this transition occurred. Braginton-Smith and Oliver state that a variety of "accounts confirm that whaleboats were double-ended from at least 1696 on." Braginton-Smith, *Cape Cod Shore Whaling*, 37. However, Kugler claims that "in 1750, the boats in use reflect and an early stage of development . . . about twenty-five feet in length, with sharp bows, rounded bottoms, clinker planking, and square sterns." Kugler, "The Whale Oil Trade," 157.

17. Reginald B. Hegarty, *Birth of a Whaleship* (New Bedford: NBFPL, 1964), 135.

18. Commenting on this phenomenon, a Boston paper in 1737 said, "There are now fitting out from this place [Provincetown] a dozen sail of Vessels . . . bound for the Davis Streights on the Whaling Design, and are just ready to sail; So many of our people are now bound on this Voyage, that there will not be left behind above a Dozen or Fourteen men in the Town." "Province-Town, April 5," *New England Weekly Journal*, Apr. 19, 1737.

19. It is not clear exactly when or why this tradition originated, although the general claim is that it was done to "keep the most experienced man at the position of greatest responsibility." Ashley, *The Yankee Whaler*, 6.

20. Obed Macy claimed that up through 1760, "not a single white person [from Nantucket] was killed or drowned in the pursuit" of whales, and judging by the placement of this comment in his text, he was referring to shore-whaling operations only, not at-sea whaling. Macy, *The History of Nantucket*, 44. This claim, even if restricted to shore-whaling, is subject to question because shore-whaling was very dangerous, and whalemen in other locales that pursued this form of employ did die on occasion.

21. Starbuck, *History of Nantucket*, 356–357n. In 1724 Dinah petitioned the General Court of Massachusetts to grant her permission to marry again, and was apparently given leave to, becoming Mrs. Williams soon thereafter.

22. Starbuck, *History of Nantucket*, 358–59; and Starbuck, *History of the American Whale Fishery*, 34. For another account from the same era see, "Newport Rhode Island, July 27," *American Weekly Mercury* (Aug. 2–Aug. 9, 1744).

23. Benjamin Bangs Diary, MHS (4 vols., 1742–65). All the quotes in the text, as well as the information about Bangs, come from the first volume of this diary, unless otherwise noted. The Bangs family was one of the first to settle in the colony, tracing its lineage back to 1623, when Edward Bangs, Benjamin's great-great-grandfather, stepped off the Pilgrim ship *Anne* and took up residence in Plymouth. Benjamin was born on June 24, 1721, in modern-day Brewster, Massachusetts, on Cape Cod, which during his life was part of Harwich. A genealogist who wrote a book about the Bangs family in 1896 said that Benjamin "was a very active, enterprising merchant and shipmaster, succeeding in nearly all his undertakings, of high and noble character, and possessing excellent literary tastes." When Benjamin launched his diaries, however, all that success still lay before him. Dean Dudley, *History and Genealogy of the Bangs Family in America* (Montrose, MA: Published by the author, 1896), 4, 65.

24. There is some confusion in Bangs's entries, with the earliest entries in book 1 having dates that jump back and forth between 1742 and 1743. It is clear, how-

ever, from the text of the entries themselves and the flow of the diary which dates are in error. I have made the corrections where needed, and in only two instances that are relevant to the story told here.

25. Levi Whitman, "A Topographical Description of Wellfleet," in *Collections of the MHS for the Year 1794*, vol. 3 (New York: Johnson Reprint Corporation, 1968), 121.

26. "Boston," *Boston Weekly News-Letter* (Nov. 19–Nov. 26, 1741).

27. Schneider, *The Enduring Shore*, 151.

28. Josiah Paine, *A History of Harwich, Barnstable County, Massachusetts: 1620–1800* (Rutland, VT: Tuttle, 1937), 436.

29. Ibid., 419, 422, 424, 430, 434, 436, 438.

30. Macy, *Whale Fishery at Nantucket*, 161; Hutchinson, *The History of the Colony and Province of Massachusetts-Bay*, vol. 2, 341; and Arthur M. Schlesinger, *The Birth of the Nation* (New York: Alfred A. Knopf, 1969), 48. In 1728 a Mr. Thomas Amory wrote the following in a letter to England: "You will find good encouragement in the whale-fishery—many here and at Nantucket are engaged in it and there is a great deal of money made in it." William B. Weeden, *Economic and Social History of New England, 1620–1789*, vol. 1 (Williamstown, MA: Corner House Publishers, 1978), 441. To get an idea of the scope of the transatlantic trade, in July 1730, London received shipments of 154 tons of whale oil from the American colonies, and 9,200 pounds of whalebone. Abiel Holmes, *American Annals or A Chronological History of America*, vol. 2 (Cambridge, MA: W. Hilliard, 1805), 125.

31. The following discussion about the attempted revival of the British whale fishery is based largely on David Macpherson, *Annals of Commerce, Manufactures, Fisheries, and Navigation*, vol. 3 (London: Mundell and Son, 1805), 130–35, 141, 155–56, 160, 167, 178–80.

32. Scoresby, *An Account of the Arctic Regions*, vol. 2, 104.

33. MacPherson, *Annals of Commerce*, vol. 3, 198–99; and Scoresby, *An Account of the Arctic Regions*, vol. 2, 105–6, 108.

34. Comparing the Nantucket whalemen with the Dutch, Jefferson observed, "Their economy was more rigorous than that of the Dutch. Their seamen, instead of wages, had a share in what was taken. This induced them to fish with fewer hands, so that each had a greater dividend in the profit. It made them more vigilant in seeking game, bolder in pursuing it, and parcimonious [sic] in all their expences." Jefferson, "Observations on the Whale Fishery," 380.

35. William Edward Hartpole Lecky, *A History of England in the Eighteenth Century*, vol. 2 (New York: D. Appleton and Company, 1892), 110; Alfred W. Crosby, *Children of the Sun: A History of Humanity's Unappeasable Appetite for Energy* (New York: W. W. Norton, 2006), 87; and Gerald S. Graham, "The Migrations of the Nantucket Whale Fishery: An Episode in British Colonial Policy," *New England Quarterly* 8 (June 1935), 179.

36. Lecky, *A History of England in the Eighteenth Century*, vol. 2, 105.

37. Graham, "The Migrations of the Nantucket Whale Fishery," 179; Lecky, *A History of England in the Eighteenth Century*, vol. 2, 110–11; Edouard A. Stackpole, "Nantucket Whale Oil and Lighting," *Rushlight* 48 (Sept. 1982), 3.

38. Macy, *History of Nantucket*, 62–63. There are, it should be noted, references in various places to a small quantity of Nantucket whale oil being shipped to England in the *Hanover* in 1720. One is in *Nantucket Argument Settlers: Island History at a Glance, 1602–1993* (Nantucket: Inquirer and Mirror, 1994), 13–14.

39. The following discussion of Thomas Hancock's first foray into the whaling

business is based largely on W. T. Baxter, *The House of Hancock, Business in Boston 1724–1775* (Cambridge: Harvard University Press, 1945), 48–51.

40. Thomas Hancock to Francis Wilkes, November 4, 1737, Hancock Family Collection, BLHBS.

41. Some authors have claimed that it was a Basque whaling captain by the name of François Sopite, who made the first use of on-board tryworks at the end of the sixteenth century. However, even Sanderson, the most ardent supporter of this notion admits that "we have no written record of this event." And if Sopite did do this, it is odd that no other whalemen, Basque or otherwise, used on-board tryworks until the American colonists did so in the middle of the eighteenth century. It seems more likely, then, as Ellis argued, that Sopite's "'invention may have been the invention of some creative authors." Sanderson, *A History of Whaling*, 129; and Ellis, *Men and Whales*, 46.

CHAPTER SEVEN: Candle Wars

1. Quoted in James B. Hedges, *The Browns of Providence Plantations* (Cambridge: Harvard University Press, 1952), 89; and Kugler, "The Whale Oil Trade," 155.

2. "An Act for Granting Unto Benjamin Crabb the Sole Priviledge [*sic*] of Making Candles of Coarse Spermaceti Oyl," in *The Acts and Resolves, Public and Private, of the Province of the Massachusetts Bay*, vol. 3 (Boston: Albert Wright, 1878), 546–47.

3. Quoted in Kugler, "The Whale Oil Trade," 160–61.

4. Quoted in Dow, *Every Day Life in the Massachusetts Bay Colony*, 127–28.

5. Ephraim Chambers, *Cyclopædia or an Universal Dictionary of Arts and Sciences Containing an Explication of the Terms, and an Account of the Things Signified Thereby, in the Several Arts, Both Liberal and Mechanical and the Several Sciences, Human and Divine . . . extracted from the best Authors, Dictionaries, Journals, Memoirs, Transactions, Ephemerides &c. in Several Languages . . . by E. Chambers F.R.S. . . . . In Two vols. MDCCXLIII* (London: 1743).

6. Quoted in Hedges, *The Browns of Providence Plantations*, 89.

7. For good descriptions of the spermaceti candlemaking process, see Elmo Paul Hohman, *The American Whalemen* (New York: Longmans, Green and Co., 1928), 334–35; Patty Jo Rice, "Beginning with Candle Making, A History of the Whaling Museum," *Historic Nantucket* 47 (Winter 1988); and Kugler, "Whale Oil Trade," 164. For an excellent, in-depth discourse on the names and uses for all the various oils and waxes that were extracted from whales, see David Littlefield and Edward Baker, "Oil from Whales," in Wilson Helflin, *Herman Melville's Whaling Years*, edited by Mary K. Bercaw Edwards and Thomas Farel Heffernan (Nashville: Vanderbilt University Press, 2004), 231–40.

8. Hedges, *The Browns of Providence Plantations*, 76–77, 90.

9. Benjamin Franklin to Susanna Wright, November 21, 1751, in *The Papers of Benjamin Franklin*, vol. 4, edited by Leonard W. Labaree (New Haven: Yale University Press, 1959), 211. Long after Franklin penned this letter, the superior illuminating power of spermaceti candles was put to use in creating the definition for the term "candlepower." According to a nineteenth century book on physics, "The candle-power is the amount of light given by a spermaceti candle burning 2 grains per minute, and of such size that 6 weigh 1 pound." Fred J. Brockway, *Essentials of Physics, Saunders Question—Compends, No. 22* (Philadelphia: W. B. Saunders, 1892), 144.

10. Quoted in Hedges, *The Browns of Providence Plantations*, 90.

11. Ibid., 93.

12. Quoted in ibid., 96. See also Kugler, "The Whale Oil Trade," 168.

13. Hedges, *The Browns of Providence Plantations*, 97; Peter Tertzakian, *A Thousand Barrels a Second: The Coming Oil Break Point and the Challenges Facing an Energy Dependent World* (New York: McGraw-Hill, 2006), 11.

14. Hedges, *The Browns of Providence Plantations*, 98–100, 103.

15. The trust's plan to keep the price of head matter from rising too fast was spectacularly unsuccessful. In 1761 the maximum price for head matter had been pegged at six pounds per ton above the price of "Brown oil." By 1774 that number had risen to forty pounds per ton. At the same time, the price of candles rose hardly at all. In Boston, for example, spermaceti candles commanded a little less than 20 percent more in 1774 than they had a decade earlier. Ibid., 112, 114–15.

16. Joseph Lawrence McDevitt, Jr., *The House of Rotch: Whaling Merchants of Massachusetts, 1734–1828* (University Microfilms International, PhD diss. American University, Washington, DC, 1978), 1–2, 41–42.

17. Kugler, "The Whale Oil Trade," 172; and Leonard Ellis Bolles, *History of New Bedford and its Vicinity, 1602–1892* (Syracuse: D. Mason & Co., 1892), 57–59; Daniel Ricketson, *The History of New Bedford* (New Bedford, 1858), 58; and McDevitt, *The House of Rotch*, 137–38.

18. For sperm whales there were three grades to consider. The clearest, whitest, and sweetest-smelling oil, which was rendered from the freshest blubber, commanded the highest price. The next lower grade was the yellow, more odiferous, thinner oil rendered from slightly stale blubber that had "aged" in casks or had not been properly tried out in the first place. At the bottom of the sperm-whale-oil hierarchy was the brown oil, rendered from the oldest, rottenest blubber, brought to port after long trips during the summer months in the North or in the warmer latitudes of the South, during which time the blubber, stored in casks in the steamy and dark hold, began to decompose into a stinking stew. The great value of sperm whale oil becomes clearer when one considers that the oil rendered from right whales, simply called whale oil in the trade, was usually no more valuable than the brown oil of the sperm. McDevitt, *The House of Rotch*, 55–69; Kugler, "The Whale Oil Trade," 159; and Hedges, *The Browns of Providence Plantations*, 88.

19. Henry Cruger to Aaron Lopez, July 28, 1776, in *Commerce of Rhode Island, 1726–1800*, vol. 1, edited by Worthington Ford, *MHS Collections*, 7th Series, vols. 9–10 (Boston: Published for the Society, 1914–15), 165.

20. Quoted in Hedges, *The Browns of Providence Plantations*, 112–13.

CHAPTER EIGHT: Glory Days

1. These fashions were not always welcomed. The hoop petticoat, which toward the middle of the eighteenth century had, in many instances, achieved truly gargantuan proportions, led one irritated man to write a pamphlet in 1745 titled, "The Enormous Abomination of the Hoop-Petticoat," in which he complained, "of late ... [the hoop-petticoat] has spread itself to so enormous a circumference that there is no enduring it any longer.... The very sight of those cursed hoops is enough to turn one's stomach." "Crinoline and Whales," *Eclectic Magazine* (Feb. 1859), 230; and Elizabeth Ewing, *Dress and Undress: A History of Women's Underwear* (New York: Drama Book Specialists, 1978), 41–45. For back-

ground on whaling and the lighting of the era, see William T. O'Dea, *The Social History of Lighting* (London: Routledge and Kegan Paul, 1958), 200.

2. John J. McCusker and Russell R. Menard, *The Economy of British America, 1607–1789* (Chapel Hill: University of North Carolina Press, 1985), 108. McCusker and Menard make an excellent point about our relative lack of knowledge when it comes to understanding all the linkages between whaling and the economy in the years prior to the Revolutionary War: "Cod may have been king for the fishermen, but whaling was the prince of professions. . . . Centered in southern New England and the eastern end of Long Island, the whaling industry promoted the development of the region by providing the stimulus for a variety of linked enterprises, thus directly employing the capital, labor, and talent of the area. It was very big business indeed, about which we know far too little." Ibid., 312. And one major area of such linkages where we are particularly ignorant pertains to the trade that went within and between the colonies, as opposed to between the colonies and England. As Shepherd and Williamson note, "The coastal trade of the British North American colonies, as well as the coastal trade among the American states and the remaining British colonies after the American Revolution and well into the nineteenth century, remains one of those areas in North American economic history about which we know very little." James F. Shepherd and Samuel H. Williamson, "The Coastal Trade of the British North American Colonies, 1768–1772," *The Journal of Economic History* 32 (Dec. 1972), 783.

3. The productivity of the cod and whale fisheries was a topic that greatly interested Thomas Jefferson, who noted that, in the early 1770s, while cod fishing generated £250,000 per year, whaling's tally was £100,000 more. Thomas Jefferson, "Report on Cod and Whale Fisheries, February 1, 1791," in Saul K. Padover, *The Complete Jefferson* (New York: Duell, Sloan & Pearce, Inc., 1943), 330.

4. "Newbern in North Carolina," *Boston Chronicle* (July 11–18, 1768), 286.

5. Warren Barton Blake, in the introduction to Crèvecoeur's *Letters from an American Farmer*, viii.

6. Crèvecoeur, *Letters from an American Farmer*, 86–88, 124, 126–27, 141–42.

7. Joseph C. Hart, *Miriam Coffin or The Whale-Fishermen* (1834; reprint, San Francisco: H. R. Coleman, 1872), 58.

8. Macy, *The History of Nantucket*, 57–58; Philbrick, *Abram's Eyes*, 196–98; and Elizabeth A. Little, "The Nantucket Indian Sickness," in *Papers of the Twenty-First Algonquian Conference*, edited by William Cowen (Ottawa: Carleton University, 1990), 181–96.

9. Despite increasing lays, it was not always easy for whaling captains to get good help. The captain of the whaleship *Doler*, who went on a couple of short, consecutive cruises in 1763, offered the following observations in his log. After returning to port one time, "4 of our hands left us & run a Way like Roges as they are and We must go to ye *vinyard* for more hands & ye 30 Day of july We Went to Sea With a fool crew." This journal is in rough shape, and some have commented that the whaleship might have been *Dolen* or *Dollar*, not *Doler*. Log of the *Doler* of Dartmouth, Massachusetts, International Marine Archives Log #880B.

10. Daniel Vickers, "Nantucket Whalemen in the Deep-Sea Fishery: The Changing Anatomy of an Early American Labor Force," in *Journal of American History* 72 (Sept. 1985), 291.

11. Ibid., 295.

12. *Free Negroes and Mullatoes, Massachusetts General Court House of Representatives* (Boston: True & Green Printers, 1822), 11–12; George H. Moore, *Notes on the History of Slavery in Massachusetts* (New York: Negro Universities Press, 1968), 117; and McKissack and McKissack, *Black Hands, White Sails*, 18–19.

13. Quoted in Nathaniel Philbrick, "'I Will Take to the Water": Frederick Douglass, the Sea, and the Nantucket Whale Fishery," *Historic Nantucket* 40 (Fall 1992), 50.

14. Jackson, *The British Whaling Trade*, 55; and MacPherson, *Annals of Commerce*, 511–12.

15. Jackson, *The British Whaling Trade*, 55–64.

16. Quoted in ibid., 65. See also George Bancroft, *A History of the United States*, vol. 7, 12th ed. (Boston: Little, Brown and Company, 1875), 185.

17. "Accounts; Whaling; Vessels; Labrador Coast; Difficulties; Consequences; Orders," *Boston Evening Post* (Aug. 26, 1765); and Starbuck, *History of the American Whale Fishery*, 45.

18. William H. Whiteley, "Governor Hugh Palliser and the Newfoundland and Labrador Fishery, 1764–1768," *Canadian Historical Review* 50, no. 2 (June 1969): 142.

19. "Boston, August 21," *Connecticut Courant* (Sept. 1, 1766), 1; and Spears, *The Story of The New England Whalers*, 80–81.

20. "By Order of His Excellency the Governor," *Massachusetts Gazette and Boston News-Letter* (Jan. 8, 1767).

21. "Boston, August 25," *Georgia Gazette* (Oct. 15, 1766); and Scoresby, *An Account of the Arctic Regions*, vol. 2, 135.

22. Starbuck, *History of the American Whale Fishery*, 53–54. Colonial whalemen weren't always on the losing side of their encounters with enemies. In 1771, for example, two whaling sloops from Nantucket were anchored at the mouth of Abaco Harbor in the West Indies, when another ship came into view showing the colors for distress. One of the Nantucket captains, along with a small crew, rowed to the ship to offer assistance. As soon as the captain climbed aboard, the commander of the ship placed a pistol to the captain's temple and demanded that he pilot the ship into the harbor. The captain claimed ignorance of the port's underwater topography but said that there was a man in his crew who could perform the task. That man was summoned, and on successfully piloting the ship into the harbor, he, his captain, and other crew members were allowed to return to their sloop.

While on board the "distressed" ship, the Nantucketers had noticed that all the men were armed and that there was a man pacing back and forth in the cabin. When the captains of the two Nantucket sloops considered this information, they concluded that the ship had been taken over by pirates and that the man in the cabin was the deposed captain. The Nantucketers immediately devised a plan to retake the vessel and liberate the crew. They invited the pirate captain to dine on board one of the sloops, and he came with his boatswain as well as the real captain of the ship, who was introduced as one of the passengers. Rather than serve dinner the Nantucketers tied up the pirate captain and his boatswain, then listened to the real captain tell them what had happened. His ship had sailed from Bristol, Rhode Island, he said, to the coast of Africa, where it picked up a cargo of slaves. On the way to the West Indies, part of his crew mutinied with the intention of becoming pirates; thus the pirate captain was really one of the original crew. The Nantucketers offered the boatswain a deal, which he accepted. If he returned to the ship, freed the chief mate, brought him back to the sloop, and then helped to liberate the ship, the Nantucketers would attempt to have the mutiny charges that would certainly be leveled against him dropped. To encourage his cooperation the Nantucketers also lied, telling the boatswain that there was a British man-of-war not far off that could be called on to retake the mutinous ship if a particular signal were given.

As soon as it became clear that the boatswain had failed to keep his side of the bargain, one of the Nantucket sloops weighed anchor and sailed with a bearing that would bring it alongside the pirated ship. The mutineers moved their cannons to that side, expecting to blast the sloop when it came within range. But the Nantucket captain was too smart to sail into that trap. At the last moment, he had his sloop tack and come up on the opposite side of the ship. The mutineers repositioned their cannons, but the sloop was well out of range before they could fire. Once the sloop sailed out of view of the ship, it came hard about and set aloft the signal that had been shared with the boatswain. When the sloop came back into view and the boatswain saw the signal, alarm spread among the mutineers, thinking that a British man-of-war would soon be attacking them. Rather than stand and fight, they fled to shore where they were quickly apprehended. The Nantucket whalemen boarded the ship, freed the chief mate, and sailed the ship and the mutineers, now in irons, to New Providence, where the whalemen witnessed the hanging of the chief mutineer and received "about 2,500 dollars . . . for their good conduct and bravery." "Newport, April 15, 1771," *Boston Evening Post,* Apr. 22, 1771.

23.   *Massachusetts Gazette and Boston News-Letter,* July 26, 1764.

24.   "Boston, October 2," *Boston News-Letter and New-England Chronicle,* Oct. 2, 1766, 3; and *Boston Post Boy,* Sept. 29, 1766.

25.   Banks, *The History of Martha's Vineyard,* vol. 1, 445; Emma Mayhew Whiting and Henry Beetle Hough, *Whaling Wives* (Boston: Houghton Mifflin Company, 1953), 1.

26.   Peleg Folger, *Journal of the Ship* Seaflower *of Nantucket,* entry for July 25, 1752 (bound with journal of the ships *Grampas, Mary, Seaflower, Greyhound, Phebe* of Nantucket, NA Special Collection, NA).

27.   *Massachusetts Gazette and Boston Post Boy and the Advertiser,* Oct. 14, 1771.

28.   Henry T. Cheever, *The Whale and his Captors; or, The Whalemen's Adventures, and the Whale Biography, as gathered on the homeward cruise of the "Commodore Preble"* (1850; reprint, Fairfield, WA: Ye Galleon Press, 1991), 175–80; and Gustav Kobbe, "The Perils and Romance of Whaling," *The Century* 40 (Aug. 1890), 515.

29.   A contemporary whaling song gave voice to the importance of this dark and powerful drink.

> *For killing northern whales prepar'd,*
>   *Our nimble boats on board,*
> *With craft and rum, (our chief regard,)*
>   *And good provisions stor'd.*

A portion of John Osborne's "whaling song," quoted in Frederick Freeman, *The History of Cape Cod: The Annals of the Thirteen Towns of Barnstable County,* vol. 2 (Boston: Printed for the Author by Geo. C. Rand & Avery, 1862), 89.

30.   Peleg Folger, *Journal of the Ship* Grampas *of Nantucket,* entry for May 11, 1751 (bound with journal of the ships *Grampas, Mary, Seaflower, Greyhound, Phebe* of Nantucket, NA Special Collection, NA)

31.   Peleg Folger, *Journal of the Sloop* Phebe *of Nantucket,* entry for Aug. 18, 1754

(bound with journal of the ships *Grampas, Mary Seaflower, Greyhound, Phebe* of Nantucket, NA Special Collection, NA). Another way that Folger distinguished himself from his peers was by inserting Latin phrases and sayings into his musings, a peculiarity that led one of his shipmates to scribble in the margins of Folger's journal, "Old Peleg Folger is a Num Skull for writing in Latin." Peleg Folger, *Journal of the Sloop* Mary *of Nantucket*, entry for May 16, 1752 (bound with journal of the ships *Grampas, Mary, Seaflower, Greyhound, Phebe* of Nantucket, NA Special Collection, NA.

32.   Benjamin Franklin, "A Letter from Benjamin Franklin to Mr. Alphonsus le Roy, Member of Several Academies at Paris, Containing Sundry Maritime Observations," in *Transactions of the American Philosophical Society held at Philadelphia*, vol. 2 (Philadelphia: Robert Aitken, 1786), 314–17; Captain John Lacouture, "The Gulf Stream Charts of Benjamin Franklin and Timothy Folger," *Historic Nantucket* 3 (Fall 1995), 82–86; and H. A. Marmer, "The Gulf Stream and Its Problems," *Geographical Review* 19 (July 1929), 457–78. Ponce de Leon encountered and puzzled over the Gulf Stream in 1513, while sailing from Puerto Rico to Cape Canaveral. His three ships were often pushed back by the current. In the early 1500s Spanish ships used the gulf to their advantage, choosing to sail with it up the coast on their returns to Europe. In 1612 Lescarbot thought about the Gulf Stream, and noted the dividing line between cold and warm water. "I have found something remarkable upon which a natural philosopher should meditate. On the 18th of June 1606, in lattitude 45° at a distance of six times twenty leagues east of the Newfoundland Banks, we found ourselves in the midst of very warm water despite the fact that the air was cold. But on the 21st of June all of the sudden we were in so cold a fog that it seemed like January and the sea was extremely cold too." Quoted in Henry Stommel, "The Gulf Stream, A Brief History of the Ideas Concerning its Cause," *Scientific Monthly* 70 (Apr. 1950), 242–43; and Henry Stommel, *The Gulf Stream, A Physical and Dynamical Description*, 2nd ed. (Berkeley: University of California Press, 1965), 1–4.

33.   Quoted in Esmond Wright, *Franklin of Philadelphia* (Cambridge: Belknap Press of Harvard University Press, 1986), 57.

34.   Franklin, "A Letter from Benjamin Franklin to Mr. Alphonsus le Roy," 315.

35.   Ibid.; and Benjamin Franklin, *The Works of Benjamin Franklin*, vol. 6 (Louisville: C. Tappan, 1844), 497.

36.   Franklin, "A Letter from Benjamin Franklin to Mr. Alphonsus le Roy," 315; Ronald L. Clark, *Benjamin Franklin, A Biography* (New York: Random House, 1983), 205–7; and Philip L. Richardson, "Benjamin Franklin and Timothy Folger's First Printed Chart of the Gulf Stream," *Science* 207 (Feb. 1980), 643. As Richardson points out, the chart that Franklin had printed was done in 1769 or 1770, but the chart that most people have seen is the 1786 version—a "copy of a copy" of the original. The earlier version was "lost" until Richardson rediscovered it in the collection of the Bibliothèque Nationale in Paris.

37.   This account based largely on Baxter, *The House of Hancock*, 168–76, 223–31, 243–46.

38.   John Hancock to Harrison & Barnard, September 2, 1767, Hancock Family Collection, BLHBS.

CHAPTER NINE: On the Eve of Revolution

1. Starbuck, *History of the American Whale Fishery*, 57.
2. Bruce Catton and William B. Catton, *The Bold and Magnificent Dream, America's Founding Years, 1492–1815* (New York: Doubleday & Company, 1978), 236; and William Edward Hartpole Lecky, *The American Revolution, 1763–1783* (New York: D. Appleton and Company, 1932), 9–10.
3. Benjamin Franklin, *The Works of Benjamin Franklin*, edited by Jared Sparks, vol. 4 (Boston: Hilliard, Gray and Company, 1840), 42.
4. Samuel Eliot Morison, Henry Steele Commager, and William E. Leuchtenburg, *A Concise History of the American Republic*, 2nd ed., vol. 1 (to 1877) (New York: Oxford University Press, 1983), 68; James K. Hosmer, *American Statesman, Samuel Adams* (Boston: Houghton Mifflin and Company, 1885), 78–79; and Lecky, *The American Revolution*, 105–6.
5. Thomas O'Connor, *The Hub, Boston Past and Present* (Boston: Northeastern University Press, 2001), 55; Garraty, *The American Nation*, 84; and George Bancroft, *The History of the United States of America, from the Discovery of the Continent*, abridged and edited by Russel B. Nye (Chicago: University of Chicago Press, 1966), 184–85.
6. Ward, *Colonial America*, 94, 366; Allan Nevins and Henry Steele Commager, *A Short History of the United States* (New York: Alfred A. Knopf, 1966), 37, 66–67; Catton and Catton, *The Bold and Magnificent Dream*, 249.
7. Quoted in Edmund S. Morgan, *The Birth of the Republic, 1763–89* (Chicago: University of Chicago Press, 1977), 46.
8. David McCullough, *John Adams* (New York: Simon & Schuster, 2001), 65; and Lecky, *The American Revolution*, 128.
9. Quoted in Hiller B. Zobel, *The Boston Massacre* (New York: W. W. Norton, 1970), 195.
10. Kwame Anthony Appiah and Henry Louis Gates, *Africana: The Encyclopedia of the African and the African-American Experience* (Philadelphia: Running Press, 2003), 48.
11. Quoted in McCullough, *John Adams*, 65–66. See also O'Connor, *The Hub*, 54–55; and Hutchinson, *The History of the Colony and Province of Massachusetts-Bay*, vol. 3, 194–96.
12. Quoted in Lecky, *The American Revolution*, 127–28.
13. O'Connor, *The Hub*, 56–67; and Morgan, *The Birth of the Republic*, 57–58.
14. Ibid.; and Stackpole, *The Sea-Hunters*, 62–65.
15. Quoted in O'Connor, *The Hub*, 59.
16. Quoted in Bancroft, *A History of the United States*, vol. 7, 222, 239.
17. *The Annual Register or a View of the History, Politics, and Literature, for the Year 1775* (London: Printed for J. Dodsley in Pall Mall, 1776), 85.
18. Quoted in Bancroft, *A History of the United States*, vol. 7, 239.
19. *The Annual Register or a View of the History, Politics, and Literature, for the Year 1775*, 80, 87.
20. Starbuck, *The History of Nantucket*, 179n.
21. David Barclay, in *The Parliamenatary Register, or History of the Proceedings and Debates of the House of Commons*, vol. 1 (London: J. Walker, R. Lea, and J. Nunn, 1802), 284.
22. *The Annual Register or a View of the History, Politics, and Literature, for the Year 1775*, 85.

23. Stanley Ayling, *Edmund Burke, His Life and Opinions* (New York: St. Martin's Press, 1988), 80; and Edmund Burke, *Burke's Speech on Conciliation With America*, edited by Charles R. Morris (New York: Harper & Brothers, 1945), 103.

24. Burke, *Burke's Speech on Conciliation*, 14, 21–23.

25. Bancroft, *History of the United States from the Discovery of the American Continent*, vol. 7, 270; and M. Garnier to Count de Vergennes, March 20, 1775, in *Naval Documents of the Revolution*, vol. 1 (Washington, DC: Government Printing Office, 1968), 438.

26. *The Parliamentary Register of History of the Proceedings and Debates of the House of Commons, During the First Session of the Fourteenth Parliament of Great Britain*, vol. 1 (London: T. Gillet, 1802), 423.

CHAPTER TEN: Ruin

1. Macy, *The History of Nantucket*, 88.

2. Starbuck, *History of Nantucket*, 182. For an excellent discussion of how whaleboats were used to further the war, see John Gardner, "Whaleboat Warfare on the Sound," *Log of the Mystic Seaport* 28 (July 1976), 59–68; Overton, *Long Island's Story*, 136–39; and Richard Cranch to John Adams, in *Naval Documents of the Revolution*, vol. 3 (Washington, DC: Government Printing Office, 1968), 958–60.

3. "Journal of the Continental Congress, May 29, 1775," in *Naval Documents of the Revolution*, vol. 1, 565–66.

4. *The Journals of Each Provincial Congress of Massachusetts in 1774 and 1775, and of the Committee of Saftey* (Boston: Dutton and Wentworth, 1838), 470.

5. Kezia Coffin Fanning Papers, MS 2, folder 4, diary entry for May 23, 1775, NHA.

6. Nevins and Commager, *A Short History of the United States*, 71; Schlesinger, *The Birth of the Nation*, 243; As Lecky noted, "In almost every part of the States—even in New England itself—there were large bodies of devoted loyalists." Lecky, *The American Revolution*, 275.

7. Henry Ward to Samuel Ward, May 30, 1775, in *Naval Documents of the Revolution*, vol. 1 (Washington, DC: Government Printing Office, 1964), 571; and Byers, *The Nation of Nantucket*, 211.

8. Quoted in Alexander Starbuck, "Nantucket in the Revolution," *Nantucket Inquirer*, July 18, 1874.

9. William Rotch, *Memorandum Written by William Rotch in the Eightieth Year of his Age* (Boston: Houghton Mifflin Company, 1916), 2–5.

10. Letter from Jonathan Jenkins to Dr. Nathaniel Freeman, September 1, 1775, in *Naval Documents of the Revolution*, vol. 3, 1283–84.

11. The reference to the "Nation of Nantucket" comes from a journal entry that Ralph Waldo Emerson wrote on May 23, 1847, quoted in Everett U. Crosby, *Nantucket in Print* (Nantucket: Tetaukimmo, 1946), 151.

12. Quoted in Starbuck, *The History of Nantucket*, 189n.

13. Rotch, *Memorandum*, 6.

14. McDevitt, *The House of Rotch*, 209, 205–18.

15. "Broadside," Massachusetts General Court, Watertown (Aug. 10, 1775), digital copy accessed Apr. 14, 2006, from Library of Congress, American Memory online collection of broadsides, leaflets, and pamphlets from America and Europe, portfolio 38, folder 27j, digital I.D., rbpe 0380270j http://hdl.loc.gov/loc.rbc/rbpe.0380270j.

16. For an example of such a bond, see Master's Bond for the Massachusetts Whaling Brig *Fox*, in *Naval Documents of the Revolution*, vol. 3, 765.

17. Francis Rotch to Lord North, 9 January 1776, Rotch Family Papers, MHS; and Byers, *The Nation of Nantucket*, 212–13.

18. Rotch, *Memorandum*, 5.

19. "Boston, January 21," *Continental Journal and Weekly Advertiser*, Jan. 21, 1779.

20. *The Annual Register or a View of the History, Politics, and Literature, for the Year 1776* (London: Printed for J. Dodsley in Pall Mall, 1777), 118.

21. Quoted in Irwin Shapiro and Edouard Stackpole, *The Story of Yankee Whaling* (New York: Harper & Row, 1959), 82.

22. John Adams to the Massachusetts Council, September 13, 1779, in *Papers of John Adams*, edited by Gregg L. Lint, Robert J. Taylor, Richard Alan Bryerson, Celeste Walker, and Joanna M. Revelas, vol. 8, March 1779–February 1780 (Cambridge: Belknap Press of Harvard University Press, 1989), 146.

23. McCullough, *John Adams*, 174, 187, 207.

24. Letter from John Adams to Daniel McNeill, October 9, 1778, *Papers of John Adams*, edited by Robert J. Taylor, vol. 7, September 1778–February 1779 (Cambridge: Belknap Press of Harvard University Press, 1989), 121–22.

25. John Adams to the Massachusetts Council, September 13, 1779, 145–47.

26. Quoted in Stackpole, *The Sea Hunters*, 82.

27. John M. Bullard, *The Rotches* (New Bedford: Self-published 1947), 19.

28. Banks, *The History of Martha's Vineyard*, vol. 1, 380–81.

29. Stackpole, *The Sea Hunters*, 85–86.

30. NHA Research Library, Kezia Coffin Fanning Papers, MS 2, folder 4, diary entry for May 23, 1775.

31. Quoted in McDevitt, *House of Rotch*, 248; and Starbuck, *History of Nantucket*, 210.

32. Stackpole, *The Sea Hunters*, 86; and Byers, *The Nation of Nantucket*, 219.

33. Starbuck, *The History of Nantucket*, 211n.

34. Quoted in McDevitt, *The House of Rotch*, 250; and Byers, *The Nation of Nantucket*, 219.

35. Rotch, *Memorandum*, 9–10.

36. Quoted in Macy, *The History of Nantucket*, 100.

37. Quoted in Edouard A. Stackpole, *Nantucket in the Revolution* (Nantucket: NHA, 1976), 68–70.

38. Nantucket Town Meeting Records, July 7, 1779, Office of the Town Clerk, Nantucket Town and County Building.

39. Quoted in Stackpole, *The Sea Hunters*, 86.

40. Quoted in Starbuck, *The History of Nantucket*, 215, 217.

41. Macy, *The History of Nantucket*, 112.

42. Rotch, *Memorandum*, 25.

43. Quoted in Starbuck, *The History of Nantucket*, 252–53.

44. Rotch, *Memorandum*, 33.

45. Most historians cite Obed Macy's numbers, which claim that 134 ships were captured and another 15 were lost during the war, which, when subtracted from the 150 whaleships Jefferson said Nantucket owned in 1775, leaves only 1 Nantucket whaleship still afloat at the war's end. See Macy, *The History of Nantucket*, 122; and Starbuck, *History of the American Whale Fishery*, 77.

    But as McDevitt notes, although the records make it impossible to get an accurate number, Nantucket certainly had more than one whaleship at the close of the Revolutionary War. Indeed, just before the war ended, Nantucket whaling merchants had asked for and received thirty-five whaling permits, and it is unlikely that they would have done so had they only had one vessel ready to sail. McDevitt, *The House of Rotch*, 279–81. Also Zaccheus Macy, a Nantucketer who was writing in 1792, claims that at the end of the war Nantucket's whaling fleet had been reduced to "thirty old hulks." Two other written accounts, one from 1785 and the other from 1790, claim that the number was nineteen. Macy, "A Short Journal of the First Settlement of the Island of Nantucket," 157; and Jefferson, *The Papers of Thomas Jefferson*, 173n, 231. Finally, Daniel Webster claimed in one of his speeches, that there were fifteen whaleships left on Nantucket at the end of the war. Daniel Webster, *Speeches and Forensic Arguments* (Philadelphia: Perkins & Marvin, 1835), 436. See also "The Whale Fishery, by a Citizen of Philadelphia—1785" (from the American Museum, Philadelphia, 1789), quoted in Crosby, *Nantucket in Print*, 87.

46. Starbuck, *History of the American Whale Fisheries*, 77.

CHAPTER ELEVEN: Up from the Ashes

1. "The Whale Fishery," *North American Review*, 38 (Jan. 1834), 102; Stackpole, *The Sea Hunters*, 95; Starbuck, *History of the American Whale Fishery*, 77–78; Bullard, *The Rotches*, 35; and Zepheniah W. Pease, "The Brave Industry of Whaling," *Americana* 12 (Jan.–Dec. 1918), 83.

2. Derek Jarrett, *Pitt the Younger* (New York: Charles Scribner's Sons, 1974), 64; David Wallechinsky and Irving Wallace, *The People's Almanac #3* (New York: William Morrow & Company, 1981), 264; Douglas Southall Freeman, *George Washington: A Biography*, vol. 5 (New York: Charles Scribner's Sons, 1952); 388n; Arthur Shrader, " 'The World Turned Upside Down,' A Yorktown March, or Music to Surrender By," *American Music* 16 (Summer 1998), 180–215; George Washington, *The Diaries of George Washington*, vol. 3, edited by Donald Jackson and Dorothy Twohig (Charlottesville: University of Virginia Press, 1978), 432n; and the following Web sites, which were accessed on May 13, 2006: http://www.americanrevolution.org/upside.html; http://www.contemplator.com/england/worldtur.html; http://writersalmanac.publicradio.org/programs/2000/10/16/index.html; http://www.orionsociety.org/pages/oo/sidebars/America/Telleen.html.

3. A humorous and perhaps apocryphal anecdote involving a hunchbacked crewman on the *Bedford* shows how the end of the war had dramatically changed the relationship between the United States and England. When that crewman went ashore, he was approached by a British sailor who slapped him on the back saying, "Hello, Jack, what have you got here?" The none-too-pleased and fiercely proud American responded, "Bunker Hill, and be damned to you!" Rotch, *Memorandum*, vi–vii.

4. Byers, *The Nation of Nantucket*, 232; and *The Annual Register or a View of the History, Politics, and Literature, for the Year 1775*, 113.

5. Rotch, *Memorandum*, 36.

6. Quoted in Edouard A. Stackpole, *Whales & Destiny, The Rivalry between America, France, and Britain for Control of the Southern Whale Fishery, 1785–1825* (Amherst: University of Massachusetts Press, 1972), 19.

7. John Adams letter to John Jay, August 25, 1785, in *The Works of John Adams, Sec-*

ond President of the United States, compiled by Charles Francis Adams (1850–56; reprint, Freeport, NY: Books for Libraries Press, 1969), 307–9.

8. Quoted in Macy, *The History of Nantucket,* 130.

9. Starbuck, *History of the American Whale Fishery,* 79.

10. Quoted in McDevitt, *The House of Rotch,* 311.

11. Quoted in Stephen B. Miller, *Historical Sketch of Hudson* (Hudson, NY: Byan & Webb, 1862), 103.

12. Margaret B. Schram, *Hudson's Merchants and Whalers: The Rise and Fall of a River Port 1783–1850* (New York: Black Dome, 2004), 16–43, 136–47.

13. Two of the most patriotic Nantucket Navigators were the Jenkins brothers, Seth and Thomas. When Parliament was debating the passage of the Restraining Act in 1775, one provision of which would prohibit Americans from whaling in the North Atlantic Ocean, it was Captain Seth Jenkins of Nantucket who stood before the legislators and pleaded the island's case, arguing that if Nantucketers could not whale, they would survive as best they could, and possibly "emigrate to the continent," but would not, under any circumstances, live under the "military government" of Halifax. See Seth Jenkins, in *The Parliamentary Register, or History of the Proceedings and Debates of the House of Commons,* vol. 1 (London: J. Walker, R. Lea, and J. Nunn, 1802), 283.

And during the war Thomas Jenkins, who had lost a considerable amount of property during George Leonard's notorious raid on Nantucket, accused five of the island's most prominent residents, including William Rotch, of aiding and abetting Leonard, and labeled them "as persons dangerous and inimical to the freedom and Independence of this and the other United States of America." Seth Jenkins, in *The Parliamentary Register, or History of the Proceedings and Debates of the House of Commons,* vol. 1 (London: J. Walker, R. Lea, and J. Nunn, 1802), 283.

14. Quoted in Graham, "The Migrations of the Nantucket Whale Fishery," 188; and Stackpole, *Sea Hunters,* 105.

15. Quoted in McDevitt, *The House of Rotch,* 305.

16. Quoted in Graham, "The Migrations of the Nantucket Whale Fishery," 193–94.

17. Quoted in Stackpole, *The Sea Hunters,* 115.

18. Quoted in McDevitt, *The House of Rotch,* 326. See also ibid., 328.

19. Rotch, *Memorandum,* 40–41.

20. Byers, *The Nation of Nantucket,* 233.

21. Rotch, *Memorandum,* 42–43.

22. Ibid., 42–43, 45; and McDevitt, *The House of Rotch,* 337–38.

23. George Washington to Marquis de Lafayette, September 1, 1785, in *The Writings of George Washington,* edited by Jared Sparks, vol. 9 (Boston: Little, Brown and Company, 1855), 129–30.

24. Dumas Malone, *Jefferson and His Time: Jefferson and the Rights of Man,* vol. 2 (Boston: Little, Brown and Company, 1951), 45; and William Cutter, *The Life of General Lafayette* (New York: George F. Cooledge & Brother, 1849), 161–62.

25. Macy, *The History of Nantucket,* 249–50.

26. Jefferson, "Observations on the Whale Fishery," 381–82.

27. Jefferson, "Report on the Fisheries," 216.

28. Rotch, *Memorandum,* 50.

29. Jefferson, "Observations on the Whale Fishery," 383.

30. Jefferson, "Report on the Fisheries," 214–15; Starbuck, *History of the American Whale Fishery,* 88–91; Thomas Jefferson to John Adams, in *Memoirs, Correspon-*

dence and Private Papers of Thomas Jefferson, Late President of the United States, edited by Thomas Jefferson Randolph (London: Henry Colburn and Richard Bentley, 1829), 412–14; and Thomas Jefferson to John Jay, November 19, 1788, in *The Writings of Thomas Jefferson*, edited by H. A. Washington, vol. 2 (New York: Derby & Jackson, 1859), 511–13.

31. Jefferson, "Observations on the Whale Fishery," 386. Jefferson's tally focuses exclusively on the Massachusetts fishery, neglecting to take into account the whaling vessels coming from Long Island and Rhode Island, which, if added, would have brought the number of American whaleships operating prior to the revolution up to around 360. Starbuck, *History of the American Whale Fishery*, 89n.

32. Quoted in William John Dakin, *Whalemen Adventurers* (1934; reprint, Sydney: Sirius Books. 1963), 1.

33. Christopher Gore to Tobias Lear, December 10, 1790, cited in Jefferson, *The Papers of Thomas Jefferson*, 200–204; and Graham, "The Migrations of the Nantucket Whale Fishery," 197–99.

34. Quoted in McDevitt, *House of Rotch*, 376, 368, and 383; and Stackpole, *Whales & Destiny*, 211–12.

35. Quoted in McDevitt, *House of Rotch*, 386.

36. Crosby, *Children of the Sun*, 89; and Byers, *The Nation of Nantucket*, 247.

37. One of the reasons that Americans felt the need to find new whaling grounds, including those in the Pacific, was that the whaling grounds in the North Atlantic were becoming severely depleted. As Edward Augustus Kendall observed in the early 1800s:

> The comparatively total disappearance of the whale, in the Atlantic, is an unquestionable fact; and the naturalist has his choice, between the attributing the phenomenon to the destruction of the animal, or to its flight: he may believe that the whales of the northern latitudes of the east coast of America had perished by the harpoon, before the fishermen thought of stretching to the Western Islands; or he may believe that they have retired from their pursuers. The numbers, in which they were formerly known as high as Davis's Straits, would perhaps appear to be exaggerated by historians, were they not supported by modern descriptions of the new seats of the fishery.

Edward Augustus Kendall, Esq., *Travels Through the Northern Parts of the United States in the Years 1807 and 1808*, vol. 2 (New York: I. Riley, 1809), 206.

38. Rhys Richard, *Into the South Seas: The Southern Whale Fishery Comes of Age on the Brazil Banks, 1765–1812* (Parameta, New Zealand: self-published, 1993), 26; and Stackpole, *Whales & Destiny*, 130. Some have claimed that the *Rebecca* was the first American whaleship to round Cape Horn, but that doesn't appear to be the case. That honor appears to go the *Beaver* of Nantucket ("Who Sent the First American Whaler to the Pacific," *Nantucket Inquirer*, Nov. 21, 1874; and Daniel Ricketson, *New Bedford of the Past* (Boston: Houghton, Mifflin and Company, 1903), 113).

39. Washington is often quoted as having said, "be wary of foreign entanglements," but although that was his sentiment, those weren't his words. William Safire, *Lend Me Your Ears: Great Speeches in History* (New York: W. W. Norton, 1997), 393.

40. Benjamin W. Labaree, William M. Fowler, Jr., John B. Hattendorf, Jeffrey J. Safford, Edward W. Sloan, and Andrew W. German, *America and the Sea: A Maritime*

History (Mystic: Mystic Seaport, 1998), 182; and Robert W. Love, Jr., *The History of the U.S. Navy* (Mechanicsburg, PA: Stackpole Books, 1992), 57.

41. Quoted in McCullough, *John Adams*, 495.

42. Quoted in Richard B. Morris and Jeffrey B. Morris, *Great Presidential Decisions, State Papers that Changed the Course of History from Washington to Reagan* (New York: Richardson, Steirman & Black, Inc., 1988), 49.

43. Quoted in Mellen Chamberlain, *John Adams: The Statesman of the American Revolution, With Other Essays and Addresses Historical and Literary* (Boston: Houghton, Mifflin and Company, 1899), 241.

44. Labaree et al., *America and the Sea*, 184; and Macy, *The History of Nantucket*, 150.

45. Labaree et al., *America and the Sea*, 198; and Robert Leckie, *The Wars of America* (New York: Harper & Row, 1968), 230–31.

46. Leckie, *The Wars of America*, 231.

47. Labaree et al., *America and the Sea*, 207.

48. Quoted in Leckie, *The Wars of America*, 232.

49. Labaree et al., *America and the Sea*, 212; "Remarks (On Board the USF President, Commodore Rodgers) Made by M.C. Perry," in *Proceedings of the United States Naval Institute*, vol. 15 (Annapolis: United States Naval Institute, 1889), 339–42; and Samuel Maunder, *The History of the World*, vol. 2 (New York: Henry Bill, 1854), 474.

50. Quoted in Macy, *The History of Nantucket*, 163.

51. Labaree et al., *America and the Sea*, 213.

CHAPTER TWELVE: Knockdown

1. Washington Irving, *The Works of Washington Irving*, vol. 1 (New York: J. B. Lippincott & Co., 1869), 123, 230; and Frances Diane Robotti and James Vescovi, *The USS* Essex *and the Birth of the American Navy* (Holbrook, MA: Adams Media Corporation, 1999), 141–49.

2. "The Salem Frigate," *Salem Gazette*, Nov. 23, 1798.

3. *Salem Gazette*, Oct. 1, 1799.

4. Labaree et al., *America and the Sea*, 213; and Robotti and Vescovi, *The USS* Essex, 152–53, 158–62.

5. Captain David Porter, *Journal of a Cruise* (1815; reprint, Annapolis: Naval Institute Press, 1986), 73.

6. Porter, *Journal of a Cruise*, 82.

7. One old Nantucket saying claimed that gales off the Cape blow "so hard it takes two men to hold one man's hair on." Macy, *The Nantucket Scrap Basket*, 10.

8. Porter, *Journal of a Cruise*, 91–93.

9. Ibid., 116, 126.

10. Ibid., 134.

11. Ibid., 136–37.

12. Ibid., 163, 174–75.

13. Charles Haskins Townsend, "The Whaler and the Tortoise," *Scientific Monthly* 21 (Aug. 1925), 166–72.

14. Porter, *Journal of a Cruise*, 176.

15. Ibid., 200–1.

16. Ibid., 201–2.

17. Ibid., 230, 233.

18. Ibid., 253–54.

19. Ibid., 266–67, 452.
20. Ibid., 300–446.
21. Ibid., 452–62; and James Barnes, *Naval Actions of the War of 1812* (New York: Harper & Brothers, 1896), 175–86.
22. Porter, *Journal of a Cruise*, 273–74.
23. Theodore Roosevelt, *The Naval War of 1812*, with new introduction by H. W. Brands (1882; reprint, New York: Da Capo Press, 1999), 166.
24. Washington Irving, quoted in David F. Long, "David Porter: Pacific Ocean Gadfly," in *Command Under Sail*, edited by James C. Bradford (Annapolis: Naval Institute Press, 1985), 179.
25. Thomas Hart Benton, *Thirty Years' View; or A History of the Working of the American Government for Thirty Years From 1820 to 1850*, vol. 2 (New York: D. Appleton and Company, 1857), 498.
26. Robotti and Vescovi, *The* USS Essex, 202.
27. J. Fred Rippy, *Joel R. Poinsett: Versatile American* (New York: Greenwood Press Publishers, 1968), 31.
28. *Inquirer and Mirror*, Sept. 14, 1872; *Inquirer and Mirror*, Sept. 7, 1872; and Starbuck, *History of the American Whale Fishieries*, 93–94.
29. Rippy, *Joel R. Poinsett*, 49.
30. JUSTICE, *The Nantucket Inquirer*, Aug. 9, 1824; and Ann Belser Asher, "The Talcahuano Incident" *Historic Nantucket* (Oct. 1989), 13–18. Poinsett went on to notoriety as a U.S. minister to Mexico, a congressman representing South Carolina, and the secretary of war under President Martin Van Buren. But, perhaps Poinsett's most lasting claim to fame is in his popularization of a colorful plant that bears his name—the poinsettia.
31. Quoted in Macy, *The History of Nantucket*, 170–71.
32. Ibid., 191–204; and Reginald Horseman, "Nantucket's Peace Treaty with England in 1814," *The New England Quarterly* 54 (June 1981), 186–97.

CHAPTER THIRTEEN: The Golden Age

1. Elmo Paul Hohman, *The American Whalemen*, 41; David Moment, "The Business of Whaling in America in the 1850s," *Business History Review* (Winter 1988), 263; William H. Seward, *The Works of William H. Seward*, edited by George E. Baker, vol. 1 (New York: Redfield, 1853), 242.
2. Few topics in whaling have engendered more variations on a theme than the number of whales that American whalemen killed. Using different assumptions about the barrels of oil and pounds of baleen produced per whale, and the number of whales struck but not killed, different authors have produced different numbers. One of the best estimates is Scammon's, who estimated that for the thirty-eight years beginning in 1835 and ending in 1872, 292,714 whales were "captured or destroyed by the American whaler's lance," making for an annual average of 7,703. The number of whales killed includes those that were mortally wounded but were not secured by the whalemen—in other words, they were lost at sea. Scammon estimates that for sperm whales, 10 percent of the whales so wounded were lost; while for right, bowhead, humpback, and gray whales, the number is 20 percent. Charles M. Scammon, *The Marine Mammals of the Northwestern Coast of North America, Together with an Account of the American Whale Fishery* (1874; reprint, New York: Dover Publications, 1968), 244. For a good discussion of various estimates, see Lance E. Davis, Robert E. Gallman,

and Karin Gleiter, *In Pursuit of Leviathan: Technology, Institutions, Productivity, and Profits in American Whaling, 1816–1906* (Chicago: University of Chicago Press, 1997), 133–49.

3. Davis et al., *In Pursuit of Leviathan*, 4; Samuel Eliot Morison, *The Maritime History of Massachusetts* (Boston: Houghton Mifflin Company, 1921), 317–18; and Seward, *The Works of William H. Seward*, 244.

4. Clark, "The Whale-Fishery," 145; John G. B. Hutchins, *The American Maritime Industries and Public Policy, 1789–1914* (Cambridge: Harvard University Press, 1941), 269.

5. Scammon, *The Marine Mammals of the Northwestern Coast of North America*, 243–44.

6. Macy, *The History of Nantucket*, 205.

7. Quoted in the *New Bedford Mercury*, Nov. 10, 1815.

8. Macy, *The History of Nantucket*, 209, 211.

9. *Nile's Register*, Dec. 2, 1820, 212.

10. Jared Sparks, "A Visit to Nantucket in 1826," *Historic Nantucket* 24 (Apr. 1977), 7.

11. "Greatest Voyage Ever Made," *Nantukcket Inquirer*, Sept. 11, 1830; and Starbuck, *History of the American Whale Fishery*, 270–71.

12. "Greatest Voyage Ever Made," *Nantucket Inquirer*.

13. "Festival," *Nantucket Inquirer*, Sept. 25, 1830.

14. Philbrick, *Away Off Shore*, 181.

15. "Festival," *Nantucket Inquirer*, Sept. 25, 1830.

16. A. Hyatt Verrill, *The Real Story of the Whaler* (New York: D. Appleton and Company, 1923), 217; Starbuck, *History of The American Whale Fishery*, 260–61 (Starbuck says the voyage ended in 1827, but that is an error); and Judith Navas Lund, *Whaling Masters and Whaling Voyages Sailing from American Ports, A Compilation of Sources* (New Bedford: NBWM, KWM, and Ten Pound Island Book Co., 2001), 652.

17. William Comstock, *Voyage to the Pacific Descriptive of the Customs, Usages, and Sufferings on Board of Nantucket Whale-Ships* (Boston: Oliver L. Perkins, 1838), 3–4.

18. Macy, *The History of Nantucket*, 153–55; Starbuck, *The History of Nantucket*, 324; Douglas-Lithgow, *Nantucket, A History*, 353–54; Edouard A. Stackpole, "Peter Folger Ewer: The Man Who Created the 'Camels,'" *Historic Nantucket* 33 (July 1985), 19–30; and Harry B. Turner, *The Story of the Island Steamers* (Nantucket: Inquirer and Mirror Press, 1910), 102–13.

19. Typewritten manuscript of the letter, signed by J. A. B., in the manuscript collection of the NHA. The Camel Collection, 1842–1850, folder 317; *Boston Daily Advertiser*, quoted in "The Nantucket Camels," *New Bedford Mercury*, Oct. 21, 1842.

20. Hohman, *The American Whaleman*, 11; Nathaniel Philbrick, *In The Heart of the Sea* (New York: Viking, 2000), 221.

21. Starbuck, *The History of Nantucket*, 337–41.

22. James K. Polk, "Fourth Annual Message to Congress, December 5, 1848," in *A Compilation of the Messages and Papers of the Presidents, 1789–1897*, vol. 4, edited by James D. Richardson (Washington, DC: Published by Authority of Congress, 1899), 636.

23. Southampton, for example, lost roughly 250 seaman to gold fever. Adams, *History of the Town of Southampton*, 236.

24. Carpenters were commanding twelve to fourteen dollars, and regular laborers could get between five and eight dollars. Hawes, *Whaling*, 192.

25. "Memoranda," *Whalemen's Shipping List and Merchants' Transcript*, Feb. 20, 1849. Another whaling captain, whose crew abandoned him after the ship docked at Monterey, informed his owners that "all hands have left me but two. . . . As for the ship she will lay here for a long time, for there's not the least chance of getting a crew. . . . You probably have heard the situation of things here. A sailor will be up at the mines for two months, work on his own account, and come down with from two to three thousand dollars, and those that go in parties do much better. . . . It is impossible for me to give you any idea of the gold that is got here." "Gold Hunting in California," *Whalemen's Shipping List*, Dec. 5, 1848.

26. By January 1, 1850, 650 Nantucketers went to California, according to "A List of Persons from Nantucket now in California or on their way whither; Including the names of the vessels in which they sailed, the time of their sailing, and of their arrival there; also, Persons returned, &c." (Nantucket: Jethro C. Brock, Jan. 1, 1850). According to Philbrick, "Soon after the Great Fire of 1846, virtually all able-bodied men evacuated the island in the mad rush for gold; in just nine months the town lost a quarter of its voting population." Philbrick, "Every Wave a Fortune," 445. See also Macy, *The Story of Old Nantucket*, 136.

27. *Nantucket Inquirer*, Dec. 6, 1848.

28. "G. M. E.," *Whalemen's Shipping List*, June 15, 1852.

29. Macy, *The History of Nantucket*, 91, 293–94; Starbuck, *History of the American Whale Fishery*, 633. The *Oak* did manage to send 60 barrels of sperm whale oil and 450 barrels of whale oil back to Nantucket before it was sold in Panama in 1872.

30. Ellis, *History of New Bedford*, 227.

31. An even better measure of the growing disparity between these two ports comes from the number of voyages they sent forth. During the 1820s Nantucket and New Bedford were both whaling titans competing in the same league, with the former posting a respectable 280 whaling voyages to the latter's 354. But by the 1850s Nantucket's 114 voyages fell far short of New Bedford's 915. Davis et al., *In Pursuit of Leviathan*, 43. See also Clark, "The Whale-Fishery," 171–72; Hohman, *The American Whalemen*, 42; and Lance E. Davis, Robert E. Gallman, Teresa D. Hutchins, "Risk Sharing, Crew Quality, Labor Shares and Wages in the Nineteenth Century American Whaling Industry," *National Bureau of Economic Research, Inc., Working Paper* 13 (May 1990), 3.

32. Quoted in Morison, *Maritime History of Massachusetts*, 315.

33. Thomas Jefferson, writing in 1790, cited a means of protecting wooden hulls from boring worms, which did not require the application of copper. He mentioned an engineer who had "observed that the whaling vessels would be eaten to a honey-comb, except a little above and below water, where the whale is brought into contact with the vessel, and lies beating against it till it is cut up." That engineer, desirous of keeping the submerged timbers at one of his mills from being riddled by worms, had soaked his timbers in oil—cod oil in this instance—and found that it did indeed protect the wood from the worms. Whether impregnating the hulls of whaling ships with whale oil on a regular basis would have been practical or even useful on this score is not known. Jefferson, *The Writings of Thomas Jefferson*, 157–58.

34. Transcribed by author on a visit to the Seamen's Bethel in New Bedford.

35. Melville, *Moby-Dick*, 40.

36. According to Hayward, "The whale fishery has proved very lucrative, and New Bedford is thought to be one of the richest cities in proportion to the number of

its inhabitants any where to be found." John Hayward, *A Gazetteer of the United States of America* (Hartford: Case, Tiffany, and Company, 1853), 471. See also Charles Slack, *Hetty: The Genius and Madness of America's First Female Tycoon* (New York: Ecco, 2004), 5; Percy Wells Bidwell, "Population Growth in Southern New England, 1810–1860," *American Statistical Association* 120 (Dec. 1917), 826; and Herbert L. Aldrich, "New Bedford" *New England Magazine* 4 (May 1886), 440.

37. Green's fortune at the time of her death in 1916 was estimated at $100 million, which, according to Slack, would be worth about $1.6 billion in 2004 dollars. Slack, *Hetty*, ix, 18.

38. Samuel Rodman, *The Diary of Samuel Rodman: A New Bedford Chronicle of Thirty-Seven Years*, edited by Zephaniah W. Pease (New Bedford: Reynolds Printing Company, 1927), 37, 39; and Kathryn Grover, *The Fugitive's Gibralter* (Amherst: University of Massachusetts Press, 2001), 106.

39. "To the Public," *Whalemen's Shipping List*, March 17, 1843.

40. The number of American ports that pursued whaling (or sent out whaleships) during the golden age depends on who is doing the counting. Many sources state that around thirty-eight ports were thus engaged. Walter S. Tower, *A History of the American Whale Fishery* (Philadelphia: Publications of the University or Pennsylvania, 1907), 51. But the most comprehensive accounting of those ports concludes that between the 1820s and the 1850s, a total of sixty-three different cities and towns sent out at least one whaleship. See Davis et al., *In Pursuit of Leviathan*, 43–44.

     If one looks more expansively at all the American cities and towns that ever sent out a whaleship throughout entire the history of American whaling, the number rises to 104. Lund, *Whaling Masters and Whaling Voyages*, 723–24.

41. Clark, "The Whale-Fishery," 171–72.

42. New London's whaling lineage reaches back to the late 1600s, when small-scale shore whaling operations sprang up along the coast, but it wasn't until toward the end the next century that New Londoners began heading out to sea to catch whales. In 1784 the whaleship *Rising Sun* returned from a successful voyage, leading the editor of the local paper to encourage his readers to become whalemen: "Now, my horse jockeys, beat your horses and cattle in to spears, lances, and harpoons and whaling gear, and let us all strike out; many spouts ahead! Whales aplenty, you have them for catching." Despite such rousing calls to action, New London sent out only a handful of whaleships up through the early 1820s, when whaling really began to take off. Quoted in Dulles, *Lowered Boats*, 202.

43. Robert Owen Decker, *The Whaling City* (Chester, CT: Pequot Press, 1976), 74–75, 82, 89; C. A. Williams, "Early Whaling Industry of New London," in *Records and Papers of the New London County Historical Society*, part 1, vol. 2 (New London: New London County Historical Society, 1895), 3–8; and Barnard L. Colby, *Whaling Captains of New London County for Oil and Buggy Whips* (Mystic: MSM, Inc., 1990), 1.

44. Quoted in Henry Howe, *Adventures and Achievements of Americans* (New York: Geo. F. Tuttle, 1859), 645; and Sidney Withington, "The George Henry and the Salvage and Restoration of the H.M.S. Resolute," in *Two Dramatic Episodes of New England Whaling* (Mystic: Marine Historical Association, Inc., July 1958), 29.

45. Barnard L. Colby, *New London Whaling Captains* (Mystic: Marine Historical Association, Inc., Nov. 25, 1936), 18; and Decker, *The Whaling City*, 84.

46. Dorothy Ingersoll Zaykowski, *Sag Harbor: The Story of an American Beauty* (Sag Harbor: Sag Harbor Historical Society, 1991), 81–83. Sag Harbor began open-ocean whaling in 1760, with the *Dolphin,* the *Success,* and the *Goodluck* leading the way. The town's whaling fleet grew steadily until it was shut down by the War of 1812, only to reemerge slowly in subsequent years.

47. James Fenimore Cooper, *The Sea Lions: Or, The Lost Sealers,* vol. 1 (London: Richard Bentley, 1849), 7–9.

48. For an excellent case study of one of these minor ports (Portsmouth, NH), see Kenneth R. Martin, *"Heavy Weather and Hard Luck," Portsmouth Goes Whaling* (Portsmouth: Peter E. Randall, Portsmouth Marine Society, 1998).

49. "Whaling," *Gloucester Telegraph,* May 4, 1833.

50. All of the background for the following section on Delaware whaling, except where noted, comes from Kenneth R. Martin, *Delaware Goes Whaling, 1833–1845* (Greenville, DE: Hagley Museum, 1974).

51. Quoted in ibid., 12.

52. Quoted in Margaret S. Creighton, *Dogwatch & Liberty Days: Seafaring in the Nineteenth Century* (Peabody, MA: Peabody Museum of Salem, 1982), 44.

53. Freeman Hunt, "Progress of the Oil Trade and Whale Fishery," *Merchants' Magazine, and Commercial Review* 9 (July to Dec. 1843), 381.

54. *Hansard's Parliamentary Debates: Third Series, Commencing with the Accession of William IV,* vol. 99, fifth vol. of the session (London: G. Woodfall and Son, 1848), 57; Jackson, *The British Whaling Trade,* 119; and Lance E. Davis and Robert E. Gallman, "American Whaling, 1820–1900: Dominance and Decline," in *Whaling and History,* edited by Bjørn L. Basberg, Jan Erik Ringstad, and Einar Wexelsen (Sandefjord, Norway: Kommander Chr. Christensens Hvalfangstmusuem, 1993), 58–59.

55. Quoted in Robert W. Kenny, "Yankee Whalers at the Bay of Islands," *American Neptune* 12 (Jan. 1952), 32–33.

56. Charles Nordhoff, *Whaling and Fishing* (1856; reprint, New York: Dodd, Mead & Company, 1895), 11–12.

57. According to one source from 1840, many "hundreds [of drunkards] are sent on whaling voyages, or on board of other vessels, to keep them out of the reach of temptation—but ship-board, is but a poor school, for those who lack decision of character, and yield easily to the gratification of their appetites." Ralph Barnes Grindrod, *Bacchus: An Essay on the Nature, Causes, Effects, and Cure, of Intemperance* (New York: J. & H. G. Langley, 1840), 496.

58. Stackpole, *The Sea Hunters,* 471.

59. "The Whale Fishery," *North American Review,* 108.

60. Hohman, *The American Whalemen,* 90.

61. Quoted in Hershel Parker, *Herman Melville: A Biography,* vol. 1, 1819–1851 (Baltimore: Johns Hopkins University Press, 1996), 182.

62. Morison, *The Maritime History of Massachusetts,* 322.

63. J. C. Mullett, *A Five Years' Whaling Voyage, 1848–1853* (1859; reprint, Fairfield, CT: Ye Galleon Press, 1977), 9–10.

64. As Lisa Norling notes, most of the literature on whaling agents has focused on "the often brutally exploitative relationship of agents to the sailors themselves," but at the same time "virtually no attention has been paid to the connections between the industry and seamen's kin and dependents." This book adds nothing to an understanding of those connections, other than to indicate that Norling's work points to a more nuanced view of agents and their role in whaling.

Lisa Norling, "Contrary Dependencies, Whaling Agents and Whalemen's Families, 1830–1870," *The Log of Mystic Seaport* 42 (Spring 1990), 3–11.

65. Brown, "The Whalemen, Vessels and Boats," 218.

66. W. Jeffrey Bolster, "'To Feel Like a Man': Black Seaman in the Northern States, 1800–1860," *Journal of American History* 76 (Mar. 1990), 1173–99.

67. Quoted in W. Jeffrey Bolster, *Black Jacks: African American Seamen in the Age of Sail* (Cambridge: Harvard University Press, 1997), 176–77.

68. Bolster, *Black Jacks*, 161.

69. Browne, *Etchings of a Whaling Cruise*, 108.

70. Lorin Lee Cary and Francine C. Cary, "Absalom F. Boston, His Family, and Nantucket's Black Community," in *Historic Nantucket* 25 (Summer 1977), 15, 17; Frances Ruley Kartunnen, *The Other Islanders: People Who Pulled Nantucket's Oars* (New Bedford: Spinner Publications, 2005), 65, 68.

71. Quoted in Bolster, *Black Tars*, 162–63.

72. Quoted in Cary and Cary, "Absalom F. Boston," 18.

73. John Thompson, *The Life of John Thompson: A Fugitive Slave* (Worcester: Published by the author, 1856), 110.

74. Decker, *The Whaling City*, 86; Kevin S. Reilly, "Slavers in Disguise: American Whaling and the African Slave Trade, 1845–1862," in *American Neptune* 53 (Summer 1993), 178.

75. Reilly, "Slavers in Disguise," 177–89; and Verrill, *The Real Story of the Whaler*, 236–39.

76. Over the eighty years of its service, the structure and the layout of the *Charles W. Morgan* was modified many times. This description includes the ship's general form and highlights many of the features that would not have changed too dramatically over time. For excellent descriptions of the *Morgan* and its history, see John F. Leavitt, *The Charles W. Morgan* (Mystic: Mystic Seaport, Marine Historical Association, 1973), and Edouard A. Stackpole, *The* Charles W. Morgan, *The Last Wooden Whaleship* (New York: Meredith Press, 1967).

77. Quoted in Stackpole, The Charles W. Morgan, 32.

78. Elizabeth A. Little, "Live Oak Whaleships," in *Historic Nantucket* 19 (Oct. 1971), 24.

79. On a successful voyage, as more whales were killed, the hold's space would be increasingly given over to the casks of oil and bundles of baleen, as the food supplies dwindled. The oil casks, which had been built on the mainland and broken down at the outset of the voyage into bundles of staves, called shooks, to save space, were set up by the cooper as needed. The casks came in many different sizes and fit together like a jigsaw puzzle to ensure that every inch of the curved hull was used to full advantage. The amount of supplies that a ship like the *Morgan* would bring on a voyage was truly astounding, both in variety and bulk. One list of such supplies, which was used by shipowners and officers to ensure that they had everything they needed on board before setting out, ran to forty-eight pages, and included more than nine hundred different articles. Among the necessary particulars were shirts, trousers, jackets, hats, needles, thread, blankets, tobacco, pipes, hatchets, sperm candles, iron spoons, tin pots, thermometers, opera glasses, charts, lead pencils, bills of sale, copies of shipping papers, trypots, and as many as nine extra spars, ten sizes of casks, eleven different weights of sheathing copper, nineteen types of nails, twenty-six spare sails, twenty-seven forms of crockery, fifty-eight varieties of food and cabin stores, eighty-odd kinds of whalecraft (harpoons, lances, and the like), and three hun-

dred carpenter's tools and items of assorted hardware. When one considers that many hundreds of ships had to be thus provisioned, the true scope of the whaling industry during the golden age becomes even more apparent. To supply just sixty-five whaleships leaving New Bedford in 1858, it took, in part, roughly 14,000 pounds of flour, 18,000 pounds of coffee, 26,000 pounds of potatoes, 10,000 casks of beef, 100,000 gallons of molasses, 65,000 feet of pine boards, 750,000 pounds of cordage, 33,000 casks of water, 450 whaleboats, 52,000 pounds of copper nails, 1,000 tons of hoop iron, and 1,000,000 staves. The price tag for all of the provisions purchased that year came to $1,950,000. Hohman, *The American Whalemen*, 331-32; and Starbuck, *History of the American Whale Fishery*, 111n.

80. Quoted in Paul Giambarba, *Whales, Whaling, and Whalecraft* (Centerville, MA: Scrimshaw Publishing, 1967), 38. Whalemen were well aware of the merchantmen's disdain for them. Writing in his journal, John Randall of the whaleship *California* bitterly noted the passing of a merchant ship at sea. "About sunset saw a sail off our starboard bow she proved to be a large Merchant man we hove our yard aback but she passed us too big to speak with us Blubber Hunters we braced the yards and stood on." John Randall, log of the whaleship *California*, entry for Nov. 30, 1849, ODHS log 698.

81. Hohman, *The American Whaleman*, vii.

82. Richard Henry Dana, Jr., *Two Years Before the Mast* (1840; reprint, New York: Penguin Books, 1981), 281.

83. Starbuck, *History of the American Whale Fishery*, fn96, 222-23.

84. Ashley, *The Yankee Whaler*, 41.

85. Quoted in Frederick P. Schmidt, Cornelius de Jong, and Frank H. Winter, *Thomas Welcome Roys: America's Pioneer of Modern Whaling* (Charlottesville: University Press of Virginia, 1980), 23.

86. Quoted in John R. Bockstoce, *Whales, Ice & Men, The History of Whaling in the Western Arctic* (Seattle: University of Washington Press, 1986), 23.

87. Schmidt et al., *Thomas Welcome Roys*, 11-12.

88. Quoted in ibid., 24.

89. Quoted in Bockstoce, *Whales, Ice & Men*, 23-24.

90. "From the Far North," *Whalemen's Shipping List*, May 14, 1849; Schmidt et al., *Thomas Welcome Roys*, 25; and Bockstoce, *Whales, Ice & Men*, 24.

91. "New Whaling Ground," *Whalemen's Shipping List*, Feb. 6, 1849.

92. Logbook for the *Ocmulgee*, ODHS logbook #204; and Arthur C. Watson, *The Long Harpoon: A Collection of Whaling Anecdotes* (New Bedford: George H. Reynolds, 1929), 49.

93. The average number of barrels yielded by different types of whales is a difficult if not impossible number to pin down with certainty. The estimates used here are taken from Bockstoce and Scammon. But depending on how one performs the calculations, the number of barrels produced by an average sperm or right whale will vary. Bockstoce, *Whales, Ice & Men*, 95; Scammon, *Marine Mammals*, 244; and Davis et al., *In Pursuit of Leviathan*, 135, 140.

94. The bowhead's reign as baleen king was confirmed in 1883, when a single whale brought in by an American whaler yielded 3,100 pounds of baleen, the all-time record for the industry. Brandt, *Whale Oil*, 28.

95. *The Friend*, Oct. 15, 1850.

96. Quoted in Robert Lloyd Webb, *On the Northwest: Commercial Whaling in the*

Pacific Northwest, 1790–1967 (Vancouver: University of British Columbia Press, 1988), 81.

97. To New Bedford whaling captain Daniel McKenzie the trend was clear. "When, half a century ago," he wrote in 1849, "our ships first ventured into the Pacific in quest of sperm whales, the coasts of Chili and Peru abounded in them; and our hardy pioneers in this daring occupation, were there enabled to fill their ships, without the necessity of penetrating further. But the whaling fleet increased extensively; the persecuted whales were in a measure killed and driven from their haunts; so that later voyages, to insure success, have been compelled to push their adventures into still farther and comparatively unknown seas. . . . there is scarce a spot of any extent but what has been furrowed by the keels of a whaler, and been a place of privation to her enduring crew." Quoted in M. F. Maury, *Explanations and Sailing Directions to Accompany the Wind and Current Charts,* 6th ed. (Philadelphia: E.C. Biddle, 1854), 373–74.

98. Quoted in Ashley, *The Yankee Whaler,* 103.

99. There is, however, one story of a whaling captain who returned from a four-year cruise with nothing to show for his efforts, and remarked that although he and his men had a miserable time whaling, "We had a *damn fine sail.*" Macy, *Nantucket Scrap Basket,* 21–22.

100. Leonard Gifford to Lucy Roberts, 10 November 1853, Leonard S. and Lucy Gifford Papers, ODHS Mss. 98, Subgroup 1, Series A, Folder 2; Starbuck, *History of the American Whale Fishery,* 478–79; and Charles T. Congdon, *Reminiscences of a Journalist* (Boston: James R. Osgood and Company, 1880), 16.

101. "Noble Project," *Nantucket Inquirer,* Nov. 26, 1822.

102. Quoted in Stackpole, *The Sea Hunters,* 458.

103. A. B. C. Whipple, *Vintage Nantucket* (New York: Dodd, Mead & Company, 1978), 136.

104. Nathaniel Hawthorne, "Chippings With a Chisel," in Nathaniel Hawthorne, George Parsons Lathrop, Julian Hawthorne, *The Complete Works of Nathaniel Hawthorne* (Boston: Houghton Mifflin Company, 1887), 460.

105. Eliza Brock Diary, February 1855, Logbook 136, NHA.

106. Lisa Norling, *Captain Ahab Had a Wife: New England Women and the Whalefishery, 1720–1870* (Chapel Hill: University of North Carolina, 2000), 263. The poem was written in February 1855, by Martha Ford, a doctor's wife in New Zealand who had been hosting a group of whaling wives. The poem was transcribed into the journal of Eliza Brock, one of the whaling wives, who at the time was most decidedly not living out the fantasy praised in the song but rather had joined her husband on board his ship, the *Lexington* of Nantucket, and that is how she found herself in Martha Ford's house being entertained that February day.

107. Quoted in David Cordingly, *Women Sailors and Sailors' Women* (New York: Random House, 2001), 122. Many other whaling wives expressed similar sentiments. Just after her husband had shipped out, Susan Snow Gifford wrote in her diary, "I felt very bad after you had gone and I did not know what to do with myself. I went upstairs and cried till my head ached and I felt most sick." Another wife wrote a letter to her husband complaining, "We have been married five years and lived together ten months. It is *too bad, too bad.*" Susan Snow Gifford Diary, November 13, 1859, manuscript on deposit at the NBWM; and Mary Chipman Lawrence, *The Captain's Best Mate: The Journal of Mary Chipman*

Lawrence on the Whaler Addison, *1856–1860,* edited by Stanton Garner (Providence: Brown University Press, 1966), xvi.

108. Charles Pierce to Eliza Tobey Pierce, Mar. 30, 1860, B85–411, NBWM.

109. Joan Druett, *"She Was a Sister Sailor": The Whaling Journals of Mary Brewster, 1845–1851* (Mystic: MSM, 1992).

110. Joan Druett, *Petticoat Whalers, Whaling Wives at Sea, 1820–1920* (Hanover, NH: University Press of New England, 2001), 19.

111. Benjamin Morrell, *A Narrative of Four Voyages to the South Sea, North and South Pacific Ocean, Chinese Sea, Ethiopic and Southern Atlantic Ocean, Indian and Antarctic Ocean, from the Year 1822 to 1831* (New York: J. & J. Harper, 1832), 337–38; and Abby Jane Morrell, *Narrative of a Voyage to the Ethiopic and South Atlantic Ocean, Indian Ocean, Chinese Sea, North and South Pacific Ocean, in the Years 1829, 1830, and 1831* (New York: J. & J. Harper, 1833), 16–18.

112. Morrell, *A Narrative of Four Voyages,* 338–39.

113. "Forty-two Wives of Whaling Captains in the Pacific," *The Friend,* Nov. 8, 1858; and "Lady Whalers," *Whalemen's Shipping List,* Feb. 1, 1853.

114. "A Journal of a Whaling Cruise," *Whalemen's Shipping List,* Mar. 27, 1855. Loneliness on board whaleships was a companion that visited women and men alike. Edwin Pulver, on the whaleship *Columbus,* wrote in his diary, "This evening I feel very lonesome. I am all alone there is several natives sitting at my door talking what is the topic of their conversation is more than I can tell. But I almost wish I was one of them they have no trouble, that is much more than I can say." Journal on board the whaleship *Columbus* of Fairhaven, entry for Nov. 24, 1852, log 167, PPL.

115. Lawrence, *The Captain's Best Mate,* xix.

116. Elizabeth A. Little, "The Female Sailor on the *Christopher Mitchell:* Fact and Fantasy," *American Neptune* 54 (Fall 1995), 252.

117. Nelson Cole Haley, *Whale Hunt: The Narrative of a Voyage by Nelson Cole Haley, Harpooner in the Ship Charles W. Morgan, 1849–1853* (New York: Ives Washburn, Inc., 1948), 60–70; and Jacqueline Kolle Haring, "Captain, the Lad's a Girl!" *Historic Nantucket* 40 (Winter 1992), 72–73.

118. Haley, *Whale Hunt,* 61–62, 64, 67.

119. "A Story with a Touch of Romance in It," *Nantucket Inquirer,* Aug. 16, 1849.

120. Ibid.

121. "A Female Sailor," Article from the *New York Herald* reprinted in the *Nantucket Inquirer,* Jan. 25, 1850. For a tale of another woman whaler, who signed on to the whaleship *America* in 1862, see Suzanne J. Stark, "The Adventures of Two Women Whalers," *American Neptune* 44 (Winter 1984), 22–24.

122. Jules Michelet, *The Sea* (London: T. Nelson and Sons, 1875), 209.

123. S. Whitemore Boggs, "American Contributions to Geographical Knowledge of the Central Pacific Islands," *Geographical Review* 28 (Apr. 1938), 185; "Voyage of Exploration," *Nantucket Inquirer,* Mar. 22, 1828); and "The Whale Fishery," *North American Review,* 113. The whalemen's logbooks also helped them become better hunters by enabling navy lieutenant Matthew Fontaine Maury to provide them with a guide to the haunts of whales. In the mid-1800s, Maury, who has been called the father of oceanography and the "pathfinder of the seas," launched a major effort to map the world's oceans, the main goal being to improve navigation by identifying the quickest routes for commercial and naval mariners to get where they were going. Rather than rely on government-sponsored explorations to supply this information, Maury, who was at the time head of the

navy's Depot of Charts and Instruments, distributed specially designed log-books and asked mariners to keep a daily record of the weather, winds, currents, and water temperatures they encountered on their trips, and then return the logbooks to him so that he and his staff could mine them for data to construct the maps.

One of the main reasons so many mariners aided Maury in his quest was because of the quid pro quo he offered. You provide me the data, Maury said, and I will provide you with maps that will help you do your jobs better. Maury was especially keen on getting whalemen to participate because he knew they trav-eled more widely than any other mariners and that they kept particularly detailed daily logs of the weather and ocean conditions. And Maury could use the whalemen's dedication to recording where they saw whales to glean further information on water temperatures by employing the crude but powerful rela-tionship that sperm whales tend to swim in warm waters, while right whales pre-ferred the cold. In return for the whalemen's participation, Maury promised to supply them with charts that showed "at a glance" where the whales "have been most hunted;—when, in what years, and in what months it has been most fre-quently found—whether in shoals, as stragglers;—and whether sperm or right."

Numerous mariners, including hundreds of whalemen, sent Maury logs, from which he and his team produced more than seventy charts, including track charts, trade-wind charts, pilot charts, thermal charts, and storm and rain charts. But the chart that most excited the whalemen was, of course, the whale chart, which, Maury proudly proclaimed, "cannot fail to prove of great impor-tance to the whaling interests of the country,—an interest . . . which fishes up annually from the depths of the ocean, property, in real value of which far exceeds that of the gold mines of California." As he had promised, Maury sent his whalemen contributors copies of the chart, and they couldn't have been hap-pier. "The Whale Chart," one whaling captain effused, "is a precious jewel; it seems to have *waked* up the merchants and masters to the practical utility of your researches in their behalf; there is not, and cannot be but one opinion, and that highly favorable: it is sought for by all interested in whaling." Charles Lee Lewis, *Matthew Fontaine Maury: The Pathfinder of the Seas* (Annapolis: United States Naval Institute, 1927); and Edmund Blair Bolles, *The Ice Finders: How a Poet, a Professor, and a Politician Discovered the Ice Age* (Washington, DC: Coun-terpoint Press, 2000), 5; M. F. Maury, *Explanations and Sailing Directions to Accompany the Wind and Current Charts*, fifth edition (Washington: C. Alexander, 1853), 289, 291, 301, and 314; and Mawer, *Ahab's Trade*, 261.

124. "Voyage of Exploration," *Nantucket Inquirer*, Mar. 22, 1828.
125. Stackpole, *The Sea Hunters*, 460.
126. For an excellent book on the U.S. Exploring Expedition, see Nathaniel Phil-brick, *Sea of Glory* (New York: Viking, 2003).
127. Charles Wilkes, U.S.N., *Narrative of the United States Exploring Expedition During the Years 1838, 1839, 1840, 1841, 1842*, vol. 5 (Philadelphia: Lea and Blanchard, 1845), 485.
128. Ibid.
129. Melville, *Moby-Dick*, 108.
130. C. F. Winslow, "Some Account of Capt. Mercator Cooper's visit to Japan in the whale ship *Manhattan*, of Sag Harbor," *The Friend*, Feb. 2, 1846,17–20; Letter from Mercator Cooper to Jospeh C. Delano, February 8, 1851, from Joseph C. Delano Papers, Mss. 64, Ser. D, S-S 19, folder 4, Old Dartmouth Historical Soci-

ety; and Aaron Haight Palmer, *Documents and Facts Illustrating the Origin of the Mission to Japan, Authorized by the Government of the United States, May 10th, 1854* (Washington, DC: Henry Polkinhorn, 1857), 15–16.

131. Winslow, "Some Account of Capt. Mercator," 18.

132. Letter from Mercator Cooper to Jospeh C. Delano, February 8, 1851.

133. Winslow, "Some Account of Capt. Mercator," 18.

134. Ibid., 20.

135. Peter Booth Wiley, *Yankees in the Land of the Gods, Commodore Perry and the Opening of Japan* (New York: Viking, 1990), 22–25; and "Japan," *The Friend*, Oct. 1, 1849.

136. Quoted in Jo Ann Roe, *Ranald MacDonald, Pacific Rim Adventurer* (Pullman: Washington State University Press, 1997), 102.

137. The most unusual of the former prisoners rescued by the *Preble* was undoubtedly Ranald MacDonald. He was an American whalemen, but not one of the *Lagoda*'s crew. MacDonald was a crewman on the whaleship *Plymouth*, which in June 1848 was off the coast of Japan. That was when MacDonald made the most unusual request. He asked the captain if he could take one of the whaleboats and make his way to the Japanese coast. Obsessed with Japan since he was very young, MacDonald wanted to make contact with the Japanese, regardless of the serious risk that entailed. The captain reluctantly consented and sent him on his way, sure that MacDonald would never be heard from again. MacDonald was captured and imprisoned, and during his confinement he taught English to Japanese translators, who would later serve as interpreters during Commodore Perry's visit to Japan in the early 1850s. For more on MacDonald see Roe, *Ranald MacDonald*; and Ranald MacDonald, *Ranald MacDonald: The Narrative of His Life, 1824–1894* edited by William S. Lewis and Naojiro Murakami (1923; reprint, Portland: Oregon Historical Society Press, 1990).

138. Quoted in Wiley, *Yankees in the Land of the Gods*, 29.

139. Quoted in Samuel Eliot Morison, *"Old Bruin": Commodore Mathew Calbraith Perry* (Boston: Little, Brown and Company, 1967), 285; and George Lynn-Lachlan Davis, *A Paper Upon the Origin of the Japan Expedition* (Baltimore: John Murphy & Co., 1860), 9–10.

140. Henry L. Bryan, *Compilation of Treaties in Force* (Washington, DC: U.S. Government Printing Office, 1899), 326.

141. Rhys Richards, *Honolulu Centre of Trans-Pacific Trade* (Honolulu: Pacific Manuscripts Bureau and Hawaiian Historical Society, 2000), 9; Maxine Mrantz, *Whaling Days in Old Hawaii* (Honolulu: Aloha Graphics, 1976), 9; and Gavan Daws, *Shoal of Time: A History of the Hawaiian Islands* (New York: Macmillan Company, 1968), 169. In the mid-1830s there were as many as three thousand Hawaiians on American whaleships. Steven Roger Fischer, *A History of the Pacific Islands* (New York: Palgrave, 2002), 100–101.

142. Quoted in Chester S. Lyman, *Around the Horn to the Sandwich Islands and California, 1845–1850*, edited by Frederick J. Teggart (New Haven: Yale University Press, 1924), 179.

143. Ernest S. Dodge, "Early American Contacts in Polynesia and Fiji," *Proceedings of the American Philisophical Society* 107 (Apr. 15, 1963), 105.

144. "The Morality of Whaleship Captains," *Whalemen's Shipping List*, Jan. 5, 1858.

145. Quoted in Dulles, *Lowered Boats*, 243.

146. William C. Park, *Personal Reminiscences of William Cooper Park, Marshall of the Hawaiian Islands, From 1850–1884* (Cambridge: Harvard University Press,

1891), 36—44; Briton Cooper Busch, *"Whaling Will Never Do for Me," The American Whaleman in the Nineteenth Century* (Lexington: University Press of Kentucky, 1994), 177—83; and W. D. Alexander, *A Brief History of the Hawaiian People* (New York: American Book Company, 1899), 274.

147. Lyndall Baker Landauer, *Scammon: Beyond the Lagoon* (San Francisco: Associates of the J. Porter Shaw Library), 11—39.

148. Scammon, *Marine Mammals*, 263.

149. Quoted in Dick Russell, *Eye of the Whale* (New York: Island Press, 2001), 39; and John Dean Caton, "The California Gray Whale," *American Naturalist* 22 (June 1888), 511.

150. Scammon, *Marine Mammals*, 263—64.

151. Ibid., 33.

152. Daniel Francis, *History of World Whaling* (New York: Viking, 1990), 116.

153. Lytle, *Harpoons and Other Whalecraft*, 14—59.

154. Sidney Kaplan, "Lewis Temple and the Hunting of the Whale," *New England Quarterly* 26 (Mar. 1953), 79.

155. Ashley, *The Yankee Whaler*, 86.

156. Quoted in Hershel Parker, *Herman Melville, A Biography*, vol. 2, *1851—1891* (Baltimore: Johns Hopkins University Press, 2002), 18.

157. "Moby-Dick; or the Whale," *United States Democratic Review* 30 (Jan. 1852), 93.

158. Andrew Delbanco, *Melville: His World and Work* (New York: Alfred A. Knopf, 2005), 320.

159. Not everyone, of course, thinks highly of *Moby-Dick*. Philip Roth, in his fictional account *The Great American Novel*, has one of his characters comment on the book in the following less-than-glowing terms. *"Moby-Dick* is a book about blubber, with a madman thrown in for excitement. Five hundred pages of blubber, one hundred pages of madman, and about twenty pages on how good niggers are with the harpoon." Philip Roth (New York: Holt, Rinehart and Winston, 1973), 27.

160. Samuel Eliot Morison, *Whaler Out of New Bedford* (New Bedford: Old Dartmouth Historical Society, 1963), 10; and Robert L. Carothers and John L. Marsh, "The Whale and the Panorama," *Nineteenth Century Fiction* 26 (December 1971), 319—28.

161. Elton W. Hall, *Panoramic Views of Whaling by Benjamin Russell* (New Bedford: Old Dartmouth Historical Society, 1981), 1—2.

162. Quoted in Morison, *Whaler Out of New Bedford*, 8.

163. Quoted in Carothers and Marsh, "The Whale and the Panorama," 320. See also, *New Bedford Mercury*, January 17, 1848.

CHAPTER FOURTEEN: "An Enormous, Filthy Humbug"

1. W., "A Chapter on Whaling," *The New-England Magazine* 8 (June 1835), 445.

2. "The Story of the Whale," *Harper's New Monthly Magazine*, 12 (Mar. 1856), 466—67.

3. William B. Whitecar, *Four Years Aboard the Whaleship* (Philadelphia: J. B. Lippincott, 1860), 413; Ben-Ezra Stiles Ely, *"There She Blows:" A Narrative of a Whaling Voyage* (1849; reprint, Middletown, CT: Wesleyan University Press, 1971), 118; Nordhoff, *Whaling and Fishing*, 136; and George Whitefield Bronson, *Glimpses of the Whaleman's Cabin* (Boston: Damrell & Moore, Printers, 1855), 8, 12. Another whalemen, trying to dissuade his brother from following in his footsteps, wrote

to him, "that it would be better . . . to be painted black and sold to a southern planter rather than to be doomed to the forecastle of a whale ship. It is not only unpleasant but very uncertain and dangerous, exposed to all kinds of weather and the toughest kind of living and compelled to associate with the very scum and off-scourings of infamy and to sum the whole up it is the most dogish life that ever fell to the lot of mortal man." Justin Martin to Charles Martin, November 29, 1844, VFM 246, Manuscript Collection of the G.W. Blunt Library, MSM, Inc.

4. Robert Weir, log of the bark *Clara Bell*, of Mattapoisett, Massachusetts, for cited entries, log 164, Manuscripts Collection, G.W. Blunt White Library, MSM, Inc.; Tamara K. Hareven, "The Adventures of a Haunted Whaling Man," *American Heritage* 28 (Aug. 1977), 48; and Starbuck, *The American Whale Fishery*, 528–29.

5. Captain Edward S. Davoll, "The Captain's Specific Orders on the Commencement of a Whale Voyage to his Officers and Crew," *Old Dartmouth Historical Sketches Number 81* (June 5, 1981), 5, 8–11.

6. Quoted in A. B. C. Whipple, *The Whalers* (Alexandria, VA: Time-Life Books, 1979), 64.

7. Quoted in Parker, *Herman Melville*, vol. 1, *1819–1851*, 183. The captain didn't only lord over the men but occasionally the animals on board as well. Consider the observations of William Allen, a crewman on the New Bedford whaleship *Samuel Robertson*, which he recorded in his journal:

> This day is a day ever to be remembered on board our ship a day in which the power and authority of the capt was shone forth with blazing splendor. . . . [it was a pleasant day] when our pet . . . boar jack the sailor who had been playing forward came aft and went the quarter deck in sight of the capt which so enraged him that he kicked him into his pen and not satisfied with that he called two of the sailors and made them haul him out and fetch him aft where he began bashing him the poor fellow crying for mercy till he got to the wheel when he could stand no longer but fell down in a kind of fit . . . his mouth covered with foam in this situation he lay for a few moments and then staggered along . . . and then fell again into another fit, the capt then gave him another severe kick saying if you do not get over this after breakfast, I will cut your throat—but he was saved that job the poor creature died . . . the foregoing needs no comment—but it is plain to be seen if a man would use a poor dumb beast in that way he would not be very careful of the backs or feelings of his men as he has often proved.

William Alfred Allen, Journal, entry for August 3, 1842, ODHS 1039.

8. As Busch points out, "Use of the 'cat' was abolished in 1850 on American merchant vessels, a category that included whaleships as far as the courts were concerned." *Whaling Will Never Do for Me*, 25. For a tally of floggings on American whaleships between 1820 and 1920, see Busch, 26–27.

9. Hohman claims that some of the particularly horrid treatment of whalemen in the golden age was necessitated by the nature of the men themselves. "It should be stated, in partial extenuation, that the character of the men in the forecastle often suggested, if it did not necessitate, stern and rigorous treatment. The deck of a whaler at sea was no place for soft words or an appearance of timidity. Rigid and unquestioning discipline was imperative in order to insure both success and safety; and the human scourings which comprised a large percentage of the mid-

century whaling crews were not amenable to subtle suggestion." Hohman, *The American Whalemen*, 14.

10. Cushman v. Ryan, C.C. Mass. 1840, 1 Story 91, 6 F. Cas. 1070, No. 3515. For a good description of judicial involvement in whaling cases, see Gaddis Smith, "Whaling History and the Courts," *Log of the Mystic Seaport* 30 (Oct. 1978), 67–80.

11. Ashley, *The Yankee Whaler*, 54.

12. Browne, *Etchings of a Whaling Cruise*, 24, 43.

13. To get an idea of how important such longevity was, consider that on June 14, 1853, the *Whalemen's Shipping List* ran a short article on a new product, which the paper called the "Imperishable Potato," especially designed for "long voyages." "Imperishable Potato," *Whalemen's Shipping List*, June 14, 1853.

14. Charles L. Newhall, *The Adventures of Jack: Or, A Life on the Wave*, edited by Kenneth R. Martin (1859; reprint, Fairfield, CT: Ye Galleon Press, 1981, 10.

15. Sandra L. Oliver, "What Is Lobscouse Anyway?" *Mystic Seaport Log* 43 (Spring 1991) 18–19; and Hohman, *The American Whalemen*, 131.

16. Nordhoff, *Whaling and Fishing*, 71.

17. Quoted in Margaret S. Creighton, *Rites & Passages: The Experience of American Whaling, 1830–1870* (Cambridge, England: Cambridge University Press, 1995), 2, 125.

18. Ely, *"There She Blows,"* 9.

19. *Speech of Mr. Grinnell, of Massachusetts, on the Tarriff, with Statistical Tables of the Whale Fishery of the United States* (Washington, DC: Gales & Seaton, 1844), 5, 14.

20. Entries for June 3–5, 1854, logbook of the *Morea* of New Bedford, 1853–56, ODHS logbook #135.

21. There was a not inconsiderable number of whalemen whose limbs got caught in the line playing out, and were pulled to their death. One might reasonably ask if such men could have been saved by the quick action of one of their mates, who, cutting the line with a hatchet, might loosen the rope's coil about the submerged man and, possibly, let him live to see another day. As Sir Arthur Conan Doyle observed, even the quickest of reflexes in such a situation might not have had any effect. "If the loop catches the limbs of any one of the boat's crew, that man goes to his death so rapidly that his comrades hardly know that he has gone. It is a waste of fish to cut the line, for the victim is already hundreds of fathoms deep." Doyle, *Memories and Adventures*, 37.

22. Macy, *The History of Nantucket*, 244–45.

23. Eleanora C. Gordon, "The Captain as Healer: Medical Care on Merchantmen and Whalers, 1790–1865," *American Neptune* 54 (Fall 1994), 265.

24. Sometimes the treatments proscribed appeared to be worse than the diseases they were meant to attack. Thus, a "shipmaster's medical directory" published in 1854 recommends that a patient with a cold follow a two-day regimen that begins with his feet being immersed in warm water, followed in order by the swallowing of "three purging pills [to induce vomiting] . . . a dose of epsom salts . . . or castor oil, . . . an eighth of a grain of tartar emetic [to induce more vomiting, and] . . . ten or fifteen drops of antimonial wine [to cause yet more vomiting] . . . several times during the day, in a little warm water . . . [and if the captain felt it was needed,] a teaspoonful of elixir paregoric, with the antimony . . . [could] be given at night." *The Shipmaster's medical directory: prepared and selected from the most approved medical works, for John G. Nichols by An Experienced*

Physician (Boston: John G. Nichols, Ship and Family Medicine Chests, 1854), 42–43.

25. Whitecar, *Four Years Aboard the Whaleship*, 358; Hohman, *The American Whalemen*, 139; "Cure for Scurvy," *Whalemen's Shipping List*, Apr. 1, 1845; and Joan Druett, *Rough Medicine* (New York: Routledge, 2000), 144–45.

26. William F. Macy, *The Nantucket Scrap Basket* (Boston: Houghton Mifflin Company, 1930), 13.

27. Davis, *Nimrod of the Sea, or The American Whalemen*, 194–96.

28. *In a Sperm Whale's Jaws*, edited by George C. Wood (Hanover: Friends of the Dartmouth Library, 1954), 8–9, 15–16.

29. Walt Whitman, "Song of Joys," in *Leaves of Grass*, edited by Harold W. Blodgett and Sculley Bradley (New York: New York University Press, 1965), 180.

30. "Aboard a Sperm Whaler," *Harper's New Monthly Magazine* 8 (Apr. 1854), 673.

31. Browne, *Etchings of a Whaling Cruise*, 115–21.

32. Ely, *"There She Blows*," 48–49.

33. Davis, *Nimrod of the Sea*, 77. For an excellent discussion of how the pattern of cutting in evolved over time, see Michael P. Dyer, "The Historical Evolution of the Cutting-In Pattern, 1798–1967," *American Neptune* 59 (Spring 1999), 137–48.

34. As Bennett notes, "It is a somewhat curious fact, that notwithstanding the myriads of sharks which assemble during the pursuit and cutting in of a Sperm Whale, it but seldom if ever occurs that whalers receive any personal injury from their attacks, although their disasters so frequently plunge them into the sea, and at times when these dangerous fish are not only numerous around them, but also display a most active and ferocious disposition." Bennett, *Narrative of a Whaling Voyage*, vol. 2, 222.

35. Jacob A. Hazen, *Five Years Before the Mast* (Philadelphia: Wills P. Hazard, 1854), 86.

36. Browne, *Etchings of a Whaling Cruise*, 129; and Davis, *Nimrod of the Sea*, 81.

37. Melville, *Moby-Dick*, 384–85.

38. Quoted in Dulles, *Lowered Boats*, 129.

39. Browne, *Etchings of a Whaling Cruise*, 63.

40. William A. Abbe, logbook of the *Atkins Adams*, Oct. 10, 1858 to Sept. 26, 1859, entry for Jul. 17, 1859, in the collection of NBWM, ODHS logbook 485. Charles Dickens, not unaware of the rigors of whaling, wrote, "A whale ship presents a strange scene during the process of trying out. The decks are literally swimming in oil. . . . The white sails are blackened by the smoke, and the neat trim ship of yesterday has suddenly become a floating mass of dirt and grease enveloped on thick, black, and stinking clouds." In the early 1800s a story made the rounds about a British man-of-war that came upon a whaleship in the South Seas trying out a whale. The captain of the warship was distressed by the sight of flames dancing on the deck and smoke rising into the rigging, and when his ship came alongside the whaleship he demanded to know what the bloody hell was going on. We're "trying" came the response. "Trying!" said the annoyed and somewhat mystified Brit. "Trying what, Sir?—to set your ship on fire?" Charles Dickens, *Household Words: A Weekly Journal*, vol. 6 (New York: Dix & Edwards Publishers, 1853), 403; and Bennett, *Narrative of a Whaling Voyage*, vol. 2, 211–12n.

41. Nordhoff, *Whaling and Fishing*, 131.

42. Harry Morton, *The Whale's Wake* (Dunedin, NZ: University of Otago Press, 1982), 56; Brown, "The Whalemen, Vessels and Boats," 234.

43. Quoted in Stephen Currie, *Thar She Blows: American Whaling in the Nineteenth Century* (Minneapolis: Lerner Publications Company, 2001), 6; and *Meditations from Steerage: Two Whaling Journal Fragments*, edited by Stuart M. Frank (Sharon, MA: KWM, 1991), Introduction.

44. Richard Boyenton, Logbook of the *Bengal*, May 29, 1834, PEM.

45. Making conclusive statements about the average profitability of whaling voyages during the golden age of whaling (or any other time, for that matter), is a risky undertaking, given how many factors have to be taken into account and how huge of an accounting exercise would be required to support such statements adequately. Hohman is one person who thoroughly studied this issue, and his general conclusion on the matter bears repeating. "In sum, then, the financial results of whaling voyages covered the whole range between ruinous losses and magnificent profits. But, tho the available figures do not warrant precise and conclusive assertion, it is evident that the cases at each extreme offset each other so effectually that the long-run, normal rate of profit for the industry as a whole was an essentially modest one." Elmo P. Hohman, "Wages, Risks, and Profits in the Whaling Industy," *Quarterly Journal of Economics* 40 (Aug. 1925), 668. See also, Hohman, *The American Whalemen*, 217–43; Moment, "The Business of Whaling," 274; Norling, *Captain Ahab Had a Wife*, 135; "Notes on Nantucket, Aug. 1, 1807," in *Collections of the MHS*, vol. 3 of the second series (Boston, 1815), 30; and Davis et al., "Risk Sharing, Crew Quality," 7–11.

46. Hohman, *The American Whalemen*, 240.

47. Davis et al., *In Pursuit of Leviathan*, 177.

48. Morison, *The Maritime History of Massachusetts*, 319.

49. "Successful Shipping Adventure," *Boston Daily Advertiser* (Jan. 9, 1851); Kobbe, "The Perils and Romance of Whaling," 523; and Starbuck, *History of the American Whale Fishery*, 453.

50. John C. Sullivan, A Voyage on *New Holland*, Marble Family Papers, Kendall Collection, NBWM, 2–3; and Mary Malloy, "Whalemen's Perceptions of the 'High & Mighty Business of Whaling,'" *Log of the Mystic Seaport* 41 (Summer 1989), 65.

51. Richard Boyenton, Logbook of the *Bengal*, Feb. 28, 1834, PEM.

52. Browne patterned his book after Richard Henry Dana's *Two Years Before the Mast*, which detailed problems in the merchant marine and had a positive impact on improving the situation for sailors in that line of service.

53. Browne, *Etchings of a Whaling Cruise*, iii–iv.

54. Christopher Slocum, Journal on the whaleship *Obed Mitchell* of New Bedford, undated entry near end of journal, log 514, PPL.

55. Hohman, *The American Whalemen*, 62; "Review of the Whale Fishery for 1850," *Whalemen's Shipping List*, Jan. 7, 1851.

56. Letter from Fayette M. Ringgold to John Appleton, September 1, 1858, in *State Department, Dispatches from United States Consuls in Paita, Peru, 1833–1874*, vol. 3 (June 30, 1851–Dec. 31, 1864).

57. Hohman, *The American Whalemen*, 63.

58. Deserters who decided to live on the tropical Pacific islands were often viewed with derision by other whalemen. John F. Martin, of the ship *Lucy Ann* out of Wilmington, described the scene that greeted the ships when they stopped off at one of those islands, and in the process paints a none-too-flattering picture of deserters. "When a ship comes in the white men flock on board they are called beach combers & a regular set of scoundrels they are, they are too lazy too work

at home for a living & prefer staying here where the living grows to their hands without having to work for it. Their object in coming to the ship was to beg clothes as they can not go naked like the natives their skin will not stand the sun, old trousers patches and took articles that the natives would not touch with one of their spears." Log of the *Lucy Ann* of Wilmington, entry for February 19, 1843, KWM, log 434.

59. A Friend to Whalemen, "Three young men drowned in Gray's Harbor, Northwest Coast," *The Friend*, Mar. 14, 1846.

CHAPTER FIFTEEN: Stories, Songs, Sex, and Scrimshaw

1. Although most whalemen looked forward to gamming and enjoyed these ocean-borne gatherings, there were at least a few whalemen who either grew weary of them, or just weary of gamming so often with the same ships over and over. One whaleman in the mid-1800s wrote in his journal that "he was 'getting sick' of gamming. 'It is impossible to get any sleep,' he declared. 'when you have a boats crew gamming in the forecastle.'" Quoted in Creighton, *Dogwatch & Liberty Days*, 59.

   Another whaleman wrote, "Spoke that Confounded ship again the Lion i wish to the Lord She was somewhere else. Well, well, we must do the best we can." Sylvanus Tallman, log of the *Canada*, entry for Jan. 11, 1848, ODHS log 200.

2. Robbins, *The Gam*, xii; and John Frost, *The Panorama of Nations: comprising the characteristics of courage, perseverance, enterprise, cunning, shrewdness, vivacity, ingenuity, contempt of danger and of death exhibited by people of the principal nations of the world, as illustrated in narratives of peril and adventure* (Auburn, NY: Beardsley, 1852), 61. During gams, one whaleman wrote, "The time is jenerally spent by the Capts in spinning the greatest lies about their personal engagements with whales how far they can throw the lance and kill a whale. In the forecastle [the crewman talk] . . . about those of their acquaintances who had been killed or maimed by whales . . . [describe] the different islands and ports they had visited [and share bawdy reminiscences] of women & wine [and] whoring & hard drinking." William Alfred Allen, journal entry for September 18, 1842, ODHS 1039.

3. Parker, *Herman Melville*, vol. 1, 184.

4. An excellent account of the sinking of the *Essex* is Nathaniel Philbrick's *In The Heart of the Sea*.

5. Quoted in Thomas Faral Heffernan, *Stove by a Whale* (Middletown, CT: Wesleyan University Press, 1981), 190–91.

6. Quoted in Gale Huntington, *Songs the Whalemen Sang* (New York: Dover Publications, 1970), 42–46.

7. Edwin Pulver, Journal on board the whaleship *Columbus* of Fairhaven, entry for October 15, 1852, log 167, PPL.

8. Francis Allyn Olmsted wrote that the whaleship *North America* had a "library . . . consisting of about two hundred volumes." Francis Allyn Olmsted, *Incidents of a Whaling Voyage* (1841; reprint, New York: Bell Publishing Company, 1969), 52.

9. Typed transcript of the Journal kept on board the *Mt. Wollaston*, 1853–1856, owned by the NBFPL.

10. Stuart M. Frank, *Dictionary of Scrimshaw Artists* (Mystic, CT: MSM, 1991), xxvii. The earliest known piece of American scrimshaw is a busk (a rigid ele-

ment used to stiffen a corset) carved out of baleen and signed in 1766 by Alden Sears, a whaling captain from Harwich, who presumably made the piece for his wife around the time that he moved back to Massachusetts after spending five years in Nova Scotia. The Sears busk was discovered by Stuart M. Frank and Don Ridley as part of their ongoing effort to write the definitive catalog of the world's largest collection of scrimshaw, which is housed at the NBWM. As they dig deeper into the holdings of the museum, it is certainly possible that they will uncover even earlier pieces of American scrimshaw. The first known American reference to scrimshaw comes from George Attwater, a crewman on the *Henry* of New Haven. On a foggy, windless day in late May, 1823, when the prospects for whaling were dim, Attwater wrote in his journal that, "the boatsteerers & most of the Ship's company are employed working bone evry opertunity they can get. This scrimpshawing buissness gose by fits & starts but I think the jagging falk [fork] feavour has not raged so strong as it does at present." As for the honor of being the first known American to carve images onto the teeth of a sperm whale, that goes to Nantucketer Edward Burdett, whose earliest effort dates to around 1825.

Discoveries of scrimshaw are continually being made, and there is certainly the possibility, if not the inevitability, that other pieces will be found that will cast doubt on the observations made here. The same goes for references to scrimshaw in American journals, and there might come a time when Attwater has to relinquish his crown. Frank, *Dictionary of Scrimshaw Artists*, 23, 118; Charles H. Carpenter, Jr., "Early Dated Scrimshaw," *Antiques* 102 (Sept. 1972), 414; personal communication with Michael P. Dyer, librarian and maritime historian at the NBWM, on June 26, 2006; George Attwater, entry for May 30, 1823, in George Attwater, *The Journal of George Attwater Before the Mast on the Whaleship Henry of New Haven, 1820–1823*, edited by Kevin S. Reilly (New Haven: New Haven Colony Historical Society, 2002), 405; personal communication with David Littlefield, museum interpreter and whaling historian, Mystic Seaport, the Museum of America and the Sea, June 17, 2006; and Joshua Basseches and Stuart M. Frank, *Edward Burdett, 1805–1833, America's First Master Scrimshaw Artist*, KWM Monograph Series No. 5 (Sharon, MA: KWM, 1991).

11. High-quality scrimshaw from the whaling era is extremely valuable. The highest price ever paid for a scrimshawed whale tooth came in August 2005, at an auction in New England, where an eight-inch tooth sold for $303,000. One side of the tooth is carved a with a striking image that includes five sperm whales, albatrosses flying overhead, a whaleship under full sail, and whaleboats in the water, one of which has just been upset by the flick of a whale's tail. The other side is equally impressive, with a Federal-style house, surrounded by plants, with a slivered moon and a star in the sky, and a sunburst design at the tip of the tooth. The artist of the tooth is unknown and is referred to as the "Pagoda/Albatross artist." The year 2005 was a phenomenal one for scrimshaw sales, with record prices being set three times. The first record fell in May, when an Edward Burdett tooth sold for $182,250, then another Burdett tooth brought $193,000 in August. But this last record was held for just a few minutes, as right after that sale was made, the tooth of the Pagoda/Albatross artist was bought by a highly "sophisticated" collector. See David Hewett, "Northeast Auctions Completes the Season with a $9.7 million Harvest in Portsmouth," *Maine Antique Digest* 33 (Nov. 2005), 36C–39C; and

Jeanne Schinto, "Scrimshaw Record is Unexpectedly Smashed by a Burdett Tooth," *Maine Antique Digest* 33 (July 2005), 1–3B.

12. Quoted in Frank, *Dictionary of Scrimshaw Artists*, 96–97. One particularly enterprising whaleman carved the following into a piece of a sperm whale's jawbone, no doubt gaining great pleasure from imagining the ultimate resting place of his gift.

> *Accept, dear Girl this busk from me;*
> *Carved by my humble hand.*
> *I took it from a Sparm Whale's Jaw,*
> *One thousand miles from land!*
> *In many a gale*
> *Has been the Whale,*
> *In which this bone did rest,*
> *His time is past,*
> *His bone at last*
> *Must now support thy brest.*

Quoted in Ashley, *The Yankee Whaler*, 114.

13. A. B. C. Whipple, *Yankee Whaler in the South Seas* (Rutland, VT: Charles E. Tuttle Company, 1973), 183. As Foster Rhea Dulles wrote, "The American could not resist the proffered charms of these dusky beauties of the tropics . . . the foremast hand so long cooped up in the narrow confines of a whaler's forecastle, took his fun where he found it." Dulles, *Lowered Boats*, 63.

14. Log of the ship *Samuel Robertson*, November 11, 1843, ODHS 1039; and Busch, *"Whaling Will Never Do for Me,"* 144.

15. Busch, *"Whaling Will Never Do for Me,"* 136–37.

16. Ernest S. Dodge, *New England and the South Seas* (Cambridge: Harvard University Press, 1965), 45. For a less damning view of whalemen and their use of alcohol while in port, see "Judge Andrew's Address," *The Friend*, Jan. 1, 1848.

17. Busch, *"Whaling Will Never Do for Me,"* 187.

CHAPTER SIXTEEN: Mutines, Murders, Mayhem, and Malevolent Whales

1. "Trial of the Junior Mutineers," *Republican Standard*, Nov. 25, 1858; "Trial of the Mutineers of the Ship Junior, for the Murder of Captain Archibald Mellen," *Boston Daily Journal*, Nov. 18, 1858; "Trial of the Junior Mutineers," *New Bedford Weekly Mercury*, Nov. 12, 1858; "Trial of the Junior Mutineers," *Republican Standard*, Nov. 16, 1858; and Sheldon H. Harris, "Mutiny on the Junior," *American Neptune* 21 (Apr. 1961), 112–13.

2. "The Junior Mutiny," *Republican Standard*, Jul. 1, 1859; "Trial of the Junior Mutineers," *Republican Standard*, Nov. 25, 1858; and "The Junior Mutiny," ibid., July 7, 1859. Although many newspaper articles at the time spelled Plumer's name "Plummer," I have gone with one *m* since that is the way it is spelled in the log of the *Junior*.

3. "The Junior Mutiny," *Republican Standard*, July 1, 1859; "The Junior Mutiny," ibid., July 7, 1859.

4. "Trial of the Junior Mutineers," *New Bedford Weekly Mercury*, Nov. 12, 1858.

5. Ibid.

6. "United States Circuit Court," *Boston Daily Advertiser*, Nov. 10, 1858; "Trial of the Junior Mutineers," *Republican Standard*, Nov. 18, 1858.

7. "Mutiny and Murder on Board the Ship Junior of this Port," *Whalemen's Shipping List*, Apr. 6, 1858.

8. "United States Circuit Court," *Boston Daily Advertiser*, Nov. 10, 1858; "The Mutiny on Board the Ship Junior," *Republican Standard*, Apr. 29, 1858; and "Arrival of Ship Junior with Her Mutineers," ibid., Aug. 26, 1858.

9. Alonzo D. Sampson, *Three Times Around the World, Life and Adventures* (Buffalo: Express Printing Company, 1867), 122.

10. Sampson, *Three Times Around the World*, 123.

11. Ibid.

12. "Trial of the Junior Mutineers," *Republican Standard*, Nov. 18, 1858; "Trial of the Junior Mutineers," *New Bedford Weekly Mercury*, Nov. 12, 1858.

13. "Trial of the Junior Mutineers," *New Bedford Weekly Mercury*, Nov. 12, 1858.

14. "The Junior Mutineers," *Republican Standard*, Sept. 2, 1858.

15. Sampson, *Three Times Around the World*, 125.

16. "The Mutiny and Murder on Board the Whale-Ship Junior—Sydney News," *Republican Standard*, Apr. 8, 1858.

17. Text taken from transcription of the *Junior* logbook, by William H. Tripp. The logbook is in the collection of the NBFPL. Text also found in "The Mutiny and Murder on Board the Junior," *New Bedford Weekly Mercury*, Apr. 23, 1858.

18. "Mutiny and Murder on Board Ship Junior, of This Port," *Whalemen's Shipping List*, Apr. 6, 1858.

19. Sampson, *Three Times Around the World*, 127.

20. Ibid.

21. Ibid., 128.

22. "Ship Junior," *Whalemen's Shipping List*, Apr. 20, 1858.

23. Sampson, *Three Times Around the World*, 131–33, 143.

24. Although Sampson claims that his boat had only four men, not six, given the bulk of the available contemporary evidence he must have been mistaken (perhaps because he wrote his account nearly ten years after the fact). Virtually all the newspaper reports agree that Plumer, Cartha, Stanley, and Rike were caught near Twofold Bay, in southern New South Wales, early in February. None of those accounts mentions, or even offers a hint, that there were two other men traveling with this group. Similarly the newspaper accounts show that Sampson was apprehended near Port Albert, in southern Victoria, by the local police with three others—Brooks, Canel, and Herbert. If Sampson's boat had had only four passengers, than one wonders how he could claim that two of the men he traveled with simply disappeared, yet when he was captured by the police there were three other men with him. And those same accounts that have Sampson being taken into custody with three other men, also state that at the time of these arrests, the Victorian police were still looking for Burns and Hall—this all at a time that was many weeks after Plumer, Cartha, Stanley, and Rike had already been captured. To complicate matters further, a few newspaper accounts talk of there being five men in each boat. In the end, regardless of which distribution of men between the two boats is correct, the basic outlines of the story remain the same. For some of the articles alluded to see: "Ship Junior," *Whalemen's Shipping List*, Apr. 20, 1858 (which copies an article from the *Sydney Morning Herald*); "The Mutiny and Murder on Board the Junior," *New Bedford Weekly Mercury*, Apr. 23, 1858; "The Whaleship Junior," *Whalemen's Shipping List*, Apr. 27, 1858; "The Mutineers of the Ship Junior," *Republican Standard*, July 15, 1858; "Ship Junior," *Republican Standard*, May 20, 1858; "The Mutiny on Board Ship Junior,"

Republican Standard, May 27, 1858; "Eight of the Mutineers of the Ship Junior Captured," ibid., Apr. 22, 1858; "Later.—Only Four Captured," *Republican Standard*, Apr. 22, 1858; "The Mutiny and Murder on Board the Whale-Ship Junior—Sydney News," ibid., Apr. 8, 1858; and Harris, "Mutiny on the Junior," 120.

25. "The Mutiny on Board Ship Junior," *Republican Standard*, May 27, 1858; "The Mutineers of the Ship Junior," ibid., July 15, 1858; and "Arrival of Ship Junior with her Mutineers," *Republican Standard*, Aug. 26, 1858.

26. "The Mutineers of the Junior," *New Bedford Daily Mercury*, Aug. 6, 1858; "The Mutineers of the Junior," *Republican Standard*, Aug. 5, 1858; "Arrival of the Ship Junior with the Mutineers," *New Bedford Daily Mercury*, Aug. 27, 1858; and "The Whaleship Junior," *Whalemen's Shipping List*, Jul. 13, 1858.

27. *New Bedford Daily Mercury*, Oct. 5, 1858.

28. "Arrival of Ship Junior With Her Mutineers," *Republican Standard*, Aug. 26, 1858.

29. "United States District Court," *Boston Daily Advertiser*, Nov. 10, 1858.

30. "Court Calendar," *Boston Daily Advertiser*, Dec. 1, 1858; and "The Junior Mutineer Case," *Boston Daily Advertiser*, Dec. 6, 1858.

31. "Conclusion of the Junior Trial," *New Bedford Evening Standard*, Dec. 1, 1858.

32. "Sentence of the Junior Mutineers," *Republican Standard*, Apr. 28, 1859.

33. Ibid; and "Sentence of Plummer for Murder," *Boston Courier*, Apr. 22, 1859.

34. Quoted in Chester Howland, *Thar She Blows!* (New York: Wilfred Funk, 1951), 223.

35. "The Junior Mutineer," *Whalemen's Shipping List*, July 12, 1859.

36. "Disclosure Concerning the Junior Mutiny," *Boston Journal*, May 4, 1859; "The Junior Mutiny," *Boston Journal*, May 23, 1859; "Cyrus W. Plumer," *Boston Journal*, June 25, 1859; and "The Plumer Case," *Boston Journal*, Jun. 30, 1859.

37. Howland, *Thar She Blows*, 216; "Plummer's Sentence Commuted," *Republican Standard*, July 14, 1859; *Republican Standard*, Mar. 31, 1859.

38. Quoted in Howland, *Thar She Blows*, 218.

39. "Plummer's Sentence Commuted," *Republican Standard*, July 14, 1859; "Plummer's Commutation," *Boston Daily Courier*, Jul. 9, 1859; "The Junior Mutineers," *Whalemen's Shipping List*, July 12, 1859; and Harris, "Mutiny on the Junior," 128.

40. Ulysses S. Grant, Pardon, July 16, 1874, in the records of the National Archives and Records Administration, Northeast Region, 75–76: and Howland, *Thar She Blows!* 223.

41. Silas Jones, "Narrative of Silas Jones, from the log of the *Awashonks*," *Atlantic Monthly* (Sept. 1917), 314.

42. Jones, "Narrative of Silas Jones," 316, 319.

43. The background for and quotes about this native attack comes from Haley, *Whale Hunt*, 136–42. Sydenham is one of the Gilbert Islands in the central Pacific.

44. Browne, *Etchings of a Whaling Cruise*, 263.

45. Beyond the three instances cited in the following pages—that of the *Union*, the *Essex*, and the *Ann Alexander*—there is at least one other instance of a whale sinking an American whaleship. On March 17, 1902, the New Bedford whaleship *Kathleen* was rammed and sunk by a sperm whale about one thousand miles off Brazil. The captain and the crew, along with the captain's wife, were saved by a passing steamer. While whales had, to be sure, a very good reason for attacking whaleships—after all, they were attacking them—whaleships were not the only seagoing vessels that whales rammed and sunk, either intentionally or by

accident. For example, when Francis Marion, who would later gain fame as an American Revolutionary War hero, was fifteen he shipped out on a schooner involved in the West Indian trade. On returning from those islands, the schooner was struck by a "whale with such violence as to loosen a plank," and the ship quickly foundered, leaving the men on board barely enough time to escape on one of the schooner's boats. And the *New Bedford Medley* reported on July 1, 1796, that a ship out of Rochester, New York, the *Harmony*, "was run foul of by a whale . . . stove, and sunk." There are also other instances of whales sinking ships outside of the American experience. For example, in 1855 a British ship, the *Waterloo*, was sunk by a whale in the North Sea. One newspaper report of the disaster stated that, "The leviathan who caused the disaster is supposed to have been a *Russian* whale, on a privateering cruise." Another British ship, the *Crusader*, was also sunk by a whale in 1852. Thomas H. Jenkins, *Bark Kathleen Sunk by a Whale* (New Bedford: H. S. Hutchinson & Co., 1902); Robert D. Bass, *Swamp Fox: The Life and Campaigns of General Francis Marion* (Orangeburg, SC: Sandlapper Publishing Co., Inc., 1959), 6; "New Bedford Marine Journal," *New Bedford Medley*, July 1, 1796; "A Vessel Sunk by a Whale," *Whalemen's Shipping List*, Apr. 24, 1855; and "A Ship Sunk at Sea by a Whale," *Whalemen's Shipping List*, July 20, 1852.

46. If American whaleships were constructed as Marco Polo claimed some ships in the thirteenth century were constructed, the ramming of a whale and the breaching of the hull might not have led inevitably to the sinking of the ship. "Some of the ships," wrote Polo, "that is the bigger ones, have also thirteen bulkheads or partitions made of stout planks dovetailed into one another. This is useful in case the ship's hull should chance to be damaged in some place by striking on a reef or being rammed by a whale in search of food—a not infrequent occurrence, for if a whale happens to pass near the ship while she is sailing at night and churning the water to foam, he may infer from the white gleam in the water that there is food for him there and so charge full tilt against the ship and ram her, often breaching the hull at some point." Polo and Rustichello of Pisa, *The Travels of Marco Polo*, 241.

47. Edmund Gardner, *Captain Edmund Gardner of Nantucket and New Bedford, His Journal and His Family*, edited by John M. Bullard (New Bedford: Bullard, 1958), 11.

48. Owen Chase, *The Wreck of the Whaleship Essex* (1821; reprint, San Diego: Harcourt Brace & Company, 1965), 9.

49. Quoted in Philbrick, *In the Heart of the Sea*, 81.

50. Chase, *The Wreck of the Whaleship Essex*, 11–12.

51. Philbrick, *In the Heart of the Sea*, 83.

52. Chase, *The Wreck of the Whaleship Essex*, 16.

53. Clement Cleveland Satwell, *The Ship Ann Alexander of New Bedford, 1805–1851* (Mystic: Marine Historical Association, 1962); "Thrilling Account of the Destruction of a Whale Ship by a Sperm Whale—Sinking of the Ship—Loss of the two of the boats and miraculous Escape of the Crew," *Whalemen's Shipping List*, Nov. 4, 1851; and "A Ship Sunk by A Whale," *Living Age* 31 (Nov. 29, 1851), 415–16.

54. John Scott DeBlois, "A Fighting Whale's Triumph," *The Mercury*, Newport Rhode Island, February 5, 1881.

55. Ibid.; and "Thrilling Account of the Destruction of a Whale Ship by a Sperm Whale," *Whalemen's Shipping List*, Nov. 4, 1851.

56. DeBlois, "A Fighting Whale's Triumph," *The Mercury*, Newport, Rhode Island, Feb. 5, 1881.

57. Ibid., Feb. 12, 1881.

58. Ibid., Feb. 19, 1881; ibid., Feb. 26, 1881; and William Chambers, *Chambers' Home Book or Pocket Miscellany*, vol. 1 (Boston: Gould and Lincoln, 1853), 163–64.

59. Quoted in Parker, *Herman Melville*, vol. 1, 878.

60. "Decidedly Incredulous," *Whalemen's Shipping List*, Nov. 18, 1851.

CHAPTER SEVENTEEN: Stones in the Harbor and Fire on the Water

1. Tower, *A History of the American Whale Fishery*, 121.

2. Letter from Gideon Welles to George D. Morgan, October 17, 1861, in *Official records of the Union and Confederate Navies in the War of the Rebellion, series I, vol. 12, North Atlantic Blockading Squadron (February 2, 1865–August 3, 1865); South Atlantic Blockading Squadron (October 29, 1861–May 13, 1862)* (Washington, DC: Government Printing Office, 1901), 416–17.

3. Sidney Withington, "The Sinking of Two 'Stone Fleets' at Charleston, S.C. during the Civil War," in *Two Dramatic Episodes of New England Whaling* (Mystic: Marine Historical Association, Inc., July 1958), 45; Arthur Gordon, "The Great Stone Fleet, Calculated Catastrophe," *United States Naval Institute Proceedings* 94 (Dec. 1968), 76; and letter from George D. Morgan to S. F. DuPont, November 18, 1861, in *United States Naval War Records Office, Official Records of the Union and Confederate Navies in the War of the Rebellion, series I, vol. 12*, 418. Some people called the Stone Fleet the "Rat Hole Squadron," being sent as they were to plug the harbors so the rats, that is, the Confederates, couldn't get out. "The Rat Hole Squadron," *New Bedford Evening Standard*, Dec. 10, 1861.

4. Frank P. McKibben, "The Stone Fleet of 1861," *New England Magazine* 24 (June 1898), 486; and John E. Woodman, Jr., "The Stone Fleet," *American Neptune* 21 (Oct. 1961), 236.

5. *United States Naval War Records Office, Official records of the Union and Confederate Navies in the War of the Rebellion, Series I, vol. 12*, 418–19.

6. Pardon B. Gifford, "The Story of the Stone Fleet," in *Famous Fleets in New Bedford's History* (New Bedford: Reynolds Printing, 1935), 7.

7. "The Stone Fleet," *New Bedford Mercury*, Nov. 25, 1861.

8. "The Great Stone Fleet," *New York Times*, Nov. 22, 1861.

9. Letter from J. S. Misroon to S. F. DuPont, December 5, 1861, in United States Naval War Records Office, *Official Records of the Union and Confederate Navies in the War of the Rebellion, series I, vol. 12*, 419.

10. Gordon, "The Great Stone Fleet," 79.

11. Letter from J. S. Misroon to S. F. DuPont, December 5, 1861, 419; Gordon, "The Great Stone Fleet," 78; Withington, "The Sinking of Two 'Stone Fleets,'" 50–51; Woodman, "The Stone Fleet," 239; and "Arrival of the Stone Fleet," *New Bedford Evening Standard*, Dec. 20, 1861.

12. Quoted in Withington, "The Sinking of Two 'Stone Fleets,'" 51.

13. Quoted in ibid; and Gordon, "The Great Stone Fleet," 80.

14. Letter from Charles Henry Davis to S. F. DuPont, December 21, 1861, *United States Naval War Records Office, Official records of the Union and Confederate Navies in the War of the Rebellion, series I, vol. 12*, 422.

15. Howard P. Nash, Jr., "The Ignominious Stone Fleet," *Civil War Times Illustrated*,

3 (June 1964), 48; and *United States Naval War Records Office, Official records of the Union and Confederate Navies in the War of the Rebellion*, series I, vol. *12*, 510–11.

16. "The Sunken Fleet," *New York Times*, Dec. 26, 1861.

17. See, for example, A. Dudley Mann to President Jefferson Davis, February 1, 1862, in *Official Records of the Union and Confederate Navies in the War of the Rebellion*, series *2*, vol. *3* (Washington, DC: Government Printing Office, 1922), 323–25.

18. Letter from Robert E. Lee to Judah P. Benjamin, December 20, 1861, in *United States Naval War Records Office, Official records of the Union and Confederate Navies in the War of the Rebellion*, series I, vol. *12*, 423.

19. Quoted in Withington, "The Sinking of Two 'Stone Fleets,'" 63; and *The Times* (of London), Dec. 19, 1861.

20. John Morley, *The Life of Richard Cobden* (Boston: Roberts Brothers, 1881), 574–75.

21. Quoted in Gordon, "The Great Stone Fleet," 82.

22. J. E. Hilgard, *On Tides and Tidal Action in Harbors* (Washington, DC: Government Printing Office, 1875), 17–18; Woodman, "The Stone Fleet," 254; letter from Thomas M. Wagner to Leo D. Walker, February 12, 1862, in *United States Naval War Records Office, Official records of the Union and Confederate Navies in the War of the Rebellion*, series I, vol. *12*, 423–24; Withington, "The Sinking of Two 'Stone Fleets,'" 68; and McKibben, "The Stone Fleet," 488.

23. Herman Melville, *Battle Pieces and Aspects of War*, edited by Sidney Kaplan (Amherst: University of Massachusetts Press, 1972), 31–32.

24. James D. Bulloch, *The Secret Service of the Confederate States in Europe* (1883; reprint, New York: Modern Library, 2001), 17.

25. Charles M. Robinson III, *Shark of the Confederacy* (Annapolis: Naval Institute Press, 1995), 16; and William M. Fowler, *Under Two Flags: The American Navy in the Civil War* (New York: W. W. Norton & Company, 1990), 282–83. Bulloch's nephew, Theodore Roosevelt, would later become president of the United States.

26. Quoted in Robinson, *Shark of the Confederacy*, 35.

27. Raphael Semmes, *Service Afloat or, The Remarkable Career of the Confederate Cruisers Sumter and Alabama* (1869; reprint, Baltimore: Baltimore Publishing Company, 1887), 421.

28. Ibid., 423.

29. Quoted in Warren Armstrong, *Cruise of a Corsair* (London: Cassell, 1963), 42.

30. Quoted in Shapiro and Stackpole, *The Story of Yankee Whaling*, 85.

31. Semmes, *Service Afloat*, 424, 432–33, 449.

32. Raphael Semmes, *Memoirs of Service Afloat, During the War Between the States* (Baltimore: Kelly Piet & Co., 1869), 611.

33. Quoted in Robinson, *Shark of the Confederacy*, 69.

34. "The Sinking of the Alabama, Full Account of the Action," *Farmer's Cabinet*, July 14, 1864, 2.

35. Bulloch, *The Secret Service*, 401.

36. James I. Waddell, *C.S.S. Shenandoah, The Memoirs of Lieutenant Commanding James I. Waddell*, edited by James D. Horan (New York: Crown Publishers, Inc., 1960), 66, 94.

37. Bulloch, *The Secret Service*, 412; John Thomson Mason, "The Last of the Confederate Cruisers," *Century Magazine* 56 (Aug. 1898), 602; and James D. Bulloch to S.R. Mallory, in *Official Records of the Union and Confederate Navies in the War of*

the Rebellion, series I, vol. 3 (Washington, DC: Government Printing Office, 1896), 757–59.

38. James D. Bulloch to James I. Waddell, October 5, 1864, in *Official Records of the Union and Confederate Navies in the War of the Rebellion, series I, vol. 3*, 749.

39. "Destruction of Bark Edward, of This Port, by a Rebel Pirate," *Whalemen's Shipping List*, Mar. 7, 1865.

40. Mason, "The Last of the Confederate Cruisers," 605.

41. Cornelius E. Hunt, *The Shenandoah or the Last Confederate Cruiser* (New York: G.W. Carleton & Company Publishers, 1867), 59–60.

42. "Destruction of Bark Edwards, of This Port, by a Rebel Pirate," *Whalemen's Shipping List*, Mar. 7, 1865.

43. Hunt, *The Shenandoah*, 95.

44. Ibid., 97; and "William A. Temple, Affadavit," in *Correspondence Concerning Claims Against Great Britain Transmitted to the Senate of the United States*, vol. 3 (Washington, DC: Philip & Solomons, Booksellers, 1869), 481.

45. Waddell, *C.S.S. Shenandoah*, 140.

46. Burns, *The Shenandoah*, 114.

47. Mason, "The Last of the Confederate Cruisers," 607; and Burns, *The Shenandoah*, 115.

48. Waddell, *C.S.S. Shenandoah*, 145.

49. "E. V. Joice, Notary Public, testimony taken," *Correspondence Concerning Claims Against Great Britain*, vol. 3, 382–83.

50. Quoted in Bockstoce, *Whales, Ice & Men*, 111.

51. Waddell, *C.S.S. Shenandoah*, 158.

52. Spunky, *Republican Standard*, Aug. 24, 1865.

53. Burns, *The Shenandoah*, 164; and Temple, Affadavit, in *Correspondence Concerning Claims Against Great Britain*, vol. 3, 482.

54. "The Late Destruction of Whalers," *Whalemen's Shipping List*, Aug. 22, 1865.

55. Waddell, *C.S.S. Shenandoah*, 166.

56. "News from the Shenandoah: Wholesale Destruction of American Whalers," *The Friend*, Sept. 1, 1865.

57. Hunt, *The Shenandoah*, 175.

58. Waddell, *C.S.S. Shenandoah*, 167.

59. "The Pirate Shenandoah Still at Work," *Republican Standard*, Aug. 31, 1865.

60. Hunt, *The Shenandoah*, 191–92, 194.

61. "Further Destruction of Whaleships!" *Whalemen's Shipping List*, Aug. 29, 1865.

62. Waddell, *C.S.S. Shenandoah*, 168–69.

63. Hunt, *The Shenandoah*, 199.

64. Ibid., 200.

65. "The Man Who Defied Waddell the Pirate," *Whalemen's Shipping List*, Sept. 26, 1865.

66. Hunt, *The Shenandoah*, 201–2.

67. Hunt, *The Shenandoah*, 202.

68. Ibid., 204.

69. Waddell, *C.S.S. Shenandoah*, 171, 173.

70. Bockstoce, *Whales, Ice & Men*, 122.

71. Hunt, *The Shenandoah*, 217.

72. Waddell, *C.S.S. Shenandoah*, 176.

73. Bulloch, *The Secret Service*, 417, 427. In June 1865 Bulloch had tried to communicate with Waddell while the latter was still at sea, sending him a letter, which

was distributed to British consuls in the Pacific, informing Waddell that the war was over and what his options might be, but since Waddell didn't head into any ports prior to returning to England, he never got the communication. James D. Bulloch to James I. Waddell, June 19, 1865, in *Official Records of the Union and Confederate Navies in the War of the Rebellion, series II, vol. 2*, 811–12.

74. Mason, "The Last of the Confederate Cruisers," 609.
75. THE PIRATE SHENANDOAH! SHE STEERS IN THE TRACK OF WHALERS, TERRIBLE HAVOC EXPECTED, *Whalemen's Shipping List and Merchants' Transcript*, July 25, 1865; DESTRUCTION OF WHALESHIPS BY THE PIRATE SHENANDOAH! *Whalemen's Shipping List and Merchants' Transcript*, Aug. 1, 1865; "The Late Destruction of Whalers," ibid., Aug. 22, 1865; FURTHER DESTRUCTION OF WHALESHIPS! *Whalemen's Shipping List and Merchants' Transcript*, Aug. 29, 1865; and "The Pirate Shenandoah Still at Work," *Republican Standard*, Aug. 31, 1865.
76. "The Pirate Shenandoah," *New York Times*, Aug. 27, 1865.
77. "Wholesale Piracy," *Republican Standard*, Aug. 31, 1865.
78. Quoted in Bockstoce, *Whales, Ice & Men*, 125; and *Papers Relating to the Treaty of Washington, Geneva Arbitration*, vol. 1, (Washington, DC: Government Printing Office, 1872), 178.
79. Bockstoce, *Whales, Ice & Men*, 126.
80. "Capt. Waddell Dead," *New York Times*, Mar. 17, 1886.
81. Waddell, *C.S.S. Shenandoah*, 184.

CHAPTER EIGHTEEN: From the Earth

1. Leroy Thwing, *Flickering Flames, A History of Domestic Lighting Through the Ages* (Rutland, VT: Charles E. Tuttle Company, 1974), 55; and Charles Louis Flint, Charles Francis McCay, John C. Merriam, Thomas Prentice Kettell, and L. P. Brockett, *One Hundred Years' Progress of the United States* (Hartford: L. Stebbins, 1870), 163.
2. "Oil!" *New Bedford Mercury*, June 24, 1842; and "Hogs Superseding the Whale Fisheries!" *New Bedford Weekly Mercury*, Mar. 11, 1842.
3. "Spermaceti v. Lard," *New Bedford Weekly Mercury*, Sept. 23, 1842; "Hog vs. Whale" *New Bedford Weekly Mercury*, Oct. 7, 1842.
4. "Oil," *Whalemen's Shipping List and Merchants' Transcript*, May 2, 1843.
5. Many lard-oil detractors chose to lampoon this form of lighting in verse. See, for example, "Oil Song," *New Bedford Weekly Mercury*, Oct. 28, 1842; and "Oil Song," ibid., Nov. 4, 1842.
6. "Another Camphene Explosion!" ibid., Oct. 7, 1842; and "Another Beauty of Camphene," *Whalemen's Shipping List and Merchants' Transcript*, July 13, 1852.
7. "Camphene Lamp Exploded," *Nantucket Inquirer*, Sept. 17, 1842.
8. The *Whalemen's Shipping List* offered the following rationale for government intervention vis-à-vis camphene: "We have often thought that the State, which recently seems to take such care of what we shall eat, and what we shall drink, ought to interfere in this matter. We have statutes for the storage of gunpowder. It is put away, out of reach of hap and hazard. Yet every day we hear of this house burned, of that child killed, by the explosion of what is called 'Camphene.' It seems to us that the State might find some ground for its legislation, even here." "Camphene, Burning Fluid, Etc.," *Whalemen's Shipping List*, May 25, 1852.
9. "Patent Oils, &c.," *Nantucket Inquirer*, Apr. 14, 1841. At least one observer of the

whaling industry's apparent concern for the safety of those who used camphene wryly wondered if the concern was misplaced. "The *Nantucket Inquirer*," noted a brief piece in a Boston paper, "speaking of 'Camphene,' asks with much sympathetic humanity, 'Why will persons be so venturesome as to use this dangerous article?' This is a very natural question for those who have been so 'venturesome' as to undertake to catch whales, a matter we supposed to be quite as dangerous as burning camphene." "A Fellow Feeling Makes Us Wondrous Kind," *Morning News* (excerpting from the *Boston Daily Advertiser*), May 8, 1845.

10.   In England, the introduction of gas into the cities in the early nineteenth century, counterintuitively perhaps, contributed to the increased demand for whale oil, because once people saw the shops and streets being so beautifully lit with gas, their own desire for lighting their homes was correspondingly increased, and the best way to do that was to burn sperm whale oil. Bennett, *Narrative of a Whaling Voyage*, vol. 2, 188.

11.   O. Fogy, "Gas in New Bedford," *Whalemen's Shipping List*, June 29, 1852.

12.   "Diary of Rev. Moses How," no. 59 in *Series of Sketches of New Bedford's Early History* (1931), 28.

13.   Kendall Beaton, "Dr. Gesner's Kerosene: The Start of American Oil Refining," *The Business History Review* 29 (Mar. 1955), 38, 43; Catherine M. V. Thuro, *Oil Lamps* (Paducah: Collector Books, 1976), 15–16. Although the base cost of kerosene was not much lower, and at times was higher than the cost of equivalent amounts of other illuminants, kerosene lasted far longer and produced much more light than its competitors, thereby greatly reducing its cost per unit of light.

14.   Ibid., 28; "Coal Oil Manufacture," *Republican Standard*, Feb. 2, 1860; and Tertzakian, *A Thousand Barrels a Second*, 18.

15.   Tower, *A History of the American Whale Fishery*, 128.

16.   "The Oil Market," *Republican Standard*, Mar. 25, 1858.

17.   Amory B. Lovins, E. Kyle Datta, Odd-Even Bustnes, Jonathan G. Koomey, and Nathan J. Glasgow, *Winning the Oil Endgame, Innovation for Profits, Jobs, and Security* (Snowmass, CO: Rocky Mountain Institute, 2005), 4–5; and Davis et al., *In Pursuit of Leviathan*, 352–54, 361–62.

18.   With respect to the impact of petroleum on the whale oil industry, Starbuck observed:

> The increase in population would have caused an increase in consumption [of whale oil] beyond the power of the fishery to supply, for even at the necessarily high prices people would have had light. But other things occurred. The expense of procuring oil was yearly increasing when the oil-wells of Pennsylvania were opened, and a source of illumination opened at once plentiful, cheap, and good. Its dangerous qualities at first greatly checked its general use, but, these removed, it entered into active, relentless competition with whale-oil, and it proved the more powerful of the antagonistic forces.

Starbuck, *History of the American Whale Fishery*, 109–10.

19.   Daniel Yergin, *The Prize, The Epic Quest for Oil, Money & Power* (New York: Simon & Schuster, 1991), 25.

20.   A contemporary booster of oil-derived kerosene called it "the light of the age," and unstintingly extolled its virtues. "Those that have not seen it burn, may rest assured its light is no moonshine; but something nearer the clear, strong, brilliant light of day, to which darkness is no party . . . [it] emits a dainty light; the

brightest and yet the cheapest in the world; a light fit for Kings and Royalists and not unsuitable for Republicans and Democrats." Quoted in Yergin, *The Prize*, 28.

21. Ibid., *The Prize*, 30; E. V. Smalley, "Striking Oil," *The Century* 26 (July 1883), 326; and Davis et al., *In Pursuit of Leviathan*, 379–80.

22. Log of the *Nimrod*, July 13, 1860, ODHS Log 946.

23. Edmund Morris, *Derrick and Drill or An Insight Into the Discovery, Development, and Present Condition and Future Prospects of Petroleum* (New York: J. Miller, 1865), 124. Morris claimed that an old whaling captain offered the following hypothesis to account for the existence of petroleum deposits in Pennsylvania: "A large shoal of whales were stranded in Western Pennsylvania, at the time of the subsidence of the flood, and that the oil-borers are now sinking holes in the blubber." Morris added that this theory was "not generally accepted, save among brother whalers" (124). See also S. J. M. Eaton, *Petroleum: A History of the Oil Region of Venango County, Pennsylvania* (Philadelphia: J. P. Skelly & Co., 1866), 284.

24. Tower, *A History of the American Whale Fishery*, 128.

25. "Year in Review," *Whalemen's Shipping List*, Jan. 31, 1871.

CHAPTER NINETEEN: Ice Crush

1. "Honolulu Harbor," *The Polynesian*, Oct. 19, 1850.

2. "Letters About the Arctic, No. II," *Whalemen's Shipping List and Merchants' Transcript*, May 10, 1853.

3. Quoted in Everett S. Allen, *Children of the Light, The Rise and Fall of New Bedford Whaling and the Death of the Arctic Fleet* (Orleans, MA: Parnassus Imprints, 1983), 202, 204–5.

4. William F. Williams, "Loss of the Arctic Fleet," in *Famous Fleets in New Bedford's History*, 3.

5. Bockstoce, *Whales, Ice & Men*, 152.

6. "Polar Sea Perils," *New York Times*, Nov. 14, 1871; and "Crushed Among Icebergs," *Harper's Weekly* (Dec. 2, 1871), 1130.

7. Timothy Packard, log of the *Henry Taber*, entry for Aug. 31, 1871, ODHS Log 455.

8. Log of the bark *Eugenia*, entry for September 1, 1871, NBFPL.

9. "Polar Sea Perils," *New York Times*; and Bockstoce, *Whales, Ice & Men*, 154.

10. "Polar Sea Perils," *New York Times*; and Allen, *Children of the Light*, 226; and Bockstoce, *Whales, Ice & Men*, 154–55.

11. William Earle, log of the *Emily Morgan*, entry for Sept. 9, 1871, NBFPL.

12. Quoted in Allen, *Children of the Light*, 231.

13. James Dowden, unidentified news clipping, scrapbook 2, NBWM, p. 77.

14. "Polar Sea Perils," *New York Times*.

15. Quoted in Frank P. McKibben, "The Whaling Disaster of 1871," *New England Magazine* 24 (June 1898), 492; and Allen, *Children of the Light*, 242.

16. William Earle, log of the *Emily Morgan*, entry for Sept. 14, 1871, NBFPL. According to Robert P. Gifford, a mate on board the *Gay Head*, the whaleboats were loaded with supplies to last for "40 days." Log of the *Gay Head*, entry for Sept. 14, 1871, ODHS Log 962.

17. Williams, "Loss of the Arctic Fleet," 10.

18. Quoted in Starbuck, *History of the American Whale Fishery*, 108.

19. "Polar Sea Perils," *New York Times*.

20. "Terrible Disaster to the Arctic Fleet, Thirty-Three Vessels Lost," *Whalemen's Shipping List and Merchants' Transcript*, November 7, 1871; and "The Arctic Disaster," *Whalemen's Shipping List and Merchants' Transcript*, November 14, 1871.

21. "Loss of the Arctic Fleet, from Our Own Correspondent," *New York Times*, Nov. 7, 1871.

22. Bockstoce, *Whales, Ice & Men*, 161.

23. Williams, *Loss of the Arctic Fleet*, 9.

24. Allen, *Children of the Light*, 265.

25. Bockstoce, *Whales, Ice, & Men*, 165.

26. Quoted in Allen, *Children of the Light*, 266.

27. Quoted in ibid., 272.

28. Bockstoce, *Whales, Ice & Men*, 152; and Allen, *Children of the Light*, 269.

29. "Disastrous News From the Whaling Fleet," *Whalemen's Shipping List*, Oct. 24, 1876; and "The Arctic Disaster," *Whalemen's Shipping List and Merchants' Transcript*, Nov. 7, 1876.

30. "Caught in the Ice," *Boston Globe*, Oct. 23, 1876.

CHAPTER TWENTY: Fading Away

1. N. T. Hubbard, *Autobiography of N.T. Hubbard, with Personal Reminiscences of New York City from 1789 to 1875* (New York: J.F. Trow & Son, 1875), 26–27.

2. Tower, *A History of the American Whale Fishery*, 121.

3. "Whaling Enjoys a New Life," *New York Times*, Sept. 14, 1902. These prices for sperm and whale oil were taken from Tower for the years up through 1905, and then *Whalemen's Shipping List* until 1914. See Tower, *A History of the American Whale Fishery*, 128; and Davis et al., *In Pursuit of Leviathan*, 368–75. Similarly whale oil, which sold for thirty-five cents in 1888, sank to twenty-eight cents in 1895, and stayed below forty cents from then on.

4. "Review of the Whale Fishery for 1872," *Whalemen's Shipping List*, Feb. 4, 1873.

5. Lloyd C. M. Hare, *Salted Tories: The Story of the Whaling Fleets of San Francisco* (Mystic, CT: Marine Historical Association, Inc., 1960), 105.

6. Starbuck, *History of the American Whale Fishery*, 155–56n; and Webb, *On the Northwest*, 47. One of the most unusual uses for whalebone that I chanced upon was as an applicator of iodine to the cervix, as part of the treatment for fibroid tumors of the uterus. See Fleetwood Churchill, *On the Diseases of Women; Including Those of Pregnancy and Childhood* (Philadelphia: Blanchard and Lea, 1857), 251.

7. Tower, *A History of the American Whale Fishery*, 72, 128.

8. "To Cruise for Whalebone," *New York Times*, July 18, 1889.

9. Bockstoce, *Whales, Ice & Men*, 95; Webb, *On the Northwest*, 116; and "Great Catch of Whales," *New York Times*, Nov. 6, 1898.

10. Renny Stackpole, *American Whaling in Hudson Bay, 1861–1919* (Mystic, CT: Munson Institute of American Maritime History, 1969).

11. Stackpole, *American Whaling in Hudson Bay*, 20; and Bockstoce, *Whales, Ice & Men*, 271–72.

12. Quoted in Hare, *Salted Tories*, 93.

13. Mark Twain, "The Whaling Trade," in *Mark Twain, Letters From Honolulu* (Honolulu: Thomas Nickerson, 1939), 58–59.

14. Although the cost of labor was key to Twain's position, there were other consid-

erations, he pointed out, that had to be taken into account. "In facilities for shipping crews," Twain continued, "in economy of time and distance of travel of a voyage, in facilities for insuring, in cheapness of money, in facilities for transshipping cargoes, ditto ditto for chartering and equipping vessels, and ditto ditto for communicating with owners, Honolulu cannot begin to compete with San Francisco." Twain, "The Whaling Trade," 62–63, 65–67.

15. Personal communication with Michael P. Dyer, librarian and maritime historian, NBWM. June 9, 2006.

16. Hare, *Salted Tories*, 56.

17. A *New York Times* article in 1895, observed:

    The rapid decline of the American whaling industry is causing no little worry to those still interested in this once important business. The sun of its destiny is moving rapidly toward its western horizon. Whether some modern Joshua shall command it to stand still, or whether it shall move still nearer its full setting, is yet uncertain. Some oil and bone will still be used until their perfect substitutes are produced at so low a cost that the expense of whaling will entirely absorb its profits. Few persons . . . have any idea of the former size and importance of this industry.

    "Whaling Not What It Was," *New York Times*, Feb. 17, 1895.

18. Jenkins, *Bark Kathleen Sunk by a Whale*, advertisement on last page of the pamphlet.

19. "Whaling Enjoys a New Life" *New York Times*, Sept. 14, 1902.

20. "Made $40,000 in 17 Months," *Boston Daily Globe*, Dec. 28, 1902.

21. Bockstoce, *Whales, Ice & Men*, 335.

22. Quoted in Ellis, *Men and Whales*, 138.

23. "The Anti-Corset Law," *Whalemen's Shipping List*, Apr. 1, 1902.

24. In *Catherine: A Story*, originally serialized in 1839–40, William Makepeace Thackeray uses the term "whalebone prison" in a rather steamy passage: "The great Galgenstein descended towards Mrs. Catherine. Her cheeks glowed red-hot under her coy velvet mask, her heart thumped against the whalebone prison of her stays. What a delicious storm of vanity was raging in her bosom! What a rush of long-pent recollections burst forth at the sound of that enchanting voice!" William Makepeace Thackerary, "The Adventures of Philip on his way Through the World, to which is now prefixed A Shabby Genteel Story, Catherine: A Story," in *Thackeray's Complete Works*, Cambridge edition, vol. 2 (Boston: Estes and Lauriat, 1881), 378.

25. Elizabeth Ewing, *Dress and Undress: A History of Women's Underwear* (New York: Drama Book Specialists, 1978), 113.

26. Bockstoce, *Whales, Ice & Men*, 337.

27. *Whalemen's Shipping List and Merchants' Transcript*, Dec. 29, 1914.

28. Judith Boss, *New Bedford, A Pictorial History* (Norfolk: Denning Company, 1983), 68.

29. Tower, *A History of the American Whale Fishery*, 121.

30. "Alcoholic Liquors," *Whalemen's Shipping List and Merchants' Transcript*, Jan. 30, 1912; "Vacations in the Country," ibid., Apr. 16, 1912; and "African Ants," ibid., July 29, 1913.

31. Elmo P. Hohman, "American and Norwegian Whaling: A Comparative Study of Labor and Industrial Organization," *Journal of Political Economy* 43 (Oct. 1935), 629; Davis et al., *In Pursuit of Leviathan*, 502–3; Webb, *On the Northwest*, 143–44; and Jackson, *The British Whaling Trade*, 178–80.

32. In 1937–38, for example, nearly 55,000 whales were killed worldwide. Robert Cushman Murphy, "Lo, The Poor Whale," *Science* 91 (Apr. 19, 1940), 374. According to one estimate, during the twentieth century roughly two million whales were killed in the Southern Hemishpere alone. C. Scott Baker and Phillip J. Clapham, "Modeling the past and future of whales and whaling," *Trends in Ecology and Evolution* 19 (Jul. 2004), 366.

33. "Whaling Still Profitable," *New York Times*, Oct. 13, 1918; and "Whaler Has Cargo Valued at $72,000," *Boston Daily Globe*, Aug. 1, 1917.

34. Quoted in "Whaling Still Profitable," *New York Times*, Oct. 13, 1918.

35. "Three Whalers Safe in Port," *New Bedford Evening Standard*, Jul. 10, 1918.

36. Frank G. Carpenter, "Whales and Sharks Help to Win the War," *Boston Daily Globe*, Jan. 20, 1918.

37. "Whale Meat Lunch to Boost New Food," *New York Times*, Feb. 9, 1918.

38. "Tons of Food Going to Waste," *Boston Daily Globe*, Feb. 22, 1914.

39. During the war roughly 1.6 million pounds of gray-whale meat was sold, which is the equivalent of 25,000 head of cattle. Most of the meat was marketed in California. Ommanney, *Lost Leviathan*, 63; and Robotti, *Whaling and Old Salem*, 52–53.

40. E. Keble Chatterton, *Whalers and Whaling* (New York: William Farquhar Payson, 1931), 129.

41. "World Premiere, Elmer Clifton's 'Down To The Sea In Ships,'" Olympia, New Bedford, MA, Sept. 25, 1922, playbill.

42. Marjory Adams, "New Bedford's Aristocracy Goes in for Movie Acting," *Boston Daily Globe*, Aug. 27, 1922.

43. In 1916 the *Charles W. Morgan* had been hired by a motion picture company to be in the silent movie *Miss Petticoats*, featuring one of the era's rising stars, Alice Brady.

44. Z. W. Pease, "Back From a Whale Hunt with a Whale!," *Boston Daily Globe*, Apr. 30, 1922.

45. Ibid.

EPILOGUE: Fin Out

1. "Wanderer Sails on Whaling Cruise," *New Bedford Mercury*, Aug. 26, 1924; "Last Old Whaler Fitting for Sea at New Bedford," *Boston Herald*, Aug. 24, 1924; and Ralph Woodward, Jr., "The Bark Wanderer Soon to Sail for Whales," *New Bedford Times*, Aug. 16, 1924.

2. "Picturesque Service on the Eve of Whaler's Departure," *New Bedford Mercury*, Aug. 25, 1924.

3. Reprinted in "Wanderer," ibid., Aug. 26, 1924.

4. *New Bedford Mercury*, Aug. 26, 1924.

5. Alexander Crosby Brown, "Reminiscences of the Last Voyage of the Bark Wanderer," *American Neptune* 9 (Jan. 1949), 19.

6. Brown, "Reminiscences of the Last Voyage," 25.

7. "Whaling Bark Wanderer Lost on the Rocks at Cuttyhunk," *New Bedford Mercury*, Aug. 27, 1924; "Wanderer," *Republican Standard*, Aug. 27, 1924; "Wanderer's Lost Men Safe on Lightship," ibid.; "Wanderer's Crew Safe," *New Bedford Mercury*, Aug. 28, 1924); and Brown, "Reminiscences of the Last Voyage of the Bark Wanderer," 26.

8. "Whaling Bark Wanderer Lost on the Rocks at Cuttyhunk," *New Bedford Mercury*, Aug. 27, 1924.
9. Quoted in Brown, "Reminiscences of the Last Voyage," 27–28.
10. "Wanderer's Crew Safe," *New Bedford Mercury*.
11. "Souvenir Hunters Raid the Wanderer," *New Bedford Mercury*, Sept. 3, 1924.
12. Ibid.
13. The *Wanderer* was not, however, the very last American wooden whaleship to go to sea. That distinction goes to the *John R. Manta*, a small schooner out of New Bedford, which sailed in 1925 and again in 1927, bringing back three hundred barrels of sperm oil on its first voyage and only itself—just barely—on the second. Although there would continue to be sporadic, small-scale, shore-based whaling operations in America up through the early 1970s, particularly in California, the *Wanderer* and the *John R. Manta*'s voyages truly did signal the end of the great era of American whaling. William Henry Tripp, *"There Goes Flukes"* (New Bedford: Reynolds Printing, 1938).

Select Bibliography

This bibliography contains a fraction of the sources cited in this book. It is intended as a starting point for those who want to learn more about whaling in America, or whaling in general. For more information about specific topics covered in the text, please refer to the endnotes.

Adams, James Truslow. *History of the Town of Southampton.* Port Washington, NY: Ira J. Friedman, Inc., 1962.

Allen, Everett S. *Children of the Light: The Rise and Fall of New Bedford Whaling and the Death of the Arctic Fleet.* Orleans, MA: Parnassus Imprints, 1983.

Attwater, George. *The Journal of George Attwater Before the Mast on the Whaleship Henry of New Haven, 1820–1823*, edited by Kevin S. Reilly. New Haven: New Haven Colony Historical Society, 2002.

Banks, Charles Edward. *The History of Martha's Vineyard Dukes County Massachusetts.* 3 vols. Edgartown, MA: Dukes County Historical Society, 1966.

Beale, Thomas. *The Natural History of the Sperm Whale.* 1839. Reprint, London: Holland Press, 1973.

Bennett, Frederick D. *Narrative of a Whaling Voyage Round the Globe from the Year 1833–1836.* 2 vols. 1840. Reprint, New York: Da Capo Press, 1970.

Berzin, A. A. *The Sperm Whale.* Washington, DC: National Marine Fisheries Service, 1971.

Bockstoce, John R. *Whales, Ice & Men, The History of Whaling in the Western Arctic.* Seattle: University of Washington Press, 1986.

Bolster, W. Jeffrey. *Black Jacks: African American Seaman in the Age of Sail.* Cambridge: Harvard University Press, 1997.

Braginton-Smith, John, and Duncan Oliver. *Cape Cod Shore Whaling, America's First Whalemen.* Yarmouth, MA: Historical Society of Old Yarmouth, 2004.

Brandt, Karl. *Whale Oil, An Economic Analysis.* Palo Alto, CA: Food Research Institute at Stanford University, 1940.

Breen, T. H. *Imagining the Past.* Reading, MA: Addison-Wesley Publishing, 1989.

Bronson, George Whitefield. *Glimpses of the Whaleman's Cabin.* Boston: Damrell & Moore, Printers, 1855.

Browne, J. Ross. *Etchings of a Whaling Cruise*, edited by John Seelye. 1846. Reprint, Cambridge: Belknap Press of Harvard University Press, 1968.

Bullard, John M. *The Rotches.* New Bedford: self-published, 1947.

Bullen, Frank T. *The Cruise of the Cachalot.* New York: D. Appleton and Company, 1899.

Bulloch, James D. *The Secret Service of the Confederate States in Europe.* 1883. Reprint, New York: Modern Library, 2001.

Busch, Briton Cooper. *"Whaling Will Never Do for Me": The American Whaleman in the Nineteenth Century.* Lexington: University Press of Kentucky, 1994.

Byers, Edward. *The Nation of Nantucket: Society and Politics in an Early American Commercial Center, 1660–1820*. Boston: Northeastern University Press, 1987.

Chase, Owen. *The Wreck of the Whaleship Essex*. 1821. Reprint, San Diego: Harcourt Brace & Company, 1965.

Chatterton, E. Keble. *Whalers and Whaling*. New York: William Farquhar Payson, 1931.

Cheever, Henry T. *The Whale and His Captors: Or, The Whalemen's Adventures, and the Whale Biography, as gathered on the homeward cruise of the "Commodore Preble."* 1850. Reprint, Fairfield: Ye Galleon Press, 1991.

Clapham, Phil. *Whales of the World*. Stillwater, MN: Voyageur Press, 1997.

Coarse, Robert. *The Seafarers: A History of Maritime America 1620–1820*. New York: Harper & Row, 1964.

Colby, Barnard L. *New London Whaling Captains*. Mystic: Marine Historical Association, Inc., 1936.

Creighton, Margaret S. *Dogwatch & Liberty Days: Seafaring in the Nineteenth Century*. Peabody: Peabody Museum of Salem, 1982.

———. *Rites & Passages: The Experience of American Whaling, 1830–1870*. Cambridge, England: Cambridge University Press, 1995.

Crèvecoeur, J. Hector St. John de. *Letters from an American Farmer*. 1782. Reprint, New York: E.P. Dutton & Co., Inc., 1957.

Dakin, William John. *Whalemen Adventurers*. 1934. Reprint, Sydney: Sirius Books, 1963.

Dannenfeldt, Karl H. "Ambergris: The Search for Its Origin." *Isis* 73 (Sept. 1982): 382–97.

Davis, Lance E., Robert E. Gallman, and Karin Gleiter. *In Pursuit of Leviathan: Technology, Institutions, Productivity, and Profits in American Whaling, 1816–1906*. Chicago: University of Chicago Press, 1997.

Davis, William M. *Nimrod of the Sea or the American Whaleman*. 1874. Reprint, North Quincy: The Christopher Publishing House, 1972.

Decker, Robert Owen. *The Whaling City*. Chester, CT: Pequot Press, 1976.

Dodge, Ernest S. *New England and the South Seas*. Cambridge: Harvard University Press, 1965.

Douglas-Lithgow, R. A. *Nantucket, A History*. New York: G.P. Putnam & Sons, 1914.

Dow, George Francis. *Whale Ships and Whaling: A Pictorial History*. New York: Dover Publications, 1985.

Druett, Joan. *Petticoat Whalers: Whaling Wives at Sea, 1820–1920*. Hanover, NH: University Press of New England, 2001.

Dulles, Foster Rhea. *Lowered Boats: A Chronicle of American Whaling*. New York: Harcourt, Brace and Company, 1933.

Dyer, Michael P. "The Historical Evolution of the Cutting-In Pattern, 1798–1967." *The American Neptune* 59 (Spring 1999): 137–48.

Edwards, Everett J., and Jeannette Edwards Rattray. *"Whale Off!" The Story of American Shore Whaling*. New York: Coward McCann, Inc., 1932.

Ellis, Leonard Bolles. *History of New Bedford and its Vicinity, 1602–1892*. Syracuse: D. Mason & Co., 1892.

Ellis, Richard. *The Book of Whales*. New York: Alfred A. Knopf, 1980.

———. *Men and Whales*. New York: Alfred A. Knopf, 1991.

Ely, Ben-Ezra Stiles. *"There She Blows": A Narrative of a Whaling Voyage*. 1849. Reprint, Middletown, CT: Wesleyan University Press, 1971.

Francis, Daniel. *A History of World Whaling*. New York: Viking, 1990.

Frank, Stuart M. *Dictionary of Scrimshaw Artists*. Mystic: Mystic Seaport Museum, 1991.

Freeman, Frederick. *The History of Cape Cod: The Annals of the Thirteen Towns of Barnstable County.* Vol. 2. Boston: Printed for the Author by Geo. C. Rand & Avery, 1862.

Gardner, Edmund. *Captain Edmund Gardner of Nantucket and New Bedford, His Journal and His Family,* edited by John M. Bullard. New Bedford: self-published, 1958.

Gifford, Pardon B. "The Story of the Stone Fleet," in *Famous Fleets in New Bedford's History.* New Bedford: Reynolds Printing, 1935.

Goode, George Brown. *The Fisheries and Fishery Industries of the United States, Section V, History and Methods of the Fisheries.* Washington, DC: Government Printing Office, 1887.

Gordon, Arthur. "The Great Stone Fleet: Calculated Catastrophe." *United States Naval Institute Proceedings* 94 (Dec. 1968): 72–82.

Gordon, Eleanora C. "The Captain as Healer: Medical Care on Merchantmen and Whalers, 1790–1865." *American Neptune* 54 (Fall 1994): 265–77.

Gordon, Jonathan. *Sperm Whales.* Stillwater, MN: Voyageur Press, 1998.

Graham, Gerald S. "The Migrations of the Nantucket Whale Fishery: An Episode in British Colonial Policy." *New England Quarterly* 8 (June 1935): 179–202.

Haley, Nelson Cole. *Whale Hunt: The Narrative of a Voyage by Nelson Cole Haley, Harpooner in the Ship Charles W. Morgan, 1849–1853.* New York: Ives Washburn, Inc., 1948.

Hare, Lloyd C, M. *Salted Tories: The Story of the Whaling Fleets of San Francisco.* Mystic: Marine Historical Association, Inc., 1960.

Hart, Francis Russell. *New England Whale-Fisheries.* Cambridge, England: John Wilson and Son, The University Press, 1924.

Hawes, Charles Boardman. *Whaling.* Garden City, NY: Doubleday, Page & Company, 1924.

Hazen, Jacob A. *Five Years Before the Mast.* Philadelphia: Wills P. Hazard, 1854.

Hedges, James B. *The Browns of Providence Plantations.* Cambridge: Harvard University Press, 1952.

Hegarty, Reginald B. *Birth of a Whaleship.* New Bedford: New Bedford Free Public Library, 1964.

Hohman, Elmo Paul. *The American Whalemen: A Study of Life and Labor in the Whaling Industry.* New York: Longmans, Green and Co., 1928.

Howland, Chester. *Thar She Blows.* New York: Wilfred Funk, 1951.

Hunt, Cornelius E. *The Shenandoah or the Last Confederate Cruiser.* New York: G.W. Carleton & Company Publishers, 1867.

Huntington, Gale. *Songs the Whalemen Sang.* New York: Dover Publications, 1970.

Jackson, Gordon. *The British Whaling Trade.* Hamden, CT: Archon Books, 1978.

Jefferson, Thomas. "Observations on the Whale Fishery (1788)." In Merrill D. Peterson, *Thomas Jefferson, Writings.* New York: Library of America, 1984.

———. "Report on Cod and Whale Fisheries, February 1, 1791." In Padover, Saul K., *The Complete Jefferson.* New York: Duell, Sloan & Pearce, Inc., 1943.

Jenkins, J. T. *A History of the Whale Fisheries.* 1921. Reprint, Port Washington, NY: Kennikat Press, 1971.

Kaplan, Sidney. "Lewis Temple and the Hunting of the Whale." *New England Quarterly* (Mar. 1953): 78–88.

Kartunnen, Frances Ruley. *The Other Islanders: People Who Pulled Nantucket's Oars.* New Bedford: Spinner Publications, 2005.

Kittredge, Henry C. *Cape Cod: Its People and Their History.* Boston: Houghton Mifflin Company, 1968.

Kugler, Richard C. "The Whale Oil Trade, 1750–1775." In *Seafaring in Colonial Massachusetts*. Boston: Colonial Society of Massachusetts, 1980.

Kurlansky, Mark. *The Basque History of the World*. New York: Penguin, 1999.

Lawrence, Mary Chipman. *The Captain's Best Mate: The Journal of Mary Chipman Lawrence on the Whaler* Addison, *1856–1860*, edited by Stanton Garner. Providence: Brown University Press, 1966.

Leavitt, John F. *The Charles W. Morgan*. Mystic: Marine Historical Association, 1973.

Lipton, Barbara. "Whaling Days in New Jersey." *Newark Museum Quarterly* (Spring/Summer 1975).

Lockley, Ronald M. *Whales, Dolphins and Porpoises*. New York: W. W. Norton & Co. Inc., 1979.

Lovins, Amory B., E. Kyle Datta, Odd-Even Bustnes, Jonathan G. Koomey, and Nathan J. Glasgow. *Winning the Oil Endgame, Innovation for Profits, Jobs, and Security*. Snowmass, CO: Rocky Mountain Institute, 2005.

Lund, Judith Navas. *Whaling Masters and Whaling Voyages Sailing from American Ports: A Compilation of Sources*. New Bedford: New Bedford Whaling Museum, Kendall Whaling Museum, and Ten Pound Island Book Co., 2001.

Lytle, Thomas G. *Harpoons and Other Whalecraft*. New Bedford: Old Dartmouth Historical Society Whaling Museum, 1984.

Macy, Obed. *The History of Nantucket*. 1835. Reprint, Clifton, NJ: Augustus M. Kelley, 1972.

Martin, Kenneth R. *Delaware Goes Whaling, 1833–1845*. Greenville: Hagley Museum, 1974.

Matthews, Leonard Harrison. *The Whale*. New York: Simon & Schuster, 1968.

Mawer, Granville Allen. *Ahab's Trade: The Saga of South Seas Whaling*. New York: St. Martin's Press, 1999.

McDevitt, Joseph Lawrence Jr. *The House of Rotch: Whaling Merchants of Massachusetts, 1734–1828*. University Microfilms International: PhD diss. American University, Washington, DC, 1978.

McKissack, Patricia C., and Frederick L. McKissack. *Black Hands, White Sails: The Story of African-American Whalers*. New York: Scholastic Press, 1999.

Melville, Herman. *Moby-Dick*. 1851. Reprint, New York: Bantam Books, 1986.

Miller, Pamela A. *And the Whale Is Ours: Creative Writing of American Whalemen*. Boston: David R. Godine, 1979.

Morison, Samuel Eliot. *The Maritime History of Massachusetts*. Boston: Houghton Mifflin Company, 1921.

Morrell, Benjamin. *A Narrative of Four Voyages to the South Sea, North and South Pacific Ocean, Chinese Sea, Ethiopic and Southern Atlantic Ocean, Indian and Antarctic Ocean, from the Year 1822 to 1831*. New York: J. & J. Harper, 1832.

Mrantz, Maxine. *Whaling Days in Old Hawaii*. Honolulu: Aloha Graphics, 1976.

Mulford, David E. "The Captain and the King." *Awakening the Past, The East Hampton 350th Anniversary Lecture Series, 1998*. New York: Newmarket Press, 1999.

Mullett, J. C. *A Five Years' Whaling Voyage, 1848–1853*. 1859. Reprint, Fairfield, CT: Ye Galleon Press, 1977.

Murphy, Robert Cushman. "Floating Gold." *Natural History* 3 (March-April, 1933): 117–30.

———. "Lo, The Poor Whale." *Science* 91 (Apr. 19, 1940): 374.

———. *Logbook for Grace*. New York: Time Incorporated, 1947.

Newhall, Charles L. *The Adventures of Jack: Or, A Life on the Wave*, edited by Kenneth R. Martin. 1859. Reprint, Fairfield, CT: Ye Galleon Press, 1981.

Nordhoff, Charles. *Whaling and Fishing.* 1856. Reprint, New York: Dodd, Mead & Company, 1895.

Norling, Lisa. *Captain Ahab Had a Wife: New England Women and the Whalefishery, 1720–1870.* Chapel Hill: University of North Carolina, 2000.

Olmsted, Francis Allyn. *Incidents of a Whaling Voyage.* 1841. Reprint, New York: Bell Publishing Company, 1969.

Ommanney, F. D. *Lost Leviathan.* New York: Dodd, Mead & Company, 1971.

Palmer, William R. *The Whaling Port of Sag Harbor.* PhD diss. Columbia University, 1959.

Parker, Hershel. *Herman Melville: A Biography.* Vol. 1, *1819–1851,* Baltimore: Johns Hopkins University Press, 1996.

———. *Herman Melville: A Biography.* Vol. 2, *1851–1891.* Baltimore: Johns Hopkins University Press, 2002.

Parr, Charles McKew. *The Voyages of David de Vries, Navigator and Adventurer.* New York, Thomas Y. Crowell Company, 1969.

Philbrick, Nathaniel. "'Every Wave Is a Fortune': Nantucket Island and the Making of American Icon." *New England Quarterly* 66 (Sept. 1993): 434–47.

———. *Away Off Shore, Nantucket Island and Its People, 1602–1890.* Nantucket: Mill Hill Press, 1994.

———. *Abram's Eyes: The Native American Legacy of Nantucket Island.* Nantucket: Mill Hill Press, 1998.

———. *In the Heart of the Sea.* New York: Viking, 2000.

———. *Sea of Glory.* New York: Viking, 2003.

Porter, David. *Journal of a Cruise.* 1815. Reprint, Annapolis: Naval Institute Press, 1986.

Proulx, Jean-Pierre. *Whaling in the North Atlantic from the Earliest Times to the Mid-19th Century.* Ottawa: Parks Canada, 1986.

Reeves, Randall R., and Edward Mitchell. "The Long Island, New York, Right Whale Fishery: 1650–1924." In *Right Whales: Past and Present Status, in the Proceedings of the Workshop on the Status of Right Whales, New England Aquarium, June 15–23, 1983.* International Whaling Commission Special Report 10, edited by Robert L. Brownell, Jr., Peter B. Best, and John H. Prescott. Cambridge, England: International Whaling Commission, 1986: 201–20.

Reilly, Kevin S. "Slavers in Disguise: American Whaling and the African Slave Trade, 1845–1862." *American Neptune* 53 (Summer 1993): 177–89.

Reynolds, J. N. "Mocha Dick: or the White Whale of the Pacific: A Leaf from a Manuscript Journal." *Knickerbocker* 13 (May 1839): 377–92.

Robbins, Charles Henry. *The Gam, Being a Group of Whaling Stories.* Salem, MA: Newcomb & Gauss, 1913.

Robotti, Frances Diane. *Whaling and Old Salem.* New York: Bonanza Books, 1962.

Robotti, Frances Diane, and James Vescovi. *The USS Essex and the Birth of the American Navy.* Holbrook, MA: Adams Media Corporation, 1999.

Rotch, William. *Memorandum Written by William Rotch in the Eightieth Year of his Age.* Boston: Houghton Mifflin Company, 1916.

Sampson, Alonzo D. *Three Times Around the World: Life and Adventures.* Buffalo: Express Printing Company, 1867.

Scammon, Charles M. *The Marine Mammals of the Northwestern Coast of North America, Together with an Account of the American Whale Fishery.* 1874. Reprint, New York: Dover Publications, 1968.

Schmidt, Frederick P., Cornelius De Jong, and Frank H. Winter. *Thomas Welcome Roys: America's Pioneer of Modern Whaling*. Charlottesville: University Press of Virginia, 1980.

Schneider, Paul. *The Enduring Shore*. New York: Henry Holt and Company, 2000.

Schram, Margaret B. *Hudson's Merchants and Whalers: The Rise and Fall of a River Port 1783–1850*. New York: Black Dome, 2004.

Scoresby, William. *An Account of the Arctic Regions with a History and Description of the Northern Whale-fishery*. Vol. 1 and 2, *The Arctic* and *The Whale-Fishery*. Devon, England: David & Charles Reprints, 1969.

Semmes, Raphael. *Service Afloat or, The Remarkable Career of the Confederate Cruisers Sumter and Alabama*. Baltimore: Baltimore Publishing Company, 1887.

Shapiro, Irwin, and Edouard Stackpole. *The Story of Yankee Whaling*. New York: Harper & Row, 1959.

Sherman, Stuart. *The Voice of the Whaleman*. Providence: Providence Public Library, 1965.

Shoemaker, Nancy. "Whale Meat in American History." *Environmental History* 10 (Apr. 2005): 269–94.

Simpson, Marcus B. Jr., and Sallie W. Simpson. *Whaling on the North Carolina Coast*. Raleigh: Division of Archives and History, North Carolina Department of Cultural Resources, 1990.

Slijper, E. J. *Whales*. New York: Basic Books, Inc., 1962.

Smith, Bradford. *Captain John Smith: His Life & Legend*. Philadelphia: J. B. Lippincott Company, 1953.

Smith, Gaddis. "Whaling History and the Courts." *Log of the Mystic Seaport* 30 (Oct. 1978): 67–80.

Smith, John. *The Complete Works of Captain John Smith (1580–1631)*. 3 vols. edited by Philip L. Barbour. Chapel Hill: University of North Carolina Press, 1986.

Spears, John R. *The Story of New England Whalers*. New York: Macmillan Company, 1922.

Stackpole, Edouard A. *The Sea-Hunters*. Philadelphia: J. B. Lippincott Company, 1953.

————. *The Charles W. Morgan, The Last Wooden Whaleship*. New York: Meredith Press, 1967.

————. *Whales & Destiny, The Rivalry between America, France, and Britain for Control of the Southern Whale Fishery, 1785–1825*. Amherst: University of Massachusetts Press, 1972.

————. *Nantucket in the Revolution*. Nantucket: Nantucket Historical Association, 1976.

Starbuck, Alexander. *History of the American Whale Fishery*. 1878. Reprint, Secaucus, NJ: Castle Books, 1989.

————. *The History of Nantucket, County, Island and Town*. Boston: C. E. Goodspeed, 1924.

Stommel, Henry. "The Gulf Stream: A Brief History of the Ideas Concerning Its Cause." *Scientific Monthly* 70 (April 1950): 242–53.

Tower, Walter S. *A History of the American Whale Fishery*. Philadelphia: Publications of the University of Pennsylvania, Series on Political Economy and Public Law 20, 1907.

Tripp, William Henry. *"There Goes Flukes."* New Bedford: Reynolds Printing, 1938.

True, Frederick W. *The Whalebone Whales of the Western North Atlantic*. Washington, DC: Smithsonian Institution Press, 1983.

Twain, Mark. "The Whaling Trade." In *Mark Twain, Letters From Honolulu*. Honolulu: Thomas Nickerson, 1939.

Verrill, A. Hyatt. *The Real Story of the Whale*. New York: D. Appleton and Company, 1923.

Vickers, Daniel. "The First Whalemen of Nantucket." *William and Mary Quarterly* 40 (1983): 560–83.

———. "Nantucket Whalemen in the Deep-Sea Fishery: The Changing Anatomy of an Early American Labor Force." *Journal of American History* 72 (Sept. 1985): 277–96.

Waddell, James I. *C.S.S. Shenandoah, The Memoirs of Lieutenant Commanding James I. Waddell*, edited by James D. Horan. New York: Crown Publishers, Inc., 1960.

Webb, Robert Lloyd. *On the Northwest: Commercial Whaling in the Pacific Northwest, 1790–1967*. Vancouver: University of British Columbia Press, 1988.

Whipple, A. B. C. *Yankee Whalers in the South Seas*. Rutland, VT: Charles E. Tuttle Co., 1973.

———. *The Whalers*. Alexandria, VA: Time-Life Books, 1979.

Whitecar, William B. *Four Years Aboard the Whaleship*. Philadelphia: J. B. Lippincott & Co., 1860.

Wilkes, Charles. *Narrative of the United States Exploring Expedition During the Years 1838, 1839, 1840, 1841, 1842*, Vols. 1 and 5. Philadelphia: Lea and Blanchard, 1845.

Winslow, C. F. "Some Account of Capt. Mercator Cooper's visit to Japan in the Whale Ship *Manhattan*, of Sag Harbor." *The Friend*, Feb. 2, 1846.

Withington, Sidney. *Two Dramatic Episodes of New England Whaling*. Mystic: Marine Historical Association, Inc., July 1958.

Zaykowski, Dorothy Ingersoll. *Sag Harbor: The Story of An American Beauty*. Sag Harbor: Sag Harbor Historical Society, 1991.

Illustration Credits

JACKET IMAGE: Detail from an 1834 print titled *Pêche du Cachalot (Cachalot Fishery)*, based on a painting by Ambroise-Louis Garneray. Courtesy of New Bedford Whaling Museum

Frontispiece: *Pêche de la Baleine (Whale Fishery)*, print based on a painting by Ambroise-Louis Garneray. Courtesy of New Bedford Whaling Museum

Page 11: Courtesy of New Bedford Whaling Museum

Pages 14–15: This 1620 painting of Dutch bay whaling in the Arctic, by Cornelis Claeszoon van Wieringen, shows the extent to which whaling had already progressed by the time the Pilgrims landed in America. Whaleboats are hauling whales to shore, where the blubber is cut and placed in try-pots for rendering. Courtesy of New Bedford Whaling Museum

Page 17: This item is reproduced by permission of the Huntington Library, San Marino, California.

Page 30: Courtesy of New Bedford Whaling Museum

Page 41: Courtesy of East Hampton Library, Long Island Collection

Page 63: Courtesy of Nantucket Historical Association

Page 75: © Flip Nicklin / Minden Pictures

Page 90: Courtesy of New Bedford Whaling Museum

Page 109: Courtesy of John Carter Brown Library at Brown University

Page 119: Courtesy of New Bedford Whaling Museum

Pages 136–37: *Capturing a Sperm Whale*, painted by William Page, based on a sketch by Cornelius B. Hulsart, a whaleman who lost an arm while on the whaleship *Superior*. Created in 1835, this is believed to be the first American whaling print. Courtesy of New Bedford Whaling Museum

Page 139: Courtesy of Boston Athenæum

Page 149: Courtesy of New Bedford Whaling Museum

Page 165: Courtesy of New Bedford Whaling Museum

Page 188: Courtesy of U.S. Naval Historical Center

Page 205: Courtesy of Berkshire Athenaeum, Pittsfield, MA

Page 253: Courtesy of New Bedford Whaling Museum

Page 275: Courtesy of New Bedford Whaling Museum

Page 282: Courtesy of New Bedford Whaling Museum

Pages 306–7: Courtesy of New Bedford Whaling Museum

Page 309: Courtesy of New Bedford Whaling Museum

Page 335: Courtesy of New Bedford Whaling Museum

Page 342: Courtesy of New Bedford Whaling Museum

Page 353: Courtesy of New Bedford Whaling Museum

Page 370: Courtesy of New Bedford Whaling Museum

Acknowledgments

I enjoyed writing this book, in large part because of the many people and organizations that helped me along the way. All of them have my sincerest thanks, but a few merit special recognition. The Nantucket Historical Association awarded me an E. Geoffrey and Elizabeth Thayer Verney Fellowship, making it possible for me to spend two wonderful weeks on Nantucket, learning about the island's illustrious whaling past and drafting chapters. My time on Nantucket was made more pleasant by Research Associate Elizabeth Oldham, who steered me through the association's library, and by Photograph Archives Specialist Marie Henke, who served as my source for images.

Michael P. Dyer, the librarian and maritime historian at the New Bedford Whaling Museum (NBWM), was a phenomenal source of information and support, and never failed to challenge me and help me find materials, always with a sense of humor and spirit of adventure. His positive response to, and comments on, the manuscript were much appreciated. Laura Pereira, the assistant librarian at the NBWM, also reviewed the manuscript and was equally supportive. I was amazed by her ability to answer numerous, often obscure questions quickly and accurately. And the NBWM's curator of photography, Michael Lapides, diligently helped me gather the bulk of the photos and artwork that grace the pages of this book.

Many other individuals and institutions provided critical support. David Littlefield, museum interpreter and whaling historian at Mystic Seaport—the Museum of America and the Sea, critically reviewed the manuscript and provided numerous valuable suggestions for improvement. Paul A. Cyr, the curator of special collections and whaling expert at the New Bedford Free Public Library, always had entertaining stories to share, and pointed me to key texts. In my hometown of Marblehead, Ann Connolly, Sudha Newman, and Jonathan Randolph, all of whom work at the Abbot Public Library, were ever willing to help me track down sources within the library and through interlibrary loan, which offers researchers a most wonderful bibliographical lifeline to the holdings of scores of regional libraries.

The staffs of the following institutions were also a joy to work with: the American Antiquarian Society, the American Philosophical Society, the Berkshire Athenaeum (Pittsfield, MA), the Boston Athenæum, the Boston Public Library, the East Hampton Public Library, the G. W. Blunt White Library at Mystic Seaport, the Historical Collections Department at Baker Library (Harvard Business School), the Huntington Library, the John Carter Brown Library at Brown University, the Massachusetts Historical Society, the Massachusetts State Archives, the Nantucket Atheneum, the National Archives and Records Administration (Northeast Region), the Newport Public Library, the Providence Public Library, the Sag Harbor Whaling and Historical Museum, the Salem State College library, the San Francisco Maritime National Historic Park Library, and the State Library of Massachusetts.

Others who assisted me include Patricia Boulos, Georgen Charnes, David Cory, Doug Christel, James A. Craig, Susan Danforth, Kimberly Drooks, Allan Eaton, Leigh Fought, Amy German, Joan Gearin, Francois Gohier, Walter Hickey, Frances Karttunen, Peter Kelliher, Paul Maltacea, Kimberly Nusco, Hugh Parker, Niles Parker, Paul Perra, Nathaniel Philbrick, Andy Price, Wendy Schnur, Doug and Jodi Smith, Zachary N. Studenroth, Lincoln J. Thurber III, Melanie Tossell, Thomas Warren, Marci Vail, Lisa Walling, and Louisa Watrous. I also want to thank George Darcy and Hannah Goodale of the National Marine Fisheries Service for giving me an opportunity to take a limited but much appreciated amount of time off from my regular job to work on the book.

When I began this project, I was overwhelmed by the sheer volume of books, journals, and articles written about whaling. But over time this surfeit of materials proved to be a most welcome associate, providing me with valuable information and insights. I owe a great debt to all the writers whose names and works are cited in the endnotes and the bibliography, and I hope that my efforts will be viewed by future researchers and writers in the same way.

Russell Galen, my trusted agent, helped me hone my proposal, offered encouragement, and taught me about the intricacies of publishing. The first proposal I submitted to Russ had the book ending with the American Revolution. Russ responded that my view was too narrowly focused, that he thought the book had to span the entire history of American whaling. Initially I balked at this suggestion. After all, I argued, relatively few people had written extensively about the colonial period, while many had written about the golden age of whaling during the nineteenth century and the industry's demise in the early twentieth. Furthermore, I thought that a book encompassing all of American whaling would be too much like a whale, and a bit overwhelming. On further reflection, however, I agreed with Russ, and given the book that resulted, I thank him for pushing me to think more expansively about the project.

Working with W. W. Norton was a true pleasure. My editor, Bob Weil, with his deft pen and keen advice, vastly improved the manuscript and gave me the greatest gift a writer can receive—lessons on improving one's craft. Bob's assistant, Tom Mayer, patiently explained the mechanics of preparing the manuscript and helped me successfully travel the path to publication. Managing editor Nancy Palmquist oversaw the editing and indexing process, and made the excellent choice of selecting Sue Llewellyn to copyedit the book, a task she performed with skill and humor. Production manager Julia Druskin did a fantastic job pulling everything together to create the book you are holding in your hands.

OF ALL WHO DESERVE THANKS, none are more important than my family. My dad, Stanley Dolin, read the manuscript, and his positive feedback gave me confidence that I was headed in the right direction. My mother, Ruth, was equally encouraging and interested in the project. Jennifer, my wife, and my children, Lily and Harry, were there every step of the way, and they never failed to provide support and make me laugh, often at myself. Jennifer was not only a sounding board for ideas, but she also read the manuscript numerous times and was characteristically direct, thoughtful, and insightful in her comments. My children kept tabs on my progress by often visiting me in the basement and asking how the "whale book" was going, and finally, toward the end of the project asking me, "When are you going to be done with that book?" If it weren't for Jennifer, Lily, and Harry, I could not have written *Leviathan*.

Index

Page numbers in *italics* refer to illustrations. Page numbers beginning with 375 refer to notes.

About the Author

ERIC JAY DOLIN, who grew up near the coasts of New York and Connecticut, graduated from Brown University, where he majored in biology and environmental studies. After getting a master's degree in environmental management from the Yale School of Forestry and Environmental Studies, he received his PhD in environmental policy and planning from the Massachusetts Institute of Technology, where his dissertation examined the role of the courts in the cleanup of Boston Harbor.

Dolin has worked as a program manager at the U.S. Environmental Protection Agency, an environmental consultant stateside and in London, an intern at the National Wildlife Federation and on Capitol Hill, an American Association for the Advancement of Science Mass Media Science and Engineering Fellow at *BusinessWeek*, a curatorial assistant in the Mollusk Department at the Harvard Museum of Comparative Zoology, and a fisheries policy analyst at the National Marine Fisheries Service. Currently, he is a full-time writer.

Much of Dolin's writing reflects his interest in wildlife and environmental history. His books include the *Smithsonian Book of National Wildlife Refuges*, *Snakehead: A Fish Out of Water*, and *Political Waters*, a history of the degradation and cleanup of Boston Harbor. He has been fascinated by whales and the history of whaling since he was a boy.

Dolin and his family reside in Marblehead, Massachusetts, a coastal community with a rich maritime history.